The Palgrave Handbook of Violence in Africa

Obert Bernard Mlambo · Ezra Chitando
Editors

The Palgrave Handbook of Violence in Africa

Volume 2

Editors
Obert Bernard Mlambo
Classical Studies Section
School of Languages and Literatures
Rhodes University
Makhanda, South Africa

Ezra Chitando
Department of Philosophy
Religion and Ethics
University of Zimbabwe
Harare, Zimbabwe

ISBN 978-3-031-40753-6   ISBN 978-3-031-40754-3 (eBook)
https://doi.org/10.1007/978-3-031-40754-3

© The Editor(s) (if applicable) and The Author(s), under exclusive license to Springer Nature Switzerland AG 2024

This work is subject to copyright. All rights are solely and exclusively licensed by the Publisher, whether the whole or part of the material is concerned, specifically the rights of translation, reprinting, reuse of illustrations, recitation, broadcasting, reproduction on microfilms or in any other physical way, and transmission or information storage and retrieval, electronic adaptation, computer software, or by similar or dissimilar methodology now known or hereafter developed.
The use of general descriptive names, registered names, trademarks, service marks, etc. in this publication does not imply, even in the absence of a specific statement, that such names are exempt from the relevant protective laws and regulations and therefore free for general use.
The publisher, the authors, and the editors are safe to assume that the advice and information in this book are believed to be true and accurate at the date of publication. Neither the publisher nor the authors or the editors give a warranty, expressed or implied, with respect to the material contained herein or for any errors or omissions that may have been made. The publisher remains neutral with regard to jurisdictional claims in published maps and institutional affiliations.

Cover credit: Jürgen Schott/Alamy Stock Photo

This Palgrave Macmillan imprint is published by the registered company Springer Nature Switzerland AG
The registered company address is: Gewerbestrasse 11, 6330 Cham, Switzerland

Paper in this product is recyclable.

Foreword

This compendium (in 2 volumes) shows that violence is not a "special practice" but that nearly every human practice can be turned into something violent. Correspondingly, this book traces the "violent turn" in human society across a great diversity of cultural settings and domains. The human is the one living being we should be most careful about since no other living species on earth causes more deaths in the human population. And with every new human practice, there is potential for new violence to emerge. The compendium is therefore also a guide for recognizing and documenting when ordinary things (including well-intended actions) turn violent. If we want to change the course of things for the better and if we want to be prepared to prevent and prosecute violence, we need to recognize it in its many possible manifestations. We need to understand its recurrent and underlying structures (for instance, in patriarchy) as this volume convincingly shows.

This collection focuses on Africa, but without entrenching the stereotype of Africa as a particularly violent place, because wherever there is violence, there are also people who seek to stop it. The many examples of ways of dealing with conflicts in non-violent ways and of turning away from violence are testimony to that. As the contributions to the book show, the human condition is never innocent and harmless—but it is not hopeless either.

Thomas Widlok
University of Cologne
Cologne, Germany

Contents

Violence in Africa: A General Introduction   1
Obert Bernard Mlambo and Ezra Chitando

Conceptualizing Violence in Africa

Violence in Africa: Reflecting on a Broad Concept   23
Ezra Chitando and Obert Bernard Mlambo

The Rate of Oppression (ROp): The Apartheid Studies Approach to the Study of Harm   53
Nyasha Mboti

On Systemic and Epistemic Violence in Africa   77
Patricia Pinky Ndlovu and Sabelo J. Ndlovu-Gatsheni

Technologies of Violence in Africa   99
Wesley Mwatwara and Obert Bernard Mlambo

Border Violence in Africa   119
Rachel Ibreck and Souhayel Weslety

Diaspora and the Afterlife of Violence: Eritrean National Narratives and What Goes Without Saying   141
Victoria Bernal

The Chemical Violence of Colonial Encounters in Africa:
Historiographical Reflections and Theoretical Perspectives   167
Elijah Doro

Epistemic Violence in the Postcolony: Interrogating
the Colonial Legacy and War in Francophone African Literature   183
Gibson Ncube

Geographies of Violence and Informalization: The Case
of Mathare Slums in Nairobi, Kenya   203
Maurice Omollo and Solomon Waliaula

Through the Afrocentricity Lens: Terror, Insurgency
and Implications for Regional Integration in Southern Africa
from Cabo Delgado Province, Mozambique   221
*Daniel Nkosinathi Mlambo, Victor H. Mlambo,
and Mandla Mfundo Masuku*

The State and Violence in Africa

Discourses on Political Violence and the Mechanics
of Legitimation in Official Commissions of Inquiry in Africa   243
Claire-Anne Lester

Party Politics, Violence, Impunity, and Social Injustices
in Zimbabwe (1980–2022)   265
Vellim Nyama and Pedzisai Ruhanya

Preventing Electoral Violence in Africa: Towards Sustainable
Peace   285
Khabele Matlosa

"Dirge to Slit Bodies": EndSARS, Police Brutality,
and Nigerian Dystopia in Jumoke Verissimo and James Yéku's
Soro Soke: When Poetry Speaks Up   307
Ayokunmi Ojebode

The Resource Curse and Structural Violence in Angola: A Path
for Perpetual Conflicts   329
Jeremiah Bvirindi

Electoral Violence in Ghana's Fourth Republic: The Case
of Party Vigilantism   347
*Emmanuel Debrah, Isaac Owusu-Mensah, Sampson Danso,
and Gilbert Arhinful Aidoo*

Investigating the Causes and Impact of Electoral Violence in Nigeria 367
Usman Sambo, Babayo Sule, and Mohammed Kwarah Tal

Ungoverned Space and National Security in Nigeria 387
Arinze Ngwube

Children, Youth and Violence

Trauma, Violence, and Memory in African Child Soldier Memoirs 409
Stacey Hynd

Africa and Violence: The Metamorphosis and Participation of Child Soldiers in Conflict Zones 437
Toyin Cotties Adetiba

Youth, Violence, and Political Accumulation: Urban Militias in Zimbabwe 459
Simbarashe Gukurume and Godfrey Maringira

Youth, Proliferation of Small Arms and Light Weapons, and Conflicts in 21st Century Africa 479
Babayo Sule, Ibrahim Kawuley Mika'il, and Mohammed Kwarah Tal

Violence Against Children on the Streets in Sub–Saharan Africa: An Overview 501
Witness Chikoko

Violence Against Disabled Children in Botswana 521
Thabile Anita Samboma

Nature, Religion and Cultural Violence in Africa

Violence against Nature in African Traditional Thought and Practice 541
Obert Bernard Mlambo and Kudzanai Melody Mlambo

Yearning for Old Time Religion in the Face of Globalization? Interpreting Fundamentalisms and Violent Extremism in Africa 559
Ezra Chitando

In God's Name: Violent Extremism in North East Nigeria 575
Jacinta Chiamaka Nwaka

Beyond Ethnicity: Reflections on the History and Politics
of Violence in Uganda   601
Evarist Ngabirano

The Intersectionality Between Violence and Poverty in Africa:
Sketching the Prevalence of Various Forms of Violence
in South Africa   619
Rabson Hove

Violence Against Nature in Africa: A Historical Assessment   639
Marlino Eugénio Mubai

Xenophobia, Afrophobia, or Promoting Xenophilia? Semantic
Explorations of Violence and Criminality in South Africa   661
Martin Mujinga

Enchanted Worldviews and Violence Against Persons
with Albinism in Sub-Saharan Africa   677
Francis Benyah

Violence Against Persons with Albinism in Malawi   699
Jones Hamburu Mawerenga

Globalization, Islamic Fundamentalism and Violence Through
the Youth in Kenya   721
Susan M. Kilonzo

Gender and Violence in Africa

Sexual Violence Against Girls and Women in African Conflict   745
Veronica Fynn Bruey

The Cost of Violence Against Women in Africa   779
Tshenolo Jennifer Madigele and Mutsawashe Chitando

Violence against Women in Egypt: A Closer Look at Intimate
Partner Violence and Female Genital Mutilation   795
Yasmin M. Khodary

"Wait, Let's Talk About It": A Feminist Assessment
of the Response of the Church of the Cross Hayfield
(NELCSA) to Gender-Based Violence in Pietermaritzburg,
South Africa   819
Lindiwe Princess Maseko

Breaking The Silence: Exploring the Challenges and Support
Mechanisms for Male Survivors of Gender-Based Violence
in Sub-Saharan Africa — 849
Susan Monyangi Nyabena

Gender Violence: A Portrait of Women for Change's Fight
Against Gender-Based Violence in Zambia — 865
Nelly Mwale and Joseph Chita

Persisting Inequalities: An Intersectional View of Climate
Change, Gender and Violence — 879
Mary Nyasimi and Veronica Nonhlanhla Jakarasi

"Women's Sexuality Captured": Another Form
of Gender-Based Violence (GBV) in the Swati Patriarchal Space — 893
Sonene Nyawo

Changing Contexts, Changing Violence Patterns? The Case
of African Diaspora Women — 909
Nomatter Sande and Amos Muyambo

Adolescent Boys, Young Men, and Mental Health in Southern
Africa — 925
Mutsawashe Chitando

Towards a Reconstruction of Sacralized Traditions to Avert
Gender-Based Violence Prevalent in Girl-Child Marriages
Amongst the Akamba — 941
Telesia Kathini Musili

Violence, Memory and the Law in Africa

Pre-colonial and Colonial Violence in Zimbabwe:
A Literary-cultural Exegesis — 961
Oliver Nyambi

"Living in the Shadow of Death": Understandings of Political
Violence and Its Aftermath in the Zimbabwean Context — 979
Chenai Matshaka and Ruth Murambadoro

Forgetting as a Psychological Weapon? Critiquing the Call
to Forget in a Zimbabwe Founded and Ruled by Violence — 1001
Collium Banda

Incest as Dismissal: Anthropology and Clinics of Silence 1019
Parfait D. Akana

Preventing Violent Conflict in Africa

Confronting Military Violence in Africa's Electoral Spaces:
Law, Institutions, and Remedies 1033
James Tsabora

Managing Conflict in Africa: Challenges and Opportunities
for the African Union 1051
Victor H. Mlambo, Ernest Toochi Aniche, and Mandla Mfundo Masuku

Beyond Xenophobia or Afrophobia: Strategies and Solutions 1071
Nomatter Sande and Martin Mujinga

Violent Piracy off the Coast of Nigeria: A Theoretical Analysis 1087
Kalu Kingsley Anele

Insurgency in Mozambique: Can SADC's NATO's Article 5
Treaty Address Future Insurgences in the Region 1111
*Victor H. Mlambo, Mandla Mfundo Masuku,
and Daniel Nkosinathi Mlambo*

Mediatized Conflict: A Case of Nigerian Media Reportage
of Farmer-Herder Conflict 1133
Ridwan Abiola Kolawole and Babatunde Raphael Ojebuyi

Conclusion 1151
Obert Bernard Mlambo and Ezra Chitando

Index 1155

Notes on Contributors

Toyin Cotties Adetiba is Associate Professor and Head of the Department of Political and International Studies, University of Zululand, South Africa. He has published extensively in accredited peer-reviewed journals and book chapters and co-authored a book. Adetiba is an NRF reviewer apart from reviewing for several number of accredited journals. His research interests include Political Science, International Relations, Conflict Resolution, Diplomacy, and Migration.

Gilbert Arhinful Aidoo is a Lecturer in the Department of Political Science at the University of Education, Ghana. His research domain includes democracy and electoral violence, terrorism, security governance, human rights, and regionalism in Africa. He has produced a few publications on democracy and electoral violence, terrorism, regionalism, and human rights in Africa.

Parfait D. Akana is a sociologist and anthropologist. He is founder and Executive Director of the Muntu Institute Foundation (African Humanities and Social Sciences) and teaches at the University of Yaounde II. He holds a Ph.D. in Sociology from École des Hautes Études en Sciences Sociales (Paris). He worked for CODESRIA (2014–2017) and has been Visiting Fellow for Nantes Institute of Advanced Studies (2017–2018) and Stellenbosch Institute for Advanced Study (2019). His areas of research include mental health, gender, sexual violence, digital and popular cultures. His publications include *Se mobiliser pour le football en Afrique. Une sociologie du* *supportérisme* (Muntu Institute Press, 2023), *Affects* (Muntu Institute Press, 2022), *Réflexivités africaines* (Muntu Institute Press & Jimsaan, 2021).

Kalu Kingsley Anele is a Lecturer in Cultural Heritage at the Preservation Research Institute, Pusan National University, South Korea.

Ernest Toochi Aniche Ph.D. is a Senior Lecturer and the Acting Head of theDepartment of Political Science, Federal University Otuoke, Bayelsa State, Nigeria. He earned B.Sc., M.Sc., and Ph.D. degrees from the Department of Political Science, University of Nigeria with emphasis on international relations. He belongs to various professional associations. His research interests include African regionalism, comparative regionalism, migration and border studies, conflict and peace studies, security studies, and international political economy.

Collium Banda is an Extraordinary Research Fellow in the Unit for Reformational Theology and the Development of the South African Society, Faculty of Theology, North-West University, South Africa, and adjunct lecturer at Theological College of Zimbabwe, Bulawayo, Zimbabwe. His research interests include African Pentecostalism, Christian doctrines in the African public space, African traditional religions, African indigenous knowledge systems, and Christianity in African contexts of suffering.

Francis Benyah is a Ph.D. candidate in the Study of Religions at the Åbo Akademi University, Turku, Finland. His research interests focus on pentecostal/charismatic theology and African pentecostal Christianity with a special interest in how it intersects and interacts with public life in areas such as media, politics, health, and human rights.

Victoria Bernal is a Cultural Anthropologist whose scholarship in political anthropology contributes to media studies, diaspora studies, gender studies, and African studies. Her work addresses questions relating to politics, digital media, migration and diaspora, war, globalization, transnationalism, civil society and activism, gender, development, and Islam. Dr. Bernal's research is particularly concerned with relations of power and inequality and the dynamic struggles of ordinary people as they confront the cruel and absurd contradictions arising from the concentration of wealth and political power locally and globally. She has carried out ethnographic research in Sudan, Tanzania, Eritrea, Silicon Valley, and cyberspace. She is the author of *Nation as Network: Diaspora, Cyberspace, and Citizenship*, and *Cultivating Workers: Peasants and Capitalism in a Sudanese Village* as well as numerous articles. She is co-editor of anthologies on *Cryptopolitics: Exposure, Concealment and Digital Media*, and *Theorizing NGOs: States, Feminisms, and Neoliberalisms*.

Professor Bernal has received fellowships from the Fulbright Foundation, the Catholic University of Leuven, Belgium, the Center for Advanced Studies in the Behavioral Sciences at Stanford, the American Philosophical Society, and the Rockefeller Foundation. She is a Professor at the University of California, Irvine where she teaches courses on Digital Media and Culture, Global Africa, Nations, States and Gender, and Security, Secrecy, and Surveillance, among others.

Veronica Fynn Bruey is a multi-award winner and a passionate academic-advocate. Holding six academic degrees from four continents, she has researched, taught, consulted, and presented at conferences in over 30 countries. She's authored five books, several book chapters, and journal articles. She is the founder/editor-in-chief of the *Journal of Internal Displacement*; the co-lead of Law and Society's Collaborative Research Network (CRN-11): "Displaced Peoples"; the lead of Law and Society Association's International Research Collaborative (IRC-10): "Disrupting Patriarchy and Masculinity in Africa"; and the founder of the Voice of West African Refugees in Ghana at the Buduburam Refugee Settlement in Ghana. She is also the Australian National University International Alumna of the Year, 2021, the president of the International Association for the Study of Forced Migration, and a Co-Chair of the Africa Interest Group, American Society of International Law. Currently, she is the Director of Flowers School of Global Health Sciences, and an Assistant Professor in Legal Studies at Athabasca University. Veronica is a born and bred Indigenous Liberian war survivor.

Jeremiah Bvirindi (Ph.D.) is the director of Evaluations and Research Solutions Africa (Pvt) Ltd (EARS-AFRICA). He is a holder of two earned doctorates, a Doctor of Philosophy in Peace, Leadership, and Governance from Africa University and a Doctor of Philosophy in Public Policy Evaluation, from the Swiss School of Management, Switzerland. He is a Lecturer at Midlands State University and Africa University (part-time) and a notable scholar who has published a number of academic papers in the field of governance, peace, and public policy effectiveness.

Witness Chikoko is a Senior Lecturer in the Department of Social Work, University of Zimbabwe. He is currently a Research Fellow with University of Johannesburg's Department of Social Work in South Africa. He holds a D.Phil. in Social Studies, a Master's in Social Work, a Postgraduate Diploma in Project Planning and Management, and a Bachelor degree (Honours) in Social Work, all from the University of Zimbabwe. His research interests are childhood studies and social protection.

Joseph Chita is a Lecturer in the Department of Religious Studies at the University of Zambia. His research interests are in religion and society, and some of his publications cut across disciplines. He is a member of the African Association for the Study of Religions (AASR), and the Association for the Study of Religion in Southern Africa (ASRSA).

Mutsawashe Chitando is a Ph.D. candidate in the Public Health and Health Economics Unit and Division, School of Public Health and Family Medicine, Faculty of Health Sciences, University of Cape Town, South Africa.

Ezra Chitando serves as Professor in Religious Studies at the University of Zimbabwe and has served as the Desmond Tutu Extraordinary Professor for Social Justice at the University of Western Cape, South Africa. He has a wide range of research and publication interests, including violence against women, political violence, and peace-building. He co-edited the volume *Justice Not Silence: Churches Facing Sexual and Gender-Based Violence*.

Sampson Danso is a Political Science Lecturer with the Department of Distance Education, University of Ghana, Legon and a Ph.D. candidate at the University of South Africa. His research areas are inter-party dialogue, voting patterns, and elections in Ghana.

Emmanul Debrah is Associate Professor in the Department of Political Science, He has published extensively in the areas of party politics, elections and democratic development.

Elijah Doro is an environmental historian and Research Fellow at Agder University in Norway. He has written on the environmental history of tobacco farming in Zimbabwe. His interests are histories of pollution and contamination in southern Africa and medical histories.

Simbarashe Gukurume is a social scientist whose work lies at the intersection of Sociology and Social Anthropology. Currently serving as a Senior Lecturer at Sol Plaatje University, he also holds a research associate position at Stellenbosch University within the Department of Sociology and Social Anthropology. Simbarashe's research interests revolve around the overarching theme of youth subjectivities and their intricate connections with various aspects of everyday life, including politics, livelihoods, and transitions. His scholarly pursuits delve into the realms of informality, religiosity, displacement, and the political expressions of youth in the midst of enduring economic and political crises. Simbarashe is a former awardee of the African Peacebuilding Network Research Fellowship (2021–2022) and the African

Humanities Programme Fellowship awarded by the American Learned Societies and the Carnegie Corporation in New York, USA.

Rabson Hove is a Practical Theologian. He holds a Ph.D. in Ministerial Studies from the University of KwaZulu Natal. He is a Post-Doctoral Fellow in the Research Institute for Theology and Religion (RITR) at University of South Africa (UNISA). Dr. Hove is also an ordained minister and chaplain of the Evangelical Lutheran Church in Zimbabwe (ELCZ), Diaspora His research interests include ecumenism, pastoral care, and community development.

Stacey Hynd gained her D.Phil. in History from the University of Oxford in 2008. She lectured at the University of Cambridge and is now Senior Lecturer in African History and Co-Director of the Centre for Imperial and Global History at Exeter. Her previous research has focused on crime, violence, the death penalty, and gender in colonial Africa, with a focus on Malawi, Kenya, and Ghana. Her current research is on the histories of child soldiering and humanitarianism in Africa.

Rachel Ibreck is a Senior Lecturer in Politics and International Relations at Goldsmiths, University of London. Her research interests include human rights and legal activism in atrocity, conflict, and displacement settings in Africa. She has published in academic journals including the *Journal of Intervention and Statebuilding*, the *Journal of Civil Society*, and *African Affairs*. She is author of *South Sudan's Injustice System: Law and Activism on the Frontline* (Zed Books, 2019). She is co-investigator on the Fondazione Compagnia di San Paulo research project: *Traces of Mobility, Violence and Solidarity: Reconceptualizing Cultural Heritage Through the Lens of Migration*.

Veronica Nonhlanhla Jakarasi is a Chartered Development Finance Analyst and the Head of Climate Finance at the Africa Enterprise Challenge Fund. She leads climate finance resources mobilization to support small and growing businesses to respond to climate change challenges and accelerate the deployment of climate-smart technologies to rural, marginalized, and vulnerable communities. She also supports SMEs to develop and implement climate-smart investment plans and prioritize climate actions. Veronica has over 15 years of experience in climate finance and diplomacy, and environment and natural resources management, having led the establishment of the Climate Change Management Department in 2014, and served as the Manager for Climate Finance and Sustainability at the Infrastructure Development Bank in Zimbabwe (IDBZ). She supports the African Group of Lead Negotiators on Mitigation issues and the Group of 77 and China on Gender and Climate

Change Issues under the UNFCCC process. She has authored different academic papers and book chapters, including on climate finance, gender, and disaster management. Veronica serves on different national and regional boards and is currently the Board Chair of the Forestry Commission in Zimbabwe.

Yasmin M. Khodary is Professor of Political Science at the British University in Egypt. She has been working in the development field for the past 15 years. She is the winner of the Abdelhameed Shoman Prize for Arab Researchers and the Ahmed Bahaa-eldin Research Award for Young Authors. She also won the UNDP Project-Award on Corruption Risks in Health and Education, the UNDP Project-Award on Youth Engagement, the UNDP Project-Award on Fighting Corruption and the BUE Young Investigators' Project-Award on Gender in Peacebuilding. Her fields of interest include governance, social accountability, corruption, gender and peacebuilding. Her key publications include: "Middle Eastern Women between Oppression and Resistance" in the *Journal of International Women's Studies;* "FGM in Egypt" in the *Journal of Aggression, Conflict and Peace Research;* "Assessing the Impact of Gender Equality and Empowerment in Matters of Inheritance in Egypt" in the *Journal of the Middle East and Africa;* and "Women and Peace Building in Iraq" in the *Journal of Peace Review.*

Susan M. Kilonzo is Associate Professor in the Department of Religion and Philosophy at Maseno University, Kenya. She is a research methodology specialist. She has held the Alexander Von Humboldt Research Fellowship in Germany. Her research and publication interests include religion and violence, gender, development, peacebuilding and method and theory.

Ridwan Abiola Kolawole teaches journalism and communication in the Department of Mass Communication, Fountain University, Osogbo, Nigeria. His research interest covers Applied Communication. He is a 2022–2023 Doctoral Dissertation Completion Fellow of the Next Generation of the Social Science Research Council (SSRC), New York. Kolawole is a Research Associate of the *Youth Aspirations and Resilience* project of the Partnership for African Social and Governance Research (PASGR), funded by the MasterCard Foundation.

Claire-Anne Lester is a Lecturer in Sociology in the Department of Sociology and Social Anthropology at Stellenbosch University, South Africa. Her research concentrates on state violence, commissions of inquiry investigating violence in the South African mining sector, critical legal theory, and political economy.

Tshenolo Jennifer Madigele (B.A., M.A. and Ph.D.) is a Theology Lecturer at the University of Botswana. Her teaching areas include practical theology and systematic theology. Her research interests include human sexuality, with a particular focus on the LGBTI (lesbian, gay, bisexual, transgendered and the intersexed) communities, gerontology, gender and community building, health and spirituality and both pastoral care and counselling. One of her publications is "Homes as 'Cages of Violence and Abuse for Women' During Covid-19 Pandemic: A Pastoral Care Approach to the Case of Botswana and South Africa" (Madigele and Baloyi 2022) which appeared in the journal *HTS Teologiese Studies/Theological Studies*.

Godfrey Maringira is Associate Professor of Anthropology at Sol Plaatje University, Kimberley, Northern Cape, South Africa. He is a National Research Foundation C2 rating. He is a senior Volkswagen Stiftung Foundation research fellow and is also a Principal Investigator of the International Development Research Center (IDRC) research on gang violence in South Africa. He is an active board member of the Social Sciences Research Council—Next Generation Social Sciences in Africa. His areas of research include armed violence in Africa with a specific focus on the military in post-colonial Africa. His 2017 *African Affairs* Journal article "Politicisation and Resistance in the Zimbabwe National Army", was awarded the Best Author Prize in 2018. In 2020 he was awarded the Benedict Vilakazi Best Author Prize, *African Studies Journal* (Routledge) for his article titled: "When Combatants Became Peaceful: Azania People Liberation Army Ex-Combatants in Post-Apartheid South Africa". He is the author of *Soldiers and the State in Zimbabwe*, Routledge, 2019.

Lindiwe Princess Maseko is a Ph.D. student in Gender and Religion in the School of Religion, Philosophy, and Classics, at the University of KwaZulu Natal in South Africa. Her areas of interest are reproductive health and rights, reproductive justice, and African women's identity.

Mandla Mfundo Masuku is an Associate Professor in the School of Built Environment and Development Studies at the University of KwaZulu-Natal. His research areas include inclusive education, food security, scholarship of teaching and learning, African studies, and gender.

Khabele Matlosa is a political economist and an independent policy analyst with speciality in democracy, elections, governance, conflict prevention, management and resolution, constitutionalism, human rights, migration, and socio-economic development. He has researched and written widely on these areas over the years. He possesses enormous experience working in multicultural settings with the United Nations (UN) and the African Union (AU). Through the AU, he has worked closely with Regional Economic Communities and Regional Mechanisms in Africa. He has access to networks of innovation, knowledge, practice, lobby, and advocacy cutting across various sectors in Africa including governments, civil society, private sector, political parties, media, faith-based organizations, academia and think tanks, women's groups, youth groups, and traditional governance institutions among others.

Chenai Matshaka is a researcher at the University of Pretoria, Centre for Mediation in Africa. She writes on transitional justice and women in mediation in Africa, as well as civil society and its role in peace processes in Africa. She has worked with diverse research institutions and Non-Governmental Organizations (NGOs) in South Africa and Zimbabwe on human rights and security, and transitional justice, as well as migration and refugee issues, all of which also form part of her research interests.

Jones Hamburu Mawerenga is a Lecturer in Systematic Theology, Christian Ethics, and African Theology at the University of Malawi. He holds a Ph.D. from Mzuzu University. He is the author of *The Homosexuality Debate in Malawi* (2018) and *Systematic Theology* (2019). His current research interest on the topic of discourses of albinism in Malawi was motivated by the desire to curb violent attacks and gross human rights violations against persons with albinism in the country.

Nyasha Mboti is the pioneer and founder of Apartheid Studies, a new interdisciplinary field of study from the Global South which utilizes the notion of "apartheid" as a paradigm by which to understand the confounding persistence and permanence of harm, oppression, and injustice. This account is articulated in *Apartheid Studies: A Manifesto* (Africa World Press, 2023). Mboti is an Associate Professor and Head of the Department of Communication Science at the University of the Free State, Bloemfontein, in South Africa. He lives in Johannesburg.

Ibrahim Kawuley Mika'il is a Senior Lecturer in the Department of International Relations, Institute for Transport Technology, Zaria, Kaduna State, Nigeria. He has published extensively on corruption, Nigerian political economy, and good governance. He is a leading advocate of the strategies of combating corruption in the Nigerian political system.

Victor H. Mlambo is a Lecturer at the University of Johannesburg, School of Public Management, Governance and Public Policy. Victor's research interests include conflict and migration studies, political geography, regionalism, and security studies.

Obert Bernard Mlambo is Associate Professor of Classical Studies and History, formerly based at the University of Zimbabwe, Zimbabwe. His research interests involve Roman History, Classics and Colonialism, Postcolonial Classics, and the issues of Violence, Gender, Politics, and Land in ancient Rome and Zimbabwe. Obert Mlambo now teaches Roman history in a global context at Rhodes University. He is a former Humboldt Fellow at the Institute of African Studies and Egyptology, University of Cologne, Germany, and a Guest Scholar at the Global South Studies Centre of the University of Cologne, Germany.

Daniel Nkosinathi Mlambo Ph.D., holds a Postgraduate Diploma in Teacher Education from the Haaga-Helia University of Applied Sciences School of Vocational Teacher Education (Finland), a Ph.D. and Master's degree in Public Administration, an Honours in International Relations, and a junior degree in Development Studies, all from the University of Zululand. His research focuses on African political economy, regional integration, governance and democracy, migration, and security studies.

Kudzanai Melody Mlambo is an independent scholar whose research interests include climate change, natural resources management, and food security studies.

Marlino Eugénio Mubai is Lecturer and Chair, Department of History, Eduardo Mondlane University, Mozambique. His research areas are warfare, environment, and society. He also explores various layers of politics, society, and culture including religion.

Martin Mujinga is the General Secretary of the Methodist Church in Zimbabwe and the General Secretary Elect of the Africa Methodist Council. He is also a Research Fellow of the Research Institute for Theology and Religion at the University of South Africa. Dr. Mujinga is an Adjunct Lecturer at the Midlands State University and United Theological College. His research interests are in the fields of Methodist history and theology,African spirituality, the role of religion in transforming societies, theologies of migration, women and religion, human trafficking, chaplaincy, African theology, liberation theology, political theology, Pentecostal theologies and ecotheology.

Ruth Murambadoro is an African feminist who writes on women, transitional justice, gender justice, and the politics of the Global South. Based at the Centre for Feminist Research, York University, her work explores the gendered nature of the post-colonial state to broaden understandings of violence perpetrated against women in Zimbabwe. She holds research affiliations with the Harriet Tubman Institute, and Wits School of Governance. Her long-term project involves working with emerging and seasoned African artists to build a digital repository (re)presenting African women's resistance in the postcolony.

Telesia Kathini Musili is a lecturer at the Department of Philosophy and Religious Studies, University of Nairobi, Kenya. She is also a research fellow at the University of South Africa. Her research interests revolve around the intersection of religion, ethics, media, and environment, focusing on the response to contemporary issues affecting women and society at large.

Amos Muyambo is a Theologian Educator and Researcher, currently affiliated to the University of Botswana in the Department of Student Welfare in the Disability Support Services. Research interests are African spirituality, gender disability. and religion and development.

Nelly Mwale (Ph.D.) is a Senior Lecturer in the Department of Religious Studies at the University of Zambia. Her research interests include religion in the public sphere, religion and higher education, church history, and African indigenous knowledge systems.

Wesley Mwatwara is Assistant Professor in Global Economic and Social History at Vrije University Amsterdam and a research associate at Walter Sisulu University. His areas of research include socio-environmental history, animal history, sustainability, and peace and conflict studies. His articles appear in journals such as the *South African Historical Journal*, *Journal of Southern African Studies*, *Kronos*, *Historia*, *Global Environments*, *Environment and History*.

Gibson Ncube lectures at Stellenbosch University. He has held fellowships supported by the Stellenbosch Institute for Advanced Study, the National Humanities Center (USA), and Leeds University Centre for African Studies (UK). He has published widely in the fields of comparative literature, gender, and queer studies, as well as cultural studies. He co-convened the Queer African Studies Association (2020–2022) and was the 2021 Mary Kingsley Zochonis Distinguished Lecturer (African Studies Association, UK). He currently sits on the editorial boards of the following journals: *Journal of Literary Studies*, the *Canadian Journal of African Studies*, the *Nordic Journal of African Studies* as well as *Imbizo: International Journal of African Literary* *and Comparative Studies*. He holds a C1 NRF rating. He is the author of the book *Queer Bodies in African Films* (2022).

Patricia Pinky Ndlovu is a Doctoral Fellow at the Chair of Sociology of Africa at the University of Bayreuth in Germany and her doctoral study is on violence and gender in the taxi industry in South Africa.

Sabelo J. Ndlovu-Gatsheni is Professor and Chair of Epistemologies of the Global South with Emphasis on Africa, as well as Vice-Dean of Research in the "Africa Multiple Cluster of Excellence" at the University of Bayreuth in Germany. He has published extensively on epistemic violence in Africa and is a leading advocate of decolonization.

Evarist Ngabirano is a Senior Lecturer and Dean of the Faculty of Humanities and Social Sciences at Mountains of the Moon University, Fort Portal, Uganda. He holds a PhD in Social Studies from Makerere University. He received the SSRC—Next Generation Social Sciences in Africa programme fellowship. His research interests focus on issues of nationalism, culture, politics, and religion.

Arinze Ngwube is a Lecturer in the Department of Political Science of Federal University, Oye-Ekiti State, Nigeria. He has contributed articles and book chapters on international affairs.

Susan Monyangi Nyabena is a Masters' student at the University of Nairobi. Her key research interests are sexual and reproductive health rights, gender equality, and transformative masculinities. She is a gender and human rights consultant at Gender Ink.

Vellim Nyama is a Development Practitioner who holds a Ph.D. in Human Geography from the University of the Free State in South Africa (SA). He has worked for a number of development organizations in Zimbabwe and Africa. His research interests focus on governance, participatory democracy, and peace building. He has published on the local governance process in Zimbabwe.

Oliver Nyambi is Associate Professor of English literature and cultural studies in the Department of English, University of the Free State in South Africa. His research focuses on crisis literatures, visual cultures of the Zimbabwean crisis, onomastics, indigenous environmentalisms, and political discourse. His latest books are *Cultures of Change in Contemporary Zimbabwe* (2021), co-edited with Tendai Mangena and Gibson Ncube, *The Zimbabwean Crisis after Mugabe* (2021), co-edited with Tendai Mangena and Gibson Ncube, and a sole-authored monograph *Life-Writing from the Margins in Zimbabwe:*

Versions and Subversions of Crisis (2019). His most recent book: *Contested Liberations and Transitions in Zimbabwe: (Counter)Cultures of Crisis Post-2000* is forthcoming with Brill.

Mary Nyasimi is a renowned scientific expert in the field of gender equality, social inclusion and climate change. Dr. Nyasimi holds a Ph.D. in Sustainability Agriculture and Ecological Anthropology from Iowa State University. With over 15 years of experience in the research and development, Mary has been actively working towards promoting policies and systems that support gender equality, social inclusion and climate change adaptation and mitigation in Africa. Her extensive knowledge and expertise make her a sought-after consultant, and she has worked with various national and international organizations. Through her work, Mary continues to be a staunch advocate for marginalized communities, particularly women, girls, youth, people with disability and indigenous people ensuring their voices are heard, and decisions impacting their lives are made with their participate and engagement.

Sonene Nyawo is a Senior Lecturer in the Department of Theology and Religious Studies at the University of Eswatini. She has published widely in the following areas of her research interests: new religious movements in Africa, traditional ritualization, women's fertility, climate change, religion and gender, and women and peacebuilding.

Jacinta Chiamaka Nwaka holds a Ph.D. in African History, from the University of Ibadan and is an Associate Professor of Peace History in the Department of History and International Studies, University of Benin, Benin City, Nigeria. She was an IDRC/UPEACE doctoral fellow (2008–2010). Dr. Nwaka was also a Post-Doctoral Fellow of the American Council of Learned Societies (ACLS) under its African Humanities Programme (AHP), and a 2016 recipient of IRG of Social Science Research Council New York under the African Peacebuilding Network (APN). She recently won the African Guest Researcher's visiting scholarship at the Nordic African Institute Uppsala Sweden. Her research interests are peace history with a focus on the intersections of religion and peace/conflict, humanitarian interventions, and women's studies.

Ayokunmi Ojebode is a Lecturer at SOAS, University of London, and a Fellow at the Institute for Name-Studies (INS), School of English, University of Nottingham, England. His areas of expertise are African literature, Cultural Studies, Health Humanities, and Literary Onomastics. He co-authored "Name as National Archive: Capturing of Yoruba Masculinist

Names in Tunde Kelani's Saworoide" in *The Cinema of Tunde Kelani: Aesthetics, Theatricalities and Visual Performance, Cambridge Scholars*, 2021.

Babatunde Raphael Ojebuyi is a Senior Faculty Member in the Department of Communication and Language Arts, University of Ibadan, where he teaches journalism, media ethics, digital media, and language use. His research focuses on these areas. Ojebuyi is the Principal Investigator of the *Youth Aspirations and Resilience* project of the Partnership for African Social and Governance Research (PASGR), funded by the MasterCard Foundation.

Maurice Omollo holds a Ph.D. from Kenyatta University, Kenya. He is a lecturer at the Department of Environmental Studies, Geography and Agriculture of Maasai Mara University in Kenya. Previously he taught at Kenyatta University in the Department of Geography for seven years. He is a settlement geographer with special interest in urban studies, with focus on informal settlement, and on issues including environmental, economic, and social welfare. The informality of the settlements provides an avenue towards understanding poor people's circumstances and struggles since the majority of the urban poor reside in these structures. Dr Omollo has written on the slum area of Mathare Valley of Nairobi, Kenya, touching on coping strategies relating to diverse issues that work against the residents. Currently he is involved in a study on entrepreneurial masculinity in the informal settlements of Nairobi City of Kenya.

Isaac Owusu-Mensah is a Senior Lecturer at the Department of Political Science, University of Ghana. He has extensive publications on various spheres of Ghanaian democracy.

Pedzisai Ruhanya is a lecturer at the Department of Creative Media and Communication at the University of Zimbabwe. He is also a founder and director at the Zimbabwe Democracy Institute. He holds a Ph.D. in Media and Democracy from the University of Westminster in London. He is a former Post-Doctoral Research Fellow with the University of Johannesburg's School of Media and Communication. He has more than 20 publications in peer-reviewed journals, book chapters and two co-edited books. His research interest is in the role of the media in political transitions.

Usman Sambo is a Senior Lecturer in the Department of Public Administration, Yobe State University Damaturu, Nigeria. He has published extensively on Nigerian governance, politics and administration in both local and international reputable journals and book publishers. He is a leading advocate of good governance and peacebuilding in Northeast Nigeria.

Thabile Anita Samboma is a Research Fellow under the Governance and Administration Unit at Botswana Institute for Development Policy Analysis (BIDPA). Her research interests are in policy analysis, gender, children's rights, disability, and education. She has authored several journals and a book chapter.

Nomatter Sande holds a Ph.D. in Religion and Social Transformation from the University of KwaZulu Natal (South Africa). Nomatter is a Practical Theologian. He is a Research Fellow at the Research Institute for Theology and Religion (RITR) in the College of Human Sciences, University of South Africa (UNISA). His research interests include disability studies, pentecostal theology, religious violence, peace, and gender.

Babayo Sule is a Senior Lecturer in the Department of International Relations, Federal University of Kashere Gombe State Nigeria. He has published extensively on the Nigerian electoral process, political parties, and party financing as well as conflict and peacebuilding in Nigeria and Africa. He is an advocate of peacebuilding in Northeast Nigeria, and transparent and violent-free election, as well as the liberation of Africa from neo-colonial chains.

Mohammed Kwarah Tal is a Lecturer in the Department of Political Science, Federal University of Kashere, Gombe State, Nigeria. He has published on political behaviour and voting culture in the Nigerian democratic process. He is an advocate of good governance and electoral integrity and transparency.

James Tsabora is a Senior Lecturer in Law in the Faculty of Law at the University of Zimbabwe, and senior research consultant in human rights and democratic governance, constitutionalism, rule of law, and natural resource governance.

Solomon Waliaula holds a Ph.D. in literature from Moi University, Kenya and is an Associate Professor in Literature and Cultural Studies at Maasai Mara University in Kenya. He is currently a Research Fellow at the Department of Anthropology and African Studies at Johannes Gutenberg University of Mainz, as well as Research Associate at University of the Witwatersrand, Department of African Literature. His research interests are in popular culture and cultural studies.

Souhayel Weslety is based in Sociology at the Université Tunis Carthage. He is a researcher in Migration and Political Science and a university instructor holding the Cambridge Delta. He is involved in a number of research programmes including the Fondazione Compagnia di San Paulo—funded research project *Traces of Mobility, Violence and Solidarity, Tunisian Democracy Lab* with the Friedrich Ebert Foundation and a first-of-its-kind study programme within the *Migrants* project.

List of Figures

Geographies of Violence and Informalization: The Case of Mathare Slums in Nairobi, Kenya

Fig. 1　The Slum Villages of Mathare Valley in Nairobi, Kenya (*Source* Extracted and modified from Data Exchange Platform for Horn of Africa [DEPHA, 2008])　205

Preventing Electoral Violence in Africa: Towards Sustainable Peace

Fig. 1　Electoral cycle　296
Fig. 2　Homicide rate by continent, 2017 (*Source* UNIDOC [2019: 11])　300

Ungoverned Space and National Security in Nigeria

Fig. 1　Nigeria's security threats (*Source* Armed Conflict Location and Event Project 2021)　399

Youth, Proliferation of Small Arms and Light Weapons, and Conflicts in 21st Century Africa

Fig. 1　Youth population increase in Africa (*Source* Sow, Brookings 2018)　483
Fig. 2　Total value of global arms trade in USD in 2018 2019 (*Source* SIPRI)　485
Fig. 3　Flow of weapons in the Sahel 2011–2017 (*Source* DW, 2019)　487

Violence against Women in Egypt: A Closer Look at Intimate Partner Violence and Female Genital Mutilation

Fig. 1	The social characteristics of the sample (education)	801
Fig. 2	Sample distribution by age group	801

"Women's Sexuality Captured": Another Form of Gender-Based Violence (GBV) in the Swati Patriarchal Space

Fig. 1	Reported abuse based on type form 2014–2018	896

Adolescent Boys, Young Men, and Mental Health in Southern Africa

Fig. 1	Social ecological model adapted to mental health in Africa (*Source* Davids et al. [2019])	935

List of Tables

Preventing Electoral Violence in Africa: Towards Sustainable Peace

Table 1	Pre-voting phase	297
Table 2	Voting phase	297
Table 3	Post-voting phase	298
Table 4	Public trust in institutions in Africa	299

In God's Name: Violent Extremism in North East Nigeria

Table 1	Poverty index of Nigeria (CBN, 2006)	589

Violence against Women in Egypt: A Closer Look at Intimate Partner Violence and Female Genital Mutilation

Table 1	The actual distribution of inhabitants in Qalyoubia and Minia	800
Table 2	The sample distribution according to gender and urban/rural division	801
Table 3	IPV by gender	804
Table 4	FGM by gender	805
Table 5	IPV by residence	806
Table 6	FGM by residence	806
Table 7	IPV by wealth	808
Table 8	FGM by wealth	809
Table 9	IPV by education	810
Table 10	FGM by education	812

Table 11	The consequences of the January uprisings by gender and residence	813
Table 12	The consequences of the 25 January uprisings by wealth	813
Table 13	The consequences of the 25 January uprisings by education	814

"Wait, Let's Talk About It": A Feminist Assessment of the Response of the Church of the Cross Hayfield (NELCSA) to Gender-Based Violence in Pietermaritzburg, South Africa

| Table 1 | A comparison of the degree of gender-based violence affecting women and men | 840 |

Managing Conflict in Africa: Challenges and Opportunities for the African Union

| Table 1 | Patterns of Conflict in Africa since 1975 | 1058 |

Violent Piracy off the Coast of Nigeria: A Theoretical Analysis

| Table 1 | Actual and attempted piracy attacks, 1 January 2019–31 December 2022 | 1089 |
| Table 2 | Actual and attempted piracy incidents | 1090 |

Mediatized Conflict: A Case of Nigerian Media Reportage of Farmer-Herder Conflict

Table 1	Audience perception of parties being supported by the media in relation to rating of the reportage	1142
Table 2	Audience believability of media reportage and stakeholders held responsible	1143
Table 3	Audience victimhood by government's attitude and efforts towards resolving the conflict	1144
Table 4	Association between the rating of the reportage (partisan, unfair and fair) and media contribution to the escalation of the conflict	1144
Table 5	Percentage of the audience who believe in media contribution to the escalation of the percentile	1145

Gender and Violence in Africa

Sexual Violence Against Girls and Women in African Conflict

Veronica Fynn Bruey

1   Introduction

The continent of Africa has seen sustained elevation of both violent and low-grade conflicts since the mid-1950s, when Ghana was one of the first African countries to gain independence from colonial rule on 6 March 1957. Whether an increased level of conflict is an indicator of poor leadership, a study done by Yiew et al. suggests that good governance contributes to reduced armed conflict (Yiew et al., 2016: 3741). The violence associated with conflict compels people to leave their places of habitual residence. The entire process of forced movement is awash with vulnerabilities that expose girls and women to sexual violence and exploitation. A long-standing orthodoxy of classical migration theorists is that migration is mainly determined by economic and labour market forces, and, thus, people move to maximize their individual utility (Bean & Brown, 2015: 70; Borjas, 1989: 458). Neoclassical theorists extend individual risk and collective decision-making to the reasons why people migrate (Massey et al., 1993: 436). Myron Weiner argues that migrants are not just isolated individuals who react to economic stimuli but are also social beings who seek to achieve better outcomes for themselves, their families, and their communities by actively shaping forced migration patterns (Weiner, 1995: 21–29). Conflict in Africa is inextricably tied to forced migration. It is this very act of being compelled to leave one's

V. F. Bruey (✉)
Athabasca University, Athabasca, AB, Canada
e-mail: vfynnbruey@athabascau.ca

habitual place of residence that inherently creates dangerous journeys. The fatality associated with mass movement predisposes girls and women to all sorts of vulnerabilities with sexual violence being the most common attack (V. P. Fynn, 2011: 30–32).

Scholars have pointed to the legacy of colonialism as the impetus for conflicts in Africa. Some blames the proliferation of stockpiling light weapons which has fallen into the hands of emerging violent nonstate groups through the porous borders of Mali, Niger, Algeria, and Tunisia (for example) (Method, 2018; Staff Reporter, 2018). While others argue that it is the curse, rather than the blessing, of natural resources—particularly oil—that gravitate Africans toward conflict and violence (Bekele, 2017). Nonetheless, the practice of colonialism is undeniably chronic, persistent, and violent (Chinweizu, 1987; wa Thiong'o, 1986: 9), encumbered with poverty, political, social, and economic inequalities (Stewart, 2002: 342). Here, V. Y. Mudimbe's and Olufemi Taiwo's definitions of colonialism are paraphrased as a complex process of organizing and transforming African territories into European constructs where those settling (the colonists) exploit the region by dominating the local majority (Mudimbe, 1988: 14; Taiwo, 2010: 34–35). Whether as a civilizing or Christianizing mission, (Achebe, 1959: 49; Gray, 1982: 59; Nunn, 2010: 147) an ethical science/medicine project, (Fanon & Chevalier, 1965: 121–126) a land dispossession operation (Rugege, 2004: 283), an imposition of political power (Mamdani, 2001a), or vast economic control over African territories (Rodney, 1972), the repercussion of colonialism arrested Africa's growth by "spread[ing conflicts] into the new sovereign multi-ethnic states" (Bariagaber, 2016: 16–17).

The legacy of colonization as a "divide and conquer" apparatus is directly entwined with the occurrence of conflicts in Africa. For instance, the genocide in Rwanda, hinged on Belgian colonists' division of the Hutus from Tutsi based on physical appearance (Aremu, 2010: 551; Pumphrey & Schwartz-Barcott, 2003: 23). This subjugation that is rooted in the belly of colonialism, necessitated the germination and intensity of violent conflict/warfare throughout the decolonization period. Here decolonization literally means the independence of African states from colonial rule. Newly independent states in Africa, even after more than six decades, epitomize neocolonial architecture: dictatorship, one-party state, oligarchy, and military rule sprinkled with repressive regimes, nepotism, and elitism—an adulterated leadership scheme, mainly perpetrated by men (Fynn, 2011: 32). As Frantz Fanon aptly reasoned, "decolonization is always a violent phenomenon" (Fanon, 1963: 35). To the extent that men are involved and dominate the decolonization regime via conflict and armed struggle, girls and women remain violated physically, emotionally, and sexually (Fynn Bruey, 2016: 100–168).

During the colonial era across Africa, the colonialists fused traditional ethnic boundaries and amalgamated language groups that were once considered rivals, which partly fostered bickering that spun into violent conflicts (Bulcha, 1988: 19–21). Prior to, and 25 years immediately after, the first African country gaining its independence from colonial British rule, some 40 conflicts of varying magnitudes were recorded (Marshall, 2006: 41–42). For example, between 1955 and 1984, some 101 (attempted) coups, internal conflicts, and full-blown wars occurred across the continent (Fynn, 2011: 192). Violent interstate conflicts gradually declined to 21 conflicts from 1976 to 1984 (Marshall, 2006: 42–43), in other words, towards the end of the Cold War. This downward trend in conflict only lasted for a brief moment (World Bank Group & United Nations, 2018: 15). The 1990s saw a heightened conflict level in Africa, peaking at 23 by the end of 1989 (Marshall, 2006: 43). A similar trend continued throughout the first ten years of the twenty-first century with violent conflicts as low as seven, recorded in 2005 (Gleditsch et al., 2002: 621–624; Pettersson & Wallensteen, 2015: 539; Raleigh & Moody, 2017: 2) to a substantial upturn with as many as 21 conflicts in 2018—"the highest number of civil conflicts since 1946" (Bakken & Rustad, 2018: 1; Rustad & Bakken, 2019: 2).

Violent conflict in Africa increased exponentially after the supposed "decolonization" period. Having endured the trans-Atlantic slave trade for over 400 years (1430s–1833), the Berlin Conference of 1844 ushered the continent into another 70+ years of repressive colonial regimes leading to a constant rise in violent conflicts and civil wars. Even 57 years after the founding of the Organization of African Unity (now the African Union), the continent is still ravaged with violent conflicts with 11 of the 15 world's most fragile states in Africa (Rosenthal, 2021).

The following examples are illustrative, contextual, and instructive. The First Civil War in Sudan from 1955–1972 attests to the fact that the reasons behind racial, ethnic, cultural, and religious conflicts are centuries old, occurring long before postcolonial violence (Poggo, 2011: 14–15). Six years after independence from Britain, Nigeria experienced its first coup d'état on 15 January 1966—the origin of the Biafra War (Achebe, 2012: 58–60; Forsyth, 2015: 1–35; Moses & Heerten, 2018: 3–43; Venter, 2016: 40–41, 44). Other postcolonial conflicts include (but are not limited to): Uganda ethnic warfare during Idi Amin's regime, 1971–1978; (Mamdani, 1983: 35–41; Nyombi & Kaddu, 2015: 6–7, 17–20) the Ethiopia-Eritrea war, 1974–1991 (Gebru Tareke, 2009: 56–65); the Mauritania-Morocco colonial war over Sahrawi Arab Democratic Republic, though ongoing, intensified 1975–1981 (Fynn, 2011: 5); the Angola civil war involvng the National Union for the Total Independence of Angola (UNITA), Cabinda, and the Front for the Liberation of the Enclave of Cabinda (FLEC), 1975–2006 (James III, 2011: 1, 41; Koloma Beck, 2012: 21–23); the Mozambique Civil War with RENAMO, 1981–1992 (Cabrita, 2000: 127–212; Isaacman & Isaacman, 1983: 79–108) the Sudan ethnic war, 1983–2002 (Deng, 1995: 9–32, 135–184; Jok, 2001: 21); Liberia's civil war, 1989–2003 (Ellis, 2007: 31–74); Sierra Leone's civil-ethnic conflict between the RUF and the Mende, 1991–2001 (Kaifala, 2017: 185–212); and Burundi/Rwanda, ethnic violence—Hutus target Tutsis, 1994–1998 (Mamdani, 2001b: 76, 185; Mwakikagile, 2013: 27).

Although some of the deadliest conflicts in Africa (e.g., in Liberia, Sierra Leone, Rwanda, Burundi, and La ô d'Ivoire, to name a few) have ended, a number of violent conflicts and warfare still linger across the continent. For example, the Lord's Resistance Army in Uganda is responsible for many children born of conflict-related violence (Denov & Lakor, 2019: 211). The "Great Africa War" in the Democratic Republic of Congo (DRC) has not only resulted in over five million lives lost, but "whenever there is fighting there is systematic rape in villages" (Masisi, 2018). Ongoing insurgency attacks in politically fragile Somalia over the past eight years enable conflict-related sexual violence and trafficking for exploitation to flourish and persist. With the crises in Somalia reported as the most active conflict followed by Nigeria, South Sudan, and Libya, and, more recently, internal conflicts in Zimbabwe (Fitiwi, 2018: 1–13), Kenya (Mueller-Hirth, 2019: 163–165), Chad (Al Jazeera News, 2019a; Boutellis, 2013), the Central African Republic (Carayannis & Lombard, 2015: 3; Check, 2014; Lombard, 2016: 14; Murray & Sullivan, 2019; Ochab, 2018), Guinea Bissau (International Crisis Group, 2012: 3; Odigie, 2019: 1–19), The Gambia (Hartmann, 2017: 85–99), Mali (Benjaminsen & Ba, 2019: 1–20; Boeke & de Valk, 2019: 1–20) Cameron (Chothia, 2018; International Crisis Group, 2018; Kuwonu, 2018a), and Niger (Save the Children, 2013: v; Simić, 2009: 395; United Nations High Commissioner for Refugees & Save the Children UK, 2002: 2) are sweltering. As stated earlier, this long list of persistent and protracted conflicts in Africa is not only strongly correlated with the mass movement of people, but it is also directly proportional to the entrenched gross sexual violence against girls and women.

This chapter adopts a discursive approach to examining sexual violence in African conflict. Since sexual violence in African conflict has multiple meanings and diverse conceptual interpretations, utilizing a discursive approach is important to subjectively analyse and explain the myriad viewpoints on the topic. Starting with an introduction, the chapter highlights the historical backdrop of colonization as a nexus to relatively high occurrence of conflict across the continent. A definition of key terms incorporates a literature review, elaborating on conceptual and theoretical frameworks to explain the reasoning behind the persistent, chronic, and widespread conflict in African and sexual violence in African conflict. Next, the prevalence, cause, and impact of sexual violence in African conflict is discussed. A select few synopses are cited to contextualize the enormity and severity of sexual violence, the chapter argues that girls and women are disproportionately affected by sexual violence in conflict. The chapter then concludes by underscoring some best practices as a way forward in the response to, and prevention of, sexual violence against girls and women in African conflict.

2 Key Terms Explained

For the purposes of this chapter, conflict is defined as "a particular relationship between states or rival factions within a state which implies subjective hostilities or tension manifested in subjective economic or military hostilities (Ajayi & Buhari, 2014: 140). The phrase "African conflict" or "conflicts in Africa" is operationalized in this chapter to denote the complex, collective, and diverse forms of conflicts in Africa. Inherently uncontrollable and unsolvable, violence, whether sexual or physical, is an immanent risk in conflict (Aremu, 2010: 551; Bujra, 2002: 2–5). Conflict in Africa is a complex variation (Aall, 2015: 1; Mekonnen Mengistu, 2015: 29–30) including, but not limited to, the following: (1) conventional warfare (e.g., Ethiopia and Eritrea); (2) factional warfare (e.g., Liberia); (3) genocide, ethnic and religious violence (e.g., Nigeria); (4) coup d'état (e.g., Guinea Bissau, 1998); and (5) regional conflict involving insurgency/rebel groups (e.g., Boko Haram, Al-Shabaab, and the Lord's Resistance Army).

Boko Haram means "Westernization is Sacrilege" in Hausa, Jamāʿat Ahl al-Sunnah li-l-Daʿawah wa al-Jihād in Arabic (which means "People committed to the Prophet's Teaching for propagation and Jihad"), or Islamic State's West African Province was founded by Muhammed Yusuf in north-eastern Nigeria. Since its founding in 2002, the Islamic State of West Africa has displaced nearly 2.4 million people, killed thousands, and abducted, raped, and forcibly married hundreds of schoolgirls in the impoverished region of Lake Chad covering areas of Cameroon, Chad, Niger, and Nigeria (Amnesty

International, 2021: 269; Check, 2014: 3–4; Prieto Curiel et al., 2020: 1–3; Solomon, 2014: 1–7). Affiliated with Al Qaeda, the Somalian-based Al Shabaab (which means "The Youth" in Arabic) was formed in 2006 with a primary goal of overthrowing the Somalia government (Mapping Militant Organizations, 2019: 3).

Since 2010, Al Shabaab attacks, especially against civilians, Somalia government targets, diplomats, and aid workers in Somalia, Kenya, Uganda, and Djibouti have resulted in at least 4,500 deaths, and the abduction and forced marriages of many schoolgirls and young women (Hansen, 2014: 73–102; 39–66; Maruf & Joseph, 2018: 1–66; Singh et al., 2022: 2; Solomon, 2015: 39–66). Led by Joseph Kony, the Lord's Resistance Army (LRA) was created in 1987 following the downfall of Alice Lakwena's Holy Spirit Army in neighbouring Uganda.[1] While the Lord's Resistance Army maintains strong ties in Uganda, its activities now extend to South Sudan, the eastern Democratic Republic of Congo, and Central African Republic (Ahere & Maina, 2013: 1–11; Allen & Vlassenroot, 2010: ix; Eichstaedt, 2009: xvii–xx).

The Lord's Resistance Army is notorious for abducting nearly 100,000 youths and children to abuse them as child soldiers, porters, and sex slaves. The stories of Richard and Evelyn Amony personalize such hideous war crimes against humanity. Richard, a 17-year-old child soldier of the LRA, was commanded to use the blunt end of an axe to crush the skulls of his parents as they lay on the ground with their hands tied (Eichstaedt, 2009: 1). In her book, Evelyn Amony recounts her ordeal of being abducted by the LRA when she was 11 years old, where she spent more than a decade training as a fighter, becoming Kony's wife at 14, and mothering three of his children (Amony & Baines, 2015: 20–21). These personal stories and regional conflicts, termed Africa's "New War" (Ellis, 2003: 29–30; Kaldor, 2013: 1–3),[2] continue to pose grave challenges to the continent's peace and security, especially for girls and women.

Article 1 of the Convention on the Elimination of All Forms of Discrimination against Women (CEDAW), 1979 defines "discrimination against women" as:

---

[1] Based in Acholi-speaking region of northern Uganda, the goal of Lakwena's Holy Spirit Movement, was to oust Yoweri Museveni's National Resistance Movement. Though successful in gaining support from the Acholi people, the Holy Spirit Movement was defeated by Museveni's National Resistance Army in 1988.

[2] According to Stephen Ellis, Africa's so-called "new wars" in a perceptual diversion from post-modern/post-independence degenerate war towards a more recent eruption of unofficial militarised/guerilla/ethnic warfare occurring after the cold war era.

any distinction, exclusion or restriction made on the basis of sex which has the effect or purpose of impairing or nullifying the recognition, enjoyment or exercise by women, irrespective of their marital status, on a basis of equality of men and women, of human rights and fundamental freedoms in the political, economic, social, cultural, civil or any other field.

Gender-based violence (GBV) is an umbrella term for any harmful act that is perpetrated against a person's will and that is based on socially ascribed (i.e., gender) differences between males and females. The term is primarily used to accentuate the structural, cultural, and institutional gender-based power differentials between males and females, which place females at risk for multiple forms of violence (Fynn Bruey, 2016: 28).

Article 1 of the United Nations Declaration on the Elimination of Violence Against Women (DEVAW), 1993 defines violence against women (VAW) as

any act of gender-based violence that results in, or is likely to result in, physical, sexual or psychological harm or suffering to women, including threats of such acts, coercion or arbitrary deprivation of liberty, whether occurring in public or in private life. (Inter-Agency Standing Committee, 2015: 322)

The DEVAW's definition of violence against women includes sexual and gender-based violence, and constitutes state or institutional, structural, or cultural, and community or interpersonal infliction of harm against girls and women (whether by commission or omission) (Fynn Bruey, 2016: 28).

Child sexual abuse is generally used to refer to any sexual activity between a child and closely related family member (incest) or between a child and an adult or older child from outside the family. It involves either explicit force or coercion or, in cases where consent cannot be given by the victim because of his or her young age, implied force. Sexual Exploitation and Abuse (SEA) is a common acronym in the humanitarian world referring to acts of sexual exploitation and sexual abuse committed by United Nations, NGOs (non-governmental organization), and inter-governmental organizations (IGOs) peacekeepers and personnel, mainly against women and adolescent females (Inter-Agency Standing Committee, 2015: 322). Claiming its commitment to zero tolerance for sexual exploitation and abuse, the United Nations defines sexual exploitation as:

the actual or attempted abuse of a position of vulnerability, differential power, or trust, for sexual purposes, including, but not limited to, profiting monetarily, socially or politically from the sexual exploitation of another," and sexual abuse as "the actual or threatened physical intrusion of a sexual nature, whether by force or under unequal or coercive conditions. (Nordås & Rustad, 2013: 512; United Nations Secretary General, 2003, sec. 1)

Sexual and gender-based violence (SGBV): The United Nations High Commissioner for Refugee's SGBV Prevention and Response Training Package states that SGBV "refers to any act perpetrated against a person's will, based on gender norms and unequal power relationships. It encompasses threats of violence and coercion. It inflicts harm on women, girls, men and boys" (United Nations High Commissioner for Refugees, 2016: 15). There are different perspectives regarding what constitutes or should be counted as sexual violence, SGBV or VAW in African conflicts. The legal definition of sexual violence may be different from the survivor viewpoint or feminist understanding. The Office of the United Nations High Commissioner for Human Rights (OHCHR) defines sexual violence as:

> a form of gender-based violence and encompasses any sexual act, attempt to obtain a sexual act, unwanted sexual comments or advances, or acts to traffic, or otherwise directed against a person's sexuality using coercion, by any person regardless of their relationship to the victim, in any setting. Sexual violence takes multiple forms and includes rape, sexual abuse, forced pregnancy, forced sterilization, forced abortion, forced prostitution, trafficking, sexual enslavement, forced circumcision, castration and forced nudity.

The World Health Organization suggests that the term sexual and other forms of gender-based violence comprise rape, attempted rape, sexual abuse, sexual exploitation, early forced marriage, domestic violence, marital rape, trafficking, and female genital mutilation (World Health Organization, 2019). The Inter-Agency Standing Committee defines sexual violence as:

> any sexual act, attempt to obtain a sexual act, unwanted sexual comments or advances, or acts to traffic a person's sexuality, using coercion, threats of harm or physical force, by any person regardless or relationship to the victim, in any setting, including but not limited to home and work.

Sexual violence takes many forms, including rape, sexual slavery and/or trafficking, forced pregnancy, sexual harassment, sexual exploitation and/or abuse, and forced abortion (Inter-Agency Standing Committee, 2015: 322). Sexual and gender-based violence in conflict can also take the form of sexual slavery, sexual harassment, femicide, and harmful traditional practices (Mohammed, 2018: 5).

Without denying the existence of sexual violence against boys and men, sexual violence in this chapter is focused on all forms of sexual violence against girls and women committed by individuals and members of armed groups, peacekeepers, and personnel of the United Nations, NGOs, and IGOs during the conduct of war in continental Africa. Such violence includes, but is not limited to, rape, attempted rape, forced nudity, sexual mutilation, sexual slavery, forced prostitution, transactional sex, forced marriage, and forced abortion (Meger, 2010: 103). Conflict-related sexual violence refers to incidents of rape, sexual slavery, forced prostitution, forced pregnancy, enforced sterilization, or any other form of sexual violence of comparable gravity, against women, men, girls or boys in conflict or post-conflict settings or other situations of concern (e.g., political strife) (Inter-Agency Standing Committee, 2015: 321). Sexual violence is not confined to the physical aspects of combat or battle. Targeted incidents of GBV against girls and women which could trigger violent conflict between warring factions and the community at large are also cause of rampant sexual violence. Occurrences of sexual violence tend to feed into the broader cycles of generalized violence by reinforcing the root causes of regional conflict (Thompson, 2013: 8).

Therefore, a legacy of sexual violence in conflict could carry over to peace time and may translate into a "normal state of affairs" within families and communities (Thompson, 2013). The continuation of sexual violence from peace time to during and after conflict underscores the persistent cycle of intergenerational trauma well beyond the active period conflict (Ghobarah et al., 2004: 869). Pursuant to CEDAW's definition of discrimination against women and since girls and women are mostly affected by sexual violence perpetrated by males, this chapter uses "sexual and gender-based violence" (SGBV) specifically and "violence against women (VAW)" generally to collectively describe violence targeted at females pre-, during and post-conflict situations in Africa. Sexual violence, sexual and gender-based violence and VAW are also used interchangeably throughout the chapter to refer to the widespread and indiscriminate forms of abuse, exploitation, and cruelty against girls and women in African conflict.

3 Theorizing Sexual Violence in African Conflict

Poverty is a nexus of conflict in Africa as it compounds the vulnerability to ethnic, religious and political insurgency especially when there are high rates of unemployment, unequal access to public good, opportunities and resources (Marks, 2016: 1). Africa is home to the world's largest arable landmass, second largest (the Nile) and longest rivers (the Congo) and contains the second largest tropical forest in the world, while containing 30% of all global mineral reserves, 8% of the world's stock of oil reserves, 7% of natural gas, and 70% of exported minerals (African Development Bank Group, 2016: 3). African countries whose economies rely on oil and other minerals are most likely at risk for violent conflict because exploitation of such rich resources can attract rogue international plunderers who support belligerent groups or corrupt leaders in Africa (Department for International Development, 2001: 13).

Although rich in natural resources, Africa is one of the poorest continents of the world, mainly due to corrupt leadership. And it is this chronically poor leadership that stimulates economic, social, and political inequality between groups, which eventually increases the prospect of conflict (Addison et al., 2002: 365; Aremu, 2010: 552; Department for International Development, 2001: 13) Aloa argues that "[t]he conflicts and political instability that have characterized the [the DRC]'s history cannot be separated from its abundant natural resources…as copper, diamonds, uranium, cobalt, silver, gold, etc., have all contributed to the conflict in the DRC" (Alao, 2007: 112). In Sierra Leone, "[d]iamonds… have been implicated in terrible wars and have compounded the corruption and misrule that have had such corrosive effects [on states]" (Alao, 2007: 112). Daniel Bekele asserts that, "[a]t the turn of the century, Angola's development indicators remained among the worst in the world, while $4.2bn in oil revenues illegally bypassed Angola's central bank and disappeared without explanation from 1997 to 2002" (Bekele, 2017). Undeniably, the extremely high demand for oil, especially from Western countries, features prominently in African conflict, which is encouraged by multinational corporations' exploitation of poor governance in African oil-producing states (Alao, 2007: 158).

Indisputably, conflict is widespread on the African continent, especially since independence from colonial rule started back in the mid-1950s. Decolonization is a fundamental element of political violence (either perpetrated by the colonized or the colonizers) and is tightly associated with the liberation and self-determination revolution and process (Fanon, 1963: 35). As a matter of fact, cathartic violence necessitates African freedom from the colonial system (Celucien, 2012: 1). As discussed above, violence in and of itself—a core characteristic of African conflict—is not limited to the African liberation movement. Instead, systematic violence functions at three levels: (1) institutional or state (e.g., slavery and genocide); (2) structural or cultural (e.g., polygyny and female genital cutting); and (3) interpersonal or community (rape and forced marriage) (Fynn Bruey, 2016: 102–104). An examination of these three interconnecting levels of systematic violence through the lens of case examples below promises to explicate the complex layers of violence with respect to the mechanism for justice, equality, and fairness.

To survive African conflict means to personally and collectively deal with its horrific impact of trauma to the body, psyche, and soul, in addition to the effects on quality of life as a result of communities' destruction (McKay & Mazurana, 2004: 33). Yet, as noted elsewhere, even after the conflict is over, girls and women are still required and expected to resume their traditional gender roles in spite of the abuse, violence, and trauma they are carrying (McKay & Mazurana, 2004: 15). In African conflict, the roles often demanded of girls and women by society are conflicting. On one hand, women are invited to participate in nation and community building. At the same time, the social construct of females as "mothers" subjects them to male intensified use of power and violence to "protect" them. Obviously, males' responsibility to "protect" girls and women in African conflict does not materialize, especially where public displays of physical and sexual violence, such as rape, occur. To some extent such societal expectation can also been seen as a weapon of war in terms of emasculating husbands, fathers, brothers, and sons by showing that they are not able to protect. Sexual acts, which disproportionately affect women, are sometimes committed in full view of family and community, thereby making girls and women unworthy of protection (El Jack, 2003: 11).

Indeed, sexual violence is a global scourge and certainly not endemic to conflicts in Africa. Yet, from North, South, East, West and Central Africa, girls and women continuously suffer sexual violence. For far too long sexual violence has been left unexposed and considered a natural or unavoidable aspect of war. However, sexual violence is not just a side effect of African conflict. Rather, in the time of peace, societal custom allows men to have access to women's bodies and labour through the institution of marriage. During conflict, when institutions and structures are broken down or weakened, boys' and men's desires to control the female body and reproductive capacities are heightened, and sexual violence becomes a relatively easy avenue. In other words, sexism, especially sexual violence, is intensified through extreme violence specifically perpetrated by boys and men against girls and women (McKay & Mazurana, 2004: 15).

Based on a research study of 60 children born in Lord's Resistance Army (LRA) captivity, reveals the stigma associated with such sexual violence persists after the conflict in Uganda. Children born in LRA's captivity endure multiple hardships as secondary and intergenerational survivors of sexual violence that require legal protection as well as social support (Denov & Lakor, 2019: 211). So, how do we reverse the damage done to the thousands (if not millions) of girls and women survivors of sexual violence in African conflict? The permanent damage of trauma endured by survivors of sexual violence in African conflict is problematic. For instance, indigenous health rituals might be used that incorporate a series of symbolic meanings to sever a survivor's link with their history of violence in order to cleanse and purify them for restoration back to their families and communities. Nonetheless, girls and women gravely affected by sexual violence in African conflict are resilient and strong. Focusing attention on how survivors, especially children, cope, build attachments and relationships, connect with family, receive peer social support, and make meaning of their individual experience are crucial for healing and renewal (Betancourt & Khan, 2008: 317).

4 Sexual Violence in Conflict: Prevalence, Causes, and Impact

Is sexual violence in African conflict a cause for serious concern? Would the relatively frequent occurrences of sexual violence against girls and women stop if there were no conflict(s) happening in Africa? Obviously, the answer is emphatically "yes" to the former and "no" to the latter. Categorically, conflict-related sexual violence is not endemic to Africa and the sincere goal here is not to run the risk of essentializing the African continent, even considering the vastness of the issue at stake. However, the frequency with which conflict occurs across the continent, largely explains the astronomical increase in sexual violence, particularly against girls and women. Evelyn Kamau argues that the existence and notoriety of sexual violence during peace time provides an impetus and launching pad for its frequent occurrence during armed conflict (Kamau, 2011: 86). Unequivocal empirical research shows that conflict in Africa exacerbates the incidence and prevalence rates of sexual violence against girls and women who are most in need of assistance and, hence, at greater risk of sexual exploitation and abuse. Children and women most at risk in African conflict are representatives of the elderly, single mothers, people with disability, orphans, unaccompanied minors, separated family members, pregnant women, and neonates. Despite the variations of the type of conflict happening in Uganda, Côte d'Ivoire, and Liberia, empirical research shows that the higher levels of sexual violence observed are related to girls' and women's exposure to conflict (Kelly et al., 2018).

Sexual violence in conflict falls under the umbrella of gender-based violence and is not necessarily limited to violence against women as boys, men, and transgender people are also targets of gender violence (Bastick et al., 2007: 18). Forms of violence against boys and men in African conflict range from forced conscription, sex-selective massacre (especially after mass incidence of sexual abuse), imprisonment and forced labour (Carpenter, 2006: 88; Touquet & Gorris, 2016: 36–38). Notwithstanding, both boys and girls are used as child soldiers and children associated with armed forces and armed groups with some serving as porters, cooks, guards, messengers, or spies (Human Rights Watch, 2008; UNICEF, 1997: 1, 2007: 7). For instance, an estimated 40% of the 12,500 girls in armed groups in the Democratic Republic of Congo (DRC) were girls (Coulter et al., 2008: 19). Research with 224 former combatants (222 men and two women) in Goma, DRC may appear to infer that more female combatants experience sexual violence compared to civilian women and girls. A study of female fighting forces in Sierra Leone, Uganda and Mozambique reveals that girls are systematically abducted and recruited by males to provide sexual service (McKay & Mazurana, 2004: 28). These findings must be carefully examined given the lack of comprehensive research data on the topic. To be clear, in the DRC conflict, particularly in the North Kivu region, sexual violence is perceived as a "plague" where an estimated 80% of girls and women have been raped (Haer et al., 2015: 618).

Synonymous with the term "conflict," sexual violence is broad and wide. According to the Inter-Agency Standing Committee, sexual violence is:

> any sexual act, attempt to obtain a sexual act, unwanted sexual comments or advances, or acts to traffic a person's sexuality, using coercion, threats of harm or physical force, by any person regardless of relationship to the victim, in any setting, including but not limited to home and work.

In this chapter, the forms of sexual violence considered include, but are not limited to the following: sexual abuse, sexual harassment, sexual abuse and exploitation, domestic violence, trafficking, female genital cutting, rape, attempted rape, gang rape, sexual slavery, forced pregnancy, forced abortion, forced marriage, and forced prostitution.

As indicated above, rape is perceived as a "weapon of war," girls and women are sexually violated with family, friends, and strangers as witnesses. Rifles, knives, sticks, and other objects are inserted into pregnant women which may lead to miscarriage (Kuloglu, 2008: 228); sometimes survivors' breasts are mutilated, their genital organs are severed during (mass) rapes and at times, they are shot in the vagina (Mechanic, 2004: 17). Thirteen-year-old Félicité from DRC implores that, "I want to tell the world that we need peace—stop the war. We need to make sure children and women are protected. People who rape need to be arrested" (Save the Children UK, 2013: v).

The incidence and prevalence rates of sexual violence in African conflict are relatively troubling. Consider the following situation which typifies the severity and enormity of the situation. In 1988, the National Resistance Army in Uganda did not only massacre some 300,000 people and bury many alive, it also sexually abused women while their family stood by in order to humiliate and denigrate the Acholi people (Katumba-Wamala, 2000: 160; Nasong'o, 2015: 48). In the DRC, rape is considered the "worst in the world" where approximately 200,000 girls and women were sexually assaulted during a 10-year period of the civil war (Kelly, 2010: 2). "After publicly raping fifteen women, [the soldiers] whipped them until there was no more skin on their buttocks. One victim ... begged them to shoot her in the head... and they refused," said a Congolese doctor (Mechanic, 2004: 17). In Mali, the resurgence of rebel attacks, combat, and aerial bombardments in January 2013 led to damage of local schools. Salif, a 13-year-old, whose story was reported by Save the Children, sighed: "[t]he day the rebels came, they destroyed the school. I saw them. They went inside the school. They went into the headmaster's office and destroyed everything. They destroyed the students' papers and folders" (Save the Children, 2013: 14).

Some 68% of women younger than 18 years old were forcibly married in the Central African Republic. In Liberia, a survey of 1,666 adults found that 32.6% of male combatants experienced sexual violence while 16.5% were forced to be sexual servants (Johnson et al., 2008: 676). In Sierra Leone, 74% of a sample of 388 Liberian refugee women living in camps reported being sexually abused prior to being displaced while 55% experienced sexual violence during displacement (Inter-Agency Standing Committee, 2015: 8). Of 64 women with disabilities interviewed in post-conflict Northern Uganda, one-third reported experiencing some form of GBV and several had children as a result of rape (Inter-Agency Standing Committee, 2015: 15). In a 2011 assessment, Somali adolescent girls in the Dadaab refugee complex in Kenya explained that they are in many ways "under attack" from violence that includes verbal and physical harassment; sexual exploitation and abuse in relation to meeting their basic needs; and rape, including in public and by multiple perpetrators. Girls reported feeling particularly vulnerable to violence while accessing scarce services and resources, such as at water pumps or while collecting firewood outside the camps (Inter-Agency Standing Committee, 2015: 15).

When fleeing violence in search of safety, girls and women vulnerabilities multiply as the risk of being sexually assaulted and violated increases. The story of 17-year-old Tatiana from the DRC epitomizes the threat of sexual violence in African conflict:

> Tatiana was eight-and-a-half-months pregnant when her husband and her two-year-old son were hacked to death by irregular/rogue militia in May 2003. When she, her mother and two younger sisters heard that the same militia intended to raid the district of Bunia, where they lived, they fled. Six days later, they reached a militia checkpoint, but her mother could not pay the US$100 demanded. The militia cut her throat, killing her. When Tatiana's 14-year-old sister began to cry, she was shot in the head. Her other sister, aged 12, was taken to a nearby clearing and gang-raped. Tatiana was told to leave at once or suffer the same fate. After six days walking, she went into labour and gave birth to a girl. Although she had lost a lot of blood, she had to take to the road again the following day. The baby later died.

At the core of African conflict is human tragedy and casualty. Civilians, especially children and women, increasingly suffer death, famine, and epidemic disease post-independence. It is estimated that some eight million people have died as a result of conflicts in Africa (Department for International Development, 2001: 10). In 2014 alone, 92% of all fatalities recorded as a result of political conflict in Africa occurred in nine countries, namely, Nigeria, South Sudan, Somalia, Sudan, the CAR, Libya, Egypt, Cameroon, and the DRC (Cilliers, 2015: 7). The catastrophic impact of conflict in Africa is seen in the millions that are uprooted and forcibly displaced internally and internationally. According to the United Nations High Commissioner for Refugees (UNHCR), by the end of 2020, 82.4 million people were forcibly displaced as a result of persecution, conflict, violence, human rights violations, and events seriously disturbing public order (The United Nations High Commissioner for Refugees, 2021: 6). Similarly, of the 55 million people internally displaced at the end of 2020, 48 million are displaced due to conflict and violence (Internal Displacement Monitoring Group, 2021). The conflict in the Central African Republic alone, has left an estimated 2.5 million people relying on humanitarian assistance and 690,000 internally displaced

(Danziger, 2018). In eastern Chad and Central African Republic intensified fighting forced an estimated 200,000 Sudanese refugees to cross the border from Darfur (Boutellis, 2013: 121). A low-grade conflict in Cameroon that has killed 2,000 Cameroonians and displaced 437,000 is feared to result in destabilizing Central and West Africa even as Boko Haram insurgency "lays low" in the Lake Chad Basin (Chothia, 2018; Kuwonu, 2018a: 29; Malley, 2018).

The roots of sexual violence in African conflict are also deeply embedded in the social construct of gender norms which define and determine roles, responsibility, opportunities, privileges, and limitations of girls and boys. Social constructs of gender norms that are taught and reinforced by a culture predict and assume authority, power relationship, and dominance of males over females throughout life (United Nations High Commissioner for Refugees, 2016: 11). Generally, societal expectation and gender roles of girls and women in conflict do not change, wherein girls are seen as passive and relegated to providing care, mothering, and submitting to the vices of boys and men. On top of fulfilling their expected roles as mothers, daughters, wives, and caregivers; conflict amplifies gender roles for girls and women, putting demands on them to provide care and support. Therefore, irrespective of how chaotic the environment that conflict creates, girls and women are still the ones who collect water, gather firewood, cook, and bear children (Martin, 2004). Boys and men often capitalize on the mechanism and operation of these stereotypical gender roles to effectuate and worsen sexual abuse and violations. Apart from the usual dominant-male desire to exert power and control over the "weaker sex," girls and women are often perceived as inevitable "spoils of war," "weapons of war," or "collateral damage." Thus, sexual violence against girls and women is methodically used as a tactic of war and terrorism in African conflict.

Without a doubt, the effect of conflict is grim and incessant. Conflicts in Africa destroy lives and property, forcibly displace people internally and internationally, worsen proliferation of illicit small arms and light weapons trade, amplify poverty, disease and hunger, increase drug and human/child trafficking, and, of course, subject girls and women to sexual exploitation and abuse (Annan, 2014: 1; Brown-Eyeson, 2003: 33–53). For instance, the rise of religious/jihadist terrorist attacks in Burkina Faso, Chad, Côte d'Ivoire, Kenya, Mali, Nigeria and Somalia has killed thousands of civilians, while continuously undermining any political, economic, and social development (Basedau, 2017: 2; Hendrix, 2015: 1; Lado et al., 2014).

Forced displacement due to conflict, whether within country or across African borders, predisposes girls and women to sexual abuse and exploitation by insurgents claiming to be "freedom fighters," peacekeepers, humanitarian workers, paramilitary personnel, state officials, United Nations staff and others. Rebel groups, paramilitaries, United Nations (UN) peacekeeping forces and other humanitarian workers in Liberia, Guinea, Sierra Leone, Côte d'Ivoire, Mali, Somalia, South Sudan and Democratic Republic of Congo (DRC) have all been implicated in sexually exploiting and abusing girls and women during conflict. A young adolescent girl in Liberia insists how "[i]t's difficult to escape the trap of those (NGO) people; [because] they use the food as bait to get you to have sex with them." The earliest report by the United Nations High Commissioner for Refugees (UNHCR) and Save the Children-UK lamented that,

> Agency workers with special responsibilities for children, such as caring for children with disabilities, providing accelerated learning programmes, and loans for the vulnerable, were allegedly using the very same resources intended to improve children's lives and reduce their vulnerability, as a tool of exploitation. Frequent reports were received…on how agency workers give these services to girls in exchange for sex.

The act of constantly fleeing to new environments under duress to avoid conflict can impose unbearable challenges on girls and women. In addition to experiencing survival guilt, inability to return home, loss of loved ones, lack of access to education, being isolated, exposure to over-crowdedness, living poor sanitary conditions, no access to safe drinking water, and inadequate food supply (Blavo, 2018: 20–45); girls and women are also susceptible to forced marriage, forced prostitution, sexual enslavement, trafficking, becoming pregnant, and contracting sexually transmitted diseases (STDs) such as HIV/AIDS, gonorrhoea, chlamydia, hepatitis B, genital warts, herpes, and syphilis (V. P. Fynn, 2011: 34–35). Sexual violence in African conflict is horrific leaving survivors with harmful and permanent damage to girls and women's genitals and internal reproductive organs (e.g., fistula) (Haer et al., 2015: 611). Survivors are denigrated, shamed, and rejected by their communities, families, and friends. The story of Gunya exemplifies the severe impact of sexual violence on girls and women in African conflict:

> Gunya is a woman in her late twenties. Soldiers of the Lord's Resistance Army (LRA) abducted her when she was eleven years old and forcefully conscripted her into the rebel ranks. Gunya spent a little over a decade with the rebels before deserting. While there, she gave birth to a son with Onen, an LRA soldier. Though abducted, she expresses her continued support for the LRA and their tactics, admitting that she sometimes thinks of going back to the

lum [bush] when life becomes hard as a civilian at home… Short on cash and without other support, she was also keen for his [Onen] family to pay the fine due for unsanctioned sex (*luk*) for the children, who were born outside of formal marriage. (Hansen, 2014: 1–3)

The impact of conflict in Africa continues long after the conflict is over. Grace Maina cautions that "[f]or most women, the end of war and conflict is marked by the excessive effects of trauma and shame" (Maina, 2012: 1). Mathilda Lindgren argues that impunity for past violations is a recipe for persistence of sexual violence beyond conflict termination (Lindgren, 2011: 1). As more boys and men end up dying in conflicts, an increased number of girls and women survivors of sexual violence become orphans. Unemployed women who become single head of families turn to prostitution, which intensifies their risks of contracting HIV/AIDS (Mindzie & Stone, 2006: 6).

5 Contextualizing Sexual Violence in African Conflict: Short Synopsis

It is impossible to carry out a comprehensive assessment of sexual violence in African conflict. A brief overview of the four country examples below illustrates the severity and enormity of sexual violence in conflicts across the northern (Libya), southern (Democratic Republic of Congo), eastern (South Sudan), and western (Mali) regions of the continent. Partly informed by the United Nations Secretary-General Report on Conflict-Related Sexual Violence (United Nations, 2017) and the Secretary General Report for Children and Armed Conflict (United Nations General Assembly, 2021), the goal here is to contextualize the theoretical and practical significance of sexual violence in African conflict, the impact it has on the real lives of girls and its implication for social justice, equality and fairness. These documents report an increase of up to 70% of rape and other forms of sexual violence in armed conflict-ridden countries, including the four highlighted below (United Nations General Assembly, 2021: 3).

Mali

In 2012, a separatist Tuareg uprising launched a coup d'état and evicted security forces from the north of Mali. The Tuareg rebels later saw their political struggle hijacked by three Salafi-jihadist groups, who then attacked southern

Mali in January 2013. Following this, an intervention led by France raised €3.25 billion with the deployment of 12,000 United Nations Multidimensional Integrated Stabilization Mission in Mali (MINUSMA) (Boeke & de Valk, 2019: 1). The crisis, combined with a lack of services, limited humanitarian access, stigma and fear of reprisals continues to impede reporting of conflict-related sexual violence. In January 2017, a Report of the United Nations Secretary General on Conflict-Related Sexual Violence noted that a suspect in a case concerning the alleged sexual assault of 19 children was released from custody (United Nations, 2017: 23). In the same year, the United Nations peacekeeping force, MINUSMA investigated 23 cases of conflict-related sexual violence, including rape, gang rape, forced prostitution, sexual slavery and forced marriage. One of the cases was perpetrated by three members of the Malian Defense and Security Forces, four by elements of the *Groupe d'autodéfense des Touaregs Imghad et leurs alliés*, and the others by civilians (United Nations, 2017: 23). Humanitarian service providers also recorded five sexual assaults by elements of the Malian Defence and Security Forces, a case of sexual violence by members of the *Mouvement pour l'unicité et le jihad en Afrique de l'Ouest*, and another by the *Mouvement national pour la libération de l'Azawad* (United Nations, 2017: 23). In 2018, conflict-related sexual violence remained underreported owing to high levels of insecurity, the unwillingness or failure to investigate and prosecute cases, and the stigmatization of survivors. Of 22 reported incidents two were rapes and 20 were gang rapes, which included 13- and 9-year-old girls (United Nations, 2017: 23).

Democratic Republic of Congo

In 2016, the United Nations Organization Stabilization Mission in the Democratic Republic of the Congo (MONUSCO) verified 514 cases (340 women, 170 girls, three men, and one boy) of conflict-related sexual violence. During the same period, the United Nations Population Fund (UNFPA) reported 2,593 cases of sexual violence in conflict-affected provinces (United Nations, 2017: 16). The *Force de résistance patriotiques de l'Ituri* was responsible for 20% of incidents; the Mai Mai Raia Mutomboki combatants, 18%; and the Mai Mai Simba factions 4% (United Nations, 2017: 16). In 2017, *Médecins Sans Frontières* treated 2,600 people, of which 32 were men who had been forced under armed threat to rape members of their own community. Some 162 were children under the age of 15, including 22 children below the age of five who were also treated for rape (Jackson, 2002). A survivor testifies, "I was raped in my home, next to my husband's body, in the presence of my children. It was last year, during the violence. I had five children. They killed three of them, leaving me with just two. They raped my three oldest girls before killing them" (Jackson, 2002). In 2018, MONUSCO documented 1,049 cases of conflict-related sexual violence against 605 women, 436 girls, 4 men, and 4 boys. In most incidents, women and girls were targeted while walking to school, or collecting firewood or water, or under police custody (United Nations, 2017: 23).

Libya

Ongoing conflict in Libya and acute political instability continues to exacerbate civilians and migrants' vulnerability to sexual violence. In November 2017, a CNN documentary revealed that African migrants seeking to get into Europe were being sold as slaves by some criminal gangs in Libya (Mafu, 2019: 1). The migrants have been subjected to beatings, starvation, denial of food and water, gang rapes, and the renting out of women to armed men for sexual abuse. In 2018, the United Nations Secretary-General report on Conflict-Related Sexual Violence affirmed that, migrant women and girls are particularly vulnerable to rape with many being exposed to forced prostitution and sexual exploitation (United Nations, 2017: 21). In particular, many Nigerian women and girls are vulnerable to trafficking by both armed groups and multinational criminal networks. The hopes of 17 women and girls who suffered sexual violence at the Surman detention centre were crushed as Mamduh Miloud Daw, the head of the detention centre refused to transfer them to protection agencies (United Nations, 2017: 21).

South Sudan

In 2016, the United Nations Mission in South Sudan (UNMISS) documented 577 incidents of conflict-related sexual violence, including rape, gang rape and sexual slavery (United Nations, 2017: 28). The survivors included 57 girls, several were below 10 years of age and two were less than one year old. Of 376 cases of sexual violence recorded by service providers, 157 were forced into marriage allegedly to both State and non-State armed actors. On 10 July 2018, UNMISS and the Office of the High Commissioner for Human Rights (OHCHR) found at least 120 women and girls (some as young as 4 years) were raped and gang-raped with 132 abducted for sexual slavery (Secretary-General, 2019: 29). In September, a special military court convicted 10 rank-and-file soldiers of the South Sudan People's Defence

Forces and sentenced them to between 10- and 14-years' imprisonment for committing sexual crimes (Secretary-General, 2019: 29).

6 Conclusion: The Way Forward in Addressing Sexual Violence in African Conflicts

It is always difficult to write about sexual violence as a survivor of war and abuse. Sexual violence in African conflict is disturbing and sometimes seems a hopeless situation. Therefore, addressing conflict-related gender-based violence means "getting the past right," as well as recognizing broader structural injustices that should be transformed through the peace and rebuilding process (Thompson, 2013: 6). In spite of the challenges associated with curbing sexual violence in African conflict, significant progress has been made by individuals and institutions both locally and international. Unfortunately, it is the persistence of impunity for sexual violence that continues to allow men to perpetrate violence against women.

Then UN High Commissioner for Human Rights, Louise Arbour, said that "women's oppression and abuse had occurred particularly in times of conflict when the rule of force obliterated the rule of law" and that "[c]onflict exacerbated gender-based violence and the likelihood of impunity" (UN Security Council, 2004). Margot Wallström, former Secretary-General's Special Representative on Sexual Violence in Conflict affirms that, "Women have no rights, if those who violate their rights go unpunished." Ending impunity for sexual violence is a critical part of the Council's broader mandate to shepherd situations "from might to right, from rule of war to rule of law, from bullets to ballots," she noted. "If women continue to suffer sexual violence, it is not because the law is inadequate to protect them, but because it is inadequately enforced" (UN News, 2010).

Michael Flood, a leading expert and feminist on preventing violence against women, suggests that research evidence shows that: (1) men's beliefs about violence against women are shaped by perceptions of their male peers' attitudes and behaviours; (2) men's willingness to intervene in sexual violence is shaped by perceptions of their male peers' willingness to do so; and (3) men leveraging their own social, professional, and familial ties make it easy to access social circles, potentially recruit, see the movement as relevant, and perceive the "messenger" as credible (Flood, 2019: 171). Therefore, in order to sustain male prevention of violence against women, advocates must extend beyond the social networks of existing advocates and allies (Flood, 2019: 171), which is the case of Denis Mukwege.

In October 2018, Denis Mukwege (and Nadia Murad), a world renowned Congolese gynaecologist from Bukavu won the Nobel Prize "for [his] efforts to end the use of sexual violence as a weapon of war and armed conflict" (Nobel Prize Organisation, 2018). Mukwege, who is fondly referred to as "the man who mends women" runs the Panzi Hospital in Bukvu, South Kivu where he has provided care for some 45,000 women wounded by rape and other violent assaults (Kuwonu, 2018b: 6). It must be emphasized that none of the above efforts would be possible without genuine support for regional integration and promotion of mutual security based on migration and economy. Engaging boys and men in violence prevention, harnessing regional collaboration on migration and economic growth and mainstreaming gender equality will go a long way toward sustainable development.

Sadly, violent conflict is an impediment to sustainable development, peace and prosperity on the continent. In particular, conflict in Africa prevents girls and women from fully engaging in society, scars posterity, and costs millions of dollars in health expenses, job losses, and debt (Mohammed, 2018: 5). Therefore, curbing sexual violence in conflict must start with exposing and challenging the pervasive culture of conflict in Africa and corresponding impunity that allow such mayhem rape, torture, and other forms of sexual violence to persist by heeding to women's stories/voices.

Today, many international, regional, and national laws and policies exist to protect the rights of girls and women from sexual violence in conflict. However, there is no simple or easy solution to ending conflict in Africa and thus curbing sexual violence in African conflicts. Nevertheless, efforts and attempts to address the situation must adopt a sustainable approach that first, provides a sophisticated understanding of country-specific concern (Grono, 2011), and second, builds on African capacity and leadership to tackle socio-economic issues (e.g., poverty, housing, education, and health). Conflict should never be a means for obtaining self-determination or political independence (Kitenge, 2017) because its ability to violate girls and women and, hence, destroy the lifeblood (girls and women) of African societies is unforgiving.

Bibliography

Aall, P. R. (2015). *Conflict in Africa* (p. 20). Centre for International Governance Innovation.

Achebe, C. (1959). *Things Fall Apart*. Anchor Books.

Achebe, C. (2012). *There Was a Country: A Personal History of Biafra*. Viking Penguin.

Addison, T., Le Billon, P., & Murshed, M. (2002). Conflict in Africa: The Cost of Peaceful Behaviour. *Journal of African Economics, 11*(3), 365–386. https://doi.org/10.1093/jae/11.3.365

African Development Bank Group. (2016). *African Natural Resources Center*. African Development Bank Group. https://www.afdb.org/fileadmin/uploads/afdb/Documents/Publications/anrc/AfDB_ANRC_BROCHURE_en.pdf

Ahere, J., & Maina, G. (2013). *The Never-ending Pursuit of the Lord's Resistance Army: An Analysis of the Regional Cooperation Initiative for the Elimination of the LRA* (p. 11). The African Centre for the Constructive Resolution of Disputes.

Ajayi, A. T., & Buhari, L. O. (2014). Methods of Conflict Resolution in African Traditional Society. *African Research Review, 8*(2), 138. https://doi.org/10.4314/afrrev.v8i2.9

Al Jazeera News. (2019a, August 18). Chad Declares Emergency in East After Ethnic Killings. *Al Jazeera*. https://www.aljazeera.com/news/2019/08/chad-declares-emergency-east-ethnic-killings-190818142801954.html. Accessed 30 December 2019.

Al Jazeera News. (2019b, December 28). Dozens Killed in Mogadishu Car Bomb Attack. *Al Jazeera*. https://www.aljazeera.com/news/2019/12/dozens-killed-mogadishu-car-bomb-attack-police-191228072334950.html. Accessed 30 December 2019.

Alao, A. (2007). *Natural Resources and Conflict in Africa: The Tragedy of Endowment*. Rochester Press (*Rochester Studies in African History and the Diaspora*, Vol. 29).

Allen, T. (1991). Understanding Alice: Uganda's Holy Spirit Movement in Context. *Africa, 61*(3), 370–399. https://doi.org/10.2307/1160031

Allen, T., & Vlassenroot, K. (Eds.). (2010). *The Lord's Resistance Army: Myth and Reality*. Zed Books.

Amnesty International. (2021). *Amnesty International Report 2020/21* (p. 408). Amnesty International. https://www.amnesty.org/en/wp-content/uploads/2021/06/English.pdf

Amony, E., & Baines, E. K. (2015). *I Am Evelyn Amony: Reclaiming My Life from the Lord's Resistance Army*. University of Wisconsin Press.

Annan, N. (2014). Violent Conflicts and Civil Strife in West Africa: Causes, Challenges and Prospects. *Stability: International Journal of Security & Development, 3*(1), 16. https://doi.org/10.5334/sta.da

Aremu, J. O. (2010). Conflicts in Africa: Meaning, Causes, Impacts and Solution. *African Research Review, 4*(4), 549–560.

Bakken, I. V., & Rustad, S. A. (2018). *Conflict Trends in Africa, 1989–2017*. Peace Research Institute Oslo. https://reliefweb.int/report/world/conflict-trends-africa-1989-2017

Bariagaber, A. (2016). *Conflict and the Refugee Experience: Flight, Exile, and Repatriation in the Horn of Africa*. Routledge. https://www.taylorfrancis.com/books/e/9781315573373. Accessed 19 December 2019.

Basedau, M. (2017). *The Rise of Religious Armed Conflicts in sub-Saharan Africa: No Simple Answers*. GIGA German Institute of Global and Area Studies.

Bastick, M., Grimm, K., & Kunz, R. (2007). *Sexual Violence in Amed Conflict: Global Overview and Implications for the Security Sector*. Geneva Centre for the Democratic of Armed Forces.

Bean, F. D., & Brown, S. K. (2015). Demographic Analyses of Immigration. In C. B. Brettell & J. F. Hollifield (Eds.), *Migration Theory: Talking Across Disciplines* (pp. 67–89). Routledge.

Bekele, D. (2017, April 12). Africa's Natural Resources: From Curse to a Blessing. *Al Jazeera*. https://www.aljazeera.com/indepth/opinion/2017/04/africa-natural-resources-curse-blessing-170409121054152.html. Accessed 2 January 2019.

Benjaminsen, T. A., & Ba, B. (2019). Why Do Pastoralists in Mali Join Jihadist Groups? A Political Ecological Explanation. *The Journal of Peasant Studies, 46*(1), 1–20. https://doi.org/10.1080/03066150.2018.1474457

Betancourt, T. S., & Khan, K. T. (2008). The Mental Health of Children Affected by Armed Conflict: Protective Processes and Pathways to Resilience. *International Review of Psychiatry, 20*(3), 317–328. https://doi.org/10.1080/09540260802090363

Blavo, E. Q. (2018). *The Problems of Refugees in Africa: Boundaries and Borders*. Routledge. https://public.ebookcentral.proquest.com/choice/publicfullrecord.aspx?p=5839110. Accessed 30 December 2019.

Boeke, S., & de Valk, G. (2019). The Unforeseen 2012 Crisis in Mali: The Diverging Outcomes of Risk and Threat Analyses. *Studies in Conflict & Terrorism, 1–20*. https://doi.org/10.1080/1057610X.2019.1592356

Borjas, G. J. (1989). Economic Theory and International Migration. *The International Migration Review, 23*(3), 457–485.

Boutellis, A. (2013). Chad and Central African Republic. In J. Boulden (Ed.), *Responding to Conflict in Africa: The United Nations and Regional Organizations* (pp. 121–144). Palgrave Macmillan.

Brown-Eyeson, A. (2003). *Protecting Children from Exploitation in West African: Illusion or Reality?* Master of Laws. University of Georgia.

Bujra, A. (2002). *African Conflicts: Their Causes and Their Political and Social Environment* (p. 49). Private Document 4. Development Policy Management Forum.

Bulcha, M. (1988). *Flight and Integration: Causes of Mass Exodus from Ethiopia and Problems of Integration in the Sudan*. Scandinavian Institute of African Studies.

Cabrita, J. M. (2000). *Mozambique: The Tortuous Road to Democracy*. Palgrave. http://site.ebrary.com/id/10045573. Accessed 29 December 2019.

Carayannis, T., & Lombard, L. (Eds.). (2015). *Making Sense of the Central African Republic*. Zed Books.

Carpenter, R. C. (2006). Recognizing Gender-based Violence Against Civilian Men and Boys in Conflict Situations. *Security Dialogue, 37*(1), 83–103. https://doi.org/10.1177/0967010606064139

Celucien, J. (2012). Prophetic Religion, Violence, and Black Freedom: Reading Makandal's Project of Black Liberation Through a Fanonian Postcolonial Lens of Decolonization and Theory of Revolutionary Humanism. *Journal of Race, Ethnicity, and Religion, 3*(4), 1–30.

Check, N. A. (2014). The Rise of Radical and Asymmetric Armed Insurgents in the Central African Sub-region: A Causal Analysis. *African Institute of South Africa, 113*, 1–8. https://www.africaportal.org/publications/the-rise-of-radical-and-asymmetric-armed-insurgents-in-the-central-african-sub-region-a-causal-analysis/. Accessed 4 December 2018.

Chinweizu. (1987). *Decolonizing the African Mind*. Pero Press.

Chothia, F. (2018, October 4). Cameroon's Anglophone Crisis: Red Dragons and Tigers—The Rebels Fighting for Independence. *BBC News*. https://www.bbc.com/news/world-africa-45723211. Accessed 2 January 2019.

Cilliers, J. (2015). Future (Im)Perfect? *Institute for Security Studies, 287*, 1–24.

Coulter, C., Persson, M., & Utas, M. (2008). *Young Female Fighters in African Wars: Conflict and Its Consequences*. Nordiska Afrikainstitutet.

Danziger, R. (2018, December). Confronting the Challenges of Migration in West and Central Africa. *Africa Renewal Online* (pp. 13–14). https://www.un.org/africarenewal/magazine/december-2018-march-2019/confronting-challenges-migration-west-and-central-africa. Accessed 29 December 2018.

Deng, F. M. (1995). *War of Visions: Conflict of Identities in the Sudan*. Brookings Institution.

Denov, M., & Lakor, A. A. (2019). Post-war Stigma, Violence and "Kony Children": The Responsibility to Protect Children Born in Lord's Resistance Army Captivity in Northern Uganda. In B. D'Costa & L. Glanville (Eds.), *Children and the Responsibility to Protect* (pp. 211–232). Brill Nijhoff.

Department for International Development. (2001). *The Causes of Conflict in Africa*. Department for International Development. https://webarchive.nationalarchives.gov.uk/www.dfid.gov.uk/pubs/files/conflict-africa.pdf

Eichstaedt, P. H. (2009). *First Kill Your Family: Child Soldiers of Uganda and the Lord's Resistance Army*. Lawrence Hill Books.

El Jack, A. (2003). *Gender and Armed Conflict: Overview Report* (p. 50). Institute of Development Studies.

Ellis, S. (2003). The Old Roots of Africa's New Wars. *Internationale Politik Und Gesellschaft, 2*, 29–43.

Ellis, S. (2007). *The Mask of Anarchy: The Destruction of Liberia and the Religious Dimension of an African Civil War*. New York University Press.

Fanon, F. (1963). *The Wretched of the Earth* (C. Farrington, Trans.). Grove Press.

Fanon, F., & Chevalier, H. (1965). *A Dying Colonialism*. Grove Press.

Fitiwi, M. (2018). *Zimbabwe Conflict Insight* (Vol. 2, pp. 1–13). Institute for Peace and Security Studies, Addis Ababa University. https://www.africaportal.org/documents/18475/zimbabwe_conflict_insight_final_13.09.2018.pdf

Flood, M. (2019). Reaching and Engaging Men. *Engaging Men and Boys in Violence Prevention* (pp. 115–182). Palgrave Macmillan. https://doi.org/10.1057/978-1-137-44208-6. Accessed 13 April 2019.

Forsyth, F. (2015). *The Biafra Story: The Making of an African Legend*. Pen & Sword Military.

Fynn, V. (2011). Africa's Last Colony: Sahrawi People—Refugees, IDPs and Nationals? *Journal of Internal Displacement, 1*(2), 40–58.

Fynn, V.P. (2011). *Legal Discrepancies: Internal Displacement of Women and Children in Africa*. Flowers Books. https://www.amazon.com/Legal-Discrepancies-Internal-Displacement-Children/dp/1453873414

Fynn Bruey, V. (2016). *Systematic Gender Violence and the Rule of Law: Aboriginal Communities in Australia and Post-War Liberia* (PhD Thesis). Australian National University. http://hdl.handle.net/1885/159520

Gebru Tareke. (2009). *The Ethiopian Revolution: War in the Horn of Africa*. Yale University Press (The Yale Library of Military History).

Ghobarah, H. A., Huth, P., & Russett, B. (2004). The Post-war Public Health Effects of Civil Conflict. *Social Science & Medicine, 59*(4), 869–884. https://doi.org/10.1016/j.socscimed.2003.11.043

Gleditsch, N. P., et al. (2002). Armed Conflict 1946–2001: A New Dataset. *Journal of Peace Research, 39*(5), 615–637. https://doi.org/10.1177/0022343302039005007

Gray, R. (1982). Christianity, Colonialism, and Communications in Sub-Saharan Africa. *Journal of Black Studies, 13*(1), 59–72.

Green, E. C., & Honwana, A. (1991). *Indigenous Healing of War-Affected Children in Africa* (p. 4). World Bank Group.

Grono, N. (2011, March 2). What Are Some of the Challenges for Conflict Prevention and Resolution Over the Next Two Decades? *Global Conflict—Future Trends and Challenges Toward the 21st Century*.

Haer, R., Hecker, T., & Maedl, A. (2015). Former Combatants on Sexual Violence During Warfare: A Comparative Study of the Perspectives of Perpetrators, Victims and Witnesses. *Human Rights Quarterly, 37*, 609–628.

Hansen, S. J. (2014). *Al-Shabaab in Somalia: The History and Ideology of a Militant Islamist Group, 2005–2012*. Oxford University Press. http://www.mylibrary.com?id=557262. Accessed 31 December 2019.

Hartmann, C. (2017). ECOWAS and the Restoration of Democracy in the Gambia. *Africa Spectrum, 52*(1), 85–99. https://doi.org/10.1177/000203971705200104

Haynes, J. (2007). Religion, Ethnicity and Civil War in Africa: The Cases of Uganda and Sudan. *The Commonwealth Journal of International Affairs, 96*(390), 305–317.

Hendrix, C. (2015). *When and Why Are Nonviolent Protesters Killed in Africa?* Sie Center, Josef Korbel School of International Studies, Univerity of Denver.

Hoeffler, A. (2017). *Post-conflict Stabilization in Africa*. African Economic Research Consortium. https://www.africaportal.org/publications/post-conflict-stabilization-africa/. Accessed 4 December 2018.

Human Rights Watch. (2008). *Coercion and Intimidation of Child Soldiers to Participate in Violence*. Human Rights Watch. https://www.hrw.org/news/2008/04/16/coercion-and-intimidation-child-soldiers-participate-violence. Accessed 6 January 2019.

IASC Task Force on Gender and Humanitarian Assistance. (2005). *Gender-based Violence Interventions in Humanitarian Settinggs: Focusing on Prevention of and Response to Sexual Violence in Emergencies* (p. 101). Inter-Agency Standing Committee.

Inter-Agency Standing Committee. (2015). *Guidelines for Integrating Gender-Based Violence Interventions in Humanitarian Action: Reducing Risk, Promoting Resilience and Aiding Recovery*. Inter-Agency Standing Committee. https://interagencystandingcommittee.org/working-group/iasc-guidelines-integrating-gender-based-violenceinterventions-humanitarian-action-2015

Internal Displacement Monitoring Group. (2021). *Global Report on Internal Displacement 2021* (p. 122). NGO Report. Internal Displacement Monitoring Centre of the Norwegian Refugee Council. https://www.internal-displacement.org/global-report/grid2021/. Accessed 5 January 2019.

International Crisis Group. (2012). *Beyond Turf Wars: Managing the Post-Coup Transition in Guinea-Bissau* (p. 24). International Crisis Group.

International Crisis Group. (2018). *Cameroon, Crisis Group*. https://www.crisisgroup.org/africa/central-africa/cameroon. Accessed 2 January 2019.

Isaacman, A. F., & Isaacman, B. (1983). *Mozambique: From Colonialism to Revolution, 1900–1982*. Westview Press.

Jackson, R. (2002). Violent Internal Conflict and the African State: Towards a Framework of Analysis. *Journal of Contemporary African Studies, 20*(1), 29–52. https://doi.org/10.1080/02589000120104044

James III, W. M. (2011). *A Political History of the Civil War in Angola, 1974–1990* (Paperback). Transaction Publishers.

Johnson, K., et al. (2008). Association of Combatant Status and Sexual Violence with Health and Mental Health Outcomes in Postconflict Liberia. *Journal of American Medical Association, 300*, 676–690.

Jok, J. M. (2001). *War and Slavery in Sudan*. University of Pennsylvania Press. http://site.ebrary.com/id/10491935. Accessed 29 December 2019.

Kaifala, J. (2017). *Free Slaves, Freetown, and the Sierra Leonean Civil War*. Palgrave Macmillan (African Histories and Modernities).

Kaldor, M. (2013). In Defence of New Wars. *Stability: International Journal of Security and Development, 2*(1), 4. https://doi.org/10.5334/sta.at

Kamau, E. W. (2011). Domestic Adjudication of Sexual and Gender-Based Violence in Armed Conflict: Considerations for Prosecutions and Judges. *African Journal of Legal Studies, 4*(1), 85–122.

Katumba-Wamala, E. (2000). The National Resistance Army (NRA) as a Guerrilla Force. *Small Wars & Insurgencies, 11*(3), 160–171. https://doi.org/10.1080/09592310008423293

Kelly, J. (2010). *Rape in War: Motives of Militia in DRC* (p. 16). United States Institute of Peace.

Kelly, J. T. D. et al. (2018). From the Battlefield to the Bedroom: A Multilevel Analysis of the Links Between Political Conflict and Intimate Partner Violence in Liberia. *British Medical Journal Global Health, 3*(2), p. e000668. https://doi.org/10.1136/bmjgh-2017-000668

Kitenge, S. (2017, April 26). *Transforming Violent Conflicts in Africa—Challenges and Strategies*. African Network of Youth Policy Experts.

Koloma Beck, T. (2012). *The Normality of Civil War: Armed Groups and Everyday Life in Angola*. Campus-Verl (Mikropolitik der Gewalt, 7).

Kuloglu, C. (2008). Violence Against Women in Conflict Zones. In *Women in the Military and in Armed Conflict* (pp. 226–238). VS Verl. für Sozialwiss.

Kuwonu, F. (2018a). Crisis Worsens in Cameroon. *Africa Renewal Online* (pp. 28–29).

Kuwonu, F. (2018b). Plaudits for the Man Who Mends Women. *Africa Renewal* (p. 6).

Lado, L., Lynch, T., & Muyangwa, M. (2014, June 17). Religious Violence in Sub-Saharan Africa and the Future of the Secular State. *Conflict Resolution and Peacebuilding*. Woodrow Wilson Center.

Lindgren, M. (2011). *Sexual Violence Beyond Conflict Termination: Impunity for Past Violations as a Recipe for New Ones* (p. 8). The African Centre for the Constructive Resolution of Disputes. https://www.africaportal.org/publications/sexual-violence-beyond-conflict-termination-impunity-for-past-violations-as-a-recipe-for-new-ones/

Lombard, L. (2016). *State of Rebellion: Violence and Intervention in the Central African Republic*. Zed Books.

Lombardo, E., & Meier, P. (2016). *The Symbolic Representation of Gender: A Discursive Approach*. Routledge.

Mackenzie, M. (2010). Securitizing Sex? Towards a Theory of the Utility of Wartime Sexual Violence. *International Feminist Journal of Politics, 12*(2), 202–221. https://doi.org/10.1080/14616741003665250

Mafu, L. (2019). The Libyan/Trans-Mediterranean Slave Trade, the African Union, and the Failure of Human Morality. *SAGE Open, 9*(1), 1–10. https://doi.org/10.1177/2158244019828849

Maina, G. (2012). An Overview of the Situation of Women in Conflict and Post-conflict Africa. In *Convention on the Elimination of All Forms of Descrimination Against Women Committee's Regional Consultation*. The Proposed General Recommendation on Human Rights of Women in Situations of Conflict and Post-conflict (p. 12). The African Centre for the Constructive Resolution of Dispute.

Malley, R. (2018, December 28). *10 Conflicts to Watch in 2019*. Crisis Group. https://www.crisisgroup.org/global/10-conflicts-watch-2019. Accessed 2 January 2019.

Mamdani, M. (1983). *Imperialism and Fascism in Uganda*. Heinemann Educational Books.

Mamdani, M. (2001a). Beyond Settler and Native as Political Identities: Overcoming the Political Legacy of Colonialism. *Comparative Studies in Society and History, 43*(1), 651–664.

Mamdani, M. (2001b). *When Victims Become Killers: Colonialism, Nativism, and the Genocide in Rwanda*. Princeton University Press.

Mapping Militant Organizations. (2019). *Al Shabaab*. Stanford University. https://cisac.fsi.stanford.edu/mappingmilitants/profiles/al-shabaab

Marks, Z. (2016). *Poverty and Conflict* (pp. 1–5). University of Birmingham.

Marshall, M. G. (2006). *Conflict Trends in Africa, 1946–2004: A Macro-Comparative Perspective* (p. 83). Department for International Development, Government of the UK.

Martin, S. F. (2004). *Refugee Women* (2nd ed.). Lexington Books.

Maruf, H., & Joseph, D. (2018). *Inside al-Shabaab: The Secret History of al-Qaeda's Most Powerful Ally*. Indiana University Press.

Masisi, J. B. (2018, April 3). "The Wars Will Never Stop"—Millions Flee Bloodshed as Congo Falls Apart. *The Guardian*. https://www.theguardian.com/world/2018/apr/03/millions-flee-bloodshed-as-congos-army-steps-up-fight-with-rebels-in-east. Accessed 30 December 2019.

Massey, D. S., et al. (1993). Theories of International Migration: A Review and Appraisal. *Population and Development Review, 19*(3), 431–466.

McKay, S., & Mazurana, D. E. (2004). *Where Are the Girls? Girls in Fighting Forces in Northern Uganda, Sierre Leone and Mozambique: Their Lives During and After War*. Rights & Democracy.

Mechanic, E. (2004). *Why Gender Still Matters: Sexual Violence and the Need to Confront Militarized Masculinity, A Case of the Conflict in the Democratic Republic of the Congo* (p. 39). NGO Report. Partnership Africa Canada. https://www.africaportal.org/publications/why-gender-still-matters-sexual-violence-and-the-need-to-confront-militarized-masculinity-a-case-study-of-the-conflict-in-the-democratic-republic-of-the-congo/

Meger, S. (2010). Rape of the Congo: Understanding Sexual Violence in the Conflict in the Democratic Republic of Congo. *Journal of Contemporary African Studies, 28*(2), 119–135. https://doi.org/10.1080/02589001003736728

Mekonnen Mengistu, M. (2015). The Root Causes of Conflicts in the Horn of Africa. *American Journal of Applied Psychology, 4*(2), 28. https://doi.org/10.11648/j.ajap.20150402.12

Method, S. (2018, August 6). Stemming the Tide: African Leadership in Small Arms and Light Weapons Control. *OEF Research*. https://oefresearch.org/think-peace/african-small-arms-control. Accessed 9 January 2019.

Mindzie, M. A., & Stone, L. (2006). *Women in Post-conflict Societies in Africa* (p. 66). https://www.africaportal.org/publications/women-post-conflict-societies-africa/. Accessed 4 December 2018.

Mohammed, A. (2018, December). *Ending Violence Against Women and Girls in the Sahel: Crucial for Sustatinable Development*. Africa Renewal Online (pp. 4–5).

Moses, A. D., & Heerten, L. (Eds.). (2018). *Postcolonial Conflict and the Question of Genocide: The Nigeria-Biafra War, 1967–1970*. Routledge. The Routledge Global 1960s and 1970s.

Mudimbe, V. Y. (1988). *The Invention of Africa: Gnosis, Philosophy, and the Order of Knowledge*. Indiana University Press (African Systems of Thought).

Mueller-Hirth, N. (2019). Women's Experiences of Peacebuilding in Violence-affected Communities in Kenya. *Third World Quarterly, 40*(1), 163–179. https://doi.org/10.1080/01436597.2018.1509701

Murray, E., & Sullivan, R. (2019). *Central African Republic Struggles to Implement Peace Deal* (pp. 1–5). United States Institute of Peace. https://www.usip.org/publications/2019/10/central-african-republic-struggles-implement-peace-deal. Accessed 30 December 2019.

Mwakikagile, G. (2013). *Civil Wars in Rwanda and Burundi: Conflict Resolution in Africa* (1st ed.). New Africa Press.

Nasong'o, S. W. (2015). *The Roots of Ethnic Conflict in Africa: From Grievance to Violence*. http://public.eblib.com/choice/publicfullrecord.aspx?p=4082569. Accessed 23 November 2018.

Nobel Prize Organisation. (2018). *The Nobel Peace Prize 2018*. NobelPrize.org. https://www.nobelprize.org/prizes/peace/2018/mukwege/facts/. Accessed 1 January 2019.

Nordås, R., & Rustad, S. C. A. (2013). Sexual Exploitation and Abuse by Peacekeepers: Understanding Variation. *International Interactions, 39*(4), 511–534. https://doi.org/10.1080/03050629.2013.805128

Nunn, N. (2010). Religious Conversion in Colonial Africa. *American Economic Review, 100*(2), 147–152. https://doi.org/10.1257/aer.100.2.147

Nyombi, C., & Kaddu, R. (2015). *Ethnic Conflict in Uganda's Political History*.

Ochab, E. (2018). *The Religious War in the Central African Republic Continues*. UNICEF USA.

Odigie, B. (2019). *ECOWAS's Efforts at Resolving Guinea-Bissau's Protracted Political Crisis, 2015–2019* (p. 19). African Centre for the Constructive Resolution of Disputes. https://www.accord.org.za/conflict-trends/ecowass-efforts-at-resolving-guinea-bissaus-protracted-political-crisis-2015-2019/. Accessed 30 December 2019.

Office of the High Commissioner for Human Rights. (2014). *Sexual and Gender-based Violence in the Context of Transitional Justice*. UN Office of the High Commissioner for Human Rights.

Pettersson, T., & Wallensteen, P. (2015). Armed conflicts, 1946–2014. *Journal of Peace Research, 52*(4), 536–550.

Poggo, S. S. (2011). *The First Sudanese Civil War: Africans, Arabs, and Israelis in the Southern Sudan, 1955–1972*. Palgrave Macmillan. http://public.eblib.com/choice/publicfullrecord.aspx?p=455389_0. Accessed 28 December 2019.

Prieto Curiel, R., Walther, O., & O'Clery, N. (2020). Uncovering the Internal Structure of Boko Haram Through Its Mobility Patterns. *Applied Network Science, 5*(1), 28. https://doi.org/10.1007/s41109-020-00264-4

Pulvirenti, R., & Abrusci, E. (2019). Prosecuting Trafficking Crimes for Sexual Exploitation in Times of Conflict: Challenges and Erspective'. *Journal of Trafficking and Human Exploitation, 3*(1), 97–120. https://doi.org/10.7590/245227719X15476235096562

Pumphrey, C. W., & Schwartz-Barcott, R. (Eds.). (2003) *Armed Conflict in Africa*. Scarecrow Press.

Raleigh, C., & Moody, J. (2017). *Real-time Analysis of African Political Violence* (p. 17). Armed Conflict Location and Event Data Project.

Rodney, W. (1972). *How Europe Underdeveloped Africa*. Bogle-L'Ouverture.

Rosenthal, J. (2021, November 8). Africa Will Continue to Suffer Coups and Civil Wars in 2022. *The Economist*. https://www.economist.com/the-world-ahead/2021/11/08/africa-will-continue-to-suffer-coups-and-civil-wars-in-2022. Accessed 28 March 2022.

Rugege, S. (2004). Land Reform in South Africa: An Overview. *International Journal of Legal Information, 32*(2), 283–312. https://doi.org/10.1017/S0731126500004145

Rustad, A. S., & Bakken, I. V. (2019). *Conflict Trends in Africa, 1989–2018* (pp. 1–4). Peace Research Institute Oslo.

Save the Children. (2013). *Attacks on Education: The Impact of Conflict and Grave Violations on Children's Futures* (p. 38). NGO. Save the Children—UK. https://www.savethechildren.net/sites/default/files/Attacks%20on%20Education_0.pdf#overlay-context=

Save the Children UK. (2013). *Unspeakable Crimes Against Children: Sexual Violence in Conflict* (p. 50). Save the Children Fund. http://www.savethechildren.org.uk/resources/online-library/unspeakable-crimes-against-children. Accessed 1 June 2013.

Secretary-General. (2019). *Special Measures for Protection from Sexual Exploitation and Abuse*. Sexual Exploitation and Abuse: Implementing a Zero-Tolerance Policy A/73/744 (pp. 1–22). United Nations.

Simić, O. (2009). Who Should be a Peacekeeper? *Peace Review, 21*(3), 395–402. https://doi.org/10.1080/10402650903099492

Singh, R., Goli, S., & Singh, A. (2022). Armed Conflicts and Girl Child Marriages: A Global Evidence. *Children and Youth Services Review, 137*, 106458. https://doi.org/10.1016/j.childyouth.2022.106458

Solomon, H. (2014). *Nigeria's Boko Haram: Beyond the Rhetoric* (p. 7). The African Centre for the Constructive Resolution of Disputes.

Solomon, H. (2015). *Terrorism and Counter-Terrorism in Africa: Fighting Insurgency from Al Shabaab, Ansar Dine and Boko Haram*. Palgrave Macmillan.

Staff Reporter. (2018, February 22). Africa: The Influx of Small Arms, Light Weapons. *The Guardian (Lagos)*. https://allafrica.com/stories/201802220192.html. Accessed 9 January 2019.

Stewart, F. (2002). Root Causes of Violent Conflict in Developing Countries. *BMJ, 324*(7333), 342–345. https://doi.org/10.1136/bmj.324.7333.342

Taiwo, O. (2010). *How Colonialism Preempted Modernity in Africa*. Indiana University Press.

The United Nations High Commissioner for Refugees. (2021). *Global Trends: Forced Displacement in 2020* (p. 72). United Nations High Commissioner for Refugees. https://www.unhcr.org/flagship-reports/globaltrends/

Thompson, S. (2013). *Addressing Gender-based Violence in West African Peace Processes: A Guidance Note for Mediators* (p. 20). Martti Ahtisaari Centre. http://cmi.fi/wp-content/uploads/2016/09/GBV_Guidance_Note.pdf

Touquet, H., & Gorris, E. (2016). Out of the Shadows? The Inclusion of Men and Boys in Conceptualisations of Wartime Sexual Violence. *Reproductive Health Matters, 24*(47), 36–46. https://doi.org/10.1016/j.rhm.2016.04.007

UN News. (2010, April 27). Tackling Sexual Violence Must Include Prevention, Ending Impunity—UN Official. *UN News*. https://news.un.org/en/story/2010/04/336662. Accessed 13 April 2019.

UN Security Council. (2004, October 28). *Day-long Security Council Debate on Issue of Women, Peace, Security; Problems on Oppression, Exploitation Stressed*. Security Council. https://www.un.org/press/en/2004/sc8230.doc.htm. Accessed 13 April 2019.

UNICEF. (1997). *Cape Town Principles and Best Practices on the Prevention of Recruitment of Children into the Armed Forces and Demobilization and Social Reintegration of Child Soldiers in Africa*. Jean Claud Legrand. https://openasia.org/en/wp-content/uploads/2013/06/Cape-Town-Principles.pdf

UNICEF. (2007). *Principles and Guidelines on Children Associated with Armed Forces or Armed Groups*. United Nations Children's Fund. https://www.unicef.org/mali/media/1561/file/ParisPrinciples.pdf

United Nations. (2017). *Report of the Secretary-General on Conflict-Related Sexual Violence*. UN S/2017/249 (p. 27). Office of the Special Representative of the Secretary-General on Sexual Violence in Conflict. http://www.un.org/en/events/elimination-of-sexual-violence-in-conflict/pdf/1494280398.pdf

United Nations General Assembly. (2021). *Report of the Special Representative of the Secretary-General for Children and Armed Conflict*. A/17/263. United Nations (p. 18). https://www.un.org/ga/search/view_doc.asp?symbol=A/76/231&Lang=E&Area=UNDOC

United Nations High Commissioner for Refugees. (2016). *SGBV Prevention and Response: Training Manual*. UNHCR.

United Nations High Commissioner for Refugees and Save the Children UK. (2002, October 22–November 30). *Sexual Violence and Exploitation: The Experience of Refugee Children in Guinea, Liberia and Sierra Leone—Based on Initial Findings and Recommendations from Assessment Mission* (p. 19). UN Report. United

Nations High Commission for Refugees. https://www.savethechildren.org.uk/sites/default/files/docs/sexual_violence_and_exploitation_1.pdf

United Nations Secretary General. (2003). *Special Measures for Protection from Sexual Exploitation and Sexual Abuse*. ST/SGB/2003/13. https://hr.un.org/sites/hr.un.org/files/1/documents_sources-english/08_secretary-.

Venter, A. J. (2016). *Biafra's War 1967–1970: A Tribal Conflict in Nigeria That Left a Million Dead*. Helion & Company. http://VH7QX3XE2P.search.serialssolutions.com/?V=1.0&L=VH7QX3XE2P&S=AC_T_B&C=Biafra%27s%20War%201967-1970%20:%20A%20Tribal%20Conflict%20in%20Nigeria%20That%20Left%20a%20Million%20Dead&T=marc&tab=BOOKS. Accessed 28 December 2019.

Ward, J. et al. (2007). *The Shame of War: Sexual Violence Against Women and Girls in Conflict* (UN Report) (p. 139). Office for the Coordination of Humanitarian Affairs & Integrated Regional Information Network. http://lastradainternational.org/lsidocs/IRIN-TheShameofWar-fullreport-Mar07.pdf

wa Thiong'o, N. (1986). *Decolonising the Mind: The Politics of Language in African Literature*. J. Currey.

Weiner, M. (1995). *The Global Migration Crisis: Challenge to States and to Human Rights*. HarperCollins College Publishers (The HarperCollins Series in Comparative Politics).

World Bank Group and United Nations. (Eds.). (2018). *Pathways for Peace: Inclusive Approaches to Preventing Violent Conflict*. World Bank.

World Health Organization. (2019). *Sexual and Other Forms of Gender-based Violence in Crises, Technical Guidance*. https://www.who.int/hac/techguidance/pht/SGBV/en/

Yiew, T. H., et al. (2016). Does Bad Governance Cause Armed Conflict? *International Journal of Applied Business and Economic Research, 14*(6), 3741–3755.

Young, J. (2019). *South Sudan's Civil War: Violence, Insurgency and Failed Peacemaking*. Zed Books.

The Cost of Violence Against Women in Africa

Tshenolo Jennifer Madigele and Mutsawashe Chitando

1 Introduction

Violence is not neutral. There is a high price to be paid at various levels, including at the personal, family, community, national and continental levels whenever violence of any type is perpetrated. While it would be a fallacy to ascribe all of Africa's challenges with development to violence, it remains true that violence must feature in explanations of Africa's struggles for peace, prosperity, and progress. As with other parts of the world, violence against women is a major concern in Africa. It is perpetrated both in war situations and beyond. This echoes what Sachseder (2023) has presented with reference to Black and Indigenous women in Colombia, where the perpetrators of violence are able to get away with it very easily. Violence against women in politics (Krook, 2020; Manyonganise, 2023) prevents many women from making significant contributions to the development of their communities and nations. The COVID-19 situation witnessed a sharp increase in cases of violence against women globally. Africa was also affected, with recommendations being made for governments and other actors to invest in providing effective responses (African Union Commission—Women, Gender and Development Directorate [AUC-WGDD] et al., 2020).

T. J. Madigele
University of Botswana, Gaborone, Botswana

M. Chitando (✉)
University of Cape Town, Cape Town, South Africa
e-mail: chtmut001@myuct.ac.za

While recognizing the dangers of generalizing about Africa, we also appreciate the value of adopting a perspective that seeks to have a broader view of (the cost of) violence against women in diverse African settings (see e.g. Muluneh et al., 2020). Such an approach is useful in that it has the potential of mobilizing African governments and other strategic actors to realize the urgency of collective action in responding to violence against women. Regional Economic Communities (RECs) and the continental body, the African Union (AU), can play a more effective role in responding to violence against women when they have been sensitized regarding the cost of violence against women beyond national concerns. In this chapter, we draw attention to the occurrence of various forms of violence against women in Africa. This presents the platform for examining the cost of such violence. We close by appealing for cultures of peace in Africa. We argue that there is a sound business case for investing in cultures of peace in Africa, as this ensures that the costs accompanying violence against women are minimized, thereby creating more fiscal space for other initiatives that will promote the continent's development.

2 Violence Against Women in Africa: An Overview

Violence against women is a pervasive and deeply rooted problem in Africa, affecting millions of women and girls across the continent. Violence against women manifests in various forms, including physical, sexual, psychological, and economic violence. The prevalence of violence against women in Africa can be attributed to a complex interplay of cultural, social, economic, and political factors (WHO, 2012). In this section, we will provide an overview of the different forms of violence against women in Africa, as well as the underlying causes and consequences. However, we acknowledge that the key terms used sometimes overlap. We, therefore, approach the term "violence against women" as an elastic concept.

Gender-based violence is a significant contributor to economic violence against women in Africa. Gender-based violence refers to any harmful act that is perpetrated against an individual based on their gender. It encompasses a range of behaviours that are intended to exert power and control over someone because of their gender identity or perceived gender roles. This type of violence can take many forms, including physical, sexual, emotional, and psychological abuse. It is a pervasive problem that affects people of all ages, races, and socioeconomic backgrounds (WHO, 2012). According to a report by the World Health Organization ([WHO] 2013), more than one-third of women in Africa have experienced either physical or sexual violence at some point in their lives. The causes of gender-based violence are complex and multifaceted, but can be attributed to factors such as poverty, inequality, and cultural norms that perpetuate gender stereotypes.

One factor that contributes to gender-based violence in Africa is the prevalence of patriarchal attitudes and beliefs. In many African societies, men are seen as superior to women and are granted more power and authority. This power dynamic can lead to men feeling entitled to control and dominate women, which can manifest in abusive behaviour (Jewkes & Morrell, 2012). Another factor is poverty, which can create conditions that make women more vulnerable to violence. Women who live in poverty may lack access to education and economic opportunities, making it difficult for them to escape abusive situations (Kabeer, 2001).

3 Forms of Violence Against Women in Africa

Physical violence is one of the most common forms of violence in Africa. Physical violence refers to the use of force or aggression to cause harm to individuals or groups (Alesina et al., 2021: 72). This violence can take many forms, including domestic violence, sexual violence, political violence, and inter-communal violence. Physical violence in Africa is often associated with poverty, inequality, and political instability, and it has significant social, economic, and health consequences for the affected individuals and communities (Krook, 2017: 78). Physical violence in Africa is, therefore, influenced by a complex interplay of different factors. It includes acts such as beating, slapping, punching, kicking, burning, or using weapons to inflict harm on women. In some African countries, harmful traditional practices such as female genital mutilation (FGM) are still prevalent, causing physical harm to women.

Sexual violence is another significant form of physical violence against women in Africa. It includes acts such as rape, attempted rape, unwanted sexual touching, and other forms of non-consensual sexual contact (Dartnall & Jewkes, 2013: 4). In conflict-affected regions like the Democratic Republic of Congo (DRC), South Sudan and Nigeria, sexual violence has been used as a weapon of war to terrorize communities and exert power over women (Alesina et al., 2021: 102). In these countries, rape has been systematically employed by armed groups to terrorize and subjugate communities. Sexual violence not only inflicts physical and psychological harm on the victims, but also serves to destabilize families and communities by breaking social bonds and stigmatizing survivors. The prevalence of sexual violence varies across African countries but remains alarmingly high in many regions. Factors contributing to sexual violence include gender inequality, harmful cultural practices, and weak legal systems that fail to protect victims and hold perpetrators accountable (Kalra & Bhugra, 2013: 245).

Psychological violence is another form of violence against women in Africa. It involves emotional abuse, threats of harm or abandonment, humiliation, intimidation, and controlling behaviour (WHO, 1997). This form of violence can have long-lasting effects on a woman's mental health and well-being. Psychological violence against women in Africa is a pervasive and complex issue that encompasses various forms of emotional and mental abuse (Fawole & Dagunduro, 2014). This type of violence can manifest in several ways, including verbal abuse, humiliation, manipulation, control, isolation, and threats. Psychological violence has severe consequences on the mental health and well-being of women, often leading to depression, anxiety, post-traumatic stress disorder (PTSD), and even suicide (Fawole & Dagunduro, 2014: 300). In many African countries, deeply rooted cultural norms and traditions contribute to the prevalence of psychological violence against women. Patriarchal societies often perpetuate gender inequality and condone harmful practices that subject women to emotional abuse. Some of these practices include female genital mutilation (FGM), child marriage, and polygamy.

Female Genital Mutilation (FGM) is a harmful traditional practice that involves the partial or total removal of the external female genitalia for non-medical reasons (Alesina et al., 2021: 103). Female genital mutilation is prevalent in several African countries and is often justified as a rite of passage or a means to preserve a girl's purity. The psychological impact of FGM on women includes feelings of shame, humiliation, betrayal by family members, and fear of intimacy (Kalra & Bhugra, 2013: 245). Child marriage is another harmful practice that disproportionately affects girls in Africa. Early marriage often results in girls being forced into relationships with older men who may exert control over their lives. This power imbalance can lead to psychological violence in the form of verbal abuse, manipulation, and isolation from friends and family (Alesina et al., 2021: 106). In addition to cultural factors, other factors contributing to psychological violence against women in Africa include poverty, lack of education, and weak legal frameworks. Poverty can exacerbate gender inequality and make women more vulnerable to abuse. Lack of education may limit women's awareness of their rights and access to resources that could help them escape abusive situations. Weak legal frameworks often fail to protect women from psychological violence or hold perpetrators accountable (Alesina et al., 2021: 100).

Moreover, cultural norms and gender inequality play a significant role in perpetuating domestic violence in Africa. Domestic violence encompasses various forms of abuse, including physical, emotional, sexual, and economic violence perpetrated by intimate partners or family members (Bassey & Bubu, 2019: 21). The prevalence of domestic violence in Africa is influenced by a range of factors, such as cultural norms, gender inequality, poverty, and weak legal frameworks (Alesina et al., 2021). Poverty is another factor that exacerbates domestic violence in Africa. Financial stress can lead to increased tension within households and may result in violent behaviour. Moreover, impoverished communities often lack access to resources and support services for victims of domestic violence (WHO, 2012). Weak legal frameworks also contribute to the prevalence of domestic violence in Africa. In many countries, laws addressing domestic violence are either inadequate or poorly enforced. This lack of legal protection can leave victims vulnerable and discourage them from seeking help (Bassey & Bubu, 2019: 21).

Domestic violence can be exacerbated by tensions between different ethnic or religious groups. In some cases, women may be targeted for abuse because of their perceived affiliation with a rival community. For example, during the Rwandan genocide in 1994, many Tutsi women were subjected to brutal acts of sexual violence by Hutu perpetrators as part of a broader campaign of ethnic cleansing (Moore, 2008: 778). In many African societies, traditional beliefs about gender roles and the status of women contribute to the normalization of violence against women. For example, some cultures may view wife-beating as an acceptable form of discipline or a husband's right (Alesina et al., 2021). Forced marriage is another manifestation of violence against women in Africa. In some regions, girls are forcibly married off to members of rival communities as a means of forging alliances or settling disputes (Haffejee et al., 2020: 20). This practice does not only violate the girls' rights to bodily autonomy and self-determination; it also exposes them to increased risks of domestic violence and sexual assault within their new households.

Additionally, women's economic dependence on their partners can make it difficult for them to leave abusive relationships (Tenkorang et al., 2021). Intimate Partner Violence (IPV) is one of the most common forms of physical violence against women in Africa. It refers to any behaviour within an intimate relationship that causes physical, psychological, or sexual harm to those in the relationship (WHO, 2012). About 36.6% of African women have experienced physical and/or sexual IPV in their lifetime. This prevalence varies across countries, with some regions such as Central African Republic reporting rates as high as 65.64%, Botswana at 65% and others such as Tunisia as low as 20.85% (Tenkorang et al., 2021). Several factors contribute to the high prevalence of IPV in Africa, including gender inequality, poverty, lack of education, and cultural norms that perpetuate male dominance and control over women.

Political violence is another form of violence against women common in the African continent. It is a pervasive and complex issue that encompasses various forms of violence, including physical, sexual, psychological, and economic. This violence occurs in different contexts, such as during elections, political protests, and within political parties. It is driven by multiple factors, including patriarchal norms, gender inequality, and the lack of legal frameworks to protect women's rights (Krook, 2017; True, 2012). Women in politics often face physical attacks, such as beatings, abductions, and assassinations. These attacks are intended to intimidate and silence them or to punish them for their political activities. Women also face sexual assault and rape which are used as weapons of political violence against women. This form of violence is often used to humiliate and degrade women and to assert power over them. Women in politics are also frequently subjected to threats, harassment, and intimidation. This can take the form of verbal abuse, online trolling, or stalking. They are also facing economic violence as a form of political violence. Women's access to resources are restricted as a form of political violence. This may include withholding financial support or denying them opportunities for employment or education (Krook, 2017; True, 2012).

Factors contributing to political violence against women include patriarchal norms found in African societies. Patriarchal norms refer to the societal expectations and values that prioritize male dominance and control over women. These norms are deeply ingrained in many cultures and have been perpetrated through generations. Patriarchal norms can manifest in various ways, such as limiting women's access to education and job opportunities, restricting their freedom of movement, and promoting traditional gender roles. Traditional gender roles and expectations often perpetuate the belief that women should not be involved in politics. This can lead to hostility and violence against women who challenge these norms. Gender inequality is another factor which leads to violence against women in Africa. Gender inequality refers to the unequal treatment of individuals based on their gender, particularly in terms of access to resources, opportunities, and social status. It is a pervasive issue that affects individuals across the globe and has significant impacts on social, economic, and political outcomes. Women's unequal status in society can make them more vulnerable to political violence.

This includes limited access to education, employment, and resources, as well as social and cultural barriers that prevent women from participating in politics. In many African countries, there is a lack of comprehensive legislation to protect women's rights and address gender-based violence. This can make it difficult for women to seek justice and protection from political violence (Alesina et al., 2021).

Economic violence is another form of violence prevalent in Africa. It includes denying women access to financial resources or employment opportunities, controlling their income or assets, and restricting their ability to make decisions about household finances. Economic violence in the African context is a multifaceted issue that encompasses various forms of discrimination, exploitation, and abuse (Tenkorang et al., 2021). It refers to the systemic and structural barriers that prevent women from accessing resources, opportunities, and services, which ultimately perpetuates gender inequality and hinders their economic empowerment (True, 2012: 10). Economic violence against women in Africa manifests in several ways, including wage discrimination, limited access to education and training, restricted property rights, lack of access to credit and financial services, and gender-based violence in the workplace.

Some women in Africa often face wage discrimination, earning less than their male counterparts for the same work. Wage discrimination refers to the unfair treatment of employees based on their gender, race, or other personal characteristics, resulting in unequal pay for the same work. This can occur through direct discrimination, where an employer pays different wages to employees who are doing the same job but belong to different groups, or through indirect discrimination, where certain policies or practices have a disproportionate impact on certain groups and result in lower pay (Goldin, 2018). This pay gap is attributed to various factors such as occupational segregation, undervaluation of women's work, and discriminatory practices by employers. Wage discrimination not only affects women's income but also contributes to the feminization of poverty (Fisher et al., 2021). Moreover, some African girls face barriers to education due to cultural norms that prioritize boys' education over girls', early marriage, and gender-based violence in schools. Limited access to education results in lower literacy rates among women compared to men, which further restricts their employment opportunities and economic independence. Additionally, in many African countries, customary laws and patriarchal norms limit women's property rights. Women often have limited or no rights to inherit or own land, housing, or other assets. This lack of property rights not only undermines women's economic security but also increases their vulnerability to domestic violence and other forms of abuse. Women in Africa are also vulnerable to various forms of gender-based violence in the workplace, including sexual harassment, exploitation, and abuse. This not only affects their mental and physical well-being but also creates a hostile work environment that hinders their career advancement and economic opportunities (Fisher et al., 2021).

Harmful traditional practices are also a form of gender-based violence in Africa. Female genital mutilation, for example, is a widespread practice that can cause physical and psychological harm to girls and women (UNICEF, 2016). Child marriage is another harmful practice that puts young girls at risk of violence and exploitation. Cultural violence against women in Africa is a complex issue with deep roots in traditional beliefs and practices. These cultural practices often reinforce gender inequality and perpetuate harmful attitudes towards women, resulting in various forms of violence. Some of the causes of cultural violence against women in Africa are patriarchal norms. Patriarchy is deeply entrenched in many African societies, where men hold power and authority over women (Lorber, 2019). This power dynamic is reinforced through cultural practices such as female genital mutilation (FGM), child marriage, and bride price, which are all forms of violence against women (Alesina et al., 2021: 103). Additionally, many African societies have traditional beliefs that view women as inferior to men and assign them subordinate roles in society. These beliefs are often used to justify violence against women, such as wife-beating or the practice of widowhood rites, where widows are subjected to various forms of abuse and humiliation (Lorber, 2019). Lack of legal protection leaves women vulnerable to abuse and violence without any recourse. Women who have limited access to education are more likely to be subjected to cultural violence as they lack the knowledge and skills to challenge harmful practices or seek help.

Social violence against women in Africa is a persistent problem that has deep roots in cultural, social, economic, and political factors. The causes of social violence against women in Africa are complex and multifaceted. Patriarchal culture perpetuates gender inequality and reinforces the belief that men are superior to women. This belief system creates an environment where violence against women is accepted as normal and justified. Poverty is another form of social violence. Women who live in poverty are more likely to experience violence because they lack economic resources and are dependent on their partners or family members for survival. Conflict and war exacerbate social violence against women in Africa. During times of conflict, women become vulnerable to sexual violence, rape, and other forms of abuse. However, many African countries lack effective legal frameworks to protect women from violence (Lorber, 2019). Laws that do exist are often not enforced, leaving women without recourse when they experience violence. Some traditional practices in Africa perpetuate violence against women. They can lead to physical and psychological harm.

4 The Cost of Violence Against Women in Africa

Having examined the various forms of violence against women in Africa in the foregoing section, this section analyses the cost of this violence. Violence against women, like other forms of violence, comes at a great cost to Africa. Recognizing the value of the concept of intersectionality, where variables such as race, gender, class, sexuality and others (Meer & Müller, 2017) coalesce and engender multiple forms of oppression, in this chapter we acknowledge that, given the diversity among women, the cost of violence is not uniform. In particular, Black and Indigenous women in Africa tend to carry the greatest burden of the costs of violence. We admit, however, that there is no unanimity regarding the most effective way of calculating the cost of violence against women (see e.g. Vyas et al., 2023). Data from national demographic and health surveys are mostly used in such studies, although this has its own challenges (see e.g. Alesina et al., 2016; Breuer, 2021). Nonetheless, it is possible to outline some of the approaches that have been adopted, particularly in relation to categorizing the types of costs. The following example, with particular reference to Kenya, is helpful:

> The costs can be classified as directly tangible, indirectly tangible, directly intangible and indirectly intangible. Directly tangible costs represent actual money spent, expenditure on prevention and service provision including legal, health, social services and counselling. Indirectly tangible costs are measured as a loss of potential and income. Directly intangible costs result from the GBV, but have no monetary value, for example psychological trauma, pain and suffering. Indirectly intangible costs result from the GBV but have no monetary value. This includes negative psychosocial effects on witnesses of violence, especially children. Unless checked and monitored, GBV has the potential to become a heavy burden on Kenya's Gross Domestic Product (GDP) and have a negative impact on the attainment of universal healthcare. (Kenya Institute for Public Policy Research and Analysis, 2021: 3)

Another example, drawn from a study on the cost of violence against women in Lesotho, is also useful. The Commonwealth Secretariat notes the following:

The methodology includes three types of costs:

- Direct costs: including the cost of medical treatment for physical and sexual abuses—doctors/hospital bills for physical injuries; the cost of psychosocial care; the cost of law enforcement/the police; and loss of earned income due to absence from work, as well as loss of imputed earnings from being unable to attend to household activities, including childcare etc.
- Indirect costs: which measures reduced gross domestic product (GDP) because of the decline in private consumption due to loss of female earnings. Reduced private consumption expenditure leads to a decline in effective demand and subsequently gross domestic product—because of their interdependence in the circular flow of income generation in an economy (in economic literature, these effects are known as the "first round impacts" of any shock or intervention).
- Induced costs: capture the further reduction (i.e. the "second round effects") in GDP due to loss of demand for the products (unaffected in the first round) which are linked with the products that are affected indirectly. (Commonwealth Secretariat, 2020: xi–xii)

The citations above show the diverse costs of violence against women in Africa. Such an approach is useful as it goes beyond the simple accounting method. It assists women activists, policy makers, progressive politicians and other strategic individuals and institutions in Africa to appreciate the cost of violence against women. While the use of figures should not be understood as a tactic to shock casual policy makers and politicians into action, it is valuable in taking violence against women from the domain of being a "private issue" into a serious human development issue. Given that both the African Union's Agenda 2063 and the United Nation's 2030 Sustainable Development Goals seek to achieve gender equality, understanding the cost of violence against women in Africa is critical for progress (see e.g. Moyo & Dhliwayo, 2019).

Asante et al. (2019: 16) have developed a comprehensive conceptual framework for the social and economic impacts of violence against women. In relation to the economic dimension, they reflect on the impact on an individual or the household. Thus, there is loss of income, loss of consumption/welfare, out-of-pocket expenditure accessing health/legal services, impact on children and health status/trauma. They refer to the business/community and draw attention to costs relating to NGO services, loss of business output, loss of productivity/profit and workplace prevention programmes. The costs borne by the government relate to service provision, social transfers and expenditure on prevention. The social impact is on both individuals and households and is felt in the loss of quality of life and decreased participation. Social cohesion is compromised, resulting in loss of trust. As highlighted in the introduction, the social cost at the national level is felt through a decrease in women's political participation and an increase in collective violence. The net cost has been expressed in a recent study as follows:

> We find that violence against women and girls has a negative effect on economic activity. The results show that when the percentage of women subject to domestic violence declines by 1 percentage point, per capita nightlights-based economic activities increase by 8 percent. Our results provide empirical support for the channel through which violence against women and girls can affect economic activity, as we find that more violence is associated with a significant drop in female employment. Our results also show that violence against women is more detrimental to economic development in countries without protective laws against domestic violence, natural resource rich countries, where women are deprived of decision-making power and during economic downturns such as this pandemic crisis. In addition, we find that the economic cost of violence against women is higher in countries where the gender gap in education between partners is high. The results are robust to several alternative specifications. The findings imply that sub-Saharan African countries should strengthen laws to combat violence against women and reinforce women's decision-making power. Furthermore, promoting women's education will be key to reduce the gender gap in education and the influence and control by men. Sub-Saharan African countries should also address the increased levels of domestic violence during the COVID-19 crisis to bolster the economic recovery. (Ouedraogo & Stenzel, 2021: 4)

The passage cited above presents the economic impact of violence against women in Africa in a very clear way. It lays bare the cost of violence against women and the contexts in which women's vulnerability to violence is pronounced. Calculating the cost of violence against women challenges duty bearers to acknowledge the seriousness of the issue. This is due to the fact that many of them are only persuaded by arguments that prioritize economic consequences. The following citation on the cost of intimate partner violence (IPV) in Ethiopia illustrates the impact of this approach:

> The aggregate cost of IPV in Ethiopia, including costs for women and households, as well as the potential cost of service provision, comes to 68,154,357,585 Birr (USD 1,312,652,927). In sum, this cost of IPV is equivalent to 1.21% of 2020 GDP. It demonstrates in clear terms the significant economic drain that IPV places on the economy, thus affecting the economic security and well-being of women and households. (UN Women Ethiopia 2022: 11)

Finally, although it might seem unsavoury, there is a need to also factor in the costs that perpetrators of violence against women face, particularly when they are arrested. In those contexts where the law is effective, they must pay fines, or they are imprisoned. Imprisonment also burdens the taxpayer as the perpetrator, who might have been more productive, would now need to be looked after while in prison. There are costs involved in programmes that seek to prevent perpetrators from performing acts of violence against women. However, there are currently only very few studies that have sought to present the cost of popular prevention interventions in specific African contexts (see e.g. Michaels-Igbokwe et al., 2016) or the cost of prevention in a number of African countries (see e.g. Torres-Rueda et al., 2020).

5 Conclusion

In order for Africa to avoid paying the hefty price of violence against women, it is important for the continent to invest in cultures of peace. Cultures of peace for development in Africa involve the creation of an environment where individuals, communities, and nations can interact peacefully and resolve conflicts without resorting to violence. This approach emphasizes the importance of cultural diversity, dialogue, and cooperation in promoting peace and development (Adebayo, 2016). In such an environment, women can flourish by bringing all their gifts and talents to their families, communities, countries, and the continent. They will not be constrained by the fear of violence in personal relationships and in the wider society. Nurturing cultures of peace in Africa will minimize the cost of violence against women. In particular, it will reduce the pain and suffering, as well as premature mortality that are associated with violence against women. Promoting cultures of peace in African homes, schools, the media, religious institutions, and other spaces will spare the continent costs relating to violence against women and free the continent to redirect scarce financial and other resources towards other development endeavours.

References

Adebayo, A. (2016). Cultures of Peace for Development in Africa: The Role of Education. *Journal of Education and Practice, 7*(26), 77–84.

African Union Commission—Women, Gender and Development Directorate (AUC-WGDD), et al. (2020). *Gender-Based Violence in Africa During the COVID-19 Pandemic* (Policy Paper). African Union Commission—Women,

Gender and Development Directorate (AUC-WGDD). https://au.int/sites/def ault/files/documents/39878-doc-final-final-policy_paper-_gbv_in_africa_during_ covid-19_pandemic.pdf. Accessed 9 July 2023.

Alesina, A., Brioschi, B., & La Ferrara, E. (2021). Violence Against Women: A Cross-Cultural Analysis for Africa. *Economica, 88*(349), 70–104.

Alesina, A., et al. (2016). *Violence Against Women: A Cross-Cultural Analysis for Africa* (NBER Working Paper No. 21901). https://www.nber.org/system/files/working_ papers/w21901/w21901.pdf. Accessed 9 July 2023.

Asante, F., et al. (2019). *Economic and Social Costs of Violence Against Women and Girls in Ghana: Country Technical Report*. NUI Galway.

Bassey, S. A., & Bubu, N. G. (2019). Gender Inequality in Africa: A Re-examination of Cultural Values. *Cogito: Multidisciplinary Research Journal, 11*(3), 21–36.

Breuer, S. (2021). *Economic Analyses on the Cost of Gender-Based Violence in Namibia* (ZÖSS Discussion Paper, No. 86). Universität Hamburg, Zentrum für Ökonomische und Soziologische Studien (ZÖSS).

Commonwealth Secretariat. (2020). *The Economic Cost of Violence Against Women and Girls: A Study of Lesotho*. Commonwealth Secretariat. https://production-new-commonwealth-files.s3.eu-west-2.amazonaws.com/migrated/inline/The_ Economic_Cost_of_Violence_Against_Women_and_Girls_UPDF%5B3%5D. pdf. Accessed 9 July 2023.

Dartnall, E., & Jewkes, R. (2013). Sexual Violence Against Women: The Scope of the Problem. *Best Practice & Research Clinical Obstetrics & Gynaecology, 27*(1), 3–13.

Fawole, O. I., & Dagunduro, A. T. (2014). Prevalence and Correlates of Violence Against Female Sex Workers in Abuja, Nigeria. *African Health Sciences, 14*(2), 299–313.

Fisher, B., et al. (2021). *Gender Wage Discrimination in South Africa Within the Affirmative Action Framework* (EDWRG Working Paper Number 01-20).

Goldin, C. (2018). A Grand Gender Convergence: Its Last Chapter. *American Economic Review: Papers & Proceedings, 108*(5), 109–113.

Haffejee, S., Treffry-Goatley, A., Wiebesiek, L., & Mkhize, N. (2020). Negotiating Girl-Led Advocacy: Addressing Early and Forced Marriage in South Africa. *Girlhood Studies, 13*(2), 18–34.

Jewkes, R., & Morrell, R. (2012). Gender and Sexuality: Emerging Perspectives from the Heterosexual Epidemic in South Africa and Implications for HIV Risk and Prevention. *Journal of the International AIDS Society, 15*(Suppl. 2), 17411.

Kabeer, N. (2001). Conflicts over Credit: Re-evaluating the Empowerment Potential of Loans to Women in Rural Bangladesh. *World Development, 29*(1), 63–84.

Kalra, G., & Bhugra, D. (2013). Sexual Violence Against Women: Understanding Cross-Cultural Intersections. *Indian Journal of Ppsychiatry, 55*(3), 244–249.

Kenya Institute for Public Policy Research and Analysis. (2021). KIPPRA Discussion Paper No. 261. KIPPRA.

Krook, M. L. (2017). Violence Against Women in Politics. *Journal of Democracy, 28*(1), 74–88.

Krook, M. L. (2020). *Violence Against Women in Politics*. Oxford University Press.
Lorber, J. (2019). *Gender Inequality: Feminist Theories and Politics*. Oxford University Press.
Manyonganise, M. (2023). *Daring Patriarchy? A Biblical Engagement with Gender Discourses on Political Participation in Post-colonial Zimbabwe*. University of Bamberg Press.
Meer, T., & Müller, A. (2017). Considering Intersectionality in Africa. *Agenda, 31*(1), 3–4. https://doi.org/10.1080/10130950.2017.1363583
Michaels-Igbokwe, C., et al. (2016). Cost and Cost-Effectiveness Analysis of a Community Mobilization Intervention to Reduce Intimate Partner Violence in Kampala, Uganda. *BMC Public Health, 16*, 196. https://doi.org/10.1186/s12889-016-2883-6
Moore, A. R. (2008). Types of Violence Against Women and Factors Influencing Intimate Partner Violence in Togo (West Africa). *Journal of Family Violence, 23*, 777–783.
Moyo, T., & Dhliwayo, R. (2019). Achieving Gender Equality and Women's Empowerment in Sub-Saharan Africa: Lessons from the Experience of Selected Countries. *Journal of Developing Societies, 35*(2), 256–281.
Muluneh, M. D., et al. (2020). Gender-Based Violence Against Women in Sub-Saharan Africa: A Systematic Review and Meta-Analysis of Cross-Sectional Studies. *International Journal of Environmental Research and Public Health, 17*(3), 903. https://doi.org/10.3390/ijerph17030903
Ouedraogo, R., & Stenzel, D. (2021). *The Heavy Economic Toll of Gender-Based Violence: Evidence from Sub-Saharan Africa* (IMF WP/21/277).
Sachseder, J. C. (2023). *Violence Against Women in and Beyond Conflict: The Coloniality of Violence*. Routledge.
Tenkorang, E. Y., Asamoah-Boaheng, M., & Owusu, A. Y. (2021). Intimate Partner Violence (IPV) Against HIV-Positive Women in Sub-Saharan Africa: A Mixed-Method Systematic Review and Meta-Analysis. *Trauma, Violence, & Abuse, 22*(5), 1104–1128.
Torres-Rueda, S., et al. (2020). What Will It Cost to Prevent Violence Against Women and Girls in Low- and Middle-Income Countries? Evidence from Ghana, Kenya, Pakistan, Rwanda, South Africa and Zambia. *Health Policy and Planning, 35*(7), 855–866.
True, J. (2012). *The Political Economy of Violence Against Women*. Oxford University Press.
United Nations Children's Fund (UNICEF). (2016). *Female Genital Mutilation/Cutting: A Global Concern*. https://data.unicef.org/resources/female-genital-mutilationcutting-global-concern/. Accessed 9 July 2023.
UN Women Ethiopia. (2022). *Economic Costs of Intimate Partner Violence Against Women in Ethiopia: Technical Report*. UN Women Ethiopia.
Vyas, S., et al. (2023, January). The Economic Cost of Violence Against Women and Girls in Low- and Middle-Income Countries: A Systematic Review of the

Evidence. *Trauma Violence Abuse, 24*(1), 44–55. https://doi.org/10.1177/15248380211016018. Epub 2021 May 17. PMID: 33998339.

World Health Organization. (1997). *Violence Against Women* (No. WHO/FRH/WHD/97.8). World Health Organization.

World Health Organization. (2012). *Understanding and Addressing Violence Against Women: Intimate Partner Violence* (No. WHO/RHR/12.36). World Health Organization.

World Health Organization. (2013). *Global and Regional Estimates of Violence Against Women: Prevalence and Health Effects of Intimate Partner Violence and Non-partner Sexual Violence.* https://apps.who.int/iris/handle/10665/85239

Violence against Women in Egypt: A Closer Look at Intimate Partner Violence and Female Genital Mutilation

Yasmin M. Khodary

1 Introduction

In 1995, the Beijing Declaration and Platform of Action for Equality, Development and Peace noted that "in all societies, to a greater or lesser degree, women and girls are subjected to physical, sexual, and psychological abuse that cuts across lines of income, class, and culture." More than 28 years later, violence against women (VAW), which is a clear manifestation of gender inequality, remains a widespread world phenomenon further exacerbated by existent social, economic, and overall gender inequality. African women are definitely no exception. From female genital mutilation or cutting (FGM/C), child marriage, honour crimes, and intimate partner violence (IPV) in the private space, to sexual harassment and state violence in the public space, African women are exposed to several forms of violence across their lifetime. The scope of these forms of violence is hardly documented or reported accurately as a result of cultural restrictions and traditions.

In Egypt, around 7.8 million women are exposed to at least one form of violence annually, whether perpetrated by an intimate partner, close relatives, or strangers in the public space. According to the latest survey conducted by the Ministry of Health and Population in 2015, around 26% of ever-partnered women aged 15–49 years old experience physical and/or sexual violence from their partner at least once in their lifetime. However, very

---

Y. M. Khodary (✉)
Professor of Political Science, The British University in Egypt, El Shorouk, Egypt
e-mail: yasmin.khodary@bue.edu.eg

limited updated information is available on the scope of VAW in Egypt and the associated factors. This chapter aims to map the different forms of VAW in Egypt with a special focus on FGM and IPV. It also aims to answer the following question: To what extent do factors such as gender, residence, wealth, and education shape women's exposure to violence and increase the risk of their exposure to certain forms of VAW in Egypt? This chapter relies on data collected from a representative sample of 400 Egyptian men and women in Qalyoubia Governorate (Lower Egypt) and Minia Governorate (Upper Egypt) not only to provide an overview of the prevalence of FGM and IPV but, most importantly, also to test the significance of various categories of inequalities, such as gender, urban–rural division, wealth, and education, for the prevalence of FGM and IPV in Egypt.

2 An Overview of Intimate Partner Violence and Female Genital Mutilation in Egypt

Intimate partner violence is perpetuated against women by their intimate partners. According to the World Health Organization (2010), IPV is defined as any "behaviour within an intimate relationship that causes physical, sexual or psychological harm, including acts of physical aggression, sexual coercion, psychological abuse, and controlling behaviors."[1] Despite being criminalized by various international human rights conventions, such as the Universal Declaration of Human Rights, the Declaration on the Elimination of Violence Against Women, and the Platform for Action of the Fourth World Conference on Women, one in every three women around the world remains subjected to physical or sexual violence by their intimate partners (World Health Organization, 2016). According to the 2014 Egyptian Demographic Health survey, 36% of married women in Egypt aged between 15 and 49 years experience physical violence perpetrated by their partners. In patriarchal and conservative cultures, such as in Egypt, IPV poses a particularly serious challenge, given women's reluctance or inability to expose their partners or call for professional help from social workers, psychologists, physicians, or the police force.

Considerable literature investigates the risk factors associated with women's increased likelihood of experiencing IPV. Scholars identify three groups of risk factors, including: individual/personal, relationship/relational and community/societal factors. Individual factors, such as exposure to previous

---

[1] A special thanks to Nehal Hamdy and Nour Kamel for their help with the literature review.

abuse and normalization of violence, are found to increase the risk of women experiencing violence (Abramsky et al., 2011). In a meta-analytical review of 85 studies to identify risk factors related to physical IPV, Stith et al. (2004) identify many risk factors for perpetration of physical IPV, which are mostly individual and relational factors. They find large effect sizes between perpetration of physical IPV and five risk factors, including illicit drug use and attitudes condoning marital violence. They also find moderate effect sizes between perpetration of physical IPV and six risk factors, including traditional sex-role ideology, anger, depression, alcohol use, history of partner abuse, and career/life stress. Researchers identify further individual factors, such as specific age groups, carry a higher risk of domestic victimization. For example, Greenfeld and Craven (1998) found females in the USA in the age group from 16 to 24 to have been at high risk of domestic violence.

Community and societal factors, including low socio-economic status, also play a role in increasing the likelihood of women's exposure to IPV (Heise & Gracia-Moreno, 2002). According to the Australian Bureau of Statistics (2013), low socio-economic status is an influential aspect to the occurrence of family violence. Jewkes (2002) refers to poverty as the most important social and demographic IPV risk factor. Women lacking access to regular sources of income or having financial problems witness increasing likelihood of being trapped in abusive relationships (Jewkes, 2002). Stark (1987), Sampson and Groves (1989) and Krivo and Peterson (1996) assert that social conditions such as poor housing, distressed neighbourhood, and disrupted families have a positive relation to domestic violence. In addition, Ozer et al. (2003) and Ullman (2005) found that social reasons, such as lack of social support, are correlated with potential victimization. Women who feel isolated from friends and family are at higher risk of witnessing IPV and remaining in violent relationships. These feelings occur most readily for immigrant women as many have left behind families and friends (Menjivar & Salicido, 2002). Cutrona et al. (2008) also explain that in poor communities, such as slums, there are very few role models for healthy competent marriage relations. Because of the daily stressors and life frustrations, couples in poor communities tend to blame each other for their low-quality conditions, which in the long term cause them to have less warmth for each other.

A series of studies on IPV in Egypt were also carried out in the past decades referring to a combination of risk factors. In 1979, a study was conducted by Malek Zaghloul on intimate partner abuse in Egypt and its key motives using 50 cases of women who had been physically abused by their husbands in Abdin, Egypt. The study found that the likelihood of women's physical abuse increases with lack of financial resources and persistent psychological stress as a result of economic burdens and low quality of life (Al-Magdoub, 2003). Polygamy, which resulted in additional burdens on men and their inability to provide for their households, was also identified as another risk factor associated with IPV. In 1989, another study was carried out investigating the factors related to married couples' homicides. The study revealed that relationships that ended with an act of homicide were built on years of abusive and aggressive behaviour from the men's side. Women who killed their husbands tolerated years of physical and sexual violence. In addition, the study found that these homicides took place among middle and lower classes and that social and economic frustrations increased the risk of exposure to IPV among couples, leading ultimately to murder. In 1994, a third study was conducted by Abdel-Wahab on family violence in Egypt using a sample of 224 cases in order to identify the most significant reasons behind the spread of IPV in Egyptian society. The study found that economic conditions came at the top of the reasons that stimulated the use of violence against women in the family, followed by low educational and social status of both the husband and the wife. The study also highlighted that IPV levels was evidently higher among couples in poor communities than among those in affluent communities. Similarly, Habib (2009) revealed in a summary report on violence against women in Egypt that IPV mostly prevailed among couples that had low educational status and belonged to low socio-economic class.

Similarly, a set of socio-cultural factors were found to increase women's exposure to FGM in Egypt. Female genital mutilation is defined by WHO as "all procedures that involve partial or total removal of the external female genitalia, or other injury to the female genital organs for non-medical reasons" (WHO, 2023). A very common cultural notion associated with FGM is that it ostensibly controls women's sexuality and protects girls until their marriage time (Barsoum et al., 2011: 10; UNICEF, 2014). According to Kaplan et al. (2011), FGM is considered as an effective way to reduce women's sexual feelings, maintain virginity, and reduce the likelihood of prostitution. It also enhances marriage opportunity and ensures the female identity as she becomes a pure female not a male. Furthermore, FGM is perceived to enhance girls' marriage opportunities and ensure the female identity. Some families believe that this practice is essential for girls before marriage to protect them (Yount, 2002). In some cultural contexts, FGM is considered a necessity to protect women from sexual assault. Women who did not undergo FGM are considered prostitutes in both behaviour and profession (Yount, 2002). Therefore, FGM is applied against the will of females for protection of their virginity and family honour. In addition, in some circumstances, FGM can be interpreted as a manifestation of men's insecurity. Men use violence as a way of emphasizing their masculine role, and consequently assume the power to dominate (Heise et al., 1995).

According to Packer (2005), FGM is practised in Egypt because of sociocultural notions and persistent inequalities, which defy existent legislation. Egyptian women have usually been constrained by customs and traditions to a subsidiary role. Egyptian society generally embraces a rigid patriarchal structure, and Egyptian men generally understand manhood, *Quama* in Arabic, as "superiority," "responsibility," and "duty to protect the family." This perception tends to shape men's attitudes, especially towards their close family members and particularly their daughters. Thus, fathers believe that it is their duty to deliver their girls "protected" and "chaste" to their future husbands (El-Zanaty & Way, 2003). According to El-Mouelhy et al. (2013), such analysis of men's perceptions regarding their role in the family is necessary to understand their perceptions of FGM. A very common cultural notion is that FGM is deemed to control women's sexuality and protect girls until their marriage (Barsoum et al., 2011; UNICEF, 2014).

In addition to cultural notions, the prevalence of FGM is correlated also with social factors in Egypt, such as lack of education. A study conducted by Badawi (1989) asserts that the majority of women who had undergone FGM come from modest and low socio-economic backgrounds, such as having illiterate or poorly educated parents. To eradicate FGM, international organizations usually emphasize female empowerment, through improving women's position in society and reducing gender inequality. Education constitutes a cornerstone in this process; as women's social position is often measured by their education (WHO, 2008). According to Jejeebhoy (1995), education plays a crucial role in enhancing a woman's position. It does not only ensure economic and social independence for women, but it also provides an alternative path to status, which has a positive effect on their psychological and cultural lives. Furthermore, it is argued that education positively impacts women's ability to make healthy reproductive choices and increase the likelihood of their opposition to FGM.

This study provides a more recent account of the significance of various categories of inequalities, such as gender, urban–rural division, wealth, and education on the prevalence of FGM and IPV in Egypt. It also investigates the perceptions of the risk factors that increase their exposure to such violence, particularly FGM. As noted by Spruin et al. (2015), there has been limited attention to investigating women's perceptions and personal accounts of the risk factors, which they believe increases their exposure to such violence. It remains important to investigate the factors which society sees are crucial in increasing their likelihood of being exposed to IPV. Investigating these personal views and perceptions may provide further understanding of the phenomenon from the perspective of women and can, ultimately, contribute to the making of informed decisions by government or societal actors.

3 Research Methods

The study employs a quantitative method for data collection and analysis. A survey was carried out with a random sample of 400 from upper Egypt (Minia) and lower Egypt (Qalyoubia), also representing rural and urban areas of Egypt. In Qalyoubia; the field work was done in Qalyoub (Markez) representing the urban areas and Abou Senh (village) representing the rural areas. On the other hand, in Minia, the field work was carried out in Abou Kurkas (Markez) representing the urban areas and Mansafis (village) representing the rural area, as appears in Table 1.

According to the CAPMAS census, there are 2.4 million inhabitants in urban areas in Qalyoubia and 3.3 million inhabitants in the rural areas. On the other hand, there are one million inhabitants in urban areas in Minia and 4.5 million distributed in the rural areas. The equation of: $E = 1.96 * \sqrt{P(1-P)} / \sqrt{n}$ was then edited so that the size of the sample was calculated according to the equation: $(N-n) / (N-1)$.

Given the available cost and resources, data were collected from sample of 400,[2] representative of rural and urban areas, as well as males and females, including 200 women and 200 men and, at the same time, 200 urban and 200 rural, as appears in Table 2.

The sample reflects a wide range of demographic features as appears in Figs. 1 and 2, representing the nature of the communities in Qalyoubia and Minia Governorates. The education of the majority of the sample is intermediate education (41%) followed by basic education (27%). Egypt's K–12 education system includes six years of primary and three years of preparatory

Table 1 The actual distribution of inhabitants in Qalyoubia and Minia

Qalyoubia		Minia	
Markez	Village	Markez	Village
121,000	329,734 (17 villages)	604,230	25,000 (47 village)
384	377	374	378

---

[2] All participants took part in the interviews voluntarily. Confidentiality was maintained throughout this research. Pseudonyms were used to protect participants' identities.

Table 2 The sample distribution according to gender and urban/rural division

Urban		Rural	
Males	Females	Males	Females
100	100	100	100

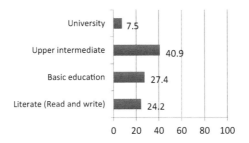

Fig. 1 The social characteristics of the sample (education)

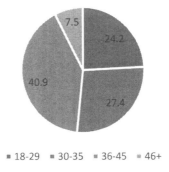

Fig. 2 Sample distribution by age group

education as well as three years of secondary education, together constituting basic education. Students who reach the secondary school level are often referred to as holding intermediate education. The age group of the majority of the sample is between 36 and 46 years (41%) followed by the age group between 30 and 35 years (27%). These are also age groups of men and women who have been in relationships for a fairly long period, which allows for a better profile of VAW, particularly IPV.

The survey, which primarily included closed questions, aimed at investigating the prevalence of different forms of VAW, particularly IPV (including physical, psychological, sexual, and economic violence by intimate partners) and FGM, as well as the factors associated with VAW. Questions (to male and female respondents) about physical violence inquired about incidents where women were slapped, pushed, kicked, dragged, beaten, or strangled among others. On the other hand, questions about psychological violence inquired about incidents where women were insulted or humiliated, threatened with harm, forbidden from visiting their families, or deprived from going out or participating in social activities. Questions about sexual violence inquired about incidents where women were being forced to have sex against their will. Finally, questions about economic violence inquired about incidents where women were forced to give their husbands their financial resources or where the husband refused to support their families financially. Other questions were focused on FGM as a form of VAW. This section on FGM explored women's exposure to forms of FGM and the perceptions around this. It inquired about whether or not FGM was conducted by a doctor, if the respondents received any awareness information about FGM, if they think FGM should continue, if they believe FGM prevents adultery, if they believe FGM leads to social and psychological problems, and if their daughter was exposed to/will be exposed to FGM. In addition, questions about FGM's relation to religion, education, tradition, or socio-economic status were also asked.

Finally, some questions were asked about the different economic, political, and socio-cultural impacts—if any—for the 25 January 2011 uprisings in Egypt on the spread of VAW in Egypt. The Egyptian uprisings, which raised the slogan of "Bread, liberty, and social justice," have led to a societal shift as well as having economic and political repercussions. These include the spread of individualism and individual as well as group violence, the increase in economic pressures and the unemployment rate under the new government's austerity measures, and political polarization and instability (Abd-Elmoteleb, 2017). It is, thus, intriguing to see the impact of these forces on VAW, particularly IPV and FGM.

The survey was then statistically analysed using SPSS. Data were not only analysed to reflect frequencies, but also to test the influence of assumed associated risk factors, such as gender (males and females),[3] residence (rural and urban), wealth (poorest, middle, rich, richest) as well as education (literate, basic education, upper intermediate, and university) on VAW, particularly IPV and FGM. To provide different levels of wealth, a factor analysis was made based on a variety of factors, including: ownership of house, fridge, television, personal computer or laptop, washing machine, and the number of persons per room. Based on the factor analysis, four lines were drawn where the wealthiest were labelled "richest," the following "rich," then "middle" and "poorest."

---

[3] For cultural purposes, the questions followed a binary understanding of gender through female/male division.

4 Findings on Factors Influencing the Prevalence of IPV and FGM

More than 85% of the women in the sample were exposed to at least one form of violence against women, including IPV or FGM. The vast majority of the sample, whether women (95%), and even more the men (96%), believed that women's exposure to violence negatively impacts the quality and nature of their participation in the family, public space, and political arenas. Here, there is a marginal statistically significant difference between the rural and urban responses, where a relatively greater percentage of the responses from rural areas (98%) than responses from urban areas (94%) were confident of the negative impact of VAW on women's participation. Despite such negative consequences, various forms of VAW are still prevalent in Egypt. The following sections explain the findings regarding factors associated with VAW, particularly IPV and FGM.

Gender and Women's Exposure to IPV and FGM

Overall, the majority of answers by female respondents' revealed a higher level of IPV than the male partners reported they exercised against women. As appears in Table 3, the female respondents revealed higher levels of physical violence in terms of: use of force against them by their partners (21%), being slapped (21%), and having their arms or hair pulled (10%). The difference between the responses of women and men here was found highly statistically significant as highlighted in grey in the Table 3 (and all tables). Women also reported higher levels of psychological violence in terms of being threatened to be hurt (7%), being insulted or humiliated (23%), and being forbidden from contacting their female friends (11%). In addition, they reported higher levels of sexual violence (8%) than men (1%). The difference between the responses of women and men here was also found highly statistically significant.

While reporting acts of IPV against women is expected to be higher by women than what their male partners report exercising, some acts of violence were reported by male respondents more frequently than women reported. This includes acting nervously when women speak to other men and stalking women or insisting on knowing where women are all the time, which 71 and 37% of the men reported occurring respectively compared to 68 and 27% of the females. The difference between women's and men's responses when it came to stalking women or insisting on knowing where women are all the time, in particular, was found highly statistically significant. Both actions are

Table 3 IPV by gender

Exposure to kinds of IPV	Females (%) (Yes)	Males (%) (Yes)
Acts nervously when you speak with another man	68	71
Prevents you from any contact with your female friends	11	5
Prevents you from contacting your family	8	5
Stalks you or insists on knowing where you are all the time	27	37
Threatens to hurt you	7	0
Insults you/demeans you	23	1
Threatens to cut financial resources	7	7
Forces you to have sex with him	8	1
Uses force against you or throws things at you	13	5
Slaps you on the face	21	5
Pulls your arm or hair	10	4
Burns you or tries to strangle you	0.5	0.5

associated with masculinity or manhood in Egypt and justified through men's *Quama* or "responsibility" to oversee and protect women and family (Packer, 2005; UNICEF, 2014).

On the other hand, when it comes to FGM, as appears in Table 4, around 83% of the women in the sample reported going through FGM. The differences between the responses of women and men in most of the survey questions on FGM was found highly statistically significant. Regardless of the information they received, a considerable percentage of men and, even more women still believe FGM should prevail. Despite the majority of the female respondents (92%), and even more of the male respondents (94%), receiving awareness sessions and information on FGM's negative consequences and root causes, 34% of the female respondents and 20% of the male respondents believe that FGM should continue. Around 38% of the female respondents and 21% of the male respondents exposed/will expose their daughters to FGM, which is a sign of the continuing belief in FGM regardless of awareness campaigns.

Female genital mutilation seems to be deeply rooted in the minds and practices of Egyptian society. As explained earlier by Packer (2005), more than any other factor, socio-cultural notions explain the persistence of the FGM practice in Egypt defying existent legislation and make it harder for awareness campaigns to spread information to eradicate the practice of FGM. Both female respondents (65%) and male respondents (76%) believe Egyptian traditions are the major root cause for the spread of FGM. Fewer

Table 4 FGM by gender

Undergoing FGM	Females (%) (Yes)	Males (%) (Yes)
Exposed to any form of FGM	83	59
The procedure was conducted by a doctor	47	19
Received information about FGM	92	94
FGM is related to religion	26	16
FGM is related to lack of education	5	8
FGM is related to tradition	65	76
FGM is related to socio-economic status	4	1
FGM should continue	34	20
Husbands want their wives to undergo FGM	36	40
FGM prevents adultery	34	41
Your daughter was exposed to/will be exposed to FGM	38	21
FGM leads to social and psychological problems	62	62

female respondents (26%) and male respondents (16%) associate this practice with religion, despite the idea that women seem to suffer this confusion more. Traditions and patriarchal cultural norms support the existence and continuation of FGM.

Residence (Rural–Urban) and Women's Exposure to IPV and FGM

There was a statistically significant difference between rural and urban responses on a variety of forms of IPV. As highlighted in dark grey in Table 5, this includes stalking women or insisting on knowing where their female partners are all the time as well as pulling women's arms or hair, where the number of responses of rural participants confirming these practices (41 and 10% respectively) were twice those of urban participants (23 and 5% respectively). On the other hand, there was a high statistically significant difference between urban and rural responses regarding economic violence or threatening women by saying one would cut the financial resources provided to them. As highlighted in light grey in Table 5, a marginal statistically significant difference was also found regarding sexual violence or forcing women to have sex with them, where the urban affirmative responses were higher (10 and 6%) than rural affirmative responses (4 and 3% respectively).

When it comes to FGM, as highlighted in grey in Table 6, the differences between almost all rural and urban responses were statistically significant. The only response where there was no difference between rural and urban

Table 5 IPV by residence

Exposure to kinds of IPV	Rural (%)	Urban (%)
Acts nervously when you speak with another man	72	76
Prevents you from any contact with your female friends	6	10
Prevents you from contacting your family	5	8
Stalks you or insists on knowing where you are all the time	41	23
Threatens to hurt you or to hurt someone close to you	4	4
Insults you/demeans you	11	12
Threatens to cut the financial resources	4	10
Forces you to have sex with him	3	6
Uses force against you or throws things at you	10	8
Slaps you on the face	15	11
Pulls your arm or hair	9.5	4.5
Burns you or tries to strangle you	0	1

Table 6 FGM by residence

Undergoing FGM	Rural (%) (Yes)	Urban (%) (Yes)
Exposed to any form of FGM	84	58
The procedure was conducted by a doctor	35	36
Received information about FGM	95	90
FGM is related to religion	22	20
FGM is related to education	3	10
FGM is related to tradition	73	68
FGM is related to socio-economic status	2	3
FGM should continue	33	22
Believe that husbands want their wives to undergo FGM	51	25
FGM prevents adultery	47	28
Your daughter was exposed to/will be exposed to FGM	34	25
FGM leads to social and psychological problems	51	73

participants was how the FGM procedure was conducted. Nearly the same percentage of rural participants (35%) and urban participants (36%) reported that this procedure was conducted by a doctor. Despite Egyptian laws which impose a high penalty on doctors, in particular, who operate such procedures on women and girls, whether for financial remuneration or for holding the same beliefs and cultural notions around this act, many still carry out FGM.

Except for the above question, the difference between the responses of rural and urban participants in the remaining questions were statistically significant. Very statistically significant differences between high affirmative responses for rural participants and urban participants were shown in the questions related to the exposure to FGM, receiving information, the belief that FGM must continue and insisting on conducting FGM on daughters.

A higher percentage of rural participants (95%) than urban participants (90%) reported that they had received information about FGM reflecting the efforts exerted by government and local NGOs in running awareness campaigns and disseminating information about the problem of FGM in rural areas, where FGM is most prevalent. Nonetheless, around 84% of the rural participants reported that they themselves or their wives were exposed to FGM, compared to 58% of the urban participants, suggesting that limited improvement had been achieved. Also, a lower percentage of rural participants (51%) were convinced FGM leads to social and psychological problems compared to urban participants (73%). As a result, 33% of the rural participants still believe FGM should continue compared to 22% of the urban participants. This also reflected their responses about proceeding or planning to proceed with FGM on their daughters, where 34% of rural participants reported that they had or would do, compared to 25% of the urban participants.

This can be explained by looking at perceptions around FGM, as well as the factors associated with it. Around 51% of the rural participants reported that they believe that husbands want their wives to undergo FGM and 47% were still convinced that FGM prevents adultery compared to 25 and 28% of the urban participants. These higher responses by rural participants than urban responses were found highly statistically significant. When it comes to why these perceptions exist in the first place, 73% of the rural participants believed FGM is rooted in tradition and 20% believed it is rooted in religion, reflecting confused understanding of religion influenced by culture and traditions, compared to 68 and 20% of the urban participants respectively. These higher responses by rural participants than urban participants were found marginally statistically significant. On the contrary, marginally statistically significant higher responses by urban participants than rural participants were found with regard to the belief that FGM is associated with education (10%) and socio-economic factors (3%) compared to 3 and 2% of the rural participants.

Wealth and Women's Exposure to IPV and FGM

Examining how the participants' answers were influenced by wealth reveals women's exposure to different forms of violence regardless of their wealth status. Every wealth category, however, was more inclined to practise certain forms of IPV over others, as appears in Table 7. The rich category witnessed

Table 7 IPV by wealth

Exposure to kinds of IPV	Poorest (%)	Middle (%)	Rich (%)	Richest (%)
Acts nervously when you speak with another man	67	65	78	67
Prevents you from any contact with your female friends	11	6	9	6
Prevents you from contacting your family	9	4	10	3
Stalks you or insists on knowing where you are all the time	46	36	25	18
Threatens to hurt you or to hurt someone close to you	7	1	4	3
Insults you/demeans you	14	9	15	8
Threatens to cut the financial resources	9	5	9	3
Forces you to have sex with him	9	3	4	0
Uses force against you or throws things at you	14	9	10	1
Slaps you on the face	18	10	16	8
Pulls your arm or hair	10	4	11	3
Burns you or tries to strangle you	1	0	0	1

the highest rates of acting nervously when women speak to other men, preventing women from contacting their families, insulting or demeaning women, pulling women's arms or hair, and threatening to cut women's access to financial resources. Yet this category came second in preventing women from any contact with their female friends, threatening to hurt women or to hurt someone close to them, and even using force against women or throwing something at them, slapping women on the face, and forcing women to have sex with them. This reflects the practice of a combination of physical, psychological, and even economic and sexual forms of IPV among the rich class.

The poorest class, on the other hand, witnessed the practice of different forms of IPV against women over others. This includes preventing women from any contact with their female friends, stalking women or insisting on knowing where they are all the time, threatening to hurt women or hurt someone close to them, using force against women or throwing something at them, slapping women on the face, and forcing women to have sex with them. The poorest class also came second in acting nervously when women speak to other men (equal to the richest), preventing women from contacting their families, insulting or demeaning women, and pulling their arms or hair.

Overall, the rich and poorest classes seem to reflect the highest levels of IPV compared to the middle and richest class, which still reported forms of IPV but with relatively lower rates. The middle class still came second in stalking women or insisting on knowing where they are all the time. The richest class also came second in acting nervously when women speak to other men. Equal to the poorest class, the richest class also witnessed the one-time incident of attempting to burn or strangle a woman. Other than these forms of IPV, the middle and richest class came last in the remaining forms of IPV.

When it comes to wealth and FGM, similar to IPV, all classes showed high levels of practising FGM. However, as appears in Table 8, there seems to be a more clearly systematic pattern of responses among classes on many of the questions about FGM, unlike IPV. There seems to be an increase in the exposure to FGM and the supporting perceptions with the decrease in wealth. The poorest class seem to have the highest rates of: undergoing FGM, believing husbands want their wives to undergo FGM, believing that FGM prevents adultery, and attempting to expose the daughters to FGM, if they have not exposed them already to FGM. It is also the class least likely to have received information about FGM and least likely to think FGM leads to social and psychological problems.

With the increase in wealth from middle to rich and richest classes, the exposure to FGM and the spread of FGM-supportive ideas decrease, especially with the increase in the information these groups have on FGM and their rising belief of the social and psychological consequences of FGM as appears in Table 8. All classes, however, agree that FGM is related to tradition above other factors, with a relatively higher percentage of the richest class believing FGM is related to education (or the absence of quality education) more than the rest of classes.

Table 8 FGM by wealth

Undergoing FGM	Poorest (%)	Middle (%)	Rich (%)	Richest (%)
Exposed to any form of FGM	76	73	75	60
The procedure was conducted by a doctor	28	36	40	40
Received information about FGM	89	93	94	95
FGM is related to religion	21	24	25	12
FGM is related to education	6	6	6	8
FGM is related to tradition	72	66	68	76
FGM is related to socio-economic status	2	4	1	3
FGM should continue	30	28	30	17
Husbands want their wives to undergo FGM	49	41	35	25
FGM prevents adultery	41	40	43	26
Your daughter was exposed to/will be exposed to FGM	32	32	31	21
FGM leads to social and psychological problems	48	57	66	80

Education and Women's Exposure to IPV and FGM

Examining how the participants' answers were influenced by education reveals women's exposure to different forms of violence regardless of education. Acting nervously when women speak to other men is the most common form of IPV among all levels. However, other than this, every level of education was more inclined to practice certain forms of IPV over others as appears in Table 9. Among the literate groups—like the poorest classes in the previous section—the most common forms of IPV are stalking women or insisting on knowing where they are all the time, threatening to hurt women or hurt someone close to them, using force against women or throwing something at them, and forcing women to have sex with them. This reflects the practice of a combination of physical, psychological, and even economic and sexual forms of IPV among the literate group.

Table 9 IPV by education

Exposure to kinds of IPV	Literate (%)	Basic Education (%)	Intermediate Education (%)	University Education (%)
Acts nervously when you speak with another man	63	74	62	67
Prevents you from any contact with your female friends	5	8	15	5
Prevents you from contacting your family	5	6	11	5
Stalks you or insists on knowing where you are all the time	45	36	29	23
Threatens to hurt you or to hurt someone close to you	8	4	2	3
Insults you/demeans you	8	12	14	11
Threatens to cut the financial resources	11	5	8	7
Forces you to have sex with him	11	4	5	2
Uses force against you or throws things at you	11	12	9	3
Slaps you on the face	13	16	15	7
Pulls your arm or hair	5	10	8	2
Burns you or tries to strangle you	0	1	0	1

The basic education group on the other hand witnessed the highest rates of acting nervously when women speak to other men, using force against women or throwing something at them, slapping women on the face, and even pulling their hair or arms. This group came second (with still high rates) in preventing women from any contact with their family and female friends, stalking women, or insisting on knowing where they are all the time, threatening to hurt women or to hurt someone close to them, insulting and demeaning women and burning or strangling women.

Lower levels of IPV are, however, found among intermediate and university educated groups. The intermediate education group has the highest rate of preventing women from any contact with their family (11%) and female friends (15%) as well as insulting or demeaning women (14%). Equal to the basic education group, the university group also witnessed the one-time incident of attempting to burn or strangle a woman. Other than these forms of IPV, the university group came last in the remaining forms of IPV.

When it comes to wealth and FGM, similar to IPV, all classes showed high levels of practising FGM. However, as appears in Table 10, there seems to be a more clearly systematic pattern of responses among classes on many of the questions about FGM, unlike IPV. There seems to be an increase in the exposure to FGM and the supporting perceptions with the decrease in education. The hardly literate group seem to have the highest rates of: undergoing FGM, believing husbands want their wives to undergo FGM, believing that FGM prevents adultery, and, thus, advocating the continuation of FGM and attempting to expose the daughters to FGM, if they have not exposed them already to FGM. It is also the class least likely to think FGM leads to social and psychological problems despite receiving information about FGM the most. With the increase in the level of education from basic education to intermediate and university levels, the exposure to FGM and the spread of FGM-supportive ideas decrease as well as the rising belief of the social and psychological consequences of FGM increases as appears in Table 10. All classes, however, agree that FGM is related to tradition above other factors, with a relatively higher percentage of the university groups believing FGM is related to education (or the absence of quality education) more than the rest of classes.

The Interplay of Other Factors in VAW: The Economic and Political Context

When asked about the most influential reason for the increase in VAW, the economic circumstances after the 25 January uprisings were identified by all

Table 10 FGM by education

Undergoing FGM	Literate (%)	Basic Education (%)	Intermediate Education (%)	University Education (%)
Exposed to any form of FGM	90	73	74	59
The procedure was conducted by a doctor	26	32	38	45
Received information about FGM	95	92	94	92
FGM is related to religion	26	18	35	16
FGM is related to education	3	7	2	9
FGM is related to tradition	71	72	62	73
FGM is related to socio-economic status	0	3	2	3
FGM should continue	63	27	30	12
Husbands want their wives to undergo FGM	75	39	36	26
FGM prevents adultery	66	39	41	24
Your daughter was exposed to/will be exposed to FGM	61	29	33	16
FGM leads to social and psychological problems	21	63	64	73

four categories (gender, residence, wealth, and education) as the most influential reason. According to the UN report (2017), "while the revolution of 2011 brought millions of Egyptian men and women together in a common cause, conservative forces continue to constrain the lives of women and girls and reinforce rigid ideas about manhood". As appears in Table 11, the sociocultural impact of the uprisings was recognized, particularly by the males and rural participants in the sample from all wealth categories alike. The difference between males and females and rural and urban areas when it comes to

Table 11 The consequences of the January uprisings by gender and residence

Factors in the interplay	Females (%)	Males (%)	Rural (%)	Urban (%)
Political circumstances after the 25 January uprisings are the reasons for the increase in IPV	37	47	41	43
Economic circumstances after the 25 January uprisings are the reasons for the increase in IPV	88	92	93	88
The change in socio-cultural conditions after the 25 January uprisings are the reasons for the increase in IPV	51	81	70	62

Table 12 The consequences of the 25 January uprisings by wealth

Factors in the interplay	Poorest (%)	Middle (%)	Rich (%)	Richest (%)
Political circumstances after the 25 January uprisings are the reasons for the increase in IPV	42	42	43	42
Economic circumstances after the 25 January uprisings are the reasons for the increase in IPV	96	95	86	81
The change in socio-cultural conditions after the 25 January uprisings are the reasons for the increase in IPV	67	68	66	63

the impact of the change in socio-cultural conditions after the 25 January as the reason for the increase in IPV was found highly significant.

However, it seems that the importance of the economic circumstances after the 25 January uprisings is associated negatively with the levels of wealth and education. As appears in Table 12, while the poorest and middle classes (96 and 95% respectively) place more emphasis on the economic circumstances, the rich and richest classes (86 and 81% respectively), which do not struggle financially, place less emphasis on the economic factor.

Similarly, as appears in Table 13, while the literate and basic education groups (97 and 94% respectively) place more emphasis on the economic circumstances, the intermediate education and university groups place less emphasis on the economic factor (86 and 84% respectively). The political factor, however, seems to have the least influence on VAW, according to the respondents from all wealth and education groups.

Table 13 The consequences of the 25 January uprisings by education

Factors in the interplay	Literate (%)	Basic Education (%)	Intermediate Education (%)	University Education (%)
Political circumstances after the 25 January uprisings are the reasons for the increase in IPV	34	39	50	45
Economic circumstances after the 25 January uprisings are the reasons for the increase in IPV	97	94	86	84
The change in socio-cultural conditions after the 25 January uprisings are the reasons for the increase in IPV	71	66	64	66

5 Conclusion

Despite the widespread belief that women's exposure to violence negatively impacts the quality and nature of their participation in the family, public space, and political arenas, VAW remains prevalent in Egypt. Gender, residence, wealth, and education tend to shape women's exposure to IPV and FGM, but in different ways and not necessarily through a clear pattern. Some final remarks can be drawn in this regard.

The majority of answers by female respondents revealed higher levels of violence, except for actions that are associated with masculinity and can be justified through the lens of men's *Quama* or "responsibility" to oversee and protect women. These actions include acting nervously when women speak to other men and stalking women or insisting on knowing where the women would be. Statistically significant differences were also found between rural and urban study participants in acts of intimate partner violence, such as stalking women, pulling women's arms or hair, threatening to cut financial resources provided to women, which were found to be higher among rural participants than urban ones.

Socio-cultural notions explain the persistence of FGM in Egypt, defying existent legislation and making it harder for awareness campaigns to spread information to eradicate the practice of FGM. A considerable percentage of men and, even more women still believe FGM should prevail. The differences between the responses of women and men and the rural and urban areas in most of the survey questions on FGM were found to be highly statistically significant, referring to stronger perceptions around FGM as well as the factors associated with it among men and rural residents than women and urban residents. The practice of FGM, however, remains widespread among both rural and urban residents.

Examining how the participants' answers were influenced by wealth and education reveals women's exposure to different forms of violence regardless of wealth and educational status. Every wealth and education group, however, was more inclined to practise certain forms of IPV over others. Though a particular pattern was absent, the richest class and the university groups were the least likely to commit forms of violence.

Respondents from all education and wealth strands agree FGM should prevail. However, unlike IPV, there seems to be a more clearly systematic pattern of responses among different wealth and education groups about FGM, unlike IPV. There seems to be an increase in the exposure to FGM and the supporting perceptions with the decrease in wealth and education.

To conclude, VAW is deeply rooted in the traditions of men and women from different residential, wealth, and educational backgrounds in Egypt. Enforcing legislation without addressing the root causes behind VAW or without carrying out awareness campaigns against VAW is not the best strategy to fight VAW. But as noted in the chapter, too, despite the high rate of information received by many groups, the practice of FGM and IPV remains highly prevalent among these same groups receiving such information. This shows the need for more efforts from the government and civil society to combat different forms of VAW, using non-conventional awareness activities to disseminate information. Examples of such activities include door-knocking activities, interactive local theatre, and awareness through sports activities. These activities have to target both men and women in addressing and resolving women's issues and in fighting VAW. The 2009 Rio de Janeiro conference calls for the inclusion of men into the activities that address women's issues and that aim to change attitudes and behaviours towards greater gender equality (Barker et al., 2011). Similarly, women should be targeted because, as mothers and grandmothers, they are the cornerstone behind the perpetuation of misguided traditions for the future generations (Khodary, 2018). It is only through integrating both men and women into the fight for gender equality and using unconventional and locally tailored solutions that attitudes and behaviours can change.

References

Abd-Elmoteleb, S. (2017). The January Revolution and its Repercussions on the Egyptian Personality: A Field Study. *Faculty of Arts Journal, Mansoura University, 60*(1015), 1149.

Abramsky, T., et al. (2011). What Factors are Associated with Recent Intimate Partner Violence? *Findings from the WHO Multi-Country Study on Women's Health and Domestic Violence, BioMed Central Public Health, 11*(109), 1–17.

Al-Magdoub, A. (2003). *The Phenomenon of Violence in the Egyptian Family*. The National Center for Criminal and Social research.

Australian Bureau of Statistics. (2013). *Defining the Data Challenge for Family, Domestic and Sexual Violence*. Australia: The Australian Bureau of Statistics.

Badawi, M. (1989). *Epidemiology of female sexual castration in Cairo Egypt*. [Unpublished] 1989. Presented at the First International Symposium on Circumcision Anaheim California, 1–2 March 1989.

Barker, G., Contreras, M., Heilman, B., Singh, A., Verma, R., & Nascimento, M. (2011). Evolving Men: Initial Results from the International. *Men and Gender Equality Survey*.

Barsoum, G., Rifaat, N., El-Gibaly, O., Elwan, N., & Forcier, N. (2011). *National Efforts Toward FGM-Free Villages in Egypt: The Evidence of Impact*. National Council of Childhood and Motherhood.

Cutrona, C. E., Wallace, G., & Wesner, K. A. (2008). Neighborhood Characteristics and Depression: An Examination of Stress Processes. *Current Directions in Psychological Science, 15*(4), 188–192.

El-Mouelhy, M. et al. (2013). Men's Perspectives on the Relationship between Sexuality and Female Genital Mutilation in Egypt. *Sociology Study, 3*(2). 104–13.

El-Zanaty and Associates and ICF International. (2015). *Egypt Health Issues Survey 2015*. Ministry of Health and Population.

El-Zanaty, F. (2015). Factors and Determinants of FGM/C of girls aged 0–17 years: A Secondary Analysis of the Egypt Demographic and Health Surveys 2005, 2008 and 2014.

El-Zanaty, F., & Way, A. (2003). *Egypt Interim Demographic and Health Survey*. Ministry of Health and Population/Egypt, National Population Council/Egypt, El-Zanaty and Associates/Egypt, and ORC Macro.

George, J., & Stith, S. M. (2014). An Updated Feminist View of Intimate Partner Violence. *Family Process, 53*(2), 179–193.

Greenfeld, L., & Craven, D. (1998), *Violence by Intimates: Analysis of Data by Current or Former Spouses, Boyfriends and Girlfriends*, US Department of Justice Office of Justice Programs.

Habib, S. (2009). *Egypt Violence against Women Study Summary of Findings*. National Council for Women.

Heise, L., & Gracia-Moreno, C. (2002). Violence by Intimate Partners. In E. G. Krug, L. L. Dahlberg, J. A. Mercy, A. B. Ziwi, & R. Lozano (Eds.), *World Report on Violence and Health* (pp. 87–121). WHO Press.

Heise, L., Moore, K., & Toubia, N. (1995). *Sexual Coercion and Reproductive Health: A Focus on Research*. The Population Council.

Jejeebhoy, S. J. (1995). Women's Education, Autonomy, and Reproductive Behaviour: Experience from Developing Countries. *OUP Catalogue*.

Jewkes, R. (2002). Intimate Partner Violence: Causes and Prevention. *Violence against Women, 359*(9315), 1423–1429.

Kaplan, A., et al. (2011). Health Consequences of Female Genital Mutilation/cutting in the Gambia: Evidence into Action. *Health Report, 8*, 26.

Khodary, Y. (2018). What Difference can it Make? Assessing the Impact of Gender Equality and Empowerment in Matters of Inheritance in Egypt. *The Journal of the Middle East and Africa, 9*(2), 173-193.

Krivo, L. J., & Peterson, R. D. (1996). Extremely Disadvantaged Neighborhoods and Urban Crime. *Social Forces, 75*(2), 619–648.

Menjivar, C., & Salicido, O. (2002). Immigrant Women and Domestic Violence: Common Experiences in Different Countries. *Gender & Society, 16*(898), 898–920.

Ministry of Health and Population, El-Zanaty and Associates, and ICF International. (2015). *Egypt Demographic and Health Survey 2014*. Cairo, Egypt and Rockville, Maryland.

Ozer, E. J., Best, S. R., Lipsey, T. L., & Weiss, D. S. (2003). Predictors of Post-traumatic Stress Disorder and Symptoms in Adults: A Meta-analysis. *Psychological Bulletin, 129*(3), 5273.

Packer, C. (2005) Circumcision and Human Rights Discourse, in Nnaemeka, O. and Ezeilo, J. (Eds) *Engendering Human Rights: Cultural and Socio-Economic Realities in Africa*, pp. 223–248, Palgrave Macmillan.

Sampson, R. J., & Groves, W. B. (1989). Community Structure and Crime: Testing Social-disorganization Theory. *American Journal of Sociology, 94*(4), 774–802.

Spruin, E., Alleyne, E., & Papadaki, L. (2015). Domestic Abuse Victims' Perceptions of Abuse and Support: A Narrative Study. *Journal of Criminological Research, Policy and Practice, 1*(1), 19–28.

Stark, R. (1987). Deviant Places: A Theory of the Ecology of Crime. *Criminology, 25*(4), 893–910.

Stith, S. M., et al. (2004). Intimate Partner Physical Abuse Perpetration and Victimization Risk Factors: A Meta-analytic Review. *Journal of Aggression and Violent Behavior, 10*, 65-98.

Ullman, S. E. (2005). Interviewing Clinicians and Advocates who work with Sexual Assault Survivors: A Personal Perspective on Moving from Quantitative to Qualitative Methods. *Violence against Women, 11*(9), 1113–1139.

UNICEF (2014) "*Media Backgrounder: Female Genital Mutilation/Cutting (FGM/C).*

World Health Organization. (2008). *Eliminating Female Genital Mutilation: An Interagency Statement*. WHO.

World Health Organization. (2023). *Female Genital Mutilation*. WHO.

Yount, K. M. (2002). Like Mother, like Daughter? Female Genital Cutting in Minia. Egypt. *Journal of Health and Social Behavior, 3*, 336–358.

"Wait, Let's Talk About It": A Feminist Assessment of the Response of the Church of the Cross Hayfield (NELCSA) to Gender-Based Violence in Pietermaritzburg, South Africa

Lindiwe Princess Maseko

1 Introduction

"Wait...Let's Talk About It".[1]
Does it make you angry?
Does it make you feel sad?
Feeling scared, turning away your face...
What is it about, what about it?
"Wait, let's talk about it".
Does your family know?
Your fellow, your fellas?
Your diary you signed about it?
What about yourself, what about me?
Together let's talk about it.
Ought it to be normal, a culture of violence?
Ought it to be normal, a culture of silence?

---

[1] An original poem by Lindiwe Princess Maseko.

An unpublished version of this paper was originally presented at the Tumaini University Makumira, Tanzania in February 2023, where the author was enrolled as one the pioneer students for the Helene Ralivao Fund on Research Program on Theology, Gender Justice and Leadership in Africa.

L. P. Maseko (✉)
School of Religion, Philosophy, and Classics University of KwaZulu Natal, Pietermaritzburg, South Africa
e-mail: lindyprincessmaseko@gmail.com

> Embracing death in our faces?
> Charity begins at home.
> Think the talk, to walk the talk.
> With compassion, passion.
> Let's talk about it, Gender-Based Violence!

This piece is a combination and a collection of voices from the members of The Church of The Cross (Hayfields) Northeastern Evangelical Lutheran Church (NELCSA) as a concerned faith community. It expresses their voices that have found another way to talk about gender-based violence for the first time. These are the voices that have taken me so far with this matter of concern. As a young woman in the African context within this faith community, exposed to a context like South Africa, I cannot overlook the prevalence of Gender-Based Violence (GBV) that is reported time and again on the daily news. Having participated in Silent Protest and Praxis Reflection on Gender-Based Violence and Faith as a gender and religion student at the University of KwaZulu-Natal, Pietermaritzburg, together with Ujamaa Trust, "AIDS Health Care Foundation", "We Will Speak Out South Africa," and "Act Ubumbano" in South Africa using the hashtag #silencing the silence in 2019, I feel that there is still more need for hearing the voice (in another way) of the church in addressing GBV in South Africa. The church has Christ's mandate which stands for issues of social justice and is a prophetic voice to attend to the oppressed in society. Christ's mission is seen in the gospel of Luke:

> The spirit of the Lord is upon me because he has anointed me to proclaim good news…he has sent me to proclaim freedom for the prisoners…to set the oppressed free. (Jesus in Luke 4:18)

Gender-Based Violence has become the new pandemic in the twenty-first century and a Sexual and Reproductive Health Rights (SRHR) concern around the globe and contextually, that continues to receive attention. Decker et al. (2015) underscore that GBV is a global health and human rights issue with individual and social factors. Each year, countries across the world observe the 16 Days of Activism against GBV, as an international awareness-raising campaign that promotes no violence against women. Recent research proves that GBV is now a twin, or more than, to some pandemics such as Covid-19 (Dlamini, 2021: 583). On a global scale, prior to Covid-19, research recorded that one in three women who have been in a relationship had experienced physical or sexual violence by an intimate partner (García-Moreno et al., 2013; World Bank, 2019). John et al., (2020: 65) clarify that these statistics have been researched in 80 countries. In detail, the statistics record that, globally, 7% of women have been sexually assaulted by someone other than a partner. Further, 38% of murders of women are committed by an intimate partner, and 18% of women and girls aged 15 to 49 years who have been in a relationship with a man, had experienced physical and sexual violence by an intimate partner in the previous 12 months (United Office on Drugs and Crime—UNODC, 2018). In recent history, UN Women (2020) records that 87,000 women were killed internationally, and many of these killings were committed by an intimate partner or a family member, which implies that GBV is not performed by strangers. Economically, it has been estimated that the cost to the economy can be up to 3.7% of some countries' GDP, and the global cost of violence against women and girls, before Covid-19, stood at US $1.5 trillion, which is approximately 2% of global domestic product, (UN Women, 2020).

Gender-based violence is not a one-size-fits-all; it is accompanied by a constellation of ideas. Primarily, in most cases it is rooted in gender norms and roles assigned to women, and, thus, most women are excluded from GBV response processes (John et al., 2020). In this case, it has been proven that women are at the receiving end of this harsh reality, and, hence, they experience GBV in all the stages of their lives. Dlamini states that they suffer across the life cycle: girlhood, adolescence, adulthood, and old age. However, it is also a pity to know that women remain silent or are silenced from speaking out about GBV. Dlamini observes that less than 40% of women report having experienced violence, and most of those who do, seek help from a family or friend (Dlamini, 2021: 583). UN Women (2020), states that less than 10% of women who seek help go to the police.

In Africa, as a continent, GBV is a lived reality as well. The 58 studies on GBV that involve intimate partner violence (IPV) and non-IPV among women in sub-Saharan Africa (SSA), and research studies published in English from 2008–2019 through a random effect meta-analysis show that the prevalence of IPV among women was 44% and non-pooled prevalence was 14%. The highest prevalence rates of IPV that were reported included 29.40% emotional, 25.87% physical, and 18.75% sexual violence in sub-Saharan Africa (Muluneh et al., 2020).

In the context of South Africa, GBV has reached pandemic levels. In fact, one in four women is involved in an abusive relationship (Jewkes & Abrahams, 2002), and every sixth hour a woman is killed by her intimate partner (Matthew et al., 2004). Darong (2020) states that 30 to 60% of women have experienced or have been exposed to GBV in Pietermaritzburg, South Africa. However, it is also a sad reality that GBV does not only affect the survivor and those who have succumbed, but also their families. Another effect shows that children who grow up with violence are more likely to become perpetrators (Dlamini, 2021). This also causes unwanted and adverse maternal and new-born baby health outcomes, as well as long- and short-term physical, psychological and social impacts (SAMJ, 2016). While GBV is a web of many connected factors, another reality is that South Africa is a religious nation and if 90% of people are religious, then who is responsible for violence against women? Is it the 10% unaffiliated to any religious group? In this way, the GBV statistics and the number of religious people in South Africa speak the same language. Thus, the dialogue and action on GBV should include religious and faith contexts, since the church is regarded and perceived as a safe space, there is a need to know its position on GBV.

2 Gender-Based Violence (GBV) as a Contextual Lived Reality

To understand GBV as a contextual reality in South Africa, and in particular in Pietermaritzburg, it is essential to acknowledge GBV as a global lived reality, based on some academic scholarly and scientific research. This section presents a variety of literature and a point of departure, and provides a working definition(s). It shows a case of the causality, influencing factors, and consequences, in particular the intersectionality characterizing this reality and the reproductive health of individuals. This section will look closely into gaps to be addressed within the existing given literature in this study.

As previously noted, GBV is a global phenomenon (Mampane, 2020). According to the United Nations (UN General Assembly, 1993) and United States Agency for International Development (USAID, 2014: 3) GBV is "any act of violence that results in or is likely to result in physical, sexual, mental harm or suffering to women including threats such acts like coercion, or arbitrary deprivation of liberty whether occurring in public or in private life". Gender-based violence is also violence that is directed at an individual based on biological sex, gender, and identity or perceived adherence to socially defined norms of masculinity and femininity, (USAID, 2014). Gender-based violence depends on a perpetrator and "victim" and includes Intimate Partner Violence (IPV) or non-Intimate Partner Violence or is classified by the type of activity, like sexual, physical, or emotional (USAID, 2010). On that note, GBV is regarded as a form of human rights violation and is part of the UN gender equality agenda of the 17 Sustainable Development Goals (SDGs) to be achieved by 2030 (Mampane, 2020). Thus, GBV is a human rights abuse that cuts across all contexts, whether developed or developing, despite culture, socio-economics, class or religion (Abraham et al., 2014; USAID, 2010; World Bank 2019). Exploring the experiences of women in Pietermaritzburg, South Africa, Shabalala (2020) records that 30 to 65% of women have experienced or have been exposed to GBV in their lifetime so far. Although studies prove that women can also be the perpetrators of violence, research proves that women are the most affected "victims" and are affected at a higher magnitude because of their gender (Allen, 2018; Sikweyiya et al., 2017).

3 Causes of Gender-Based Violence

Rachel Jewkes (2002:1 6185), describes GBV as a web of associated and mediating factors and processes which are centrally influenced by ideas about masculinity and the position of women in society and ideas about the use of violence. The implication is that GBV reality is complex and must be approached from the prism of intersectionality.

Allen (2018) argues that GBV in the context of South Africa is a result of an "intersectionality" of many oppressions. "Culture of violence," patriarchy, the idea of masculinity, economic injustice, poverty, societal norms, lack of awareness of available resources, and lack of law enforcement are some of the factors that make GBV a reality (Allen, 2018; Mampane, 2020; Muluneh et al., 2020). Writing from an intersectional approach to GBV in the context of South Africa, Allen (2018) further explains that the "culture of violence" is perpetuated by necessary roles of patriarchy that leave women suppressed and as subordinates. Further, economic injustice, or poverty per se, has caused some women, in South Africa generally, and contextually in the rural Eastern Cape of South Africa to engage in "transactional sex" which involves sex with a non-primary male partner in exchange for material goods or money, (Allen, 2018). Mampane (2020) argues that GBV is fundamentally caused by societal norms and different power relations, where men are usually perceived to be superior to women.

Further, silence, especially among women, is reported to be another significant cause of the persistence of GBV. Palermo et al. (2014) and WHO (2012) record that GBV is considered the "tip of the iceberg or silent epidemic," since "victims" are hesitant to reveal their experience of violence due to several reasons. Many women find it difficult to communicate their experiences on GBV, even in health centres, as these are often experienced as shameful, hence, the need for training about GBV that would be beneficial in these health centres (Allen, 2018). Muluneh et al. (2020) state that women are afraid of the stigma, shame, financial barriers, revenge, and sometimes actions and attitudes surrounding violence as a normal component of life. In the context of Pietermaritzburg, South Africa, Ellsberg and Heise (2002) make reference to women reporting fewer GBV issues because of their fear of society. The authors further point out that society can take a stand for the abuser by believing that the abuser is "a good or church-going person" and is unlikely to violate an individual. Since men are seen as the controllers and breadwinners within the family or in a relationship, it becomes very difficult for the "victim" to speak out for fear of losing financial support (Ellsberg & Heise, 2002). In Pietermaritzburg, there is a lack of support and a lot of assault from people who are close to the "victims" such that it is difficult to disclose violence to the person one is close to (Shabalala, 2020).

4 Effects of Gender-Based Violence

There are many negative effects of GBV, including poor mental and physical health (Campbell, 2002; Levi & Pen-Kekara, 2022). Thus, GBV has been pointed out as a global health problem with a higher prevalence in developing countries (Pallitto et al., 2006; Moreno et al., 2013). Gender-based violence affects the health status of women and children (Moreno, 2013). According to Allen (2018), mental health issues also affect women who suffer from GBV. Campbell (2002) adds that GBV also has caused or resulted in depression, and severe post-traumatic disorders as the most two widespread mental health diseases.

Apart from mental-health-related issues, research proves that GBV has drastic consequences for the reproductive health of individuals, especially women. The World Health Organization (2013) reports that multi-country studies prove that women of "reproductive age" who have verbally revealed the prevalence of IPV range between 15% in urban areas in countries like Japan and 71% in other countries like Ethiopia. Kishor and Johnson (2005) maintain that research shows that poor levels of reproductive health are more highly connected to the frequency of domestic violence than to poverty. Mampane (2020) in her work on GBV, women, and HIV in a rural community in South Africa, notes that rape has been identified as a major contributor to HIV infection risk factors, hence, such gender-based power inequalities pose barriers to the adoption of safer sexual practices in relationships (Allen, 2018). Jewkes (2016) also adds that reproductive-health-related issues in the context of GBV lower access to contraceptives and result in a higher risk of sexually transmitted infections (STIs). Research done in the context of South Africa records that higher rates of HIV and AIDS in women are particularly connected to the experience of GBV (Guedes, 2004; Jewkes et al., 2010; Kishor & Johnson, 2005). Allen (2018) also adds that transactional sex is associated with HIV infection in Soweto in South Africa.

5 The Research Gap

This chapter reflects how reflects how feminist scholarly work contributes to responding holistically to GBV. There is a need for reflections that focus on GBV in faith communities such as NELCSA. First, although GBV seems to have a greater impact on women than men, the literature lacks an affirming action-oriented approach to the feminization of this reality and how men can be fully involved to actively participate in the GBV roundtable (although they are an advantaged gender). Second, the discussion of religion or faith spaces' action in this literature is thin. There is a need for faith communities to reclaim their position to sustain themselves as safe spaces for GBV roundtable discussions. Third, the literature lacks affirmative use of terminology that continues to be used and adopted daily in faith spaces and adopted beyond. For example, the term "victim" lacks a holistic approach to addressing this lived reality for women who are still surviving "physically." Thus, this chapter adopts a better terminology that encompasses hope and life affirmation for young women and girls. Fourth, the literature does not include the view and the response of specific church denominations such as The Church of The Cross (Hayfields) NELCSA on GBV in South Africa.

The questions I seek to answer in this chapter are: What is the social context of GBV in Pietermaritzburg, South Africa? What is The Church of the (Hayfields) NELCSA's response to GBV as a religious institution in Pietermaritzburg city? How can a feminist assessment of The Church of The Cross (Hayfields) NELCSA's response to GBV contribute to affirming the reproductive health of and justice for young women in Pietermaritzburg? It is against such a reality and background that in this study, I adopt a Reproductive Justice Framework to critically assess the response of The Church of the Cross (Hayfields) NELCSA (as a member and a young adult in this congregation) to GBV in Pietermaritzburg, South Africa.

6 Research Methodology

This chapter adopts a qualitative action-oriented research method that studies human problems through social analysis of humans by observing the way in which they live, and how they are conditioned within their diverse worldviews (Creswell, 2013, 2014; Swinton & Mowat, 2016; Yin, 2011). As a point of departure, I engaged with the gatekeepers, in this case, the two pastors serving in this congregation, to seek permission to conduct this research. I presented an introductory letter from Tumaini University, Makumira as evidence of the research that was needed. The pastors gave me permission to conduct research and they suggested effective methods for me as a researcher, for the leadership, and for the participants. The study observed all the necessary ethical principles. I used focus-group discussions to collect data. Breen (2007) indicates that focus-group discussions are used to explore a group's experiences and generate ideas for the group and give a deeper understanding of the phenomenon for the purpose of hearing their common experiences, within a social context. These groups were categorized as young adults, youths, and a random selection of elderly members. The young adult group had six participants (three women and three men), the youths were twelve (seven girls and five boys) and the other members ten (women only) to discuss eight guiding questions. I categorized the participants according to their relevant groups so that they could share their reflections with a deeper understanding and provided a social environment where they were comfortable. I adopted this method to attain a diverse appreciation of the contextual reality of GBV from three groups (both men and women), and how they situated themselves to collectively contribute to the GBV response process. This method was relevant for this feminist study as it allowed me to listen to the voices of people of faith and the extent to which both men and women are impacted by this reality.

I also adopted in-depth one-on-one interviews to collect data. Breen (2007) states that one-on-one interviews ought to probe individual experiences encouraging self-reflection on issues that could be distorted if social pressure were placed on individuals. Hence, I selected four women within the same context of Pietermaritzburg who are also members of The Church of The Cross (Hayfields) NELCSA. However, they had different occupations. The aim was to get unique information about the extent to which GBV affects women in terms of their health, specifically reproductive health-related issues, and how feminist work can apply the Reproductive Justice approach to bring life affirmation to women in Pietermaritzburg. Additionally, I carried out key informant interviews with the two pastors as the leadership of The Church of the Cross (Hayfields) NELCSA, to get some unique information from the leadership.

Feminist cultural hermeneutics is used as a specific study resource. This resource examines and interprets how culture "conditions" people's understanding in a time and location, (Kanyoro, 2002: 9). Culture is addressed as a concept that cuts across to normalize and romanticize Gender-Based Violence, because of the "culture of violence" in a context like Pietermaritzburg, South Africa. This tool interrogates the patriarchal nature of culture that afflicts women more than men. Thus, it uses gender as a cultural analysis to assess the extent to which culture influences men and women in The Church of the Cross (Hayfields) NELCSA to be concerned about GBV.

Thus, this study is not only about the context of Pietermaritzburg but is also a project where lessons of women's vulnerability can be drawn from the assessment of GBV in this context. Kanyoro (2002), argues that cultural hermeneutics views gender as a concept for cultural analysis. This is because mostly it has become a reality that GBV is not an easy issue to disclose, and especially to speak about, from the context of women more than men because of culture. Thus, this feminist hermeneutical tool undresses "culture" so that GBV can be easily critically approached and spoken about as a way of responding to it. Further, it exposes the culture of silence in the so-called safe spaces like the faith community so that women, in this specific reality, are able to vent their feelings towards their experiences of GBV. The following section explores the Reproductive Justice framework.

7 The Reproductive Justice Framework

The Reproductive Justice lens is used to frame the argument of this research. Reproductive Justice was birthed in 1994 by feminists of colour who were already working on the conception of reproductive health and rights (Ross & Solinger, 2017: 290). It is a political movement that knits together reproductive rights and social justice, to attain reproductive justice (Ross & Solinger, 2017: 9), and, thus, a human right. Chrsitle et al. (2017: 243–250) assert that the Reproductive Justice framework displays ideas of social justice and reproductive inequalities that seek to bring justice to women's reproductive-related issues beginning from the grassroots level. It identifies gendered heteropatriarchal relations in socio-economic and political contexts that extend to reproduction. This frame is relevant in this study as it perceives GBV as a constellation of different factors like patriarchy, poverty, unemployment, and as part of the SRHR landscape. It explores how social injustice between men and women influences the prevalence of GBV, which results in more vulnerability in young girls and women, which later affects their reproductive health. Reproductive justice, therefore, enables this research to enhance the agency in the church to challenge structural power inequalities that construct GBV culture in young women and girls in South Africa, even though GBV is not gender selective.

8 Overview of the Church of the Cross (Hayfields) NELCSA

Prior to the data presentation and the response of this congregation to GBV, it is vital to present a brief background to the Church of the Cross (Hayfields). The Church of the Cross (Hayfields) congregation is a member of the Northeastern Evangelical Lutheran Church in South Africa (NELCSA), which is the Southern Circuit. It is located in Pietermaritzburg, KwaZulu-Natal province in South Africa. The Church of the Cross (Hayfields) is over 100 years old and consists of 420 members: 228 women and 192 men. Previously, it was mostly a German-speaking congregation, although now it is mostly an English-speaking congregation despite the fact that for most of the members, English is not their mother-tongue. They speak other languages like IsiZulu, Afrikaans, Shona, German, Swathi, Venda, Setswana and so forth. However, English is the common language that is spoken by everyone in the congregation. (Interview 1, by the researcher on September 15, 2022, with Pastors in the congregation). This congregation is diverse in terms of age, gender, cultural, linguistic, and socio-economic aspects. It is served by two pastors who are also a couple. These pastors had served for nine years at the time the study was conducted. The leadership structure includes the Congregational Council that leads the congregation together with the two pastors. There are six congregational councillors, elected democratically in a general meeting of the congregation for a period of three years and who can be re-elected for another period of three years.

Gender-Related Issues in the Congregation

It is worth noting that The Church of the Cross (Hayfields) NELCSA talks about gender-related issues though it tries not to have traditional gender roles. For example, when a woman or women are supposed to work in the church preparing tea, both men and women do prepare tea together. The congregation adopted this intentional process to have a representative of each gender and age in all duties in the church (Interviewee 2, 15 September 2022). The congregation has also adopted the idea of selecting women to be members of the Council. The Bible translation is always intended to produce inclusive language. More so, the congregation does not have specific women's or men's leagues or prayer groups, but they try to invite everyone to participate. The congregation synod has a code of conduct whereby individuals can report to three individuals of their choice if they are treated in a manner that makes them feel unsafe. Importantly, the Church of the Cross (Hayfields) NELCSA, uses a theological point of view that strives to put men and women at the same level. For example, during a pre-counselling session of marriage, couples are taught that marriage is a partnership on an equal basis. There are a few sessions on marriage preparation, communication in marriage, and biblical bases of marriage for the couples. The way marriage is also addressed in the sermons is on an equal basis without bias towards or against any gender, showing men and women are created in God's image and, hence, addressing gender injustice through the sermon.

9   NELCSA Social Reality of Gender-Based Violence in Pietermaritzburg

Definitions of Gender-Based Violence

A total of 27 participants from this congregation (8 men and 18 women) participated in three focus group discussions and four participants (1 man and 3 women) participated in in-depth interviews. Participants were of diverse races, including black Africans, white South Africans, and coloured, all using different languages. Participants described GBV as a major theme throughout the research which manifested in different perspectives. The general point of view portrayed GBV as any form of abuse (physical, sexual, emotional, verbal, and psychological) of an individual because of their gender or their sex. Therefore, it was discussed as abuse towards a different gender/sex or the same gender/sex. Some participants stressed that it is generally a mistreatment of the "female" gender. Overall, GBV was portrayed as an "epidemic"—a widespread experience that could occur in any space, to anyone, whether poor, rich, or from a developing, or developed context, as discussed in the following unfolding results.

The Church Pastors as Eyewitnesses of GBV

The reality of GBV was first discussed in the church leadership space, through in-depth interviews. The leadership participants openly discussed that GBV was a reality where both women and men, but mostly women, have been approaching the leadership about GVB experiences. However, it has not been easy for such individuals to talk about it after having undergone such experiences. They shared this reality as something that the congregants face in their daily lives and as an ongoing challenge.

> During the Covid time, there was a cry for help from someone who felt she was, as well as her children, in danger and she had no work and her husband got very aggressive and in such a way we had to look for a safe place for them…" (Interview 15 September 26, 2022).

Overall, one of the challenges that was discussed was the fact that GBV is not easy to see since some of the individuals suffer from emotional abuse. The leadership also reviewed the challenge of finding a place to which they could refer the survivors but said sometimes they had involved a family member. (Interview 15 September 26, 2022).

Congregation Women as Witnesses and "Surviving Individuals" of Gender-Based Violence

Quite a number of women turned out to be witnesses and surviving individuals of GBV, showing diverse experiences in contexts such as workplaces like high schools, hospitals, the church, social working areas, trauma centres, and counselling centres. Abuse between children, siblings, and parents, and mostly towards girls and women, was detected in poor homes in Pietermaritzburg where some participants do charity work. To emphasize this, one female participant (Participant 1) testified: "What I have come across now is people who are women are suffering a lot. Every time I give them the food parcels for the family." Another female participant witnessed a female teacher at a high school being violated by her male partner, sadly to the point of death. Moreover, GBV was closely studied through the personal stories of the female participants during this research. Three women participants shared their stories as shown below.

Participant 1 shared her childhood experience of GBV involving her relative, Participant 2 shared her experience of the reality of GBV during her marriage, and Participant 3 shared her concerns about a fellow woman who has been silent in an abusive marriage:

1. **Female Participant 1**

Growing up, I never knew what abuse was. I had an aunt, once a week she would always have a blue eye and she would wear shades… when my uncles see her, they would go somewhere and talk to her… when we go to visit her place, the doors had punches on them…I now recall it now that was abuse…-sometimes he would beat her, drag her through the passage to the bedroom …after all that fighting there was always that 'sexing', I don't know whether he was raping her…when I see her now she is damaged…that was only the living example at my early age.

2. **Female Participant 2**

In my first marriage, when I was unemployed, my husband used to abuse me verbally and emotionally … saying: "You are a parasite, I am feeding you that is why you are so thin" When I got the job, he was so frustrated because I was not asking for anything, he said to me: "Please resign I am going to give you R15 000 per month." And I said, "You failed to give me R10 how are you going to give R15 000?" That is when the conflict started … Every time I would go to work, (I am a field worker), I would go to Pongola[2] he would phone me where I was at, 2 a.m. and instruct me what to say. He would say "Say I love you," … He would beg me to resign…saying "You can have my bank cards, you can keep everything," but I knew I wouldn't fall for it, I had an experience of not working over a period of 12 months.

3. **Female Participant 3**

Somebody now is getting a divorce after 25 years of marriage and there was verbal abuse over 25 years, and "she" did not say a word to anybody and now it is enough. Their child is finishing school and now it's just enough.

---

[2] Pongola is a town on the north bank of the Phongolo River, in a fertile valley on the N2, near the Lubombo Mountains, in the valleys of Zululand, easily accessible from the Eswatini border post.

Congregation Women Witnessing the Context of GBV and Their Reproductive Health

A collection of voices agreed on the fact that many women who have suffered from GBV have had STIs, with some being infected with HIV, due to rape or unprotected forced sex. One participant woman explained: "The last thing a rapist thinks is to protect himself when having forced sex" and this illustrates the degree of the lack of consent and protection during sexual activity. It worried women that, when their fellow women go to the clinic, they do not get adequate help as they are belittled by other women, hence, they end up not going until their reproductive system deteriorates. Facing physical abuse by other women, like being beaten during their pregnancy, compromises their health, as they suffer abdominal pains.

Another reproductive health issue that was discussed was teenage pregnancy, which brings rape into focus. The participants discussed that there is always a question around teenage pregnancy as they feel that most girls do not actually consent to sexual intercourse or lack contraceptives they can use. Women in the focus group discussion stressed that girls and young women are mostly blamed by their partners and face accusations about the pregnancy, namely, that it is "their fault" to fall pregnant, hence, their partners beat them to get rid of the pregnancy.

Congregation Young Adults and Youth as Witnesses of the Reality of Gender-Based Violence

Young adult and youth focus groups of both young women and men considered the reality of GBV in the context of *umjolo*.[3] They related this topic to their relationships and to the experiences of their friends and peers. Emotional abuse was singled out among female friends of the participants in their relationships, where a boyfriend tells a girl what to do, what to wear and always blames her. However, it was highlighted that in such cases a girl finds it difficult to leave the relationship. The female participants in this group often found themselves in an uncomfortable situation where they could not pass by a group of young men freely without receiving any comments about their bodies. Violence in families where parents fight, or one parent is abused, was noted as a difficult emotional state for some young people within the church,

---

[3] Zulu slang for courtship.

and outside as well. It was emphasized that this state leaves a girl in a situation where she can dislike being at home at all. One young adult also testified that GBV had also been experienced in bars and restaurants.

10 A Comparison of the Degree of Gender-Based Violence Between Women and Men

Throughout the focus group discussions and interviews, participants debated whether women are more affected by GBV than men. Several participants agreed that this reality had much more effect "obviously" on women in South Africa. However, the argument was that society is more aware of the problem with women because they were more vulnerable and quicker to be identified, unlike men who submit to the violence and hold themselves together, as they are not supposed to be "cry-babies" because of what society perceives of them. Female participants argued that it did not always mean that women were quick to identify or strong to be in this situation; it was because women have come to terms with it. Some male participants pointed out the societal expectations imposed on them make it difficult for them to speak about their GBV experiences, thus, "men too" suffer emotional abuse to a certain extent. One female participant explains how men can be vulnerable to women's violence:

> In a normal household you find siblings, boys, and girls, and normally the boys are treated superior to the girls, like the brother can hit her sister.... When these girls grow up that is why they abuse their men because they grew up in that situation and they can always try to defend themselves...something that could be resolved verbally...they always strike first.

The following monologue, however, discloses that even if women's stories of GBV are more publicized, there are still a large number of victims: "…it doesn't really matter like if men come out and talk or not, but it's the numbers which speak…yeah, they do talk…. obviously, it's going to be 'females' that are more affected by GBV because of the societal expectations."

11 NELCSA Practical Responses to Gender-Based Violence

A Realistic Way of Thinking

Young adult participants from this congregation admitted that there is a need to have realistic thinking on approaches to GBV. Instead of focusing on the whole city (Pietermaritzburg), which can seem hopeless and overwhelming, young adults and youths suggested that there is a need to have self-awareness as individuals first. For one to create awareness in others, they should be aware of themselves: "starting by yourself will help others to follow what you do, for example, 'monkey see monkey do,' other individuals will notice you and what is within your power as a young woman or a young man."

Charity Begins at Home

The participants discussed that as people of faith, they must teach their children ways of communicating with the other gender. For example, they spoke about three terms that a boy child should know when interacting with girls. One female participant in the elderly focus group says: "I always tell my boys…I am raising boys, I want you to grow up knowing that a 'No' is a 'No,' there is 'please' and 'thank you'". The participants in the elderly group of women felt that boy children need to be taught and socialized in a way that will make them respect women throughout their lifetime. It starts at home, so families and parents have a big responsibility. On this note, other participants felt like it can also be difficult to raise children in a way that will contribute to less violence against the other gender. One female participant said, "I also feel like a mother who has been abused for a very long does not have the strength to do that… you feel so worthless… you are so broken down…" Maybe the families need to talk about it with a different approach.

Creating the Church as a Safe Space

It was discussed that to help women (in the context of female "victims") there is a need to make it easier for them to come forward and speak out without feeling judged, for example by being asked questions such as: "How could you stay with that man for so long?" If they only receive counselling, it does not always help them, as after counselling they may go back home to a man who throws a cup at them again. So, it would be better if such individuals are given assistance like accommodation to which they can relocate for a while for respite from the horrific situation. Another action to consider would be that young people could also come to church where youth, young adult, and confirmation classes provide safe spaces to talk about it. As a church or as a faith community, there is a need to do more for people, to participate in charity groups, and create safe spaces.

Roundtable Dialogue on Gender-Based Violence

The participants felt there was a need to collectively learn to talk diligently about GBV, however, they were confused about where to start. The following comment from one female participant (Participant 1) vividly shows this: "What is a little bit lacking for me is I am not sure where to send people…I am not sure where the safe spaces are…".

Another participant, Participant 2, said:

> It is time when we should get involved and avoid saying 'I don't want to get involved.' We all have a responsibility to speak out, to get involved. There is a need to stop saying 'it's not my child, it's not my problem.' The community should not turn an eye away from an individual who is suffering from GBV.

From the elderly group of women, one female participant in the church, who is also a counsellor in different organizations in Pietermaritzburg, shared her encounter with one young man who is a co-worker. In her encounter she explains what she thinks can be a life-affirmative approach toward violence in relationships. She explains:

> He said to me "Gogo,[4] how do I love my girlfriend she really loves me." I said "Why do you want to know, what is the problem?" He said, "but, when she doesn't pick up her phone when I phone her, I get so angry… I just want to fight, and she fights back, she doesn't want to see me, and I don't want to see her for about a week… and then we miss each other, and we come back together. It goes on and on…" I said to him, "Try and talk about it, just use **your finger**" and say **"wait**, no fighting I am talking **let's talk about it**, I am at work…" I told him, "**My finger**" is very powerful, it seems to diffuse everything.

The participants then discussed this idea of educating members in the church and even outside the faith community to learn to "talk about it," be it an

---

[4] Zulu term for grandmother.

issue, a problem, or a misunderstanding; being patient with each other when others are talking to resolve issues before they escalate into violence.

The dialogue stressed that people must learn to confide in other people and for some reason, burdensome problems can become lighter and they can get some views, although sometimes maybe not a solution. The participants suggested that the church should embrace many people who are facing GBV. People of faith in the church and in other spaces should familiarize themselves with the situation. The need for one person to start a conversation so that others join was discussed as a strategy, for example, inviting others to participate in a roundtable discussion. The participants worried about one strategy which has been used time and again, of the publicizing of the issue by the government and civil societies, instead of "talking about it" as a faith community and with the "victims."

Diffusing Socially Constructed Gender Roles

Despite a difference in the degree of GBV between women and men, participants felt that both genders should participate together in church. Normalized duties like making tea are moving from being women's duties to becoming a whole family duty. If a man is not married, he should be paired with another gender. Also, anyone should have the opportunity to be a counsellor or a children's church teacher.

Towards a Combined Response

From focus groups to in-depth interviews, participants agreed that there must be a collective resource-based approach, thus, sharing ideas from congregation to congregation, from different churches. Gender-based violence is a dire reality in South Africa generally, thus, the leadership in the government, and different organizations should not neglect the church in working collaboratively on this rising concern. Men should also join with women and be concerned about supporting them when they are responding to GBV. The church should include or educate men to speak out against GBV. The church should embrace individuals who talk about GBV and who can afford to talk outside of the church.

12 Theologically Affirmative Response to Address Gender-Based Violence

Accompaniment

Accompaniment was discussed as a theological response to a person after the separation from an abusive relationship or marriage. Participants felt that the pastors should accompany such individuals by praying together with them, talking to and with them, encouraging them, and making them feel they are integrated into the congregation and they have support from them. This can be done through pastoral visits and support groups where individuals with common challenges meet and discuss how they cope with similar realities. The participants discussed how this would mean involving those affected by GBV to address the issues rather than individuals who are outside of the GBV experience.

13 A Feminist Assessment of The Church Of The Cross (Hayfields) NELCSA's Response to Gender-Based Violence

The section above constitutes the social context of GBV in South Africa, especially in Pietermaritzburg, and how The Church of the Cross (Hayfields) intends to respond to GBV. It traces the trend of this pandemic from a grassroots approach of causality, the factors behind it, and practical steps to be taken by the church to address this situation. Thus, GBV from these diverse perspectives seems to be affecting more women and their physical and reproductive health more than men, which is less spoken about in faith spaces. It is, therefore, the aim of this section to acknowledge the current response of the NELCSA on GBV, but also to critically interrogate whether their intended response affirms young women's well-being and reproductive health. This section acknowledges GBV as a pandemic that affects both men and women, however, a woman's reproductive health issues must be looked at through reproductive justice which examines how social injustice between men and women is played out and where patriarchy is a root cause. It utilizes feminist cultural hermeneutics as a study resource that investigates how the lives of individuals, especially women, are conditioned in the context of GBV, where culture as a concept, the culture of violence, and culture of silence are the main contributing factors.

To employ this study resource, it is important to initiate this assessment with "culture" and how it involves and conditions the lives of people. At this point, I want to acknowledge culture because Africa is a cultural continent and South Africa is a context where a diversity of cultures are shared and celebrated for a positive life to some extent. However, apart from this, critically assessing how culture has been captured by the patriarchy in the context of GBV is worth noting. Culture is a key element in understanding GBV. Some traditional cultural practices and ideas of femininity, the culture of violence, and the culture of silence must be interrogated. There is a need to review the cultural context and probe who is behind it: is it culture or culture captured by patriarchy? Patriarchy seems to have romanticized culture and (ab) uses it to justify GBV.

The second critical assessment is the representation of gender in the Church of the Cross (Hayfields) NELCSA. Thus, gender in this context is assessed using the prism of cultural hermeneutics (Kanyoro, 2002). The response of church members to gender-related themes like GBV is significant. To give details, in an expected focus group of ten elderly members, only ten women showed up. In a youth focus group of twelve, only five boys showed up, and seven girls. Although the young adult focus group of six participants had a balanced number of three young women and three young men, the general gender disparity portrays that GBV reality is a feminized issue for some members coming from different spaces. Thus, first of all, women are more concerned about "talking about it," to share their experiences, perpetuating patriarchy in the absence of men who appear to benefit from patriarchy. Second, it suggests a frame of unconcerned masculinities in this congregation who cannot be part of roundtable discussions of how much this reality affects them as well as women. In highlighting this, Chitando and Chirongoma (2012: 1) talk about redemptive masculinities as "supermen who intervene swiftly and decisively to save women and children..." Hence, aside from the NELCSA's affirmative ways to address this reality, there is a need for educating men to be part of GBV dialogues as quickly as possible, to become more concerned and be more responsive. There is a need for this congregation to encourage men to talk about GBV in Pietermaritzburg rather than feminizing or masculinizing gender and GBV. The gender-balance approach should start in the church, through the text, and in men's mindsets, thus, reshaping men to be more responsive to gender and GBV.

In assessing this congregation's response to GBV, it is essential to emphasize the acknowledgment that women are more vulnerable in the face of GBV. Besides the comparison approach in this reality, I want to clarify that GBV is not an issue for women only. To illustrate this, some examples from the written literature and from direct and partly indirect quotations from the focus group are noted in Table 1.

Out of the 26 direct and indirect quotations in the table above, 20 of them illustrate that women are affected by GBV and 4 of the quotations show that "men too" are affected by this pandemic. The picture provided by this table does not only show the impact of GBV on women, but it extends to the effects on their reproductive health as shown earlier. Whilst women are affected at a social level where social inequalities characterize their lives, this trend is extended to their reproductive health. As shown above, the teenagers tend not to actually consent to sex, including protected sex. Physical attacks on pregnant women lead to long effects and damages, whilst economic injustice might lead pregnant women to starvation which can affect their health. This assessment invites this faith community to educate their members to acknowledge this reality so that sexual and reproductive health becomes an open subject in the church and the larger community. If church members (men) lack knowledge of gender imbalance at a social level, it is impossible for them to understand how that affects women's reproductive health in a patriarchal context.

14 Negative Terminology about "Surviving Individuals" of GBV

Inasmuch as this research acknowledges the response in this congregation, the terminology in addressing surviving individuals of GBV was not affirming. During the data-gathering the term "victim" was used eight times to address situations where individuals are affected by GBV and are still alive "physically." Whilst I concur that there are some individuals who have succumbed to death, or mental-related realities like depression, it is life-giving to use the phrase "surviving individuals" as it gives hope to those still surviving physically after this reality. Calling them "victims" portrays them as losers, thus, "victimizing the victim." Using affirmative words when addressing this issue at a faith community level shows the concern and sensitive response of the church in dealing with GBV. Thus, this research appreciates the response of The Church of The Cross (Hayfields) NELCSA, however, it also acknowledges a need to resist using shaming and naming terminology about the individuals who experienced or are experiencing GBV.

Table 1 A comparison of the degree of gender-based violence affecting women and men

Showcase of GBV affecting women	Showcase of GBV affecting men
"30% of women so far have experienced GBV at the age of 15 in their lifetime." (Moreno et al., 2013)	"Unlike men who submit and hold themselves together, as they are not supposed to be "cry-babies" because of what the society perceives of them."
"Exploring the experiences of women in Pietermaritzburg, South Africa, Shabalala (2020) records that 30 to 65% of women have experienced or have been exposed to GBV in their lifetime so far...."	"… 'men too', suffer emotional abuse to a certain extent."
"…fundamentally caused by societal norms and different power relations where men are usually perceived to be more superior to women."	"….I always tell my boys…I am raising boys, I want you to grow up knowing that a 'No' is a No, there is please and thank you,"
"During the Covid time, there was a cry for help of somebody where she felt in danger and her children as well, there was no work…her husband got very aggressive and in such a way we had to look for a safe place for them...."	"How do I love my girlfriend she really loves me…. I just want to fight, and she fights back, she doesn't want to see me, and I don't want to see her for about a week…"
"What I have come across now is people who are women are suffering a lot, every time I give them the food parcel for the family"	
"….I had an aunt, once a week she would always have a blue eye and she would wear shades… now recall it now that was abuse……after all that fighting there was always that 'sexing', I don't know whether he was raping her….when I see her now, she is damaged…"	
"In my first marriage, when I was unemployed, my husband used to abuse … me verbally and emotionally to say "You are a parasite, I am feeding you that is why you are so thin'…. I had an experience of not working over a period of 12 months…"	

Showcase of GBV affecting women	Showcase of GBV affecting men
"…Somebody now is getting a divorce after 25 years of marriage and there was verbal abuse over 25 years, and 'she' did not say a word to anybody and now it is enough"	
"…The female participants in this group, found themselves often in an uncomfortable situation where they could not pass by a group of young men freely without receiving any comments about their bodies…"	
"…the society knows much about women as they are vulnerable and quick to be identified…"	
"…it doesn't really matter like if men come out and talk or not, but it's the numbers which speak…yeah, they do talk…. obviously, it's going to be females that are affected"	
"Let's say you are married to someone who is rich or someone who is well developed and has money, yeah like…. he can afford stuff…. and you have not gone to school and your job does not give you a lot of money to live properly and you are married to this person, if he abuses you, you won't leave because you can't start on your own…"	
"…your boyfriend buys you flowers and then you forgive him because you think he is going to change."	
"…if a woman wears clothes in a certain way, she kind of represents the 'asking for it'."	
"…in our generation we think that being in a toxic relationship is cool, we think that is love…"	
"Normally a man would just start the fight for no good reason and substance abuse plays a role."	

(continued)

Table 1 (continued)

Showcase of GBV affecting women	Showcase of GBV affecting men
"...a young girl walking to school and then being approached and raped, forcefully asked on a date by men..." "...young woman who died due to severe beating from her boyfriend, but her family felt guilty to report it." "...women blaming themselves as the problem, feeling less worthy as 'sexual objects'." "...for women, when they get abused, maybe once, all of a sudden they start to hate men and say, 'men are trash,' because of anxiety and fear." "...He beats her almost to death... I could see her ribs. She thinks she is broken; she can't have medical attention...her family has written [her off...]" "Young women are mostly blamed by their partners and face accusation that it is 'their fault' to fall pregnant, hence this is when their partners beat them to get rid of the pregnancy." "The last thing a rapist thinks is to protect himself when having forced sex." "...most of the girls do not actually consent to sexual intercourse..." "I also feel like a mother who has been abused for a very long does not have the strength to do that... you feel so worthless... you are so broken down..." "How could you stay with that man for so long?"	

15 Conclusion

This study assessed The Church of The Cross (Hayfields) NELCSA's response to GBV in Pietermaritzburg, from a feminist perspective. It examined this by tracing the social context of GBV in Pietermaritzburg through focus group discussions and in-depth interviews with members of the church. This study has acknowledged the current response of the congregation to addressing GBV, which includes affirmative biblical interpretation through preaching and the diffusing of gendered-socially constructed ideas during church duties. It also noted the intended practical responses to GBV which include: a realistic way of thinking towards addressing GBV; "charity begins at home"; creating and sustaining the church as a safe space; roundtable dialogues on GBV; a combined response of the church, community, and government to GBV; and accompaniment as a theological response.

Based on the findings and the assessment of this study, GBV is a constellation of factors that are somehow related. These include patriarchal culture, ideas of real masculinity, ideas of proper femininity, context, societal norms, the culture of silence, inequality, and so forth. To exemplify this concept, in some African patriarchal contexts like South Africa, if a young woman is deprived of further education because of her gender, she is, first, likely to lack the ability to stand on her own, or to gain employment. Second, she is likely to stay in an abusive relationship for economic survival reasons. Third, even if she is abused, she is likely to remain silent as she is afraid to expose her partner to society as some cultures suggest "silence" denotes "respect." Parkes (2015: 7) underscores that "poverty and inequality are deeply implicated in violence, and violence associated with poverty can lead to children and women finding themselves as outcasts, marginalized, silenced, and damaged by violence." GBV is not only a "theoretical subject" but a reality that is not easily spoken about or responded to in faith communities and beyond. Although GBV is likened to some 21st-century pandemics like Covid-19, it is a kind of disease for which there is no vaccination. Gender-based is not gender, class, status, or age selective. It is a reality that can be faced by anyone within the church and beyond. Although GBV is not gender selective, it is a reality that is marginalized and feminized because of the ideas of masculinity. Thus, some men consider "gender-related issues like GBV as 'women's issues'" and therefore not a serious reality where "real men" can gather and talk. Gender-based violence is a disease, causing a new public health pandemic. While it affects both men and women, it has an impact on the SRHR of young women to a greater extent. Forced sex, deprivation of health, and medical decision-making continue to threaten women's reproductive health and rights. However, gender-based violence surviving individuals are still named and shamed as the term "victim" is used to address their experience of this reality in the faith community and beyond.

While this chapter appreciates the work done and proposed to be done by the congregation under study, it raises three recommendations to this faith community. First, written from a feminist perspective and through a Reproductive Justice Framework, this chapter recommends a balanced gender representation. The faith community should invite and include more men to be part of the GBV conversation so that they become responsible and concerned about masculinities in pandemics like GBV that affect them. It is strategic to introduce a gender policy within the congregation that will help the congregants to understand issues of gender and how they condition men and women. Through such a policy, there should be an admission from both men and women of all age groups in this congregation that GBV is a reality, and it affects both men and women. However, this policy should also help the congregants to understand that more women are affected by GBV. Women are vulnerable and at risk of sexual, reproductive-related diseases. Conducting seminars can combine knowledge of GBV and reproductive health rights, as well as conducting Contextual Bible Studies on GBV. The Church of The Cross (Hayfields) NELCSA pastors should conduct Contextual Bible Studies frequently. This is vital to the congregation as CBS is a product of praxis—a circle of reflection and action (West, 2007). The Bible can be used as a resource to transform a context, in this case, the prevalence of GBV in Pietermaritzburg, and resisting negative language and terminology (like "victim") that is often used when addressing the subject of GBV and individuals who have lived the reality. Doing CBS will allow the congregation to (SEE), that is identify GBV as a theme, (JUDGE) that is to identify a biblical text that might address GBV; formulate questions by analysing and linking text and context, articulating, and owning the bible study; and finally, developing a plan of action to address GBV as a congregation. Through some biblical stories where mostly (women) are surviving individuals of GBV, a CBS can educate and inform church members to understand that GBV is not a femininized issue but a reality that negatively impacts on women's sexual and reproductive health.

Further, formal training to respond to GBV should begin as this is vital for (women and men) pastors, youth, young adults, and the elderly to receive formal training through a course with guidelines on how to handle the GBV reality within the church and outside. For example, in Pietermaritzburg, there is "LIFELINE", a ten-day Gender-Based Violence Counsellor training, a course that is designed to equip social workers, social auxiliary workers, teachers, pastors, child and youth care workers, psychologists, counsellors and other health care professionals with the knowledge to understand the root causes of GBV. Also, the course develops skills to identify and prevent GBV incidents. The course is consistent with the latest World Health Organization guidelines and the South African legal framework on GBV. The course is a competency-based curriculum; it enables the development of the knowledge and skills to provide comprehensive and high-quality care to people subjected to GBV. The church should support the members to join such a course as it brings an understanding of key concepts including GBV, domestic violence, Intimate Partner Violence, child abuse, non-partner sexual violence, increased knowledge of GBV, its root causes and how these root causes can be addressed, increased knowledge of the cycle of violence, and application of GBV-related counselling skills.

Since GBV is a constellation of ideas that include poverty and economic injustice, it is vital for The Church of the Cross (Hayfields) to begin and sustain projects that fund specific surviving individuals of GBV so that they can resist violence and become resilient in this situation. We cannot separate gender from "our" bodies because violence has been taking place on women's and men's bodies. When women and men speak about their experiences, there should be a concerned community that listens and believe in these embodied realities. The church should accept the stories of violence as a source of theology. At the core of these experiences, there is still the battle and need to survive physically, psychologically, socially, and spiritually. It is now high time for this congregation, and for other faith communities in the context of South Africa, to talk about GBV and to listen to surviving individuals of GBV, with empathy and compassion. They should be doing this together as women and men, to save mostly women!

Bibliography

Abrahams, N., Devries, K., Watts, C., Pallitto, C., Petzold, M., Shamu, S., & García-Moreno, C. (2014). Worldwide Prevalence of Non-partner Sexual Violence: A Systematic Review. *Lancet, 383*, 1648–1654.

Allen, S. (2018). *The Importance of an Intersectional Approach to Gender-based Violence in South Africa* (p. 526). University Honors Theses. https://doi.org/10.15760/honors.531

Breen, R. L. (2006). A Practical Guide to Focus-group Research. *Journal of Geography in Higher Education, 30*(3), 463–475.

Campbell, J. C. (2002). Health Consequences of Intimate Partner Violence. *The Lancet, 359*(9314), 1331–1336.

Chiweshe, M., Mavuso, J., & Macleod, C. (2017). Reproductive justice in context: South African and Zimbabwean women's narratives of their abortion decision. *Feminism & Psychology, 27*(2), 203–224.

Chitando, E., & Chirongoma, S. (2012, Eds.). *Redemptive Masculinities, Men, HIV, and Religion*, Geneva: World Council of Churches Publications.

Creswell, J. W. (2014). *Research Design: Qualitative, Quantitative, and Mixed Methods Approach*. Sage.

Creswell, J. W. (2013). *Qualitative Inquiry & Research Design: Choosing among Five Approaches*. Sage.

Darong, G. G. (2020). Exploring the Experiences of Women in the Fight against Gender-based Violence in Scottsville, Pietermaritzburg. Submitted in fulfilment of the requirement for Research Plus Special Topic -ANTH302 - project College of Humanities, School of Social Sciences University of KwaZulu-Natal, Pietermaritzburg Campus.

Decker, M. R., Latimore, A. D., Yasutake, S., Haviland, M., Ahmed, S., Blum, R. W., Sonenstein, F., & Astone, N. M. (2015). Gender-based Violence Against Adolescent and Young Adult Women in Low and Middle Income Countries. *Journal of Adolescent Health, 56*(2), 188–196.

Dlamini, N. J. (2021). Gender-based Violence, Twin Pandemic to COVID-19. *Critical Sociology, 47*(4–5), 583–590.

Dunkle, K. Jewkes, R. Brown, H. McIntyre, J. Gray, G., & Harlow, S. (2003). Gender-based Violence and HIV Infection among Pregnant Women in Soweto. *Gender and Health Group, Men on Relationships with and Abuse of Women, Medical Research Council Technical Report*, Medical Research Council, Tygerberg.

Enaifoghe, A., Dlelana, M., Durokifa, A. A., & Dlamini, N. P. (2021). The Prevalence of Gender-based Violence Against Women in South Africa: A Call for Action. *African Journal of Gender, Society & Development, 10*(1), 1117.

Ellsberg, M., & Heise, L., (2002). Bearing Witness: Ethics in Domestic Violence Research. *The Lancet, 359*(9317), 1599–1604.

García-Moreno, C., Pallitto, C., Devries, K., Stöckl, H., Watts, C. & Abrahams, N., (2013). *Global and Regional Estimates of Violence Against Women: Prevalence and Health Effects of Intimate Partner Violence and Non-partner Sexual Violence*. World Health Organization.

Guedes, A. (2004). *Addressing Gender-Based Violence from the Reproductive Health/ HIV Sector: A Literature Review and Analysis*. Population Technical Assistance Project.

John, N., Casey, S. E., Carino, G., & McGovern, T. (2020). Lessons Never Learned: Crisis and Gender-based Violence. *Developing World Bioethics, 20*(2), 65–68.

Jewkes, R., & Abrahams, N. (2002). The Epidemiology of Rape and Sexual Coercion in South Africa: An Overview. *Social Science & Medicine, 55*(7), 1231–1244.

Kanyoro, R. A. (2002). *Feminist Cultural Hermeneutics: An African Perspective, Introductions in Feminist Theology*. The Pilgrim Press.

Kishor, S., & Johnson, K., (2005). Profiling Domestic Violence: A Multi-country Study. *Studies in Family Planning, 36*(3), 259–261.

Mampane, J. N. (2020). Susceptible Lives: Gender-based Violence, Young Lesbian Women and HIV Risk in a Rural Community in South Africa. *Journal of International Women's Studies, 21*(6), 249–264.

Matthews, S. Abrahams, N. Martin, L. J. Vetten, L. Van der Merwe, L., & Jewkes, R. (2004). Every Six Hours a Woman is killed by her Intimate Partner. *A National Study of Female Homicide in South Africa*. MRC Brief No. 5.

Moreno, G. C., & Pallitto, C. (2013). *Global and Regional Estimates of Violence against Women: Prevalence and Health Effects of Intimate Partner Violence and Non-Partner Sexual Violence*. WHO.

Muluneh, M. D., Stulz, V., Francis, L., & Agho, K. (2020). Gender-based Violence against Women in Sub-Saharan Africa: A Systematic Review and Meta-analysis of Cross-sectional Studies. *International Journal of Environmental Research and Public Health, 17*(3), 903. https://doi.org/10.3390/ijerph17030903.PMID:32024080;PMCID:PMC7037605

Palermo, T., Bleck, J., & Peterman, A. (2014). Tip of the Iceberg: Reporting and Gender-based Violence in Developing Countries. *American Journal of Epidemiology, 179*(5), 602–612.

Pallitto, C. C., Jansen, H. A., Ellsberg, M., Heise, L., & Watts, C. H. (2006). WHO Multi-country Study on Women's Health and Domestic Violence against Women Study Team. Prevalence of Intimate Partner Violence: Findings from the WHO Multi-country Study on Women's Health and Domestic Violence. *Lancet, 368*, 1260–1269.

Parkes, J. (2015). *Gender Violence in Poverty Contexts*. Taylor & Francis.

Ross, L., & Solinger, R. (2017). *Reproductive Justice: An introduction* (Vol. 1). University of California Press.

Sikweyiya, Y. Nduna, M. Shai, N. & Jewkes, R. (2017). Motivations for Participating in a Non-interventional Gender-based Violence Survey In A Low-income Setting in South Africa. *BMC Public Health*, 17, 605. https://doi.org/10.1186/s12889-017-4525-z

Swinton, J., & Mowat, H. (2016). *Practical Theology and Qualitative Research*. SCM press.

The World Bank. (2019). *Gender-Based Violence (Violence against Women and Girls)*. https://www.worldbank.org/en/topic/socialsustainability/brief/violence-against-women-and-girls

USAID, IGWG, PRB, (2010). Gender-based Violence: Impediment to Reproductive Health. In *Population Reference Bureau. USAID*.

United Nations Office on Drugs and Crime (UNODC). (2018). *Global Study on Homicide: Gender Related Killing of Women and Girls, Vienna*. https://www.unodc.org/documents/data-and-analysis/GSH2018/GSH18_Gender-related_killing_of_women_and_girls.pdf

UN Women. (2020). *The Shadow Pandemic: Violence against Women and Girls and COVID-19.* https://www.unwomen.org/en/digital-library/multimedia/2020/4/infographic-ccovid19-violence-against-women-and-girls

UN General Assembly. (1993). In *Declaration on the Elimination of Violence against Women.*

West, G. (2007). *Doing Contextual Bible Study: A Resource Manual.* Ujamaa Center.

World Bank. (2019). Violence against Women and Girls. https://www.worldbank.org/en/topic/socialdevelopment/brief/violence-against-women-and-girls

World Health Organization. (2013). *Global and Regional Estimates of Violence against Women: Prevalence and Health Effects of Intimate Partner Violence and Non-partner Sexual Violence.* Geneva: World Health Organization

Yin, R. (2011). *Qualitative Research from Start to Finish.* Guilford Press.

Breaking The Silence: Exploring the Challenges and Support Mechanisms for Male Survivors of Gender-Based Violence in Sub-Saharan Africa

Susan Monyangi Nyabena

1 Introduction

Gender-based violence (GBV) is a widespread problem impacting people globally, with significant consequences for society, the economy, and health (UNICEF, 2020). Although the discussion on gender-based violence has mainly centred on female survivors and victims, there is a growing acknowledgment that men also encounter violence and confront distinct obstacles in obtaining support services (Bates & Taylor, 2023; Carpenter, 2006). In sub-Saharan Africa, the experiences of male survivors of GBV have mainly remained invisible, perpetuating a culture of silence and hindering their access to much-needed assistance (Carpenter, 2006).

Male survivors of GBV in sub-Saharan Africa face numerous socio-cultural barriers that impede their recognition, reporting, and access to support services (Nakalyowa-Luggya et al., 2022). Many of these barriers are also experienced by male survivors of GBV in other parts of the world. Traditional gender roles and patriarchal masculinity discourage men from seeking help, as disclosing their experiences of violence can be perceived as a violation of societal expectations of strength and self-reliance (Hlavka, 2017). Additionally, cultural beliefs and stigmatization surrounding male victimization may perpetuate shame and silence, further marginalizing male survivors.

S. M. Nyabena (✉)
University of Nairobi, Nairobi, Kenya
e-mail: Nyabena@africa-union.org

Most male survivors face additional challenges due to the lack of knowledge and understanding about their victimization among healthcare providers, legal professionals, and the wider community (Nakalyowa-Luggya et al., 2022). According to Jewkes et al. (2015), many support services do not have gender-responsive approaches that can fully support male survivors. There is a lack of specialized programmes and inadequate funding for comprehensive support. Furthermore, legal frameworks and policies addressing GBV may not fully recognize or provide adequate protection for male survivors, leaving them without avenues for justice and redress (Stemple, 2009).

Over time, men have traditionally enjoyed advantages conferred by gender roles and societal norms; however, there is an emerging recognition of the detrimental effects these norms can have on the male survivors of violence. The increasing awareness of how these gender norms operate against victims sheds light on the oppressive nature of such norms. Attitudes and expectations towards individuals who have experienced victimization, regardless of gender, are closely intertwined with prevailing gender norms (Mankowski & Maton, 2010).

Although the term "gender-based violence" may intuitively encompass both sexes, international human rights law, as currently formulated, specifically pertains to female victimization (Gorris, 2015: 415). Consequently, this narrow conceptualization perpetuates the notion that sexual violence and gender-based violence exclusively apply to female survivors and victims, resulting in the invisibility, limited research, and insufficient addressing of men and boys as survivors and victims (Linos, 2009: 1549; Stemple, 2009: 636–637). This exclusionary practice impacts significantly on the provision of protection and existing programmes, as support services are primarily tailored to meet the needs of female survivors and victims, leaving men with limited access to adequate assistance (SVRI (n.d.); UNHCR & RLP, 2012). The representation of violence against men is predominantly confined to conflict settings, neglecting the experiences of civilian men. A disproportionate focus on female victimization leads to inadequate comprehension of men's victimhood and the broader context of violence (Conroy, 2013).

2 Methodology

This chapter employed a desk review methodology to investigate male survivors of GBV challenges and support mechanisms in sub-Saharan Africa. The desk review process involved extensively searching relevant literature using various online databases, academic journals, and institutional websites. The search focused on publications spanning the period from 1988 to 2023, utilizing keywords such as "male survivors of gender-based violence," "GBV against men," "challenges," "support mechanisms," and "sub-Saharan Africa." The extracted data involved meticulously examining and evaluating selected articles and reports, then categorizing information into key themes. The synthesized findings were subsequently interpreted to discern patterns, trends, and overarching arguments within the literature.

Through a thematic organization of the findings, this research aimed to identify salient arguments, debates, and challenges related to GBV against men. Key themes and sub-topics encompassed the prevalence and manifestations of GBV against men, socio-cultural factors contributing to underreporting and stigma, barriers impeding access to support services, strategies for promoting inclusive support mechanisms, and policy and legal framework considerations. However, it is crucial to acknowledge the limitations associated with this methodology. As a secondary research approach, its efficacy is contingent upon the availability and quality of existing literature, potentially omitting recent advancements or unpublished studies. Ethical considerations were addressed through proper citation and acknowledgment of authors' work.

The methodology employed in this research offers a comprehensive approach to investigating the challenges and support mechanisms for male survivors of GBV. By systematically searching for relevant literature, extracting and analysing data, and synthesizing the findings, this study contributes to the existing knowledge base concerning GBV against men and their support mechanisms. The outcomes of this research will inform future studies and potential interventions aimed at recognizing and eradicating violence against men, promoting inclusive support mechanisms, and considering the policy and legal frameworks surrounding this issue.

3 Gender-Based Violence Against Men

The documentation of male sexual violence can be classified into three distinct categories: (1) instances where it is acknowledged but not explicitly classified as sexual violence, (2) cases where it is appropriately identified and characterized but lacks subsequent accountability, and (3) situations where it is explicitly recognized as sexual violence, leading to consequential actions (Sivakumaran, 2010).

The occurrence of GBV against men encompasses a spectrum of abusive behaviours. Hines and Douglas (2009) found that men experienced various forms of violence, encompassing physical, psychological, and sexual violence, as well as abusive and controlling behaviours that align with the definition of intimate partner violence (IPV) provided by the World Health Organization. According to the WHO (2010) definition, physical violence involves slapping, hitting, kicking, and beating. Men who have experienced IPV have reported instances of being pushed, shoved, grabbed, shaken, slapped, hit, kicked, bitten, scratched, and threatened or harmed with a knife or other objects (Scott-Storey et al., 2023). Similarly, sexual violence involving nonconsensual sexual acts, forced sexual acts, and rape, are prevalent among male survivors. Additionally, emotional and psychological abuse, manifested through threats, humiliation, and control, constitute other forms of GBV experienced by men (Scott-Storey et al., 2023).

Intimate partner violence emerges as a significant form of GBV, wherein men endure physical, sexual, and emotional abuse from their intimate partners (Scott-Storey et al., 2023). Notably, family-related violence, characterized by acts of mistreatment perpetrated by family members or relatives, also impacts men, resulting in detrimental consequences for their physical and psychological well-being (Scott-Storey et al., 2023). Moreover, men may encounter violence within community settings, spanning public spaces and situations of conflicts or emergencies (Dienye & Gbeneol, 2009). The classification of "women and children" perpetuates a depiction portraying women as akin to children, rendering them vulnerable and needing protection. Meanwhile, instances where boys experience sexual violence are often regarded as a precursor to their eventual manhood, thus potentially warranting separate categorization or inclusion within the broader framework of sexual violence against men (Russell, 2007).

Despite the perception that GBV primarily affects women, studies have shown that men experience violence across different contexts and societies. Research conducted in sub-Saharan Africa has revealed alarming rates of GBV against men. A study conducted in South Africa found that 17% of men reported experiencing physical violence from an intimate partner, while 3% reported experiencing sexual violence (Jewkes et al., 2015). Similarly, a study in Nigeria reported that the prevalence of IPV among men stood at 42.5% during the COVID-19 pandemic (Oloniniyi et al., 2023). One in five men in Somalia reported physical or sexual violence victimization during childhood (Wirtz et al., 2018). The Kenya National Bureau of Statistics (KNBS & ICF, 2023) has reported that many men aged 15–49 in Kenya have experienced physical and sexual violence at some point. Specifically, the data reveals that around 27% of men in this age bracket have been victims of physical violence, while 6% have reported incidents of sexual violence. Understanding the prevalence and various forms of GBV experienced by men is crucial in recognizing the extent and nature of their victimization.

4 Socio-cultural Factors Contributing to Underreporting and Stigma

Cultural traditions and societal norms significantly influence the abuse men experience at home, with acts of violence perpetrated against men often not culturally supported, leading to public intimidation and amusement (Steinmetz & Lucca, 1988). Men believe that society expects them to embody traits such as courage, strength, dominance, power, and self-reliance while dismissing the notion that they can be victims of violence (Steinmetz & Lucca, 1988). These gendered beliefs and societal expectations shape the perceptions and experiences of men regarding their vulnerability to violence. The prevailing social construction of masculinity often discourages men from acknowledging and seeking support as survivors and victims of violence. The cultural pressure to conform to traditional gender roles reinforces the perception that men should not be seen as victims but instead maintain an image of invulnerability. These deeply ingrained beliefs contribute to the underreporting and stigmatization of male violence survivors. The societal narrative that men should be strong and impervious to harm creates significant barriers for male survivors in recognizing, disclosing, and accessing support services.

Gender norms and expectations in sub-Saharan African societies contribute to the underreporting and stigma of GBV against men. Traditional notions of masculinity often emphasize strength, power, and invulnerability, creating a societal construct that discourages men from disclosing their experiences as victims of violence (Hlavka, 2017). Fear of being perceived as weak or emasculated, as well as the anticipation of social judgment and ridicule, further contribute to the reluctance of male survivors to come forward and share their stories (Douglas & Hines, 2011). These deeply rooted socio-cultural norms and attitudes surrounding masculinity create a barrier that inhibits male survivors from seeking help and hinders efforts to address GBV against men.

Moreover, societal perceptions of gender roles and power dynamics can perpetuate a culture of victim-blaming and denial of male victimization. Prevailing beliefs that men are inherently strong and invulnerable make it challenging for others to acknowledge that they can also experience violence

(Hlavka, 2017). Consequently, male survivors may encounter scepticism, disbelief, or accusations of fabricating their experiences when they attempt to disclose their victimization (Douglas & Hines, 2011). Such reactions reinforce the stigma associated with GBV against men, discouraging survivors from seeking support and perpetuating the cycle of silence.

Reliance on traditional conflict resolution mechanisms, such as family or community mediation, can also contribute to underreporting and perpetuating the stigma surrounding GBV against men. These mechanisms often prioritize preserving family or community harmony over addressing the rights and needs of individual survivors (Hlavka, 2017). Consequently, male survivors may hesitate to report their experiences or seek justice due to concerns about disrupting social relationships or facing additional stigmatization within their communities. Furthermore, cultural norms surrounding privacy, family honour, and reputation can deter male survivors from reporting GBV. Concerns about social consequences, including the potential for family disruption or negative community perceptions, may discourage disclosure and prevent access to support services (Dienye & Gbeneol, 2009). Fear of retaliation or further harm can also contribute to the underreporting of GBV against men, as perpetrators may employ intimidation tactics to maintain control over their victims (Stark, 2012).

Promoting gender-transformative approaches that challenge harmful masculinity norms, promote gender equality, and encourage help-seeking behaviours can play a pivotal role in breaking the silence (Jewkes et al., 2015). Sensitizing healthcare providers, legal professionals, and the broader community to the experiences and needs of male survivors can help reduce stigmatization and improve access to support services. Furthermore, fostering inclusive and non-judgmental environments that validate the experiences of male survivors, regardless of their sexual orientation, can help create safe spaces for disclosure and healing (Hlavka, 2017).

5 Barriers to Accessing Support Services

Accessing support services is paramount for male survivors of GBV in the sub-Saharan African context. Nonetheless, the journey to seek help is often hindered by various barriers that impede their ability to access the necessary support. A critical obstacle lies in the limited awareness and knowledge surrounding available support services tailored to male survivors of GBV. Many men may ignore such services or erroneously assume they are exclusively intended for women (Douglas & Hines, 2011). This lack of awareness acts as a deterrent, preventing male survivors from actively seeking help as they struggle to identify appropriate channels for assistance and are uncertain about the individuals or organizations they can approach in times of need.

Cultural and social norms surrounding masculinity discourage men from seeking help and disclosing their encounters with GBV. Within numerous sub-Saharan African societies, traditional perceptions of masculinity emphasize strength, self-reliance, and emotional stoicism (Adamson, 2017). Consequently, male survivors often fear disclosing their victimization would result in being perceived as weak or stripped of their masculine identity. The prevailing cultural perspective, which traditionally assigns men a non-victim status in domestic settings, hinders the implementation of protective measures for male individuals ensnared in abusive relationships (Ayodele, 2017). The pressure to conform to these norms hinders their willingness to seek support services or even acknowledge their victimhood.

Furthermore, the prevalence of stigma and societal attitudes towards male victimization exacerbate barriers when attempting to access support services. In many communities, male survivors encounter scepticism, disbelief, or blame upon disclosing their experiences of GBV (Chynoweth et al., 2020). Societal perceptions that men should be capable of protecting themselves or that violence against men is of less significance can lead to victim-blaming and trivializing their experiences. Such stigmatization perpetuates a culture of silence, rendering it arduous for male survivors to step forward and avail themselves of the support they require.

The presence of stigma and societal attitudes hinders access to support services for male survivors of GBV. These barriers are rooted in cultural beliefs that associate masculinity with strength and invulnerability, challenging the perception that men can be victims of violence and discouraging them from seeking help (Wright, 2016.). The fear of judgment, ridicule, or disbelief upon disclosing their experiences further exacerbates the reluctance of male survivors to access support services (Chynoweth et al., 2020). Additionally, as noted earlier, the apprehension of retribution or retaliation from perpetrators is a deterrent, impeding male survivors from reaching out for assistance. Perpetrators often employ intimidation tactics, threats, or acts of violence to maintain control over their victims and dissuade them from seeking help (Stark, 2012).

Furthermore, the potential disruption of familial or community dynamics and the fear of further harm contribute to the complexity of accessing support services for male survivors. Dienye and Gbeneol (2009) conducted a study that revealed a low prevalence of reported cases of GBV among men. The authors attribute this phenomenon to men's reluctance to involve law enforcement agencies or seek medical assistance, even in situations involving physical injuries, due to feelings of shame associated with disclosing familial violence. Additionally, this reluctance may be intensified by a perceived inability to exercise control over their wives (Dienye & Gbeneol, 2009).

An additional impediment arises from the constrained availability and accessibility of support services catering to male survivors. Within numerous sub-Saharan African nations, support services addressing GBV predominantly prioritize women, leaving male survivors with limited resources (Ayodele, 2017). According to Douglas and Hines (2011: 7), many male victims who sought assistance from domestic violence agencies encountered a disheartening response, being told, "We only help women." This dearth of dedicated services engenders feelings of marginalization and neglect among male survivors, perpetuating underreporting and stigmatization. Furthermore, the absence of tailored support systems and resources specifically designed to meet the unique needs of male survivors constitutes a substantial barrier. According to a study done by Ayodele (2017), no institutional structures on the ground were found to support male victims, even in environments in which social provisions are assumed to be in abundance. The scarcity of such services reinforces the invisibility of male victimization and perpetuates the notion that GBV is predominantly a women's issue. Furthermore, a notable disparity exists between the number of male survivors who experience violence and those who seek healthcare services, indicating a low utilization rate among the former. This suggests that most men who undergo sexual violence avoid seeking medical care (Gatuguta et al., 2018.) Consequently, the lack of acknowledgment and support exacerbates feelings of isolation and hampers male survivors' propensity to seek help.

Structural and logistical barriers present significant challenges when accessing support services for male survivors of GBV. According to Christian et al. (2011), men often miss out on treatment due to stigmas, shame, and various barriers. These barriers may include high treatment costs, limited access to services, transportation limitations, long waiting lists, and inadequate service provision in rural or remote areas. Insufficient allocation of funding and resources targeted explicitly at support services for male survivors exacerbates these barriers, undermining their ability to seek and obtain the necessary assistance. The scarcity of financial resources allocated to GBV interventions adversely affects the availability of support services, particularly in less populated or geographically isolated regions (Christian et al., 2011). The constrained availability of services in such areas poses significant challenges for male survivors. Financial constraints, impeding their ability to afford transportation or meet other associated costs, further hinder access to support services.

Moreover, long waiting lists exacerbate the difficulties faced by male survivors, delaying their access to crucial support and care. Furthermore, the absence of male-friendly spaces or specialized counselling services compounds the challenges encountered by male survivors seeking support (Christian et al., 2011). The lack of tailored services that address male survivors' specific needs and experiences can discourage them from seeking help, as they may feel that the available services are ill-suited to their requirements, limiting their opportunities for healing and recovery.

6 Promoting Inclusive Support Mechanisms

By developing support systems that recognize and respond to male survivors' unique experiences and challenges, we can create an environment that fosters healing, empowerment, and resilience.

An effective strategy for fostering inclusive support mechanisms entails the implementation of gender-transformative programming. Such interventions challenge detrimental gender norms and foster equality and respectful relationships (Jewkes et al., 2015). By engaging men and boys in meaningful dialogues and educational activities centred on gender equality, these interventions can create a shift in societal attitudes, mitigate stigmatization, and encourage male survivors to seek the support they require. Notably, initiatives like the "Soul City + " programme in South Africa have effectively leveraged media campaigns and community involvement to challenge traditional masculinity norms and promote positive gender attitudes (Gibbs et al., 2020).

An additional strategy involves providing comprehensive training and sensitization programmes for service providers, aiming to enhance their understanding and response to the unique needs of male survivors. Healthcare professionals, counsellors, and legal personnel should undergo targeted training on gender-responsive approaches that acknowledge the specific experiences of male survivors of GBV. This training should encompass a range of topics, including trauma-informed care, a nuanced understanding of male victimization, and the establishment of safe and non-judgmental environments conducive to disclosure and healing. Organizations such as "Men Can Stop Rape" in Uganda have successfully implemented training initiatives for service providers, strengthening their capacity to effectively support male survivors of GBV (Jewkes et al., 2015). The "Padare/Enkundleni: Men's

Forum on Gender" organization in Zimbabwe also addresses sensitive topics such as gender identity, sexuality, HIV/AIDS, and violence against women and girls by facilitating open discussions with traditional and religious leaders, abusers, and everyday men (Minnings, 2014).

Establishing dedicated support services and helplines tailored to the specific needs of male survivors assumes great significance in fostering inclusivity within the context of addressing GBV. By creating specialized services that cater specifically to the unique challenges faced by male survivors, the barriers to seeking assistance can be effectively dismantled, granting male survivors a safe and inclusive space where their specific needs can be addressed effectively. An example of such an initiative is the "Brothers for Life" campaign implemented in South Africa. This campaign developed a toll-free helpline and support network explicitly targeting men affected by GBV, providing them with essential services such as counselling, referrals, and legal advice (Jewkes et al., 2015).

The active involvement of the community and the establishment of secure environments where male survivors can freely express their experiences can foster inclusivity within the context of GBV. Community-based initiatives that offer platforms for men to gather, exchange narratives, and provide mutual assistance can play a pivotal role in breaking the prevailing silence surrounding GBV and mitigating associated stigmas (Douglas & Hines, 2011). Peer-support groups, survivor networks, and men's forums are community-oriented approaches that facilitate healing processes and empower male survivors. An example of such initiatives is the "Sonke Gender Justice" programme in South Africa, which has effectively implemented community mobilization strategies to engage men in combating GBV and providing support for male survivors (Jewkes et al., 2015). By actively engaging men in challenging harmful gender norms, fostering dialogue, and promoting empathy, this programme has fostered community-level change and facilitated the creation of safe spaces for male survivors to share their experiences and seek support.

Acknowledging that promoting inclusive support mechanisms necessitates sustained collaboration among government agencies, civil society organizations, and other relevant stakeholders within the field is imperative. This collaborative effort serves to develop comprehensive policies and guidelines that ensure the provision of support services tailored to the needs of male survivors in a gender-responsive manner. A key element of this collaboration involves meaningful engagement with male survivors, whose perspectives, voices, and lived experiences are central to designing and implementing support mechanisms (Hlavka, 2017). Creating specialized services can dismantle these barriers, ensuring male survivors have equitable access to the required support. Moreover, the active involvement of male survivors in decision-making processes facilitates the identification and understanding of their specific needs, thereby enabling the tailoring of support systems to meet their needs effectively.

7   Policy and Legal Frameworks

The perpetuation of GBV against men often goes unrecognized and lacks meaningful consequences, as highlighted by Sivakumaran (2010). In certain instances, incidents of male sexual violence are depicted but fail to result in repercussions for the accused for various reasons (Sivakumaran, 2010). According to Sivakumaran (2010), a concerning trend emerges wherein the occurrence of male sexual violence is disregarded when considering the legal implications associated with such findings. This disregard perpetuates the misconception that men and boys are not susceptible to sexual violence, reinforcing the prevailing notion that sexual violence solely affects women and girls. By characterizing sexual violence against men and boys solely within the framework of torture, there is a risk of further marginalizing their experiences and overlooking the need for comprehensive attention to their victimization (Sivakumaran, 2010).

According to the Centre for African Justice, Peace, and Human Rights (2023), Uganda is among the African nations where instances of male victims of sexual violence have been reported. However, it is noteworthy that Uganda's existing domestic criminal law primarily recognizes sexual violence against women, focusing on cases of rape perpetrated against females (Sivakumaran, 2010). Consequently, the courts predominantly handle more sexual violence cases involving female victims. This disparity in reported cases does not necessarily imply that instances of sexual abuse against males are non-existent. Instead, it reflects the reluctance of male victims to report such offences, mainly due to the absence of specialized facilities and legal frameworks tailored to addressing and adjudicating sexual violence against men.

An effective response to GBV against men necessitates establishing a robust policy framework. Such policies should explicitly acknowledge male victims of GBV and their distinct needs while guaranteeing the availability and accessibility of services, support mechanisms, and resources tailored to male survivors. By adopting policy frameworks that comprehensively address GBV, irrespective of gender, inclusivity is promoted, ensuring that male survivors are neither overlooked nor excluded from support initiatives (Gibbs et al., 2017). An exemplary instance of such comprehensive legislation is the "Domestic Violence Act" in South Africa, which safeguards all victims of domestic violence, regardless of their gender, and facilitates the procurement of protection orders and access to support services (Gibbs et al., 2017). Legal frameworks are pivotal in the comprehensive response to GBV perpetrated against men, establishing the necessary foundations for accountability and justice. Laws must encompass all forms of GBV, encompassing violence directed towards men, and ensure the culpability of perpetrators. Moreover, legal frameworks should ensure the efficacy of the justice system in addressing the specific needs and experiences of male survivors. This entails providing appropriate protective measures, legal representation, and comprehensive support throughout the legal process.

8 Conclusion

The comprehensive and multifaceted addressing of challenges and support mechanisms for male survivors of GBV in sub-Saharan Africa is paramount. The prevalence and various forms of GBV against men in the region cannot be overlooked, as evidenced by research findings. Underreporting and stigma associated with socio-cultural factors present considerable obstacles that hinder male survivors from coming forward and seeking support (Hlavka, 2017). Additional barriers, such as societal expectations of masculinity, the fear of judgment, and the absence of appropriate services, further impede their access to much-needed support (Douglas & Hines, 2011).

Nevertheless, there is a growing acknowledgment of the imperative to address GBV against men. Policy and legal frameworks serve as critical foundations for intervention and support. Developing comprehensive policies that explicitly recognize male victimization, ensure inclusivity, and provide avenues for accessing justice and support is indispensable (Gibbs et al., 2017). Legal frameworks should encompass the criminalization of all forms of GBV and ensure perpetrators' accountability while catering to the specific needs of male survivors.

Efforts to surmount barriers and foster inclusivity have given rise to various support mechanisms. Gender-transformative programming emerges as a powerful approach that challenges harmful gender norms and engages men and boys in promoting gender equality and preventing violence (Jewkes et al., 2015). The training and sensitization of service providers enhance their capacity to respond effectively to the unique needs of male survivors.

Furthermore, the establishment of dedicated support services, helplines, and community-based initiatives create safe spaces for male survivors to seek support, share experiences, and access resources (Douglas & Hines, 2011).

By breaking the silence surrounding GBV and recognizing the plight of male survivors, societies can work towards creating an environment that not only supports and protects them but also empowers them. Only through collective efforts and an unwavering commitment to gender equality can we break the silence against GBV perpetrated against men.

References

Adamson, A. (2017). *Divergent Masculinity Discourses among Stellenbosch Student Males: Traditional Masculinity and the Progressive Male/New Man Discourse* (Doctoral dissertation, Stellenbosch: Stellenbosch University).

Ayodele, J. O. (2017). The Socio-cultural Causes of Male Victimisation in Domestic Contexts in A Qualitative Analysis. *International Journal of Criminal Justice Sciences, 12*(2), 252–269

Bates, E. A., & Taylor, J. C. (Eds.). (2023). *Domestic Violence Against Men and Boys: Experiences of Male Victims of Intimate Partner Violence.* Routledge.

Carpenter, R. C. (2006). Recognizing gender-based Violence against Civilian Men and Boys in Conflict Situations. *Security Dialogue, 37*(1), 83–103.

Centre for African Justice, Peace, and Human Rights. (2023) Men And Boys As Hidden Victims Of Sexual Violence: A Conversation On Sexual Violence Perpetrated Against The Male Gender Organised By Centre For African Justice, Peace And Human Rights. https://centreforafricanjustice.org/men-and-boys-as-hidden-victims-of-sexualviolence-a-conversation-on-sexual-violence-perpet rated-against-the-male-genderorganised-by-centre-for-african-justice-peace-and-human-rights/#:~:text=Male%20victims%20are%20discouraged%20from,not%20want%20to%0be%20scorned

Christian, M., Safari, O., Ramazani, P., Burnham, G., & Glass, N. (2011). Sexual and Gender-based Violence against Men in the Democratic Republic of Congo: Effects on Survivors, their Families and the Community. *Medicine, Conflict and Survival, 27*(4), 227–246.

Closson, K., Hatcher, A., Sikweyiya, Y., Washington, L., Mkhwanazi, S., Jewkes, R., Dunkle, K., & Gibbs, A. (2020). Gender Role Conflict and sexual Health and Relationship Practices amongst Young Men Living in Urban Informal Settlements in South Africa. *Culture, Health & Sexuality, 22*(1), 31–47.

Conroy, A. A. (2014). Gender, Power XE "Power", and Intimate Partner Violence: A Study on Couples from Rural Malawi. *Journal of Interpersonal Violence, 29*(5), 866–888.

Chynoweth, S. K., Buscher, D., Martin, S., & Zwi, A. B. (2020). A Social Ecological Approach to Understanding Service Utilization Barriers among Male Survivors

of Sexual Violence in Three Refugee Settings: A Qualitative Exploratory Study. *Conflict and Health, 14*(1), 1–13.
Dienye, P. O., & Gbeneol, P. K. (2009). Domestic Violence against Men in Primary Care in Nigeria XE "Nigeria." *American Journal of Men's Health, 3*(4), 333–339.
Douglas, E. M., & Hines, D. A. (2011). The Helpseeking Experiences of Men who Sustain Intimate Partner Violence: An Overlooked Population and Implications for Practice. *Journal of Family Violence, 26*(6), 473–485.
Gatuguta, A., Merrill, K. G., Colombini, M., Soremekun, S., Seeley, J., Mwanzo, I., & Devries, K. (2018). Missed Treatment Opportunities and Barriers to Comprehensive Treatment for Sexual Violence Survivors in Kenya: A Mixed Methods Study. *BMC Public Health, 18*(1), 1–18.
Gibbs, A., Jacobson, J., & Kerr Wilson, A. (2017). A Global Comprehensive Review of Economic Interventions to Prevent Intimate Partner Violence and HIV risk Behaviours. *Global Health Action, 10*(sup2), 1290427. https://doi.org/10.1080/16549716.2017.1290427
Gibbs, A., Washington, L., Abdelatif, N., Chirwa, E., Willan, S., Shai, N., Sikweyiya, Y., Mkhwanazi, S., Ntini, N., & Jewkes, R. (2020). Stepping Stones and Creating Futures Intervention to Prevent Intimate Partner Violence among Young People: Cluster Randomized Controlled Trial. *Journal of Adolescent Health, 66*(3), 323–335.
Gorris, E. A. P. (2015). Invisible Victims? Where are Male Victims of Conflict-related Sexual Violence in International Law and Policy? *European Journal of Women's Studies, 22*(4), 412–427.
Hines, D. A., & Douglas, E. M. (2009). Women's Use of Intimate Partner Violence Against Men: Prevalence, Implications, and Consequences. *Journal of Aggression, Maltreatment & Trauma, 18*(6), 572–586.
Hlavka, H. R. (2017). Speaking of Stigma and the Silence of Shame: Young Men and Sexual Victimization. *Men and Masculinities, 20*(4), 482–505.
Jewkes, R., Flood, M., & Lang, J. (2015). From Work with Men and Boys to Changes of Social Norms and Reduction of Inequities in Gender Relations: A Conceptual Shift in Prevention of Violence against Women and Girls. *The Lancet, 385*(9977), 1580–1589.
KNBS and ICF. (2023). *Kenya Demographic and Health Survey 2022. Key Indicators Report. Nairobi, Kenya, and Rockville, Maryland*, USA: KNBS and ICF.
Linos, N. (2009). Rethinking Gender-based Violence During war XE "War" : Is Violence against Civilian Men a Problem Worth Addressing? *Social Science & Medicine, 68*(8), 1548–1551.
Mankowski, E. S., & Maton, K. I. (2010). A Community Psychology of Men and Masculinity: Historical and Conceptual Review. *American Journal of Community Psychology, 45*, 73–86.
Minnings, A. (2014). How Men are Transforming Masculinities and Engaging Men and Boys to End Violence against Women and Girls in Zimbabwe: A Case Study.
Nakalyowa-Luggya, D., Lutwama-Rukundo, E., Kabonesa, C., & Kwiringira, J. (2022). It is Such a Shameful Experience... Barriers to Help-Seeking among Male

Survivors of Intimate Partner Violence (IPV) in Uganda XE Uganda. *Gender and Behaviour, 20*(4), 20502–20517.

Oloniniyi, I. O., Ibigbami, O., Oginni, O. A., Ugo, V., Adelola, A., Esan, O. A., Amiola, A., Daropale, O., Ebuka, M., Esan, O., & Mapayi, B. (2023). Prevalence and Pattern of Intimate Partner Violence during COVID-19 Pandemic among Nigerian Adults. *Psychological Trauma, 15*(5), 868–876. https://doi.org/10.1037/tra0001335. Epub 2022 Aug 18.

Russell, W. (2007). Sexual Violence against Men and Boys. *Forced Migration Review, 27*, 2223.

Scott-Storey, K., O'Donnell, S., Ford-Gilboe, M., Varcoe, C., Wathen, N., Malcolm, J., & Vincent, C. (2023). What about the Men? A Critical Review of Men's Experiences of Intimate Partner Violence. *Trauma, Violence, & Abuse, 24*(2), 858–872.

Sivakumaran, S. (2010). Lost in Translation: UN Responses to Sexual Violence against Men and Boys in Situations of Armed XE "Armed" Conflict. *International Review of the Red Cross, 92*(877), 259–277.

Social Stigma Silences Male Domestic Abuse Victims. [online]. https://edubirdie.com/examples/social-stigma-silences-male-domestic-abuse-victims/. Accessed 19 June 2023.

Steinmetz, S. K., & Lucca, J. S. (1988). Husband Battering. *Handbook of Family Violence*, pp. 233–246.

Stemple, L. (2008). Male Rape and Human Rights. *Hastings LJ, 60*, 605.

Stark, E. (2012). Looking Beyond Domestic Violence: Policing Coercive Control. *Journal of Policecrisis Negotiations, 12*(2), 199–217.

SVRI (Sexual Violence Research Initiative) (n.d.) Care and Support of Male Survivors of Sexual Violence. Briefing paper. www.svri.org/CareSupportofMaleSurviv.pdf

UNICEF. (2020). Gender-based Violence in Emergencies: Gender-based Violence Reaches every Corner of the Globe. Emergency Settings, GBV soars.

UNICEF. (2012). Violence against Children in Kenya: Findings from a 2010 National Survey. United Nations Children's Fund Kenya Country Office, Division of Violence Prevention, National Centre for Injury Prevention and Control, U.S. Centers for Disease Control and Prevention, Kenya National Bureau of Statistics: Nairobi, Kenya.

UNHCR and RLP (UN High Commissioner for Refugees and Refugee Law Project). (2012). Working with Men and Boy Survivors of Sexual and Gender-based Violence in Forced Displacement. www.stoprapenow.org/uploads/advocacyresources/1343219299.pdf

Wirtz, A. L., Perrin, N. A., Desgroppes, A., Phipps, V., Abdi, A. A., Ross, B., Kaburu, F., Kajue, I., Kutto, E., Taniguchi, E., & Glass, N. (2018). Lifetime Prevalence, Correlates and Health Consequences of Gender-based Violence Victimisation and Perpetration among Men and Women in Somalia XE "Somalia." *BMJ Global Health, 3*(4), e000773.

Wright, C. (2016). The Absent Voice of Male Domestic Abuse Victims: The Marginalisation of Men in a System Originally Designed for Women. *Plymouth Law and Criminal Justice Review* 8: 333–350.

Gender Violence: A Portrait of Women for Change's Fight Against Gender-Based Violence in Zambia

Nelly Mwale and Joseph Chita

1 Introduction

This chapter explores the work of women-led initiatives that promote gender equality in Zambia in order to show their contribution to the fight against gender-based violence. The chapter is premised on the long-standing challenge of violence against women, which takes different forms worldwide. Globally, violence against women is recognized as a complex phenomenon that has implications for policymakers and justice systems within countries (Bradbury-Jones et al., 2019; Heise et al., 2002; Jewkes et al., 2000). Gender-based violence against women has been acknowledged as a violation of basic human rights worldwide. Global research has also shown the health burdens, intergenerational effects, and demographic consequences of violence against women (United Nations (UN), 2006). In Zambia, the Central Statistics Office (2018: 311) reported that more than one-third of women aged between 15 and 49 had experienced physical violence at least since the age of 15 (Nkana, 2020; UN Women, UN General Assembly Report on Zambia, 2011). In 2015, Zambia reaffirmed its commitment to fighting the scourge of gender-based violence against women and girls by including trafficking and forced early and child marriages (Global Leaders' Meeting on 27 September 2015). Gender-based violence has, thus, been linked to poor health, insecurity, and inadequate social mobilization among women (Central Statistical

N. Mwale (✉) · J. Chita
Department of Religious Studies, University of Zambia, Lusaka, Zambia
e-mail: nelly.mwale@unza.zm

Office, 2014). Based on this, the chapter seeks to interrogate the contribution of women to curbing gender-based violence against women in Zambia.

The chapter is indirectly anchored on the concerns of the UN Women (a global champion for gender equality, working to develop and uphold standards of women and girls) that Zambia had one of the highest rates of sexual and gender-based violence in the world (Nkana, Zambia Daily Mail, 28 October 2020). Gender Links also reported that Zambia had the highest cases of gender-based violence (GBV) in southern Africa in 2013 (Lusaka Times, 10 December 2013). Similarly, the Zambia National Assembly (2022) report by the Committee on National Guidance and Gender Matters on the performance audit report of the Auditor General on the management and disposal of gender-based violence cases in Zambia from 2017 to 2022 affirmed that cases of gender-based violence in Zambia had been on the rise. For example, in 2019, a total of 25,121 cases of gender-based violence were reported compared to the 22,073 cases reported in 2018, translating into an increase of 3,048 cases, representing 14%. In 2020, a total of 26,370 cases were reported from 1 January to 31 December 2020, representing a percentage increase of 5% (Zambia National Assembly Report, 2022: 2). These high figures for cases of gender-based violence against women were/are contrary to the peaceful nature of Zambia, as the country is often described as the beacon of peace.

Accordingly, different governments and concerned organizations have initiated various strategies to deal with gender-based violence against women. For example, women's advocacy groups have attempted to highlight the consequences of gender-based violence against women and called for change. In Zambia, one such organization is Women for Change (WfC), a Lusaka-based non-governmental organization (NGO) which has been in existence for over 25 years. WfC was born in 1992 out of a Canadian Universities Services Overseas (CUSO) project after CUSO phased out its Women's Economic Empowerment project in Zambia. Since then, the organization has grown into an internationally recognized Zambian NGO promoting the rights of women and men, benefiting over 330,000 rural Zambians, as described by the Social Watch News (21 March 2013). In Zambia, WfC works directly with women in the community with the intent to empower them to recognize their own concerns and analyse causes and effects using participatory methods.

As it is among the oldest women-led initiatives in gender justice in the country, WfC has been purposively selected as a unit of inquiry in this chapter. The organization is also a pro-rural initiative working in rural communities in Zambia, focusing on social and economic changes that empower women and children. The main objective of such interventions is to contribute to the creation of sustainable economic and social systems which are controlled by rural communities, and which respond to their needs (Women for Change (n.d.) Strategic Plan, 2018–2022). It has since grown into one of the most influential indigenous NGOs in Zambia through its thematic areas which include women's access and control over productive resources, children's rights to education, and women's access to comprehensive reproductive health rights and services. This is achieved through values such as gender sensitivity, rural focus, participatory approaches, transparency and accountability, social justice and human dignity, mutual respect and women's rights and solidarity.

The chapter is also directly linked to the aspirations of the UN's Sustainable Development Goals (SDGs) in which gender-based violence against women is identified as having implications on the attainment of the SDG Number 5. The SDG Number 5 seeks to achieve gender equality and empower all women and girls, by ending all forms of discrimination against all women and girls everywhere; eliminating all forms of violence against all women and girls in public and private spheres, including trafficking and sexual and other types of exploitation; and eliminating all harmful practices such as child, early, and forced marriage and female genital mutilation (UN Women Strategic Plan 2022–2025, 2021).

Additionally, the chapter is driven by lapses in scholarship on gender-based violence and women-led initiatives in Zambia. Thus, although the work of women-led initiatives in addressing gender-based violence is topical in the public sphere, little scholarly attention is given to this dimension, as the focus tends to be on the nature and effects of gender- based violence (Chibesa, 2017; Ngonga, 2016). The few studies on WfC have tended to dwell on human rights (Hansungule, 1996) to the neglect of the broader ways in which the organization has addressed gender-based violence in a holistic manner. Therefore, the chapter seeks to map out the ways in which WfC has been addressing gender-based violence against women in Zambia and indirectly contributing towards the UN agenda of promoting gender equality, empowering all women and girls, and ending violence against women and girls (UN Women Strategic Plan, 2021). The chapter unfolds by conceptualizing gender-based violence and providing a policy context before focusing on the work of WfC in response to gender-based violence in Zambia.

2   Conceptualizing Gender-Based Violence

The Zambia Gender Status Report (2021: 12) defines gender as the socially constructed traits attributed to being female or male. These attributes involve the roles and responsibilities assigned to men and women by society. The attributes also include expected, allowed, valued, and accepted behaviour and conduct among men and women. Further, gender is interpreted as "the roles, duties and responsibilities which are culturally or socially ascribed to men, women, girls and boys" (Gender Equity and Equality Act, 2015 No. 22 of 2015, 463).

Accordingly, gender-based violence has multi-dimensional definitions that are used to capture violence that transpires due to the role expectations related to each gender and unequal power relationships. Gender-based violence is, therefore, linked to violence which takes place on the basis of one's gender. This chapter draws on the understanding of gender-based violence as stipulated in the Zambia Anti-Gender-Based Violence Act, No. 1 of 2021. In this regard, gender-based violence is any act that results in or is likely to result in, physical, sexual, or psychological harm or suffering to a person, including threats of such acts, coercion, or arbitrary deprivations of liberty, whether occurring in public or private life. This definition of gender-based violence is closely related to the understanding of gender-based violence by the UN (CSO, 2018: 311).

Gender-based violence takes different forms, for example, Fonck (2005) affirms that gender-based-violence can include physical, sexual, psychological, or other forms of violence.

Zulu (2022) affirms that gender-based violence in Zambia takes the form of physical, mental, social, or economic abuse against a person because of that person's gender. As such, women in Zambia experience a variety of forms of violence, including battery, sexual abuse, and exploitation, rape, defilement (rape of a child), and incest.

Given the multiple dimensions of gender- based violence, the chapter pays attention to the violence against women in general. It is assumed that one form of violence is more likely to be linked to other forms of abuse. Therefore, the interest is in showing how WfC addresses all the different forms of gender-based violence in their work in rural Zambia.

3   Brief Policy Context of Gender-Based Violence Against Women in Zambia

Gender-based violence in Zambia is given attention through different pieces of legislation and policies which seek to enhance women empowerment. At the international level, Zambia has signed and ratified all the major international instruments and is also a signatory to the African Charter on Human and People's Rights (ACHPR). At regional level, Zambia signed the Gender and Development Declaration of the Southern African Development Community (SADC) in 1997, in which the government pledged to take urgent measures to prevent and deal with increasing levels of violence against women and children (SADC, Gender, and Development, 1997).

At national level, the notable policies include the Gender Equity and Equality Act No.22 of 2015, which is aimed at domesticating international human rights instruments such as the Convention on the Elimination of All Forms of Discrimination Against Women (CEDAW) (adopted in 1979); the SADC Protocol on Gender and Development (2008); and the Protocol to the African Charter on Human and Peoples' Rights on the Rights of Women in Africa (2003) (Ministry of Gender, 2021). The Gender Equity and Equality Act gives effect to CEDAW and is intended to implement women's empowerment targets that meet the international standards of the SDGs, as well as Zambia Vision 2030. Other policies and strategies include the National Child Policy (aimed at promoting and protecting children's rights) and the Re-Entry Policy (aimed to promote gender mainstreaming to attain equality and equity). The Adolescent Sexual and Reproductive Health Policy, the Comprehensive Sexuality Education Curricula for In-School and Out-of-School Adolescents, and the Ending Child Marriage Strategy, are also in place to promote gender equality and equity.

Besides the policy framework, the work on gender-based violence is informed by the Republican Constitution. In this regard, in 2016, the Zambian Constitution was amended to include critical and progressive articles for gender equality. The amended Constitution acknowledges that every citizen, man or woman, has equal rights to participate in, determine, and build a sustainable political, legal, and socio-economic order freely. The Constitution further provides for human dignity, equity, social justice, equality, and non-discrimination among the national values and principles (Article 8 of the Constitution of the Laws of Zambia). The Republican Constitution CAP 1 Article 23 also condemns various acts which cause physical, sexual, or psychological harm or suffering to women and children. The Constitution also provides that nominations to public office must ensure

50% representation of each gender category and mandates the Human Rights Commission to take necessary steps to appropriately redress the rights of all persons, which includes women, children, and people with disabilities.

The Gender Equity and Equality Commission, which was created to further enhance the protection of women's rights, also promotes gender equality and equity. This is through its mandate which is to promote the mainstreaming and attainment of gender equality (Article 246 of the Constitution).

Additionally, Zambia has established various institutions which include Zambia Women's Parliamentary Caucus (ZWPC), the Gender Forum, the Permanent Human Rights Commission (PHRC), and the Victim Support Unit. The Victim Support Unit was established in 1994 by the Zambia Police Service in almost all police stations and became operational in 1996. It is charged with the responsibility of addressing violation of human rights that are gender-based. Besides government initiatives, NGOs are also key players in gender-based violence against women. For example, the establishment of the Non-Governmental Organizations Coordinating Council (NGOCC) in 1985 by Zambian women has been a milestone in the promotion of gender equality and equity. The NGOCC was born out of the realization that the process of empowering women needed concerted efforts. Suffice to state that the Zambian government has established strategic partnerships with local, regional, and global institutions and organizations for enhancement and acceleration of gender mainstreaming in the country.

As was reported by Manjoo in her report to the UN General Assembly, the Zambia government "secured a number of important legal and institutional achievements in the area of gender, equality, and protection from violence against women in the context of complex and difficult social and economic challenges" (Manjoo, 2011: 19). The major burden highlighted by the Mission to Zambia was the limitation of translating the country's achievements into concrete improvements in the lives of the majority of women. In as much as the government of Zambia is committed to finding lasting solutions to issues surrounding GBV, efforts of stakeholders like WfC cannot be overlooked because they are aimed at complementing the State's efforts to fight the scourge of gender-based violence against women and girls including trafficking and forced, early, and child marriages (Global Leaders' Meeting on 27 September 2015).

4 Women for Change's Immersion in Gender-Based Violence Work

The forward strides of WfC in gender-based violence can be examined using themes, which range from advocacy against gender-based violence (through gender-based violence specific projects) to service provision for GBV survivors, promotion of behaviour changes, and women's empowerment.

Advocacy Against Gender-Based Violence

This has largely been done via anti-gender-based-violence projects. For example, among the many projects implemented by WfC is the community-led Anti-GBV project. Through this project, community facilitators (volunteers) were trained whose role was to provide legal and psychosocial counselling services to their communities on a voluntary basis. Additionally, the community facilitators were taught on how to increase access to justice for GBV survivors (Social Watch News, 2013).

WfC also established anti-GBV One-Stop-Shops in some of the operational areas. This was with the view to help women to claim their rights and seek paralegal justice when faced with GBV in rural areas. The focus on rural communities could be understood in relation to the fact that gender-based violence was also rampant in rural communities due to the harmful social, cultural, and religious practices, which undermine the dignity, health, or liberty of a person. As such, with help from the UN, and Irish Aid, among others, WfC opened up an Anti-GBV One-Stop-Shop (Women for Change, 2017). The One-Stop-Shops are equipped with paralegals, counsellors, and staff that are trained in processing and preserving evidence. In this project, WfC organized a five-day community workshop to train community members that would form part of the staff to run One-Stop-Shops. This strategy does not only foster community-driven initiatives to curb GBV but also promotes self-sustaining intervention. As a result of the success of the village-led model in Petauke, WfC was asked to replicate it in the rest of the country and, later on, to train other NGOs in implementing it (Women for Change, 2017).

The One-Stop-Centre (OSC) approach has been adopted as a national strategy in dealing with gender-based violence. The OSCs incorporate a physical examination room and several interview rooms, and the focus is on enhancing survivor safety and perpetrator accountability by planning and coordinating core centre services, including providing prompt, immediate, and longer-term health care, easy access to police and legal services, and counselling services (Zambia National Assembly report, 2022).

The setting up of one stop centres was significant given that the key driver for gender-based violence is linked to inequality for women and the associated violence and harmful and controlling aspects of masculinity that result from patriarchal power imbalances embedded in many of Africa's traditional and cultural beliefs (Mashiri, 2013). This imbalance often leads to pervasive cultural stereotypes and attitudes that perpetuate the cycle of gender violence and in turn prevent women from accessing much-needed help. These efforts were also in line with the aspirations of the Anti-Gender-Based-Violence Act (Anti-GBV Act) of Zambia which seeks to enhance gender justice by safeguarding the warfare against pervasive violence that has its roots in social and gender exclusion and power imbalance, horizontal inequalities, and poverty (Hapinga, 2021).

Behaviour Change

WfC was also spearheading and fostering behaviour change as a strategy to curb GBV. Influenced by behaviour change theories, WfC worked with different stakeholders especially active actors at community level, and in turn they were agents of change in GBV. The narrative of some participants in the WfC project attests to this:

> I was notorious for excessive drinking and dagga smoking, I also constantly fought physically with other community members. One time I was sent to deliver cooked chicken to the chief but on the way I ate it. [I was fond of] abusing my wife and neglecting my children. I would not give my wife any money but would come home, usually late at night, and demand food. If there was none this would lead to fighting. One day, in the process of fighting, one of our children was burnt by hot porridge. After the child was burnt, my wife called on the paralegals for help. They intervened by providing counselling and mentoring for change. I realised that at the rate I was going I would end up either in prison or dead. My wife did not leave me because one of our children has epilepsy and there is stigma in our community on this matter. I am now a changed man. I am now also providing advice and counselling to others and public testimonies on my change. My wife has become a paralegal helping other women who find themselves in similar situation to hers. (Women for Change, 2017: 31)

Using a multifaceted approach like One-Stop-Centre and behaviour change initiatives, WfC has been able to play a significant role at community level. Suffice to note that these efforts have rural women at heart. This is because in rural Zambia, most people are poor, and women are the majority of the poor. Poverty is not simply about income, but social exclusion and accessing healthcare which requires travel over long distances (and even clinics that are accessible have perhaps one health provider, who is always overwhelmed) (Central Stastical Office, 2014). Similarly, access to education remains a challenge. For the most part, women carry a disproportionate burden of the daily workload as they spend hours each day, walking perhaps ten kilometres, to fetch clean drinking water and gather firewood to use as fuel for cooking. The place of women in this context also has a cultural and social injustice dimension, especially in that women are often socialized not to speak out, even when they are being abused or burdened with work. For example, some communities, especially in the rural areas, tend to embrace negative cultural beliefs in which gender-based violence is seen as a norm. Examples of these teachings include sayings that stress that if a man does not beat his wife, it is taken to mean he does not love her.

Other cultural practices include *lobola* (bridewealth) as revealed in a study by Moono et al. (2020) on married women in Lusaka's Kamanga compound. The study demonstrated that paying *lobola* translated into buying a wife and as such, a wife became a husband's property. This is because *lobola* is thought to give the man or husband powers to treat his wife as he wishes, including subjecting her to sexual and other forms of abuse and, in turn, taking away a wife's rights to make decisions on matters that affect her own life. While Moono et al. drew these conclusions, it is imperative to indicate that the commercialization of *lobola* was a significant contributing factor to gender-based violence (Mwale and Chita, 2021).

This focus on behaviour change adopted by WfC is also emphasized by Lwatula (2019) when she observes that the law cannot work in isolation. Since the subordination of women is institutionalized and deep-rooted and, for greater progress to be made towards gender justice in Zambia, there must be a change in social attitudes together with a review of existing legal provisions with a view to improving the law, Lwatula (2019) argues. Banda (2019) also concluded that poverty, substance abuse and inactive law enforcement directly enhanced acts of violence.

The focus on behaviour change is also significant as it was in line with the work of the government. The Zambia National Assembly (2022) report showed that mass campaigns were a strategy that had been adopted to address gender-based violence in the country. These mass campaigns were carried out in schools, communities, workplaces, and churches to sensitize people and increase awareness to reduce GBV incidents in the country (Zambia National Assembly, 2022). Therefore, the enactment of laws on gender-based voices in Zambia is one way in which gender-based violence is resented as a public issue that needs to be treated as a public crime rather than a private problem which requires private solutions. By and large, the success of this intention is dependent on behaviour change.

Women's and Girls' Empowerment

WfC also worked to address the numbers of girls dropping out of school in rural districts in Zambia. This was against the backdrop of social norms which often lead to an understanding that the appropriate role for girls is to be a good wife and mother, and cultural norms dictate that education is not necessary for that role (Women for Change, 2014). In a context of poverty, some families would opt to keep boys in school and arrange marriages for the girls. Through working with adolescent girls aged 10–18 (who often drop out of secondary school because of early marriage, teen pregnancy or lack of water and sanitation), the girls are offered with incentives to re-enrol in school. Teachers are also trained to help support the girls in their return to school. Parents and traditional leaders are also included in this work to build awareness of the importance of education in reducing poverty and improving day-to-day lives for women and children (Firth, 2020). WfC target girls using the empowerment initiative realizing that girls who are neglected today are the abused women of tomorrow, as such certain interventions to end GBV are better started early, so as to make future interventions possible.

Besides empowering females through education, WfC also offered training for community members from the surrounding villages of Chongwe in sexual reproductive health. Through these workshops, explanations on how gender equality and sexual reproductive health are intertwined are provided. Community members' capacities are also built in gender and human rights issues. For example, workshops on gender and human rights were conducted for adults and youth in Kapiri Mposhi in Central Zambia, among other areas. This is significant in that WfC employs a model that requires trained participants to go to train others in their communities. This strategy is underpinned by the understanding that sustainability of actions and improvement in gender equality, human rights, and sustainable development can only be achieved if the community are part and parcel of the development of their communities and are drivers of change. Existing studies have also shown that gender-based violence against women has numerous effects, including psychological trauma, death, and disfigurement as well as serious injuries (GIDD, 2008). Researchers such as Skinner (2001), Coombe (2002), and Mabula-Kankasa and Chondoka (1996) concur that gender-based violence portrays unequal or inconsistent power relations. As such, a holistic approach is required to mitigate gender violence.

Furthermore, WfC has been involved in environmental care projects for the benefit of women. For example, working in partnership with Caritas Kabwe, WfC conducted gender-mainstreaming workshops which targeted female farmers, field facilitators, teachers, and learners. Such workshops were aimed at providing reliable and accessible information to build a better understanding of gender equality as a core value in the communities. The trainings also addressed aspects on gender-based violence and the gap that exists between men and women, boys and girls in terms of access to and control over productive resources. The intent of workshops of this nature was to mould boys and girls into gender champions (Women for Change, Facebook post, https://web.facebook.com/WFCZambia).

Similar agriculture-related workshops were conducted in the rural district of Rufunsa in Lusaka province where women were growing assorted crops and rearing livestock. This interest in women was driven by the idea that women's empowerment was a yardstick for rural women improving their livelihood (Hamabuyu, 14 April 2023). Women are at the centre of these efforts because, as Sisselman (2009) notes, men are not excluded from domestic violence, but the most common victim and the most socially injured party is usually a woman.

All these initiatives were done through community-led interventions. These included role plays, songs, drama, and participatory training sessions that helped to illustrate the negative impact of discrimination on women and on the community. This is because WfC does not want to speak for rural women, but to amplify their voice by teaching skills so that they able to stand up for themselves and take collective action to address the problems that they face: they want to challenge the cultural practices that inhibit women from progressing in life, as noted by Lyamba Siyanga, (Noble Women's Initiative, 2016). The work of WfC also resonates with the feminist stance of seeking to help women to increase their awareness of ascribed gender roles and oppressive social status through increased feminist movements and social action with the aim of producing a better world for them (women) (Partab, 2011).

5 Conclusion

The chapter explored gender-based violence from the perspective of the work of women-led organizations in Zambia. Given that WfC was involved in efforts to address gender-based violence against women in a holistic manner, the chapter concludes that women have their own agency and their efforts have had an impact in the Zambia context. This has been seen through the ways in which strategies adopted by WfC have had a bearing on the national agenda of dealing with gender violence. The chapter also concludes that participatory methods proved significant for dealing with gender-based violence as communities drove the efforts to curb gender-based violence. This brings to the fore the lesson that gender-based violence is often a product of social construction, and, hence, requires concerted societal efforts to address it. The chapter also concludes that women-led initiatives such as WfC are an important source for scholars and stakeholders to find best practices that could enhance gender equality and equity. By and large, the chapter concludes that efforts from a single entity such as WfC, although not generalizable, demonstrate that all efforts of goodwill in addressing gender-based violence against women had the ultimate goal of attaining the Sustainable Development Goal Number 5.

References

Anti-Gender-Based Violence Act, No. 1 of 2021. Details.

Banda, B. M. (2019). Socio-cultural Factors Associated with Gender-based Violence in Chipata city, Zambia. *Texila International Journal of Public Health, 7*(4), 232–243.

Bradbury-Jones, C., Appleton, J. V., Clark, M., & Paavilainen, E. (2019). A Profile of Gender-based Violence Research in Europe: Findings from a Focused Mapping Review and Synthesis. *Trauma, Violence, & Abuse, 20*(4), 470–483.

Central Statistical Office. (2014). *Demographic and Health Survey 2013–14*. CSO.

Chibesa, F. (2017). Effects of Gender-based Violence among Couples: A Case of Shapande Compound in Choma District. *Journal of Humanities and Social Science, 22*(11), 53–61.

Firth, E. (2020). *Women For Change—Zambia*, UCW Western Ontario: Waterways.

Fonck, K. (2005). Increased Risk of HIV in Women Experiencing Physical Partner Violence in Nairobi. *Kenya. AIDS and Behaviour, 9*(3), 335–339.

Government of the Responsibility of Zambia. (2015). Gender Equity and Equality Act, No. 22 of 2015. Lusaka. Government Printer.

GIDD. (2008). The Report of the Technical Committee on the Strengthening of laws; Enforcement Mechanism and Support Systems Relating to Gender-based Violence, Particularly against Women and Children. Lusaka, Cabinet Office

Haipinge, M. (2021). *A Critique on Gender-based Violence Legislation in Namibia and Zambia.* Doctoral dissertation, Cavendish University.

Hansungule, M. (1996). *Position of Women's Rights in Zambia as Seen by Women for Change.* Lusaka, Women for Change.

Heise, L., Ellsberg, M., & Gottmoeller, M. (2002). A Global Overview of Gender-based Violence. *International Journal of Gynecology & Obstetrics, 78,* S5–S14.

https://womenforchangezambia.weebly.com/organisational-structure.html

Jewkes, R., Watts, C., Abrahams, N., Penn-Kekana, L., & Garcia-Moreno, C. (2000). Ethical and Methodological Issues in Conducting Research on Gender-based Violence in Southern Africa. *Reproductive Health Matters, 8*(15), 93–103.

Lusaka Times (2013, December 10). Zambia has the Highest Cases of Violence against Women in Southern Africa.

Lwatula, M. (2019). *Gender-based Violence in Zambia: A Postcolonial Feminist Critique.* Doctoral dissertation, University of Sussex.

Manjoo, R. (2011). Report of the Special Rapporteur on Violence against Women, its Causes and Consequences: Mission to Zambia United Nation General Assembly. https://evaw-global-database.unwomen.org/-/media/files/un%20women/vaw/country%20report/africa/zambia/zambia%20srvaw.pdf?vs=2110

Mashiri, L. (2013). Conceptualisation of Gender-based Violence in Zimbabwe. *International Journal of Humanities and Social Science, 3*(15), 94–103.

Moono, P., Thankian, K., Menon, G., Mwaba, S., & Menon, J. A. (2020). Bride Price (Lobola) and Gender-based Violence among Married Women in Lusaka. *Journal of Education, Society and Behaviour Science, 33*(8), 38–47.

Mwale, N., & Chita, J. (2021). Commercialisation of Marriage Rites and Commodification of Women in Contemporary Times: The Discourse of *Lobola* in the Public Sphere in Zambia. Togarasei L and Chitando E(eds). In *Lobola (Bridewealth) in Contemporary Southern Africa: Implications for Gender Equality.* pp. 263–281. Palgrave.

Ngonga, Z. (2016). Factors Contributing to Physical Gender-based Violence Reported at Ndola Central Hospital, Ndola, Zambia: A Case Control Study. *Medical Journal of Zambia, 43*(3), 145–151.

Nkana, M. (2020, October 28). Zambia on Global GBV top list. *Daily Mail.* http://www.daily-mail.co.zm/zambia-on-global-gbv-top-list/

Nobel Women's Initiative. (2016). Meet Lumba Siyanga, Zambia. https://www.nobelwomensinitiative.org/meet-lumba-siyanga-zambia

Partab, R. (2011). Why do Violent Men Do What They Do? Dialoguing on Privileges of Patriarchy and Domestic Violence. *Journal of Gender & Religion in Africa, 17*(1), 96–113.

Social Watch News (2013) Emily Sikazwe: A Woman to Celebrate. 21 March

Women for Change (n.d) Strategic Plan 2018–2022. Lusaka, WfC.

Women for Change. (2017). *A Critical Reflection of Women for Change as a Learning Organisation.* WfC.

Zambia National Assembly. (2022). Committee on National Guidance and Gender Matters on the Performance Audit Report of the Auditor General on the Management and Disposal of Gender Based Violence Cases in Zambia from 2017 to 2022 Report. Lusaka.

Zulu, B. (2022). Zambia: Fighting Gender Based Violence as Fresh Cases Continue to Emerge. *United Nations Africa Renewal.* https://www.un.org/africarenewal/news/zambia-fighting-gender-basedviolence-fresh-cases-continue-emerge. Accessed 20 March 2023.

Persisting Inequalities: An Intersectional View of Climate Change, Gender and Violence

Mary Nyasimi and Veronica Nonhlanhla Jakarasi

1 Introduction

Climate change poses a significant threat to global sustainable development. In Africa, its impacts undermine socio-economic progress and exacerbate inequality and poverty (Cevik & Jalles, 2022; Nyiwul, 2021). Developing nations are particularly vulnerable to climate change due to their high exposure, escalating severity of climate-related extremes, and limited adaptive capacity (Ayal, 2021; Filho et al., 2019, 2021). Africa is widely recognized as the continent most susceptible to climate risks (Quirico & Boumghar, 2015). The climate change indicators in Africa are characterized by persistent temperature increases, accelerated sea-level rise, altered precipitation patterns, and a rise in extreme weather events like floods, storms, and droughts (Dresser & Balsari, 2024; IPCC, 2022; van Niekerk et al., 2022). These effects have heightened the frequency and intensity of droughts in certain regions, jeopardized human health and safety, impeded animal growth rates and productivity in pastoral systems, and adversely impacted food and water

M. Nyasimi · V. N. Jakarasi
Iowa State University, Ames, IA, USA

V. N. Jakarasi
Africa Enterprise Challenge Fund, Nairobi, Kenya

M. Nyasimi (✉)
Natural Science, UNESCO, Nairobi, Kenya
e-mail: mnyasimi@gmail.com

security in arid areas (Adhikari et al., 2015; Buma & Lee, 2019; Camberlin, 2018; Chiang et al., 2021). One of the contributing factors to these circumstances is the heavy reliance on weather-dependent activities, such as rain-fed agriculture, livestock management, or fishing for livelihoods, and persisting gender inequalities (Mugandani et al., 2022; Jaka et al., 2021; Olumba et al., 2022; Onwutuebe, 2019; Ide et al., 2021).

The consequences of climate change continue to exert pressure on various communities and individuals, but its effects disproportionately affect women and men. Women and girls, in particular, face greater vulnerability due to their reliance on natural resources for livelihoods and income (Ayanlade et al., 2022; Call & Sellers, 2019; Partey et al., 2020; Phiri et al., 2022). They engage with the environment daily through household management and are active participants during and after climatic disasters (Nyasimi & Huyer, 2017; Nyasimi et al., 2017) When access to natural resources is strained, women and girls often experience distinct forms of gender-based violence that differ from those faced by men and boys (Caridade et al., 2022; Njikho, 2020; Ovenden et al., 2022). These gender-specific vulnerabilities to both climate change and violence arise from inequalities within local power structures and socio-cultural norms and practices, including those concerning social reproductive labour (Filomina, 2014).

Recognition of these power dynamics is key to understanding and promoting resilience in the context of violent and non-violent conflicts and climate change. These associated gendered impacts continue to stand in the way of achieving Sustainable Development Goals (SDGs) across Africa, particularly goals 1 (Poverty), 5 (Gender equality) and, 13 (Climate action) (Karla et al., 2019; Ramutsindela & Mickler, 2020). The interaction between gender and other intersecting aspects of identity plays a crucial role in shaping individuals' experiences, responses, and recovery from the adverse impacts of climate change (Ayanlade et al., 2022; Versey, 2020). Moreover, the compounding risks associated with security and climate further exacerbate governance challenges and reinforce existing gender and structural inequalities, thus increasing violence (Fletcher & Reed 2022; Lawson et al., 2020). Consequently, women, girls, and already vulnerable populations find themselves at the forefront of interconnected crises. The pervasive nature of gender inequality significantly hinders females' ability to adapt and build resilience. This inequality exposes women to heightened risks of gender-based violence, while girls are less likely than boys to continue their education amidst climate-related events and other forms of insecurity, including conflicts. Moreover, individuals with disabilities or belonging to ethnic or religious minorities face additional obstacles in these circumstances (Ayanlade et al., 2022; Mikulewicz et al., 2023).

2 Understanding the Intersection between Climate Change, Gender and Violence

For the purpose of this discussion, climate change refers to the long-term alterations in climate patterns within a particular location, region, or the planet as a whole (UN, 2022). These changes are measured by shifts in various elements associated with typical weather conditions, such as temperature, wind patterns, and rainfall. Climate change is linked to extreme weather events like floods, storms, heatwaves, and droughts, all of which have significant negative impacts on livelihoods and other economic sectors (Asadnabizadeh, 2021; Clarke et al., 2022; Majedul, 2022; Sillmann et al., 2021). In addition, we define gender as the socially constructed norms, roles, attitudes, and characteristics attributed to individuals based on their perceived sex, as well as the dynamics and interactions among different gender groups (Lindqvist et al., 2021). Gender relations greatly influence power dynamics and are closely intertwined with prevailing norms of femininity and masculinity. These norms play a pivotal role in shaping the emergence, evolution, and experiences of crises, including armed conflicts and disasters, for individuals from diverse backgrounds.

As stated by the World Health Organization (2002), violence refers to the intentional use of physical force or power, either threatened or actual, against oneself, another individual, or a group or community. This force has the potential to cause injury, death, psychological harm, maldevelopment, or deprivation. In contrast, gender-based violence specifically targets individuals based on their gender. Violence against women is defined as "any form of gender-based violence that is likely to cause physical, sexual, or psychological harm or suffering to women. This includes acts of threat, coercion, or arbitrary deprivation of liberty, irrespective of whether these acts occur in public or private life" (WHO, 2021).

In Africa, various forms of violence against women and girls are prevalent and frequently reported. These include intimate partner violence, which encompasses physical, sexual, or psychological abuse by a partner. Female genital mutilation, a cultural practice found in certain parts of Africa, is also a significant issue. Early child and forced marriages, where girls under 18 are coerced into marriage, are another form of violence. Additionally, sexual violence in conflict situations is a grave concern, involving acts such as rape, sexual assault with physical violence, abduction, sexual slavery, and forced prostitution. Furthermore, the concept of intersectionality recognizes that individuals' unique lived experiences are shaped by multiple identities and their interactions with marginalizing structures, norms, and narratives. Gender intersects with other socio-cultural characteristics, including race, ethnicity, disability, sexual orientation, and age, resulting in a distinct set of norms and experiences (SIDA, 2015). In some vulnerable regions, climate change has contributed to intra-state conflicts, which further exacerbate existing gender imbalances and other political, social, and economic stresses, leading to instances of gender-based violence (GBV). An example of this is the civil conflict in Darfur, Sudan, often referred to as the world's "first climate change conflict," driven by water scarcity, which is a known risk factor amplifying GBV against women (WFP, 2017).

Africa is already experiencing the tangible effects of climate change through a range of events, including the rising waters in the Eastern Rift Valley lakes, locust invasions in the Horn of Africa, and severe drought conditions in southern Africa. These calamities have contributed to an increase in violent conflicts at the household and community levels, stemming from heightened food and water insecurity, loss of livelihoods, growing water scarcity, and climate-induced displacements. The deteriorating conditions of people's lives exacerbate social, economic, and political grievances, particularly affecting marginalized groups such as women, the elderly, individuals with disabilities, and the youth. The adverse impacts of climate change further magnify the risk of violence between groups dependent on climate-sensitive sectors like agriculture, pastoralism, and fishing, especially in the absence of alternative livelihood options. This creates a greater likelihood of people resorting to violence in order to protect or access natural resources. These developments clearly illustrate the interconnectedness of climate change, gender, and violence, with the convergence of these factors resulting in various vulnerabilities that disproportionately affect men and women (Alam et al., 2015).

For instance, during periods of prolonged droughts and increased temperatures leading to crop failure, livestock losses, and food insecurity, women are often compelled to travel longer distances in search of food and water or engage in bartering services for sustenance. This puts them at a higher risk of experiencing sexual assault and other forms of abuse.

There is a growing global recognition of the interconnection between climate change and the escalation of GBV through various underlying mechanisms. As previously mentioned, when access to natural resources becomes strained, women and girls become more susceptible to GBV as a consequence of their efforts to secure access (Isola & Tolulope, 2022). The impacts of climate change in vulnerable environments can further widen gender inequalities, heighten the vulnerability of women and sexual minorities, and indirectly intensify instances of sexual and GBV (Camey et al., 2020). As competition over increasingly scarce resources intensifies, violence is exacerbated, and existing inequalities are deepened, as GBV often becomes a means to reinforce power dynamics and maintain control over resources. In some communities, child forced marriages have unfortunately emerged as a survival strategy, serving as a coping mechanism in the face of adversity (Lwanga-Ntale & Owino, 2020; McLeod et al., 2019).

The Convention on the Elimination of All Forms of Discrimination Against Women (CEDAW) Committee emphasized in its General Recommendation No.37 (2018) that women and girls are often at a heightened risk of experiencing violence in the aftermath of disasters, particularly when faced with food insecurity and the absence of social protection programmes. Understanding the connections between climate change and GBV becomes crucial as the latter imposes extensive economic and social burdens on society. It further amplifies existing inequalities and vulnerabilities within communities, including poverty and the violation of children's rights. Simultaneously, GBV negatively impacts the social, economic, and cultural rights of women, such as their rights to work and education. By exploring these correlations, we can address the multifaceted impacts of GBV and climate change on individuals and societies.

3 Differentiated Impacts of Climate Change and How They Have Contributed to Violence

While climate change is non-discriminatory, affecting one and all, the nature of its impacts are not gender neutral. Its effects are felt most acutely by those segments of the population that are already in vulnerable and marginalized situations, thereby worsening the risk of violence (IPCC, 2019). Climate change affects women and girls disproportionately, leaving them among the most vulnerable to its assortment of impacts. Women and men are impacted differently due to differences in their traditional roles, societal expectations, power structures, and livelihoods. Socially based roles and responsibilities ascribed to men and women within a given society lead to inequalities in the access to resources affected by environmental change, to barriers to participation, and to unequal adaptive capacities. Additionally, women and other socially excluded groups often have fewer rights and limited decision-making power in comparison to men (Muluneh et al., 2021; Nyahunda et al., 2021).

As climate change is being recognized as a serious aggravator of all types of GBV against women and girls, it is poised to exacerbate the already increasing number of complex emergencies, which disproportionately affect women and girls. Thus, disasters such as floods, droughts, storms and other extreme events triggered by climate change often cause surges in GBV due to competition over scarce livelihood resources. For women living in rural areas and belonging to indigenous peoples, the disadvantages derived from the impacts and effects of climate change, on account of natural disasters, are greater, as they are more dependent on the natural and environmental goods and services. While changing climatic conditions can amplify the risk of domestic and intimate partner violence by creating the conditions for disrupting traditional gender norms, they can also increase competition and tensions over access and use of scarce resources, which in some instances may turn violent (Fjelde & von Uexkull, 2012; Raleigh, 2010). Sadly, despite being the guardians of natural resources and repositories of traditional ecological knowledge in many cultures, women often lack the voice to provide solutions to resource scarcity. This lack of participation can compound gender inequalities in the allocation of scarce resources. (In fact, this lack of participation can be seen as an effect of structural violence).

Resource scarcity and the disruption of traditional gender roles and norms due to loss of livelihoods heighten the risk of intra-household conflicts. These consequences might affect different groups of women to different degrees depending on intersecting vulnerabilities and power structures. Women and girls revealed that the gendered division of labour, particularly around the collection of water and fuelwood, heightened gendered-climate risks, including increased risk of sexual and GBV (was this from a focus group discussion?). For example, failure to ensure household water security elicited disappointment and acts of physical violence from husbands as the role of managing household water is ascribed to females. Thus, in periods of prolonged drought, women and girls are forced to make more frequent and longer journeys to obtain food or water for their families, which makes them vulnerable to sexual exploitation and other forms of violence compared to women not living in drought conditions. Girls in Mozambique reported that they endured sexual violence at the hands of older men who lured them with gifts as they engaged in water collection activities far away from home

(FGD?). Several other examples revealed that women and girls disproportionately suffer from verbal, physical, and sexual violence both within and outside the household as a spill-over effect of water insecurity. Such situations are not only destructive, but perpetual as they place an economic burden on the women and girls through increasing their workload, which in some cases has resulted in girls missing or dropping out of school.

A study analysing the data of nearly 84,000 women taken from 19 Demographic and Health Surveys in sub-Saharan Africa found that women living in severe drought had higher risk of experiencing physical and sexual violence by intimate partners compared with women not living in drought conditions (Epstein et al., 2020). In addition, the 2021 Global Report on Food Crises revealed that Africa remained the continent most affected by food crises. The report noted three major, intertwined drivers of the acute food insecurity, namely, conflict, weather extremes, and economic shocks, including those from the Covid-19 pandemic. In families where men left home to seek a living elsewhere, women and children were left to fend for themselves, which made them vulnerable to violence and sexual exploitation.

The widespread drought and famine in many of the African countries has seen an upward trend in the number of girls who are minors being sold into early forced marriages in exchange for food and livestock to help their families survive. Child marriage is another manifestation of gender inequalities and violation of children's rights that increases in times of crisis and that has been observed in disaster-affected areas such as in Zimbabwe, Malawi, Uganda, Mozambique, Ethiopia, and South Sudan. The practice has been explained by some as a survival strategy to obtain cattle among pastoralist groups, money, and other assets via the traditional practice of transferring wealth through the payment of dowries, in the absence of other viable alternatives. The associated impacts of such coping strategies on young women's and girls' security are likely to become more prevalent with climate change resulting in increased drought frequency and livelihood pressures (McLeod et al., 2019).

In other instances, girls are pulled out of school to cope with food and income insecurity. For many of these girls, life has not been easy as they experience different forms of abuse, including sexual violence and physical abuse at the hands of either their partner or non-partner. Again, many women who derive their livelihoods from selling fish along the coastal regions and on inland water bodies reported that they have suffered sexual exploitation as fish supply has become scarce, mainly attributed to climate change and overharvesting. A case in point is Kenya, where fishermen are now not only expecting money as payment but are also demanding sexual favours from women (Kwena et al., 2012).

Climate impacts and related security risks, such as displacement, food insecurity, and health risks, are also not gender neutral. In the aftermath of extreme weather events and climate change-induced societal and economic shocks, women are at a higher risk of being victims of sexual exploitation, domestic violence and human trafficking. Climate change drives migration, both internally and externally, which increases the risk of being victim to GBV. For instance, intimate partner violence rates rose in Malawi, Mozambique and Zimbabwe after Cyclone Idai in 2019 (UNFPA, 2021). Overcrowded and unsafe conditions in disaster shelters and climate refugee camps also disproportionately exposed women, the elderly, people with disabilities, and girls to gender-based violence (Freedman, 2016; Jensen, 2019; Muuo et al., 2020).

While acknowledging the intersection of gender inequality, climate change, and violence, it is essential to recognize that men can also be victims, just as women can be agents. Men may fall victim to violence influenced by socio-cultural and political disparities. Disasters can disrupt a sense of control for men, leading to acts of violence against vulnerable individuals, such as women and children within households. Instances have been reported where men, faced with crop failure, loss of livestock, and food insecurity, turn to alcohol and violence as maladaptive coping mechanisms, driven by the perceived failure to fulfil traditional roles as breadwinners and providers for their families (Khan et al., 2022). Furthermore, the persistent droughts being experienced in most parts of Africa such as Kenya, Uganda, and South Sudan tend to accelerate tensions among pastoralists, and between pastoralists and farmers. The scarcity of fodder and water force pastoralists to move their cattle into border regions or even territories traditionally used by other groups, hence increasing the likelihood for violent confrontations. In extreme cases, the adverse impact of climate change can result in direct violent competition over water or grazing areas. Moreover, raiding neighbouring groups is a frequently used measure to re-stock cattle when a significant portion of the herd perishes during a drought.

Another case in point is the farmer-herder violence in the Lake Chad region (Chad, Cameroon, Nigeria and Niger) where competition for natural resources such as water, pasture and land is rife. The diminishing water resources and the decline in the lake's ecosystem have sparked resource-based conflicts of a violent nature. Women and girls in those areas continue to face daily human rights violations and violence, including child, early, and forced marriage, denied access to resources, home eviction, and domestic sexual violence. On the other hand, violence against women and sexual exploitation, in some instances, are found to intensify conflict dynamics as masculine norms compel men to retaliate when their families' well-being is endangered. Thus, GBV is not only devastating to the survivors but to the families at large.

4 Addressing the GBV and Climate Change Nexus

Given that that environmental conflicts often breed a culture of violence and that the most vulnerable are more likely to be victimized, addressing the nexus between climate, gender, and violence becomes critical to both peacebuilding efforts and developing strong communities resilient to climate change impacts. This requires looking beyond the characterization of women as victims and recognizing their significant role in responding to climate change. They engage in a range of strategies to minimize negative impacts and they adopt several survival strategies to respond to environmental conflicts. These strategies, including those that have used collective action, have contributed towards household and community level resilience in the form of enhanced food security, increased capacity, and leadership. For instance, women often assume active roles in responding to the various climate change and natural disaster impacts, undertaking evacuations, food collection, road clearance, health care, and more, making them well-positioned to identify climate change solutions from a gender perspective. By empowering women with decision-making power on climate change issues, risks that may give rise to GBV can be addressed proactively, and where they do arise, local women are better placed to advance appropriate redress measures. Moreover, when women and girls are excluded from climate action, this action becomes less effective and climate harms are exacerbated.

Despite their vulnerabilities to climate change, rural women can be important agents of change and innovators. Considering that women have proactively adopted many different types of specific climate-smart practices, technologies, and livelihood changes as coping strategies, it is imperative to acknowledge the contribution towards household and community-level resilience in the form of enhanced food security, increased capacity, and leadership. Hence, new strategies for integrating their knowledge and strategies into more formal natural resource management policies and practices are essential. More important is making certain that there are spaces created and resources allocated to ensure effective and meaningful participation of women.

While there is a growing recognition of the climate crisis's impact on women and girls and efforts to incorporate gender equality and their participation in adaptation and mitigation policies, the connection between the climate crisis and the exacerbation of GBV against women and girls receives comparatively less attention in international, regional, and domestic processes. Compounding the issue is the lack of available data on the consequences of the climate crisis concerning GBV. In 2017, the Gender Action Plan was established under the UN Framework Convention on Climate Change (UNFCCC) to enhance gender mainstreaming within its work. However, the integration of existing policies and guidelines on gender equality into climate change and gender-based policies is often inadequate, resulting in a disconnect between these issues and the corresponding policy commitments when applied to relevant contexts. While various policies exist on different thematic areas in certain countries, what is needed is the harmonization of policy frameworks and strategy documents.

5 Concluding Remarks

Given the mounting evidence linking climate change, gender, and violence, it is imperative to conduct further research aimed at comprehending the intricate interconnections and effective strategies for addressing these issues within specific national contexts. Emphasizing the significance of collecting and disseminating sex-disaggregated data, particularly in contexts of climate vulnerability and state fragility, is crucial. Moreover, it is essential to synchronize local and global initiatives to tackle these challenges and translate political commitments into tangible actions. Progressing with political commitments and integrating policy frameworks hinges on comprehensive and pertinent scientific evidence that illuminates the multifaceted dynamics at the intersection of climate, gender, and violence. To achieve this, it is necessary to develop gender-sensitive conceptual frameworks and methodologies that specifically centre on women and violence concerning environmental conflicts.

References

Adhikari, U., Nejadhashemi, A. P., & Woznicki, S. A. (2015). Climate Change and Eastern Africa: A Review of Impact on Major Crops. *Food and Energy Security, 4*(2), 110–132. https://doi.org/10.1002/fes3.61

Asadnabizadeh, M. (2021). Status of Impacts of Extreme Climate Events at the UN Climate Change Conference (COP25). *International Journal of Climate Change: Impacts & Responses, [s. l.], 13*(1), 1–11. https://doi.org/10.18848/1835-7156/CGP/v13i01/1-.

Ayal, D. Y. (2021). Climate Change and Human Heat Stress Exposure in Sub-Saharan Africa. *CABI Reviews.* https://doi.org/10.1079/PAVSNNR202116049

Ayanlade, A., Smucker, T., Nyasimi, M., Sterlya, H., Weldemariam, L. F., & Simpson, P. (2022). Complex Climate Change Risk and Emerging Directions for Vulnerability Research in Africa. *Climate Risk Management, 40*(100497), 1–10. https://doi.org/10.1016/j.crm.2023.100497

Boluk, K. A., Cavaliere, C. T., & Higgins-Desbiolles, F. (2019). A Critical Framework for Interrogating the United Nations Sustainable Development Goals 2030 Agenda in tourism. *Journal of Sustainable Tourism, 27*(7), 847–864. https://doi.org/10.1080/09669582.2019.1619748

Buma, W. G., & Lee, S.-I. (2019). Multispectral Image-Based Estimation of Drought Patterns and Intensity around Lake Chad. Africa. *Remote Sensing, 11*(21), 2534. https://doi.org/10.3390/rs11212534

Call, M., & Sellers, S. (2019). How does Gendered Vulnerability Shape the Adoption and Impact of Sustainable Livelihood Interventions in an Era of Global Climate Change? *Environmental Research Letters, 14,* 083005. https://doi.org/10.1088/1748-9326/ab2f57

Camberlin, P. (2018). *Climate of Eastern Africa.* (Vol. 1). Oxford University Press. https://doi.org/10.1093/acrefore/9780190228620.013.512

Caridade, S. M. M., Vidal, D. G., Dinis, M. A. P. (2022). Climate Change and Gender-Based Violence: Outcomes, Challenges and Future Perspectives. In Leal Filho, W., Vidal, D.G., Dinis, M.A.P., Dias, R.C. (Eds.), *Sustainable Policies and Practices in Energy, Environment and Health Research.* World Sustainability Series. Springer. https://doi.org/10.1007/978-3-030-86304-3_10

Cevik, S., & Jalles, J. T. (2022). *For Whom the Bell Tolls: Climate Change and Inequality.* IMF.

Chiang, F., Mazdiyasni, O., & AghaKouchak, A. (2021). Evidence of Anthropogenic Impacts on Global Drought Frequency, Duration, and Intensity. *Nature Communications, 12,* 2754. https://doi.org/10.1038/s41467-021-22314-w

Clarke, B., et al. (2022). Extreme Weather Impacts of Climate Change: An Attribution Perspective. *Environmental Research: Climate, 1,* 012001. https://doi.org/10.1088/2752-5295/ac6e7d

Dresser, C., & Balsari, S. (2024). Disaster Medicine in a Changing Climate. In G. Ciottone (Ed.), *Ciottone's Disaster Medicine* (3rd ed., pp. 51–57). Elsevier. https://doi.org/10.1016/B978-0-323-80932-0.00008-2

Epstein, et al., (2020). Drought and Intimate Partner Violence towards Women in 19 Countries in Sub-Saharan Africa during 2011–2018: A Population-Based Study. https://journals.plos.org/plosmedicine/article/file?id=10.1371/journal.pmed.1003064%26type=printable

Filho, W., Balogun, A., Olayide, O. E., Azeiteiro, U. M., Ayal, D. Y., Muñoz, D. C., Nagy, G. J., Bynoe, P., Oguge, O., Toamukum, N. Y., Saroar, M., & Li, C. (2019). Assessing the Impacts of Climate Change in Cities and Their Adaptive Capacity: Towards Transformative Approaches to Climate Change Adaptation and Poverty Reduction in Urban Areas in a Set of Developing Countries. *Science of the Total Environment, 692*, 1175–1190. https://doi.org/10.1016/j.scitotenv.2019.07.227

Filho, W., Krishnapillai, M., Sidsaph, H., Nagy, G. J., Luetz, J. M., Dyer, J., Otoara Ha'apio, M., Havea, P. H., Ra, K., Singh, P., et al. (2021). Climate Change Adaptation on Small Island States: An Assessment of Limits and Constraints. *Journal of Marine Science and Engineering, 9*, 602. https://doi.org/10.3390/jmse9060602

Filomina, C. S. (2014). Women, Climate Change and Liberation in Africa. *Race, Gender and Class, 21*(1/2), 312–333.

Fletcher A. J., & Reed, M. G. (2022). *Different Experiences, Diverse Knowledges Gender, Intersectionality, and Climate Change in Rural and Resource Contexts.* Taylor & Francis. eBook ISBN 9781003089209.

Freedman, J. (2016). Sexual and Gender-Based Violence Against Refugee Women: A Hidden Aspect of the Refugee "Crisis." *Reproductive Health Matters, 24*, 18–26.

Ide, T., et al. (2021). Gender in the Climate-Conflict Nexus: "Forgotten" Variables, Alternative Securities, and Hidden Power Dimensions. *Politics and Governance, 9*(4), 43–52.

Isola, A. A., & Tolulope, A. (2022). Women, Security, and Gender-Based Violence in the Northeast, Nigeria. *Journal of International Women's Studies, 24*(4), Article 6. https://vc.bridgew.edu/jiws/vol24/iss4/6

Jaka, et al. (2021). Rural Women and Livelihoods: Options For Poverty Alleviation In Drought Risk Areas Of Bikita District, Zimbabwe. *European Journal of Social Sciences Studies*, [S.l.] *6*(1). ISSN 25018590. https://oapub.org/soc/index.php/EJSSS/article/view/992

Jensen, M. A. (2019). Gender-Based Violence in Refugee Camps: Understanding and Addressing the Role of Gender in the Experiences of Refugees. *Inquiries Journal, 11*(02). http://www.inquiriesjournal.com/a?id=1757

Khan, A. R., et al. (2022). Men and Climate Change: Some Thoughts on South Africa and Bangladesh. *NORMA*. https://doi.org/10.1080/18902138.2022.2077082

Kwena, Z. A., et al. (2012). Transactional Sex in the Fishing Communities along Lake Victoria, Kenya: A Catalyst for the Spread of HIV. *Africa Journal of AIDS Research, 11*(1), 9–15.

Lawson, E. T., Alare, R. S., Salifu, A. R. Z., et al. (2020). Dealing with Climate Change in Semi-Arid Ghana: Understanding Intersectional Perceptions and Adaptation Strategies of Women Farmers. *GeoJournal, 85*, 439–452. https://doi.org/10.1007/s10708-019-09974-4

Lindqvist, L., Sendén, G., & Renström, E. A. (2021). What is Gender, Anyway: A Review of the Options for Operationalising Gender. *Psychology & Sexuality, 12*(4), 332–344. https://doi.org/10.1080/19419899.2020.1729844

Lwanga-Ntale, C., & Owino, B. O. (2020). Understanding Vulnerability and Resilience in Somalia XE "Somalia. *Jamba, 12*(1), 856. https://doi.org/10.4102/jamba.v12i1.856.PMID:33408804;PMCID:PMC7768599

Majedul, M. M. (2022) Threats to Humanity from Climate Change. In Bandh, S. A. (Ed.), *Climate Change*. Springer. https://doi.org/10.1007/978-3-030-86290-9_2.

McLeod, C., Barr, H., & Rall, K. (2019). Does Climate Change Increase the Risk of Child Marriage: A Look at What We Know—And What We Don't—With Lessons from Bangladesh and Mozambique. *Columbia Journal of Gender & Law, 38*, 96.

Mikulewicz, M., Caretta, M. A., Sultana, F., & Crawford, N. J. W. (2023). Intersectionality & Climate Justice: A Call for Synergy in Climate Change Scholarship. *Environmental Politics*. https://doi.org/10.1080/09644016.2023.2172869

Mugandani, R., Muziri, T., Murewi, C. T. F., Mugadza, A., Chitata, T., Sungirai, M., Zirebwa, F. S., Manhondo, P., Mupfiga, E. T., Nyamutowa, C., et al. (2022). Mapping and Managing Livelihoods Vulnerability to Drought: A Case Study of Chivi District in Zimbabwe. *Climate, 10*(12), 189. https://doi.org/10.3390/cli10120189

Muluneh, M. D., Francis, L., Agho, K., & Stulz, V. A. (2021). Systematic Review and Meta-Analysis of Associated Factors of Gender-Based Violence against Women in Sub-Saharan Africa. *International Journal of Environmental Research and Public Health, 18*, 4407. https://doi.org/10.3390/ijerph18094407

Muuo, S., Stella, K. M., Martin, K. M., Alys, M., Loraine, J. B., Hope, O., Martin, B., Mazeda, H. & Chimaraoke, I. (2020). Barriers and Facilitators to Care-Seeking Among Survivors of Gender-Based Violence in the Dadaab Refugee Complex. *Sexual and Reproductive Health Matters, 28*(1). https://doi.org/10.1080/26410397.2020.1722404

Njikho, S. F. (2020) *How Are Climate Change-Related Events Causing Increased Hardships Leading to Violence Against Rural Women in Malawi?* University ProQuest Dissertations Publishing.

Nyahunda, L., Makhubele, J. C., Mabvurira, V., & Matlakala, F. K. (2021). Vulnerabilities and Inequalities Experienced by Women in the Climate Change Discourse in South Africa's Rural Communities: Implications for Social Work," 51(7), 2536–2553. https://doi.org/10.1093/bjsw/bcaa118

Nyasimi, M., & Huyer, S. (2017). Closing the Gender Gap in Agriculture Under Climate Change. *Agriculture Development, 30*, 37–40.

Nyasimi, M., Kimeli, P., Sayula, G., Radeny, M., Kinyangi, J., & Mungai, C. (2017). Adoption and Dissemination Pathways for Climate-Smart Agriculture Technologies and Practices for Climate-Resilient Livelihoods in Lushoto. *Northeast Tanzania. Climate, 5*, 63. https://doi.org/10.3390/cli5030063

Nyiwul, L. (2021). Climate Change Adaptation and Inequality in Africa: Case of Water, Energy and Food Insecurity. *Journal of Cleaner Production, 278*, 123393. https://doi.org/10.1016/j.jclepro.2020.123393

Olumba, E. E., et al. (2022). Conceptualising Eco-Violence: Moving Beyond the Multiple Labelling of Water and Agricultural Resource Conflicts in the Sahel. *Third World Quarterly, 43*(9), 2075–2090.

Onwutuebe, C. J. (2019). Patriarchy and Women Vulnerability to Climate Change in Nigeria. *SAGE Open* January–March: 1–7.

Ovenden, N., & Van Daalen, K. (2022). Apollo-University Of Cambridge Repository. *Lancet Planet. Health* (https://www.safetylit.org/week/journalpage.php?jid=25603) (ePub).

Partey, S. T., Dakorah, A. D., Zougmoré, R. B., et al. (2020). Gender and Climate Risk Management: Evidence of Climate Information Use in Ghana. *Climatic Change, 158*, 61–75. https://doi.org/10.1007/s10584-018-2239-6

Phiri, A., Howele M. A. C. Toure, Oliver Kipkogei, Rokiatou Traore, Pamela M. K. Afokpe & Alemayehu Abebe Lamore. (2022). A Review of Gender Inclusivity in Agriculture and Natural Resources Management Under the Changing Climate in Sub-Saharan Africa. *Cogent Social Sciences, 8*(1). https://doi.org/10.1080/23311886.2021.2024674.

Ramutsindela, M., & Mickler, D. (2020). *Africa and the Sustainable Development Goals*. Springer.

Sillmann, J., Daloz, A. S., Schaller, N., Schwingshackl, C. (2021). Chapter 16—Extreme weather and climate change. (Eds): Trevor M. Letcher. *Climate Change* (Third Ed.). Elsevier: 359–372. https://doi.org/10.1016/B978-0-12-821575-3.00016-5

Van Niekerk, L., Lamberth, S. J., James, N. C., Taljaard, S., Adams, J. B., Theron, A. K., & Krug, M. (2022). The Vulnerability of South African Estuaries to Climate Change: A Review and Synthesis. *Diversity, 14*(9), 697. https://doi.org/10.3390/d14090697

Versey, H. S. (2020). Missing Pieces in the Discussion on Climate Change and Risk: Intersectionality and Compounded Vulnerability. *Policy Insights from the Behavioral and Brain Sciences, 8*(1), 67–75. https://doi.org/10.1177/2372732220982628

WFP. (2017). *The First Climate Change Conflict*, https://www.wfpusa.org/articles/the-first-climate-changeconflict/#:~:text=Darfur%20has%20been%20labeled%20the,political%20factors%20leading%20to%20conflict .

WHO. (2021). *Violence Against Women*. https://www.who.int/news-room/fact-sheets/detail/violence-against-women

"Women's Sexuality Captured": Another Form of Gender-Based Violence (GBV) in the Swati Patriarchal Space

Sonene Nyawo

1   Introduction

An article in the *Times of Eswatini*, on Monday, 29 May 2023, titled, "Church Discourages use of Muti, Promotes Chastity," caught my attention. Unyazi Lwezulu Shembe, the leader of the Nazareth Baptist Church (*Baka Shembe*), had a two-week long historic visit to the Kingdom of Eswatini. The article stated that the church promotes the sexual purity of girls, and that they are tested and confirmed virgins before joining the girls' regiment. They are obliged to remain virgins until the couple consummates their marriage. It was further reported in the publication that *umgidi,* which are the cultural dances performed by members, are not just for enjoyment, but has significance to church members. An *Umfundisi* (leader) was cited as saying:

> the principle of Shembe is that all men should enter into fully fledged marriages. Girls have to preserve their purity until their allotted time for marriage. A man cannot join the regiment of men without having fulfilled his marriage responsibility, which is defined by the payment of *lobola* and a wedding. (*Times of Eswatini*, Monday, 29 May, 2023)

S. Nyawo (✉)
Department of Theology and Religious Studies, University of Eswatini, Kwaluseni, Eswatini
e-mail: snyawo@uniswa.sz

Core to this chapter's discussion is the hypothesis that glorifying virginity to the extent of subjecting girls to virginity tests is a form of gender-based violence (GBV). Patriarchy, power relations, and hierarchical constructions of masculinity and femininity are presented as predominant and pervasive drivers of the violence (WHO, 2010: 6). Toxic masculinity driven by certain religio-cultural norms is harmful to society through its promotion of physical, emotional, and sexual violence, especially in social institutions like the home and the church (Nyawo et al., 2020). The cited publication presents the Nazareth Baptist Church making it compulsory for girls to preserve their virginity until marriage, hence, the virginity tests to confirm their status. Also, their virginity will accrue them *lobola* from their partners, who have an obligation to fulfil marriage responsibilities of *lobola* payment, rather than preserving purity.

In such scenarios, beneficiaries of the patriarchy are seen as using victims of violence as a means towards their own ends rather than treating them as ends in themselves (Birsch, 2014). To treat human beings as a means to an end is to show disrespect for them as autonomous and rational human beings. Human beings, regardless of gender, have a right to [life, dignity,] health, non-discrimination, freedom from "torture and cruel, inhuman and degrading treatment or punishment" (WHO, 2010: 6). It is argued in this chapter that virginity testing, which, according to the cited publication, is intended to confirm one's purity, violates the girls' right to life and dignity. Also, it is used as a means of exerting control over women and their sexuality; thus, their sexuality is captured by patriarchal constructions. This is what the chapter seeks to demonstrate, with specific reference to the violence that underlies the practice of virginity testing.

2   Outlining the Context

Swati society is patriarchal in its nature, and by extension its fundamental social units, like the church, and family, whose basis is marriage, is also patriarchal (Nyawo & Nsibande, 2014). Male dominance thriving in these institutions often fuels behaviour where women are seen as subordinate to men. Harmful customary practices, and the misuse of culture to justify harmful actions toward women, have all largely contributed to gender inequality and male superiority. Despite its exposure to modern socio-political and economic transformation, Swati society has upheld its conventional gender dynamics whereby subservience, deference towards males, and asymmetrical gender roles are purported in essentialist terms. Social agents like family and church, as Kabeer (1996) has observed, are central to the reproduction of patriarchal relations and women's subordination.

In the past few years Eswatini has witnessed unprecedented reports of gender-based violence (GBV). In response to this epidemic, a national commissioned study was undertaken.[1] It was deemed necessary to provide contextual and evidence-based knowledge (i.e. research) on sexual and gender-based violence (SGBV) in the country in order to understand and resolve the problem, which has a cost for the individual, families, and society. Sexual and gender-based violence in its three forms: physical, sexual, and emotional, is a serious health, social, and human rights problem (Ravi & Ahluwalia, 2017). Physical violence includes beating, kicking, or attacking with a weapon, whilst emotional violence involves threats, insults, and scolding. Sexual violence on the other hand may include incest, sodomy, indecent assault, and unwanted sexual contact. Statistics indicate that the three forms of violence, plus financial violence, are a persistent problem in the Kingdom of Eswatini. In particular, the United Nations Population Fund (2021) reports that at least one in three women in Eswatini experiences some form of sexual abuse by the age of 18, and 48% of women are reported to have experienced some form of sexual violence in their lifetimes. The following graph (see Fig. 1) adapted from police reports in different stations throughout the country from 2014 to 2018 indicates that there is an upward trend in all types of violence which mainly target women and children, although men are also increasingly affected (Nyawo et al., 2020).

Acknowledging the cited statistics on reported cases of violence in a period of five years, this chapter argues that male social dominance, incubated by patriarchy, also extends to subtle control of women's reproductive abilities. Studies undertaken by Ngcobo (2007), Mdluli (2007), African Women's Economic Policy Network. (AWEPON), (2005), Women and Law in Southern Africa. (WLSA), (2001), Daly (2001) and Nhlapho (1992) on the dynamics of Swati society have confirmed the Swati family as pro-natal, with the ultimate purpose of marriage to be procreation. Hence, women's fertility, which comes as a result of girls keeping their virginity, is highly valued. This chapter, therefore, advances the argument that girls keeping their virginity is an expression of male social dominance, exercised not through

---

[1] The Deputy Prime Minister's Office (DPMO), which is responsible for Social Welfare and Gender issues, commissioned the University of Eswatini (UNESWA) to examine the drivers of sexual and gender-based violence (SGBV) in the Kingdom of Eswatini, to profile its perpetrators and survivors, and to examine the perceptions of EmaSwati regarding the reasons for and the acceptability of SGBV. The intention of this study (Nyawo et al., 2020), therefore, was to develop a general overview on the current status of issues related to SGBV and to come up with recommendations on how this could be curbed in the Kingdom of Eswatini using findings based on empirical evidence.

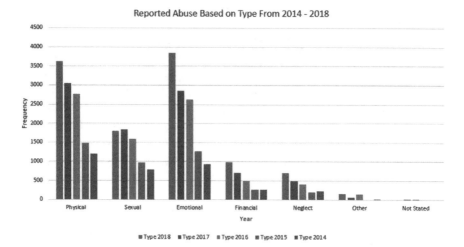

Fig. 1 Reported abuse based on type form 2014–2018

brute force, but through a religio-cultural dynamic reinforced by socialization. In a society where the woman's self-conception is developed whilst couched in patriarchal language, the young woman's virginity becomes crucial to attracting high *lobola* premium that would benefit her paternal family, and guarantee perpetual lineage for her marital family.

3 Theoretical Considerations on Gender

That women's sexuality is being captured by toxic masculinities but not by brute force, draws on theoretical outlooks on gender, echoed by sociological theories that define gender as socially constructed notions of masculinity and femininity. Many theoretical perspectives submit that gender is generally thought about in binary terms; that is, man/woman and masculine/feminine. Thus, roles, norms and expectations of women and men are marked by these binaries and are communicated through sex-role stereotyping (Nyawo & Nsibande, 2014). The stereotypes limit gender-appropriate behaviour to a range of rigid roles which are assigned to women and men on the basis of their gender. For example, "women are nurturers" and "men are aggressors" (Nyawo, 2014). It is these role expectations, which are subtle and deeply ingrained in people's attitudes, that contribute to gender inequalities. Connell (1987) gives a theoretical account on gender disparities in the book *Gender and Power and Masculinities*, where he asserts that the social power held by men creates and sustains gender inequalities. For Connell, gender relations are a product of everyday interactions and practices, and people's behaviour and actions are directly linked to collective social arrangements. These arrangements are continuously reproduced over lifetimes and generations through social agencies, but are also subject to change (Giddens, 2005). Connell, further, makes reference to a society's gender order, which he explains as the power relations between masculinities and femininities that are widespread throughout the society. He posits that gender order has three realms (labour, power, and sexual relationships) which represent the main sites in which gender relations are constituted and constrained. Labour being the sexual division of labour in social institutions like family, church, and workplace, power being social relations like authority, violence, and ideology in institutions, and sexual relationships being the dynamics within intimate relationships, are all structured in a particular gender regime, so claims Connell (1987: 74).

Sociological theories make a difference between sex and gender. They use the term sex to refer to the anatomical and physiological differences that define male and female bodies, whilst in contrast, gender relates to socially constructed notions of masculinity and femininity (Giddens, 2005). The expressions of masculinity and femininity are ordered in a hierarchy oriented around one defining premise, which is the domination of men over women. According to Connell (1987), at the top of the hierarchy is hegemonic masculinity which he defines as man's social dominance, exercised not through brute force, but through a cultural dynamic. Social agencies like family, church, school, and media then become channels that establish the hegemony where children learn gender expectations and norms that they gradually internalize. Walby (1986) views these social agencies as patriarchal cultural which produce representation of women "within a patriarchal gaze." These representations tend to influence women's identities and prescribe acceptable standards of behaviour and action. Thus, young girls feel obligated to test for their virginity and remain pure until consummation in marriage, so as to uphold hegemonic masculinity.

4 Gender, Power and Violence

Women in Law Southern Africa (WILSA) Swaziland (2001) undertook a study on domestic violence against women in the then Swaziland, where patriarchal culture was identified as the main contributing factor to domestic violence. It was established that women's minority status in Eswatini leads men to exercise control over women, thus, subjugating and violating them.

The study identified types of violence carried out in Swati homes as assault, rape, non-sexual physical domestic violence, sexual physical domestic violence, incest, and emotional abuse. The most common of these was emotional abuse, where the perpetrator inflicts non-physical pain on the victim through insults and name-calling. Participants from these studies revealed that there was a veil of secrecy around issues of violence in the homes, such that women who were courageous enough to report such cases to the police would later withdraw the charges even before the perpetrator was arrested (Zwane, 2013). The studies further linked domestic violence in the homes with the perceived minority status of the women by society, which is reinforced by the marriage contract a man and woman enter into (Convention on the Elimination of All Forms of Discrimination Against Women. (CEDAW), 2011; Mofolo, 2011; Nhlapho, 1992; Zwane, 2013). The marriage contract allows discriminating cultural practices like *kuteka* (traditional marriage), *emalobolo* (dowry), *inhlanti* (substitute wife), and *kungenwa* (wife inheritance). A close scrutiny of these practices by WLSA (2002) reveals that they expose women to various types of violence which deprive women of their dignity as human beings.

Zwane (2013) reflects on issues of assault which WLSA listed amongst the types of violence. Echoing the same views, she adds that women in Eswatini, however, have the right to charge their husbands with assault under both the Roman-Dutch and traditional legal systems. She indicates that it is mostly urban women that would do so, usually in extreme cases when mediation by senior members of the extended family have been unsuccessful in stopping such violence. On the contrary, rural women would often have no recourse if family intervention did not succeed, because traditional courts were unsympathetic to "unruly" or "disobedient" women and were less likely than modern courts to convict men of spousal abuse (Zwane, 2013: 11). Unfortunately, the Roman-Dutch legal system would often give light sentences in cases of abuse against women. Hence, a sense of helplessness would often inhibit women from reporting cases of domestic violence, including being assaulted for their infertility.

The earlier cited studies by WLSA, Nhlapho and Zwane advance the thesis that socialization is a contributory factor to violence, either in overt or covert ways. At an early age, women learn to accept their socially defined inferiority and subordination to men, and they internalize it as normal. Social norms and practices, therefore, which expose women to violence would not be questioned; instead they would be explained as *"umhambo weMaswati"* (obligatory practices for the Swati). Furthermore these studies speak at length about the payment of *emalobolo* (dowry) as one socio-cultural practice that largely contributes to domestic violence. The study by WLSA, in particular, records responses from women which reveal that the payment of dowry for a woman can have negative connotations for how the two people should treat each other within marriage.

As alluded to earlier, the perception of *lobola* as a legally accepted "price" for purchasing the women's reproductive abilities affirm that a woman is bought and is, therefore, regarded as property. The studies reveal that when she does not fulfil the obligations attached to her "purchase," physical violence can ensue. Hence *lobola* reduces the woman into an object, which then predisposes her to being a target of the man's violent behaviour (Asamoah-Gyadu, 2007; Ngcobo, 2007). The chapter argues that even before the woman suffers physical violence from the perpetrator, her sexuality being controlled through socialization is another type of violence. The next section explores the socio-cultural value attached to virginity.

5 Cultural Socialization on Virginity

Socialization, according to Clifford (2001), Riley (1989), Ruether (2002), and Lerner (1993), trains women to understand themselves in terms of patriarchal super-ordination and subordination of being in the centre or being on the margin. Further, it leads them to internalize that they have to accept and adapt to things as they are. Gendered social norms, which Namabira and Kamanzi (2013: 88) have explained as formal and informal rules which govern people's behaviour, stem from societal values of what it means to be a *"real"* woman or a *"real"* man. Virginity, therefore, is a societal value that defines an upright girl who deserves marriage. Through socialization, which is chiefly supported by biological essentialism, women are taught to accept patriarchal norms, values and beliefs as natural, divine and obligatory (Nyawo, 2014). Failure to fulfil this expectation results in social sanctions which range from verbal violence to social alienation.

Though vastly differentiated by religion, ethnicity and geography, cultures in most African traditional societies share similar attitudes towards a girl's virginity. Sexual experience is absolutely barred before marriage and, thus, virginity is eulogized and is enforced through religio-cultural institutions. Through chastity talks, young girls are socialized in the notion that the honour and shame of these institutions are so intrinsically associated with their virginity that personal affection and sexual choice do not matter much (Botting et al., 1998). Plausibly, in some African societies, virginity is not only important as a form of sexual control but also as a business asset where the girl's family would accrue some wealth through paying of *lobola* (Ritcher & Mlambo, 2005). As such, the family would use the daughter's virginity as a bargaining chip since a virgin bride would definitely fetch a higher price from the marriage negotiations, as opposed to a sexually experienced one (Le Roux, 2006). Thus, loss of virginity before marriage usually draws the wrath of the chief beneficiaries in the patriarchal system, resulting in serious repercussions like social rejection and excommunication of the girls from social institutions. However, Scorgie (2002) notes that whilst earlier injunctions regarding virginity were the consequence of a patriarchal system, now increasing health-related influences have renewed the emphasis on virginity. In response to the ravages of AIDS and teen pregnancies, some African cultures have brought virginity back into focus, with many society and culture leaders insisting that enforcing virginity before marriage is one of the ways to prevent the spread of HIV and teen pregnancies (Bhana, 2016).

Many traditional structures regard virginity testing or enforcing abstinence, as the "only way to instil what they view as the lost cultural values of chastity before marriage, modesty, self-respect and pride" (Leclerc-Madlala, 2001: 535). As the number of people dying of AIDS increased, community leaders began showing interest in reviving the old cultural tradition of virginity testing as a way to safeguard against HIV and AIDS. Kinoti (2005) argues that virginity testing is used as one method to check the onslaught of the pandemic by encouraging abstinence, which is one of the strategies for preventing the further spread of the virus. Often, those in favour of virginity testing claim that the benefits include not only the prevention of the spread of HIV and AIDS, but also teenage pregnancy and the detection of children who are sexually abused, and that it relieves the burden on pensioners who are forced to take care of unplanned babies (Le Roux, 2006). However, the practice of virginity testing has also come under heavy criticism. Some researchers argue that virginity testing is used as a means of exerting control over women and their sexuality (Nyawo, 2018).

Bower (2005) asserts that virginity testing is done in order to ensure that girls who are virgins have much broader significance. Virgins are seen as morally pure and more important because they are able to maintain their virginity up until marriage. According to Scorgie (2002) the association of female virginity with the notion of pride and dignity is commonplace in marriage, and indeed central to understanding what is at stake for the *bahloli* (testers). A girl who becomes pregnant before marriage is ostracized by girls who have passed the test for she has brought shame and disgrace both upon herself and her peers. Nowadays, the dignity and pride that virginity is believed to bestow on the individual girl continues to be linked with the avoidance of premarital motherhood (Zungu, 2000). Sexual abstinence is constructed as an end in itself, quite separate from its role in enabling fertility control and the prevention of sexually transmitted diseases and HIV transmission. Thus, "Adolescents who have sex are seen as people who have lost the vitality of youth and have become old," asserts Scorgie (2002: 10). So, if virginity is so eulogized in patriarchal spaces, how does it discriminate against women's sexuality?

It Is Another Form of Gender-Related Violence and Discrimination

Perceptions of violence differ vastly between various cultures and communities; thus, what constitutes GBV remains an issue of much debate in academic, research and support service discourse (Kabuli et al., 2013). Issues listed under the broad "violence against women" rubric include rape, sexual assault, physical assault, and domestic abuse or assault. There are also emotional abuse and economic or financial abuse, whose effects, in some cases, are as great as that associated with direct physical abuse (Kabuli et al., 2013).

Young girls having to test their virginity to confirm their purity is more of hegemonic control over their sexuality, and another form of GBV. It is *sex-based harassment*, which is explained as verbal, physical, or other non-verbal conduct of a sexual nature with the purpose or effect of violating the dignity of a person (George, 2008: 171). Giddens (2005: 119) has explained hegemony as the social dominance of a group, exercised not through brute force, but through a cultural dynamic which extends into private life and social realms. The National Gender Policy of Swaziland (2010: 10) has defined sexuality as an aspect of health that enhances personal relations, respect for the security of the person and the physical integrity of the human body, and the right to make decisions on sexuality and reproduction free of discrimination, coercion, and violence. The girls' perceptions on their sexual purity, as captured in the cited scenario in the introduction, are shaped by hegemonic constructions of sexuality that establish hierarchal relationships between femininity and masculinity. These hegemonic constructions as posited by Connell (2000) provide scaffolding for skewed relationships between women and men to be accepted as "natural" whilst inevitably legitimizing dominance and submission. Women's and girls' willingness to undergo virginity testing meets the expectations of their church and families. Such mentalities are characteristic of hegemonic control in gender regimes, whereby women live their lives to serve and satisfy the interests and ascendancy of the dominant group. This gender order is accepted by the subordinates as natural, divine, and unchangeable (Nganga, 2011; Oduyoye, 2001). As also noted by Schippers (2007: 87), hegemony legitimates ascendancy, and also inspires everyone to consent to and go along with social dominance. Failure to fit into this hegemonic "jacket" results in misery.

Women's sexual health embraces reproductive rights which are supposed to grant women freedom to decide on issues that pertain to their sexuality. However, cultural undercurrents deprive women of these rights, such that they have no control over their sexuality. It emerges in the scenario cited in the introduction that the men, who are not necessarily required to maintain purity, have the responsibility to accumulate *lobola* for their future "pure" brides. In actual fact, the *lobola* purchases her womb from her father, not the body (Nhlapo, 1992: 48), and ownership of her womb now transfers to her marital home. This is evident in the rituals families perform to redeem childless unions. For example, when elders in her marital family have proven that their son is sterile, arrangements can be made with close relatives to surreptitiously give service to their property, the "bought womb." Though not forced, the woman would submerge her dignity and ethics and comply with the deal (Nyawo, 2014).

6   Women's Sexuality Captured—A Critical Perspective

Family is a fundamental unit in Swati society, and, by extension, the church. Family is the first environment where girls and boys are oriented in gender roles that society ascribes, and they are socialized in cultural norms and values. These cultural constructs are reinforced by other social units like the church, such that they all sing from the same hymn sheet. Thus, a church would also teach young girls to preserve their virginity until marriage, which would also accrue them a high premium of *lobola*. This societal expectation is perceived and accepted as "natural, divine and unchangeable," and anyone who transgresses it is labelled a social deviant (Nyawo, 2014). Premised on this insight, I argue that the family in Swati society can be interpreted as an institutional location that creates and reproduces gender inequalities. Kabeer's (1996: 17) study on gender as an institution, defines an institution as a framework of rules for achieving social or economic goals. She further claims institutions produce, reinforce, and reproduce social relations, thereby creating and perpetuating social difference and inequality.

Confirming this assertion, Women and Law in Southern Africa, (WLSA), (2001) note that women are made to understand that *lobola* gives self-worth and respect and helps to keep marriages together. In most customary systems, paying *lobola* is portrayed as a part of a rich African heritage whose disappearance would result in people's loss of identity and sovereignty (Leclerc-Madlala, 2001). The culturally imposed "benefits" of *lobola* are so emphasized in families that young girls can view themselves as sources of wealth, and, therefore, important. Through socialization they are made to believe that, in addition to this, they are a source of wealth to their families. The number of cattle controlled by their fathers reflects his prestige and the homestead's social status and strength. Such perceptions of themselves contribute to the construction and reinforcement of their *self*.

The payment of *lobola* is, therefore, a legal obligation which marks the transfer of the woman's fertility to the husband's family. Put differently, it is the fruit of her womb that is purchased for continuity of the family name. This places a high a premium on children, making women's capabilities to beget children very crucial for the survival of every family (Mdluli, 2007; Ngcobo, 2007). Also, *lobola* is used as a control mechanism over the woman and the children that she might bear in marriage, such that she remains a permanent "stranger" in her marital family even after the death of her husband (Ngcobo, 2007: 535). Other legal tools such as the country's constitution and marriage-governing laws are also designed to put pressure on and influence the woman to accept inequalities so that she remains in the subservient position where she is meant to belong.

Moghadam (2005) points out, too, that the family is the institution where children are socialized into society's normative system of values and appropriate status expectations. She asserts that the family provides a stable emotional environment that cushions the male's ego against any harm and abuse. Conversely, such socialization renders women powerless and docile and, when internalized, it generates submissive, compliant and self-effacing behaviours (Unger, 1979: 35). From the onset girls would be socialized to accept themselves as future mothers, who should keep themselves pure until marriage commitment. Oduyoye (1995: 142) would argue, that motherhood in most African societies is a highly valued role open only to women, but desired by both women and men, as the channel by which men reproduce themselves and continue the family line. So, the actual prestige of reproduction goes to those who "own" or control the reproductive capabilities of women, such that women are not valued in themselves, but only as valuable objects or means to an end.

Notably, Rakoczy (2004: 293) challenges women not to be passive but to: affirm their bodies as intrinsically good and beautiful, in opposition to patriarchal calls to improve their bodies according to male norms; claim their right to bodily integrity, including sexual integrity, and to decisions concerning their bodies; and claim their right to health and well-being as defined by themselves. Lerner would argue that demeaning rituals and taboos related to women's sexuality are results of patriarchal concepts built into all mental constructs of societies, which have remained invisible over the centuries (1993: 3). These concepts project men as whole and powerful and females as deviant, incomplete, physically mutilated and emotionally dependent. Such an understanding is founded on the belief that men and women were created differently, and, therefore, their biology, respective needs, capacities, and functions are not the same (Lerner, 1993: 4). In a patriarchal society, men are viewed as naturally superior, stronger, and more rational, whereas women are viewed as naturally weaker, intellectually and rationally inferior, emotionally unstable, and incapable of being involved in politics (Lerner, 1993: 4). Therefore, men were designed by God to be dominant (Lerner, 1993: 4). Men, being more rational, explain and regulate the world and have control over a woman's sexuality and her reproductive functions. Women sustain daily life and are responsible for the continuation of the human race and have no rights over men. Only men can act as a go-between with God and humans; women can only mediate with God through men (Lerner, 1993: 4).

One would argue that the girls willingly participate in the testing for virginity ritual, which the cited publication makes reference to. This is what Connell (2000) labels as *emphasized* femininity, which he explains as women's compliance with their subordination, oriented to accommodate the interests and desires of men. So, whilst one admits that it is the women who eagerly embrace hegemonic masculinities, they are not beneficiaries as are the men; the reward for a girl who has preserved her purity, for instance, belongs to her father or male relatives. Thus, girls would sacrifice their dignities, and test for virginity for the benefit of men. Men usually capitalize on this women's error, accusing them of being enemies to one another. They would often defensively ask on some gender platforms, "Have you ever seen men involved in ritual performances for women? It is the women against each other." However, the issue here is not who performs what to who; it is who is meant to benefit from the performances (Nyawo, 2014). Connell observes that hegemonic masculinity ensures male dominance, whereby all men benefit on some level, though most do not have to be on the front lines or embody hegemonic masculinities (1995:187). Whether the demeaning rituals are perpetuated through *emphasized* femininity or hegemonic masculinities, the fact remains that they diminish the victim's personhood, and retard reasoning and development.

7 Conclusion

Let us conclude the chapter with a summary of the effects of virginity testing as presented by World Health Organization (World Health Organization, 2014) in its 2014 report. It causes physical, physiological, and social harm. In terms of the physical harm, virginity tests may result in physical injury to women and girls being examined, including aggravating existing injuries in the case of survivors of violence. Harm may also come from relatives who, as consequence of a perceived "failed" test may hurt or kill the woman or girl, in the name of so called "honour." Self-harm as attempted suicide has also occurred in some women or girls as a result of the "virginity testing." It may also result to psychological harm or damage. Women and girls who have been subject to virginity tests report experiencing extreme fear and anxiety before the test, and screaming, crying, and fainting during the test. Long-term effects, including self-hatred, loss of self-esteem, depression, a sense of violation of one's privacy, and re-victimization (for survivors of sexual assault) have also been reported by women and girls. Concerning its effects socially, virginity testing is often associated with harmful traditional and cultural norms that expose women and girls to stigma and perceived shame and dishonour to themselves, their families, and communities. Women or girls can be ostracized or even killed because they have had (or they are believed to have had) sexual intercourse outside of norms imposed by society before marriage. Additionally, early marriage is used in some communities as a sort of wrongly interpreted "protective" measure to avoid the shame and consequences of a girl who had sexual intercourse before marriage. Some girls may, therefore, be married off early to avoid any kind of sexual activity before marriage.

With reference to societal expectations of girls having to maintain their purity in a patriarchal space, we observe man's social dominance, exercised not through brute force, but through a religio-cultural dynamic. The chapter advances that virginity testing which reinforces this dynamic is a form of GBV; whether it is practiced against the will of the girl or not, as it controls or seizes her sexuality. Girls should, therefore, be empowered to realize that the practice of virginity testing is inhuman and unethical; it is an affront to women's and girls' dignity, and it causes physical and psychosocial distress and trauma.

Bibliography

African Women's Economic Policy Network. (AWEPON). (2005). *A Baseline Study of the Socio-Economic Impact of HIV and AIDS and the Responsiveness of Policy Framework in Swaziland*.

Asamoah-Gyadu, J. K., (2007). "Broken Calabashes and Covenants of Fruitfulness": Cursing Barrenness in Contemporary African Christianity. *Journal of Religion in Africa, 37*(4), 437–460.

Bhana, D. (2016). Virginity and Virtue: African Masculinities and Femininities in the Making of Teenage Sexual Cultures. *Sexualities, 19*(4), 465–481.

Birsch, D. (2014). *Introduction to Ethical Theories: A Procedural Approach*. Waveland Press Inc.

Botting, B., Rosato, M., & Wood, R. (1998). Teenage Mothers and the Health of their Childrsen. *Population Trends, 93*, 19–28.

Bour, D. (2002). *Fertility Desires and Perceptions of Power in Reproductive Conflict in Ghana*.

Bower, C. (2005). *Virginity Testing In Whose Interest?* Resources aimed at the Prevention of Child Abuse. RAPCAN.

Clifford, A. M. (2001). *Introducing Feminist Theology*. Orbis Books.

Connell, R. W. (1987). *Gender and Power: Society, the Person and Sexual Politics*.

Connell, R. W. (1995). *Masculinities*. Polity.

Connell, R. W. (2000). *The Men and the Boys*. University of California Press.

Convention on the Elimination of All Forms of Discrimination Against Women. (CEDAW). (2011). Gender, Leadership and Advocacy for Members of Parliament, Training Manual. Swaziland 2011–2014.

Daly, J. L. (2001). Gender Equality Rights Versus Traditional Practices: Struggles for Control and Change in Swaziland. *Development Southern Africa, 18*(1), 45–56.

George, R. P. (2008). Natural law. *Harvard Journal of Law and Public Policy, 31*.

Giddens, S. A. (2005). *Sociology (4th edition)*. Polity Press.

Kabeer. N. (1996). *Mainstreaming Gender in Social Protection for the Informal Economy*, Johnson, T. (Ed.). Commonwealth Secretariat.

Kabuli, A., Phiri, M. & Thadzi, G. N. (2013). Gender-Related Violence and the Susceptibility of Young People to HIV/AIDS in Central Malawi: Options for Public Health Policy Interventions. *Insights into Gender Equity, Equality and Power Relations in Sub-saharan Africa*, p. 221.

Kinoti, K. (2005). *Virginity Testing and the War Against Aids: A Look at the Implications of Adopting Virginity Testing as a Tool in Preventing HIV Transmission*, AWID, Young Women and Leadership.

Le Roux, L. (2006). *Harmful traditional practices, (Male Circumcision and Virginity Testing of Girls)*, University of Western Cape.

Leadership in Swaziland. (2014). *UNISWA Research Journal*, Special Volume 27 March, 2014, 45–58. University of Swaziland Research Centre.

Leclerc-Madlala, S. (2001). Virginity Testing Managing Sexuality in a Maturing HIV/AIDS epidemic. *Medical Anthropology Quarterly, 15*(4), 533–552.

Lerner, G. (1986). *The Creation of Patriarch*. Oxford University Press.

Lerner, G. (1993). *The Creation of Feminist Consciousness: From the Middle Ages to 1870*. Oxford University Press.

Mdluli, S. (2007). Voicing their Perceptions: Swazi Women's Folk Songs. *Muziki, 4*(1), 87–110.

Mofolo, T. (2011). Investigating the Factors Contributing to the Disempowerment of Women in Swaziland Perceptions of Swazi Women and Non-Governmental Organizations Operating in Swaziland. *African Insight, 41*(2).

Moghadam, V. (2005). *Globalizing Women: Transnational Feminist Networks*. Johns Hopkins University Press.

Motsa-Dladla, T. (1994). *And Still they Dance and Sing*. The Significance and Meaning of Swazi.

Namabira, J., & Kamanzi, A. Rearranging the Patriarchal Value System through Women"s Empowerment: An Experience from Tanzania. In M. Prah (Ed.), *Insights into Gender, Equity, Equality and Power Relations in Sub-Saharan Africa*, Addis Ababa: OSSREA Publications.

Namabira, J., & Kamanzi, A. (2013). *More Strategies Needed to Combat Men "Goal-Keeping"*. Presented at the conference: OSSREA's Response to the Challenges of Change.

National Gender Policy. (2010). *The Kingdom of Swaziland*.

Nganga, T. W. (2011). *Institutions and Gender Inequality: A Case Study of the Constituency Development Fund in Kenya*. Organization for Social Science Research in Eastern and Southern Africa (OSSREA). OSSREA Publications.

Ngcobo, L. (2007). African Motherhood Myth and Reality. In O. Tejumola and A. Quaysin (Eds.), *African Literature: An Anthology of Criticism and Theory*, Blackwell Publishing.

Nhlapho, T. (1992). *Marriage and Divorce in Swazi Law and Custom*. Mbabane: Websters (Pty) Ltd.

Ntawubona, J. (2013). Women's Political Participation in Uganda: A Case Study of Mbarara Municipality In M. Prah (Ed.), *Insights into Gender Equity, Equality and Power Relations in SubSaharan Africa*, Fountain Publishers.

Nyawo, S. (2014). *"Sowungumuntfukenyalo"—"You are now a real person": A Feminist Analysis of how Women's Identities and Personhood are Constructed by Societal Perceptions on Fertility in the Swazi Patriarchal Family* (Doctoral dissertation).

Nyawo, S. (2018). Socio-cultural Religious Constructions of Women and Fertility and their Implications in the Context of HIV and AIDS in Swaziland. *BOLESWA Journal of Theology and Religious Studies, 5*(1), 101–112.

Nyawo, S., & Nsibande, N. (2014). Beyond Parity: Gender in the Context of Educational Leadership in Swaziland. *UNISWA Research Journal, 27*, 45–58.

Nyawo, S., Silvane, C., Shongwe, M. N., & Khumalo, T. F. (2020). *A Situation Analysis of Sexual and Gender-Based Violence (SGBV) in Eswatini*. The Deputy Prime Minister's Office, Mbabane, Kingdom of Eswatini.

Oduyoye, M. (1995). *Daughters of Anowa: African Women and Patriarchy*. Maryknoll, Orbis.

Oduyoye, M. A. (2001). *Introducing African Women's Theology*. Sheffield Academic Press. Polity.

Railey, M. (1989). *Transforming Feminism*. Sheed and Word.

Rakoczy, S. (2004). *In Her Name: Women Doing Theology*. Cluster

Ravi, S., & Ahluwalia, S. (2017). What Explains Childhood Violence? Micro Correlates from VACS Surveys. *Psychology, Health & Medicine, 22*(S1), 17–30.

Richter, M. S., & Mlambo, G. T. (2005). Perceptions of Rural Teenagers on Teenage Pregnancy. *Health SA Gesondheid, 10*(2), 61–69.

Ruether, P. R. (1983). *Sexism and God-talk*. SCM.

Schippers, M. (2007). Recovering the Feminine Other: Masculinity, Femininity, and Gender Hegemony. *Department of Sociology, Women's Studies Program, 56*, 85–102.

Scorgie, F. (2002). Virginity Testing and the Politics of Sexual Responsibility: Implications for Aids Interventions. *African Studies, 61*(1), 55–75.

Times of Eswatini, Monday. (2023). *Church Discourages Use of Muti, Promotes Chastity*.

UNFPA. (2019). *Gender-Based Violence*. https://www.unfpa.org/gender-based-violence.

Unger, R. (1979). *Female and Male: Psychological Perspectives*. Harper & Row Publishers.

Walby, S. (1986). Gender, Class and Stratification: Toward a New Approach. In R. Crompton & M. Mann (Eds.), *Gender and Stratification*, Blackwell.

WHO. (2010). *Preventing Intimate Partner and Sexual and Sexual Violence Against Women: Taking Action and Generating Evidence*. Geneva, World Health Organization. https://www.who.int/violence_injury_prevention/publications/violence/9789241564007_eng.pdf

Women and Law in Southern Africa. (WLSA). (2001). *Multiple Jeopardy: Domestic Violence and Women's Search for Justice in Swaziland. Women and the Law in Southern Africa Research and Educational Trust*.

Women's Traditional Songs. Unpublished MA Thesis. Saint Mary's University, Halifax.

World Health Organization. (2014). Health Care for Women Subjected to Intimate Partner Violence or Sexual Violence, A Clinical Handbook. http://apps.who.int/iris/bitstream/10665/136101/1/WHO_RHR_14.26_eng.pdf [accessed 19 June 2023]

Zungu, P. (2000). *Virginity Testing as a Cultural Practice*, Richards Bay, Commission on Gender Equality.

Zwane, B. (2013). *Gender links for Equality News Services. Swaziland Office*.

Changing Contexts, Changing Violence Patterns? The Case of African Diaspora Women

Nomatter Sande and Amos Muyambo

1 Introduction

What has been popularized in most scholarship about domestic violence in Zimbabwe and other contexts is the idea of males abusing women and the picture that has been painted is that men are the sole perpetrators of violence. There is a lot of concentration on violence against women (Mukamana et al., 2020; Muyambo, 2022; Zalewski et al., 2018; Zengenene & Susanti, 2019). Women are particularly vulnerable to violence because of their relatively low status and lack of power within the family. However, in most studies, cases of violence against men (VAM) are relatively unknown. The reality is that VAM by women is prevalent. Admittedly, most societies do not talk about VAM. According to Adebayo (2014), in most societies gender violence is a serious problem, which must be understood in context, and VAM is a reality. Undoubtedly, VAM should also be considered alongside violence against women.

The patriarchal nature of most societies, including African society, and men's bloated egos cause VAM to remain unreported. The extent to which masculinities suffer from femininities through violence remains unknown,

---

N. Sande (✉)
University of KwaZulu Natal, Durban, South Africa
e-mail: pastornomsande@yahoo.com

A. Muyambo
Department of Student Welfare in the Disability Support Services, University of Botswana, Gaborone, Botswana

partly because of the way men are socialized in African communities and largely because of their portrayal as perpetrators of gender violence and women as victims in most studies that have been done. Most studies have concentrated on gender violence implicating men, and this has led to the invisibility of the prevalence of VAM in our societies (Barber, 2008; Drijber et al., 2013). Accordingly, men do suffer from Gender Based Violence (GBV) (Adebayo, 2014; Kumar, 2012; Muyambo, 2022). Men would rather suffer in silence because of their inexpressive natures or from fear of being ridiculed and, thus, emasculated. The form(s) of abuse men suffer at the hands of women may differ from those experienced by women, nonetheless this does not diminish the impact of GBV against men. While VAM happens in diverse contexts, this chapter argues that diasporic contexts are creating opportune spaces for VAM. Migration and settlement within host nations offer factors that act as key drivers for women to perpetuate VAM. This chapter stimulates this discourse by asserting that it might actually be the case that African diasporic women perpetrate VAM on a larger scale than has generally been assumed. Such a statement is not only a strong claim that may be difficult to sustain, but also puts in motion a discussion of how men are vulnerable to violence by women. We start by showing some overall statistics about violence against men by women. This is followed by positioning masculinity as a conceptual lens to understand both men and constructions of violence, and the possibilities of these views as precursors of women's VAM. Further, the chapter uses the case of Zimbabwean men in the United Kingdom (UK) to present snippets of the forms of violence perpetrated by women against men in diasporic contexts.

2 Global Statistics About Violence Against Men

Violence against men is a reality and one in six men have experienced some form of sexual violence (Greenough, 2021). Adebayo (2014) cites a global survey conducted in Canada in 2004, which found that "the percentages of males being physically or sexually victimized by their partners was 6% versus 7% for women." According to the *Nursing Standard Journal* (Barber, 2008), the following studies and statistics show evidence of VAM at almost the same levels as violence against women in Britain and America. "The 2001/2002 British Crime Survey found that 19% of domestic violence incidents affected male victims, and that about half of these incidents were committed by women" (BBC, 2005). The 2004/2005 British Crime Survey found that partner abuse was the most common form of intimate violence; 28% of women and 18% of men had experienced one or more forms of partner abuse (Finney & Development and Statistics Directorate Great Britain/Home Office/Research, 2006).

> Using time as a marker, Fontes (1999) suggested that while men abuse their female partner every 15 seconds in the United States (US), females abuse their male partner every 14.6 seconds. This male/female equality is supported by Gelles (1999), suggesting that violence between genders is equal. (Barber, 2008: 36)

Correspondingly, studies conducted in the Netherlands have also confirmed similarities with the findings of Barber (2008). According to Drijber et al. (2013: 173), "the impact is hard to deny when realizing that in the Netherlands 45% of all inhabitants have been a victim of DV at least once in their lives and 11% of this group suffers permanent physical damage". Kumar (2012) writing on experiences in India claims that role changes and power relations have brought an increase in violence against men. Kumar (2012) points out that both women and men are naturally violent and aggressive. Little information surrounds the prevalence of VAM in India, but estimation suggests that for every 100 cases of DV, 40% involve VAM (Kumar, 2012). Considering these statistics, men do suffer from gender violence at similar levels to women (Drijber et al., 2013) and cases in the West are higher than in African communities, presumably because of limited studies or the context, where men are more dominant, and their roles as providers are still highly regarded.

"The abuse of men happens in different ways which include, emotional blackmail, physical, and sexual intimidation tactics" (Mbandlwa, 2020: 6760). According to the studies that have been done, the most common types of violence suffered by men include: verbal, emotional, and psychological cruelty, including humiliation and intimidation; and physical violence, such as teeth being knocked out, slapping, biting, scratching, being seized by the throat, being kicked in the genitals, stabbing, and being threatened with a weapon, among others, enlightening us that even if men traditionally have been defined as strong and perceived as having more physical strength than women, there are other ways in which violence can be inflicted on men by women (Adebayo, 2014; Barber, 2008; Drijber et al., 2013). Some of the issues that have made it difficult to quantify VAM include failure to report cases, non-admission by men that they are being abused, inadequate support systems (as most tend to focus on women), and the tendency to focus on physical violence at the expense of emotional violence, among other factors (Barber, 2008; Zalewski et al., 2018). Violence against men is a reality, but society does not take it seriously and, therefore, VAM remains unnoticed (Zalewski et al., 2018) and a one-sided narrative, according to Mbandlwa (2020). This discussion does not approve of any form of violence and proposes that, in order to finding lasting solutions to the problems of GBV, it must be acknowledged that VAM is also a reality and strategies to end GBV must be inclusive and collaborative. Therefore, more research needs to be conducted in the subject to establish the real facts on the ground and "there is a need to holistically address domestic violence without attaching a gender to it" (Mbandlwa, 2020: 6754).

3 Masculinity as a Conceptual Framework

This chapter uses masculinity as a conceptual lens to understand the nature of men. Understanding masculinities in African communities is complex and problematic as it is influenced by diversities, social structures, and culture and mostly perceived from Western perspectives, as well as being little researched. Colonialism has peddled myths about Africa and her diverse cultural heritage; such myths have largely presented Africa, her people and culture in sadistic ways according to Makaudze and Gudhlanga (2012: 11). One thing that is clear is that gender roles are clearly defined, and male dominance is evident in most cultures. Men hold power over women in most African communities. This unequal power has often been linked to masculinities' violence (Dube, 2007).

Conversely, to understand masculinities we must deal with the actual concept of gender in African context. According to Oyewumi (2005), gender in African studies is problematic "for many feminist scholars, however the debates surrounding gender hinge not merely on difference, but on hierarchies of dominance and submission" (Oyewumi, 2005: 113). This shows that power relations are very important in understanding the concept of gender. Gender "defines the roles that our societies ascribe to us as men and women, and these relationships give more power to men than women" (Dube, 2007: 350). These roles are very strong in African communities, including in Zimbabwe, where women are defined by their domestic and care-giving roles even if they are working outside the household domain. The above definitions show that gender is not only a biological construct but also a social one. An important factor that comes out is the question of power relations and how society has given more power to males over females which has created problems in how these genders relate to one another.

Historically, interest in the study of masculinities has increased in recent years due to enhanced awareness of inequalities in society, and knowledge about masculinity, health, education, and fatherhood (Connell, 2005), diversities of masculinities and the challenges of gender-based violence's globally. According to Togarasei (2012: 149) masculinity "is a set of behaviour patterns that men ought to follow in a certain society." On the other hand, Dube points out that masculinities differ with time and takes contexts of culture, and race, among others, into consideration (Dube, 2013). In view of these assertions, we can understand that masculinities are diverse, are not fixed but change over time, and are a social construction. The study of masculinities is, therefore, a continuous task. Tognoli (1981) adds another dimension, that still remains true today, to men's crisis by explaining how men strive to find their identity in view of the social changes around them. Changing social roles, unemployment, and women taking on more previously male-only jobs has put men in a crisis. He adds that the social pressure in society for men, especially in African culture, to be in a stable relationship and not to live as single males or alone is strong (Tognoli, 1981). Early socialization has a great influence in modelling men being outside the home and women being in the domestic or home sphere, he argues (Tognoli, 1981). This assertion on the pressures of socialization as agents of society have detrimental effects as men find themselves in relationships resulting in marriage conflicts. According to Balswick (1981: 111) "much of that which constitutes masculine behaviour is presented as something males should not do rather than as something they should do." Looking at the current problems of GBV, not much has been investigated or proposed on what men should do, the factors influencing their behaviours, or how they suffer gender violence. Balswick emphasizes inexpressiveness which is a characteristic of males that has been negatively defined (Balswick, 1981). He defines an inexpressive male as one who does not verbally express his feelings, either because he has no feelings or because he has been socialized not to express his feelings (Balswick, 1981). Suggesting that the reason why men do not express their feelings is because of the role they are expected to play in society and, thus, inexpressiveness becomes a personality trait and behaviour (Balswick, 1981). He argues that inexpressiveness is a social construct (Balswick, 1981). The socialization and expectations of society play a major role especially in Africa where men are moulded not to show or express emotions in public (Chitando & Biri, 2013) as this is regarded as a sign of weakness that is associated with feminine behaviour. One becomes less of a man by expressing feelings. This has led men to view themselves as superhuman beings through societal modelling and becoming resilient. This illustrates that we do not have an actual view of what men are going through in relationships in the Zimbabwean community and beyond. What is much publicized and documented is that men are perpetrating violence against women. Masculinity is, therefore, expressed as physical courage, competitiveness, and aggressiveness (Balswick, 1981). To express gentleness and expressiveness are seen as feminine expressions (Balswick, 1981; Chitando & Biri, 2013).

4   Models of Masculinities in Context

Understanding masculinity in the Zimbabwean context is a precursor to appreciating how this may impact them in diasporic contexts like the UK. The study of masculinities is a relatively new phenomenon in the African context and there has been little study of African masculinities in specific socio-religious contexts (Chitando & Biri, 2013; Van Klinken, 2012). A man in the Zimbabwean culture is seen as strong, resilient, and inexpressive. The idiom *kufa kwemurume kubuda ura* (a man's death is seen through the coming out of intestines) shows resilience, courage and being strong willed. Men in diverse cultures such as the Shona, or Ndebele cultures are not expected to show emotions such as crying as this denotes weakness and woman-like behaviour which is felt to be shameful by many men who do not like to be compared to women as this makes them feel a loss of their manhood identity (Chitando & Biri, 2013). These characteristics of boldness, strength, and resilience are hegemonic qualities that have been seen to be the foundation of harmful behaviours and violence (Chitando & Biri, 2013).

Culture is influential and where a culture favours men, hegemonic masculinity becomes dangerous to women and other men who are in minorities (Morrell, 2001; Muyambo, 2022; Ncube & Chawana, 2018). Ncube and Chawana (2018) define hegemonic Zimbabwean masculinities as dominant and the subordination of women through sports. What are hegemonic masculinities? Chitando and Biri (2013) in their analysis of Pentecostal masculinities state that hegemonic masculinities reflect resilience, toughness, and being physically strong (Chitando & Biri, 2013). Giving examples from the Shona culture, hegemonic values show controlling behaviours where men control women, children, and property, among other things (Chitando & Biri, 2013). Closely linked to this behaviour is overseeing the house as its head and the expectation that women and children should be submissive. According to Chitando and Biri (2013), hegemonic masculinity includes inexpressiveness. Men must not show emotions in public as this is perceived as a sign of weakness and feminine behaviour. Here, a man is being modelled to be superhuman and studies show that not expressing emotions makes tension to build up in an individual, resulting in very violent behaviour in releasing this internal tension. The male supremacy or "king of the streets" (Chitando & Biri, 2013) behaviour exhibited by men can be seen here as a platform for most GBV and other violent characteristics of men in African society. To be a man is a very strong aspect of Shona culture, so that boys are groomed not to be like women and this has created a non-acceptance of female domination "*murume haatongwi nemukadzi*" (Mangena, 2021). Real manhood is fluid in Shona culture, according to Mangena (2021), and portrays masculinities as being heads of households, protectors, breadwinners, married to submissive wives, and superior to women. This fluidity of masculinities can also explain the complexities men find themselves in in maintaining these culturally defined expectations of manhood, especially in unstable spaces such as in exile. "Exile comes with obstacles for refugee men's quest to conform to culturally defined masculinity" (Jaji, 2009: 177). Mangena (2021: 3) goes on to discuss:

> how social discourses of 'being dominated by one's wife' are invoked in 'modern' contexts where anti-patriarchal successes might have provoked significant shifts of gender roles. These social discourses shape the dramas that follow when husbands fail to live up to the patriarchal expectations of being the centre of power in their families.

Zimbabwean masculinities, given the above discussion, can be seen to involve dominance, being breadwinners, and holding more power over their female counterparts and this has meant GBV usually affects more women than men. Understanding this about masculinities in Zimbabwe elucidates how it is seen as shameful and less manly for a man to admit to being violated by a woman or to report cases of VAM, and he is often met with ridicule and not taken seriously. This is further confirmed by Greenough, (2021) arguing that "the shame and stigma around male sexual abuse are interwoven with contemporary social and cultural concepts of masculinity and are also found in the ancient world and biblical texts themselves."

Besides discussing masculinity issues, there is a need to reflect about gender relations and gender-based violence in Zimbabwe. The problem of GBV is a widespread one and has greatly contributed to the violation of human rights and dignity of many in Southern Africa and elsewhere in African communities (Thompson, 2013). Thus:

> Levels of Gender Based Violence remain a concern and a major barrier to women's active participation in development. Despite the enactment of several

gender responsive laws and policies, such as the Domestic Violence Act of 2007, women and girls in Zimbabwe, continue to be the victims in 99% of GBV cases especially within the private sphere. (Ministry of Women Affairs, Gender and Community Development 2012–2015: 2)

Gender-based violence in the Zimbabwean context has been fuelled by the harsh economic conditions that have influenced many men to have more power over households as they are the source of income and breadwinners. In some households, poverty has led to a lot of substance abuse which is an instigator of GBV (Boden, 2007; Muyambo, 2018; Sweetman, 1998). Gender-based violence is rife in Zimbabwe (Chitando, 2007; Mapuranga, 2012; Muyambo, 2022). Further, "Insights into the causes of gender-based violence have been traced to the gender imbalances that exist between women and men" (Getecha & Chipika, 1995). This means that gender inequalities continue to be a key factor in understanding the GBV problem in Zimbabwe. A patriarchal Shona society is also a cause, as males are considered to be leaders of the social units. Patriarchy is the rule by the male head of social family units. Patriarchy is best defined as domination by men and how men have power and control over women. This control has led to the perpetration of GBV by men against women (Getecha & Chipika, 1995). Economic and social factors that exploit female labour and the female body are also responsible for GBV (Getecha & Chipika, 1995). Other forms of GBV occurring in Zimbabwe are economic, marital, and inheritance (Getecha & Chipika, 1995). The history of Southern Africa shows that people emerged from a hunter-gatherer pastoralist background; the ownership of livestock also defined the status and power of men as more livestock meant more power and influence (Wadley, 1997). Other aspects that defined manhood in Zimbabwe include: fatherhood, *musoro wemba* (being head of household), being the family provider, a hard worker and strong willed, as well as inexpression, sexual dominance and resilience.

5 The Case of Diasporic Zimbabwean Women Perpetrating Violence Against Men

The chapter uses the case of diasporic Zimbabwean women perpetrating VAM as a case study to show that, regardless of masculinity, men are vulnerable to women's violence. It is worth noting that this subject does not have much information as men are usually not willing to tell their stories. For this reason, what is available is critical to start the discourse about the subject matter.

Generally, there is a sudden change of economic positions between men and women on arriving in the UK. Zimbabwean men are used to conforming to the Shona proverb that asserts that *murume ndiye musoro wemba* (a man is the head of the family), which also defines a man in Shona culture (Chitando & Biri, 2013). This is a defining quality that has been central in Shona culture that makes men heirs, heads of households, leaders, decision makers, advisors, and the final disciplinarians in a family. A man is one who is a family person, married with children and who has a house and profession or trade that makes him a provider in the family. In studies and critiques that have been undertaken by scholars, men as providers and heads of households have been used by some men to wield power and use it to violate women and children in relationships (Mungwini & Matereke, 2010). Thus, a man in Zimbabwe can be identified as one who is head of a household, a provider, family man, strong, resilient, courageous, dominant, one who does not express emotions and is hypersexual (Chitando & Biri, 2013).

One might question why the particular reference to the diaspora? The socio-political situation in Zimbabwe has led to a mass movement of Zimbabweans in diaspora particularly in the UK (Mhishi, 2017) and this migration has caught scholarly attention, according to Chitando et al. (2023). This Zimbabwean exodus has seen both women and men in domestic and care industries which were traditionally female-dominated occupations in Zimbabwe. Whatever the circumstances, migration of Zimbabweans in diaspora has had an impact on their socio-religious lives and, in this particular instance, on gender. As much as we strive for sustainable gender development towards an equal society, we must be aware of the transitions caused by contemporary factors such as migration and violence and take these into consideration in mapping a way forward towards an inclusive and peaceful society. According to Chitando et al. (eds.) (2023) *Gendered Spaces, Religion and Migration in Zimbabwe*, engendering spaces that are male dominated creates places of power that exclude women. However, with migration these spaces have economically empowered women where socio-cultural definitions are redefined and this has influenced some women to perpetrate violence in intimate relationships, prompting us to be mindful of our strategies in finding lasting solutions to gender-based violence in our communities.

Comparatively, the UK context has reconstructed Zimbabwean women to become breadwinners and some women fail to manage this power. One woman in an empirical study by Pasura and Christou (2018: 529) about the experiences of men in the UK explains:

> I don't know what is happening. One of the things that is causing marriages to break down is that women who were not breadwinners suddenly they are

the main providers for families. Good marriages, people came with they were married, they were good, but they are breaking here. I have heard young wives who started having lots of money and the moment she starts having lots of money she starts saying he is having the same amount as me, they became wild, and you try to control them, and you wonder this woman tend to be so good what is the problem now.

Such an account highlights that the economic changes, gender relations, and roles in a diasporic context open avenues for women either to take revenge for abuses once done to them by men, or simply to perpetrate VAM. Due to migration, most men who were breadwinners and decision-makers and held power in the family lose this privileged status in diaspora. Such a drastic change is a key factor framing most drivers of VAM. Women occupy influential positions and control income sources. Women's professions enable them to earn more than their male counterparts. Even without professions, women are not ashamed of doing general work, unlike men.

Most men tend to return to Zimbabwe (the homeland) because of such violence or choose to suffer in silence. Other abused Zimbabweans in the UK marry women from countries like Thailand and some unfortunate individuals end up with mental health issues (The Zimbabwe Mail, 2018). Chitando and Chirongoma (2012) emphasize that the forms of masculinities that are lifegiving, that is the behaviours and attitudes of men that bring healing in a society, are reeling from the effects of violence and disease. The sexual dominance aspect of Zimbabwean masculinities has been evidenced by promiscuous behaviours, polygamy, and unofficial marriage relationships called "small houses" (Muyambo & Muyangata, 2022). African masculinities are culturally formed and socially prescribed (Chitando & Chirongoma, 2012).

Migration status has been used by many women to abuse men in the UK, especially women who receive their citizenship status before their husbands. According to Pasura (2014), how Zimbabwean women in the UK exercise power and control is equated to that of the difficult processes of the UK Home Office, as women give permission to men to either go out, socialise or do other chores, it is similar to how difficult process to get UK's settlement visa. Men suffered in silence fearing that their visa status could be revoked by women. One young man reported that,

My life has been turned upside down. My wife started not coming home saying she had long days and nights at work. She became abusive and would hit, kick, bite, punch, spit, throw things, or destroy my possessions. She would tell me that "border *ndi maenzanise*," meaning we were now equal after entering the

UK. If I tried to stand up to her, she would call the police. She would attack me while I was asleep or otherwise catch me by surprise. She started using weapons such as pots and knives or strike me with an object or threaten our children. She would tell me that if I tried to retaliate, she would take me off her visa. (Herald, 2020)

The above statement shows how men are likely to suffer in silence. Men are modelled not to show or express emotions in public (Chitando & Biri, 2013: 47). This has been problematic as very few men speak out to report gender violence. It is unheard of, or shameful to claim that one is being violated by a woman. The toughness qualities of Shona man have made them reluctant to speak out when they are victims of female violence. This has led to low levels of reporting of GBV cases, and we may never know the extent to which men have suffered from GBV. Unquestionably, masculinity makes men vulnerable to abuse by women in diasporic contexts because the male view of masculinity is shaped by the family institution, peer group, and mass media coverage and, therefore, social structures are important in our understanding of inexpressiveness as male behaviour (Balswick, 1981). Diasporic contexts like the UK do not have a competitive social support structure but offer professional counselling and support groups which are alien to many migrants.

One striking factor that has emanated from the discussion is that of gender power dynamics. The power to control (Mbandlwa, 2020) and dominate in intimate partner relationships has led to violence. It is evident that when one has power chances of abuse increase, as shown in the empowerment of Zimbabwean women in diaspora. The authors do not imply that all women in diaspora are perpetrating violence, but VAM is evident due to diaspora women gaining economic power in the UK. The one who wields power has the potential to misuse it. Understanding these gender power dynamics will inform effective programming strategies.

6   Conclusion

The argument that men are on record as perpetrating violence against women cannot be contested. Prominent reasons for such a status quo include, but are not limited to, the fact that men hold dominance in power relations, are economic holders of households, and control intimate relationships. Of course, culture has also modelled women to be submissive domestic carers, and even if women work as professionals, they are expected to play their domestic roles as housekeepers. Many men from Zimbabwe have struggled to take on domestic and care-giving occupations in the diaspora. Economic tables have been overturned, and women hold more economic power than men. Unlike what has been studied and previously established, that is: male dominance, unequal structures in society, and masculinities as perpetrators or potential perpetrators of violence, the diasporic context makes men, as well as women, more vulnerable to abuse in intimate relationships. In comparison, sometimes men are suffering more from women perpetuating violence. For the most part, the problem is how masculinity models and socializes men to be inexpressive and resilient. Diasporic context(s) are offering spaces where VAM is more common than in Zimbabwe. Dealing with gender violence needs to be collaborative: men and women trying to resolve the issues together. Snippets about how Zimbabwean men in the UK are violated by women show that when women are placed in new contexts and provided with freedom and power, some have a propensity to perpetuate violence. Further studies are needed to raise awareness and suggest interventions in the fight against violence, and such studies must be inclusive. Assuredly, the studies should not solely be aiming to curb violence against women (VAW), but violence against both women and men (VAWM).

Bibliography

Adebayo, A. A. (2014). Domestic Violence Against Men: Balancing the Gender Issues in Nigeria. *American Journal of Sociological Research, 4*(1), 14–19. https://doi.org/10.5923/j.sociology.20140401.03

Balswick, J. O. (1981). Types of Inexpressive Male Roles. In R. A. Lewis (Ed.), *Men in Difficult Times: Masculinity Today and Tomorrow* (pp. 111–119). Prentice-Hall.

BBC. (2005). *Prevalence of Male Victims*. Available at: https://www.google.com/search?q=The+2001%2F02+British+Crime+Survey+found+that+19%25+of+domestic+violence+incidents+affected+male+victims%2C+and+that+about+half+of+these+incidents+were+committed+by+women&rlz=1C5CHFA_enGB977GB977&oq=The+2001%2F02+British+Crime+Survey+found+that+19%25+of+domestic+violence+incidents+affected+male+victims%2C+and+that+about+half+of+these+incidents+were+committed+by+women&gs_lcrp=EgZjaHJvbWUyBggAEEUYOdIBCzg3NzgyMjJqMGowqAIAsAIA&sourceid=chrome&ie=UTF-8

Drijber, B. C., Reijnders, U. J. L., & Ceelen, M. (2013). Male Victims of Domestic Violence. *Journal of Family Violence, 28*, 173–178. https://doi.org/10.1007/s10896-012-9482-9

Barber, C. F. (2008). Domestic Violence Against Men. *Nursing Standard, 22*(51), 35–39.

Boden, A. L. (2007). *Women's Rights and Religious Practice Claims in Conflict*. Palgrave-Macmillan.

Carlson, K., & Randell, S. (2013). Gender and Development: Working with Men for Gender Equality in Rwanda. *Agenda: Empowering Women for Gender Equity.* https://doi.org/10.1080/10130950.2013.796075

Chitando, E. (2007). *Acting in Hope: African Churches and HIV/AIDS* (Vol. 2). WCC.

Chitando, E., & Chirongoma, S. (Eds.). (2012). *Redemptive Masculinities: Men, HIV, and Religion.* WCC Publications.

Chitando, E., & Biri, K. (2013). Faithful Men of a Faithful God? Masculinities in the Zimbabwe Assemblies of God Africa. *Exchange, 43*, 34–50.

Chitando, E., Chirongoma, S., & Manyonganise, M. (Eds.). (2023). *Gendered Spaces, Religion and Migration in Zimbabwe: Implications for Economic Development.* Routledge.

Connell, R. W. (2005). *Masculinities* (2nd ed.). University of California.

Dube, M. W. (2007). Who Do You Say That I Am? *Feminist Theology Journal, 15*(3), 346–367.

Dube, M. W. (2012). Youth Masculinities and Violence in an HIV and AIDS Context: Sketches from Botswana Cultures and Pentecostal Churches. In E. Chitando & S. Chirongoma (Eds.), *Redemptive Masculinities: Men, HIV, and Religion* (pp. 323–354). EHAIA Series. WCC.

Dube, M. (2013). Youth Masculinities and Violence in an HIV and AIDS Context: Sketches from Botswana Cultures and Pentecostal Churches. In E. Chitando & S. Chirongoma (Eds.), *Redemptive Masculinities: Men, HIV, and Religion* (pp. 323–354). EHAIA Series. WCC. Accessed 21 August 2018.

Finney, A., & Development and Statistics Directorate Great Britain/Home Office/Research. (2006). Domestic Violence, Sexual Assault and Stalking: Findings from the 2004/05 British Crime Survey (pp. 1–39). Home Office.

Getecha, C., & Chipika, J. (1995). *Zimbabwe Women's Voices.* ZWRCN.

Greenough, C. (2021). *The Bible and Sexual Violence Against Men.* Routledge.

Jaji, R. (2009). Masculinity on Unstable Ground: Young Refugee Men in Nairobi, Kenya. *Journal of Refugee Studies.* https://doi.org/10.1093/jrs/fep007

Kumar, A. (2012). Domestic Violence Against Men in India: A Perspective. *Journal of Human Behavior in the Social Environment, 22*(3), 290–296. https://doi.org/10.1080/10911359.2012.655988

Herald. (2020). Zimbabwean UK Diaspora Men Tormented by Their Wives. https://www.thezimbabwemail.com/relationships/zimbabwean-uk-diaspora-men-tormented-by-their-wives/

Makaudze, G., & Gudhlanga, E. S. (2012). The Defined Re-defined Themselves: Afro-Centered Myths for Self-Definition and Self-Analysis in Selected Postcolonial Novels. *Journal of Zimbabwe Studies, Arts, Humanities and Education, 1*(1), 1–12.

Magezi, V., & Manzanga, P. (2019). Gender Based Violence and Efforts to Address the Phenomenon: Towards a Church Public Pastoral Care Intervention Proposition for Community Development in Zimbabwe. *HTS Theological Studies Journal.* ISSN (online) 2072-8050, AOSIS 1–9.

Mangena, T. (2021). Gendering Roles, Masculinities and Spaces: Negotiating Transgression in Charles Mungoshi's and Other Writings. *African Identities*. https://doi.org/10.1080/14725843.2021.1929062

Mapuranga, T. (2012). 'Tozeza Baba,' Gender-Based Violence in Oliver Mtukudzi's Music. *Muziki: Journal of Music Research in Africa, 9*(1), 58–70.

Masengwe, G. (2012). Macho Masculinity: A Snare in the Context of HIV Among the Manyika of Zimbabwe. In E. Chitando & S. Chirongoma (Eds.), *Redemptive Masculinities: Men, HIV, and Religion* (pp. 289–304). EHAIA Series. WCC.

Mbandlwa, Z. (2020). Analysis of a One-Sided Narrative of Gender-Based Violence in South Africa. *Solid State Technology, 63*(6), 6754–6768. http://orcid.org/0000-0002-7528-3565

Mhishi, L. C. (2017). *Songs of Migration: Experiences of Music, Place Making and Identity Negotiation Amongst Zimbabweans in London* (Doctoral Thesis). Department of Anthropology and Sociology SOAS, University of London.

Ministry of Women Affairs, Gender and Community Development 2012–2015, Government of Zimbabwe.

Mukamana, I., et al. (2020). Trends in Prevalence and Correlates of Intimate Partner Violence Against Women in Zimbabwe, 2005–2015. *BMC International Health and Human Rights, 20*(2). https://doi.org/10.1186/s12914-019-0220-8

Mungwini, R., & Matereke, K. (2010, August 10). Rape, Sexual Politics and Construction of Manhood Among the Shona of Zimbabwe: Some Philosophical Reflections Thought and Practice. *A Journal of the Philosophical Association of Kenya, 2*(1), 1–19.

Muyambo, A. (2022). *Masculinities in the African Independent Churches: A Case Study of the Apostles Church of John Marange and Guta Ra Jehovha African Independent Churches* (Doctoral Thesis). Department of Theology and Religious Studies, University of Botswana, Gaborone.

Muyambo, A., & Muyangata, J. (2022). The 'Small House' Phenomenon and Its Impact on Zimbabwean Women's Sexual Reproductive Health and Rights (SRHR). In S. Chirongoma, M. Manyonganise, & E. Chitando (Eds.), *Religion, Women's Health Rights, and Sustainable Development in Zimbabwe: Volume 2* (pp. 73–88). Springer International Publishing.

Muyambo, A. (2018). *A Church's Response to Gender-Based Violence in South Africa* (Master's Research). St Augustine College SA, Linden.

Ncube, L., & Chawana, F. (2018). What Is in a Song? Constructions of Hegemonic Masculinity by Zimbabwean Football Fans. *Muziki, 15*(1), 68–88. https://doi.org/10.1080/18125980.2018.1503560

Njovana, E., & Watts, C. (1996). Gender Violence in Zimbabwe: A Need for Collaborative Action. *Reproductive Health Matters, 4*(7), 46–55. https://doi.org/10.1016/S0968-8080(96)90005-1

Oyewumi, O. (2005). *African Gender Studies*. Palgrave Macmillan.

Pasura, D. (2014). *African Transnational Diasporas: Fractured Communities and Plural Identities of Zimbabweans in Britain*. Palgrave Macmillan.

Pasura, D., & Christou, A. (2018). Theorizing Black (African) Transnational Masculinities. *Men and Masculinities, 21*(4), 521–546.

Sweetman, C. (Ed.). (1998). *Gender, Religion, and Spirituality*. Oxfam GB.

The Zimbabwe Mail. (2018). *Zimbabwean Men in UK Suffer Abuse in Silence*. https://www.thezimbabwemail.com/diaspora-news/zimbabwean-men-in-uk-suffer-abuse-in-silent/

Thompson, A. (Ed.). (2013). *What Price? Bride Price*. Uganda: MIFUMI. Accessed on YouTube 9 May 2020.

Togarasei, L. (2012). Pauline Challenge to African Masculinities: Reading Pauline Texts in the Context of HIV and AIDS. *Acta Theologica, 2012*(Suppl. 16), 148–160. https://doi.org/10.4314/actat.v32i1S.9ISSN1015-8758

Tognoli, J. (1981). Men in space. In R. A. Lewis (Ed.), *Men in Difficult Times: Masculinity Today and Tomorrow* (pp. 121–133). Prentice-Hall.

Van Klinken, A. S. (2012). Men in the Remaking: Conversion Narratives and Born-Again Masculinity in Zambia. *Journal of Religion in Africa, 42*, 175–295.

Wadley, L. (Ed.). (1997). *Our Gendered Past: Archaeological Studies of Gender in Southern Africa*. Witwatersrand University Press.

Zalewski et al. (2018). *Sexual Violence Against Men in Global Politics*. Routledge Taylor & Francis Group.

Zengenene, M., & Susanti, E. (2019). Violence Against Women and Girls in Harare, Zimbabwe. *Journal of International Women's Studies, 20*(9), 83–93. https://vc.bridgew.edu/jiws/vol20/iss9/8

Zimbabwe National Gender-Based Strategy 2012–2015. *Ministry of Women Affairs, Gender and Community Development*. Harare: UNFPA.

Adolescent Boys, Young Men, and Mental Health in Southern Africa

Mutsawashe Chitando

1 Introduction

Young people constitute the bulk of the demographic dividend in Africa. 70% of the African population are under the age of 30 (Muhia & Nanji, 2021). This group is also the fastest growing share of the African population. The United Nations defines "youth" as those between the ages of 15 and 24 (Bersaglio et al., 2015). Another important group in Africa are adolescents, who are defined as those between the ages of 10 and 19 years. Adolescence is a unique time in the developmental stages of an individual where physical, sexual, and behavioural maturation occur (Thupayagale-Tsheweage & Mokomane, 2012). It is a "multi-system transitional process involving progression from the immaturity and social dependency of childhood into adult life with the goal and expectation of fulfilled developmental potential, personal agency, and social accountability" (Curtis, 2015). It is important that young people receive the needed support to facilitate their transition from childhood to adulthood.

Investing in the health and well-being of young people is part of the Sustainable Development Agenda, as it falls under Sustainable Development Goal 3. The goal which advocates for healthy lives and well-being for everyone in all ages (Dyakova, 2017). This investment addresses the health-related challenges that deter young people from reaching their full

M. Chitando (✉)
University of Cape Town, Cape Town, South Africa
e-mail: chtmut001@myuct.ac.za

potential. The other challenges that young people battle with include unemployment, poverty, high human-immunodeficiency virus (HIV) and sexually transmitted infections burden, illicit drugs, dropping out of school, being orphaned, exposure to violence, and substance abuse, amongst others (Sharpe et al., 2021; Simegn et al., 2021; Sui et al., 2021). The emergence of COVID-19 coupled these pre-existing challenges with feelings of hopelessness, despair, and uncertainty. All these factors, when combined, render adolescents and young people vulnerable to poor mental health (Buckley et al., 2020). An estimated 10–20% of adolescents globally experience mental health disorders, depression being one of the leading causes of illness and disability in this age group, and suicide the second leading cause of death (Ouansafi et al., 2021). Gender-based violence (GBV) has been coined as a shadow pandemic during the COVID-19 pandemic. While this holds true, there is yet another shadow pandemic in the form of the mental health crisis precipitated by COVID-19. The mental health crisis is also threatening to reverse the strides made in addressing GBV and other forms of violence throughout the world.

The conditions that were put in place by most countries in Southern Africa to curb the spread of the virus resulted in the loss of jobs, loss of income, confinement to homes, and children and adolescents being kept out of school (Govender et al., 2020). Some adolescents were also reported as worrying about the loss of income of their parents because of COVID-19 (Gittings et al., 2021). Not being at work or at school and spending days on end at home also brought in feelings of a lack of purpose which has been cited as a driver for poor mental health (Gittings et al., 2021). The conditions aimed at ameliorating the coronavirus undoubtedly posed as significant stressors in the lives of those affected by the disease. People felt stressed from the fear of becoming infected, the fear of losing loved ones to infection, and the uncertainty of when it would all end. On one front, there were mental health repercussions resulting from the measures that were put in place to curb the spread of the virus (anxiety, exposure to violence, and loneliness), and on the other front there were also the mental health repercussions of the virus itself (neurological symptoms) (Rahman et al., 2020b).

At the time of writing, June 2021, COVID has been around since November 2019. While the literature around COVID-19 is growing, there is still a dearth of studies that interrogate the mental health implications of this pandemic. In addition to this, this paper capitalizes on the opportunity to contribute to the growing body of evidence on mental health in Africa. The discourse on mental health in Africa is growing in response to the COVID-19 pandemic. This chapter seeks to identify the opportunities and challenges that exist in the mental health of adolescent boys and young men in Southern Africa. It also explores the opportunities for future research while also providing recommendations on how the mental health of adolescent boys and young men could be improved. This chapter is formatted to include the introduction, methods, discussion, and the conclusion.

2 Methodology

A scoping review of the literature was conducted using different electronic databases. The electronic databases were PsycInfo, Web of Science, Medline, and PubMed. Boolean operators were used to find alternatives for the key word searches and to combine the different search terms.

We developed the following search string:

> "adolescent OR teen OR teenagers OR youth OR young people OR young adults"] AND "mental health OR mental illness OR mental disorder OR mental condition OR mental ill health OR mental ill-health OR mental wellbeing OR (mental wellness or mental well-being) OR mental health services OR mental health stigma"] AND "southern Africa OR Namibia OR Angola OR Botswana OR Lesotho OR South Africa OR Mozambique OR Zambia OR Zimbabwe OR Swaziland"] AND "covid-19 or coronavirus or 2019-ncov or sars-cov-2 or cov-19"].

Articles were included if their focus (either primary or secondary) was on adolescent boys or young men in Southern Africa. The articles needed to have a mental health component for them to be included in the scoping review. The articles were filtered by year and included articles from 2011 to 2021. The reason for this was to identify the trends in mental health for this group in the last decade. To retrieve articles which were specific to the mental health effects of the pandemic, the term "COVID-19" was added to the search string. Both grey and published literature were included in the scoping review. Only studies reported in English were included. The retrieved articles were exported to EndNote for eligibility screened. The articles were screened by title, followed by abstract screening and then finally, full-text screening. The screening was done by a single author, who would seek clarity from experts where inclusion and exclusion were unclear.

A data extraction workbook was designed in Microsoft Excel. This workbook was used to extract information for each article on author, year, population group, issue of public health concern, intervention, recommendations, and areas of future research. Data were extracted from the eligible articles followed by a thematic analysis to collate the main themes emerging from the articles. These themes will be discussed in the subsequent sections.

3 Study Limitations

The results of this study are not meant to be conclusive, rather, they are aimed at exploring the state of mental health of adolescent boys and young men in Southern Africa. It is worth noting some of the study limitations for those who might want to inform future research or decisions based on these findings, or to expand on the scope of this research. The focus on the last decade does not give an accurate depiction of the change over time in the mental health of adolescent boys and young men. The chapter does not provide a full reflection of how gender differences affect mental health. It is also focused on mental health issues related to specific group, thereby missing out on the opportunity to explore some of the mental-health-related issues emerging in children and in the elderly. The articles included were only on Southern Africa and are not a true reflection of the African continent. Furthermore, only articles which were reported in English were included in the review. The scoping review might also have benefited from having two reviewers conducting it to minimize researcher bias.

4 Study Themes

The themes identified from the articles retrieved were grouped into HIV, exposure to violence, livelihoods, COVID-19, social media, culture, and education. In this section, we draw on the findings from the scoping review to map the landscape for the mental health of adolescent boys and men in Southern Africa.

Adolescent Boys and Young Men

Adolescence is a life stage of immense biological, cognitive, emotional, and social change (National Academies of Sciences & Medicine, 2019). The second decade of life is a time in which many young people aspire to greater individual autonomy, establish a sense of self, and explore relationships beyond familial bonds with peers, romantic and sexual partners (Toska et al., 2019). As such, adolescents need all the support they can get in navigating this unique time where one is still a boy, but one's body is now resembling that of an adult. Some of these changes can be overwhelming to those experiencing them, and without the adequate guidance, adolescents might make some decisions which they might not be able to live with in their adult years. Depression is also common during this developmental stage (Beirão et al., 2020). Unfortunately there might be some adolescent boys experiencing depression during this transitional phase, struggling to share this with someone. Admitting that they are not okay might be interpreted as being weak.

According to Chinoda et al. (2020), positive mental health outcomes often lead to positive adolescence and vice versa. Having a strong support system during adolescence might positively influence the experience. Those who received this kind of support, in a study by Boyes et al. (2019) on adolescents in South Africa, were reported to have improved mental health outcomes compared to those who did not. These study findings were also consistent with those from a study by Muhia and Nanji (2021) in East and Southern Africa which revealed that psychosocial care and mental health promotion to support youth mental health can help prevent psychopathology and promote physical health amongst youths. This support can come in the form of family, friends, and the community at large.

With young men, there are also pressures associated with being a young man. They are faced with the responsibility of figuring out their employment, the pressure of starting their own families, pressure from society and friends to be a person that they might not be, and financial stress amongst others (Muhia & Nanji, 2021). Raising children, breaking chains of poverty in their family, and risky social behaviours are among some of the stressors that young men face. Being qualified and yet being unemployed, frustration at underserving governments and politicians, and judgement from religious leaders constitute some of the issues that young men are faced with. All these life pressures are enough to pose a significant strain on the mental health and well-being of the parties affected, including young men and adolescents in Southern Africa (Mngoma et al., 2021).

Socio-cultural factors can significantly influence the mental health of adolescents and young men in Southern Africa (Somefun & Simo Fotso, 2020). Of note, some traditional gender norms and expectations do not support young men in seeking help for their mental health problems. This often perpetuates a culture of silence and self-reliance (Bosco et al., 2020). This culture of silence can exacerbate distress and the risk of engaging in violent behaviour as a coping mechanism among young men and adolescent boys. Violence and mental health exist in a cyclical relationship. Exposure to violence can have severe psychological consequences, leading to mental health problems (Hinsberger et al., 2016; Monteiro, 2015). Similarly, individuals with pre-existing mental health conditions may be more vulnerable to engaging in violent behaviours or becoming victims of violence. If these challenges are not addressed, they can derail the development of the Southern African region.

Framing Mental Health

The mental health landscape in Africa is often characterized as weak, fragmented, under-resourced and under-staffed. Mental health in Southern Africa is compounded by three main factors: ignorance about the extent of mental health problems, stigma against those with mental illness and misconceptions about the disease (Kometsi et al., 2020; Mfoafo-M'Carthy & Sossou, 2017). Some Africans, if not most, do not recognize mental illnesses as the psychiatric conditions they are, rather, they view them consequences of bewitchment or evil spirits (Atilola, 2016). The stigma associated with mental illness can be attributed to a lack of education, religious reasoning, or general prejudice. Social stigma associated with mental illness has meant that most people suffer in silence, equating mental illness to a silent pandemic. In most Southern African countries, there are no clear referral pathways for mental illness (Chibanda et al., 2016). Again, this results in adolescent boys and young men suffering in silence. In these African settings, positive mental health-seeking behaviours are associated with the affluent (Khumalo et al., 2012). Those who are less well-off consider mental health seeking to be a luxury that they cannot afford. In addition, there are blurry demarcations between mental well-being and mental illness which often result in people not seeking mental health services out of the fear of being labelled (Horsfield et al., 2019; Semrau et al., 2015). An individual can be mentally healthy, have a mental health condition, or be somewhere in between. In other words, mental health is a spectrum. People with mental health conditions may recover and have moments of optimum mental health, while people without mental health diagnoses may also experience times of poor mental well-being.

While there are significant strides that are being made in advocating for mental health, there are still some gaps which exist in the financing of mental health and there are still some gaps regarding the mental health workforce. Most of the low-middle income countries (LMICs) dedicate less than 1% of government funding to mental health care (Rathod et al., 2017). Also to be considered are the high out-of-pocket payments that individuals incur while accessing mental health services (Hailemichael et al., 2019). This poses a form of structural violence considering the correlation between poverty and mental ill-health. The living conditions of people who are poor, such as living in violent communities and facing food insecurities (Jesson et al., 2021; Stansfeld et al., 2017) often predispose them to poor mental health outcomes. At the onset of poor mental health outcomes, the poor cannot readily seek mental health services in the absence of financial protection (Rathod et al., 2017). People with pre-existing mental illnesses are more likely to be impoverished due to catastrophic health expenditure while accessing mental health services (Lee et al., 2016). The unaffordability of essential mental health services might contribute to decreased capacity to function optimally for individuals, further trapping them into poverty.

It is also worth noting the disruption of mental health services that was brought about by COVID-19, where governments were re-orienting health resources to meet the demand for clinical-based healthcare services induced by COVID-19. The funds which were being channelled into COVID-19 services were mostly to secure protective wear for frontline workers and to address the physical ailments associated with the disease. Not much was allocated in view of the mental health implications of the disease for both the frontline workers, the patients, and the families of the different groups affected by COVID-19 (Kola et al., 2021).

Mental Health and Pandemics

Historically, disease outbreaks have been known to have significant impacts on the mental health of the population affected (Esterwood & Saeed, 2020). After the West African Ebola virus disease (EVD) (2014–2016), individuals affected by the disease whether survivors, family members, care-givers or health workers were more likely to present symptoms of post-traumatic stress disorder, obsessive-compulsive disorder, psychological distress, sleep disorders, suicidal ideation, substance abuse, and social anxiety (Jalloh et al., 2018). There were reports of violence and civil unrest in some affected areas. These instances of violence were often fuelled by fear, misinformation, and mistrust between affected communities and healthcare workers, as well as government authorities. Additionally, the implementation of quarantine measures, contact tracing, and restrictions on movement sometimes led to social and economic disruption, exacerbating existing tensions within communities. It, therefore, suffices to say that acts of violence were not caused by the virus itself, but were a culmination of complex social, cultural, and economic factors that were amplified by the outbreak.

Similar trends were observed for HIV as there have been instances where violence and discrimination have affected young people living with or at risk of HIV. Young people living with HIV may face stigmatization, discrimination, and violence due to the persistent misconceptions and fears surrounding the virus (Jeffries et al., 2015). This can include verbal abuse, physical violence, exclusion from social activities, and even rejection by family and friends. Such experiences can lead to low self-esteem, mental health challenges, and reluctance to seek HIV-related services (Skovdal et al., 2011). Raymond and Zolnikov (2018) noted that adolescents who were orphaned with HIV were found to exhibit some antisocial tendencies compared to their counterparts. For adolescents living with HIV, adherence to treatment was found to be correlated to mental health status in a study by Buckley et al. (2020). Studies have shown that those with pre-existing mental health conditions often face difficulties in HIV treatment adherence while poor HIV treatment adherence can result in poor mental health outcomes.

As we grapple with the concept of mental health of young people in Africa, it is also important to view the mental health landscape in the context of COVID-19. The COVID-19 pandemic has had far-reaching impacts which may influence the mental health of individuals. On one front, we explore the impact of the COVID-19 regulations on the mental health of individuals. On another front, the disease also presented some patients with neurological symptoms. For instance, many individuals with "Long COVID" reported ongoing neurological symptoms such as brain fog, memory problems, fatigue, and difficulties with concentration (Rahman et al., 2020a). Long COVID refers to persistent symptoms that extend beyond the acute phase of the illness.

Likewise, the COVID-19 restrictions resulted in elevated anxiety and depression, fears of job loss and financial insecurity, surges in cases of violence, and a shortage of caregivers (Chitando, 2020). Exposure to violence amongst adolescents was cited as a driver for mental ill-health (Sharpe et al., 2021). For adolescents, the emergence of the pandemic meant the closure of schools and having to be confined in homes, away from peers, whose relations are crucial to their development (Gittings et al., 2021). Lockdowns, social isolation, and economic stress created tense and confined environments, exacerbating existing cases of domestic violence. Victims, especially adolescent boys had difficulties in seek help or escaping abusive situations due to restricted movement and limited access to psychosocial support services. In a desk review by Muhia and Nanji (2021) on youth mental health in the context of COVID-19 in East and Southern Africa, they reported that the disruption of peer support networks due to physical distancing was reported to exacerbate youth anxieties and depression. Consequently, there was a significant rise in the number of young people resorting to illicit drug and substance abuse, despite the closure of bars and restaurants.

In the wake of these pandemics, young people have been found offering peer-support to their counterparts in need, and volunteering for those who might not be in positions to fend for themselves. A typical example is the Zvandiri Programme which was developed by the Private Voluntary Organization, Africaid in Zimbabwe. In this programme peer supporters aged 18–24 years old and living with HIV are trained and mentored (Chinoda et al., 2020). These peer supporters are known as Community Adolescent Treatment Supporters (CATS) and they are integrated within the clinics, and surrounding communities, and generate demand for HIV services across the cascade, supporting ART initiation, adherence, linkage, and retention in care for their caseload of children, adolescents, and young people (Chinoda et al., 2020). By providing peer support, reducing stigma, promoting empowerment, and delivering mental health education, the programme offers valuable mental health benefits to young people living with HIV in Zimbabwe. Similarly, during the COVID-19 pandemic, some young people were reported to find new hobbies, practise good personal hygiene to protect their loved ones, and raise awareness of COVID-19.

Social Media and Mental Health

COVID-19 also gave rise to young people practising excessive television watching and high social media usage (Muhia & Nanji, 2021). Some of the social media platforms included WhatsApp, Twitter, Instagram, TikTok, and Snapchat. Adolescents interviewed in a study by Pretorius and Padmanabhanunni (2021) indicated that they felt that it was impossible to live without social media. Regulating the use of social media in adolescents is important because it brings with it the potential for cyber-bullying, another form of violence. Admittedly, it is a convenient way of messaging and keeping in touch with loved ones, especially when physical interactions are limited. The role of social media and mass media communication channels in social and behaviour change communication in the COVID-19 response was paramount. While some of the messages that were being communicated via these channels were from credible sources, there were also fake messages that were being communicated (Ahinkorah et al., 2020). This drove a sense of unease and panic across diverse settings in Southern Africa. Since the emergence of the pandemic, the messages that were being communicated were those concerned with prevention: thorough washing of hands with soap and clean running water, wearing of masks, physical distancing, and avoiding public gatherings, among others. These messages carried within them a message of hope and light at the end of the tunnel.

This chapter is summed up by reflecting on some key issues emerging from the scoping review and providing some recommendations based on these findings in the subsequent section.

5   Conclusion

The themes which emerged from this discussion on the mental health of adolescent boys and young men in Southern Africa included the interconnectedness of violence and mental health, stigma around mental illness, poverty as a driver for mental ill-health, low-fiscal space for mental health, and the blurry demarcations between mental illness and mental wellness. These challenges are multi-layered, and the solutions, therefore, should be multi-faceted as illustrated in the socio-ecological model (see Fig. 1) to improve the mental health outcomes for adolescent boys and young men in Southern Africa.

It is critical to engage different actors at different levels to achieve the desired mental health outcomes. These actors include governments, young people, civil society organizations, healthcare providers, educators, and community leaders. This could go a long way in demystifying mental health, at the same time improving the availability of mental health services at a community level. When mental-health-related challenges are identified at a community level, and addressed at a community level, this might prove to be a more cost-effective approach in meeting community mental health needs. The integration of mental health services into primary health care, and the involvement and engagement of community leaders in responding to mental health are also ways by which access, and acceptability of mental health services can be improved. Also critical is the implementation of programmes that address the root causes of violence, promote conflict resolution skills, and provide support for at-risk individuals in communities.

The stigma associated with mental health is a major contributory factor in the health-seeking behaviours for adolescent boys and young men (Chinoda et al., 2020). Lessons from HIV show the role of advocacy and health education in challenging stigma and misconceptions around infections and illnesses. Another lesson is the need to provide youth-friendly services to increase the uptake of the services that are being offered for young people

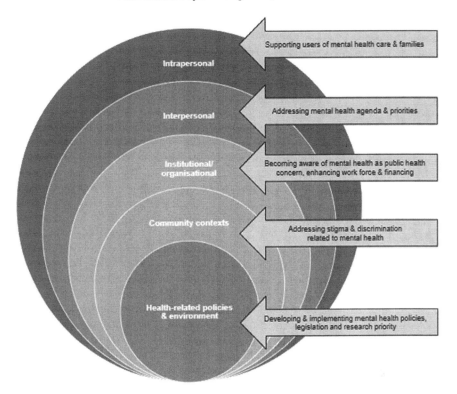

Fig. 1 Social ecological model adapted to mental health in Africa (*Source* Davids et al. [2019])

by young people. The services need to be available, affordable, and acceptable to the intended recipients (WHO, 2012). It is important to promote mental health awareness and strengthen mental health services to achieve positive-mental-health-seeking behaviours and outcomes.

References

Ahinkorah, B. O., Ameyaw, E. K., Hagan, J. E., Seidu, A.-A., & Schack, T. (2020). Rising Above Misinformation or Fake News Africa: Another Strategy to Control COVID-19 Spread. Frontiers in Communication. *5*, 45.

Atilola, O. (2016). Mental Health Service Utilization in Sub-Saharan Africa: Is Public Mental Health Literacy the Problem? Setting the Perspectives Right. *Global Health Promotion, 23*(2), 30–37.

Beirão, D., Monte, H., Amaral, M., Longras, A., Matos, C., & Villas-Boas, F. (2020). Depression in Adolescence: A Review. *Middle East Current Psychiatry, 27*(1).

Bersaglio, B., Enns, C., & Kepe T. (2015). Youth Under Construction: the United Nations' Representations of Youth in the Global Conversation on the Post-2015 Development Agenda. *Canadian Journal of Development Studies, 36*(1), 57–71.

Bosco, N., Giaccherini, S., & Meringolo, P. (2020). A Gender Perspective About Young People's Seeking Help. *Journal of Prevention & Intervention in the Community, 48*, 132–146.

Boyes, M. E., Cluver, L. D., Meinck, F., Casale, M., & Newnham, E. (2019). Mental Health in South African Adolescents Living with HIV: Correlates of Internalising and Externalising Symptoms. *AIDS Care, 31*(1), 95–104.

Buckley, J., Otwombe, K., Joyce, C., Leshabane, G., Hornschuh, S., Hlongwane, K., Dietrich, J., Grelotti, D. J., & Violari, A. (2020). Mental Health of Adolescents in the Era of Antiretroviral Therapy: Is There a Difference Between HIV-Infected and Uninfected Youth in South Africa? *Journal of Adolescent Health, 67*(1), 76–83.

Chibanda, D., Verhey, R., Munetsi, E., Rusakaniko, S., Cowan, F., & Lund, C. (2016). Scaling Up Interventions for Depression in sub-Saharan Africa: Lessons from Zimbabwe. *Global Mental Health, 3*, e13–e13.

Chitando, M. (2020). Narrowing the 'Physical Distance' Between Public Health Policies and Gender: An Analysis of Government Responses to COVID-19 in Zimbabwe and South Africa. *African Journal of Governance and Development, 9*(1.1), 352–366.

Chinoda, S., Mutsinze, A., Simms, V., Beji-Chauke, R., Verhey, R., Robinson, J., Barker, T., Mugurungi, O., Apollo, T., Munetsi, E., & Sithole, D. (2020). Effectiveness of a Peer-Led Adolescent Mental Health Intervention on HIV Virological Suppression and Mental Health in Zimbabwe: Protocol of a Cluster-Randomised Trial. *Global Mental Health, 7*.

Curtis, A. C. (2015). Defining Adolescence. *Journal of Adolescent Family Health, 7*(2), 2.

Davids, E. L., Adams Tucker, L., Wambua, G. N., Fewster, D. L., Schlebusch, L., Karrim, S. B., Attia, M., Nyoni, J., Bayouh, F. G., Kuteesa, H., & Brahim, T. (2019). Child and Adolescent Mental Health in Africa: A Qualitative Analysis of the Perspectives of Emerging Mental Health Clinicians and Researchers Using an Online Platform. *Journal of Child & Adolescent Mental Health, 31*(2), 93–107.

Dyakova, M. (2017). Investment for Health and Well-Being: A Review of the Social Return on Investment from Public Health Policies to Support Implementing the Sustainable Development Goals by Building on Health 2020.

Esterwood, E., & Saeed, S. (2020). Past Epidemics, Natural Disasters, COVID19, and Mental Health: Learning from History as We Deal with the Present and Prepare for the Future, 1–13.

Gittings, L., Toska, E., Medley, S., Cluver, L., Logie, C.H., Ralayo, N., Chen, J., & Mbithi-Dikgole, J. (2021). 'Now My Life Is Stuck!': Experiences of Adolescents and Young People During COVID–19 Lockdown in South Africa. *Global Public Health, 16*(6), 947–963.

Govender, K., Cowden, R. G., Nyamaruze, P., Armstrong, R. M., Hatane, L. (2020). Beyond the Disease: Contextualized Implications of the COVID-19 Pandemic for Children and Young People Living in Eastern and Southern Africa. *Frontiers in Public Health, 8*, 504.

Hailemichael, Y., Hailemariam, D., Tirfessa, K., Docrat, S., Alem, A., Medhin, G., Lund, C., Chisholm, D., Fekadu, A., & Hanlon, C. (2019). Catastrophic Out-of-Pocket Payments for Households of People with Severe Mental Disorder: A Comparative Study in Rural Ethiopia. *International Journal of Mental Health Systems, 13*(1), 1–13.

Hinsberger, M., Sommer, J., Kaminer, D., Holtzhausen, L., Weierstall, R., Seedat, S., Madikane, S., & Elbert, T. (2016). Perpetuating the Cycle of Violence in South African Low-income Communities: Attraction to Violence in Young Men Exposed to Continuous Threat. *European Journal of Psychotraumatology, 7*.

Horsfield, P., Stolzenburg, S., Hahm, S., Tomczyk, S., Muehlan, H., Schmidt, S., & Schomerus, G. (2019). Self-Labeling as Having a Mental or Physical Illness: The Effects of Stigma and Implications for Help-Seeking. *Social Psychiatry and Psychiatric Epidemiology, 55*, 907–916.

Jalloh, M. F., Li, W., Bunnell, R. E., Ethier, K. A., O'Leary, A., Hageman, K. M., Sengeh, P., Jalloh, M. B., Morgan, O., Hersey, S., & Marston, B. J. (2018). Impact of Ebola Experiences and Risk Perceptions on Mental Health in Sierra Leone, July 2015. *BMJ Global Health, 3*(2), e000471.

Jeffries, W. L. I., Townsend, E. S., Gelaude, D. J., Torrone, E. A., Gasiorowicz, M., & Bertolli, J. (2015). HIV Stigma Experienced by Young Men Who Have Sex with Men (MSM) Living with HIV Infection. *AIDS Education and Prevention: Official Publication of the International Society for AIDS Education, 27*(1), 58–71.

Jesson, J., Dietrich, J., Beksinska, M., Closson, K., Nduna, M., Smit, J., Brockman, M., Ndung'u, T., Gray, G., & Kaida, A. (2021). Food Insecurity and Depression: A Cross-Sectional Study of a Multi-site Urban Youth Cohort in Durban and Soweto, South Africa. *Tropical Medicine & International Health, 26*(6), 687–700.

Khumalo, I. P., Temane, Q. M., & Wissing, M. P. (2012). Socio-Demographic Variables, General Psychological Well-Being and the Mental Health Continuum in an African Context. *Social Indicators Research, 105*, 419–442.

Kola, L., Kohrt, B. A., Hanlon, C., Naslund, J. A., Sikander, S., Balaji, M., Benjet, C., Cheung, E. Y. L., Eaton, J., Gonsalves, P., & Hailemariam, M. (2021). COVID-19 Mental Health Impact and Responses in Low-income and Middle-income Countries: Reimagining Global Mental Health. *Lancet Psychiatry, 8*(6), 535–550.

Kometsi, M. J., Mkhize, N. J., & Pillay, A. L. (2020). Mental Health Literacy: Conceptions of Mental Illness Among African Residents of Sisonke District in KwaZulu-Natal, South Africa. *South African Journal of Psychology, 50*, 347–358.

Lee, S., Rothbard, A. B., & Choi, S. (2016). Effects of Comorbid Health Conditions on Healthcare Expenditures Among People with Severe Mental Illness. *Journal of Mental Health, 25*, 291–296.

Mfoafo-M'Carthy, M., & Sossou, M.-A. (2017). Stigma, Discrimination, and Social Exclusion of the Mentally Ill: The Case of Ghana. *Journal of Human Rights and Social Work, 2*(4), 128–133.

Mngoma, N. F., Ayonrinde, O. A., Fergus, S., Jeeves, A. H., & Jolly, R. J. (2021). Distress, Desperation and Despair: Anxiety, Depression and Suicidality Among Rural South African Youth. *International Review of Psychiatry, 33*(1–2), 64–74.

Monteiro, N. M. (2015). Addressing Mental Illness in Africa: Global Health Challenges and Local Opportunities. *Community Psychology in Global Perspective, 1,* 78–95.

Muhia, J., & Nanji, N. (2021). Youth Mental Health in the Context of COVID-19 in East and Southern Africa: A Desk Review.

National Academies of Sciences and Medicine. (2019). *The Promise of Adolescence: Realizing Opportunity for All Youth.* National Academies Press.

Ouansafi, I., Chibanda, D., Munetsi, E., & Simms, V. (2021). Impact of Friendship Bench Problem-Solving Therapy on Adherence to ART in Young People Living with HIV in Zimbabwe: A Qualitative Study. *PLOS ONE, 16*(4).

Pretorius, T., & Padmanabhanunni, A. (2021). A Looming Mental Health Pandemic in the Time of COVID-19? Role of Fortitude in the Interrelationship Between Loneliness, Anxiety, and Life Satisfaction Among Young Adults. *South African Journal of Psychology, 51*(2), 256–268.

Rahman, A., Niloofa, R., De Zoysa, I., Cooray, A., Kariyawasam, J. C., & Seneviratne, S. L. (2020a). Neurological Manifestations in COVID-19: A Narrative Review. *SAGE Open Medicine, 8.*

Rahman, J., Muralidharan, A., Quazi, S. J., Saleem, H., & Khan, S. (2020b). Neurological and Psychological Effects of Coronavirus (COVID-19): An Overview of the Current Era Pandemic. *Cureus, 12*(6), e8460–e8560.

Rathod, S., Pinninti, N., Irfan, M., Gorczynski, P., Rathod, P., Gega, L., & Naeem, F. (2017). Mental Health Service Provision in Low-and Middle-Income Countries, *10,* 1178632917694350.

Raymond, J. M., & Zolnikov, T. R. (2018, October). AIDS-Affected Orphans in Sub-Saharan Africa: A Scoping Review on Outcome Differences in Rural and Urban Environments. *AIDS and Behavior, 22*(10), 3429–3441. https://doi.org/10.1007/s10461-018-2134-1. PMID: 29721717.

Semrau, M., Evans-Lacko, S., Koschorke, M., Ashenafi, L., & Thornicroft, G. (2015). Stigma and Discrimination Related to Mental Illness in Low-and Middle-Income Countries. *Epidemiology and Psychiatric Sciences, 24*(5), 382–394.

Sharpe, D., Rajabi, M., Chileshe, C., Joseph, S. M., Sesay, I., Williams, J., & Sait, S. (2021). Mental Health and Wellbeing Implications of the COVID-19 Quarantine for Disabled and Disadvantaged Children and Young People: Evidence from a Cross-Cultural Study in Zambia and Sierra Leone. *BMC Psychology, 9*(1), 79.

Simegn, W., Dagnew, B., Yeshaw, Y., Yitayih, S., Woldegerima, B., & Dagne, H. (2021). Depression, Anxiety, Stress and Their Associated Factors Among

Ethiopian University Students During an Early Stage of COVID-19 Pandemic: An Online-Based Cross-Sectional Survey. *PLoS ONE, 16*(5), e0251670.

Skovdal, M., Campbell, C. M., Madanhire, C., Mupambireyi, Z., Nyamukapa, C. A., & Gregson, S. (2011). Masculinity as a Barrier to Men's Use of HIV Services in Zimbabwe. *Globalization and Health, 7*, 1–13.

Somefun, O. D., & Simo Fotso, A. (2020). The Effect of Family and Neighbourhood Social Capital on Youth Mental Health in South Africa. *Journal of Adolescence, 83*, 22–26.

Stansfeld, S. A., Rothon, C., Das-Munshi, J., Mathews, C., Adams, A., Clark, C., & Lund, C. (2017). Exposure to Violence and Mental Health of Adolescents: South African Health and Well-Being Study. *BJPsych Open, 3*(5), 257–264.

Sui, X. C., Massar, K., Kessels, L. T. E., Reddy, P. S., Ruiter, R. A. C., & Sanders-Phillips, K. (2021). Violence Exposure in South African Adolescents: Differential and Cumulative Effects on Psychological Functioning. *Journal of Interpersonal Violence, 36*(9–10), 4084–4110.

Thupayagale-Tshweneagae, G., & Mokomane, Z. (2012). Inclusiveness: A Mental Health Strategy for Preventing Future Mental Health Problems Among Adolescents Orphaned by AIDS. *Journal of Psychiatric and Mental Health Nursing, 19*(8), 746–750.

Toska, E., Hodes, R., Cluver, L., Atujunad, M., & Laurenzie, C. (2019). Thriving in the Second Decade: Bridging Childhood and Adulthood for South Africa's Adolescents. *South African Child Gauge*, 81–94.

WHO. (2012). Making Health Services Adolescent Friendly: Developing National Quality Standards for Adolescent Friendly Health Services.

Towards a Reconstruction of Sacralized Traditions to Avert Gender-Based Violence Prevalent in Girl-Child Marriages Amongst the Akamba

Telesia Kathini Musili

1 Introduction

The day was bright, as one could tell from the clear blue sky and beaming sun rays that penetrated the dry land in Kyevooa village. Despite the bright day before us, Mutunga's (not his real name) family mourned their only daughter, Muthike (not her real name). Muthike passed on while giving birth to her second child, even though she was only 15 years old. The mood in the homestead was sober as people conversed in low tones. We casually announced our arrival with "corona greetings," a middle-aged woman welcomed us warmly, handing us three-legged stools to sit on. We joined the rest, who looked suspicious of who we were. After my friend introduced herself, we were warmly welcomed into deep conversations. My daughter, now in form two, had been at school with Muthike in a nearby primary school. Though my friend and her family had relocated to the capital city, the death of Muthike had shocked her, as she was a girl who had frequented their home with her daughter. At the far corner of the homestead sat a medium-sized modern house next to the grave, where the girl's remains would lie. Muthike's mother wept uncontrollably as her close friends narrated the ordeal. Muthike had got pregnant after

T. K. Musili (✉)
Department of Philosophy and Religious Studies, University of Nairobi, Nairobi, Kenya
e-mail: telesia.musili@uonbi.ac.ke

Department of Philosophy and Religious Studies, University of Nairobi, Nairobi, Kenya

© The Author(s), under exclusive license to Springer Nature Switzerland AG 2024
O. B. Mlambo and E. Chitando (eds.), *The Palgrave Handbook of Violence in Africa*,
https://doi.org/10.1007/978-3-031-40754-3_45

her primary examination and was hurriedly married off to a wealthy elderly man away from the village in order to cover the shame she had brought to her family. The man gave Muthike's father a small amount of money and promised to follow the Kamba customs of traditional marriage later. Muthike had just sat for her primary education, but her parents could not send her to secondary school. Aged 14, Muthike had her firstborn child through a caesarian section. Months later, Muthike was pregnant again with her second child. This time, the first wife to the elderly man convinced her that she was now mature and could give birth normally. With their husband away, Muthike had to labour to bring forth her bundle of joy. Unfortunately, she did not make it and lost her life, and her baby. Amongst the Akamba, a woman cannot be buried in her husband's homestead if the dowry has not been paid in full. This fate befell Muthike's parents, as they had to plan to bury the remains of their dear daughter. Muthike's life was exchanged for a small amount of money.

Poverty in most Kenyan societies is the primary driver of forced child marriages, where girls are perceived as assets for its alleviation. Even though a boy child is treasured in most cultures, owing to the continuation of family lineage, a home that has many girls is deemed as wealthy due to the herds of cattle and money that the father would receive in exchange for their marriages (Muthiani, 1973: 32–33). On the contrary, long life is valued and treasured in our cultures, including with the Akamba. Thus, the advances to alleviate poverty through marrying off, in exchange for money, young girls who later lose their precious lives through childbirth, creates a betwixt situation. In an attempt to gain a decent living off their daughter, the parents lost her in the process, and at an early age. The girl's brittle bones and immature pelvic floor, as well as lack of access to sexual reproductive healthcare knowledge and services, all compounded and led to loss of life. The reality is that child marriage effectively ends a girl's childhood, curtails her education, increases her risk of domestic violence, and puts her at risk for early, frequent, high-risk pregnancies, and even death, which is violence.

The United Nations Children's Fund (UNICEF) (2018) defines child marriage as any legal or customary union involving a person below the age of 18. Child marriage in Kenya is a human rights violation, hence illegal (KNBS & ICF Macro, 2010), though still prevalent in some cultures. Patriarchal power and gender inequality are major drivers in fuelling girl-child marriages. Often male adult community members disregard a girl's voice and agency as they make the decisions concerning when and who she will marry (Migiro, 2017). Cast into a voiceless pit, she finds more challenges haunt her life, including and not limited to "reproductive health and psychosocial risks, maternal mortality due to postpartum haemorrhage, obstetric fistula and obstructed labour, sexually transmitted infections, and cervical cancer" (Warria, 2019: 123). These adverse effects among other deplorable conditions faced by girls in early marriages prompted a deliberate renaming of the vice to "girl-child marriages" (Eferbera & Bhabha, 2020). In agreement with Raj (2010), Eferbera and Bhabha (2020) argue that the focus on child marriages is squarely a concern directed at the health and well-being of the girl child.

Older men and boys involved in these marriages experience no or fewer life-threatening challenges than the girls. Although most of the literature and notable conventional documents use the term "child marriage," in reality, the worrying concerns addressed point to violence meted on the girl child. In the same spirit, this chapter will deliberately use "girl-child marriage" instead of "child marriage" as a girl is often the main victim in this type of marriage. A girl's lack of mobility, healthcare access, education, and economic opportunities also means that her family is more likely to be poor and unhealthy. Such perceptions and understanding reinforce power-play on limited economic opportunities and discriminatory gender norms for the girl child.

From this backdrop, the chapter prompts an intergenerational dialogue of change that forms a foundation for an inclusive society; a society that pursues self-reconstruction, respects cultures, and avoids destructive trends, especially on matters touching on sexual gender-based violence meted on girls. I took up Mugambi's (2003) reconstructive challenge by utilizing Kanyoro's (2002) cultural hermeneutic to chart ways of abandoning repressive cultural traditions, such as girl-child marriages. An embrace of change through the interpretation of negative traditional practices is anticipated as Kanyoro's analytical methodologies converse over girl-child marriages, as it flows from Muthike's story.

The chapter is divided into three sections. Section one briefly situates Mugambi's theology of reconstruction (2003) as a challenge worth pursuing, especially on this concern over girl-child marriages. Section two argues for the reconstruction guided by Musimbi Kanyoro's cultural hermeneutic to facilitate a deconstruction and reconstruction of repressive cultural norms that provide a fertile ground for girl-child marriages to thrive amongst the Akamba. In the third section, Muthike's story is analysed against some cultural beliefs and practices towards a change in dialogue that culminates in naming the injustices wrapped in girl-child marriages.

2 Jesse Mugambi's Theology of Reconstruction Challenge

Jesse Ndwiga Kanyua Mugambi is an emeritus professor at the University of Nairobi, Department of Philosophy and Religious Studies. He is a Kenyan theologian renowned for his contested theology of reconstruction. On 30th March 1990, Mugambi, while attending the All-Africa Conference of Churches (AACC), presented a paper entitled "Future of the Church and the Church of the Future in Africa" (Gathogo, 2007). In his presentation, Mugambi called for a paradigm shift within African Christianity from liberation to reconstruction. He noted that:

reconstruction was the new priority for African nations in the 1990s. The churches and their theologians will need to respond to this new priority in a relevant fashion to facilitate this reconstruction process. The process will require considerable efforts in reconciliation and confidence-building…, re-orientation and retraining (Mugambi, 1991: 36).

In his seminal chapter "Social Reconstruction of Africa: The Role of Churches" (Mugambi, 1997: 1–24), Mugambi calls for political, economic, aesthetic, moral, and theological reconstruction by Africans themselves, "irrespective of what others have to say about the continent and its people" (Mugambi, 1995: 40).

The reconstructive challenge that Mugambi poses calls for unlearning from repressing cultural socializations to re-embracing and relearning positive cultural and religious heritage foundations. Mugambi notes that "religion is the most basic stratum of these foundations" (Mugambi, 1997: 3) since being "the pillar of culture, it provides the presupposed world-view and the basic principles for the organization of society" (Mugambi, 1997: 19). He then calls on the African church to become the "lead agency" in transformative social action by "rescuing those who are perishing and caring for those who are dying" (Mugambi, 1997: 23). Further, Mugambi calls for reconstruction and re-orientation from the consumeristic and capitalist economies where maximization of profits has become the driving force in all manner of relations. Thus, the capitalist and consumeristic mentalities embedded in girl-child marriages are a challenge that all proponents of gender justice ought to undertake.

Though criticized by his contemporaries such as Wandera (2002a, 2002b) and Maluleke (1996) for such a bold move, Mugambi's theology of social reconstruction continues to stipple into minds the capabilities that are there for regaining justice-oriented African outfit (Dibeela, 2005; Gathogo, 2009; Kä Mana, 2002; Karamaga, 1997a, 1997b; Kinoti, 1997; Manus, 2003). In this spirit, I take up the challenge in the hope and conviction that God created one world, and we, therefore, need to reaffirm the need for social and gender justice for all. According to Mugambi, this social reconstruction ought to begin with the reconstruction of attitudes, to which every individual and family commits to change (Mugambi, 1997).

It is believed that the elimination of the challenge of girl-child marriages to avert shame due to teenage pregnancies or marrying them off for monetary gains can be subverted. Girl-child marriages should be acknowledged and named as a vice and a gender injustice that ought to be curbed on both a cultural and a religious front. Thus, everyone, especially the church, is invited to move forward in the agency of delivering the change. Since religion is a pillar of culture that provides worldviews, and societal and organizational principles, religion and culture become essential components in social reordering. In the following section, I delve into cultural hermeneutics as advanced by Musimbi Kanyoro to form the backbone of analysing Muthike's story of early marriage and the consequent loss of her precious life while bringing forth life to the world.

3 Musimbi Kanyoro's Feminist Cultural Hermeneutic

In taking up the reconstruction challenge, we are cognizant that religion and culture play a significant role in people's socialization in terms of morality, ethics, and gender constructions that permeate girl-child marriages. Women's life experiences (Oduyoye, 1988) are a solid foundation that African women theologians continue to build on in theologizing on matters affecting African women, which continue to perpetuate gender inequalities in societies. These experiences are narrated and analysed to make sense of prevalent conditions and are attuned to their perceptions and understanding of God. Thus, culture, religion, and other institutions that impact women's lives are scrutinized against African women's experiences. In redressing the vice of girl-child marriage, a reconstruction of drivers that fuel it is called for. This chapter adopts Musimbi Kanyoro's theory of cultural hermeneutics (2002) to shed light on religious and cultural tenets that can steer the reconstruction.

In her work on cultural hermeneutics, Kanyoro (2002) grounds the role of cultural hermeneutics in reading the Bible by explaining and analysing some cultural resources, experiences, and African women's life experiences and practices. Kanyoro (2002) utilizes culturally grounded resources such as metaphors, imageries, and naming rites, among others, to highlight women's problems from a particular cultural angle. She wittingly pinpoints destructive notions and charts how to rebuild the same positively. For example, she recounts her naming experience after giving birth to her son, whom she wanted to be named Emmanuel, for her love of the "God with us" gospel, but this was overturned by her father-in-law, who named the son after himself. Her choice of the name Emmanuel did not matter. Left with no choice, she learned the value of being granted a new title "mother" by her father-in-law, a mother of the community and a respected figure (Kanyoro, 2002: 67–68). Using cultural hermeneutics, she learned that though the naming rite gives one identity and a sense of belonging, it also tarnishes one's identity, often referring to those who are childless. From the foregoing, cultural hermeneutics can be used to liberate us within our own cultures since a critical mind can highlight the repressive components and concentrate on the positives.

Kanyoro (2002) emphasized that culture is double-edged as it can deny one the right to free agency/choice. It can also open avenues for embracing the positive components of respect, a sense of belonging, and identity. She opines that religion and the church have also used the Bible to repress women. Kanyoro calls for applying the same hermeneutic in reading the Bible to come up with conscious choices. She notes that the Bible is the tool she uses to give birth to women of critical intelligence so they can react in situations where no solution is seen in advance, as in her referral to the story of Naomi and Ruth (Kanyoro, 2002). She calls for concerted efforts between the church, the community, women's organizations, women church leaders, and African women theologians in accounting for the ills facing women and girls due to traditional repressive cultural and religious norms. Kanyoro (2002: 78) continues her concerted call with an assertion that:

> Every people must find its own way of speaking about God and of generating new symbols, concepts and models that are congenial to express their religious vision. Those who have been prevented from participating fully in this myth- and symbol-making process must claim back our right to do so. When we are able to achieve unity in diversity, then we claim to experience God's power and glory present in the community.

Women ought to, therefore, find their own way of speaking about God, reading, and interpreting from their own viewpoint, as culture and the Bible have been used to silence and oppress women. This explains why Kanyoro embraces and encourages the hermeneutic of suspicion while handling biblical texts (2002: 85). She grounds this in the fact that culture and religion emanated and thrive on androcentric tendencies that, once ignored, will continue to oppress women and girls. In agreement, Masenya (2003: 125) warns that:

The church should also critically revisit the androcentric interpretations of the Bible since these interpretations have contributed to the perpetuation of the view that the female is inferior and that the latter is God-ordained. Such a view has enabled dangerous cultural sayings, reinforced by apparently similar sayings from the Bible, to be applied indiscriminately to powerless girl children and women. These women-unfriendly Bible interpretations should be substituted with empowering, life-giving ones.

It is, therefore, the duty of every person and every social institution to take responsibility for pointing out and condemning repressive cultural and religious heritage traits and celebrating the life-affirming ones for the sake of communality and identity.

Concerning the prevalence of girl-child marriage, I follow in Kanyoro's footsteps of engaging cultural hermeneutics to interpret Akamba indigenous beliefs and traditions on marriage, which provide a fertile ground for girl-child marriages. The girl child is given precedence as the trauma of early marriage affects the girl child adversely compared to the boy child. Kanyoro (2002: 17) lauds gendered analysis in such scenarios with an assertion that:

> Gender analysis takes into account ways in which roles, attitudes, values, and relationships regarding women and men are constructed by all societies all over the world. The concepts and practices of equality and discrimination determined by social, economic, religious, and cultural factors lie at the heart of gender-sensitive perspectives. Theological engagement with gender issues seeks to expose harm and injustices that are in society and are extended to Scripture and practices of the church through culture…The fact that gender roles differ significantly from one society to another and from one historical period to another is an indication that they are socially and culturally constructed.

The call to name and challenge the oppressive aspects of religion and culture remains a challenge, though doable to all, most notably by all women, especially women theologians and the women of the altar, where all often meet to learn from God, the maker of us all. Kanyoro (2002: 17) challenges all to take up and continue with the responsibility of:

> telling these stories of dehumanizing cultural practices [though it] is still rare and a struggle… The question confronting women theologians in Africa is how can discussions on culture be incorporated into our communities so that women find it safe to speak about issues that harm their well-being?… African women theologians who have encountered feminist analysis do not quickly jump to condemn women for being custodians of dehumanizing cultural practices. It is realized that even women's actions are too deeply rooted in

patriarchal socialization and, therefore, the analysis of women's oppression has to be done in the context of gender analysis. We need to look and see how our societies are organized and how power is used by different groups, men and women, young and old, people of varying economic means, and so on. Who benefits from a particular interpretation of culture, and how is the system kept in place?

Androcentric and patriarchal socialization have continued to slow women's liberation and emancipation in decision-making, taking up or abandoning certain actions crucial to young girls' well-being. It is against this background that this chapter examines biases that support sacralizing of girl-child marriages to avert teenage pregnancies among the Akamba people.

4 Understanding the Culture of Girl-Child Marriage Among the Akamba

Child marriage is not only a contemporary ethical issue, as we may be lured to understand. Instead, it is a phenomenon that existed in the yesteryears within most traditions, including the Akamba. The Akamba are Bantu-speaking communities occupying Kitui, Makueni, and Machakos Counties of Kenya (Kiruthu et al., 2011). The Akamba community has several cultural practices, which include birth celebrations, circumcision of both boys and girls, marriage, and death. Marriage among the Akamba is a crucial social and communal marker of adulthood, where different forms of marriage have been culturally allowed (Mbiti, 1969). They include monogamous, ghost, child, and polygamous types of marriages (Kyalo, 2011). In addition, female husband-headed (*Iweto*) families were common. A woman who bore children would marry another woman to continue the family lineage by siring babies for her husband (Atanga, 2013).

Forced marriage was unheard of among the Akamba. Instead, marriage was mutual as circumcised men were allowed to seek their suitors to marry. Among the Akamba, marriage was for the circumcised boys and girls who had undergone a second initiation rite. The initiation rite is referred to as *Nzaiko*. There were two of them, *Nzaiko nini* (small/first initiation), which occurred between the ages of five and seven years old. In this initiation, cutting of the foreskin for the boys and removal of the clitoris for the girls took place. The second was *Nzaiko nene* (big/second initiation), which occurred immediately after puberty, where girls were taught how to take care of their homes and their husbands, mostly in private (Kimilu, 1962). Both initiations were paramount as women who had not been initiated were considered to be still "children," and their offspring were referred to as "children of children" (Mbiti, 1969: 130). Thus, unless a woman had gone through the ceremony, she was "nobody," "incomplete," and still a "child."

As soon as girls had gone through the two initiation ceremonies, they were free to get married. Sex and sexuality among the Akamba was taboo as it was not discussed openly, and, thus, training had to be done in a secretive space. The young men were taught provision skills such as hunting, protecting the community, and reproduction by older men, and were also provided with the secrets of their tribe and community. According to Kalule (1987: 113), in traditional Akamba culture, "sexual relation was expected to be an integral part of the young people's growth and development." Girls were mainly married between 12 and 18 years of age, while boys married later, at about 20 to 25.

Different night dances were conducted among the initiates, where sexual intercourse (complete penetration) was permitted between initiates with prospects of becoming husband and wife in the future. According to Ndeti (1972: 8), sexual acts among the initiates was allowed amongst the Akamba people but were highly regulated. *Ngomeei* is a name given to a community expert who had to be consulted in all matters involving sex. The initiates learned *mbeni*, a dance session, and music about what goes on in the secret world of men and women. After the second initiation, boys and girls were allowed to attend night song and dance events known as *kamandiko*, where they would interact with members of the opposite sex and try on/practice sexual episodes. The male and female initiates would then discuss matters of sex and, while in complete agreement, participate in a session known as *moleaga*, where they would expose their private parts to each other. *Mbalya* is another erotic dance where the initiates, now in puberty, would amuse themselves. In these kinds of dances, the boys would choose their partners, thus forming the basis of marriage. If one was mistreated or forced into sex against their will, they would report to the *Ngomeei,* and the offender would be seriously punished and even ostracized (Ndeti, 1971). It is evident that premarital sex was expected among the Akamba, but it was ironically regarded as quite shameful for an unmarried girl to become pregnant.

A perturbing aspect of this cultural tradition, which passes as a way of inculcating sexual education among the initiates, is the shame that follows an expectant unmarried girl. No mention is made of any herbal preparation for the girls before the dances to prevent them from conceiving. One wonders how the young girls were to protect themselves from becoming pregnant. Girl-child marriages, as we define them today, girls being married off or marrying below 18 years of age, mainly happened within polygamous settings among the Akamba, as expectant girls were married off to older me to avert shame. Polygamy among the Akamba was a sign of social prestige and wealth (Kyalo, 2011: 193). Kyalo further expounds on polygamous marriage among the Akamba with the assertion:

> It was and still is, only for the rich people who could afford to pay bride wealth for more than one wife. Polygamy also showed that the men could afford to keep their wives in harmony and bring up their children effectively. In the field, the researcher interviewed both polygamous and monogamous men. The polygamous [men] were asked why it was necessary for them to have more than one wife. They said that they need more children, others said that the first wife became old and could not satisfy them sexually and could not give birth any longer. In traditional Akamba marriage, the children were also a sign of wealth. It was prestigious to have more than one wife and many offspring.

Girl-child marriages occurred mostly among wealthy men, who could afford the bride's wealth, cushioning the girl's family from poverty. Men from poor backgrounds perceived girls as assets that would uplift their financial status. However, the older men arranged these kinds of marriages depriving the young girls of their moral agency. Astonishingly, older women, grandmothers, aunties, and first wives of wealthy men were involved in the marrying-off process, leaving the girl with no support system and vulnerable to violence. In most cases, arranged marriages occurred within low-income families, mostly when young girls had got pregnant or borne children out of wedlock, due to the night dance (*Kamandiko*).

Girls who became pregnant before marriage brought shame to themselves and the entire clan. Teenage pregnancies were deplored among the Kamba communities, prompting girl-child marriages to wealthy polygamous men. Controversies loom over the Akamba *Kamandiko* dance, where young men and women interacted through song and dance and in sexual escapades. A study conducted amongst the Akamba by Waila (2012: 53) best exposes the controversy with fieldwork finding that:

> traditionally, any woman who was found to be a virgin upon marriage was returned to her parents with an axe stick that had no hole put in a "*Kyondo*" for it was a sign that she was not prepared for marriage. Once she arrived at her "parents'" homestead, they understood what it meant and the father had to look for someone to deflower her, her mother then trained her on sex matters before returning her to her husband.

This is a resounding contradiction since pregnancy before wedlock was in itself a taboo and brought shame to the entire clan and community.

The grandmothers and aunties to the girl child were tasked with the duty of training the girl on how to use beads and count her safe days or take concoctions that prevented her from getting pregnant. It, therefore, goes that virginity was not a celebrated virtue among the Kamba before the coming of the missionaries. The coming of the missionaries aggravated the issue further, as expectant teen girls were paraded before church to confess of their sexual sin, without mentioning the culprit. According to Gehman (2004), every African inland church, which are widespread in Ukambani, has a "black seat of shame" where convicted converts, such as pregnant teenage girls, would sit during Sunday services. Public shame and the ethics of shame were practised even by the religious. In instances where the strong feel like they have a moral right to subjugate the weak, this denotes power-play, which most often drifts to violence.

Thus, *kamandiko, moleanga, mbalya* dances, circumcision of girls, pregnancies outside wedlock, and poverty were some of the factors that fuelled girl-child marriages among the Akamba. Wrapped within these factors are the dynamics of men's power over women's bodies. However, the men celebrated marrying a girl to older fellow men without shame or mercy. From the foregoing, it was purely the girl's and older women's responsibility (grandmother/aunties) to ensure that the girl did not conceive, even after sex during the night dances. In addition, the broad marriage age difference between girls and boys is significant, attesting to the prevalence of girl-child marriages, and thus, a gender-based violence issue among the Akamba community.

5 Towards Redressing Girl-Child Marriage Culture

Poverty and a culture of shame are the primary causative factors for girl-child marriages among the Akamba. The two factors thrive and emanate from the institutional ordering of "society's governance headed by men and women who are socialized in patriarchal and androcentric tendencies." The acquired traits of leadership and sanctions become so engrained in someone's mind that they become difficult to unlearn. Ndemanu (2018:71) expounds on these learned tenets with an assertion that:

> there is an inescapable embeddedness of traditional African religions [and culture] in people's ways of thinking and knowing to the point that it is nearly impossible to extricate oneself from it without strong feelings of stripping off a major part of one's cultural identity.

Though paramount, the essence of one's identity might deter Kanyoro from deconstructing repressive cultural practices, explaining how she opted to unearth the good aspects that defined us.

Change is, however, the only immortal constant in human lives. It is becoming evident and a reality that pregnant young girls are dying from unsafe abortions, bleeding linked to pregnancy or unsafe abortion, the frequency and number of children they bear, neglect and inadequate care, lack of access to contraceptives, and limited sexuality knowledge. Girl-child marriages are still very common in Ukambani. Even though Christianity that professes monogamous marriage and education has curtailed polygamous marriages within the three counties, economic challenges continue to be a major driver of gender-based violence. Teenage pregnancies are rising, with Machakos county, for instance, posting the latest public outcry on teen pregnancy with 3,966 cases and ranked number 14 nationally. Poverty or no poverty, and shameful as it may sound, girl-child marriage is still an option in the current times. Girl-child marriage does not cover shame; it is an injustice and celebrates men's dominance over women's sexuality. A girl becoming pregnant even from sanctioned dances was only shameful or her and her family, and nothing was said about the boy! It may have culturally worked, but it is an injustice inflicted on innocent lives.

Sex and sexuality have been taboo subjects in most cultures. However, given the advancements in technology, availability of smart gadgets, and affordable internet, sex and sexuality are no longer private subjects and have moved into the public sphere. As such, "contemporary adolescents are bereft of sexuality knowledge and this incapacitates them from making informed and responsible decisions, since the collapse of the traditional mechanisms of socializing, controlling, and checking sexual behaviour during adolescence" have collapsed or have been ignored (Kioli et al., 2012: 6). Muthike would not have lost her life if she had not been married off young.

When young girls' agency to decide on their sexual partner is infringed, violence results. The culture of shaming expectant teenage girls even in churches is disastrous. In most churches sin- and sinner-branding judgements still ensue, with the boy child left scot-free as no evidence is attached to his sexual escapades. The pregnant girl bears the entire backlash in the silence of community leaders, including the clergy. Musimbi struggles to "explain why churches and faith leaders do not do more for women, particularly women who die and suffer because they are women....I believe that God cares for these issues; God wants women to live, as the abundance of life belongs to all people, people of all faiths, and all genders" (Interview, June 20, 2011).

She rightfully criticizes the clergy's calculated silence. She asserts that "when it comes to the area of sex and reproductive consequences, faith communities cannot speak as one on the topic, even women pastors are caught up in these dictates!" (Interview, June 20, 2011). Girl-child marriages like that of Muthike should be condemned even from the pulpit. Mugambi (1997) calls on the church to take a leading role in ensuring people's decision-making agency.

Regardless of background and training, our silence, in the name of culture, patriarchy, morality, or African ethics, is our death sentence. Musimbi calls on us to redress these repressive religious and cultural tenets. She opines that premarital sex is a sin, and adultery is a sin, but speaking about sexuality is not a sin. Women theologians and women clergy are women too, and they need to speak up on sexual gender-based violence against girls. Different groups and categories of women and girls can embrace different modes of speaking out. (Interview, June 20, 2011). Traditionally, the Kamba dances and private talks trained both boys and girls on sexuality matters. However, the bias on the resulting effects stands out, as the girl was punished more harshly by the system compared to the boy. Unlearning "expectant girls" disposal to marriage in the name of shame is called for. Muthike was married off immediately after she got pregnant with her first child. It is unclear who the child's father was, though culture never considers issues of genes and paternity, as an African child is a communal child besides being prestigious. Nonetheless, marrying her off against her wish is violence worth condemning.

Girls' bodies are not merchandise for exchange in a silent black market. Dowry negotiations are usually reserved for men and older women, depriving the girl of her agency. Her consent does not matter, and her worth is quantified, yet the intrinsic value of a human person is immeasurable, unquantifiable, and inalienable. "Dowry's negotiations and honorship" (Musili, 2022) give a perception that the girl is the man's property, and he should then use her body as he so wills. Objectification of a woman's body leads to sexual gender-based violence. Muthike's dowry honourship went unattended in full, prompting the co-wives to bring her back to her parents' home for burial, as per the Akamba culture. If *ntheo* is not honoured in full, the husband is not allowed to bury the wife (Kyalo, 2011). Muthike's parents lost both their daughter and the anticipated dowry. It has been argued that dowry is a thanksgiving gesture to the girl's parents for bringing her up into a woman of character. The concept, though positive, leaves a lot to be desired, as forced marriages, and at a tender age, amount to violence.

Body ownership as a result of dowry payment is violent. It is reiterated in biblical texts, especially in the Pauline texts, when he counsels husbands and wives not to deny each other conjugal rights because each of their partner's bodies belongs to them. In her cultural hermeneutic, Musimbi Kanyoro (2002: 17) argues that even the Bible comes from a patriarchal culture, and thus exegetes and readers should be aware of the cultural imports that oppress women. Women should be critical of the culture behind and reflected in the Bible, question it, and contextualize their experiences more consciously and liberatingly (Phiri, 2007). Musimbi opined that clergy and especially women clergy should use the pulpit and a rereading of liberating texts, as well as highlighting the texts of terror in the Bible, to advocate the liberation of women (Interview, June 20, 2011).

Girl-child, non-consensual marriages with older men threaten the girls' well-being and are a resounding abuse. Backward and repressive cultural traits that forbid the schooling of a girl child ought to be challenged. Girls and young women can change the poverty narrative that has permeated all African countries. Several studies correlate the eradication of poverty with women (Moindi, 2012; Muigua, 2020; Omondi & Jagongo, 2018) with an argument that women are proactive in programmes geared toward alleviating poverty. It is time boys and men are sensitized to the value of an educated woman in society and commit to ending girl-child marriages in society. The age-old belief that women are only home-tenders and children-nurturers stands to be challenged. It is a repressive and demeaning religious and cultural trait that calls for reconstruction.

6   Conclusion

Utilizing Kanyoro's cultural hermeneutical framework, this chapter responds to Mugambi's challenge to a theology of reconstruction regarding early girl-child marriages. The chapter attests to the ideology that reconstruction theology is indeed a practical theological engagement for negotiating 21st-century challenges. Poverty, early pregnancies, and some African heritage elements such as initiation rites, songs, and dances have negative aspects that perpetuate the early girl-child marriage culture amongst the Akamba people. The chapter has foregrounded that young girls bear the brunt of the burden of girl-child marriage repercussions, which are indeed a form of gender-based violence. Depriving teenage girls of their moral agency to choose their suitors, or exchanging them to alleviate their families' poverty are injustices. The chapter concludes by proposing the need for embracing reconstructive theology of the negative cultural traits and religious texts that inhibit girls' agency and liberation.

Bibliography

Atanga, L. L. (2013). African Feminism? In L. L. Atanga, E. E. Sibonile, L. Litosseliti, & J. Sunderland (Eds.), *Gender and Language in Sub-Saharan Africa: Tradition, Struggle and Change* (pp. 301–314). John Benjamins Publishing Company.

Dibeela, M. P. (2005). Behold I Make All Things New: Exploring An Ecumenical Agenda For Reconstruction. In Wa Kasonga, K & Waruta, D (Eds.), *Revitalizing Theological Thinking in Africa: Ecumenical Thinking in Africa*. Africa Challenge: All Africa Journal of Theology, vol 1, March, 18–19.

Efevbera, Y., & Bhabha, J. (2020). Defining and Deconstructing Girl-Child Marriage and Applications to Global Public health. *BMC Public Health, 20*(1), 1–11.

Gathogo, J. M. (2007). *Liberation and Reconstruction in The Works of J. N .K. Mugambi: A Critical Analysis in African Theology*. Unpublished thesis, University of KwaZulu-Natal.

Gathogo, J. M. (2009). African Theology of Reconstruction as a Practical Theology for All. *Practical Theology in South Africa/praktiese Teologie in Suid-Afrika, 24*(2), 99–121.

Gathogo, J. M. (2020). Theology and Reconstruction in Africa. In E. K. Bongmba (Ed.), *The Routledge Handbook of African Theology* (pp. 194–209). Routledge Press.

Gehman, R. J. (2004). The Africa Inland Mission: Aspects of Its Early History. *Africa Journal of Evangelical Theology, 23*(2), 115–144.

Kalule, H. (1987). Family life. In G.Were & J.Akong'a (Eds.), *Machakos District Socio-Cultural Profile* (pp. 40–45). Ministry of planning and National Development.

Kä Mana, K. (2002). *Christians and Churches of Africa Envisioning the Future: Salvation in Jesus Christ and the Building of a New African Society*. Regnum.

Kanyoro, R. A. (2002). *Introducing Feminist Cultural Hermeneutics: An African Perspective*. Pilgrim Press.

Karamaga, A. (1997). A theology of Reconstruction. In J.N.K. Mugambi (Ed.), *Democracy and Development in Africa: The Role of the Churches*. All Africa Conference of Churches.

Kenya National Bureau of Standards. (2010). *Kenya Democratic and Health Survey 2008–2009*. Kenya National Bureau of Statistics (KNBS) and ICF Macro.

Kimilu, D. (1962). *Mukamba wa w'o*. Nairobi East Africa Literature Bureau.

Kinoti, H. W. (1997). The church in the Reconstruction of Our Moral Self. In J.N.K. Mugambi (Ed.), *The Church and Reconstruction of Africa: Theological Considerations*. All-Africa Conference of Churches.

Kioli, F. N., Were, A. R., & Onkware, K. (2012). Traditional Perspectives and Control Mechanisms of Adolescent Sexual Behavior in Kenya. *International Journal of Sociology and Anthropology, 4*(1), 1–7.

Kiruthu, F., Kapiyo, J., & Kimori, W. (2011). *The Evolving World: A History and Government Course*. Oxford University Press.

Kyalo, P. (2011). Quran and Cultural and Legal Challenges Analysis of the Practice of Islamic Law of Marriage and Divorce Among the Akamba Muslims in Kitui. *International Journal of Humanities and Social Science, 1*(8), 189–197.

Maluleke, T. (1996). Review of J. N. K. Mugambi's From Liberation to Reconstruction: African Christian Theology after the Cold War. *Missionalia, 24*(3), 472–473.

Manus, U. C. (2003). *Intercultural hermeneutics in Africa: Methods and approaches*. Acton Publishers.

Masenya, M. (2003). Trapped between two Canons: African-South African Christian Women in the HIV/AIDS Era. In I. A. Phiri, B. Haddad, & M. Masenya (Eds.), *African Women, HIV/AIDS and Faith Communities* (pp. 113–127). Cluster Publications.

Mbiti, J. (1969). *African Philosophy and Religion*. African Educational Publishers.

Migiro K. (2017). *When Women Rule: Kenyan Rebel Evades Child Marriage And Maasai Curses To Win Power*. Thomson Reuters Foundation, Thomson.

Moindi, H. N. (2012). *Factors Affecting the Economic Empowerment of Women Mvita Constituency, Mombasa County, Kenya*. Unpublished Doctoral Dissertation, University of Nairobi.

Mugambi, J. N. (1989). *African Christian Theology: An Introduction*. Heinemann Kenya

Mugambi, J. N. K. (1991). *Carry It Home*. Nairobi: Kenya Literature Bureau.

Mugambi, J. N. K. (1995). *From Liberation to Reconstruction: African Christian theology after the Cold War*, East African Educational Publishers.

Mugambi, J. N. K. (1997). Social Reconstruction of Africa: The Role of Churches. In J.N.K. Mugambi (Ed.), *The church and reconstruction of Africa: Theological considerations*. All-Africa Conference of Churches.

Mugambi, N. (2003). *Christian Theology and Social Reconstruction*. Acton Publishers.

Muigua, K. (2020). Eradicating Poverty for Inclusive Development in Kenya. *Sustainable Development, 38*, 39.

Musili, T. K. (2022). Ndwae Ngone Mwaitu: A Postmodern Cultural Phenomenon of Dowry among the Akamba and Its Influence on Spousal Violence. *Journal of International Women's Studies, 24*(4), 11.

Muthiani, J. (1973). *Akamba from Within: Egalitarianism in Social Relations*. Exposition Press

Ndemanu, M. T. (2018). Traditional African Religions and Their Influences on the Worldviews of Bangwa People of Cameroon: Expanding the Cultural Horizons of Study Abroad Students and Professionals. *Frontiers: The Interdisciplinary Journal of Study Abroad, 30*(1), 70–84.

Ndeti, K. (1971). The Institution of *kithitu* and Question of Human Justice among the Akamba. *Journal of Eastern African Research & Development, 1*(1), 69–76.

Ndeti, K. (1972). *Elements of Akamba Life*, EAPH.

Oduyoye, M. A. (1988). The Christ for African Women. In V. Fabella & M. A. Oduyoye (Eds.), *With Passion and Compassion: Third World Women Doing Theology. Reflections from the Women's Commission of the Ecumenical Association of Third World Theologians*, Orbis, Maryknoll, 35–46.

Omondi, R. I., & Jagongo, A. (2018). Microfinance services and financial performance of small and medium enterprises of youth SMEs in Kisumu County, *International Academic Journal of Economics and Finance, 3*(1), 24–43.

Phiri, I. A. (2007). *Women, Presbyterianism and Patriarchy: Religious Experience of Chewa Women in Central Malawi* (No. 4). African Books Collective.

Raj, A. (2010). When the Mother Is a Child: The Impact of Child Marriage on the Health and Human Rights of Girls. *Archives of Disease in Childhood, 95*(11), 931–935.

United Nations Children's Fund (UNICEF). (2018). Child Marriage. Online at https://www.unicef.org/protection/child-marriage.

Waila, B. N. (2012). *The Challenges of Akamba Single Mothers in Reference to Parenting the Boy Child in the Light of Christian Complementary Feminism: A Case Study of Mwala District in Machakos County*. Unpublished Doctoral dissertation, University of Nairobi.

Wandera, J. (2002). *The Voice Magazine: A Journal of St Paul's United Theological College*, vol 1. Limuru.

Warria, A. (2019). Child Marriages, Child Protection and Sustainable Development in Kenya. *African Journal of Reproductive Health/la Revue Africaine De La Santé Reproductive, 23*(2), 121–133.

Violence, Memory and the Law in Africa

Pre-colonial and Colonial Violence in Zimbabwe: A Literary-cultural Exegesis

Oliver Nyambi

Violence has, in history, pervasively attended processes, events, and ideas of making and unmaking modern nation-states, more so in previously colonized societies where colonialism manifested as brute and psychic violence, and revolutionary wars of liberation became rites and routes of passages to liberation. Theorizing the physical but mainly mental processes of traversing such routes in his chapter "Concerning Violence" in *The Wretched of the Earth* the Martinique-born liberation psychiatrist Franz Fanon (1963), famously noted that decolonization is inherently a physically and psychologically violent phenomenon. Born out of violent forces in violent conditions by violent paternalists, the postcolonial nation is inevitably entangled in precarious cycles of violence with complex roots in pre-colonial and colonial violence. The violence as well as its memory palimpsests evolutionary trajectories of becoming and being postcolonial. Creative literature has long functioned as a fascinatingly complex site from which to encounter the many dimensions and dynamics of violence in Zimbabwe. The literary archive of violence multiplies lenses into the violence and how it occurs as a performed and experienced rite of nation-ness. Using purposefully selected scenes of pre-colonial and colonial

---

This chapter forms part of funded research through the National Research Foundation (South Africa) Grant for Y-rated researchers.

O. Nyambi (✉)
Department of English, University of the Free State in South Africa, Bloemfontein, South Africa
e-mail: NyambiO@ufs.ac.za

violence from several Zimbabwean literary texts, this chapter explores their representations of violence, focusing on what they tell us about its immanence in the historical evolution of group identities and relations. Borrowing from Fanon's insights on the psychology, materiality and race of violence, the chapter centres violence as a temporal motif and concept that is fundamentally rhizomic in the social and political ordering of societies, branching out into many different leads that unravel its "necessity," causes, forms, and nature.

Walby (2013: 96) has outlined the two major ways in which violence has so far been considered in the academy. Noting that "[t]he definition and conceptualization of violence is contested," Walby argues that violence has been conceptualized in terms of other categories especially as a method and instrument of power. Walby further notes that "violence has been analysed as a distinctive phenomenon, as a non-reducible form of power, a form of practice, a set of social institutions, with its own rhythm, dynamics and practices" (2013: 96). My own approach to violence in this chapter locates it in its uses and ends and how these categories reflect on its temporal and spatial nature as a force and method of arranging power and society. There are different forms of violence that often manifest as physical and psychological violence. There is hard and soft violence. This study is about violence—all manner of violence particularly as it relates to the different ways in which society is culturally and politically structured to (dis)able certain group relations. I look at how creative literature illuminates violence as a force and method of (un)making power; of forming and deforming the powerful and the powerless for certain social and political ends. The chapter explores narratives of pre-colonial and colonial landmark events, historical figures, acts, and processes marked by or implementing violence in the creation of social, political, and cultural orders.

1 A Synoptic Overview of Violence in Zimbabwe

Violence has for long permeated Zimbabwean history as a force inhabiting events and moments of fashioning social, political, and economic orders as well as forging and organizing society under various forms and versions of nations and nationhood. We learn of this violence from many sources which include, amongst many others, names (see Dzimiri et al., 2014), praise poetry (Fortune, 1984) oral folktales, historical monuments, and written literature (Pikirayi, 2006). Toponyms are fertile epistemological sites from which to (re)know violence in history and its marks on contestations over territory, places, identities, and nations. Bulawayo—the name of Zimbabwe's second largest city, for example, is also the name of the old Matabele fortress which means "the place of slaughter" (see Dube, 2018). The name can be traced back to Kwa-Bulawayo which was the royal kraal of King Shaka of the Zulu people from where the original Matabele, led by Mzilikazi, fled during the Mfecane. "The place of slaughter," whether in south-west Zimbabwe or as the early capital of Shaka Zulu empire in KwaZulu/Zululand denotes violence and connotes a disposition to it as a social, political, and economic force, and a method and machinery of group relationality.

A brief autoethnography could be helpful in delineating pre-colonial violence as well as its historical evolution as a category of inter-group relations in territories that now form part of Zimbabwe. This writer, while growing up in the Tsonga and Ndau-speaking south-eastern lowveld of Zimbabwe, experienced the Chibhavahlengwe (Hlengwe/Tsonga/Shangani for "beat up the Hlengwe"). The Hlengwe are a Tsonga sub-group found in south-eastern Zimbabwe. The Hlengwe (who are also Tsonga) are related, by association, to the Shangani who are a Tsonga-speaking Nguni group assimilated into the Tsonga culture during the Gaza Empire established by Soshangane Manukusi in the 1800s. The Ndau, on the other hand, are found in the eastern parts of Zimbabwe. Although their Ndau language is now recognized as separate from the ChiShona language and no longer as a dialect of ChiShona, the language's significant mutual intelligibility with ChiShona reflects the close affinity between the Ndau and Shona people. The Ndau language borrows much from Hlengwe/Tsonga and Nguni languages due to widespread inter-ethnic socialization when (and after) the separate groups became subjects of the Gaza Empire (see Mathebula & Mokgoatšana, 2020). Considered amongst the Ndau/Shona people as an age-long ethnic "game" during the dry season when the Save River flow narrows, herd boys from the Ndau/Shona-speaking side of the river would cross the stream to chase, catch and beat up their Hlengwe/Tsonga/Shangani counterparts shouting "chibhavahlengwe" (we beat up the Hlengwe).

Born in a Hlengwe/Tsonga/Shangani family and raised in the Ndau/Shona side of the Save River, this writer grew up to understand that Chibhavahlengwe was but one manifestation of an entrenched Ndau/Shona superiority disposition whose performance perpetuated a spectacular tradition of ethnicized power and powerlessness and reinforced ethnic and tribal hierarchies. Perceived notions of tribal value informed a culture and tradition of performing Ndau/Shona superiority and Hlengwe/Tsonga/Shangani inferiority. Chibhavahlengwe was structured around that myth of ethnic identities and relations. The "game" was a rite of passage into an ethnic consciousness that desired the preservation of the ethnic status quo, identities, and hierarchies. Violence was the force and method that created and sustained these ethnic hierarchies which essentially valued and devalued ethnic worth.

Almost similar ethnicized power hierarchies played out between the Shona and the Ndebele in the south-western parts of the country. Having revolted from the Zulu King Shaka circa 1823, Mzilikazi ka Matshobana gathered his Khumalo clan and trooped north of what is now South Africa, initially heading to present-day Mozambique but eventually turning west into the Transvaal. Not long after establishing his initial royal town of Mhlahlandlela near modern day Pretoria around 1826, Mzilikazi's small army could not match the firepower of Boers who were buoyed by local Pedi and Tswana groups, so he fled into modern day Botswana eventually settling and establishing his Mthwakazi Kingdom in south-western Zimbabwe (c.1840). Just as they were under Shaka's Zulu empire, Mzilikazi's Matabele maintained their predatory way of life. They built the Mthwakazi state through conquering and incorporating local ethnic groups, first along the way from Zululand such as the Sotho, Pedi, and Tswana, and, upon settling, groups such as the Kalanga, Shona, and Rozvi.

Besides inter-ethnic violence, intra-ethnic violence is a dominant motif in classical Shona literature such as Chakaipa's *Pfumo reRopa* (1961) (The Spear of Blood) and *Karikoga Gumiremiseve* (1967) (The Sole "Warrior" of Ten Arrows), Mutasa's *Nhume Yamambo* (1990) (The King's Emissary) and *Misodzi, Dikita neRopa* (1991) (Tears, Sweat and Blood), Chiguvare's (1986) *Kutonhodzwa KwaChauruka* (The Pacification of Chauruka) amongst many others. These texts depict strong male heroes rising above the rest to achieve extraordinary feats through violence. The heroes' odds are usually rival warriors, and their valour leads them to successfully defend their clans as in *Pfumo reRopa* and kings (*Kutonhodzwa KwaChauruka*) or rescue their families from capture and slavery as we see in the novel *Karikoga Gumiremiseve*.

2   Colonialism and Chimurenga Violence

Colonialism is always a violent process. This is more so in the Zimbabwean context where the colonist became a settler and the colony a settler colony. The Zimbabwean history of colonialism is riddled with wars for territory, and wars of liberation that were/are known as the Chimurenga in Mashonaland and Umvukela in Matabeleland. Both terms (Chimurenga and Umvukela) refer to an uprising and are linked to legendary figures in the history of anti-colonial struggles in Zimbabwe such as Chaminuka, Murenga, King Lobengula, Lozikeyi Dlodlo, and Nehanda Charwe, who led some of the earliest uprisings against Cecil Rhodes's British South African Company settlers. While most of these figures are archived in historical narratives, myths, and legends of the nation and ethnic groups, Chaminuka and Nehanda of the Zezuru group have enjoyed wider fame and reverence. Chaminuka and Nehanda's involvement in the early years of anti-colonial uprisings is immortalized in several narrative recreations of their lives and times. Such recreations do not always realistically depict the historical figures and their encounters with colonial violence. Rather, the texts are usually structured as historical novels, that is, in the strictest sense of novels that are set in culturally and historically recognizable settings, social conditions, and situations.

Solomon Mutswairo's *Chaminuka Prophet of Zimbabwe* (1983) is perhaps the earliest of such texts to seek to preserve, in narrative form, the memory of Chaminuka and his role in the anti-colonial struggle. Violence in this text is portrayed from the vantage point of targets of violence, nevertheless Chaminuka and his people are not represented as mere hapless victims. The construction of Chaminuka as a mythical figure with divine connections to the land makes him a critical site from which to understand multiple facets of the effects of inter-ethnic and colonial violence. Chaminuka (in this text and in oral history) is a seer whose occupation of both the worldly and heavenly universes inscribe, on his violation, moral, and ethical implications that reflect on the perpetrator, the context of perpetration, and the meaning of the perpetration to both the perpetrator and the perpetrated. Violence in this text is, first and foremost, a force and statement of ascribing group agency and human worth. The following statement attributed to Chaminuka in Mutswairo's text explains how violence became a mechanism of re-stratifying people/races, cultures, beliefs, knowledges, and relations at the moment of conquest:

> Oh people of Chitungwiza, fearful of your lives and for those of your children, understand—I repeat—that there shall come from the sea a race of people without knees who are stronger than the tyrant Ndebele. They will subdue your enemies and will pursue Lobengula to his shameful death. Then these knee-less people will build white houses on the land. They will bring with them a mighty boulder, such as has never been seen before. It will roll with such force, that no one will be able to stand before it, or divert it from its course. (1983: 86)

This quotation is perhaps more popular as an etymological and onomastic source of the label "knee-less people" ("*Vasina mabvi*")—a term that would find wide usage amongst the Shona people who used it to identify the "white" colonists. There is much that can be inferred from this descriptive marker about the nature, instruments, methods of, and attitudes to colonialism and colonists but my main interest is in the philosophy of violence it engenders vis-à-vis the colonial encounter as conquest. "*Vasina mabvi*" ("knee-less people") was clearly derived from the perception that the colonists' trousers made them seem like they did not have knees. But the label meant something more in relation to race as the newest violence category of differentiating and packing humans. The marker created or rather came from a place of awareness of difference and how it (un)makes power and powerlessness. "Knee-less people" as an onomastic label is a psychosocial product of the experiential encounter with colonial conquest where the original notion of the human and humane was violently displaced and shifted to recognize not just the reality of change but also its relationship to new power hierarchies.

We can think of "*Vasina mabvi*" in this context as but one of the various psychological mechanisms of negotiating emergent group relationships in the wake of massive disruptions and destabilizations of normative hierarchies of human worth by colonialism. "*Vasina mabvi*" suggests a perception and even judgment of the colonists based on grounded relationalities, knowledges, cultures, and traditions of humanity. In this scheme of local epistemology, knees occupy the space of familiarity and normality, and their absence suggests a deformity. This deformity is thus surreptitiously linked to anticipations of difference and deviance of behaviour and disposition, hence, the warning by Chaminuka for his people to anticipate violence which is metaphorically rendered through the symbolic imagery of the unstoppable boulder.

An important dimension to difference and its link to violence in Chaminuka's prophecy above is ethnicity. The prophecy reveals, beyond the colonial violence symbolically signified by the devastation of the mighty boulder, the violence before the colonial violence. It is the violence of what Chaminuka calls "tyrant" Lobengula and the Ndebele—a reference to the Matabele kingdom. The violence of the Ndebele as evoked in Chaminuka's prophecy is an important window into the complexities and complications of statecraft in pre-colonial, colonial, and postcolonial Zimbabwe. The reference to a Ndebele "tyrant" implies Shona vulnerability. This construction of Shona ethnic subjectivity and relationality is not new. It is corroborated by early Shona narratives portraying largely ethnicized pre-colonial power struggles between the Ndebele and different sub-groups (especially the

Karanga and Zezuru) which would later on be collectively called "Shona" (see Makaudze, 2021). We can, therefore, read Chaminuka's term "tyrant" as an ethnophaulism which comes from a sense of ethnic susceptibility to Ndebele violence, and which reveals underlying group conflicts.

Many studies have enquired into the Ndebele/Shona pre-colonial violence, particularly its cultural dimensions and representations in narrative form (see Musiyiwa, 2022; Musiyiwa & Matshakayile-Ndlovu, 2005; Schmidt, 1997). Such studies have observed how anthroponyms and labelling can be utilized as critical psycho-social sites from which to understand the interplay between violence, ethnicity, and power before colonialism. A term which (amongst others) has come to archive the history and memory of this inter-ethnic pre-colonial violence is "madzviti." The term and notion of madzviti appear in written and oral stories that, one might argue, give useful backdrops to understanding the contexts in which continuing manifestations of inter-ethnic antagonisms, polarities and rivalries in modern day Zimbabwe occur. The term "madzviti" has been variously interpreted in different contexts where certain dimensions and dynamics of pre-colonial violence are considered. I referred, earlier above, to Chaminuka's term "tyrant" as an ethnophaulism that, beyond reflecting a temporal Shona disposition and attitude to the Ndebele, reveals what it meant to be powerful and powerless in the broad political scheme of ethnic identity, territory, sovereignty, and statecraft before colonialism. So, in Chaminuka's prophecy above (as in many other Shona tales of Nguni encounters (see also Musiyiwa & Matshakayile-Ndlovu, 2005), the Ndebele are othered by the Shona based on their brutality, while they othered the Shona because of their disinclination to fight. The aversion to Ndebele violence amongst the Shona was so deep that it informed a unidimensional and, at worst, stereotypical imagining of the Ndebele as synonymous with viciousness. We can infer this notion and imagining of the murderous Ndebele in Chaminuka's framing of the Ndebele king Lobengula's predicted death at the hands of the colonists as "shameful." This antipathetic characterization of Lobengula's death must be understood in the context of the onomastic category of "madzviti" and its associations of brutishness and of moral injustice, where "shame" implicitly connotes a condition of sudden incapacitation in the Ndebele to reproduce, on white colonists, the violence that they routinely meted out on the Shona.

The term "madzviti" is widely used in the context of Shona-Ndebele relations to identify the violent and the violated, hence, its collocative proximity to words such as "raids," "killings," "tyranny," and "tribute" in written and oral literature on pre-colonial society in what is now Zimbabwe. This collocative relationship between madzviti and violence suggests a psychological dimension to its coinage and usage vis-à-vis the Shona's aversion to the Ndebele warriors. While this aversion was essentially caused by feelings of victimization and loss, the fact that the victimizer had a different ethnicity made it (the aversion) acquire a strong sense of ethnic antagonism. A material conflict became an ethnic conflict with enduring implications for how the two ethnicities related as they developed into two distinct nations that would eventually be recognized by the colonists as Matabeleland and Mashonaland.

3   Pre-colonial Violence in Oral Literature

The nascent evolution of the Ndebele/Shona rivalry is archived in oral stories where the term "madzviti" functions as an onomastic mechanism of group reaction to victimization. A Ndau folktale retold by Willie Chigidi (2021) best illustrates how the expressive arts got embroiled in collective modes of archiving group experiences of violence. Chigidi (who retells the folktale as he remembers it from his childhood) makes the important point that oral storytelling was both a mechanism of preserving history—not just the history of Ndebele violence and Ndau victimization but perhaps more importantly, the history of the evolutionary path of ethnic relations informed by both the violence as well as its memory. Chigidi makes the important point that:

> to study some Ndau folktales is to be concerned at least in part with the ways in which those times when the stories were told imagine and narrate Ndau history and the history of the people they interacted with, whether on friendly or antagonistic terms. (2021: 574)

History as a product of interaction and narration reflects much more than the events that transpired in the past. Rather, as we learn from Bhabha in his aptly titled book *Nation and Narration* (1990), narration is a subjective act of inscribing vantage points and epistemes into processes of constructing a group imaginary such as the nation. The interaction between the nation and its narration in processes of its (the nation's) formation and various intervals of transitions are critical to our understanding of its being as a historical product of violent processes that are difficult to expunge from collective memory. Thus, for Bhabha,

> To study the nation through its narrative address does not merely draw attention to its language and rhetoric; it also attempts to alter the conceptual object itself. If the problematic "closure" of textuality questions the "totalization" of

national culture, then its positive value lies in displaying the wide dissemination through which we construct the field of meanings and symbols associated with national life. (1990: 3)

The nation as a "a conceptual object" (Bhabha, 1990: 3) mediated by narratives is, therefore, a site of unstable and oftentimes competing (modes of) representations. This is especially so where violence as a force and mechanism of construction forms part of the fabric of the nation's conceptual and material capillaries reinforcing both its structure and form.

Let us now look at how Chigidi's oral folktale on madzviti, circulating among the Ndau people of eastern Zimbabwe, "construct[s] the field of meanings and symbols associated with national life" (Bhabha, 1990: 3)—particularly that part of national life that is contested and volatile for the precise reason that it is born of violence. We have already seen how, as an ethnonymy conceptualizing historical moments of violence with ethnic/tribal associations, the term "madzviti" has functioned as a metaphor of collective attitudes to ethnical violence. The oral folktale retold by Chigidi reveals how, when stored in this way, the memory of this violence has the potential to destabilize essentialist imaginaries of nation, nationality, and unity that are handily created for the convenience of collectivizing people under the banner of nation. Such imaginaries are, of course, averse to fundamental differences, narratives and discourses that recall, as if to entrench, the kind of memories of ethnic violence that we see in the Ndau folktale.

In this Ndau folktale, an old woman is caught up in a raid by the madzviti whom Chigidi translates as "Nguni raiders." She and a group of other Ndau people take refuge in a cave. Mesmerized by a colony of bees working in a hive, the unnamed old lady is unable to keep quiet, so she begins to sing about how the bees were working: "Jimwe jinouya, jimwe jinoenda, jimwe jinouya, jimwe jinoenda," "Some bees are coming in, some are going out, some bees are coming in, some are going out" (Chigidi, 2021: 584–585). As the singing exposed the Ndau group, it prompted the group to move further into the cave, leaving the singing old woman at the mercy of the dzviti (one Nguni raider) who goes on to kill her with a spear. The old woman's killing, which is juxtaposed to a moment of beauty where song and admiration for the bees create an atmosphere of symbiotic cohabitation between nature and humans, is evoked as an act of senseless disruption of peace and injustice. Here is an example of this portrayal and how the imagery of violence it generates can potentially lead to an entrenchment of hostile perceptions of the Nguni raiders:

Dzviti riya rakanase kudongorera mubako muya rikaona, iya, mune munthu! Rakamirudze mukhondo waro kwaa kuti chimbuya chiya, ryu, ngepandani. Chimbuya chiya chakati pforototo, kufa, dzviti riya kwaa kuenda haro reiteera amweni aro. Chimbuya chiya ndikwo kufa kwachakaita.

The *dzviti* raider heard a voice saying, "Some bees are coming in, and some are going out." The warrior took a closer look and saw an old woman in the cave. He raised his spear and stabbed her. The warrior then walked away. That is how the old woman died. (Chigidi's translation [2021: 585])

There is, in this depiction of the violence of "Nguni raiders," an unmistakable moral dimension which qualifies the already ethnicized violence of the "Nguni raiders" and the raided and killed Ndau (old woman). Steeped in the graphic description of the killing of the innocent old woman and the naturality of the Nguni warrior's murderous disposition, this moral dimension illuminates the (un)just in a way that affectively preserves it for possible references in future Ndau/Nguni relations. Emotions are at the centre of the depiction of the Nguni warrior's natural proclivity for violence evoked in his predilection for killing the old singing Ndau woman. The killer's casual walk away from the scene of the murder ("*kwaa kuenda haro*" ("he casually walked off" (my translation) [Chigidi, 2021: 585]) demonstrates the extent to which he devalues the human worth of his victim. Archived in this way, emotions and attitudes generated by this debasement of the Ndau by the Nguni raiders create a currency of antagonistic relations and relationalities that may require a careful negotiation whenever questions of "tribe," ethnicity, origins, and autochthony arise in the process of imagining the nation and nationality.

4 Myths and Legends of Colonial Violence and Local Responses: Nehanda, Words, and Bones

Inter-ethnic conflict between the Ndebele and Shona groups decreased with the entrance of Rhodes's Pioneer Column comprising members of the British South Africa Company, to begin the initial colonial annexation of Mashonaland territories, circa 1890. Various myths and legends of process, acts, and personalities involved in the violence of the seizures have circulated in various forms and media in Zimbabwean history. Stories of the colonial invasion are recorded, archived, and circulated by different individuals, groups, and institutions with equally different motives and ends. The state, at given intervals in the postcolonial history of the nation, has retained much of the rights and mechanisms of (de)valuing resistance, resistance groups, resistance leaders, and forms of resistance to colonialism. Spurred by temporal political and hegemonic motives and ends, stories of colonialism and its resistance have been told, skipped, obfuscated, and erased depending on the overarching political objective. It is no wonder, then, that despite being one of the first fully-fledged wars of anti-colonial resistance, the so-called Matabele wars (1893–1894) are never known beyond passing anecdotes in valourized Shona resistances led by such figures as Mukwati, Murenga, Kaguvi, and Nehanda Charwe who dominate approved history textbooks in Zimbabwe today.

Nehanda Charwe—described by Mavima (2022: 40) as the "the Zezuru spirit medium commonly known today as Ambuya Nehanda and often credited with leading the 1896 anti-colonial uprisings" is the undisputed key figure in myths and legends of the anti-colonial struggle told and archived by the postcolonial state. Her arrest and execution in 1898 by the settler regime over her political mobilization have been entrenched in nationalist grand narratives of decolonization as the ultimate sacrifice for territory. In a postcolonial state where the violence of the decolonizing Chimurenga war is celebrated as the maker of national heroism and patriotism (see also Nyambi, 2022; Nyambi & Matsika, 2016), Mavima uses the concept of the ancestor to highlight the spiritual and ritual significance of Nehanda Charwe, particularly her death and the circumstances in which the death took on a politically mythical status. Invoking the popular song "*Tora gidi uzvitonge*" (Take the Gun and Liberate Yourself) which he attributes to the Zimbabwe African National Liberation Army, Mavima highlights the political fossilization, in state repositories of the liberation struggle, of the lines "*Mbuya Nehanda kufa vachitaura shuwa/kuti tinotora sei nyika/shoko rimwe ravakandiudza tora gidi uzvitonge*" (Mbuya Nehanda died uttering these words/how shall we take back this land/the one word of advice she left us/pick up the gun and liberate yourselves" (Mavima's translation [2022: 45]). This retrieval of the memory of Nehanda, guns, and words in processes of defining, characterizing, and ideologizing the struggle for its implementation in statecraft is not a new phenomenon. Death, words, and bones are critical motifs in liberation mythologies in Zimbabwe where traditional spirituality commands the undeath of the dead and wields the dead as active participants in the welfare of the living.

Yvonne Vera's novel *Nehanda* (1993) is perhaps the most eminent literary texts to recreate the story of Nehanda and to aesthetically render what is assumed to be her words and prophecy. Words and prophecy in the novel are simultaneously products and mechanisms of violence—both colonial and decolonial violence. Let us see how this is manifest in the excerpt below taken from the first few paragraphs of the beginning of the novel which is, in actual fact, its ending:

> Nehanda carries her bag of words in a pouch that lies tied around her waist. She wears some along her arms. Words and bones. Words fall into dreaming, into night. She hears the bones fall in the silence. She is surrounded by a turmoil of echoes which ascends night and sky. In the morning, a horizon of rock, of dry bones, grows into day. Nehanda carries her bag of words in a pouch that lies tied round her waist. She wears some along her arms. Words and bones. Yellow becomes crimson. She follows the crimson path that forms a meandering shape in the distance, in the world of dreams. She travels to the faraway place where her body turns to smoke. The comforting crimson brings her closer to her own death. She raises her hands above her head as though supporting a falling roof. She gestures into the sky with frantic arms. She laughs. The skin tears further away from her, and she knows that the damage to herself is now irreversible. Nothing will save her from this final crimson of death; it is too much like her inner self. (1993: 1–2)

In this excerpt, the dominant motif of words and how they are preserved in a "bag of words" and "a pouch" gestures to and, simultaneously, undermines, the political use, especially by ZANU PF, of the memory of her violent death. Words are precious to Nehanda in Vera's recreation of her life and death, and this is not least because they are the object of the death itself. Nehanda's hanging by the settler regime is a mechanism of silencing her voice which is synonymous with her anti-colonial divination and political mobilization. Her killing, seen through the lens of Western cosmology by the settlers, is believed to be her demise and that of her "inciting" voice and, hence, an "efficacious" mechanism of political control.

Unbeknown to the settlers and as slyly hinted in the excerpt above, the *svikiro* (spirit medium) in Nehanda meant that she was indestructible. It meant that although the settlers could hang and kill Charwe, they would not kill her words which were the spiritual embodiment of Nehanda. Although Nehanda would later on make the ultimate claim that her bones would rise again, it was believed amongst the Shona that her spirit would find another medium besides the demised Charwe to continue the anti-colonial struggle. Words became violence, precious violence that Nehanda Charwe "wears along her arms" (1993: 1) and in the process, becoming her. Nehanda became violence. It is no wonder, then, that besides the word being recorded and archived by the colonist, it nevertheless filtered into the consciousness of the native people who embraced its prophecy and deployed it as a site of inspiration for waging the Second Chimurenga war of circa 1964–1979. The repetition of "she wears some [words] along her arms" (1993: 1) emphasizes

Nehanda's imminent transfiguration into her own words at her death where "words and bones" (1993: 1) would become synonymous. Nehanda's bones rising would become, in the spiritual realm of the Second Chimurenga, the "word" of mobilization for the decolonization struggle.

Nehanda's words in Vera's novel above are a product of (more of a reaction to) colonial violence as much as they are violence—a liberating violence. Fanon (1963: 38) says colonial rule "is the bringer of violence into the home and into the mind of the native" but he also notes that this violence begets violence, hence his argument that "We have seen that it is the institution of the colonized masses that their liberation must, and can only, be achieved by force" (1963: 57). In Nehanda's case as portrayed in Vera's novel above, words as violence and a reaction to (colonial) violence also function as a repository for the preservation and archiving of the memory of violent encounters. This memory is carried in words and has outlived the subsequent mediums of Nehanda after the demise of Charwe. The memory has become a national legend that has survived the Second Chimurenga and is now used in various nationalist myths of autochthonous identification and disidentification as Zimbabwe and Zimbabwean.

5 Beyond Myths and Legends of Violence

Besides *Nehanda*, many literary texts have grappled with colonial violence and the responses it brewed in the colonized. Beyond portraying the historical facts of settler colonialism and violent struggles against it, the texts create lifeworlds of colonial conquest and anti-colonial struggles where events do not necessarily mimic historical facts but mirror and refract it in imaginative ways that generate alternative perspectives and discourses of oppression, violence, and liberation (struggle). It is this creative leeway produced by the imagination that allows writers to critically engage, destabilize, and test master fictions of colonialism, the liberation struggle and nation that fix certain agencies and authorizations on certain players and institutions and deny them others. Texts such as Dambudzo Marechera's *The House of Hunger* (1978), Charles Mungoshi's *Waiting for the Rain* (1975), Shimmer Chinodya's *Harvest of Thorns* (1989) amongst many others, have functioned in Zimbabwe's socio-political discourse as alternative sites from which to encounter different meanings of what colonial violence meant and could mean for the past and the present. Much has been written about how these texts reflect (on) colonial violence in its different forms (see Gwekwerere, 2018). Equally exceptional research has been done on how the literature expands horizons of where and how we can access knowledge and meanings of the different forms of resistance offered by the oppressed. From the haunting symbolic imagery of a "house of hunger" to the equally moving metaphor of "waiting for the rain," these texts locate violence in the very fibre of the native's colonial existence marked by all manner of deprivations. Beyond the now obvious symbolic metaphorization of hunger as signifying a condition of lack and its synonymity with racist and extractive settler policies, "hunger" in *The House of Hunger* is a product of strategic violence that pins the native onto the margins of means of production and, therefore, existence. In *Waiting for the Rain*, such margins engender a syndrome of identity loss and unbelonging that mark geographies and (de)limitations of humanity.

Self-constructing as the better human, the settler colonist in *Waiting for the Rain* takes upon himself the "burden" of authority over fertile land and, in the process, relegates the native to the fringes of productivity, crammed into unproductive "reserves" made up of infertile sandy soils. This violence is as physical as it is mental. Displacement is as physically painful as it is mentally deranging. This is one of the reasons why from the Americas, the Caribbean, and Africa to the Pacific and Asia, alienation has been one of the central motifs and epistemological sites from which to relearn the multifaceted and intersectional notions of colonial oppression, geographies of colonial oppression, the colonial oppressor, and the colonially oppressed. Displacement-induced alienation as embodied in the figure of Lucifer (the main character in *Waiting for the Rain*) manifests a psychic disorder that is directly and indirectly linked to failed attempts to thrive outside a familiar social habitat. Colonial material alterations to Lucifer's Mandengu family habitat unsettle and displace Lucifer's ability to relate to and identify with the land. He immediately loses his sense of self which, according to his Shona cosmology, must be grounded in the land and connected to the ancestor buried in it. In this sense, Stratton (1986: 11) observes that this human and non-human interaction in the construction and mapping of habitat "is the essence of what the old father in 'The Setting Sun and the Rolling World' is telling his son Nhamo when he says: 'Nothing is more certain to hold you together than the land and a home, a family.'" For Stratton "the land is not merely a source of physical sustenance, for the earth, of which it is a manifestation, has a central place in Shona cosmology" (1986: 11). Alienated from this pivotal structure, Lucifer and the Mandengu family lose both a source of physiological and spiritual sustenance. The resultant uprootedness in Lucifer manifests as an uncontrollable desire to be (like) the oppressor—a gesture to Fanon's notion of the "envious" native.

In his famous chapter "Concerning Violence," Fanon conceptualizes the violence of dispossession in terms of the material and physiological desires it generates in the oppressed. For him, the "native" town "is a hungry town, starved of bread, of meat, of shoes, of coal, of light ...[it] is a crouching village, a town on its knees, a town wallowing in the mire" (1963: 39). This hunger, this deprivation and lack dehumanizes the native in ways that makes re-humanization a simple matter of forceful takeover of the settler town. The unmitigated desire for the settler town cannot be divorced from this dehumanization and how it makes material the ultimate mechanics of (re)humanization. Thus, for Fanon:

> The look that the native turns on the settler's town is a look of lust, a look of envy; it expresses his dreams of possession—all manner of possession: to sit at the settler's table, to sleep in the settler's bed, with his wife if possible. The colonized man is an envious man (1963: 39).

In Lucifer's case, the physical violence of colonial dispossession and exploitation alienates him from whatever is left that humanizes the Mandengu family in the wasted Manyene Tribal Trust Land which is described as "white lands ... with the inevitable tattered scarecrow waving a silent dirge in an empty field" (1975: 39) and which he portrays as "[a] heap of dust and rubble" (1975: 52). The violence of alienation from what has come to be the familiar habitat of the native does not produce the kind of violent unmitigated desire that Fanon predicted—the craving to possess the settler town and its excesses depicted in the symbolic metaphor of the settler-owned "rolling ranches of Hampshire Estates, with their tall dry grass and the fertile soil under that grass" (1975: 52). This discrepancy in the native's reaction, disposition, and relationality vis-à-vis Fanon's teleological behaviours of the violently conditioned native can be attributed to yet another form of settler violence which is linked to Lucifer's alienation from both Manyene Tribal Trust Land and the violent desire for possession it "should" generate in him. This alienation is produced through the machinery of colonial education, particularly its systematic design to warp the native of their sense of humanity and the confidence required to match it up with any and other humanities and civilizations. The novel ends with Lucifer, scholarship in hand to study art in America, bidding goodbye to Manyene Tribal Trust land and looking over it with the eye of a tourist. Lucifer, through the scholarship and opportunity to study in the West, is thus nominally handed a sense of possession of the metropole settler town, which sense strategically mitigates material and mental sites within and about him that "should" trigger the violent disposition to possesses the Hampshire Estates.

6 Conclusion

I have not, in this chapter, tried to account for every violent literary scene set in pre-colonial and colonial times and places in what is now Zimbabwe. This is, amongst other reasons, mainly because such scenes are too many to identify let alone link to the various forms of social, tribal, and racial upheavals in the complex processes of becoming Zimbabwe. What I have done in this piece is to purposefully sample violent literary scenes in pre-colonial and colonial settings that portray imaginative life-worlds where violence, its causes, perpetrators, victims, consequences, and memories, acquire symbolic significations, meanings, and implications for how we can make sense of social, political, and economic intersections where nation and violence meet and shape each other. This chapter has demonstrated some of the ways in which "literary violence" gives (and sometimes takes from) layers of history particularly where this history or, rather, the subject of this history is shaped by violence. The violence that permeates the everyday life of pre-colonial and colonial subjects in the selected literary scenes and texts reflects on critical events, traditions, cultures, myths, legends, processes, personalities, and dispossessions involved in the formation, deformation, and reformation of what Gatsheni-Ndlovu (2009) has called "trajectories of nationalism, national identity formation and crisis." The literature reflects on the violence, unveiling temporalities that onion-layer those socio-political organizing structures that condition people, cultures, traditions, geographies, ethnicities, and races for imaginability under what Anderson (1983: 1) has called the "imagined community" that is the nation.

References

Anderson, B. (1983). *Imagined Communities: Reflections on the Origin and Spread of Nationalism*. Verso.
Bhabha, H. (1990). *Nation and Narration*. Routledge.
Chakaipa, P. (1961). *Pfumo reRopa*. Longman.
Chakaipa, P. (1967). *Karikoga Gumiremiseve*. Longman.
Chigidi, W. (2021). Matters of Survival: A Case of Heavy-Handed Didactic Moralism in Ndau Cautionary Folktales. *Journal of the African Literature Association, 15*(3), 573–589.
Chiguvare, D. (1986). *Kutonhodzwa kwaChauruka*. College Press.
Chinodya, S. (1989). *Harvest of Thorns*. Heinemann.

Dube, L. (2018). Naming and Renaming of the Streets and Avenues of Bulawayo: A Statement to the Vanquished by the Victors? *Nomina Africana: Journal of African Onomastics, 32*(2), 47–55.

Dzimiri, P., Runhare, T., Dzimiri, C., & Mazorodze, W. (2014). Naming, Identity, Politics and Violence in Zimbabwe. *Studies of Tribes and Tribals, 12*(2), 227–238.

Fanon, F. (1963). *The Wretched of the Earth* (C. Farrington, Trans.). Grove Press.

Fortune, G. (1984). Some Recurrent Structures in Shona Praise Poetry. *African Studies, 43*(2), 161–169.

Gatsheni-Ndlovu, S. (2009). *Do Zimbabweans exist? Trajectories of Nationalism, National Identity Formation and Crisis in a Post-colonial State*. Peter Lang.

Gwekwerere, T. (2018). Universal, Normative, and Indispensable: Exploring the Emphasis on Eurocentric Literary-Critical Perspectives in the Criticism of the Black Zimbabwean Novel. *Journal of Black Studies, 49*(8), 801–819.

Makaudze, G. (2021). An Eco-critical Exegesis of Shona Taboos. *Current Writing: Text and Reception in Southern Africa, 33*(2), 143–153.

Marechera, D. (1978). *The House of Hunger*. Heinemann.

Mathebula, M., & Mokgoatšana, S. (2020). The "Polyonymous Identity" of the Hlengwe People of Zimbabwe and Their Struggle for a "Collective Proper Name." *HTS Teologiese Studies/Theological Studies, 76*(4), 1–7.

Mavima, S. (2022). Raising Her Bones: Contextualising the Politicisaton of Nehanda's Legacy in the post-Mugabe Era. In T. Mangena, O. Nyambi, & G. Ncube (Eds.), *The Zimbabwean Crisis After Mugabe* (pp. 40–61). Routledge.

Mungoshi, C. (1975). *Waiting for the Rain*. Heinemann.

Musiyiwa, M. (2022). A Nation Burdened by an Unappeased Ngozi?: A "Folk" Cultural Perspective on Zimbabwe's Stagnation. In O. Nyambi, T. Mangena, & G. Ncube (Eds.), *Cultures of Change in Contemporary Zimbabwe* (pp. 202–216). Routledge.

Musiyiwa, M., & Matshakayile-Ndlovu, T. (2005). Ethnicity in Literature of Shona and Ndebele Expression. In R. Muponde & R. Primorac (Eds.), *Versions of Zimbabwe: New Approaches to Literature and Culture* (pp. 75–88). Weaver Press.

Mutasa, N. M. (1990). *Nhume Yamambo*. Mambo Press.

Mutasa, N. M. (1991). *Misodzi, Dikita neRopa*. Mambo Press.

Mutswairo, S. (1983). *Chaminuka, Prophet of Zimbabwe*. Three Continents Press.

Nyambi, O. (2022). (Un)settling Bones: Abstruse Liberations and re-gendered Commemorations in Panashe Chigumadzi's *These Bones Will Rise Again*. In T. Mangena, O. Nyambi, & G. Ncube (Eds.), *The Zimbabwean Crisis After Mugabe* (pp. 62–78). Routledge.

Nyambi, O., & Matsika, T. (2016). Re-gendering Zimbabwe's Liberation Struggle: Fay Chung's Revisionist Attitude in Re-living the Second Chimurenga: Memories from Zimbabwe's Liberation Struggle (2012). *Gender and Behaviour, 14*(2), 7379–7388.

Pikirayi, I. (2006). The Kingdom, the Power and Forevermore: Zimbabwe Culture in Contemporary Art and Architecture. *Journal of Southern African Studies, 32*(4), 755–770.

Schmidt, H. (1997). Healing the Wounds of War: Memories of Violence and the Making of History in Zimbabwe's Most Recent Past. *Journal of Southern African Studies, 23*(2), 301–310.

Stratton, F. (1986). Charles Mungoshi's *Waiting for the Rain. Zambezia, 13*(1), 11–24.

Vera, Y. (1993). *Nehanda*. Baobab.

Walby, S. (2013). Violence and Society: Introduction to an Emerging Field of Sociology. *Current Sociology, 61*(2), 95–111.

"Living in the Shadow of Death": Understandings of Political Violence and Its Aftermath in the Zimbabwean Context

Chenai Matshaka and Ruth Murambadoro

1   Introduction

Meanings of violence and trauma play an important part in how individuals and society respond to violence. These responses are central to breaking cycles of violence and building peace, hence the importance of capturing them and reflecting upon them in processes and dialogues that are inclusive. At the centre of peaceful communities are relationships between individuals and groups that make up society. When the values, structures, and systems that keep society at peace disintegrate, moving away from a violent to peaceful order becomes increasingly difficult. Breaking cycles of violence also progressively becomes complex as the essence of what brings society together is taken over by polarization. This undesirable path of polarization and trauma is what characterizes Zimbabwe's political landscape today: a landscape predicated by seemingly unending cycles of violent contestations for power.

Through the stories of Zimbabwean women and men, who have been wounded and displaced by acts of political violence, we highlight the consequences of experiences of political violence including trauma, a breakdown of family life, and a detachment from one's home and community. We draw from our ongoing research engagements that date back to 2015 involving

---

C. Matshaka (✉)
University of Pretoria, Pretoria, South Africa
e-mail: chenai.matshaka@up.ac.za

R. Murambadoro
York University, Toronto, ON, Canada

© The Author(s), under exclusive license to Springer Nature Switzerland AG 2024
O. B. Mlambo and E. Chitando (eds.), *The Palgrave Handbook of Violence in Africa*,
https://doi.org/10.1007/978-3-031-40754-3_47

interviews with more than 50 survivors of state-sanctioned violence in Zimbabwe. In these interviews we seek to link how different epochs of political strife dating back to the colonial era have shaped memories of violence and trauma in the psyche of survivors and their communities. We explore how the memory of violence remains an entrapment in the day-to-day experiences of ordinary Zimbabweans across space and time. Pseudo-names have been used in place of names of participants involved in the study to maintain confidentiality.

It is our argument in this chapter that the inability to understand and recognize the deep-rooted trauma and transcending impact of political violence in the everyday life of survivors poses a threat to transforming patterns of violent political engagement. We concur with the debates put forward by scholars such as Mlambo (2013), Ndlovu-Gatsheni (2011a), Onslow (2017) and Sachikonye (2011) amongst others that the acculturation of state-sanctioned violence in the Zimbabwean society is the biggest threat to reconciliation and rebuilding a cohesive postcolonial state.

2 Thinking of and Narrating State-Sanctioned Violence

More voices are needed to narrate and depict the lived experiences of survivors of state-sanctioned violence in colonial and postcolonial Zimbabwe because only those who have been wounded can give testimony as they are both victims of injustices and direct witnesses. While questions about the reliability of the narratives of victims and witnesses of political violence and other forms of trauma have been raised in recent scholarship on memory, there is general agreement on the need for these stories to be told. Allowing victims to tell their stories of violence and trauma helps to move them from the obscurity in which they are pushed in many societies and helps in weaving together a coherent narrative of their memories and experience of violence. The earlier this is done following violence, the greater the chances of drawing up a more coherent narrative, which is difficult to attain following traumatic experiences and after the passage of time (Saikia, 2004).

The language of "violence" is essentially relational and depicts force imposed on others, in a manner that breaks down and debases them, thereby upsetting the relations of involved parties (Cobb, 2013). Bosi et al. (2014: 1) contend that "Political violence involves a heterogeneous repertoire of actions aimed at inflicting physical, psychological and symbolic damage on individuals and/or property with the intention of influencing various audiences in order to effect or resist political, social, and/or cultural change." Political violence is synonymous with state-sanctioned violence as it is a form of domination that makes use of tangible and intangible force to achieve self-serving political goals, often violating the fundamental human rights of individuals and groups (DeMeritt, 2016; Herreros, 2006).

Agents of political violence may include, but are not exclusive to, military and paramilitary actors, the police or organized political groups, militia, as well as other groups that are seen as extensions of the government and, where the political opposition has control over means to violence, they possess a threat to the incumbent government (DeMeritt, 2016; Herreros, 2006). The tactics of those with legitimate access to repressive apparatus vary from those of opposition groups, and so do public reactions towards this action (Lupu & Wallace, 2019). These reactions to the violence are an important factor in determining how society decides to move on from the violence, or rather to move on to non-violent forms of political action. How we understand or perceive violence, therefore, determines the mechanisms adopted to address the effects of violence (Matshaka, 2022).

These mechanisms are often a source of contestation, and a direct result of the divisive nature of political violence which, as argued by Apter (1997: 1), "turns boundaries in the mind into terrains and jurisdictions on the ground." Beyond our understandings of violence, however, is the presence, or rather the ability, to sustain and keep intact structures and systems as well as relations based on particular values that allow society to deal with this violence. These structures include state legal structures as well as community structures based on cultural or religious values. This approach to thinking about violence is motivated by social movement theory that looks beyond only the perpetrators of violence to the entire system with which they interact with (Bosi & Malthaner, 2015).

Since 1900, political violence has likely killed well over 100 million people, the majority of whom were civilians (Valentino, 2014) with many survivors losing homes, livelihoods, limbs, loved ones, and even their mental health (Ghobarah et al., 2003). While political violence is undesirable, it is not an exception and is often part of a broader strategy or range of political actions used alternately and at times in combination with non-violent strategies (Bosi & Malthaner, 2015; Goodwin, 2012). For this reason, political violence needs to be understood within a broader context of political actions including those that may seem routine, such as the language of political interaction in a particular context as well as day-to-day interactions within this space (Bosi & Malthaner, 2015). This means that the decision to use violence or non-violence is "shaped by the groups' goals and identity orientation and, particularly, responds to changing environments and actions of their opponents and/or allies" (Bosi & Malthaner, 2015: 441).

Relationships between actors, diverse histories, and changes in power dynamics, among other factors, also help us to understand the nature of, and decision to use, political violence (Goodwin, 2012). Interactions within these different contexts, therefore, determine the relational dynamics within various groups, as well as between these groups and particular institutions. Further, political violence is contextualized within the broader nature of political and social conflicts existing in a particular polity, and this is key to preventing political violence (Valentino, 2014). These conflicts can include economic, ethnic, or racial inequality, and any other form of discrimination that has led society to organize or form associations on political grounds. Political parties have been a key grouping of such political interests. In African contexts these political parties have had many entanglements with various interest groups that do not necessarily seek to gain power, and this has been a source of conflict where the boundaries of political and civic spaces have been blurred.

State-sanctioned violence can be understood as both the legitimate and illegitimate use of politically sponsored power by public officials and their associates in orchestrating undue harms and manipulation on ordinary citizens (Delgado, 2020). The abuse of power by state actors in these contexts often becomes embedded in the fabric of society and occurs with impunity, rendering the abused persons subject to multiple forms of violations that strip away their dignity. This erosion of human dignity encapsulates the idea of "living in the shadow of death," a perspective that was shared by some participants in our research. Understanding the intersecting realities that fuel and sustain state-sanctioned violence in the everyday lives of ordinary citizens provides an avenue to build knowledge on the evolving nature of violence and its lasting impact on victims.

As this chapter shows, democracy in Africa is often muddled with autocracy, and its practice is often based on select rituals that are complicated by colonial histories and the nature of state formation. As such there is a constant complex connection between the need for violence as a political tool and alternative political action within movements, as well as between movements and the rest of society (Apter, 1997). More evidently, as this chapter will show, there is the need to explore how political violence impacts individuals and communities long after the fact. Some of these complexities are discussed in the following section with regard to political violence in Zimbabwe.

3   The Context

Mamdani (2003: 132) argues that "The modern political sensibility sees political violence as necessary to historical progress...moderns have come to see violence as the midwife of history." This could be argued to be the understanding of violence adopted by Zimbabwean political elites, particularly where threats to their power and hegemony have emerged. A closer reflection on the nature of violence and coercion in Zimbabwe also reflects a culture of violence that has become entrenched in the day-to-day lives of citizens and which has become part of their existence. This does not mean however, a desensitized existence in which political violence and its impacts are not fully recognized, but rather a state where encounters with this violence is almost inevitable.

Rooted in colonial struggle, embedded patterns of domination, branding, and intolerance, political violence in Zimbabwe is cyclical with seemingly unending episodes of organized violence and torture. The setting apart of different groups as enemies has been part of this embedded structure of violence with various groups emerging as foes and allies at different epochs of violence. Branding on ethnic and political party lines remains a key narrative in post-independence Zimbabwe, with language and discourse from the liberation struggle branding being perpetuated, as discussed in the following section in this chapter. Entrenched at independence, ZANU-PF hegemony remains, as rule by coercion, violence, and the threat of violence remains in the patterns of political engagement (Moore, 2008).

The hegemony and violence, though entrenched, have been met with resistance which has largely been squashed by the ZANU-PF government whenever it has emerged. Unlike African resistance to colonial rule for most parts of the early 1900s up to the 1950s, which had shifted to underground operations in the form of religious and workers' organizations that relied on peaceful engagements with the colonial administrators as a means to broker resolutions (Mlambo, 1995), resistance in postcolonial Zimbabwe has been more overt, as have been the violent responses to it.

The first decade after attaining independence from colonial rule did not bring the much-anticipated relief from state-sanctioned violence. Instead, the new independence government went to war against its citizenry, in the *Gukurahundi*[1] genocide. By the end of the second decade post-independence the

---

[1] *Gukurahundi* is a Shona term that refers to the first rain of summer that washes away the chaff from the previous season. It refers to the killing of an estimated 10,000 people belonging to the Ndebele ethnic group by the state's Fifth Brigade allegedly to suppress dissident activities in the south of Zimbabwe during the early 1980s (Nyarota, 2006: 134).

country's economy had plunged into crisis, further heightening the need for a violent state to squash dissent against it. This was fuelled in part by the government's unplanned disbursement of funds to compensate veterans of the liberation war in 1997. These demands by veterans of the liberation struggle posed a threat to the ruling elite in ZANU-PF who stood to lose electoral support from a constituency that had great influence in the political history of Zimbabwe (Kriger, 2003). In September 1997, a package was announced by the government for war veterans to receive a lump sum of Z$50 000 and a gratuity for life of Z$5 000 per month—a cost estimated at Z$4 billion, inevitably exacerbating the national debt (Kriger, 2003; Musemwa, 2011).

The resulting financial crisis was accompanied by a humanitarian crisis in which access to food, healthcare, and other basic human needs became increasingly difficult for many Zimbabweans. The government implemented budget cuts on healthcare between 1991 and 1992 and the Ministry of Health and Child Welfare retrenched an estimated 800 health workers, and abolished close to 400 nursing posts, reducing the workforce by 10% (Chimhowu & Tevera, 1991; Osika et al., 2010). In addition, a massive exodus of medical professionals seeking better remuneration and working conditions, exacerbated the challenges of the collapsing system (Gupta & Dal Poz, 2009). It is this financial crisis and growing humanitarian challenges that heightened dissent and allowed the emergence of opposition political actors in the late 1990s.

At the same time, the global community was opening up to multi-party democracy and Zimbabwe was not spared. The Movement for Democratic Change (MDC) was formed in 1999 with most of its members emerging from organized labour (Laakso, 2003). Its founding leader, the late Morgan Tsvangirai, was the former secretary general of the ZCTU that had led several protests in the 1990s challenging the government's economic policies (Onslow, 2017). This included the riots from 19–23 January 1998 following outcries over growing inflation that pushed the price of household goods such as mealie meal, rice, bread, and cooking oil exponentially (Zimbabwe Human Rights NGO Forum, 1998). Apart from the economic effects of the Economic Adjustment Programmes (ESAP), the country had been going through a tough decade marked by a series of droughts which had a huge effect on agricultural production and the agricultural-based economy (Mhone, 1995). These hardships created an opportunity for the MDC party to amass support from disenfranchised citizens, and it became a key player in the Zimbabwean political landscape, challenging the ruling ZANU-PF government to reform.

While elections in post-independence Zimbabwe have been characterized by violence at varying intensity, the stakes were substantially raised following the entry of MDC into the electoral space (Sachikonye, 2011). However, many Zimbabweans were not prepared for the aftermath of the political impasse that occurred in 2008. As one of the survivors we interviewed for this study, *Babamunini Freedom* highlighted, "What happened in 2008 was extreme brutality. Many people in my community never imagined that such display of animosity and hatred would be witnessed in our area."

A 2008 Human Rights Watch report titled "Bullets for Each of You" described the post-March 2008 electoral violence as acts of terror that were well orchestrated to ensure that the ruling ZANU-PF party retained political control in the presidential run-off that was scheduled for 27 June 2008 (Kasambala, 2008). Violence displayed during this period included bodily mutilation, murder, arson, abductions, and debilitating beatings on members and suspected supporters of the MDC. Apart from the *Gukurahundi* genocide in the early 1980s and the violent farm invasions of 2000–2003, the post-colony had not witnessed such a grandiose display of state-sanctioned violence. When such unexpected violence occurs, humanity, friendship, and kinship ties are often forgotten, and taken over by intolerance and hate. These fractures have been visible in the violence that has engulfed Zimbabwe's elections since 1980 and continues in the post-Mugabe dispensation following his dislodging from power in 2017.

4 Polarization, Intolerance, and Violence in Zimbabwe

As highlighted earlier in this chapter, the violence observed in Zimbabwe's politics after 1980 is a by-product of a divisive political culture that has polarized communities along political party lines (Ndlovu-Gatsheni, 2011a). These divisions have been decoded into the national structures of state institutions such as the police, judiciary, and military (Matsilele & Ruhanya, 2021) and in all aspects of life. Political polarization has captured all facets of Zimbabwean life creating a dangerous precedent where political affiliations and branding surface in all facets of life. The language of destroying one's enemies is part of the political rhetoric of main political parties (Mapara & Wasosa, 2012), further driving society apart. As one participant in the study, *mukoma Jacob*, stated:

The two main political parties in Zimbabwe, ZANU-PF, and MDC-T, have political slogans that teach political opponents to be intolerant. ZANU-PF's slogan says *pasi nanhingi* (bring down a particular individual), which can mean bring that person down six feet under [to the grave]. Similarly, MDC-T goes by the slogan; *isa musoro mudenga, batanidza, rovera pasi.* (take it up by the head and slam on the floor)

Political lines have been sharply drawn in Zimbabwean politics over the past few years with the MDC in its emergence emphasizing its differences from ZANU-PF and the status quo, and ZANU-PF trying to promote allegiance to it and this was done through violence and the threat of violence (Gallagher, 2015). The contest for political power by the two main political parties in Zimbabwe has cemented tensions among community members and neighbours, and has extended to the family. Sachikonye (2011) and the Zimbabwe Human Rights NGO Forum (2012) have recorded reports of over 200,000 incidents of politically related violence across the country within the first decade of the establishment of the MDC-T party. Violence witnessed is compounded by the capture of key institutions which has fuelled impunity as antagonistic political actors commit acts of violence without accountability. Some of the victims of state sanctioned violence we spoke to such as *VaChitiso*, a 52-year-old man from Buhera, have been victimized by state institutions which are meant to institute justice on their behalf. *VaChitiso* shared that,

> I was locked up for a whole month in prison without standing trial. My family did not know where I was because they had abducted me from my house, beat me up, and thrown me in prison to die from my wounds. The prison wardens used to give me pap mixed with cement in attempt to quicken my death, but I never ate their food.

These periods of violence have included unlawful detention, torture, rape, murder, electioneering, and other military operations meant to punish citizens and crush dissent. Fear, mistrust, and disunity is often churned through homilies of *Chimurenga* which hold sentiments of comrades and enemies, restricting power to a few black elites who mostly act to preserve self-interests (Makahamadze, 2018; Onslow, 2017). "*Chimurenga*" is a term that carries varying meanings that include uprising, war, resistance, struggle, and revolution. Ndlovu-Gatsheni (2011b) notes that the term "*Chimurenga*" gained prominence in the 1970s as it was largely used by the nationalists in ZANU and its fighting wing (ZANLA), meaning war against the colonial regime.

With the rise of MDC and growing opposition to the ZANU-PF government in the early 2000s, the term was used to justify any state-sponsored violence at the instigation of ZANU-PF including the violent fast-track land reform, as well as electoral violence (Ndlovu-Gatsheni, 2011b). Any threat to ZANU-PF hegemony was met with the adage of Chimurenga and a reminder that blood was spilt during the liberation war, and certainly threats that it would be spilt again should need be, to protect ZANU-PF rule (Sithole & Makumbe, 1997).

This adage of war has seen the infliction of military-style operations by the state including *Operation Chipo Chiroorwa* and *Operation Murambatsvina*, to deal with dissent and perceived opposition to a state that has been captured by the ruling party and former liberation movement—Zimbabwe African National Union-Patriotic Front (ZANU-PF) (Nyere, 2016). Those who are not victims have sadly become onlookers as the violence has become internalized as part of Zimbabwean life. This state of affairs is what Apter describes as "the hegemonic consequences of the liberating project…where it [violence] becomes self-sustaining and of long duration, people accept it, live with it, and survive in a world gone dull, nasty, brutish and short" (1997: 1–2)

Politics in Zimbabwe is a dangerous zero-sum game in which the values of respect and community are increasingly under threat. Regrettably, this culture of violence has been cemented throughout Zimbabwe's post-independence history through recurring episodes of political violence and trauma as well as the growing erosion of civic trust. While many have become observers in Zimbabwe's violent society, many have also become enablers of the system that continues to churn out this violence. These enablers of repression have included the clergy, business players, artists, and sportspersons, among other influential members of society who have fostered a deeply fractured society by aiding and propping up repression (Mutongwizo, 2016). Those in political office have amassed wealth for themselves and immediate allies, living in opulence whilst a large number of the general populace remain in poverty and uncertainty. The effect of state-sanctioned repression permeates the everyday life and day-to-day interactions of Zimbabweans in complex ways that affect those living within and outside the country.

While official figures remain contested, many Zimbabweans have been forced to leave the country in search of better living conditions as the political crisis has dampened prospects of many citizens achieving their held aspirations. Several of those in the diaspora are living as illegal immigrants, thereby facing further marginalization as they are not able to fully participate in socio-economic activities that can improve their livelihood (Dumba & Chirisa,

2010). The separation of families as some have fled the country in fear of political persecution, economic hardships, and civil unrest deepen the resentment carried by those affected by the turmoil. These extending effects of violence can be seen through the narratives of research participants such as *babamunini Freedom* who was forced into exile in 2008 after being attacked by a ZANU-PF linked militant group for being what they termed a "sellout." He was victimized following allegations of being a sympathizer with the opposition party, MDC.

The subject of witches and "sell-outs" in Zimbabwean politics is a discourse synonymous with the political contestations that flourished during the liberation struggle. The liberation struggle represents a period where the labels witches, wizards, and sell-outs were ascribed to anti-war supporters who enabled the colonial regime to suppress the interests of marginalized black people. In the context of the liberation war, witches and sell-outs were those accused of aiding, collaborating, and associating with the enemy—the Rhodesian forces and government (Marowa, 2009). Such persons had to be dealt with as part of the fight to end white supremacy and imperialism. Hence, being labelled a witch and a sell-out had dire consequences for the accused, including death. It was given as a rationale for punishments meted out to the culprits and has been extended to the post-independence political order, gaining impetus in the height of opposition politics, including the 2008 elections.

With the rise of the opposition in Zimbabwe, the discourse of "sell-outs" and witches has become synonymous with those in opposition to the state, as well as members of political parties, civil society organizations, and any entity or individual expressing disagreement with the ZANU-PF government, including those who oppose the ruling elites of the party within its ranks. Those accused of political witchcraft and selling-out, are sniffed out of the community and punished by state security agents and militia groups working for the ruling regime. It is important to note that often in the postcolonial politics of Zimbabwe, both "selling-out" and political witchcraft became tantamount and carried the same weight of offence and punishment. Those accused of this crime during the liberation struggle were reported to the freedom fighters who would hold a kangaroo court to decide the accused's fate (Machingura, 2012). During the post-2000 elections, similar control structures had been resuscitated including bases for ZANU-PF supporters that replicated the bases for liberation war fighters, and those accused of "selling-out" were reported to the ZANU-PF leaders in the area. During the liberation struggle, those accused would be tortured, maimed, or even killed (Machingura, 2012).

This was replicated during the 2008 electoral violence—a re-enactment of the glorification of violence and brutality that pervaded the liberation war and became intrenched in the country's politics. For instance, on Wednesday 21 May 2008, a group of ZANU-PF youths raided the home of *babamunini Freeman* in Uzumba and accused him of being a "sell-out." The assailants, about 20 young men, coerced him out of his home, took him to a bush that was 50 m away and brutally assaulted him. This ordeal occurred during the three months of terror that followed the 2008 harmonized elections (April to June), which have been colloquially dubbed *Operation Makavhotera Papi (Where did you put your vote?)*. The operation, led by ZANU-PF militias and state security agents including the police and army, sought to find and punish those that had voted for the opposition MDC in the first round of the 2008 harmonized elections (Bratton & Masunungure, 2008; Moore, 2008). In the 2008 harmonized elections, ZANU-PF had lost its parliamentary majority and had failed to attain an outright win in the presidential elections, leading to a run-off presidential poll (Nyere, 2016). This loss in parliamentary majority and loss in the first round of the presidential poll marked an end to electoral hegemony for ZANU-PF. The March 2008 poll results were released nearly two months after the polls with Morgan Tsvangirai of the MDC-T securing 47.9%, and Robert Mugabe of ZANU-PF 43.2% (Nyere, 2016).

Babamunini Freedom believes that his role as an educator and elections officer contributed to his targeting as a "sell-out." Teachers and other civil servants, as well as educated people in rural areas were targeted in electoral violence due to accusations of disloyalty (Pswarayi & Reeler, 2012). Teachers were accused of stealing the elections for the MDC in their capacity as electoral officers, as well "teaching politics" in schools. Being labelled *mutengesi* (sell-out /a traitor) subjected one to the threat of violence as well as loss of identity and heritage. The social construction of the idea of a sell-out or traitor is, thus, a mechanism that has been fostered and continues to be nurtured not only by the ZANU-PF regime but also in the opposition ranks to discredit those opposed to their politics.

Polarization on political lines continues to plague Zimbabwean society and has cascaded into all aspects of life, thereby threatening national cohesion and security. Points of antagonism rather than points of possible agreement and the exploitation of sources of resentment continue to be emphasized in various spaces of interaction and public discourses.

5   The Ordeal of Violence and 'Living in the Shadow of Death'

The participants in this study related their experiences of political violence during various periods including elections, "operations," protests, as well as during the war of liberation and how these experiences not only disrupted life as they knew it, but also altered their perspectives of life itself. Martín-Baró (1989) contends that war by its nature takes over all aspects of a country's state of affairs, subordinating all other spheres of life which directly and indirectly impact societal life. Similarly, political violence has a comparable trait, as it interrupts the everyday lives of individuals and the broader society in which it occurs. This form of violence draws resources by perpetrators towards the destruction of opponents, causing social polarization that sets groups on parallel positions and pressure to align with each side, as well as taking over of institutions by more powerful groups, thereby disadvantaging those labelled as the "other" (Martín-Baró, 1989). These implications of violence were highlighted in every experience narrated to us in the various interviews we conducted.

The identities of the survivors of the violence and those that inflicted the violence are clearly drawn out in the accounts given to us. They are tales of deep polarization, and in some cases despair due to the lingering fear that it will happen again. Mamdani (2003: 136) asks a pertinent question about how polarization emerges and contends that:

> If we are to make political violence thinkable, we need to understand the process by which victims and perpetrators become polarized as group identities. Who do perpetrators of violence think they are? And who do they think they will eliminate through violence?

While our research focused on those on the receiving end of the violence, these questions were answered by the victims of the violence, based on their own understandings of why they were targeted in the violence. In the narratives we captured this was expressed as patterns of domination and the power dynamics imposed by both the colonial and postcolonial state.

Despite living in the diaspora for the past 12 years, one participant in the study, *babamunini Freedom* laments that his life trajectory has not been any better than what he had escaped from in his home. In depicting the intersecting realities that forged his encounters with the state in 2008 and the afterlife of what he terms "living in the shadow of death," we expound the value of memory in navigating accounts of lived violence and trauma as well as in exacerbating political polarization. The life story shared by *babamunini*

Freedom highlights a common thread in the narratives shared by other participants such as aunty *weChitima* who survived a bullet wound during the war of liberation, *babamukuru Mavande* who narrowly escaped gunshots fired at his homestead by ZANU-PF militias in 2008, as well as *mukoma Hwande*, who was imprisoned for supporting the opposition party MDC. The narratives shared show entrenched patterns of coercion by the state across different periods and the similar implications for the victims across different geographies and temporalities. The memories of trauma are still vivid in the minds of the victims and the lines drawn between the and the perpetrators are still very clear. For example, *weChitima* expressed how her experience of violence at the hands of the colonial state had scarred her for life both physically and beyond. She narrates,

> I still remember the day. I was visiting my uncle in his village, when rumour had gone out to the Rhodesian forces that the guerrilla fighters had passed by his village. The Rhodesian forces came through and conducted a raid on the village …Yes, and l was caught up in the crossfire. The soldiers came after us, breaking doors at every hut…They got to the hut where my aunts and I were hiding…one of the soldiers got on his knees and held the gun under the door opening and made a round of shots through the opening. A bullet hit my leg. I was in so much pain and could not hold back crying. The soldiers opened the door and found me and my aunts. They took me away from the family. I had been seriously injured and my leg was torn to pieces from my knee going down. You can still see the wound here.

Such remanences of violence reared their ugly head once again during the 2008 elections, widely documented as one of Zimbabwe's most violent epochs (see for example Matyszak, 2008; Pigou, 2008). The violence of 2008 also had the trademarks of the *Gukurahundi* including arson attacks, sexual violence and torture as well as forced re-education of the masses, synonymous with how Van der Waag (2004), linked the 2000 electoral violence to the *Gukurahundi*. These shows a clearly entrenched system of brutality that has been replicated with different intensity and spread, a well-oiled machine of violence ready to be unleashed at any time. The 2008 political violence in Zimbabwe reached its peak following an electoral impasse between ZANU-PF and the larger MDC formation. The electoral impasse resulted in an election run-off which was preceded by a wave of retributive attacks largely targeting those constituencies in which MDC had won parliamentary and local government seats (Pigou, 2008). The violence was largely perpetrated by organized syndicates of ZANU-PF supporters who worked with officers of the Zimbabwe National Army (ZNA), Central Intelligence Organization

(CIO) and other state security agencies under the command of the Joint Operating Command (JOC) which was the supreme organ for coordinating state security matters and was composed of heads of Zimbabwe's key security institutions (Matyszak, 2008; Pigou, 2008).

Those who experienced the violence in rural constituencies during this time tell of how acts of terror were mostly perpetrated by the young people from the same community working on the command of leadership from the ZANU-PF party, and state security agents as coordinated by JOC. At night, homes of known and suspected MDC supporters were raided and, in some cases, burnt down with impunity. Villagers associated with the MDC were assaulted, maimed, raped, or murdered (Pigou, 2008). Day and night soon embodied a conflicting duality in the existence of the community, characterized by varying degrees of terror and turmoil as narrated by *babamunini Freedo*m. By day, the perpetrators acted as vanguards of the "moral code" of the community conducting rallies to re-educate the residents about the liberation struggle and its meaning in the political life of the community. At night, they were administrators of justice, operating raids on unsuspecting persons charged with violating the ethos of *Chimurenga* (the liberation struggle). The MDC was labelled a party of "sell-outs," "puppets of the West" and the former colonizers who, together with its supporters, deserved to be crushed by the full wrath of the state coercive machinery (Chigora et al., 2011). Food aid was used in rural constituencies as a weapon against the so-called enemies as they were denied aid if they failed to produce proof of membership to ZANU-PF in the form of party cards (Chigora et al., 2011).

Military bases or camps were set up as command centres particularly in rural areas, where the youth were rallied for *pungwes* (night vigils) and charged with the mandate to perform surveillance on community members (Museka et al., 2016). Gonye (2013: 66) describes *pungwes* as "meetings held in the bush, where guerrillas lectured the peasants (amidst song and *kongonya* dance) about the justice and necessity of the war against the Rhodesian regime." During the 2008 elections *pungwes* became meetings used by ZANU-PF to punish and re-educate alleged MDC supporters as well as to send a clear message to all villagers of their fate should they support the opposition. As such, the ZANU-PF leadership has sustained intimidation and fear in rural communities by coercing people to attend rallies where they are cautioned against supporting the opposition. The continued celebration of violence and war as a way of politicking is a great tragedy for Zimbabwean society as the implications are far reaching, particularly on the psyche of the communities that live in perpetual fear of reliving the experiences. For them it has become like "living in the shadow of death." There is certainly no doubt in their minds about the lengths that the state will go to quash dissent (Matshaka, 2022).

6 Beyond "The Shadow of Death": Moving on After Political Violence and Trauma

Moving forward after experiences of violence and torture is complex. As confirmed by Kalmanowitz and Lloyd (2005), the costs of political violence are felt over long periods of time. While there is a tendency to medicalize the trauma of political violence, Summerfield (1999) challenges the notion that this often leads to short-term responses to this trauma including counselling. When past injustices are not addressed within the home, community, and the state, survivors lose connection with the self, because trauma creates distance between the self and the past (Brison, 1999). Their bodies often collect memories of pain (Burton, 2011), and everything people do takes a meaning of its own. The recurring similarities and differences in encounters from their past produce lifelong suffering, agony, and despair. The chapter, thus, makes a case for the need to document personal narratives of survivors as a necessary step in redressing the silenced histories of survivors of state-sanctioned violence in Zimbabwe. Malathi de Alwis and Pradeep Jeganathan (2022) in *Talking About the Body in Rumours of Death* point out that multiple narratives of the past should be accommodated as lenses to understand the socio-cultural architecture of society and its effects in shaping the embodied experiences of individuals and the collective. Personal narratives are embodied with feelings, attitudes, temporality, and context, which create the living memory and history of survivors necessary in informing the remedy needed to heal their wounds.

For example, some of the participants in our study expressed how they could not separate their past encounters of violence relating to the colonial regime and those orchestrated by the post-independence regime. As their reflections showcased, there exist interconnections of multiple temporalities that have shaped their life trajectory. *Gogo Sinika* a 63-year-old woman from Masvingo shared her disappointment at the postcolonial dispensation after having suffered at the hands of the colonial government:

> Many older women in the rural areas have kept the secrets of how their bodies were violated by guerrilla fighters during the liberation struggle because we accepted that we were at war. We accepted that during the struggle our enemy was the *white man* (colonial government). Removing them would bring freedom to all, and our struggles would come to an end. But years have passed

by, and we are still poor, our life is difficult, and we are burdened with the thoughts of what happened to us. Why did we participate in the liberation struggle?

The idea of "living in the shadow of death" thus captures the living trauma embodied in the psyche of survivors of violence, whose lives are haunted by the threat of death in the hands of repressive regimes. Participants in the study shared that they have not got over the trauma of witnessing violence perpetrated on their own bodies or against family members, community members, and innocent bystanders. In a context where political violence and the threat of it recurring is a threat to the healing of victims and their ability to move forward, moving on is a difficult prospect.

Where victims of political violence are forced to remain silent and are unable to talk freely about their ordeal, feelings of polarization are exacerbated. Reporting political violence to state agents or civic groups is seen as treacherous and threatens the state's official story. The official story of political violence in Zimbabwe is often that of "enemies of the state" and a just reaction by the state to deal with threats to peace and security (Matshaka, 2022). These narratives about the victims become what Martín-Baró (1989: 10) terms "the institutionalised lie" which is threatened by the victims' speaking out about what happened to them. Hence, those who threaten the "institutionalised lie" are punished with further violence. As Martín-Baró (1989: 11) aptly contends, "What seems to be important is not whether the facts in question are true or not, which is always denied a priori; what is important is that they are stated. It is not the deeds that count, but the images." The "institutionalised lie" is, therefore, linked to denying victims of political violence a chance of getting justice and shielding the perpetrators from accountability.

The need for victims of political violence to express themselves and talk about what happened to them should, however, not only focus on the corroborated facts of history but, as Saikia (2004: 280) argues, "that personal suffering can and should be made social. Without it, extreme experiences of individual suffering will become unthinkable and therefore unknowable." Hence, the focus on giving victims of political violence an opportunity to speak about their experience should focus on healing, combating the silence, and creating narratives about the violence. While civil society groups in Zimbabwe have sought to create spaces for both social and factual accounts of political violence in Zimbabwe, the shrinking civic space in the country has made these initiatives a challenge.

While the focus by civic groups has been to engage the state and push for reforms that will enable justice and accountability for victims of political violence, there continues to be a lack of engagement between state actors and victims. One respondent in our study, a former civil society activist argued:

> The state has a wrong perception of what the people want, that is why they do not want to engage the people, they are scared of letting the victims speak out because they think they want trials and other forms of retribution.

Hence, speaking out about the violence is feared rather than accepted as a form of healing and reclaiming one's power. The "shadow of death" therefore continues to loom in the lives of those who have experienced political violence at different periods in the state's history. Their aspirations for a better future which give them hope to carry on amidst the turmoil, remain the one thing they hold on to. Whether these aspirations will be realized remains to be seen as further threats of political violence continue to loom in further contests for political power.

7 Conclusion

As shown in this chapter, violence is a relational term that affects how we relate to one another, how we see one another, and our shared future. In the case of Zimbabwe, it has led to stark polarization where even kith and kin have become foes as labels such as traitors, sell-outs, and witches have become entrenched in political discourse. This polarization, as shown in this chapter, poses a threat to peace, stability, and social cohesion among Zimbabwean communities. Polarization has engulfed all aspects of aspects of life and political labels determine access to spaces and resources.

The lingering threat of violence and persecution die to being ascribed particular labels remains pulpable among those who have suffered and witnessed political violence. The unending trauma of living in a society where violence and intolerance are entrenched is equated to "living in the shadow of death"—a constant fear of death's looming sting. Moving forward from these experiences of violence becomes almost impossible with the possibility of more violence to come and the silencing of victims, lest they dispute the official accounts of the state.

We conclude this chapter by arguing that living in a society where violence and coercion for political gains remains a threat to peace and stability in Zimbabwe. An entrenched culture of political violence with similar modus operandi across different periods in the country's history serves the passing on of general trauma and understandings of harm that make moving forward from a violent to a peaceful dispensation extremely difficult. Hence, breaking cycles of violence in Zimbabwe has to be tied with mending polarized relations among communities and individuals affected by the multiple episodes of violence and coercion in both colonial and postcolonial eras.

Acknowledgements This work (by Chenai Matshaka) is based on the research supported by the National Institute for The Humanities and Social Sciences.

Bibliography

Apter, D. E. (1997). Political Violence in Analytical Perspective. In D. E. Apter (Ed.), *The Legitimization of Violence* (pp. 1–32). Palgrave Macmillan.

Barnes, T. (1997). "Am I a Man?": Gender and the Pass Laws in Urban Colonial Zimbabwe, 1930–80. *African Studies Review, 40*(1), 59–81.

Bosi, L., Demetriou, C., & Malthane, S. (2014). A Contentious Politics Approach to the Explanation of Radicalization. In D. Chares (Ed.), *Dynamics of Political Violence* (pp. 1–24). Routledge.

Bosi, L., & Malthaner, S. (2015). Political Violence. In D. della Porta & M. Diani (Eds.), *Oxford Handbook of Social Movements* (pp. 439–451). Oxford University Press.

Bratton, M., & Eldred, N. (2008). Zimbabwe's Long Agony. *Journal of Democracy, 19*(4), 41.

Brison, S. (1999). The Uses of Narrative in the Aftermath of Violence. *On Feminist Ethics and Politics*, 200–225.

Burton, T. (2011). Painful Memories: Chronic Pain as a Form of Re-membering. *Memory Studies, 4*(1), 23–32.

Chigora, P., Guzura, T., & Mutumburanzou, J. (2011). The Challenges Facing Opposition Political Parties in Rural Zimbabwe Within 2000–2008. *African Journal of Political Science and International Relations, 5*(7), 358–366.

Chimhowu, A. O., & Tevera, D. (1991). Intra-provincial Inequalities in the Provision of Health Care in the Midlands Province of Zimbabwe. *Geographical Journal of Zimbabwe, 22*, 33–45.

Cobb, S. B. (2013). *Speaking of Violence: The Politics and Poetics of Narrative in Conflict Resolution.* Oxford University Press.

Crane, D. M., Desmond De Silva, Q. C., & Tom, Z. (2008). Seeking Justice for Zimbabwe. *The Project to End Genocide and Crimes Against Humanity.* Impunity Watch.

de Alwis, M., & Jeganathan, P. (2022). *Talking About the Body in Rumours of Death.*

Delgado, M. (2020). *State-Sanctioned Violence: Advancing a Social Work Social Justice Agenda.* Oxford University Press.

DeMeritt, J. H. R. (2016). The Strategic Use of State Repression and Political Violence. *Oxford Research Encyclopedia of Politics.*

Dumba, S., & Chirisa, I. (2010). The Plight of Illegal Migrants in South Africa: A Case Study of Zimbabweans in Soshanguve Extension 4 and 5. *International Journal of Politics and Good Governance, 1*(1.2), 1–8.

Gallagher, J. (2015). The Battle for Zimbabwe in 2013: From Polarisation to Ambivalence. *The Journal of Modern African Studies, 53*(1), 27–49.

Ghobarah, H. A., Huth, P., & Russett, B. (2003). Civil Wars Kill and Maim People—Long After the Shooting Stops. *American Political Science Review, 97*(2), 189–202.

Gonye, J. (2013). Mobilizing Dance/Traumatizing Dance: Kongonya and the Politics of Zimbabwe. *Dance Research Journal, 45*(1), 65–79.

Goodwin, J. (2012). Introduction to a Special Issue on Political Violence and Terrorism: Political Violence as Contentious Politics. *Mobilization: An International Quarterly, 17*(1), 1–5.

Gupta, N., & Dal Poz, M. R. (2009). Assessment of Human Resources for Health Using Cross-national Comparison of Facility Surveys in Six Countries. *Human Resources for Health, 7*(1), 1–9.

Herreros, F. (2006). The Full Weight of the State: The Logic of Random State-Sanctioned Violence. *Journal of Peace Research, 43*(6), 671–689.

Kalmanowitz, D., & Ho, R. T. (2016). Out of Our Mind: Art Therapy and Mindfulness with Refugees, Political Violence and Trauma. *The Arts in Psychotherapy, 49,* 57–65.

Kalmanowitz, D., & Lloyd, B. (Eds.). (2005). *Art Therapy and Political Violence: With Art, Without Illusion*. Psychology Press.

Kasambala, T. (2008). *Bullets for Each of You: State-sponsored Violence Since Zimbabwe's March 29 Elections*. Human Rights Watch.

Kriger, N. J. (1991). *Zimbabwe's Guerrilla War*. Cambridge University Press.

Kriger, N. (2003). War Veterans: Continuities Between the Past and the Present. *African Studies Quarterly, 7*(2–3), 113–137.

Laakso, L., (2003). Opposition Politics in Independent Zimbabwe. *African Studies Quarterly, 7*(2), 119–137.

Lupu, Y., & Wallace, G. P. (2019). Violence, Nonviolence, and the Effects of International Human Rights Law. *American Journal of Political Science, 63*(2), 411–426.

Machingura, F. (2012). The Judas Iscariot Episode in the Zimbabwean Religio-Political Debate of "Selling Out." In J. Kügler & M. G. Ragies (Eds.), *The Bible and Politics in Africa* (pp. 212–235). University of Bamberg Press.

Makahamadze, T. (2018). *How Do Legacies of Violence Affect Regime Stability? Nonviolent Protests and Regime Outcomes in Tunisia and Zimbabwe* (PhD Thesis). George Mason University.

Mamdani, M. (2003). Making Sense of Political Violence in Postcolonial Africa. In L. Panitch & C. Leys (Eds.), *Socialist Fighting Identities: Race, Religion and Ethno-nationalism*. Merlin Press.

Mapara, J., & Wasosa, W. (2012). Self-inflicted Tragedies: An Assessment of the Impact of Language Use by the Political Parties in Post-independence Zimbabwe. *Journal of Research in Peace, Gender and Development, 2*(13), 286–292.

Marowa, I. (2009). Construction of the 'Sellout' Identity During Zimbabwe's War of Liberation: A Case Study of the Dandawa Community of Hurungwe District, c1975–1980. *Identity, Culture and Politics: An Afro-Asian Dialogue, 10*(1), 121–131.

Martín-Baró, I. (1989). Political Violence and War as Causes of Psychosocial Trauma in El-Salvador. *International Journal of Mental Health, 18*(1), 3–20.

Matshaka, C. G. (2022). *Civil Society Narratives of Violence and Shaping the Transitional Justice Agenda in Zimbabwe*. Rowman & Littlefield.

Matsilele, T., & Ruhanya, P. (2021). Social Media Dissidence and Activist Resistance in Zimbabwe. *Media, Culture and Society, 43*(2), 381–394.

Matyszak, D. (2008). *How to Lose an Election and Stay in Power*. IDASA.

Mhone, G. (1995). Dependency and Underdevelopment: The Limits of Structural Adjustment Programmes and Towards a Pro-active State-led Development Strategy. *African Development Review, 7*(2), 51–85.

Mlambo, A. (1995). Student Protest and State Reaction in Colonial Rhodesia: The 1973 Chimukwembe Student Demonstration at the University of Rhodesia. *Journal of Southern African Studies, 21*(3), 473–490.

Mlambo, A. (2013). Becoming Zimbabwe or Becoming Zimbabwean: Identity, Nationalism and State-building. *Africa Spectrum, 48*(1), 49–70.

Moore, D. (2008). Coercion, Consent, Context Operation Murambatsvina and ZANU (PF)'s. In M. Vambe (Ed.), *The Hidden Dimensions of Operation Murambatsvina* (pp. 25–39). Weaver Press.

Msindo, E., & Nyachega, N. (2019). Zimbabwe's Liberation War and the Everyday in Honde Valley, 1975 to 1979. *South African History Journal, 71*(1), 70–93.

Murambadoro, R. (2020). *Transitional Justice in Africa*. Palgrave Macmillan.

Museka, F. Mangena, E. Chitando & I. Muwati. (2016). Sounds of "Death": The Adaptation of Madzviti-Muchongoyo Music in Silencing Dissenting Voices in Chipinge (Manicaland-Zimbabwe, 2002–2008). In F. Mangena & I. Muwati (Eds.), *Sounds of Life: Music, Identity and Politics in Zimbabwe* (pp. 114–126). Cambridge Scholars Publishing.

Musemwa, M. (2011). Zimbabwe's War Veterans: From Demobilisation to Re-mobilisation. *Transformation: Critical Perspectives on Southern Africa, 75*(1), 122–131.

Mutongwizo, T. (2016). Chipangano Governance: Enablers and Effects of Violent Extraction in Zimbabwe. *African Peace and Conflict Journal, 7*(1), 29–40.

Ndlovu-Gatsheni, S. J. (2011a). *The Zimbabwean Nation-State Project: A Historical Diagnosis of Identity and Power-based Conflicts in a Postcolonial State* (Discussion Paper 59). Nordiska Afrikainstitutet.

Ndlovu-Gatsheni, S. J. (2011b). The Construction and Decline of Chimurenga Monologue in Zimbabwe: A Study in Resilience of Ideology and Limits of Alternatives. In *4th European Conference on African Studies (ECAS4) on Contestations* over *Memory and Nationhood: Comparative Perspectives from East and Southern Africa* (pp. 15–18).

Nyarota, G. (2006). *Against the Grain: Memoirs of a Zimbabwean Newsman*. Zebra.

Nyere, C. (2016). The Continuum of Political Violence in Zimbabwe. *Journal of Social Science, 48*(1–2), 94–107.

Onslow, S. (2017). Understanding Zimbabwe: From Liberation to Authoritarianism and Beyond. *International Affairs, 93*(3), 749–751.

Osika, J., Altman, D., Ekbladh, L., Katz, L., Nguyen, H., Rosenfeld, J., Williamson, T., & Tapera, S. (2010). *Zimbabwe Health System Assessment 2010*. Maryland.

Pigou, P. (2008). *Defining Violence: Political Violence or Crimes Against Humanity*. IDASA.

Pswarayi, L., & Reeler, T. (2012). *Fragility and Education in Zimbabwe: Assessing the Impact of Violence on Education*. Research and Advocacy Unit.

Sachikonye, L. (2011). When a State Turns on its Citizens: 60 years of Institutionalised Violence in Zimbabwe. In *When a State Turns on Its Citizens*. Weaver Press.

Saikia, Y. (2004, October). Beyond the Archive of Silence: Narratives of Violence of the 1971 Liberation War of Bangladesh. *History Workshop Journal, 58*(1), 275–287.

Sithole, M., & Makumbe, J. (1997). Elections in Zimbabwe: The ZANU (PF) Hegemony and Its Incipient Decline. *African Journal of Political Science/revue Africaine De Science Politique, 2*(1), 122–139.

Summerfield, D. (1999). A Critique of Seven Assumptions Behind Psychological Trauma Programmes in War-affected Areas. *Social Science & Medicine (1982), 48*(10), 1449–1462.

Valentino, B. A. (2014). Why We Kill: The Political Science of Political Violence Against Civilians. *Annual Review of Political Science, 17*(20), 89–103.

Van der Waag, I. J. (2004). Guerrilla Veterans in Post-war Zimbabwe: Symbolic and Violent Politics, 1980–1987. *The Journal of Military History, 68*(4), 1314–1315.

Zimbabwe Human Rights NGO Forum. (1998). *A Consolidated Report on the Food Riots 19–23 January, 1998*. Zimbabwe Human Rights NGO Forum.

Zimbabwe Human Rights NGO Forum. (2012). *A Culture of Impunity in Zimbabwe: A Report on Access to Justice for Survivors of Organized Violence and Torture (OVT) in Zimbabwe*. Zimbabwe Human Rights NGO Forum.

Forgetting as a Psychological Weapon? Critiquing the Call to Forget in a Zimbabwe Founded and Ruled by Violence

Collium Banda

1   Introduction

There is a semblance of a psychological game in Emmerson Mnangagwa's call to victims of the violence of his party, ZANU-PF, to let bygones be bygones. This is because this call, which means to forgive and forget, has not been followed by a commitment to non-violent rule. While calling on the wounded masses to forgive and forget, Mnangagwa and ZANU-PF continue to use violence as an instrument in governing the country. Consequently, this chapter is a theological-ethical reflection on the question: What is a theological-ethic that the church can use to challenge Mnangagwa's use of forgetting as a psychological game to torture the victims of his violent campaign in Zimbabwe? The people I have described as "victims" in this chapter can also be described as "survivors." I have chosen to use "victims" because the campaign of violence is an ongoing process as Zimbabwe continues to be ruled by violence. Daily, citizens continue to be victimized by the state as oppressive rulers continue to entrench their brutal and unjust power each day. Therefore, I will argue in this chapter that Mnangagwa's plea to victims of his violence to let bygones be bygones is not genuine, but a psychological game of manipulating his victims to support his rule and not demand justice and accountability for their wounds. In essence, Mnangagwa manipulates the humane notion of forgiving and forgetting all wrongs in a

C. Banda (✉)
North-West University, Potchefstroom, South Africa
e-mail: collium@gmail.com

way that humanizes him as magnanimous person who forgives and forgets and portrays his victims, who demand justice for their wounds, as unforgiving, vengeful people bent on sowing seeds of discord in a peace-searching nation.

To answer the stated research question, I first describe the importance of a critical theological-ethic of memory to the church's (the universal community of believers) engagement with the political call to forgive and forget, such as one made by Mnangagwa. I then describe Mnangagwa's ironic plea to let bygones be bygones while he still subscribes to the *Chimurenga* and *Gukurahundi* "perennial paradigm war" (Ndlovu-Gatsheni & Benyera, 2015). In the following section I expound how Mnangagwa uses the notion of letting bygones be bygones as a psychological tool. This is followed by discussing how some Zimbabwean churches are so easily enticed by Mnangagwa's rhetoric of forgiving and forgetting that they end up not pressurizing him and his government to be accountable for his ruthless rule. I close the chapter by suggesting that it is the human value of victims, and not the magnanimity of perpetrators, that must inform the church's theological-ethic of engaging Mnangagwa's call to let bygones be bygones.

2 A Theological-Ethical Search for a Therapeutic View of the Memory of the Wounded

Methodologically, this chapter is a theological-ethical search for a therapeutic approach to memory of past wounds by victims of political violence in founded by violence and ruled by violence. This chapter uses theological-ethics to argue that rulers, such Mnangagwa, should not use memorial categories such as forgiving and forgetting to psychologically harm and oppress their victims, but use these categories in a just way that upholds justice and leads to healing. Kretzschmar (2021: 45) defines a theological-ethical approach as "a critical reflection from a Christian perspective on moral norms and values, as well as the perceptions, character, and behaviour of human beings—individually and collectively." Therefore, a key issue in theological-ethics is the attempt to bring biblical witness and theological perspectives to illuminate critical issues affecting the society. A theological-ethical reflection on the public function of memory is necessary in secular and multi-religious Zimbabwe because, as pointed out by Gunda (2015: 24–25), there is a widespread "biblification" of the public space through the deployment of biblically derived ideas and symbols in the Zimbabwean political space. To some extent, Mnangagwa's call to let bygones be bygones (pleading with the wounded to forgive and forget their wounds without a concrete programme of truth-telling, justice, and restitution) can be seen as an uncritical expression of the Christian view of forgiveness and not an African traditional religious approach where forgiveness requires the ceremonial appeasement of avenging spirits, known as *uzimu* in isiNdebele and *ngozi* in chiShona.

Since forgiveness and forgetting are important Christian tenets, a theological-ethical reflection on Mnangagwa's call to let bygones be bygones is necessary. Chitando and Taringa (2021: 189) highlight that although Zimbabwean churches have contributed to the occurrence of violence by alignments to identities formed on ethnic, religious, dialectics "they [still] have the capacity to provide a solid foundation for national healing and integration." However, in many situations churches fail to provide a solid foundation for national healing and integration because of a lack of a deep theological-ethic of memory that does not just uncritically quote Bible verses that command Christians to forgive. A weak theological-ethic of memory leaves churches at the mercy of manipulative rulers who use forgiveness and forgetting to maintain a political status quo instead of healing the wounded. Without a sound theological-ethic of memory, churches end up captured by politicians to promote programmes on forgiveness and forgetting that are unjust to victims who are often powerless to demand justice for their wounds. In such cases, instead of providing meaningful insights and programmes of healing and reconciliation, churches end up promoting "cheap forgiveness" that merely goes through the motions without accountability, sincere apologies, reparation, and justice. This unjustly places the burden of forgetting and forgiving onto the victims and survivors by forcing them to relate with unrepentant offenders as if they have transformed perpetrators into positive community members (Chitando & Taringa, 2021: 192). Therefore a sound theological-ethic of memory is necessary to help churches avoid being "regime enablers" (Dube, 2021; Magaisa, 2019) by using memory to perpetrate the injustices of evil regimes. As Chitando and Taringa point out, in situations of political injustices, churches must deal with forgiveness in a manner that overcomes and avoids any suspicion that they are colluding with evil civil rulers to placate restless citizens who doubt the sincerity of these authorities when they say they are willing to open dialogue on their injustices to the society. Churches need a deep theological-ethic of memory in order to lead communities to sustainable forgiveness, challenge the perpetrators to take responsibility for their wrongs, and prevent the church from ending up a servant of evil perpetrators of violence instead of a servant of God's justice.

3 Mnangagwa's Call to Let Bygones Be Bygones While Upholding a Culture of Violence

A key message by Mnangagwa was the call to forgive and forget the past and chart a new future of nonviolence. Although Mnangagwa made the call in 2017 after succeeding Robert Mugabe, that call remains alive and continues to inform his political rhetoric concerning volatile topics such as the Gukurahundi issue. In his inaugural speech as the new president in November 2017, Mnangagwa (2017) announced:

> For close to two decades now, this country went through many developments. While we cannot change the past, there is a lot we can do in the present and future to give our nation a different, positive direction.

Mnangagwa strengthened his call to leave the past and build a new future by calling the nation to forgive and forget all past wrongs, be reconciled to one another, and start a new peaceful dispensation. He stated in his appeal:

> [W]e should never remain hostages to our past. I thus humbly appeal to all of us that we let bygones be bygones, readily embracing each other in defining a new destiny. The task at hand is that of rebuilding our great country. It principally lies with none but ourselves. (Mnangagwa, 2017)

However, former president Mugabe also made a similar call in his inauguration as the founding leader of Zimbabwe, in 1980.[1] After the lengthy bloody war of independence, Mugabe's plea to let bygones be bygones endeared him to the international community as a reconciliatory and progressive leader. Similarly, Mnangagwa's promise for a new dispensation was a welcome relief to many wounded Zimbabweans. He essentially gave an impression of regret and remorse about violence, and a willingness to adopt new peaceful ways of doing politics.

It can be argued that Mnangagwa played a psychological game of wooing the wounded to let go of their anger and resentment towards him and not demand justice from him for the wounds he and his ZANU-PF party

---

[1] In his 1980 address, Mugabe stated: I urge you, whether you are black or white, to join me in a new pledge to forget our grim past, forgive others and forget, join hands in a new amity, and together, as Zimbabweans, trample upon racialism, tribalism and regionalism, and work hard to reconstruct and rehabilitate our society as we reinvigorate our economic machinery; The need for peace demands that our forces be integrated as soon as possible so we can emerge with a single national army (Mugabe, 2020).

had inflicted on them. In a way, Mnangagwa manipulated the wounded by promising them healing and transformation that are still yet to come. The call to let bygones be bygones deceptively portrayed Mnangagwa and his ZANU-PF as repentant and reformed merchants of violence.

Yet, ZANU-PF continues with its culture of violent brutalization of Zimbabweans. Since the beginning of its rule in Zimbabwe in 1980, ZANU-PF has continually employed violence to enforce its rule and authority in the country. ZANU-PF has perpetuated a culture of violence described by Ndlovu-Gatsheni (2012) as a *chimurenga* ideology that is implemented by the *Gukurahundi* strategy. In its basic form chimurenga is a chiShona word that has come to mean the struggle of resisting and overthrowing colonialism. The first African armed resistance against British colonialists in 1896–1897 is called the First Chimurenga; the armed struggle that started in the 1960s and led to the country's independence in 1980 is called the Second Chimurenga; and the economic struggle that started in 2000 characterized by the invasion and expropriation of white-owned farms is called the Third Chimurenga.[2] According to Ndlovu-Gatsheni and Benyera (2015) ZANU-PF's subscription to the chimurenga ideology means that the party is in a "perennial paradigm war." Thus, it is a party constantly waging a violent struggle. Ndlovu-Gatsheni further explains that the chimurenga ideology is implemented through a violent strategy called *Gukurahundi*. Gukurahundi is a chiShona word for the first violent storm that marks the beginning of spring and the agricultural season and washes away everything, leading to a new ecological order (Sithole & Makumbe, 1997: 134). Chitando and Taringa (2021: 191) point out that Gukurahundi "connotes violence. It suggests cleansing, the removal of undesirable elements, and it portends a (purified) new beginning (i.e., minus the "chaff")." According to Ndlovu-Gatsheni (2012: 4–5) ZANU-PF used the Gukurahundi strategy to eliminate all its opponents and party members suspected of wavering, disloyalty, or selling-out. In ZANU-PF, the chimurenga ideology is an ideology of the party's exclusive entitlement to rule Zimbabwe uncontested by claiming that it is linked to the First Chimurenga. In other words, the party constructs its legitimacy by projecting itself as a continuation of the spirit of the First Chimurenga. Thus, the party uses the violent Gukurahundi strategy to defend its exclusive claim to be the child and defender of the chimurenga.

A principal element of the chimurenga ideology is a tenet of violence expressed by the now proverbial song Zimbawe *Ndeyeropa Ramadzibaba*,

---

[2] Ndlovu-Gatsheni (2012: 3) amplifies Terence Ranger's view that the term "chimurenga" derives from Murenga, the name of a Shona pre-colonial religious leader who was actively involved in the primal 1896–1897war of resistance against British colonial settlers.

which means Zimbabwe is a product of the costly sacrificial blood of our forbearers (Chitando & Tarusarira, 2017: 9–10). The violent notion of *Zimbabwe Ndeyeropa Ramadzibaba* is complex in its claim that Zimbabwe cost the blood of the ancestors, therefore, it will be defended and ruled by blood. It basically glorifies the spilling of blood in defending and ruling Zimbabwe. It is complex, and even contradictory, in the sense it does not only mean the loss of the blood of the freedom fighters, but also the blood of enemies of the party, the blood of fellow comrades deemed to be selling out to the struggle (Chitando & Tarusarira, 2017: 10). The complexity and contradictory nature of Zimbabwe's armed struggle against colonialism led Sithole (1999) to characterize it as "struggles with the struggle."[3] Consequently, ZANU-PF rulers rise to power by killing the oppressors, rulers maintain power by killing enemies of the state, the rulers rise to the top of their ranks by killing fellow comrades who stand in their way to power, the rulers kill unwanted elements to cleanse the party, the rulers kill their followers to quell dissent, the leaders instil fear, discipline, and loyalty in their followers by killing followers who are deemed to be wavering, members of the opposition parties are killed as enemies of the struggle, and to also send a message to those who attempt to challenge the party and its leaders that their blood too will be mercilessly spilt. As explained by Chitando and Tarusarira:

> [In ZANU-PF] the identities of "heroes" and "sell-outs" are neither permanent nor static. The revolutionary icons of today can be labelled traitors tomorrow, depending on how they stand in relation to the centre of power. Factional fights within ZANU-PF have seen stalwarts of the liberation struggle demoted to traitors. (Chitando & Tarusarira, 2017: 10)

This shows the extent to which the chimurenga ideology and Gukurahundi strategy are complex and contradictory. Interestingly, the chimurenga ideology and Gukurahundi strategy were used to dethrone Mugabe in a military-led campaign coded Operation Restore Legacy. In Operation Restore Legacy, ZANU-PF demoted Mugabe from hero to traitor after accusing him of betraying the liberation struggle ethos and actors when he replaced struggle stalwarts in the party with leaders with no substantial connection to the war of independence from a faction called Generation 40 (G40) (Tendi, 2020: 66).

---

[3] Ndlovu-Gatsheni and Benyera (2015: 12) point out, "At the centre of the conflict was not only the racial question, but also the ethnic question which was subordinated to the nationalist rhetoric".

Therefore, in ZANU-PF those within and outside the party live in fear of violence after being classified as undesirable. As a sign of the deep-rootedness of the Gukurahundi strategy, even when democratic and non-violent processes of taking power, such as elections are put in place, violence is used to force people to vote for the party. The party also uses violence to reject and subvert the undesired election outcomes. Thus, the notion that *Zimbabwe Ndeyeropa Ramadzibaba* does not just mean that Zimbabwe is a product of a bloody armed struggle, but also that it is a place that spills blood: at any given time when Zimbabweans recall their past, etched in their memory is an ancestor whose blood was spilt in the name of Zimbabwe, especially those killed after being classified as sell-outs.

However, it must be noted that in some ways ZANU-PF's use of violence as a tool of governing the country is not without historical precedence. For even pre-colonial African states used violence to rise to power and maintain power. Similarly, as pointed out by Ndlovu-Gatsheni (2015: 12), "White settler colonialism was introduced through violence and was maintained through domination, repression and exploitation." Therefore Zimbabwe is a territory with a long history of the paradigm of war and violence.

Therefore, the point of great concern is that Mnangagwa's call to let bygones be bygones has not ended the perennial paradigm of war in the uses of chimurenga ideology and Gukurahundi strategy to maintain its hold on power. ZANU-PF's culture of violent rule continues to drench the memory of Zimbabweans with blood (Murambadoro, 2015: 34). Ndlovu-Gatsheni and Benyera (2015: 14) highlight that Zimbabwe remains "a society that is permeated institutionally by militarism and violence." Mnangagwa's second republic has continued the Gukurahundi culture that characterized Mugabe's first republic as evidenced by the Gukurahundi atrocities of 1983 to 1987 that claimed the lives of an estimated 20,000 unarmed civilians. Since 1987 the violent culture of Gukurahundi has continued by shifting the focus of violence from the former Patriotic Front-Zimbabwe African People's Union (PF-ZAPU) that had united with ZANU-PF, to the prominent opposition parties that emerged later such as the Zimbabwe Unity Movement (ZUM) (in 1990), the Movement for Democratic Change (MDC) (from 2000) and any prominent voice opposed to ZANU-PF's rule. Similarly, not only have elections been characterized by violence, but ZANU-PF has continuously punished citizens who vote against it, as evidenced by post-election military-backed operations against citizens such as Operation Murambatsvina (Drive Out Trash) of 2005, the 2008 post-election Operation Mavhoterapapi (Who Did You Vote For?), and Operation Chimumumu (Operation Don't Speak).

The culture of political violence has continued unabated in Mnangagwa's second republic as testified by the killing of six civilians by the army in Harare in post-election violence on the 1 August 2018. The recommendations of the Motlanthe Commission (2023), the international commission of inquiry led by former South African president Kgalema Motlanthe to investigate the incident are yet to be implemented, with Mnangagwa's government showing no appetite to implement the recommendations of the inquiry. In other contexts, the Gukurahundi strategy through withholding resources needed for human flourishing such as withholding of development, food, and agricultural inputs and implements. Therefore, remembrance stands against the pervasiveness of the Gukurahundi as ZANU-PF's political strategy of governance in Zimbabwe.

4 Mnangagwa's Use of Forgetting as a Psychological Tool

Because of Mnangagwa's continued course on the paradigm of war there is ground to be suspicious of the sincerity of his call to let bygones be bygones. There is reason to view his call to let bygones be bygones as a psychological game designed not to heal the wounded, but merely disarm their desire for justice while he and his ZANU-PF party continue to hold on to power in Zimbabwe. One can say Mnangagwa began his rule by calling for bygones to be bygones because he knew there were many Zimbabweans under the strain of grief and pain inflicted by his party who needed healing. Therefore, the message of forgiving and forgetting was convenient for him.

Despite having been the backbone of Robert Mugabe's lengthy ruthless and oppressive rule and standing accused of being the instigator of the atrocities committed by ZANU-PF, Mnangagwa has endeared himself to the troubled citizens with the promise to take the country in a new positive direction. Noyes (2020: 2) points out that although Mnangagwa played a leading role in Mugabe's government for 37 years since independence, after taking over as president, he promised a sharp departure from his erstwhile leader's brutal and authoritarian style of rule. He affirmed his commitment to his promise of a new departure by repeated slogans of ushering a "'new dispensation,' whereby he would allow political competition, cease repression, deliver free and fair elections, and invite international monitors back into the fold" (Noyes, 2020: 25). From a memorial perspective, one can say that Mnangagwa promised a new humane dispensation that would stop drenching Zimbabwe's painful memories with blood. In essence, he promised to change the meaning of the song Zimbabwe *Ndeyeropa Ramadzibaba* from a dirge that mourns Zimbabwe as a place sustained by shedding blood to its real meaning of a song of honouring the sacrifice of the sons and daughters who died in liberating the country from the colonialists.

Considering that the former leader, Mugabe had once declared, "We have degrees in violence…and it's time we should make our numbers count… by striking fear in the hearts of the white men and his running dogs of imperialism" (Mugabe, quoted in Munoriyarwa, 2021), Mnangagwa's promise for a new dispensation was a welcome relief to many wounded Zimbabweans. However, it must be noted that the same Mugabe, who declared that he had degrees in violence, and called his ZANU-PF supporters to unleash violence on the opposition, had begun his reign by calling to people to forgive and forget their past and be reconciled to one another and build a new united peaceful society. In his 1980 inaugural address, Mugabe appealed to the new nation emerging from a bitter war that divided it racially, tribally, and politically by appealing:

> I urge you, whether you are black or white, to join me in a new pledge to forget our grim past, forgive others and forget, join hands in a new amity, and together, as Zimbabweans, trample upon racialism, tribalism and regionalism, and work hard to reconstruct and rehabilitate our society as we reinvigorate our economic machinery; The need for peace demands that our forces be integrated as soon as possible so we can emerge with a single national army. (Mugabe, 2020)

Sadly, despite having pledged to forget the grim past, forgive others, forget, and join hands in a new united, peaceful, and non-discriminatory society, Mugabe would later unleash an orgy of violence. While his pledge to forgive and forget was still fresh in people's minds, he unleashed the ruthless Fifth Brigade army unit in the Gukurahundi operation. Thus, it can be said that Mnangagwa had learnt his psychological and deceptive use of memory from his former mentor, Mugabe. One can say Mugabe's passionate call to forgive and forget was not entirely sincere, it was a ploy to endear himself as a peaceful leader, while in fact he continued to build a Zimbabwe with a memory drenched in blood. That Mugabe merely used memory in a non-committal psychological manner is reflected in his unwillingness to own up and apologize for Gukurahundi. Instead of asking for forgiveness, Mugabe silenced people who wanted to press the issue of Gukurahundi by saying: "If we dig up history, then we wreck the nation, we tear our people apart into factions, into tribes, and villagism will prevail over our nationalism and over the spirit of our sacrifices" (Mashingaidze, 2010: 23). This statement shows Mugabe as a master in the psychological use of memory, for he made the wounded who wanted to press for justice, feel individualistic, factional, tribal, and villagistic in their quest for justice for their wounds. Mpofu (2021: 46) describes Mugabe's method as use of language of "grand ideal" of national unity and peace to discredit and silence people demanding justice for their wounds. The language of unity and reconciliation was employed to condemn and silence victims demanding justice for their wounds. Indeed, it has become common in Zimbabwe for people calling for the government to account for its past wrongs, such as the Gukurahundi, to be made to feel tribalistic and enemies of peace and national unity. Such people are seen as revenge-seekers. This is a form of psychological manipulation and silencing of the wounded. Ultimately, it is a psychological game that suppresses memory by replacing the need for justice for the wounded with a grand promise for development and prosperity.

Just like Mugabe, Mnangagwa has also shown himself a master in the use of memory for mere psychological purposes. Far from being therapeutic, his notion of letting bygones be bygones is designed to silence the wounded by making them feel enslaved by the past, individualistic and attention-seekers who have nothing to offer to the nation but only past wounds. Chitando and Taringa (2021: 191) call for fairness towards Mnangagwa by acknowledging that "since Mugabe's death, there has been some progress in terms of at least beginning to open conversation about Gukurahundi." Indeed, ever since he came into power, Mnangagwa has created a more open environment for talking about Gukurahundi than it was during Mugabe's days when it was a taboo (Chitando & Taringa, 2021: 190). For his part, Mnangagwa has not only opened dialogued on Gukurahundi with civic groups seeking resolution of the issue, but he also commissioned the National Peace and Reconciliation Commission (NPRC) to hold dialogues with affected communities on the issue. Mnangagwa has also held talks with traditional and community leaders such as chiefs from the regions affected by Gukurahundi and ecumenical bodies. However, some concerned civic groups complained that Mnangagwa was not meeting authentic representatives of Gukurahundi victims. While a former government minister in Mugabe's government, and political scientist professor, Jonathan Moyo (2020), commented on his Twitter account, that a group called Matabeleland Collective that had met with Mnangagwa "was neither about Matabeleland nor a collective; but a scam to cover up Mnangagwa's Gukurahundi atrocities to escape accountability." Moyo's allegation showed that Mnangagwa was not only manipulative but also deceptive by sponsoring groups to help him escape accountability over the Gukurahundi issue. Ndlovu-Gatsheni and Benyera (2015: 21) highlight that the notion of let bygones be bygones is fraught with the "death of statist justice and reconciliation mechanisms in Zimbabwe."

To Mnangagwa's credit, Gukurahundi is no longer a taboo but an open topic. Even the government-owned press now specifically uses the term Gukurahundi unlike in former times when it referred to the episode in euphemistic terms like Matabeleland disturbances. Under Mnangagwa's rule, government-owned press reports the Gukurahundi as a historical fact that needs to be addressed. Furthermore, Mnangagwa's government has discussed the issue of the reburials of Gukurahundi victims and DNA identification of people buried in mass graves (Netsianda, 2022). A senior government officer, Virginia Mabiza was quoted in the news as announcing:

> The Ministry of Home Affairs and Cultural Heritage will facilitate the issuance of birth certificates and death certificates for victims affected by Gukurahundi. It will also facilitate the exhumation and reburial of Gukurahundi victims. We're also implementing protection mechanisms for those affected by Gukurahundi to be free to discuss their experiences. (Ndlovu, 2019)

This is a remarkable shift, for formerly Mnangagwa had reinforced Mugabe's declaration that Gukurahundi was a closed chapter, yet now he was opening the closed chapter (Bulawayo24 News, 2011). The issuing of death certificates for people killed by Gukurahundi means there will be official records in official government archives of people recognized as having died from a government-sponsored programme of mass killing, therefore, Gukurahundi will no longer be merely a hearsay subject, but a government-certified fact.

Mnangagwa's opening of the closed Gukurahundi chapter should, theoretically, lead to a psychological healing of memory, yet it is a form of psychological torture that festers the wounds of his victims. Mnangagwa promises the wounded medicine that is never delivered. A great concern is that Mnangagwa openly speaks about Gukurahundi without acknowledging that ZANU-PF implemented a government programme of brutalizing citizens, on ethnic grounds. The same applies to Operation Murambatsvina that destroyed people's houses and businesses in urban areas in the name of cleaning up and reining in illegal businesses, after the party lost elections in urban areas. The government has not acknowledged that it sponsored the destruction of people's livelihoods on party political grounds. While acknowledging the historicity of Gukurahundi, Mnangagwa has refused to take personal responsibility, apologize for it, and allow the affected communities to take charge of the healing process. That his "let bygones be bygones" is a mere psychological game, is evidenced by his government's refusal to permit the affected communities to commemorate the event. Ironically, while opening discussions on Gukurahundi, Mnangagwa has embargoed commemorations by the victims. Plaques erected to mark the mass graves of victims have never seen the break of the following dawn intact, having been broken down by suspected ZANU-PF agents (Moyo, 2022). Events to commemorate the episodes have either been disrupted by the police or banned before they could start. A human rights activist, Thandekile Moyo (2022), commented that the destruction of memorial plaques erected by victims in memory of their deceased and those who were abducted during the period and have never been seen again "shows there is insincerity in the utterances by the president and the government about wanting to 'deal with the Gukurahundi genocide'." Moyo described this insincerity as the "revictimization of victims of the genocide" (Moyo, 2022). Mbuso Fuzwayo, a leader of Ibhetshu LikaZulu, the group that erected a memorial plaque that was later destroyed, was quoted as saying, "The president openly said people are free to discuss Gukurahundi. But what they are doing by stopping commemorations and destroying plaques is a high level of disrespect." (Moyo, 2022). Mnangagwa's call to Zimbabweans wounded by his party ZANU-PF's political violence to let bygones be bygones can therefore be classified as a psychological game designed to silence the wounded, preventing them from make their demand for justice.

5 The Tempting Nature of Mnangagwa's Call to the Zimbabwean Churches

Mnangagwa's call to let bygones be bygones appeals to many Christians who want to see peace prevail in Zimbabwe. Christians and churches eager for the nation to pass and forget the sad episode are easily enticed by Mnangagwa's call to forget the past, but this does not address justly the wounds of the wounded. One such group was a group of churches going by the name Faith for the Nation Campaign, led by Andrew Wutawunashe. According to a Sunday newspaper, *The Standard*, the Faith for the Nation Campaign hosted Mnangagwa in Bulawayo on 31 December 2017 to thank God for the peaceful ousting of Robert Mugabe (Ndlovu, 2017). However, in earlier times, Andrew Wutawunashe, had extolled Mugabe as God's anointed leader over Zimbabwe and even described him as Moses (Wutawunashe, 2014). Now the group celebrated Mugabe's ousting saying it had been praying for many years for a new era and that era had come in Mnangagwa (Ndlovu, 2017). However, Wutawunashe's sudden embrace of Mnangagwa can be said to have come from his being naturally pro-ZANU-PF (Ndlovu & Mwanaka, 2017). But it can also be attributed to the general tendency by churches to uncritically endorse the programmes of the governments of the day. Wutawunashe is an example of many uncritical church leaders who have avoided holding the government accountable for its abuse of the citizens.

Furthermore, Mnangagwa's call to let bygones be bygones is attractive to many church leaders because it avoids discussing sensitive topics. The human tendency is to avoid unpleasant topics and only focus on pleasant issues. Likewise, many churches prefer a semblance of positivism over negativism, even if addressing the negative elements now will lead to positive developments later. Chitando and Taringa (2021: 190) find that churches "have largely been caught up in the conspiracy of silence relating to Gukurahundi (especially during Mugabe's tenure)." They highlight that many church leaders preferred silence over Gukurahundi and were very uncomfortable, uneasy, and apprehensive about discussing the topic as highly sensitive and too political (Chitando & Taringa, 2021: 190–191). In such cases, the call to let bygones be bygones provides a convenient way of not facing the debate. Those who attempt to brook the subject are silenced by conveniently reminding them that the president has said people should forgive each other and forget the past. In so doing, the churches easily succumb to Mnangagwa's psychological use of forgiving and forgetting to silence people from holding him and his government accountable for their violence.

Furthermore, the notion of forgive and forget is attractive to churches because it provides an easy way for people to bury the past without taking personal responsibility for their own historical complicity in injustices and crimes against humanity. Chivasa and Machingura (2018: 73) point out that when one considers that close to 80% *(sic.)* of the total population in Zimbabwe claims to be Christian, it then means that the entire Christian community is involved in creating conflict in the country. Masengwe and Dube (2023: 1) add that this high population of Zimbabweans who claim to be Christian means that most conflicts in the country are between Christians. The implication of this is that the violence we attribute to Mnangagwa is actually the violence of Christians. This means in Gukurahundi atrocities, in Operation Murambatsvina, Operation Mavavhoterapapi, and in all past election violence, Christians have been brutalizing and terrorizing fellow Christians. Therefore, many Christians may find it easy and convenient to accept Mnangagwa's shallow notion of letting bygones be bygones because it saves them from the pain of self-introspection and the shame of dealing with their own hypocrisy of perpetrating violence as a Christian and victimizing fellow believers on account of ZANU-PF. It can be argued that many churches often promote "cheap forgiveness" when it comes political violence such as Gukurahundi because they do not see the role they have played as individual Christians in the wounding of other people. If churches realized their complicity in Mnangagwa's violence, true faith would compel them to think concretely and deeply about the wounds of victims.

Related to the above, some churches are easily swayed by Mnangangwa's call to forgive and forget the past, because of an uncritical understanding of forgiveness that does not pay serious attention to how Zimbabwean politicians use forgive and forget manipulatively. The politicians use forgive and forget as a psychological weapon to win votes and support, not to heal the wounded victims of their acts of violence. The very fact that Mnangagwa has spoken about letting bygones be bygones but is unwilling to apologize and compensate the victims is a clear example of him using memory as a psychological weapon to hold on to power. However, the church needs to have a deeper understanding of forgiveness to avoid co-option by the oppressive state.

6   The Human Value of Victims in Avoiding Abuse of Forgetting

What is a theological-ethic that the church can use to challenge Mnangagwa's use of forgetting as a psychological weapon to torture those he has wounded? It is suggested that an emphasis on the human value of the victims challenges Mnangagwa's use of memory to escape from accountability. One of the primary factors that seem to be driving Mnangagwa's oppressive use of forgetting is the dehumanization of people who hold different views from his party. Chitando and Taringa (2021: 191) point out that:

> This implicit dehumanization and minimization of the "other" is the first logical step in mass violence. The humanity of the "other" must be denied for his or her annihilation to be justified. In the 1994 Rwandan genocide, references to "cockroaches" were made to justify the killing of mostly the Tutsi.

This is also true in Zimbabwe, where the dehumanization of the other is prominent. During the Gukurahundi era Mnangagwa characterized the people in Matabeleland as cockroaches that needed to be exterminated by the pesticide known as DDT (Allison, 2017). Similarly, Didymus Mutasa, when he was a leading member in ZANU-PF, characterized party members of an opposing faction as weevils that needed to exterminated by a pesticide known as Gamatox (Newsday, 2014). Furthermore, scholars have described how ZANU-PF practises "patriotic history" that divides citizens into patriots and sell-outs (Ranger, 2004; Tendi, 2008). As earlier pointed out, in the chimurenga ideology anyone declared a sell-out is treated with Gukurahundi—that is, washed away. In ZANU-PF, to think differently is to become a cockroach, a weevil, and a sell-out, which essentially means to be stripped of human value and dignity. The conferring of these less-than-human terms leaves one vulnerable to the vilest form of inhuman violent punishment imaginable, including torture, rape, maiming, starvation, burning of one's property: the list is endless. It is, therefore, argued that to dehumanize people in this way and then climb onto a high platform and say "Let bygones be bygones" without any accountability for dehumanizing them, is to further dehumanize them. This is a very serious form of psychological torture and oppression of the wounded.

The church must use the theological-ethic of human dignity to challenge this dehumanization of victims that leads the perpetrators to attempt to offer their victims cheap forgiveness while refusing to take responsibility for wounds they have inflicted. There is a disdain of the human dignity of other people in both Mugabe's and Mnangagwa's refusal to openly acknowledge their role in atrocities such as Gukurahundi and to apologize for their actions. A basic theological tenet about human beings is that all human beings are created in God's image (Gen 1:27), and that they are all equal before God. Because human beings are created in God's image, the life of a human being is sacred and must be treated with respect and dignity. As Wright (2006: 421) points out, *"To be human is to be the image of God.* It is not an extra feature added on to our species; it is definitive of what it means to be human" (original italics). A central theological tenet is that all human beings are created in God's image; therefore, all human beings are precious to God. The ethical spin-off for humanity being created in God's image is that all human beings should be treated respect. We uphold the human dignity and value of other people when we take seriously the harm we have caused them and seek to make things right, instead of gaslighting them with grand nationalist ideals. Healing and reconciliation come from genuine processes that treat the wounded with dignity.

It is important for the church to prioritize the humanization of the victims. It ought to also be recognized that in Mnangagwa's notion of let bygones be bygones, he ultimately rehumanizes himself as a magnanimous forgiving leader. For Mnangagwa to announce a programme of forgiving and forgetting without acknowledging his active role in the wounding his victims is to institute a moral amnesty that promotes an amnesia of his past ruthlessness while the victims remain dehumanized by their victimhood. Ricoeur (2002: 11) tells of an ancient Greek city that had a law proclaiming that citizens should not evoke the memory of evil, or what was considered bad, and the citizens had to promise not to recall such events. However, the problem with the amnesty is that it sanitizes the record of evil leaders by cancelling all wrongs.

7 Conclusion

Memory is an important tool that politicians can use to control and manipulate for advancing their political projects. The chapter has cast doubt on the intentions of Mnangagwa's call to Zimbabweans to let bygones be bygones. Mugabe made the same call only to perpetrate heinous acts of violence against the nation. Likewise, Mnangagwa's plea for bygones to be bygones has not been followed with justice and safety for the victims of violence. Mnangagwa's notion of let bygones be bygones tramples on the human dignity of the wounded, but it does not promote justice by amnesty, and pardons, and amnesia that ultimately protect the perpetrators of violence from being held accountable for their violence that has dehumanized the victimized.

Bibliography

Allison, S. (2017). Gukurahundi ghosts haunt Mnangagwa. *The Mail & Guardian*. https://mg.co.za/article/2017-11-24-00-gukurahundi-ghosts-haunt-mnangagwa/. Accessed 04 June 2022.

Bulawayo24 News. (2011). *Gukurahundi is a Closed Chapter: Mnangagwa. Bulawayo24 News*. https://bulawayo24.com/index-id-news-sc-national-byo-5739.html. Accessed 04 June 2022.

Chitando, E., & Taringa, N. T. (2021). The Churches, Gukurahundi, and Forgiveness in Zimbabwe. *International Bulletin of Mission Research*, 45(2), 187–196.

Chitando, E., & Tarusarira, J. (2017). The deployment of a "sacred song" in violence in Zimbabwe: The case of the song "*Zimbabwe Ndeye Ropa Ramadzibaba*" (Zimbabwe was/is Born of the Blood of the Fathers/Ancestors) in Zimbabwean Politics. *Journal for the Study of Religion*, 30(1), 5–25.

Chivasa, N., & Machingura, F. (2018). "One Person's Meat is another's Poison": Developing a Theology of Conflict: The Case of the Apostolic Faith Mission (AFM) in Zimbabwe. *Journal of Religion and Theology*, 2(1), 73–84.

Dube, B. (2021). Religious Leaders as Regime Enablers: The Need for Decolonial Family and Religious Studies in Postcolonial Zimbabwe. *British Journal of Religious Education*, 43(1), 46–57.

Gunda, M. R. (2015). *On the Public Role of the Bible in Zimbabwe: Unpacking Banana's "Re-writing" Call for a Socially and Contextually Relevant Biblical Studies.* Vol. 18. (Bible in Africa Studies). University of Bamberg.

Kretzschmar, L. (2021). "What Are We Eating?" A Theological-ethical Analysis of the Effects of Food Additives on Human Beings, especially in South Africa. *Acta Theologica, 41*(2), 46–69.

Magaisa, A. T. (2019). *Big Saturday Read: The Regime and its Enablers. bigsaturdayread.* https://www.bigsr.co.uk/single-post/2019/12/14/big-saturday-read-the-regime-and-its-enablers. Accessed 28 December 2020.

Masengwe, G., & Dube, B. (2023). "Robert's Rules of Order" on Religious Conflicts in the Church of Christ in Zimbabwe. *Verbum Et Ecclesia, 44*(1), 7.

Mashingaidze, T. M. (2010). Zimbabwe's Illusive National Healing and Reconciliation Processes: From Independence to the Inclusive Government 1980–2009. *Conflict Trends. 2010*(1),19–27.

Mnangagwa, E. D. (2017). *President Mnangagwa's Inauguration speech in full.* https://www.chronicle.co.zw/president-mnangagwas-inauguration-speech-in-full-2/. Accessed 03 May 2020.

Motlanthe Commission. (2023). Report of the Commission of Inquiry into the 1st of August 2018 Post-election Violence Motlanthe Commission | veritaszim. https://www.veritaszim.net/node/3364. Accessed 13 June 2023.

Moyo, J. (2020). https://twitter.com/ProfJNMoyo/status/1226538947607760896. Accessed 16 June 2023.

Moyo, T. (2022). *ZIMBABWE IN RUINS OP-ED: Destruction of Gukurahundi Memorials Prolongs Torture of Victims and their Descendants. Daily Maverick.* https://www.dailymaverick.co.za/article/2022-01-26-destruction-of-gukurahundi-memorials-prolongs-torture-of-victims-and-their-descendants/. Accessed 17 June 2023.

Mpofu, W. J. (2021). Gukurahundi in Zimbabwe: An Epistemicide and Genocide. *Journal of Literary Studies, 37*(2), 40–55.

Mugabe, R. G. (2020). Mugabe's 1980 Independence speech that captured the nation's hope, dreams *Pindula News.* https://news.pindula.co.zw/2020/04/18/mugabes-1980-independence-speech-that-captured-the-nations-hope-dreams/. Accessed 08 May 2020.

Munoriyarwa, A. (2021). "We have Degrees in Violence": A Multimodal Critical Discourse Analysis of Online Constructions of Electoral Violence in Post-2000 Zimbabwe—Media, Conflict and Peacebuilding in Africa: Conceptual and Empirical Considerations. https://ebrary.net/173056/communication/degrees_violence_multimodal_critical_discourse_analysis_online_constructions_electoral_violence_. Accessed 03 June 2022.

Murambadoro, R. (2015). 'We Cannot Reconcile Until the Past has been Acknowledged': Perspectives on Gukurahundi from Matabeleland, Zimbabwe. *African Journal on Conflict Resolution, 15*(1), 33–57.

Ndlovu, N. (2017). *Byo churches host Mnangagwa*. The Standard. https://www.newsday.co.zw/thestandard/news/article/193766/byo-churches-host-mnangagwa. Accessed 07 June 2023.

Ndlovu, R. (2019). Zimbabwe to Compensate Victims of Genocide that Claimed 20,000 lives. *TimesLIVE*. https://www.timeslive.co.za/news/africa/2019-04-10-zimbabwe-to-compensate-victims-of-genocide-that-claimed-20000-lives/. Accessed 16 June 2023.

Ndlovu, S., & Mwanaka, H. (2017). Birth of a New Era: Wutawunashe. *NewsDay*. https://www.newsday.co.zw/news/article/72875/birth-of-a-new-era-wutawunashe. Accessed 07 June 2023.

Ndlovu-Gatsheni, S. J. (2012). Rethinking "Chimurenga" and "Gukurahundi" in Zimbabwe: A Critique of Partisan National History. *African Studies Review, 55*(3), 1–26.

Ndlovu-Gatsheni, S., & Benyera, E. (2015). Towards a Framework for Resolving the Justice and Reconciliation Question in Zimbabwe. *African Journal on Conflict Resolution, 15*(2), 9–33.

Netsianda, M. (2022). Minister Mutsvangwa on Gukurahundi burials. *The Chronicle*. https://www.chronicle.co.zw/minister-mutsvangwa-on-gukurahundi-burials/. Accessed 07 June 2023.

Newsday. (2014). Mnangagwa, Moyo Divisive Elements—Mutasa. *NewsDay Zimbabwe*. https://www.newsday.co.zw/2014/06/mnangagwa-moyo-divisive-elements-mutasa/. Accessed 06 June 2022.

Noyes, A. H. (2020). *A New Zimbabwe? Assessing Continuity and Change After Mugabe*. Rand Corporation. https://www.rand.org/pubs/research_reports/RR4367.html.

Ranger, T. (2004). Nationalist Historiography, Patriotic History and the History of the Nation: the Struggle over the Past in Zimbabwe. *Journal of Southern African Studies*, 215–234.

Ricoeur, P. (2002). Memory and Forgetting. In M. Dooley & R. Kearney (Eds.), *Questioning Ethics: Contemporary Debates in Continental Philosophy* (pp. 5–11). Routledge.

Sithole, M. (1999). *Zimbabwe: Struggles-Within-the-Struggle*. Rujeko.

Sithole, M., & Makumbe, J. (1997). Elections in Zimbabwe: The ZANU (PF) Hegemony and its Incipient Decline. *African Journal of Political Science / Revue Africaine De Science Politique, 2*(1), 122–139.

Tendi, B.-M. (2008). Patriotic History and Public Intellectuals Critical of Power. *Journal of Southern African Studies, 34*(2), 379–396.

Tendi, B.-M. (2020). The Motivations and Dynamics of Zimbabwe's 2017 Military Coup. *African Affairs, 119*(474), 39–67.

Wright, C. J. H. (2006). *The Mission of God: Unlocking the Bible's Grand Narrative*. IVP.

Wutawunashe, A. (2014). *Godly Counsel for party of Christian Values*. http://www.herald.co.zw/godly-counsel-for-party-of-christian-values/. Accessed 28 August 2015.

Incest as Dismissal: Anthropology and Clinics of Silence

Parfait D. Akana

1   Reasons for an Inquiry

How did I become interested in the issue of incest? It occurred while conducting fieldwork in a mental health facility in Yaoundé (Benoît Menni Centre) belonging to the Congregation of the Hospitaller Sisters. I built my study not only on the basis of a contract of trust with the head of this health centre and all the staff, but also on the basis of an exchange of good processes. I played, as it were, for the time of my work, the role of a consultant or a "social worker." I was the one the patients came and talked to at the end of their consultations, as a kind of "conversation officer." The instructions were always the same. For teenagers or young adults, the head of the centre would say, "Then you can go talk with your (older) brother who's in the office over there." So they came there every time to talk; to make conversation as recommended. And the inscription of such an exchange within a kind of filiality (brother, big brother) already de-formatted a framed relation because of the context. Such a position was obviously not without ambiguities. These can be seen primarily at two levels.

First, the circumstances could put me in a situation where I might react and issue, on the patient's request, a medical opinion on their condition. To

---

P. D. Akana (✉)
The Muntu Institute Foundation, Yaoundé, Cameroon
e-mail: parfait.akana@muntu-institute.africa

University of Yaounde II, Soa, Cameroon

such requests I would reply, for example, that they had first to take their medication and do what the nurses had asked them to do. It is clear that this remained a risk because it was later during my career in transcultural psychiatry in France that I was truly trained for three years in this type of listening. My basic training was that of a sociologist and anthropologist. However, without confusing a clinical interview with an ethnographic interview, one wonders about the extent to which they overlap. For example, if we look at an author such as Mike Singleton, we cannot ignore the fact that an ethnographic interview is first and foremost a work of involvement, where the researcher gives value to and takes seriously the motives of the interlocutor. Researchers do not apply their own grids of reading, to control or direct the conversation. It is always a journey with the other, concretely translated into an effort to grasp and understand, like them, their world, what is happening and what is happening to them. We find an absolutely identical approach in phenomenological psychopathology. Rudolf Bernet states on this subject that: "Any attempt to communicate with the psychotic remains vain if we are not ready to give credence to his world which for us will never be entirely real or understandable. It is only a 'normal' who goes crazy with the madman and who remains normal with the normal ones, who has a chance to open a breach in the closed world of delusion" (1992: 28). This is why we can also speak of an emotional and sensitive experience, which is certainly at the very heart of the resemblance between ethnographic interview and clinical interview.

The second level was that my intervention was seen by the administration as a way to access more information, and sometimes, in its view, information of better quality. The head of the mental health centre told me, "I can see that they do not tell me everything because I am white. But to you, they can talk to you. They are sometimes evasive with me. So try talking to them to find out after." Here we can see how difficult it is for some practitioners to work in intercultural contexts and how they get a sense of the amount of information and detail that they think may potentially be missing in the therapeutic relationship with patients. But this is not new, and religious congregations carrying out health work are constantly facing this type of difficulty. On the other hand, their "difference,"—the fact that they come from elsewhere—is sometimes perceived as a pledge of credibility and reliability and leads to the creation of a climate of trust (Kouokam Magne, 2009). There is certainly room for more in-depth investigations of the registers of trust, and the different ways in which these are built in interracial care relationships. In any case, I never shared any information with the administration—this would have amounted to betraying a secret that patients clearly described as such. One feels the embarrassment of such a position, torn between what may appear as an incentive to reveal, and the need to share information that is probably crucial in their therapeutic management. It can be assumed that it is possible, without having to betray confidences, and sometimes important because of their seriousness, to suggest in a veiled way what had happened to a patient, in order to allow the practitioners to take care of it. However, in some cases, how else to discuss rape and incest, when even the victims have chosen to share this traumatic experience with a very small number of people? How can we speak about it without knowing the details, yet knowing how serious it is? It is not possible to remain vague simply by evoking the trauma. We must understand the reasons for its emergence, the circumstances of its occurrence, and the way in which it has transformed the lives of those who have experienced it.

Whenever I had access to this information, it was incidental. As often happens over the course of investigations, the information came to me in passing. What interested me was a sociological understanding, through the use of an in-depth ethnographic and hospital-based survey, of the different stories, and the reasons that led patients, whom society labels as "crazy," to a health facility that is considered to be "the madhouse hospital." Those who came to this mental health centre, and were referred to me, came there with a socially and ontologically regressive and stigmatizing assignment. In many cases, they had already incorporated these aspects as distinctive features of their identity. It was not up to me to state a clinical judgement on such characterizations, but (always suspending my judgement) to discover the stories (given that we talk of "entry," we could adopt a spatial metaphor, perhaps "the paths" through which they entered their pathological career) from their entry into these pathological careers, but also into their lived world of affliction. This is how I managed to isolate, from the mass of data in my interviews, some constants that referred to the question of incestuous rapes and, generally, emotional and sexual disorders in the experience of mental illnesses. The case of the patient that follows is, as such, an illustration among many other cases, which I do not address here, and which speak well of the prevalence and even the endemic nature of intra-familial sexual violence. In order to carry out this work, I mainly used in-depth non-directive interviews and direct observation.

2 Reconstitution, Anthropology, and Clinics of Silence

Everything started in a "normal" way. A new patient, aged 19, came in and sat down in front of me. She was there for problems of nerves and fits. Her family had told her that she was on the road to madness, hence, her follow-up appointment in this mental health centre. Nothing, of course, foreshadowed the violence and the sudden character of the revelations she shared with me. My surprise was all the greater because she was expressing the aggression, the rape, she had been victim of five years prior with a detachment and a closure that did not show any emotion. Like a series of words flowing fluidly, without hiccups, nothing. And yet, even though she claimed that her health problems had started six months earlier with the death of her brother, she had been carrying the mark of a stain that had tainted her skin since she was 14: the age of her sacrifice and profanation.

Even though the death of her brother was the alleged reason for her health problems, it was soon evident that the rape was still having an effect. She said that she wanted to start a family later, to get married, have children, and so on. But, at the same time, she said she wanted to leave behind the "world of boys," perceived as a place of violence and defilement, where his obligatory stay, forced, translated both a primordial and definitive experience. Indeed, she asserted, she had not had sex since that event. We could talk about a round trip, but, in fact, it was just a one-way journey, followed by a difficult exit attempt: she was still wading in the muddy embraces of aggression, like an animal struggling to get out of a trap. I use the metaphor of the animal because aggression already contributes, in itself, to a denial of humanity; the refusal to recognize in the other an equal dignity that stems from a common belonging. The modalities of the aggression, the criminal technology of the rapist, and the symbolic device that he mobilizes attest to the sufficiency of the denial and the type of look that it bears on the victim: an animal, a thing of which one can dispose, without its own subjectivity.

In these words, in the course of a long conversation reflecting the depth of her affliction and painful affects, came the evocation of this awful scene:

> We were at the time at X. And they lived at Y, on the heavy axis. And, I did not have my notebooks. It was in 2005, I believe. I did not have the notebooks and we asked for books and notebooks at school. He called me. He called my grandmother; I'll go get the notebooks. I went and … his wife was at home, his wife was going to the market. I wanted to go with his wife, he refused. Well, I stayed at home with him. That's where … I went to bed because I had nothing to do. That's where he came to find me in the room. He had the

knife. He tells me (his voice at this moment is lower, like a whisper ...) that if I speak, he will kill me. He tied my hands with the rope. Yes. He began to support me everywhere, touching my buttocks and my breasts. He put his hand on my mouth. He raped me. After, he said that I do not even have to talk, that I do not have to tell anyone. He asked me not to even say. I closed my mouth until I got home. It was after, as the belly was coming out ... When the child was born, that I could say that to my parents. Because every time ... Well, there was sometimes, when with my father we go there, we are together, he has the knife, he shows me. He says that if I speak only he will stab me (she sketches at this moment the movement of a stab ...). And I did not know. I was frustrated.

In what happens, as I will show, we do not see or hear the suffering and pain that result from this trauma. The inaugural desecration of her body is accompanied by an unbelievable device of terror that is put in place by the rapist to silence her. Before her, it was her belly that spoke. The ultimate testimony of the sexual act is the belly. In this regard, a popular saying in Cameroon is: "It is when your stomach comes out that we know you were eating." Eating here connotes the sexual act. It can be compared to another saying in the Yemba language: "If you do not eat beans, your belly will not swell." Her belly came out. And she had no choice but to reveal, driven by her parents, the identity of the perpetrator of the crime.

Here, if the silence is broken, the act of speech is reduced to a fetish function. Instead of the family solidarity and outrage that would allow this word to be a force acting in the direction of the victim, we rather witness an evaluation of the crime committed as a lesser act than the losses that a trial, with its echo and its consequences, would engender. Only a few virtuous indignations subsist, and a protest for the sake of it: "Let this not be repeated!" A local expression often makes its way into conversations: "He also spoke." What does it take to hear? Let's answer with another local expression: "He still spoke." From what happened, "He also spoke," that is to say that he did not escape anyone, that there was a reaction, although verbal. The meaning of "talking," as a confession, is the pretext for an absolution and a return to the initial situation in the order of family relations. The case of this teenager offers indeed one of those eloquent examples, in which an arithmetic of alliances is accomplished. Scolding, talking too, speaking anyway, was enough to resolve this "family" dispute. It was not necessary to go further, as a denunciation in court would have greatly eroded the family ties, in the opinion of the parents of the victim. This is what the victim told me. And it was the 'solution' that prevailed in her family. The tragic essence of the initial silence was, thus, followed by a confession which was supposed to get things back in order. However, it results in an even heavier and more violent silencing of the traumatic experience of the victim. By not really taking into account its impact and its violence, the confession creates the illusion that these painful experiences were convertible into a reconciliation, by an admission, a pronounced word. What you are is the harshness of an experience, not sufficiently recognized as such. However, we must understand the extent of the damage of such a trauma that leaves a deadly mark on the victim. In this sense, Philippe Bessoles, who uses the metaphor of the devil's penis to signify sexual aggression and its devastating power, is right in saying:

> From his sordid erection, the rapist's penis condemns the victim to the hells of pathos. It eradicates the long process of ontogeny and phylogenesis slowly built since our prehistory. (…) The sperm of the devil floods with its soiling the sacred feminine. It turns it into a cloaca and a place of ease. Washing compulsions cannot purify the infamous wound. Sexual violence creates an eternal filthy face-to-face overflowing with a pestilential relent, acrid sweat. (Bessoles, 2011: 17, 18)

The result is a broken otherness, not sufficiently constituted and no longer part of the performance of the codes of a shared age group. This is the case with the stolen childhoods of teenage mothers. The transgression, especially when it is accompanied by traces (a pregnancy) as for M., gives way to another imperative that is to adapt to the psychological and physical wounds. It generates new responsibilities and makes possible, in a generational undifferentiation, the mixture of rights and duties against a background of disturbing indistinction of ages: teenager and mother at 14 years old.

One of the main consequences of this state of affairs is the debunking of the anthroposocial structures of the constitution and development of an adolescence rooted in a place signified by, for example, games and leisure, school, discovery of the other sex (or the same), and the resulting social relations. It is the adolescent dreams and carefreeness that are obliterated.

In this 19-year-old girl (at the time), a concern for her future and a fear of the "boys" were intense and expressed a deep crisis of confidence in herself and her own identity. Philippe Bessoles says: "Rape dislocates the process of identity. This annihilation concerns the shoring of the primary psychic wraps, the basal trust and the psychic containers (2011: 22). There is here, to quote Bessole's qualification, an imposture of sex: it is the occurrence of something that has no right to be in that place, which parasitizes and pollutes a land that it appropriates by force and violence and, therefore, illegitimately:

Desecration of the sacred, enjoyment of the mortifère, stain of beauty, the imprint of rape or incest reveals how much our sexuality has primitive links with cruelty, death, the original riddle, domination, subjugation, the evil, etc. A new totem erected in place of structuring exogamies, the rapist perpetuates the primitive horde of the time of fundamental violence, of totem and cannibalism. (2011: 20)

This mechanism is very clearly seen in M.'s rapist's story. This incestuous "father" tied her up like an animal and threatened her with a knife to impose silence on her, not only at the time of the act, but also in the days to come. On that bed, which represents a sacrificial scene, the place of a killing without a corpse, since the required silence announces a non-place, this bed represents a sacrificial scene, the place of a killing without a corpse, since the required silence means, according to the attacker, that nothing happened and a way of invisibilizing victim's pain. Silence is a denial and a violence. Later, he will again brandish, on various occasions, the "tool" of the silence: a knife. And what about this other heavy silence, following the unveiling of precedent and accompanied by the impunity of the executioner, because of friendship and family ties? Without spreading itself in moralistic imprecations, while strongly condemning the acts of such violence, it is necessary to analyse, if one wants to understand what is played here, the concrete situation. The unsettling conclusion is that stability and safeguarding affiliations are placed above the fate of the victims. It is as if their redemption or reparations for them would be possible only if they blend into the mould of this unitary mystique by accepting this strange compromise, where the aggressor is convicted but will never receive a punishment likely to ruin the relations that unite his family to that of the victim. In the Cameroonian context, Séverin Cécile Abega has described and analysed this situation of apparent ambiguity very well, by placing it in a context marked by corruption and a strong hatred for the judicial system, perceived as the ultimate enemy. He affirms that:

We do not always want to come to punishment, we can stop at deterrence so that the fault does not repeat itself and everyone lives in peace; and this peace, we wish it so that the unity of which we spoke at the beginning be preserved. On the other hand, if I complain to the state justice system, it can happen that my brother is sentenced, locked up. So I will have given him to a foreign force, and he is not sure that he will come back and join us in this unity. So, there is an amputation of one of the elements of the whole. It is for this reason that we tend to blame the person who was at first rather the victim. State justice is felt to be essentially violent because judicial proceedings admit inequality. It is said that everyone is equal before the law but those who have money have the best advice (lawyers). (Abega & Akana, 2012: 154)

Even worse, in the case of an incest he reports that:

> The challenge will be not only to dissuade the father from starting again and to mark the gravity of his fault, but also to safeguard his role as nurturer so as not to condemn the rest of the family to hunger, and to continue to allow him to fulfill his role as educator with respect to all his children, including the one who has suffered his aggression. Because, if his father is imprisoned, all his life it will be remembered and we will hold him responsible, especially if the brothers and sisters are poor after … This is a very complex and difficult to resolve. (Abega & Akana, 2012: 155)

In such conditions where, in addition to the traumatic violence of incest for victims and relatives, the law of silence rages against the background of food blackmail, shame is no longer a virtue. And indignation is synonymous with temerity because it announces the risk that one is committed to take, facing the possibility of being left without resources.

The situation I describe here is certainly not similar. But, in its form, and regardless of the motivations, it presents significant analogies. If in the case reported by Séverin Cécile Abega the problem is economic and financial, motivated by the fear of the children ending up on the streets, in the case I report here, it is similar. In each of the examples, the pursuit of justice brings into play a situation marked by the choice of what one commits to lose. On the one hand, the financial support of a rapist father whose imprisonment would mortgage the future of the children, including that of the victim. On the other side, the ruin of a family relationship inscribed in the time and the possibility of a conflict caused by the break. It is also striking, in the case of M., to note that despite the traumatic memory of her aggression, she still attended the funeral of her attacker. When I asked her why, she answered: "It was still the family, it was still the father of my child." What does this solicitude of victims mean to the death of their executioners? Everything happens as if satiated with her chalice, it only remained for him to rise, to realize, whatever the value, beyond the vicissitudes of his existence, the fulfilment of a certain desire for humanity which resists darkness. Louis Crocq, on this subject, can say:

> The temporality of the traumatized is deeply altered. With him, the harmonious flow of time has stopped at the frozen moment of terror or horror. The present, crystallized, static and deprived of its evanescence, is reduced to a specular image of the trauma. No longer leading to a new, fleeting present, he promises no future. (2012: 30)

But, through this sequence, we observe that in M., the achievement made possible by the aggression undergone, is rather opening up a horizon towards the future and reestablishment of an upset temporality. Even if signs and memories of this fundamental the trauma and the indelebile psychic marks of the aggression, are still present and are expressed in M's case through the way she's qualifying her "uncle", the hangman of this metamorphosis occurring with aggression, she can still say about her hangman: "It represents nothing." A whole world has crumbled. A radical change of perception. This "uncle" became nothing from the moment he profaned her.

3 Conclusion

Incestuous rape operates a transgression characterized by the indistinctness of pleasure. It is, therefore, tyrannical because it makes it possible to represent the imposture of a subject acting beyond the consecrated places where his bursting occurs through an intrusion. However, another point seems to me to be sobering. This is what I will call a predictability disorder, on which all anthropological conceptions of incest are based, and which have emphasized its entropic dimension. What is its characteristic sign? Confusion, a kind of state of inversions in which doing and saying do not intersect with common sense, but instead consecrate the advent of a great disorder. It deeply reshapes the mental map of the affected subject by shattering the codes that each individual must perform to be in synchrony with the group. A vision of the world is affected: things are not as they are expected to be. They lack an imperative of conformity that institutes a world and makes it coherent.

Here we find one of the fundamental innovations in American anthropology of communication, notably through Ray Birdwhistell, who analysed the predictability inherent in all social life and constitutive of co-belonging: "to be a member is to be predictable" (1996: 211). We expect this or that type of behaviour, because there are rules, and taboos not to be violated. Now, incestuous rape is a negation of what ought to be; what is expected. In incest, the mirror is broken, and symbols shatter with its debris. The father and the mother do not return to a predictable image that the unity of the mirror allowed to become established, but a different one that introduces confusion and blurs the path. The metaphor of the mirror is very interesting in this case. It allows us to consider this other, in a kind of dialectic, as constitutive of the mirror that reveals a "fantomal" space and the world of terror and violence to which it is linked. Achille Mbembe, inspired by the analysis of Jacques Lacan, speaks for example of "specular violence" to express such a situation of disorder that results in, inter alia, a meeting of worlds and the banishment of a certain number of limits "Essentially, these are 'extreme forms of human life'" where the backside worlds and the worlds of the place are one; the dividing line between them becoming faint (2003: 791). Transgressions such as incest and paedophilia represent this horizon of unpredictability, the occurrence of a virtuality contained in the forbidden. For victims, the consequences are notable. They are even more so as added to the trauma of sexual assault is an injunction to be silent, to silence what has happened and sometimes confront the threats or denials of adults. For example, 2002 study on child sexual abuse in Cameroon (D. Mbassa Menick) showed that 42% of cases of abuse were not reported. Also : "The rarity of legal measures and medical consultations also reflects parents' concern not to cast anathema on the victim at the risk of depriving her of the joys of marriage (...) In fact, a girl who has been raped and labelled as such has very little chance of finding a husband in the community" (2002: 61). From the foregoing, it is striking to observe that such crimes, such violence very rarely constitute, in the collective ethos, the occasion for an opportunity for transcendence through reflections likely to lead to just and effective solutions. Circumvention and avoidance clearly seem to be, sociologically, the dominant elective modalities of reaction to such crimes. I conclude that it would not be absurd to put them in deep resonance with what structures the Cameroonian collective ethos, and that Celestin Monga describes as the result of an intensive "process of unsocialization." They tend to get used to misfortune and to consider that the harm that happened is a lesser evil and could become worse if they do not get used to it; if they do not keep quiet and suffer in silence. Incestuous rapes constitute, from this point of view, an exemplary illustration of a grammar of being which affirms this: our suffering is a detail, our affections are dispensable.

Bibliography

Abega, S. C., & Akana, P. D. (2012). À propos de "Cannibales et législateurs." *Terroirs, 8*, 1–2.
Bernet, R. (1992). Délire et réalité. *Études phénoménologiques* (15).
Bessoles, P. (2011). *Le viol du féminin. Trauma sexuel et figures de l'emprise*. Champ Social Éditions, collection « Victimologie et criminologie ».
Bolya. (2005). *La profanation des vagins. Le viol, arme de destruction massive*. Éditions du Rocher/Le Serpent à Plumes.
Crocq, L. (2012). *16 leçons sur le trauma*. Éditions Odile Jacob.

Kouokam Magne, E. (2009, mai 11). *Santé et religions dans l'Extrême-Nord du Cameroun. Stratégies d'acteurs, enjeux de pouvoir et dynamiques de réseaux* (Thèse de doctorat en anthropologie). Université d'Aix-en-Provence, Marseille, 382 pp.

Mbassa Menick, D. (2002). Les abus sexuels en milieu scolaire au Cameroun. Résultat d'une recherche-action à Yaoundé. *Médecine Tropicale, 62*, 58–62.

Mbembe, A. (2003). Politiques de la vie et violence spéculaire dans la fiction d'Amos Tutuola. *Cahiers d'études africaines, 172*, 791–826.

Winkin, Y. (1996). Ray Birdwhistell (1918–1994): penser la communication autrement. *Recherches en communication* (5).

Preventing Violent Conflict in Africa

Confronting Military Violence in Africa's Electoral Spaces: Law, Institutions, and Remedies

James Tsabora

1 Introduction

The presence of the military in political spaces is a disturbing phenomenon around the world, with Africa being most affected, yet researchers have been limited by a paucity of granular data on effective institutional responses to this phenomenon. A key political process where the military has exerted their presence is the electoral space. Elections are a contested space by nature; they are a political process meant to give effect to the democratic agenda through opening a window for political change. However, in Africa, electoral contests have always been marred by vice and violence, thereby negating the democratic aspirations they are meant to advance. State and non-state actors have entered this contested space, and deployed violence to achieve political goals. Through a qualitative, comparative analysis, this chapter interrogates the form and nature of military violence in electoral spaces on the African continent with a view to suggest mechanisms that must characterize responsive, accountability and oversight mechanisms. Thus, the current chapter problematizes violence perpetrated by the military and proposes an institutional response mechanism that could be considered to address the problem.

The proposed mechanism is targeted at enhancing good governance, transparency, accountability, and justice. This model is a departure from ordinary

J. Tsabora (✉)
Faculty of Law, University of Zimbabwe, Harare, Zimbabwe
e-mail: jbtsaborah@law.uz.ac.zw

internal security structures that are operated through security-sector administrative systems. The entrance of state and non-state actors into the electoral space is not paranormal; it is their use of non-democratic means, particularly violence, when faced with the spectre of electoral damage that is condemnable. Solutions to violence in these spaces are determined by the context in which it occurs and surrounding circumstances. Understanding who perpetrates electoral violence, and why, are part and parcel of the critical dimensions to consider in the quest to curb it.

Despite an increasing number of state and non-state identities that have sought to sponsor and benefit from electoral violence, the military has dwarfed them all (Frantzeskakis & Park, 2022). The presence of these merchants of violence, functional or dysfunctional, on the democratic battlefield has not been welcome. Armed with crude force, and occasionally abusing it during election cycles, the military has proved too powerful for legal sanctions alone to intimidate (Bryden & Chappuis, 2016; Huntington, 1957; Mugari, 2021). This has resulted in injustice perpetrated against the innocent which goes unpunished even after the elections. It is against this background that the current study argues for application of new forms of accountability for security sector institutions in Africa (Bryden & Chappuis, 2016).

It is conceded that formal state institutions, such as state bodies that regulate the military, function best in a stable, functional environment. In that regard, if critical state institutions including legislatures, judiciaries, and executive organs falter in periods of crisis, the state degenerates into chaos and the military may not be easily sanctioned during such periods. Similarly, a state that is completely captured by the military, either in times of crisis or peacetime, is unable to activate mechanisms for the control of the military. This study, therefore, interrogates possible and appropriate response mechanisms for military violence in a normal, reasonably stable political environment.

2   Form and Nature of Military Violence in Electoral Spaces

Military violence during elections has taken several forms in Africa (Birch et al., 2020; Taylor, 2018). The most common form, according to Taylor (2018), is physical violence. This occurs when the military acts as an agent of incumbent leaders to spread violence against perceived political opponents. Under this form, the military takes an active partisan role, and chooses to support the political causes of one of the electoral contestants. Thus, the military utilizes its independence, and wades in the murky waters of politics.

Taylor (2018) explains how political opponents are targeted with physical violence, acts of arson, intimidation, espionage, propaganda messages, public disavowals, and digging of dirt. Birch et al. (2020) and Straus and Taylor (2012) expand on the same point, explaining how in such a form of violence supporters are harassed, political freedoms trampled upon, political rallies dispersed, and several other unlawful shenanigans are played out in an effort to destroy the political careers and prospects of opposition politicians.

The second form is psychological violence. This is also aimed at political opponents and opposition supporters. In this case, the military publicly rejects the credentials of a political opponent and promises outright war if that opponent were to win elections (Birch et al., 2020; Lupsha, 1971). Messages are carefully crafted and dispersed into the public sphere to warn citizens against voting for a particular candidate. This tactic throws the military deep into politics, and makes them lose their avowed independence, non-partisanship, and apolitical role. What is important to note is that this approach attacks and disturbs the psyche of the voter. It creates a disturbing level of uncertainty, and an expectation of chaos, violence, and any other disorders. In essence, this tactic is akin to instigating psychological warfare in the mind of the voter. It takes away rights from the voter to choose and decide on the basis of manifestos or policies of the leaders and leads them to vote on the basis of fear.

Human Rights Watch (2008) provides the best illustration for this form of violence. The first decade of the 2000s, when Zimbabwe's ZANU-PF was faced with the most serious political challenge of all time in the form of the Movement for Democratic Change, the Zimbabwe military began a direct campaign against the opposition leader, Morgan Tsvangirai. In an effort to discredit his political credentials, the military openly declared that they would not salute a person who had not participated in the liberation struggle. Another message that was spread around was that the ruling party's political power was acquired by blood, and not through the ballot, and thus the pen could not be mightier than the sword. The messages are enough to result in psychological violence as the audience are left in fear of the consequences of a party supported by the military not achieving electoral victory (Young, 2020).

Finally, another form of military violence is the subjugation of key state and electoral institutions under the direct or indirect control of the military and the abuse of such institutions to "secure the vote" mostly for the incumbent government (Birch et al., 2020). These critical institutions include the election management body, the judiciary, Parliament, and to some extent, the state media and press, or domestic electoral observer missions. The critical institutions are usually captured or subjected to extreme duress to the extent that they become nothing but the mouthpiece or the agent of the military. The judiciary and the press are similarly captured or intimidated. Spaces for independent observer missions or for civil society involvement are suppressed or constricted. The actual violence in this approach is the lack of any institution to reprimand the military, or counteract its possible use of force (Young, 2020). In fact, the potent force held by the military is usually enough to engender silence on the part of voters. The promise of violence is supremely more realistic than all the idealistic promises associated with democratic dividends such as peace and democracy.

From the above, if such violence exists in all these forms in a polity, there is effective rejection of both political transition and democratization. Further, it is also clear that this violence cannot be subdued by legal and other normal political sanctions. There is a need for other strategies. This motivates the current study which seeks to find ways of curbing unchecked military violence in election times.

3 Military Violence as Human Rights Violations

According to Davis et al. (2015), there is no doubt that aggressive actions of the military against civilians constitute gross violations of human rights. As alluded to above, military violence manifests physically through beatings, torture, abductions, arson, unlawful detentions, murder, destruction of businesses and other property, as well as physical harassment. It also results in forced disappearances and kidnappings. These actions are in direct violation of human rights recognized and guaranteed protection in terms of the constitutional system (Human Rights Watch, 2008). Significantly, these actions are a negation of political, economic, and social freedoms guaranteed to citizens under the constitution and also by national laws. In specific terms, these actions violate rights to life, property, participation in politics, liberty, privacy, freedom of assembly and association, dignity, personal security, and peace.

It must further be stated that military violence is not categorized as an offence in security-sector legislation that regulates the military (Davis et al., 2015). The command framework for military violence is often done outside the remit of the law. Consequently, military violence is difficult to sanction using internal operational structures. To this extent, it can be argued that the closed, illegal way in which military violence is done promotes impunity and defies existing institutions. In several African countries, attempts to open up the security sector to frameworks for accountability have been resisted for various reasons. From this perspective, it is clear that an external, strong oversight institution must be established to stop the trend and to communicate appropriate messages to perpetrators of military violence.

Contemporary perspectives on constitutionalism, human rights, and the rule of law suggest that the best way of ensuring that security structures operate within bounds of the law during electoral periods is to expose them to effective oversight mechanisms. As observed by Hoglund and Jarstad (2010), there are several reasons to call for a civilian oversight mechanism for the military, in particular if it has orchestrated military violence during election cycles. To begin with, civilian complaints mechanisms facilitate the exercise of democratic control over the security services. This, expressed in other words, means the mechanism subjects the military to a civilian institution not constricted by the straitjacket rules of the military (Huntington, 1957; Mugari, 2021). Such an institution also ensures respect for the rule of law in the security sector (Government of Zimbabwe, 2013) and indexes a layer of accountability.

According to UNODC (2011), accountability is defined as a system of internal and external checks and balances aimed at ensuring that members of the security services carry out their duties properly and are held responsible if they fail to do so. Another reason is that the oversight mechanism can assist in focusing attention on problems in security services practice requiring corrective action. In this way, the external independent complaints mechanism works as a catalyst for the reform of the military arm. This is of particular significance in that it combats the development of a culture of impunity by a state institution with a monopoly over the lawful use of violence.

4 The Nature of the Civilian Oversight Agency

There is no doubt of the necessity of an independent civilian oversight system to scrutinize the unlawful presence of the military in the electoral space. Debates, however, arise on the form and shape such an institution must take (Terril, 1990). Different jurisdictions have different approaches to achieving the same result. For example, in South Africa, the oversight system exists as a legislative. There is the Independent Police Investigative Directorate Act of 2011 that has a responsibility to investigate all deaths arising from police action or occurring in police custody, as well as alleged or suspected acts of brutality, criminality, corruption, and misconduct on the part of members of the South African Police Service. Its investigators have the same powers as police officers to arrest and question people and to conduct searches to unearth misconduct.

Several interventions have been put in place in different countries. In Kenya, investigative powers are given to the Independent Policing Oversight Authority (IPOA) in terms of the IPOA Act (www.policinglaw.info); in Australia, there is an Independent Broad-based Anti-Corruption Commission in Victoria (www.ibac.vic.gov.au); for Scotland, there is the Police Investigation and Review Commissioner (pirc.scotland.gov.uk); there is an Independent Complaints Authority in Denmark (www.politiklagemyndigheden.dk/english); the Enforcement Agency Integrity Commission in Malaysia (www.eaic.gov.my); the Independent Commission of Investigations in Jamaica (www.indecom.gov.jm); the Police Public Complaint Authority in Zambia; the Police Ombudsman in Northern Ireland (www.policeombudsman.org); the Civilian Complaint Review Board in New York (www.nyc.gov/html/ccrb/html/home/home.shtml); and the People's Law Enforcement Board in the Philippines (Guzman, 2007; Nalla & Mamayek 2013). These examples demonstrate attempts to provide for the independence of civilian oversight agencies.

Most jurisdictions create a system that is independent from the executive arm of the state. Worryingly, most jurisdictions establish an oversight agency for the police, and not the military. Despite this, it is clear that the agency established for the purpose must not be an internal structure within the security services sector. It must strike a balance between national security imperatives and human rights protection. It should aim at access to justice, remedies, and redress for human rights violations as well as targeting observance of the rule of law and accountability. For South Africa, the executive leadership of the agency is nominated by the Minister of Police and confirmed by a parliamentary committee (www.iol.co.za). S/he can only be suspended by a two-thirds vote in the National Assembly, thereby removing this power from the minister of police who is a member of the executive. This is seen as creating more independence for the agency.

5 Jurisdictional Aspects

The jurisdiction of the civilian oversight agency must be clarified. Comparative research illustrates that bodies of this nature possess the general jurisdiction to investigate all forms of misconduct by the security services sector

(De Angelis et al., 2016). According to Donno (2013), misconduct refers to acting in a political and or partisan manner, acting contrary to the constitution or law, violating fundamental human rights, or furthering the interests of a political party or cause.

6 Investigations

Comparative research illustrates various options in relation to powers associated with investigation (De Angelis et al., 2016). The most common approach is where the civilian oversight agency has subsidiary units or subcommittees responsible for complaints handling, investigations, remedial actions, and/or redress. Inevitably, the powers to investigate must come with corollary powers of search, entry, and seizure.

In addition to the issues discussed above, there are several other important aspects that should characterize the substantive rules and procedures of the oversight agency in relation to investigations, according to De Angelis et al. (2016). These include:

1. Definition, form, and lodging of complaints.
2. The structure of the complaints receiving and handling system.
3. The initiation and conduct of investigations.
4. The decision to investigate and refusal to institute investigations.
5. The nature of powers of entry, search, and seizure for the purposes of investigations.
6. Holding of hearings; the format of hearings, evidentiary issues, confidentiality, and protection of witnesses.
7. Procedural formalities and administrative justice aspects.

Addressing these aspects will help to ensure that the agency conducts investigations fairly, thoroughly, and transparently, and that any findings or recommendations made by the agency are based on sound evidence and in accordance with established legal principles.

7 Dispute Settlement and Administrative Issues

The dispute settlement function must be semi-judicial and quasi-adjudicatory in nature. Studies show that the civilian oversight agency incorporates dispute resolution mechanisms (De Angelis et al., 2016). Accordingly, it is suggested that where the civilian oversight agency considers it appropriate for the purpose of expediting the resolution of issues arising out of complaints and investigations of misconduct and human rights violations by the security services, it must have power to employ alternative dispute resolution mechanisms, such as mediation, conciliation, and arbitration. Further, clear provisions must be inserted in the civilian oversight agency legislation on the immunity of its personnel and staff and the contours of the relationship with sector-specific legislation or justice systems.

8 Remedies Issued by the Agency

The relationship between the civilian oversight agency and the judicial system is important (De Angelis et al., 2016). Prominently, there is a need to consider whether the power to order a particular remedy is purely administrative, or semi-judicial in nature. The question extends to enforcement of the remedy or order granted by the agency. The options revolve around direct enforceability and registration in the formal courts to make the agency remedy an order of court. Accordingly, the question is whether there is a need for "transformation" of the remedy into a court order by following a registration process, or whether the remedy is directly enforceable as if it is an order of court.

In order to arrive at the appropriate regime of remedies, the kind of remedies envisaged in the provision should have a transitional justice characteristic, rather than a judicial form of justice (McCarthy, 2009). To that extent, such remedies must be understood from a transitional justice perspective since they are based on reparative theories, and not criminal justice theory. McCarthy (2009) observes that remedies under this regime are a departure from the traditional outcomes of the criminal justice process, namely the acquittal or punishment of the accused, which are more concerned with "society's needs, most obviously for incapacitation and deterrence, than with addressing the harm suffered by victims through the transgressor's conduct." Reparative justice, he asserts, is based, on the fact that the justice process is said to take insufficient account of, and to respond inadequately to the needs of the victim, the character of the harm done to that victim and the complexity of the harm done to wider social bonds by the transgressor's conduct.

The previous discussion has emphasized the significance of granting the oversight agency the power to issue temporary or final orders. Various sources, such as kenyalaw.org, De Angelis et al. (2016), and MacCarthy (2009), recommend that the agency should have the authority to issue the following orders:

1. Direct the responsible military members to stop the violation, misconduct, or acts in question.
2. Order the responsible military members to compensate, restitute, or rehabilitate any victims of the violations, misconduct, or unlawful acts, using money, services, or other means deemed appropriate by the agency.
3. In cases where the violation, misconduct, or acts have resulted in the death of a person, direct the responsible individuals to compensate the dependents of the deceased person.
4. Order the return of any property that was unlawfully taken as a result of the violations, misconduct, or unlawful acts.
5. Order the release of any individuals who were illegally detained as a result of the violation, misconduct, or unlawful acts.
6. Direct the responsible organization to take disciplinary action against the person who committed the violation, misconduct, or unlawful acts.
7. Recommend to the Prosecutor-General that criminal proceedings be initiated against any person responsible for the violation, misconduct, or acts in question.
8. Bring the violation, misconduct, or acts in question to the attention of the government or other appropriate authorities and recommend measures to prevent its recurrence and redress its effects.
9. Take any other action that the agency deems necessary to put an end to the violation, misconduct, or acts in question or provide victims with redress or relief.

Moreover, the legislation that establishes the agency must include provisions for judicial oversight of the agency's decisions, including review and appeal processes. One common approach is to subject the oversight agency's decisions to the review and appeal powers of the Supreme Court, while enforcement of the decisions must be done through the High Court.

It is suggested that when awarding financial remedies, the oversight agency should consider several factors. These factors may include the extent of the physical harm suffered, as well as any non-material damage resulting in mental or emotional suffering. Other factors could be material damage, such as lost earnings and the inability to work, loss of or damage to property, unpaid wages or salaries, lost opportunities related to employment, education, and social benefits, loss of status, and any interference with an individual's legal rights. Additionally, the costs of legal or other relevant experts, medical services, psychological and social assistance, including for vulnerable, ill, and other disadvantaged social groups, should also be taken into account.

9 The Emerging Zimbabwean Picture: An Overview

In Zimbabwe, the legislative framework for the security services is necessarily fragmented. It finds expression in the Defence Act (Government of Zimbabwe, 1996) the Police Act (Government of Zimbabwe, 1995) and the Prisons Act (Government of Zimbabwe, 1996). Currently, there is no act of parliament for the intelligence services, despite Section 224(1) of the constitution providing that the intelligence services be established in terms of a statute or a presidential or cabinet order or directive (Government of Zimbabwe, 2013). Zimbabwe's Central Intelligence Organization is a department in the president's office that is not regulated by any specific statute. This makes it lacking in legislative accountability as it is only answerable to the state President (Desch, 1999). There is, therefore, potential for abuse and no individual complaints mechanism is provided for in any law to regulate the intelligence services www.brookings.edu. This weakens the chances of the public to have redress against the actions of the intelligence services.

Ideally, Parliament can fill the gap and chastise the military when the military enters the electoral space through the barrel of the gun. Section 207(2) of the constitution makes it clear that the security services are subject to the authority of the constitution, the president, cabinet and parliamentary oversight (Government of Zimbabwe, 2013). This essentially empowers the parliament to hold security services accountable. In Zimbabwe, this is mainly done through the Portfolio Committee on Defence, Home Affairs, and Security Services.

Ayuba (2014), however, identifies several challenges that can hinder effective parliamentary oversight. One such challenge is the lack of expertise and professionalism among parliamentarians. Additionally, security services may refuse to disclose classified information, while parliamentarians or staff members may leak sensitive security information to the media. During electoral periods, parliament may become compromised or dysfunctional as political candidates compete for the political ticket through any means necessary, including seeking endorsement or direct support from the military. As a result, parliamentary oversight may not be a viable option for checking the excesses of militarism in electoral spaces.

10 The Independent Complaints Commission

The Zimbabwean Parliament passed the Zimbabwe Independent Complaints Commission Act, Chapter 10:34 (ZICCA) in 2022, with the aim of implementing Section 210 of the Zimbabwean Constitution. Section 210 requires an independent mechanism for receiving and investigating complaints from the public about misconduct by members of the security services and for remedying any harm caused by such misconduct. The ZICCA seeks to establish an independent and fair mechanism for investigating misconduct by members of the security services, providing disciplinary recommendations based on investigations, and ensuring appropriate remedies for any harm caused. Additionally, the Act promotes accountability and transparency of the security services and their members, in accordance with constitutional principles. It is noteworthy that the Act is based on the premise of addressing security services wrongdoing.

Misconduct is defined as including the main types of violence frequently committed by the military in places where elections are held. The definition takes into account a number of factors, including: causing any death as a result of the actions of any member of a security service; unjustified use of a military firearm; rape by a member of a security service, whether the member is on duty or not; rape of a person while that person is in military custody; and the torture of, or assault on, any member of a security service in the course of the member's duties. Significantly, the Act recognizes other acts, including violations of human rights, complained of by any person, against any member of a security service in the discharge or purported discharge of the member's functions.

These actions are in addition to other actions rendered as misconduct by the Act but derived from the constitution. Thus, further forms of misconduct of the military punishable under this Act are violation of provisions of Section 208 of the constitution. Section 208 (2) of the Zimbabwe Constitution prohibits certain types of unprofessional conduct by the military (Constitution of Zimbabwe). This provision prohibits the military from acting in a partisan manner; from furthering the interests of any political party or cause; from prejudicing the lawful interests of any political party or cause; and from violating the fundamental rights or freedoms of any person. Under these provisions, military personnel are further prohibited from being active members or office-bearers of any political party or organization. Finally, serving members of the military must not be employed or engaged in civilian institutions except in periods of public emergency.

Without doubt, these provisions apply not only to cases where there is a presence of the military in electoral spaces, but also to the broader political arena. The provisions can significantly turn the tide and reverse the trend. What must, however, be remembered is that this Act, as with other ordinary pieces of legislation, is useful in a functional, stable and peaceful state. If a state descends into chaos, as has been the case with some African nations during the conduct of fierce elections in the past five decades, the law ceases to be of any practical use.

11 Functions of the Independent Complaints Commission

From the above analysis, it is clear that the constitution envisages the establishment of a properly structured independent agency usable by the public against members of the military (Brandt et al., 2011). This is significant because it indicates that the Commission which the legislation requires must be given a defined mandate, specified powers, functions, and jurisdictional limits, as well as operational and administrative procedures. In addition, the Commission needs to be viewed as an entity that handles complaints and conducts investigations and adjudications. The Commission's authority to collect, process, and question complaints must not give rise to ambiguity because the Constitution mandates that it "receives and investigates." Further, the Commission must have the authority to consider, order, or provide a set of remedies to anyone who has been wronged by security services personnel. This power is essential since without the power to order remedial measures, the Commission will not serve any purpose.

These constitutional principles are put into effect through the Act. The Commission is given investigation authority, access to evidence and information, responsibility for inspection, and, most crucially, remedial authority under Section 5 of the Act. The Commission has the authority to "make such recommendations or orders as it considers appropriate to the security service concerned or any other relevant authority, including recommendations or orders for prosecution, compensation or any other appropriate relief or internal disciplinary action," according to Section 5(2) of the Act. The remedial function is critical, and this motivated the requirement for the chairperson of the Commission to be a person "eligible for appointment as a High Court Judge or is a sitting judge or former judge."

As stated above, the fact that the Commission can make remedial orders grants it quasi-judicial power. In terms of the Act, the Commission can recommend or order several actions to be done (Section 16). These include that the Commission can recommend the immediate release of any person from unlawful detention by the military; recommend the payment of compensation to the complainant; recommend that the complainant seek redress through the courts; refer the matter to the National Prosecuting Authority for the prosecution of the member complained against; or order the appropriate security service concerned to institute appropriate internal disciplinary processes against the member complained against.

12 Principles for Remedies

The Commission is a new creature in the military space. There is no body of principles from domestic law that the Commission can embrace in granting remedies of a reparatory nature. The Commission however is at liberty to develop its own principles through considering human rights law, foreign law and international law. A number of guiding principles are provided by international human rights law, which the Commission may apply to award financial and non-financial remedies. This is due to the fact that international and regional treaty law strongly recognizes the right to a remedy. Every person has the right to an "effective remedy" for acts that violate their fundamental rights, according to Article 8 of the Universal Declaration of Human Rights. In addition, Article 6 of the International Convention on the Elimination of All Forms of Racial Discrimination recognizes the right to seek just and adequate reparations or satisfaction for any damages suffered, Article 9(5) of the International Covenant on Civil and Political Rights refers to an enforceable right to compensation. Article 14(1) of the Convention against Torture and Other Cruel, Inhuman or Degrading Treatment or Punishment provides for an enforceable right to fair and adequate compensation, including the means for as full rehabilitation as possible.

There are also important guidelines from the United Nations General Assembly Declaration of Basic Principles of Justice for Victims of Crime and

Abuse of Power (www.unodc.org), and the UN General Assembly Declaration Basic Principles and Guidelines on the Right to a Remedy and Reparation for Victims of Gross Violations of International Human Rights Law and Serious Violations of International Humanitarian Law (www.ohchr.org).

Regional treaty frameworks follow the norms of global treaty regimes. For instance, Article 21(2) of the African Charter on Human and Peoples' Rights refers to a right to recovery of property and adequate compensation. Article 63(1) of the American Convention on Human Rights calls for the situation giving rise to the breach of a right or freedom be remedied, and that fair compensation be paid to the injured party. For Zimbabwe, under Section 85 of the Constitution, violation of fundamental rights and freedoms in the Declaration of Rights, gives rise to a claim for compensation.

A study of these several treaty regimes uncovers certain common standards or values that can be regarded as principles to be followed in awarding remedies in the form of compensation, reparations, and restitution, among other similar forms. The first principle is that financial remedies such as compensation and restitution must be adequate, effective, appropriate, and prompt (www.ohchr.org). The second is the principle of non-discrimination where the remedies must be granted to victims without adverse distinction on the grounds of gender, age, race, colour, language, religion or belief, political or other opinion, sexual orientation, national, ethnic or social origin, wealth, birth or other status (www.ohchr.org) Thus, the Commission must avoid replicating discriminatory practices underlying the injustice or promoting further stigmatization of the victims.

The third principle is that the Commission must consider the need to make remedies available to direct and indirect victims, including the family members of direct victims (www.ohchr.org). This extends to those who will have suffered personal harm as a result of these offences, regardless of whether they participated in the proceedings of the Commission or not. The relationship between the direct and indirect victim is of the essence; family and cultural and social connections have to be considered. Thus, where members of the security services assault a person, leaving them disabled, the Commission must consider granting a financial remedy that benefits their dependents, as currently permissible under the law of delict (Corbett et al., 2009). This approach is entrenched in the UN Basic Principles which state that in appropriate situations and in terms of domestic law, the term "victim" also includes the immediate family or dependents of the direct victim and persons who have suffered (www.ohchr.org).

Another important principle is that priority may need to be given to certain victims who are in a particularly vulnerable situation or who require urgent assistance, such as victims of sexual or gender-based violence, individuals who require immediate medical care (especially when plastic surgery or treatment for HIV is necessary), as well as severely traumatized children, for instance following the loss of family members. This means that the Commission may need to adopt measures in terms of the concept of "affirmative action" in order to guarantee equal, effective, and safe access to reparations for particularly vulnerable victims. In the case of *The Prosecutor, ICC versus Thomas Lubanga* (www.icc-cpi.int) the International Criminal Court recommended formulating and implementing reparations awards appropriate for the victims of sexual and gender-based violence. The Court also recommended reflecting on the fact that the consequences of these crimes are complicated as they operate on a number of levels; their impact can extend over a long period of time; they affect women and girls, men and boys, together with their families and communities; and they require a specialist, integrated, and multidisciplinary approach (www.asil.org).

The principle of gender sensitivity should be mainstreamed in the award of remedies. Research advocates for a gender-sensitive approach which properly responds to challenges faced by women and girls in accessing justice in the context of harm or injury by members of the security services (Bardall, 2011, 2020). Further, the principles of participation must be respected. As Bardall (2020) observes, "victims of the crimes, their families and communities should 'participate throughout the reparations process and should receive adequate support in order to make their participation substantive and effective.'"

In situations involving children, the principle of the best interests of the child must be adopted (Constitution of Zimbabwe Section 19(1) and Section 81(2), Article 3 (1) Convention on the Rights of the Child (CRC), Guidelines on Justice in Matters involving Child Victims and Witnesses of Crime, para. 8(d)). Again, a gender-sensitive approach must be mainstreamed herein. Further, where children are concerned, the Commission system must consider providing medical services (including psychiatric and psychological care) along with assistance as regards general rehabilitation, housing, education, and training (www.icc-cpi.int).

13 Conclusion

The deployment of violence to shape and decide electoral outcomes must receive the highest condemnation from domestic and international institutions. Law, policy, and practice must reflect this condemnation. This is because military violence in electoral spaces negates the democratic agenda and nullifies the exercise of political rights and freedoms central to the legitimacy of state institutions. Several forms of military violence have been experienced in Africa. On most occasions, the law has not provided the solution since the political and security environment militates against the rule of law. Despite this reality, there is an emerging trend to subject the military to the law in cases of their sliding into electoral politics.

The current chapter thus proposed the civilian oversight institutional approach as a mechanism to ensure a stable, secure, and functional political context. This is the case when Zimbabwe has crafted a unique law to directly confront the excesses of militarism in political spaces, leading to human rights violations, criminality, and violence. This represents a massive leap in the pursuit of accountability, rule of law and constitutionalism in the military. With such a law in place, the propensity of military involvement in contentious electoral spaces may gradually die out and become a thing of the past. However, the law is not yet operational, and the jury is still discussing how best the law captures the best elements. For this reason the chapter suggests the oversight mechanism is a handy instrument in ensuring that independence, impartiality, and objectivity are realized in the absence of an active intervention.

References

Ayuba, C. (2014). *Challenges of Parliamentary Oversight of the Security Sector in a Democracy: A Case of Nigeria.* https://papers.ssrn.com/sol3/Delivery.cfm/SSRN_ID2484696_code2284210.pdf?abstractid=2484696&mirid=1

Bardall, G. (2011). *Breaking the Mold: Understanding Gender and Electoral Violence* (IFES White Paper).

Bardall, G. (2020). How Is Political Violence Gendered? Disentangling Motives, Forms, and Impacts. *Political Studies, 68*(4), 916–935.

Birch, S., Daxecker, U., & Hoglund, K. (2020). Electoral Violence: An Introduction. *Journal of Peace Research, 57*(1), 3–14. https://doi.org/10.1177/0022343319889657

Brandt, M., Cottrell, J., Ghai, J., & Regan, A. (2011). *Constitution-Making and Reform: Options for the Process.* Interpeace ISBN 978-2-8399–0871-9.

Bryden, A. & Chappuis, F. (2016). *Security Sector Governance and Reform in Africa*, https://www.academia.edu/68756900/Security_Sector_Governance_and_Reform_in_Africa1.

Corbett, M. M., Buchanan, J. M., & Gauntlett, J. (2009). *The Quantum of Damages in Bodily and Fatal Injury Cases* (p. 87). G Feltoe Guide to the Zimbabwean Law of Delict.

Davis, W. W., Mullany, L. C., Schissler, M., et al. (2015). Militarization, Human Rights Violations and Community Responses as Determinants of Health in Southeastern Myanmar: Results of a Cluster Survey. *Conflict and Health, 9*, 32. https://doi.org/10.1186/s13031-015-0059-0

De Angelis, J., Rosenthal, R., & Buchner, B. (2016). *Civilian Oversight of Law Enforcement: Assessing the Evidence NCJ Number 250287*.

De Guzman, M. C. (2007). Integrity of Civilian Review: A Contemporary Analysis of Complainants' and Police Officers' Views in the Philippines. *Police Practice and Research, 8*(1), 31–45. https://doi.org/10.1080/15614260701217966

Desch, M. C. (1999). *Civilian Control of the Military: The Changing Security Environment*. Johns Hopkins University Press.

Donno, D. (2013, September 26). *Defending Democratic Norms: International Actors and the Politics of Electoral Misconduct* (Online Ed.). Oxford Academic. https://doi.org/10.1093/acprof:oso/9780199991280.003.0003. Accessed 15 May 2023.

Frantzeskakis, N., & Park, B. B. (2022). Armed and Dangerous: Legacies of Incumbent-Military Ties and electoral Violence in Africa. *Electoral Studies, 80*, 102531.

Government of Zimbabwe. (2022). *Zimbabwe Independent Complaints Commission*.

Government of Zimbabwe. (2013). https://www.constituteproject.org/constitution/Zimbabwe_2013.pdf

Hoglund, K., & Jarstad, A. K. (2010). *Policy & Practice Brief Knowledge of durable c e ACCORD*. 001. pp. 1–5.

https://www.asil.org

https://www.icc-cpi.int/sites/default/files/CaseInformationSheets/LubangaEng.pdf

http://www.ibac.vic.gov.au

http://pirc.scotland.gov.uk/

http://www.politiklagemyndigheden.dk/english

Human Rights Watch. (2008). *All Over Again: Human Rights Abuses and Flawed Electoral Conditions in Zimbabwe's Coming General Elections, 20*, 2(A). http://hrw.org/reports/2008/zimbabwe0308/

Huntington, S. 1957. *The Soldier and the State: The Theory and Politics of Civil-Military Relations*. The Belknap Press.

International Criminal Court Rules of Procedure and Evidence. https://www.icc-cpi.int/sites/default/files/Publications/Rules-of-Procedure-and-Evidence.pdf

Justice in Matters Involving Child Victims and Witnesses of…United Nations Office on Drugs and Crime. https://www.unodc.org/documents/justice-and-prison-reform/Justice_in_matters…pdf

Lupsha, P. A. (1971). Explanation of Political Violence—Some Psychological Theories Versus Indignation *Journal of Politics and Society, 2,* 89–104.

McCarthy, J. D. (2009). From Race Riot to Collective Violence. *Contemporary Sociology, 38*(2), 118–120. https://doi.org/10.1177/009430610903800204

Mugari, I. (2021). Civilian Police Oversight: A Contemporary Review of Police Oversight Mechanisms in Europe, Australia and Africa. *Journal of Applied Security Research*.https://doi.org/10.1080/19361610.2021.1918524

Muzondidya, J. (2019). Resurgent Authoritarianism: The Politics of the January 2019 Violence in Zimbabwe. *Human Rights Reports Zimbabwe Review.* http://solidaritypeacetrust.org/zimbabwe-review/

Nalla, M. K., & Mamayek, C. (2013). Democratic Policing, Police Accountability and Citizen Oversight in Asia: An Exploratory Study. *Police Practice and Research, 14*(2), 117–129. https://doi.org/10.1080/15614263.2013.767091

Straus, S., & Taylor, C. (2012). Democratization and Electoral Violence in Sub-Saharan Africa, 1990–2008. In D. Bekoe (Ed.), *Voting in Fear: Electoral Violence in Sub-Saharan Africa* (pp. 15–38). United States Institute of Peace Press.

Taylor, C. F., Pevehouse, J., & Straus, S. (2018). Perils of Pluralism: Electoral Violence and Incumbency in Sub-Saharan Africa. *Journal of Peace Research, 54*(3), 397–411.

Terril, R. J. (1990). Alternative Perceptions of Independence in Civilian Oversight. *Journal of Police Science and Administration, 17*(2), 77–83.

UNODC. (2011). Handbook on Police Accountability, Oversight and Integrity. *Prisons Act, Chapter 7:11 Government of Zimbabwe (1996).* https://www.unodc.org/pdf/criminal_justice/Handbook_on_police_Accountability_Oversight_and_Integrity.pdf.

Young, L. E., (2020). Who Dissents? Self-efficacy and Opposition Action After State-sponsored Election Violence. *Journal of Peace Research, 57*(1), 62–76.

Managing Conflict in Africa: Challenges and Opportunities for the African Union

Victor H. Mlambo, Ernest Toochi Aniche, and Mandla Mfundo Masuku

1 Introduction

In 2019, 25 state-based conflicts were recorded in Africa, four more than in 2018. In 2019, nine countries in Africa: Cameroon, Niger, Chad, Nigeria, Libya, Burkina Faso, Mali, Somalia, and Mozambique) experienced conflicts with Islamic State within their territories (Palik et al., 2020).

Moreover, Raleigh and Kishi (2021) argue that in 2020, Africa was the sole continent where political violence rose relative to 2019. More than 17,200 distinct events of political violence were recorded in 2020, resulting in over 37,600 reported fatalities; this represents an increase of more than 4000 events from 2019, and nearly 9000 more reported fatalities. The development of postcolonial African states continues to be informed by colonial socio-economic and political governance systems. For Burimaso (2013), after the demise of colonialism, postcolonial African leaders failed to forge modern

---

V. H. Mlambo (✉)
School of Public Management, Governance and Public Policy, University of Johannesburg, Johannesburg, South Africa
e-mail: halavico@yahoo.com

E. T. Aniche
Department of Political Science, Federal University Otuoke, Otuoke, Nigeria

M. M. Masuku
School of Built Environment and Development Studies, University of KwaZulu-Natal, Durban, South Africa

© The Author(s), under exclusive license to Springer Nature Switzerland AG 2024
O. B. Mlambo and E. Chitando (eds.), *The Palgrave Handbook of Violence in Africa*, https://doi.org/10.1007/978-3-031-40754-3_51

African states which were underpinned by the need for inclusive development; rather, modern African states still relied heavily on the colonial form of governance, which was characterized by force, violence and brutality, hence the prevalence of conflicts and instability in Africa. Conflict and violence in Africa are issues that have become an impediment to inclusive development and political stability.

Joshua and Olanrewaju (2017) reflect that it seems as if the African Union (AU) lacks sufficient capacity to address these issues, which have for decades stifled Africa's potential development, although there is an urgent need to address them. Unsurprisingly, this chapter argues that the AU's apparent failure to resolve these issues cannot be viewed in isolation; rather, it is the holistic failure of African states to forge unity when faced with complex challenges. It reflects how, when faced with such challenges, African states put national interests ahead of continental considerations. Building on the above insights, this chapter acknowledges that while the AU is an important body when it comes to representing African states, nevertheless, its effectiveness is highly dependent on the level of cooperation it solicits from member states. With member states putting their national interests ahead of continental ones, the effective functioning of the AU is bound to be affected, and where there is a lack of political will and support, the AU cannot successfully carry out its mandate relating to conflict management and resolution. It is also important to note that, after colonialism, the formation of the modern Africa state did not take into consideration the values, cultures, and traditions that made up the peoples of Africa; and the apparent side-lining of these important elements means that forging unity between the different ethnic and religious peoples of Africa will remain a stumbling block in the quest to eradicate conflicts and promote continental integration.

The emergence of new conflicts has revealed the AU as a failing body and the AU has been criticized for over-relying on external donors for funds needed to finance its operations. However, this chapter argues that it is overly simplistic for African states and scholars to critique the financial shortcomings of the AU because if member states paid their dues, the AU would not need to seek external funding from abroad; hence, the demise of the AU is a direct result of member states. This chapter examines current trends in conflict and violence in Africa. It seeks to examine the role of the African Union in managing conflict in Africa and its associated challenges. The chapter is guided by the following questions: What drives conflict in Africa? How effective are AU conflict management/prevention mechanisms? What are the challenges of managing conflicts in Africa, and are there any opportunities/avenues that the AU could employ to better manage conflict in the continent?

2 Methodological Issues

To answer the research questions underpinning this chapter, a review of the literature was undertaken concerning the topic under study. This approach was key as it allowed the chapter to source data from a local, regional and international perspective, taking especially into consideration the history of conflict in Africa after colonialism. Moreover, this approach was important as it allowed for the chapter to broaden the understanding of conflict by comparing and contrasting debates and arguments in the literature, particularly since this is a contemporary issue. Political instability and governance issues are factors that have been observed as barriers to Africa's quest to eradicate widespread conflict. This chapter dwells on the debates, arguments and theoretical literature informing this contemporary issue, especially considering in particular the strides that the AU has taken in its effort to entice member states to consolidate good governance and political stability. As we take into account pre-colonial, colonial, and current narratives around the development and governance in Africa, these narratives will, therefore, become integral in allowing the chapter to reach a meaningful conclusion—hence the rationale of this methodological approach.

3 Theoretical Support

This chapter employs the assumptions of the conflict theory and the concept of state fragility to explain conflict and violence in Africa. The conflict theory was the brainchild of Muzafer Sherif, an American psychologist. For Sherif, conflicts do not come from those who are irrational or unreasonable but are driven by the competition for scarce resources (Böhm et al., 2018; Granberg & Sarup, 2012). It is called a "conflict" theory because it rejects the idea (common in the 1960s) that groups could share and cooperate. The theory rests on the premise that whenever there are two or more groups that are seeking the same limited resources, this will lead to conflict, negative stereotypes and beliefs, and discrimination between the groups (Sherif, 2015; Valentim, 2010). However, while this chapter notes the importance of cooperation within the AU, it becomes vital to reflect that the AU does not operate in isolation and that the unity of member states is vital for its success. Even though they are part of the AU, member states have national considerations which may at times supersede continental interests, resulting in reduced cooperation on continental interests. In the context of this chapter, conflicts can be described in terms of the interests of countries involved, particularly the competition over scarce water resources. The theory conceives of conflict as a consequence of competition over scarce resources. Furthermore, the chapter argues that change occurs in social relationships as a result of the competing interests of those who have the wealth and power to keep and expand their resources. However, it is the interest of those who have little political and economic power to protect their resources for the improvement of their livelihoods. Conflict can then lead to increasing animosity between opposing groups and can cause feuds to develop. Sherif further argues that when members of two groups come into contact with one another in a series of activities that embody goals which each urgently desires, but which can be attained by one group only at the expense of the other, competitive activity towards the goal changes over time to hostility (Böhm et al., 2018; Granberg & Sarup, 2012; Sherif, 2015).

There are many causes of conflict in Africa and these (as discussed in this chapter) have contributed immensely to the destabilization of Africa, they have contributed to population displacement, and civilian deaths, and compounded the status of Africa as a conflict-ridden continent. Mkandawire (2001) argues that Africa lacks the political will to spur development. African states have become obsessed with the concept of nationalism, and in the process have moved away from their continental commitments. The current governance and political structures in Africa are broken, and this is the direct result of a lack of cohesion and unity and the failure to forge one united vision for Africa's development. Supporting this notion, this chapter argues that African states are states in name only: they were not created with a fabric of unity and cohesion, but rather they were formed in a rushed process and to a great extent have not benefited the people of the continent. Rather, it is the African elites who were in the cohort of the former colonizers that have benefited from the rushed formation of the modern African state. If we consider conflicts in Africa, while the AU has limited capacity, this incapacity is further compounded by the lack of coordination among African states in collectively addressing issues that threaten the peace and stability of the continent. This chapter contends that the biggest challenge affecting the effective operation of the AU is getting political buy-in from member states, and this is not isolated as the OAU also experienced a similar challenge. Achankeng (2013) notes that many conflicts in Africa belong to the following six types: inter-ethnic conflicts, inter-state conflicts, liberation conflicts, civil rights conflicts, annexationist conflicts, and political transition conflicts. The author reveals that most, if not all, of these types of conflicts are driven by the need for power, the need to control resources, the ethnic divisions that exist, the role of external actors in African affairs, fragmented systems of governance, states not built on shared values, and the obsession with power on the part of African leaders.

This chapter also applies the concept of state fragility to make sense of the current state of conflict in Africa. The concept of state fragility is premised on the notion that without institutions anchored on good governance and the rule of law, a country is bound to witness cases of conflict and violence (Bertocchi & Guerzoni, 2011). The lack of such institutions means leaders can act with impunity, never be held accountable, and gives rise to the abuse of power by politicians; together, these issues impede development and give rise to instability. For Osaghae (2007), fragile states are countries that are extremely impoverished and have weak institutions. They have a very low capacity to fulfil the basic functions of a state, are poorly governed, and often experience political instability, including armed conflict. The African Development Bank reveals that regional Member Countries classified as fragile states include Burundi, Djibouti, Guinea, Guinea Bissau, Liberia, Sao Tome and Principe, Sierra Leone, Somalia, Sudan, South Sudan, Togo, and Zimbabwe. For Cilliers (2013) a fragile state is one in which armed conflict and violence threaten the lives of the continent's citizens and prevent them from making a decent living. It is a state where inequality and exclusion are rife, with the majority of the population remaining poor, despite its having rich natural resources in many cases. Africa is also a continent that has a record of poor governance, where the government at times is simply absent and fails to provide basic services such as schools, hospitals, and roads (Adeto, 2019; Cilliers, 2013). All these factors are often present at the same time, an explosive cocktail of problems that trap countries in constant fragility. The concept has been applied to explain conflict patterns in Somalia, Sudan, and the Central African Republic. Armed civil conflict is both a cause and consequence of state fragility.

From a colonial perspective, Pecoraro (2012) contends that the colonial state was a military and administrative entity, aimed nearly exclusively at extracting resources for the economic development of the metropolitan areas. Yet, postcolonial states inherited these structures, at the same time as the political culture was one in which the first leaders of African independence were becoming politically active. Those leaders would, after independence, keep intact the structures of coercion and administration inherited from the colonizers, while simultaneously suppressing, fervently, the pluralist institutions that had been imposed by European powers during the negotiations of independence (Tatah, 2014). In Africa, one cannot expect the AU to function optimally while member states are going through some form of socio-economic, political and governance challenges which are a result of leaders failing to put the people first and adhere to the rule of law. While external intervention might also be a contributing factor, nevertheless, the major reasons for state fragility in Africa are the obsession with power by leaders and the failure to encourage inclusive development. Instead, there has been growth in elitism, political patronage, and cronyism. This chapter concludes that fragile governance systems in Africa are a direct contributing factor to conflict and violence and without unity and consensus amongst Africa leaders, no amount of external support can help consolidate peace and stability in Africa.

4 Drivers of Conflict and Violence in Africa

Ethnic and Religious Elements

One cannot doubt that some divisions in Africa are a direct result of colonialism. Deng (1997) reveals that traditionally, African societies, and even states, functioned through an elaborate system based on the family, the lineage, the clan, the tribe, and ultimately a confederation of groups with ethnic, cultural, and linguistic characteristics in common. However, in the process of colonial state-formation, groups were divided or brought together with little or no regard to their common characteristics or distinctive attributes. Irobi (2005) argues that the countries of sub-Saharan Africa, including Sierra Leone, Ivory Coast, Liberia, and the Democratic Republic of Congo, are a volatile mix of insecurity, instability, corrupt political institutions, and poverty. This is partly due to ineffective conflict management. In postcolonial Africa, conflicts in these countries are mostly between ethnic groups, not between states. If not checked, ethnic conflicts are contagious and can spread quickly across borders like cancer cells. This chapter argues that the problem is that many African governments have failed to understand what drives ethnic conflicts and how these issues can be addressed; rather, whenever conflicts break out, they are often militarized.

Economic factors have been identified as one of the major causes of conflict in Africa. It has been argued that in multi-ethnic societies like Nigeria and South Africa, ethnic communities violently compete for property, rights, jobs, education, language, social amenities, and good healthcare facilities (Irobi, 2005). Aside from the economic factors, psychological factors as a cause of conflict are often overlooked. It has been opined that extremists build upon these fears to polarize society. Ethnic conflict is a sign of a weak state. In this case, states act with bias, favouring a particular ethnic group or region, and behaviours such as preferential treatment fuel ethnic conflicts (Irobi, 2005). However, this chapter argues that the above classification fails to reflect the integration of religious differences that have given rise to ethnic conflict. Reinforcing this assertion, Lado and Lynch (2014) contend that until just two decades ago, political-religious movements were not even a concern for the postcolonial secular state in the African region. But things may be rapidly changing. Religion has become a key contributor to conflicts in Africa. In inter-religious conflicts, the conflicting parties differ in their religious affiliation—for example, Christians and Muslims. This can overlap with ethnic identities, and it is clear that heterogeneous societies are more vulnerable to triggering conflicts along these lines.

Conflict over Resources

The abundance of literature on resource conflicts in Africa tends to conclude that Africa is suffering from a resource curse. Scholars (Graham, 2021) show that even though the continent is blessed with numerous resources, these have not been used to spur development; rather, they have given rise to conflicts and this has reinforced the notion that natural resources in Africa have been a curse rather than a vehicle for socio-economic development. At times, leaders have also been affiliated with certain groups in the fight to control resources. Tutton (2010) declares that the resource curse is by no means limited to Africa, but the continent has produced some examples of the curse at its most destructive. Government forces and armed groups have vied for control of resources, with the proceeds from their sale funding more weapons, which prolongs the violence. Conflicts that have taken place in Sierra Leone, Liberia, DR Congo, and the Ivory Coast have been to some extent fuelled by the sale of blood diamonds. Conflict can also come about when minority groups in a resource-rich area feel excluded from political power and the wealth generated by a resource. Sometimes, separatist groups try to claim ownership of the land where that resource originates—as in Angola's oil-rich Cabinda region. In Nigeria, Ejims (2013) explains that ordinary people have not benefited from oil and gas exploitation. Billions of dollars in revenue have had little positive impact on the lives of most people in recent times. Rather, there have been several armed groups that have not only targeted oil infrastructure but siphoned off the oil for sale in the black market. Angola is the second-biggest oil producer in Africa; however, the United Nations revealed that around 36% of Angolans live below the poverty line, and one in every four people is unemployed. Ben-Ari (2014) argued that, as with other oil-producing countries in Africa, oil has not proved to be a benefit to Angolans. If anything, it has produced few jobs and increased inequality and allegations of corruption. In DR Congo, abundant minerals are considered a root cause of the conflict because the mines out of which they come are believed to be controlled by armed groups who exploit the minerals (diamonds, gold, copper, cobalt, tin, tantalum, and lithium), and use the revenue to fuel their activities, earning them the label "conflict minerals" (Schouten 2019). The local population in DR Congo, and those in North and South Kivu provinces have borne the brunt of a conflict characterized by murder, rape, and displacement (Global-Witness 2015). In the context of Sudan, Ayoub (2006) illustrates that Sudan's conflicts have many causes, but at the root of each conflict are questions over the control and distribution of resources, and even though oil has been at the centre of these, the unequal distribution of land has been at the centre of the violence. In South Sudan, the world's youngest state, oil has been fuelling conflict in the country, as oil revenues have been used to fund conflicts where the government has been accused of using oil money to buy arms. This pattern of violence linked to the exploitation of natural resources can also be found in the Mano River Union countries of Liberia, Sierra Leone, and Guinea where the brutal civil wars of the 1990s and early 2000s were inextricably linked to struggles over the control of timber, diamonds, and rubber deposits (Tralac 2017) (Table 1).

However, one cannot talk about resource conflicts in Africa and neglect the role of colonialism and how it informed the current formation of the modern

Table 1 Patterns of Conflict in Africa since 1975

Country	Duration	Resources
Angola	1975–2002	Oil, diamonds
Congo, Rep. of	1997	Oil
Congo, Dem. Rep. of	1996–1997, 1998–	Copper, coltan, diamonds, gold, cobalt
Liberia	1989–1996	Timber, diamonds, iron, palm oil, cocoa, coffee, marijuana, rubber, gold
Morocco	1975–	Phosphates, oil
Sierra Leone	1991–2000	Diamonds
Sudan (Darfur)	2003	Water, Oil
South Sudan	2013–	Oil
Nigeria	2000–	Oil
Libya	2011–	Oil
Mozambique	2017–	Natural Gas

Source Tralac (2017), Mlambo and Masuku (2021), and Bulos (2019)

African state. It has been established that the primary motive of colonialism in Africa was economic gain. To achieve economic gains, basic infrastructure needed to be put in place (Adeyemo, 2019). The colonial authorities in Africa were aware of the essential role of infrastructural development in achieving maximum political, social, and economic stronghold in Africa, one might have argued that when colonialism ended, the vast network of rail, sea, and road infrastructure could be used by postcolonial African leaders to ensure that the extraction of resources benefited local communities. While in partial agreement with this position, this chapter contends that colonizers did not leave behind the skills and knowledge on how to extract resources. Thus, in modern times resource extraction in Africa is undertaken by multinational corporations and without the skills and knowledge needed for resource extraction, transportation networks alone would not have been enough. Scholars have also argued that other drivers of conflict have been issues such as colonialism, elitism, fragmentation of governance, external intervention in African affairs, terrorism, and lack of public participation in governance.

Fragmented Politics and Governance

There is no general unity in African politics; rather political power has been consolidated along the lines of religion and ethnicity. Mbaku (2020) relates that too many African countries have not yet achieved the type of reforms that can prevent dictatorship, corruption, and economic decline. Furthermore, owing to continued sectarian violence, weak and ineffective leadership, and lack of political will, countries like the Central African Republic, Eritrea, Somalia, and South Sudan have been characterized by periodic outbreaks of conflict. The Agenda 2063 of the Africa Union cannot be achieved unless urgent care is taken to address these governmental and political issues. Mbaku (2020) stresses that countries must entrench mechanisms that promote constitutionalism, accountability, democracy, and good governance if Africa is to achieve its development goals. This will in turn allow for the consolidation of popular participation in governance processes, attract investors and foreign direct investments, and strengthen Africa's resolve to consolidate peace and stability as highlighted in Agenda 2063. The link between conflict and governance is a two-way street. Security challenges can impose tough choices on governments that may act in ways that compound the problem, opening the door to heightened risks of corruption and the slippery slope of working with criminal entities. On the other hand, weak or destructive governance is sometimes the source of conflicts in the first place (Crocker, 2019). The challenge—perhaps above all others—facing Africa's leaders is how to govern under conditions of ethnic diversity. This chapter reinforces the notion that without inclusive governance, there will be no peace in Africa; rather, conflict patterns will continue to increase and compound problems in development.

5 Conflict Resolution Mechanism of the Africa Union

There is no doubt that to ensure development and political stability, there needs to be an end to widespread conflict in Africa. Even though the AU represents the interest of member states, for the AU to function optimally, it needs unparalleled support. The African Union and its history can be traced back to the formation of the Organization of African Unity (OAU) on 25 May 1963 (Mathews, 1977). The core mandate of the OAU was to ensure that every member state in Africa must contribute towards the consolidation of peace and security, ensure inclusive development, and at the same time defend the norm of non-intervention. The principle of non-intervention in the affairs of African states was driven by the OAU's respect for the sovereignty, territorial integrity, and independence of the member states (Murithi, 2008). Hence, the OAU could not intervene in conflict situations in Angola, the Democratic Republic of the Congo (DRC), Liberia, Sierra Leone, and Somalia in the 1990s. However, the formation of the African Union in 2003 changed the way conflict and violence ought to be addressed.

The key AU organ for promoting peace and security on the continent is the Peace & Security Council (PSC) which is the standing decision-making organ of the AU for the prevention, management, and resolution of conflicts (Williams, 2009). The PSC is important in terms of ensuring efficient response to *conflict and crises that have engulfed the continent. The PSC is one of the most important pillars of the African Peace and Security Architecture (APSA), which is the framework for promoting peace, security, and stability in Africa. Since its inception in 2002, the biggest challenge for the AU has been the inability to reduce conflict and prevent new conflicts from emerging. Since the emergence of the AU, the biggest change has been the shift away from the OAU's so-called non-interference stance to the AU's more interventionist approach. This is most explicitly found in Article 4 of the AU Constitutive Act. The African Peace and Security Architecture was created when the AU supported the Protocol on the Establishment of the Peace and Security Council in July 2002. It is guided by the AU's mandate and its interventionist approach. There are five pillars that are key to conflict resolution as part of the AU strategy to manage conflict.

1.1. Peace and Security Council

The standing decision-making organ of the AU for the prevention, management, and resolution of conflicts is the Peace and Security Council. The council can take decisions on a range of issues such as implementing the AU's common defence policy, performing peace-making and peace-building functions, authorizing and overseeing peace support missions, recommending Article 4(h) interventions for situations of war crimes, genocide, and crimes against humanity, and imposing sanctions for unconstitutional changes of government (African Union 1993). However, at times, the council has lacked the urgency to respond to issues in a timely manner, and Cameroon's Anglophone Crisis has been a prime example of where the council failed to react despite the conflict going on for years. Mystris (2020) argues that there is a plethora of reasons that might account for this shortcoming. First, the council, despite requiring a majority vote, is subject to political constraints that hamper its decisions. Second, there are also financial and personnel constraints. For example, mustering enough troops to fulfil a mandate can be a challenge. And third, there's the question of financing, training and equipping them. Finally, the council is also subject to external influence, and this undermines the council mandate of resolving conflict (Mystris, 2020). A case in point was NATO's intervention in Libya, which was parallel to the AU's mediation efforts.

2.2. Panel of the Wise

The Panel of the Wise is a key advisory body to the Peace and Security Council. It has the role of mediation and preventative diplomacy. The panel consists of five elders who are chosen based the basis of their contributions to peace, security, and development. The elders work at the request of the Peace and Security Council, or on the panel's initiative (Mystris, 2020). There have been successful interventions that have been attributed to the panel. Examples of their work include interventions in Kenya's post-election violence in 2008 and their reports regarding the Arab spring.

3.3. Continental Early Warning System

The objective of the Continental Early Warning System is conflict prevention and anticipating events. However, anticipating when conflict will break out and preventing it are both are notoriously difficult. Mystris, (2020) argues that prevention and anticipation rely on accurate data will to act, yet the Peace and Security Council tends to react more to conflicts rather than pre-empt them. Reports from the system inform the council and then this informs the appropriate response. However, to be effective, the systems need to work in sync with non-governmental and international organizations, academic institutions, and research centre initiatives (Mystris, 2020). The African Union notes that while this system is still impeded by funding issues, building capacity is ongoing.

4.4. African Standby Force

The mandate of the African Standby Force is solely to implement decisions made by the Peace and Security Council. This may include authorized interventions, conflict and dispute prevention, observation, monitoring, and any type of peace support mission, humanitarian assistance and peace-building (Onditi et al., 2016). However, because the force is made up of contingents from all regions of Africa, there have been considerable challenges in getting the force off the ground. Efficiently creating such a force and ensuring its optimal functionality was not going to be an easy task, because the appetite for involvement in peace support operations differs from country to country based on the different socio-economic and political conditions (Mystris, 2020). A further factor is the diverse states of readiness and capabilities of military, police, and civilians across countries and regions. While the decision to establish the force was taken in 2003, it is only in 2016 that the force was officially considered to have obtained full operational capacity. Since then, it has yet to be deployed (Mystris, 2020).

5.5. The Peace Fund

One of the most pressing challenges for the AU is the lack of funds to ensure optimal functionality. The Peace Fund is tasked with the mammoth role of ensuring the availability of funds (Mystris, 2020). It is a known fact that many member states have a history of struggling to pay their membership dues, and self-financing of the AU has yet to prove possible. This means that the fund struggles to secure support from African states. The peace fund is financed from the AU budget, fundraising, and voluntary contributions from AU members, individuals, civil society, international partners, and the private sector. While $164 million had been raised by 2020, this was well below the target of $400 million (Mystris, 2020).

The above are the most important tools available to the African Union in the matter of conflict. However, one cannot deny that the AU lacks the required institutional capacity to single-handily manage conflict. This chapter argues that if African countries supported the AU holistically, the AU would be in a better position manage conflicts.

6 Challenges of Conflict Management in Africa

The need to eradicate conflict in Africa is underpinned by the notion that in many African countries, violent conflicts have slowed down economic and social development and have even pushed it backwards. This chapter argues that the following are the major challenges to conflict management in Africa.

1.1. Political Will

One of the most pressing challenges for the African Union is the lack of unity and political will among its member states. This chapter argues that many of the AU's strategies and policies concerning conflict management are well-written on paper but are not backed by the political will to ensure their effective implementation and functioning. Ferreira-Snyman (2009) blames this on the fear of supranational institutions having too much power and authority over states. For example, the EU as a supranational institution has considerable influence and power over member states, and certain laws and policies enacted by the EU are binding on all member states. In Africa, however, the scene is different. As put by Mbaku (2020) political leadership and commitment to fight conflict at the highest levels is one of the most important preconditions for a stable Africa. Mlambo and Mlambo (2018), however, assert that the obsession with territorial sovereignty has consolidated nationalistic sentiment, which makes the state place the state and its people more important than continental considerations. Furthermore, many leaders in Africa are at the mercy of their citizens, hence focusing more on continental issues may have the appearance of neglecting issues affecting citizens, and the fear of losing power pressures leaders to pay more attention to the affairs of their states rather than those of Africa. This chapter argues that there cannot be effective continental integration and eradication of conflict if the AU is not given the necessary support.

2.2. Unequal Socio-economic Development

In a country or region, the inequality of development is bound to give rise to conflicts as the competition for resources intensifies. Even though the African Union is key to peace and stability in the continent, in reality the AU has no power to decide or influence how sovereign nation-states promote inclusive development. Guariso (2015) comments that the majority of civil conflicts that have taken place in Africa since the end of World War II were fought along ethnic lines, driven by unequal development and the apparent neglect of certain ethnic groups. In support, Odusola et al. (2017) indicate that inequalities and poverty are important drivers of social exclusion, while conflict, social unrest and instability are their manifestations. The preponderance of conflicts in poor and unequal societies has long been documented in the literature. As Nagel succinctly argues, "political discontent and its consequences – protest, instability, violence, revolution – depend not only on the absolute level of economic well-being but also on the distribution of wealth" (Odusola et al., 2017). The AU can only encourage member states to promote inclusive economic policies that contribute towards economic growth and can attract investments. Beyond that, the economic development of member states solely depends on the willingness of member states to undertake actions.

3.3. Funding

For any continental body, the ability to function optimally is highly dependent on the availability of funds, and the African Union has been struggling with this issue for years. The AU has, since its inception, always struggled to ensure the consistent inflow of funds from member states. Good Governance Africa (2017) related that in July 2016, at its summit in Kigali, Rwanda, the African Union (AU) unveiled a new funding model. The new fiscal plan was expected to raise about $1.2 billion annually—or nearly triple the AU's current budget. However, while this statement was greatly welcomed, there was a lot of doubt concerning its eventual success. Many AU member countries do not pay their annual dues or pay them late. For years most of the AU's budgets and programmes have been financed by foreign donors, including the European Union, the United States, China, the World Bank, and the United

Kingdom, according to its financial statements (Good Governance Africa, 2017). While the AU's budget grew from $278.2 million in 2013 to $393.4 million in 2015, external financing also rose from 56% to 61.7% in the corresponding years. If African nations cannot fund the AU's budget, this says something that is not complimentary and without consistent funding, one cannot expect the AU to contribute meaningfully to conflict management and resolution.

To address conflict and other pressing issues which have been affecting Africa's development, Mbaku (2020) suggests first that states which have been or are recovering from conflict should engage in process-driven constitution-making to produce an agreed-upon governing process characterized by the separation of powers, with effective checks and balances, including a robust and politically active civil society, an independent judiciary, and a viable, free, and independent press. Second, there is a need for countries to foster continuous dialogue with citizens on the importance of good governance and the need to respect human rights. Third, governments, together with civil society organizations, should put education at the centre of Africa's re-building processes (Mbaku, 2020). Fourth, each African country should engage in regular dialogue, where necessary, to revisit such important governance issues as the centrality of human rights in the structure of the country's constitution, as well as a strong and independent judiciary. Finally, all of Africa's people should work hard to ensure Africa's development and growth (Mbaku, 2020).

7 Conflict Management Africa: Opportunities for the AU

The above discussion might reinforce the idea that the AU is doomed in the matter of conflict management in the continent. However, this chapter argues that there is room to manoeuvre, however, the room for manoeuvrability is highly dependent on how African states address the current challenges that exist. This chapter identifies three opportunities which the AU can consolidate with regard to conflict management.

1.1. Consolidating Relationship with External Parties

While external actors have often been accused of intervening in the affairs of African states, this chapter argues that it would be beneficial for the African Union to consolidate good working relations with them, underpinned by equality and fairness. Countries such as the United States and the countries of the EU are well advanced in terms of intelligence gathering and could be crucial in sharing information with the AU and could help prevent conflicts even before they emerge. This would allow the AU to optimally channel resources and better respond to conflict. However, there is a great need to ensure that this relationship is kept safe to ensure that these relations are reciprocal. It is also important to take into context the emergence of new powers such as India and Brazil and how they can all contribute to helping Africa consolidate peace and stability.

2.2. Strengthening Relations with Regional Economic Communities

One of the key mandates of the African Union is to coordinate and intensify countries' cooperation and efforts to achieve a better life for the peoples of Africa. Therefore, when it comes to conflict management, regional economic communities are in a better place to promote regional peace and stability, and the AU may act as a support structure. This has been greatly observed in West Africa where the Economic Community of West African States (ECOWAS) has played a key role in maintaining peace and stability. This chapter argues that the AU cannot go it alone in the matter of conflict management and resolution; however, cooperation with regional economic communities is key to contributing to stability, further consolidating the AU's mandate to ensure peace and stability. While African regional economic communities are to a great extent overwhelmed by operational issues of their own, nevertheless, strengthening collaboration within the AU is likely to contribute towards greater coordination with regards to conflict management.

3.3. Overlooking the Principle of Sovereignty in Favour of the Greater Good

The obsession with sovereignty on the part of African states has in the past impeded any possible AU intervention in conflict management. While the principle of non-intervention was the vanguard of the OAU, this has changed under the African Union. This chapter contends that if a conflict is likely to spread beyond national boundaries, the AU ought to intervene despite any possible objection from member states. This view needs to be driven by the notion that failure to quickly react out of fear for the sovereignty of members allows a conflict to spread beyond borders, thus wreaking havoc and holding back Africa's development; hence, intervention in this regard becomes the key to protecting continental stability.

8 Concluding Remarks

This chapter has given much thought to the challenges of Africa in the matter of the widespread conflicts that exist in the continent. In a continent with such a huge reserve of natural resources, it is greatly disheartening to see such widespread events of political instability and violence. The African Union as a continental body is limited in terms of resources to effectively rein in the challenges to Africa's development. The lack of political will in Africa is reflected by the barrage of issues that are facing the African Union, issues that are hindering the AU's effectiveness in managing conflicts. Nationalist sentiments and the fear of supranational institutions have been identified as major factors. While the AU is determined to ensure peace and stability, nevertheless, with the current challenges facing the organization, it remains doubtful whether it can forge the unity needed and consolidate collective action amongst member states to bring about this peace and stability unless the right efforts are made. The 2063 Agenda of the African Union envisages a peaceful Africa, free of any form of violence and conflicts; however, one cannot deny that the realization of this target needs all role-players to be in readiness, it needs African states to commit to peace and stability, and adherence to good governance, human rights, and constitutionalism.

References

Achankeng, F. (2013). Conflict and Conflict Resolution in Africa: Engaging the Colonial Factor. *African Journal on Conflict Resolution, 13*(2), 11–38.

Adeto, Y. A. (2019). State Fragility and Conflict Nexus: Contemporary Security Issues in the Horn of Africa. *African Journal on Conflict Resolution, 19*(1), 11–36.

Adeyemo, B. A. (2019). Colonial Transport System in Africa: Motives, Challenges and Impact. *African Journal of History and Archaeology, 4*(1), 1–13.

African Union. (1993). *Protocol relating to the establishment of the Peace and Security Council of the African Union.* Available via DIALOG https://www.peaceau.org/uploads/psc-protocol-en.pdf. Accessed 15 June 2022.

Ani, N. C. (2017). Re-empowering Indigenous Principles for Conflict Resolution in Africa: Implications for the African Union. *Journal of Pan African Studies, 10*(9), 15–36.

Ayoub, M. (2006). *Land and Conflict in Sudan.* Available via DIALOG https://rc-services-assets.s3.eu-west-1.amazonaws.com/s3fspublic/Accord18_4LandandconflictinSudan_2006_ENG.pdf. Accessed 15 September 2022.

Ben-Ari, N. (2014). *Inequality Clouds Growing Economy.* Available via DIALOG https://www.un.org/africarenewal/magazine/august-2014/inequality-clouds-growing-economy/. Accessed 12 March 2022.

Bertocchi, G., & Guerzoni, A. (2011). The Fragile Definition of State Fragility. *Rivista Italiana Degli Economisti, 16*(2), 339–356.

Böhm, R., Rusch, H., & Baron, J. (2018). The Psychology of Intergroup Conflict: A Review of Theories and Measures. *Journal of Economic Behavior & Organization., 178*, 947–962.

Bulos, N. (2019). *Libya Civil War and Natural Resources Attract Mix of Nations*. Available via DIALOG https://www.latimes.com/world-nation/story/2019-08-02/libya-civil-war-and-natural-resources-attract-mix-of-nations. Accessed 11 April 2022.

Burimaso, A. (2013). *Political Leadership Crisis in the Postcolonial African States: The Case of the Democratic Republic of Congo (DRC)* (Doctoral dissertation). University of the Witwatersrand, Johannesburg.

Cilliers, J. (2013). *Africa's Fragile States Need Extra Help*. Available via DIALOG https://issafrica.org/amp/iss-today/africas-fragile-states-need-extra-help. Accessed 12 May 2022.

Crocker, C. A. (2019). *African Governance: Challenges and Their Implications*. Governance in an Emerging New World. Available via DIALOG https://www.hoover.org/research/african-governance-challenges-and-their-implications. Accessed 15 March 2022.

Deng, F. M. (1997). Ethnicity: An African Predicament. *The Brookings Review, 15*(3), 28–31.

Ejims, O. (2013). The Impact of Nigerian International Petroleum Contracts on Environmental and Human Rights of Indigenous Communities. *African Journal of International and Comparative Law, 21*(3), 345–377.

Ferreira-Snyman, A. (2009). Regional Organizations and Their Members: The Question of Authority. *Comparative and International Law Journal of Southern Africa, 42*(2), 183–209.

GlobalWitness. (2015). *Conflict Minerals in Eastern Congo*. Available via DIALOG https://www.globalwitness.org/en/campaigns/conflict-minerals/conflict-minerals-eastern-congo/. Accessed 22 January 2022.

Good Governance Africa. (2017). *The AU's Funding Woes Continue*. Available via DIALOG https://gga.org/the-aus-funding-woes-continue/. Accessed 22 January 2022.

Graham, E. (2021, March 10). Reversing the resource curse in Africa: What can be done. https://gga.org/reversingthe-resource-curse-in-africa-what-can-be-done/

Granberg, D., & Sarup, G. (Eds.). (2012). *Social Judgment and Intergroup Relations: Essays in Honor of Muzafer Sherif*. Springer Science & Business Media.

Guariso, A. (2015, December 23). *Resource Inequality and Ethnic Conflict in Africa: New Evidence Using Rainfall Data*. Available via DIALOG https://blogs.worldbank.org/impactevaluations/resource-inequality-and-ethnic-conflict-africa-new-evidence-using-rainfall-data-guest-post-andrea. Accessed 28 January 2022.

Irobi, E. G. (2005). *Ethnic Conflict Management in Africa: A Comparative Case Study of Nigeria and South Africa*. Available via DIALOG https://www.beyondintractability.org/casestudy/irobi-ethnic. Accessed 22 July 2022.

Joshua, S., & Olanrewaju, F. (2017). The AU's Progress and Achievements in the Realm of Peace and Security. *India Quarterly, 73*(4), 454–471.

Lado, L., & Lynch, T. (2014). *Religious Violence in Sub-Saharan Africa and the Future of the Secular State*. Available via DIALOG https://www.wilsoncenter.org/event/religious-violence-sub-saharan-africa-and-the-future-the-secular-state-0. Accessed 22 July 2022.

Levine, J. M., & Hogg, M. A. (2010). *Encyclopedia of Group Processes and Intergroup Relations* (Vol. 1.). Sage.

Mathews, K. (1977). The Organization of African Unity. *India Quarterly, 33*(3), 308–324.

Mbaku, J. M. (2020). Good and Inclusive Governance Is Imperative for Africa's Future. *Foresight Africa: Top Priorities for the Continent, 2030*. Available via DIALOG https://www.brookings.edu/research/good-and-inclusive-governance-is-imperative-for-africas-future/. Accessed 29 June 2022.

Mkandawire, T. (2001). Thinking About Developmental States in Africa. *Cambridge Journal of Economics, 25*(3), 289–314.

Mlambo, V. H., & Masuku, M. M. (2021). Terror at the Front Gate: Insurgency in Mozambique and Its Implications for the SADC and South Africa. *Journal of Public Affairs, 22*(1), 1–8.

Mlambo, V. H., & Mlambo, D. N. (2018). Challenges Impeding Regional Integration in Southern Africa. *Journal of Economics and Behavioral Studies, 10*(2(J)), 250–261.

Muigua, K. (2020). *The Place of Human Rights in Environmental and Natural Resources Conflicts Management in Kenya*. Available via DIALOG http://kmco.co.ke/wp-content/uploads/2020/08/The-Place-of-Human-Rights-in-Environmental-and-Natural-Resources-Conflicts-Management-in-Kenya-Kariuki-Muigua-August-2020.pdf. Accessed 9 August 2022.

Murithi, T. (2008). The African Union's Evolving Role in Peace Operations: The African Union Mission in Burundi, the African Union Mission in Sudan and the African Union Mission in Somalia. *African Security Review, 17*(1), 70–82.

Mystris, D. (2020). *The AU's Peace and Security Architecture: Filling the Gaps*. Available via DIALOG https://theconversation.com/the-aus-peace-and-security-architecture-filling-the-gaps-144554. Accessed 9 August 2022.

Odusola, A., Bandara, A., Dhilwayo, R., & Diarra, B. (2017). Inequalities and Conflict in Africa: An Empirical Investigation. In A. Odusola, A. Cornia, H. Bhorat, & P. Conceicão (Eds.), *Income Inequality Trends in SUB-Saharan Africa: Divergence, Determinants and Consequences*. United Nations Development Programme.

Ogbu, S. U. (2017). African Union and Conflict Management in Africa: The Role of Communication in the Effectiveness of Future Intervention. *International Journal of African Society, Cultures and Traditions, 5*(1), 13–27.

Onditi, F., Okoth, P. G., & Matanga, F. K. (2016). The Quest for a Multidimensional African Standby Force. *African Conflict and Peacebuilding Review, 6*(1), 69–88.

Osaghae, E. E. (2007). Fragile States. *Development in Practice, 17*(4–5), 691–699.

Palik, J., Rustad, S., & Methi, S. (2020). Conflict Trends in Africa, 1989–2019. https://reliefweb.int/report/world/conflict-trends-africa-1989-2019. Accessed 12 June 2022

Pecoraro, A. (2012, July 31). *What Are the Political Causes of Failed States in Sub-Saharan Africa.* Available via DIALOG https://www.e-ir.info/2012/07/31/what-are-the-political-causes-of-failed-states-in-sub-saharan-africa/. Accessed 9 August 2022.

Raleigh, C., & Kishi, R. (2021, February 1). *Africa: The Only Continent Where Political Violence Increased in 2020.* Available via DIALOG https://mg.co.za/africa/2021-02-01-africa-the-only-continent-where-political-violence-increased-in-2020/. Accessed 10 August 2022.

Schouten, P. (2019, April 22). *Why Responsible Sourcing of DRC Minerals Has Major Weak Spots.* Available via DIALOG https://theconversation.com/why-responsible-sourcing-of-drc-minerals-has-major-weak-spots-115245. Accessed 10 August 2022.

Sherif, M. (2015). *Group Conflict and Co-operation: Their Social Psychology.* Psychology Press.

Tatah, M. (2014). *Africa: Facing Human Security Challenges in the 21st Century.* Langaa Research and Publishing Common Initiative Group.

Tralac. (2017). *Background Paper on Natural Resource Governance in Africa Conflict, Politics and Power.* Available via DIALOG https://www.tralac.org/images/docs/11546/tana-2017-background-paper-on-natural-resource-governance-in-africa-conflict-politics-and-power.pdf. Accessed 23 September 2022.

Tutton, M. (2010). *Can Africa Break Its "Resource Curse"?* Available via DIALOG http://edition.cnn.com/2010/WORLD/africa/08/23/africa.resource.curse/index.html. Accessed 23 August 2022.

Valentim, J. P. (2010). Sherif's Theoretical Concepts and Intergroup Relations Studies: Notes for a Positive Interdependence. *Psychologica, 52*(II), 585–598.

Williams, P. D. (2009). The Peace and Security Council of the African Union: Evaluating an Embryonic International Institution. *The Journal of Modern African Studies, 47*(4), 603–626.

Beyond Xenophobia or Afrophobia: Strategies and Solutions

Nomatter Sande and Martin Mujinga

1 Introduction

Xenophobic or afrophobic attacks in South Africa are not declining; new cases are erupting from different locations and times. It is possible, therefore, that there are cases that continue to happen but are not given significant attention. In this chapter, we acknowledge the debate about whether to call the violence in South Africa xenophobia or afrophobia: we prefer to use the term afrophobia as opposed to xenophobia (details for taking this position are discussed in the section "An Overview of the Meaning and Causes of Acrophobia" below). The 2008 afrophobic attacks left 60 people dead, followed by the 2015 attacks which attracted global attention (Akinola, 2014), and in 2019 emerged yet another episode of sporadic attacks that also left some people dead. It seems there is a new dynamic to the nature of afrophobia each time the incidents happen. Perhaps, it is a failure to understand the causes and nature of afrophobia. Currently, scholars have grappled with distinguishing whether we are dealing with xenophobia, afrophobia, or criminality.

The problem of afrophobia is that it ignites multiple matters which include but are not limited to human rights, politics, economics, migration, gender, race, and identity. Mashau (2019: 8) argues:

N. Sande (✉) · M. Mujinga
University of South Africa, Gauteng, South Africa
e-mail: pastornomsande@yahoo.com

the reality is that contestation, resentment, and xenophobic violent encounters against foreign nationals continue to cloud our social discourse around migration, inclusivity, and the politics of exclusion in the global arena. If left unattended, the politics of contestation, exclusion, and marginalization will continue to divide the fragile unity of humanity in the global context.

We resonate with this argument, given that afrophobia harms nationalities. Of late, South Africa has been considered a dangerous destination for immigrants and a hostile destination (Claassen, 2017). If afrophobia continues to happen in South Africa, it is worrisome to think about the future of Africa as the continent is supposed to be united, based on the history of Africans. The problem is imagining the future of South Africa and the rest of Africa whereby African immigrants are afraid to settle in a foreign nation like South Africa. This danger of afrophobia could spread to other nations that have South Africans in their countries. This resonates with the notion that "violence begets violence." Afrophobia brings a possibility of war in Africa based on ethnic and national lines. Perhaps, this is why South African President Cyril Ramaphosa had to apologize to Zimbabweans at the funeral of former President Robert Gabriel Mugabe for the barbaric attacks on Zimbabweans and other African nationals (Chigumadzi, 2019). Besides the personal, apology by President Ramaphosa, the South African Government sent envoys to other neighbouring countries to discuss the violence against foreigners of African origin (Chigumadzi, 2019).

As authors of this chapter, we acknowledge the growing literature that scholars have contributed to researching the phenomenon of afrophobia, for example (Castillo, 2016; Chigumadzi, 2019; Long, 2015; Muzengeza, 2015; Sibeko, 2019; Tafira, 2018; Tshaka, 2016). Diverse theories and concepts have been postulated to both give the meaning and causes of afrophobia. Though understanding the causes and meaning of xenophobia is important, there is a gap when it comes to reflecting strategies and solutions for the curbing of afrophobia in South Africa and other African countries. This study resonates with Mbecke (2015: 72) who argues that "most research on xenophobia focuses mainly on its causes and consequences than on management, prevention and control policies and strategies at national and continental scales". Uniquely, we are asking how the growing literature in the discourse of afrophobia can be used to prevent future happenings. Therefore, this chapter reflects and harmonizes recommendations from both inductive and deductive research to function as strategies and solutions to move from afrophobia, criminality, and xenophobia to xenophilia.

2 Theoretical Framework

This study covers diverse disciplines; migration, sociology, and political science, therefore, it is important to use a theoretical framework based on how we understand xenophobia or afrophobia. The framework undergirding this study is the social identity theory used to interpret the meaning of afrophobia. Tajfel and Turner (1979: 40) define social theory as "the aspects of an individual's self-image that derive from the social categories to which he perceives himself belonging." Social identity theory helps us to understand how South Africans view themselves as unique and non-South Africans as the "other." An analysis of this self-image leads to the afrophobic hangover from the psychological impact of apartheid where the binary of "us" and "them" is continued. It follows, therefore, that when South Africans view foreigners they relive apartheid, yet now they are the perpetrators of the same violence they have experienced.

Remarkably, apartheid made people accept institutionalized violence as normal and part of life. In the context of identity theory, xenophobic attacks serve to protect nationalism. The studies, conducted by various scholars such as (Long, 2015; Muzengeza, 2015; Tshaka, 2016) show that violence is more afrophobic than it is xenophobic or criminality. Accepting the violence as afrophobia rationalizes it as the hangover from apartheid and identifies South Africans as socialized to violence. Henceforth, South Africans use afrophobic attacks to vindicate the notion that foreigners, in particular from elsewhere in Africa, harm them. It is possible, therefore, that social identity theory can be used to promote love as a critical tool for xenophilia and Afrophobia. This agrees with the findings by Mbecke (2015) who argues that xenophobia in South Africa is an affirmation of the societal struggle for identity. There is a need for achieving local identities within the multifaceted society of South Africa.

3 Methodology

The strategies and solutions for moving beyond afrophobia to either afrophilia or xenophilia will be explored through the use of several data sources. We sourced both theoretical and empirical-based evidence, and government policies, in particular those which recommend a solution to afrophobia. This study is not a "traditional hypothetico-deductive approach" (Dana & Dana, 2005), which simply is a qualitative methodology interested in describing and making sense of the concept of afrophobia. In this study, we will first identify literature that addresses either theoretical or conceptual perspectives of afrophobia in South Africa. This is important to put this study into context, thereby ascertaining the construction of the meanings of xenophobia and afrophobia.

What is critical to this study is that we will analyse how scholars from different disciplines and perspectives have recommended solutions to ending afrophobia. In this way, this study is qualitative because it deals with the experience of people. According to Delport et al. (2005), the goal of qualitative research is to explain peoples' lived experiences. We seek to discuss and reflect on the emerging themes from the recommendations already proffered by scholars who have researched this topic. Our self-reflection will resonate with what Brandenburg, cited in Tidwell et al. (2009: xix), calls "assumption interrogation" because it allows the researcher to cross-examine data through a reflective process to come up with new information that may emerge. Therefore, in this study, we intend to move from description to proactive engagement with strategies and solutions.

The process of reflection is "active, persistent and careful consideration of any belief or supposed form of knowledge in the light of the grounds that support it and the further conclusions to which it tends" (Dewey, 1933: 9). This study infers that harmonizing the recommendation to stop afrophobia calls for a continuous reflection and a practice that increases knowledge and transforms perspectives about afrophobia. LaBoskey (2004) argues that the purpose of reflective study is to enhance knowledge about social justice. In a similar study about afrophobia from a critical paradigm, (Kgari-Masondo & Masondo, 2019: 90) argue that "to transform how people understand the roots of afrophobia and in understanding the roots of afrophobia to safeguard peace in South Africa and globally we need to engage to the bottom line of the subject." Hence, since this study reflects on peoples' experiences to stop afrophobia, it will take a critical paradigm.

The strategies and solutions for avoiding future afrophobic attacks were analysed using the thematic method of data analysis. Thematic data analysis seeks themes, which are the dominant features of the phenomenon under study, across all types of qualitative data analysis (Tashakkori & Teddlie, 2003: 252). The two scholars further state that most qualitative data analytic techniques involve regenerating themes that evolve from the study of specific pieces of information that the investigator has collected (2009: 252). This study discusses the following emerging themes: developing government policies; embracing the reality of migration; speaking with a universal language; reviving Ubuntu philosophy; and the role of religion.

4 An Overview of the Meaning and Causes of Afrophobia

An overview of the meaning and causes of xenophobia or afrophobia is important to provide the context of this study. To clarify, how one understands something and its root cause helps in developing solutions. There is a belief that xenophobia is a global phenomenon, and the problem happening in South Africa is not unique. For example, Myambo (2019) argues that in India being darker makes being a migrant much harder. Dark skin is often associated with poverty, partially due to the hierarchical caste system. Myambo (2019) adds that in India when a migrant enters their society, the local population tends to "read" the migrant's skin tone and then assign it positive or negative associations. Myambo concludes that South Africans and Indians associate African migrants with the negative stereotype of being from less "developed" countries. Castillo (2016) gives another example of xenophobia in China where a Chinese woman shoved a black man into a washing machine only for him to emerge as shiny and clean as an Asian man. According to Castillo, the action of this woman is a typical example of how afrophobia is rampant in China as they prefer white to black foreigners (Castillo, 2016).

Neocosmos (2010) argues that xenophobia is experienced by nations in transition to post-colonization. Etymologically, the term xenophobia comes from two Greek words *xenos* (strange or foreigner) and *phobos* (fear), put together the word created means the fearing of foreign people (Crush & Ramachandran, 2009: 4). An important question to ask may be, are xenophobia and afrophobia the same? This could be answered with both yes and no. In a loose sense, some scholars like Steenkamp (cited in Tella, 2016: 145) interpret xenophobia as the same as afrophobic or negrophobic. The reason for this decision is that South Africa's isolation during the apartheid administration is the root cause for afrophobia in South Africa; also, the South Africans do not see themselves as Africans and many other African countries are war-torn zones, making it difficult for them to accept other Africans. This point is also supported by Long (2015) who confirms from a medical point of view that, while many have termed the violent attacks as "xenophobia," a more accurate term may well be "afrophobia." The justifications of Long have been discussed earlier.

Although this may be true, our view leans towards afrocentric scholars who describe the violence in South Africa as afrophobia. According to Tshaka (2016), violence in South Africa is a result of the antagonism directed by the citizens towards other fellow Africans making it afrophobia. Violence characterizes xenophobic activities which should be considered criminal. Studies show that there are killings, mass looting, and destruction of foreign-owned homes, property, and businesses (Kumalo & Mujinga, 2017: 47). Therefore, afrophobia is "criminality" against foreign nationals. According to Lazaridis (2016: 13), "Immigrants and asylum seekers are often seen as a threat to public order and stability." Therefore, the issue of accepting the violence in South Africa as afrophobia is critical in providing a solution to the violence in South Africa.

There are several theories associated with the root causes of afrophobia. For example, Long (2015) emphasizes that many factors have been put forward, ranging from macrostructural, socio-economic, and micropolitical, to psychological causes. All these factors have effects on "foreign" entrepreneurship in township economies, resulting in the possibility that some of those involved in the killings have a history of antisocial behaviour. Social causes include the behaviour of illegal and undocumented immigrants. Foreign nationals are also accused of benefiting from free government services like houses, social grants, land, and jobs (Kumalo & Mujinga, 2017: 51).

Although scholars have come up with diverse factors, this study focuses on the aftermaths of apartheid and poverty, and economic challenges resulting in racism. Internalized racism is a concept that some scholars believe is the cause of afrophobia (Tafira, 2018). As put by Tafira (2017), xenophobia is "black-on-black racism": a new form of racism. Further, Tafira justifies that South Africans have been socialized into racialized subjects. There is likely a "new racism" in South Africa because South Africans do not attack whites and other non-African nationalities.

Poverty and economic disadvantages have emerged as key causes of xenophobia (Crush & Ramachandran, 2009: 16). According to Amusan and Mchunu (2017: 4) in an environment where some segments of the population enjoy a disproportionate amount of wealth, the inequality within such an "environment builds up resentment and, eventually, someone has to pay the price for such resentment." Poverty is associated with a deep-rooted problem that is causing xenophobic attacks in South Africa. There is a link between, poverty, economics, and politics (Charman & Piper, 2012). Some people believe that South Africans are angry that the African National Congress movement has failed to provide the benefits of dealing with apartheid and the economic boom that was promised (Crush et al., 2008). We suggest, therefore that, afrophobia is a result of the displaced aggression by South Africans towards immigrants selling drugs, illegal goods, and committing crimes. These activities anger the people in host communities resulting in violence. The government affirms that criminals who want to loot goods from foreign businesses use violence to target vulnerable foreign nationals.

5 Beyond Xenophobia and Afrophobia to Xenophilia or Afrophilia: Strategies and Solutions

To establish how to prevent the future happening of afrophobia, we argue that there is a need to reflect and harmonize recommendations from both inductive and deductive research. Correspondingly, by doing so, we proffer strategies and solutions to move from afrophobia, criminality, and xenophobia to xenophilia. We resonate with Kerr et al. (2019) who suggest that scholars should understand xenophobic violence that accounts for both structure and agency: how people act and how these acts reshape and recreate social context. This chapter goes on to discuss the following emerging themes: developing government policies; embracing the reality of migration; speaking with a universal language; reviving Ubuntu philosophy; and religion.

Developing Government Policies

Developing government policies emerged as a key recommendation to solve afrophobia, given the causes of afrophobia around this subject. Solomon and Kosaka, (cited in Mngomezulu & Dube, 2019: 76) argue that in 2001 President Thabo Mbeki warned that South Africans should guard against racism and xenophobia because it undermines their democracy. In 2008, President Thabo Mbeki said, "those who wanted to use the term xenophobia were trying to explain naked criminality in the grab of xenophobia" (Essa & Patel, 2015; Tagwirei, 2019). The same point was confirmed in 2015 by President Jacob Zuma, who said the word "xenophobia" should not be used excessively because it would give the impression that most South Africans were xenophobic, yet they are not. No one can say South Africans attack foreigners only. We have a history that these things happen. There is violence here that nobody has forgotten. Political violence in South Africa could not be said to be xenophobic (du Plessis, 2015). In 2019, President Cyril Ramaphosa both perpetrated and condemned xenophobia. He perpetrated the act during a 2019 general election campaign rally, when he said, "Everyone just arrives in our townships and rural areas and sets up businesses without licenses and permits. We are going to bring this to an end. And those who are operating illegally, wherever they come from, must now know" (Ramaphosa, 2019).

He also condemned xenophobia after he was booed in Zimbabwe where he had come to the funeral of the former president Robert Gabriel Mugabe, and he apologized to Zimbabweans and also sent his envoys to some countries in Africa to discuss violence against foreigners from African origin (Chigumadzi, 2019). Mngomezulu and Dube (2019: 68) further supported the notion that the South African government unreservedly condemned these attacks and made concerted efforts to assist the victims".

In addition, the South African government has also contributed to xenophobia because of poor service delivery and should prioritize service delivery and good living conditions both for its citizens and for those who find themselves in South Africa for whatever reason. This point does not intend to endorse illegal migrants or refugees but we are pushing the idea that, as President Ramaphosa said, "South Africa like many Africa countries is a home to millions of migrants" (eNCA, 2019, September 4, 2019), and so the home must be a safe place. According to Cinnini (2019), South Africans are angry because of hardship, hence, they feel that foreigners are stealing their jobs. The spirit of pan-African ideals should be central to all African nations to fight xenophobia. South Africa has highlighted that "the political destiny of South Africa is linked to the destiny of other African states" (Phakathi, 2019: 142), and this statement brings South Africa to the spirit of brotherhood and sisterhood with other African nations.

Although the position of the South African government is to condemn afrophobia, there are no clear policies and procedures. It is possible, therefore, that regardless of this plausible action by the South African government to own up for wrongdoing by South Africa, we suggest that there should be concerted efforts by African leaders to develop their nations to help in reducing migration. It is suggested that for government policies to curb afrophobia, the solution is in building healthy relations in the political landscape of Africa. Political relations amongst African leaders open room for afrophilia among nationals. We refer to afrophilia as an affection and love towards fellow Africans. This resonates in a way, with Myambo (2019) who argues that xenophilia is the opposite of xenophobia, afrophobia, and criminality because it has aspects of love, respect, and embracing.

Embracing the Reality of Migration

This chapter has noted that to avoid further attacks on Africans, there is a need to embrace the reality of migration as a solution to afrophobia. Migration is on the increase, therefore there is a need for security and the implementation of the human rights of the migrants. Moving from xenophobia to xenophilia calls for paying attention to security. Cinnini (2019) argues that migrants are protected by International Humanitarian Law which is embedded within the international law which protects refugees:

The New York Declaration for Refugees and Migrants, adopted by the UN General Assembly in 2016, reaffirmed international refugee protection standards and provided a model for a more comprehensive response to large-scale refugee movements, based on shared global responsibility for refugees. It represented a critical development at a time when international cooperation aimed at preventing, responding to, and resolving conflicts is proving inadequate, and an increasing number of people are being internally displaced, forced across borders, or left in protracted exile as a result of conflict, violence, and persecution (Bernard, 2017: 23–24).

In general, it seems, therefore, that focusing on the 2030 Agenda for Development that is Sustainable is key to solving afrophobia in South Africa. An implication of this is the possibility that transnational and transcontinental migrations are a future reality of nations with the potential to transform both sending nations and host nations. As put by Mashau (2019), faith communities can drive the notion that all humanity should share God's world and make people feel at home wherever they find themselves. In general, therefore, it seems that Africa has to learn how the European Union has managed to enable their member nationalities to move freely in Europe. It may be the case therefore that the African Union may need to adopt this route so that Africans can appreciate and love one another.

Speaking with a Universal Language

Speaking with a universal language emerged as a key solution to stopping afrophobia because the African continent is divided by language and culture, and yet in our history, economics, and general challenges we share a lot in common. The study in this chapter showed that language is responsible for creating negative perceptions of foreigners. Music is a critical tool within African societies and helps to transform societies. Phakathi (2019) argues that music has a role in traditional African education, therefore it can be used to spread anti-xenophobia messages that may transform South Africans. Language is a tool that is used to perpetuate afrophobia in South Africa. Kgari-Masondo and Masondo (2019) argue that South Africans use indigenous language to promote exclusion and discrimination by fuelling mistrust and hatred for foreigners. It is, therefore, likely that connections exist between language and afrophilia. These findings suggest that restoring and formulating of language which enhances hospitality and solidarity with foreigners is imperative.

Reviving Ubuntu Philosophy

Reviving the Ubuntu philosophy also emerged as a key recommendation for ending afrophobia. Ubuntu values and philosophy are other strategies that emerged for dealing with xenophobia. Ubuntu is central in the South African language of togetherness. The term was championed by Desmond Tutu in 1994 since the humanity of black South Africans had been pushed to the periphery by apartheid (Tutu, 1998). For Mbaya (2010), Ubuntu entails a person's identity and fulfilment within, rather than versus the community. Ubuntu entices the identity of an individual to the society. Ubuntu values and philosophy has the potential to curb xenophobic attacks in South Africa because it is a framework of hospitality that bring people together. According to Mlambo (2019), South Africa's policy uses Ubuntu as its underpinned value. He recommended the Local Community Forums (watchdogs in particular neighbourhoods, making sure there is protection and safety) as mediators to the tensions that may arise between South Africans and foreigners. There is a better way of solving the challenges societies face than xenophobia. South Africa belongs to both the Southern Africa Development Community and the African Union and the proliferation of immigrants from other countries to South Africa can be discussed in a professional manner, rather than allowing an angry mob to exercise instant justice on those whom they think are inferior to them.

Afrophobia disrupts societies as well as works against the pan-Africanist ideal of uniting nations. Mashau (2019) suggests that tapping into the African theology of Ubuntu promotes social cohesion and helps people to practise co-existing, co-operation, co-ownership, and co-sharing. Further, although the Ubuntu philosophy promotes values that should be applied to strangers, we acknowledge that there are limits because strangers should meet certain criteria for them to receive the benefits of these good values.

Religion as a Tool to Mitigate Afrophobia

The study in this chapter found that religion has a role to play in migration and can be used as a tool to stop afrophobia. Buhle Mpofu (2015) argues that, when people move, the church also moves. In his research, Mpofu interrogates whether the church is a host, home, or hostile to migrants, in the face of a global migration crisis that has fuelled mixed reactions (2015: iv). He further argues:

> when the people move, the church moves. The church is not a temple built in local communities, but it is a lived religious experience embodied by people who belong together through a family or community called church. As people move, they do not leave behind their religious experiences (*faith/beliefs*); instead, they move with them and articulate their migration experiences in the light of these personal religious convictions and draw on them for perilous journeys and as survival strategies in host communities.

For Mpofu, migrants must be integrated into the life of the church in South Africa. Analysing Mpofu's assertion, the church becomes a home far away from home in the context of hostile xenophobia and afrophobia. Pillay (2017) buttressed Mpofu's point by arguing that churches should be proactive in the struggle against xenophobia by conducting research on the phenomenon and justifying if it is a sign of the end times. Moreover, the church should hold the government accountable for administering migration policies. The church can play the social cohesion of migrants and local communities through the teaching of love. It can, therefore, be assumed that the role of religion is important in formulating strategies and solutions for xenophobia.

6 Conclusion

This chapter was designed to reflect and harmonize recommendations from both inductive and deductive research to function as strategies and solutions to move from afrophobia, criminality, and xenophobia to xenophilia. Although xenophobia is a global phenomenon, nonetheless the violence in South Africa takes many forms. The chapter showed that there is a debate between xenophobia and afrophobia, but what is happening in South Africa is skewed towards afrophobia. Thus, South Africans seem to display a hatred for non-Africans. This chapter showed that the causes of afrophobia are diverse but, in particular, it is caused by: the hangover from apartheid which socialized South Africans to be violent subjects; the failure of economic benefits post-apartheid regime resulting in social or popular anger; and criminal activities targeting at the vulnerable foreign nationals. The chapter highlighted that the problem of afrophobia is that it poses a threat to politics, migration,

African security, and economic matters. Therefore, this chapter has identified that there is a gap when it comes to harmonizing and reflecting on the recommendations from both inductive and deductive research to solve the issue of afrophobia. The results of the study in this chapter revealed that to stop afrophobia from happening in the future, people and institutions should be intentional about: developing government policies; embracing the reality of migration; speaking with a universal language; reviving Ubuntu philosophy; and religion. It is imperative to accept that focusing on these aspects creates room to move from afrophobia to xenophilia or afrophilia; a state where there is love for one another and cementing the ideology of pan-Africanism. Taken together, the results of this study contribute not only to understanding the meaning and causes of afrophobia but how to be proactive to either minimize or stop happenings of afrophobia in the future. For future research, there is a need to focus on how the African Union can formulate policies that penalize nations that practise or instigate afrophobia.

References

Akinola, A. O. (2014). South Africa and the Two Faces of Xenophobia: A Critical Reflection. *Africa Peace & Conflict Journal, 7*(1).

Amusan, L., & Mchunu, S. (2017). An Assessment of Xenophobic/Afrophobic Attacks in South Africa (2008–2015): Whither Batho Pele and Ubuntu Principles? *South African Review of Sociology, 48*(4), 1–18.

Bernard, V. (2017). Migration and Displacement: Humanity with Its Back to the Wall. *International Review of the Red Cross, 99*(904), 1–11.

Castillo, R. (2016, August 12). Claims of "China's Afrophobia" Show We Need New Ways to Think About Race and Racism. *The Conversation.* https://africanarguments.org/2016/08/12/claims-of-chinas-afrophobia-show-we-need-new-ways-to-think-about-race-and-racism/.

Charman, A., & Piper, L. (2012). Xenophobia, Criminality, and Violent Entrepreneurship: Violence Against Somali Shopkeepers in Delft South. *South African Review of Sociology, 43*(3), 81–105.

Chigumadzi, P. (2019, October 19). *Afrophobia Is Growing in South Africa. Why? Its Leaders Are Leading It.* https://africanarguments.org/2019/10/08/afrophobia-is-growing-in-south-africa-why-its-leaders-are-feeding-it/. Accessed 15 December 2019.

Cinnini, S. F. (2019). Xenophobia in South Africa: A Human Security Perspective on African Foreign Nationals in Durban. *Journal of African Foreign Affairs, 6*(2), 51–73.

Claassen, C. (2017). *Explaining South African Xenophobia.* Available at SSRN: https://ssrn.com/abstract=2974065 or https://doi.org/10.2139/ssrn.2974065.

Crush, J., & Ramachandran, S. (2009). Xenophobia, International Migration, and Human Development. *Human Development Research Paper* (United Nations Development Programme) 47.

Crush, J., Hassim, S., Kupe, T., & Worb, E. (Eds.). (2008). *Go Home or Die Here: Violence, Xenophobia and the Reinvention of Difference in South Africa*. Wits University Press.

Dana, L. P., & Dana, T. E. (2005). Expanding the Scope of Methodologies Used in Entrepreneurship Research. *International Journal of Entrepreneurship and Small Business, 2*(1), 79–88.

Delport, C., De Vos, A., Fouche, C., & Strydom, H. (2005). *Research at Grassroots. The Place of Theory and Literature Review in the Qualitative Approach to Research.* Van Schaik.

Dewey, J. (1933). *How We Think: A Restatement of the Relation of Reflective Thinking to the Educative Process*. Heath and Company Chaik Publishers.

du Plessis, C. (2015, April 22). South Africans Have a History of Violence—Zuma. *City Press*.

eNCA. (2019, September 4). *President Cyril Ramaphosa Speaks Out Against Xenophobic Attacks*. https://www.youtube.com/watch?v=ECz3_PGiImA. Accessed 13 April 2020.

Essa, A., & Patel, K. (2015, April 2). Foreigners in S Africa Fearful After Xenophobic Attacks. *Aljazeera*. https://www.aljazeera.com/news/2015/04/foreigners-africa-fearful-xenophobic-attacks-150402090513830.html. Accessed 9 April 2020.

Kenneth, T. (2011). Is Xenophobia Racism? *Anthropology Southern Africa, 34*(3–4), 114–121.

Kerr, P., Durrheim, K., & Dixon, J. (2019). Xenophobic Violence and Struggle Discourse in South Africa. *Journal of Asian and African Studies, 54*(7), 995–1011.

Kgari-Masondo, M. C., & Masondo, S. (2019). "For Peace Sake": African Language and Xenophobia in South Africa. *Journal of African Foreign Affairs., 6*(3), 87–103.

Kumalo, S. R., & Mujinga, M. (2017). God's Hospitality Is for All: An Afro-Theological Perspective on State and Migration in South Africa. In N. Blader & K. H. Kjellin (Eds.), *Mending the World? Possibilities and Obstacles for Religion, Church and Theology* (pp. 47–61). Pickwick Publication.

LaBoskey, V. K. (2004). The Methodology of Self-Study and Its Theoretical Underpinnings. In J. J. Loughran & M. C. Hamilton (Eds.), *International Handbook of Self-Study of Teaching and Teacher Education Practices* (pp. 817–869). Dordrecht.

Lazaridis, G. (2016). *Security, Insecurity, and Migration in Europe*. Routledge.

Long, W. (2015). Anger and Afrophobia in South Africa. *South African Medical Journal, 105*(7), 510.

Mbaya, H. (2010). Social Capital and the Imperatives of the Concept and Life of Ubuntu in South African Context. *Scriptura, 104*, 367–376.

Mashau, T. D. (2019). Foreigners Go Home! Re-Imagining Ubuntology and the Agency of Faith Communities in Addressing the Migration Crisis in the City of Tshwane. In *HTS Teologiese Studies/Theological Studies* (pp. 1–8).

Mbecke, P. (2015). Anti-Afrophobia Policy Shortfalls and Dilemma in the New Partnership for Africa's Development and South Africa. *The Journal for Transdisciplinary Research in Southern Africa, 11*(4), 71–82.

Mlambo, D. N. (2019). South African Perspective on Immigrants and Xenophobia in Post-1994 South Africa. *African Renaissance, 16*(4), 53–67.

Mngomezulu, B. R., & Dube, M. (2019). Lost in Translation: A Critical Analysis of Xenophobia in Africa. *Journal of African Union Studies, 8*(2), 67–81.

Mpofu, B. (2015). *When the People Move, the Church Moves: A Critical Exploration of the Interface Between Migration and Theology Through a Missiological Study of Selected Congregations within the Uniting Presbyterian Church of Southern Africa in Johannesburg* (Pietermaritzburg: Unpublished PhD. Thesis). University of Kwa Zulu Natal.

Muzengeza, W. (2015, April 22). Xenophobia or Afrophobia in South Africa: It Is Just Convenient Amnesia. *Pambazuka News*.

Myambo, M. T. (2019, December 5). *Being Darker Makes Being a Migrant Much Harder*. https://theconversation.com/being-darker-makes-being-a-migrant-much-harder-128340. Accessed 12 April 2020.

Neocosmos, M. (2010). *From "Foreign Natives" to "Native Foreigners": Explaining Xenophobia in Post-Apartheid South Africa*. CODESRIA.

Phakathi, M. (2019). The Role of Music in Combating Xenophobia in South Africa. *African Renaissance, 16*(3), 125–147.

Pillay, J. (2017). Racism and Xenophobia: The Role of the Church in South Africa. *Verbum et Ecclesia, 33*(3), 3–17.

Sibeko, S. (2019, September 5). *South Africa Acknowledges "Afrophobia" Partly to Blame for Violence Against Foreigners*. https://af.reuters.com/article/topNews/idAFKCN1VQ0Y9-OZATP. Accessed 14 December 2019.

Solomon, H., & Kosaka, H. (n.d.). Xenophobia in South Africa: Reflections, Narratives, and Recommendations. *Southern African Peace and Security Studies, 2*(2), 5–30.

Ramaphosa, C. (2019, March 27). *ANC 2019 Elections Rally Address*. Unpublished Speech.

Tafira, H. K. (2017). *Xenophobia in South Africa: A History*. Springer.

Tafira, K. (2018). *Xenophobia in South Africa: A Brief Summary*. Macmillan.

Tagwirei, C. (2019, September 14). *A New Word Is Needed for Xenophobia, But It's Not Criminality 14 September 2019*. https://www.businesslive.co.za/bd/opinion/2019-09-14-a-new-word-is-needed-for-xenophobia-but-its-not-cr. Accessed 15 April 2020.

Tajfel, H., & Turner, J. C. (1979). An Integrative Theory of Intergroup Conflict. In W. G. Austin & S. Worchel (Eds.), *The Social Psychology of Intergroup Relations Monterey* (pp. 33–47). Brooks/Cole.

Tashakkori, A., & Teddlie, C. (2003). *Handbook of Mixed Methods in Social & Behavioral Research*. Sage.

Tella, O. (2016). Understanding Xenophobia in South Africa: The Individual, the state, and the International System. *Insight on Africa, 8*(2), 142–158.

Tidwell, D., Heston, M. L., & Fitzgerald, L. (2009). Introduction. In D. Tidwell, M. L. Heston, & L. Fitzgerald (Eds.), *Research Methods for the Self-Study of Practice* (Vol. 9, pp. xiii–xxii). Springer Science & Business Media.

Tshaka, R. (2016, November 11). *Afrophobia Versus Xenophobia in South Africa*. https://www.unisa.ac.za/sites/corporate/default/News-&-Media/Articles/Afrophobia-versus-xenophobia-in-South-Africa. Accessed 11 April 2020.

Tutu, N. (1998). *The Works of Desmond Tutu*. Hodder & Stoughton.

Violent Piracy off the Coast of Nigeria: A Theoretical Analysis

Kalu Kingsley Anele

1 Introduction

The maritime industry is crucial to the development of Nigeria. Specifically, the oil industry (Varrella, 2021; Covid-19 and the Nigerian Oil and Gas Sector—Impact on the Nigerian Economy and Key Mitigation Measures) depends on the maritime industry for its advancement and sustainability, especially in transporting crude oil and refined products, and in providing supply services to the offshore oil rigs off the coast of the country (Anele, 2020a). Aside from importation of finished goods (Adongoi et al., 2019: 75; Ugwueze & Asua, 2021), maritime industry is key in the exportation of raw materials and fishing (Adongoi et al., 2017; Anele, 2021a, 2022a, 2022b; Ezeozue, 2019; Nwokedi et al., 2020). These activities lead to heavy vessel traffic off the coast of Nigeria, thereby providing an enabling environment for pirates to operate.[1]

---

[1] Nigerian waters have been declared risky for navigation due to the incessant piracy attacks off its coast. See ICC International Maritime Bureau. 2022. Piracy and Armed Robbery against Ships, Report for the Period 1 January–31 December 2021. 22.

K. K. Anele (✉)
Business Development, GAS Entec Co., Ltd., Busan, Republic of Korea
e-mail: kkanele@gasentec.com

© The Author(s), under exclusive license to Springer Nature Switzerland AG 2024
O. B. Mlambo and E. Chitando (eds.), *The Palgrave Handbook of Violence in Africa*,
https://doi.org/10.1007/978-3-031-40754-3_53

Piracy, which is a violent[2] attack on a ship by another ship on the high sea for private ends, including armed robbery against ships in territorial waters (Law of the Sea Convention (LOSC), art 101; Convention for the Suppression of Unlawful Acts (SUA Convention) against the Safety of Maritime Navigation art 3); Suppression of Piracy and Other Maritime Offences (SPOMO) Act, ss 3–4), is rife off the coast of Nigeria; with untold physical and psychological impacts on the affected seafarers (Aleksandrov et al., 2015; Seyle et al., 2018). This definition is necessary in order to use data to analyze violent piracy attacks in Nigeria, given the fact that such attacks occur both on the high sea and in territorial waters of the country. This because the nature of piracy in Nigeria is galvanized by the fact that pirates in Nigeria are made up of resource control agitators, the Niger Delta militants, hoodlums used by politicians to wreak havoc during elections in the Niger Delta region, and transnational organized criminals. Consequently, kidnapping, hostage-taking, maiming, and sometimes death are features of violent piratical attacks in Nigerian waters (Table 2). Moreover, pirates operating in the waters of Nigeria "are often well-armed, violent and have attacked and hijacked/robbed ships/kidnapped crews along or far from the coast, rivers, anchorages, ports, and surrounding waters" (see International Maritime Bureau (IMB) Piracy Report, 2022: 22).

Data from the IMB shows that Nigerian pirates are among the most violent pirates in the world (Table 2). Also, IMB data reveals that, aside from 2021 and 2022, the number of actual and attempted piracy incidents in Nigeria (118) was more than the number in other global piracy hotspots from 2018 to 2020 (Table 1). Pointedly, the violent nature of the Nigerian pirates is bolstered by the number of times they boarded, hijacked, and fired upon vessels traversing Nigerian waters (Table 2). In terms of violence to the crew, Nigerian pirates held 12 seafarers hostage, injured 2 crew members, and kidnapped 48 seamen in 2019, and in 2020, 6 seamen were held hostage, and 62 seafarers were kidnapped by pirates in Nigerian waters (See IMB Piracy Report 2019: 11 and IMB Piracy Report 2020: 12, respectively). In all, rocket propelled grenades (RPGs), guns, and other weapons are mostly used by the pirates to engage in violent attacks against vessels plying Nigerian waters (IMB Piracy Report for 2020: 13).

---

[2] Violence means the use of physical or non-physical force, aggressive behaviour and extreme form of aggression that leads to physical or psychological harm etc. See Hamby, S. 2017. On defining Violence, and Why it Matters. *Psychology of Violence*, 7(2): 168–170. http://dx.doi.org/10.1037/vio 0000117; O'Moore, M. Defining Violence: Towards a Pupil-Based Definition. Available from: http://schoolbullying.eu/doc/Violencedefinition.pdf Accessed 20 November 2021 and What is Violence. 8. Available from: https://us.sagepub.com/sites/default/files/upm-binaries/39356_978_1_84787_036_0.pdf Accessed 16 March 2021.

Table 1 Actual and attempted piracy attacks, 1 January 2019–31 December 2022

Location	2015	2016	2017	2018	2019	2020	2021	2022
Indonesia	108	49	43	36	25	26	5	10
Philippines	11	10	22	10	5	8	5	6
Vietnam	27	9	2	4	2	4		2
Nigeria	14	36	33	48	35	35	6	
Ghana	2	3	1	10	3	9	3	7
The Congo	5	6	1	6	3	3	1	

Created by the author from IMB Reports for 2019, 2020, 2021 and 2022

Table 2 Actual and attempted piracy incidents

Year	2019				2020				2021			
	Actual Attacks			Attempted Attacks	Actual Attacks			Attempted Attacks	Actual Attacks			Attempted Attacks
Location	Boarded	Hijacked	Attempted	Fired Upon	Boarded	Hijacked	Attempted	Fired Upon	Boarded	Hijacked	Attempted	Fired Upon
Nigeria	23	2	1	9	27	7	7	4	1	1

Created by the author from IMB Reports for 2019, 2020 and 2021

This chapter dialectically analyzes the nature and consequences of piracy in Nigeria. This is done by interrogating legal instruments, reviewing case law, analyzing data, and examining scholarly publications. Further, the chapter uses theories, mostly through proxies, to analyze the causes of piracy and conceptualize the linkage between piracy and violence in Nigeria. It argues that Nigerian piracy is coterminous with the multifarious violence in the Niger Delta region of the country. Hence, attacks on offshore oil installations, violent elections, transnational organized crimes, and resource control agitations in the Niger Delta area are some of the chief causes of violent piratical attacks off the Nigerian coast. The chapter concludes that to curb violent piracy off the coast of Nigeria, the government of Nigeria must cultivate the political will to eliminate piracy in its waters, engender good governance, effectively prosecute pirates and their enablers, adequately fund, train and equip maritime enforcement agencies, and regularly promote regional cooperation.

2 Statistical Analysis of the Nature of Piracy in Nigeria

It is common knowledge that piracy is rife in Nigerian waters (Table 1). Also, Table 1 reveals that from 2016 to 2020, the annual number of actual and attempted piracy attacks in Nigerian waters has been above 30. This is significant when compared to other regional piracy hotspots. Hence, similar to the piratical acts off the coasts of Indonesia and the Philippines, piracy in the waters of Nigeria has remained consistently high (Table 1). Specifically, Table 2 shows that from 2019 to 2021, pirates boarded vessels 54 times and fired upon vessels 17 times off the Nigerian coast, indicating the violent nature of piracy in Nigeria. The heightened number of piratical acts in Nigeria has been linked to the absence of effective maritime domain awareness due to ill-equipped and ill-trained maritime enforcement agencies (Anele, 2022a; Anele, 2020b; Anele, 2022c. See NIMASA: 'Nigerian Maritime Administration and Safety Agency'. Act, s. 22; AF: 'Armed Forces'. Act, s. 1(4) (iv)). More so, the worsening economic situation in Nigeria, particularly in the Niger Delta area, and the destruction of the Niger Delta environment due to oil exploration contribute to the rising number of piratical activities off the coast of Nigeria (Anele, 2020b).

From an economic standpoint, the nature of piracy in Nigeria becomes prominent. For instance, pirates essentially attack oil and gas tankers and vessels engaged in supply service to the offshore oil rigs in Nigeria (Jacobsen,

2019–2021). Nigerian economy rely on the importation of finished goods and the exportation of raw materials for its sustenance. Thus, heavy vessel traffic is common in Nigerian waters. However, due to piracy in the country's waters, Nigeria loses about US$2.74 billion due to an increase in the insurance charges and other charges on Nigerian shipments (Anele, 2021a: 15). Piracy and oil theft have led to the loss of about US$750 million by Nigeria, and it implicates the revenue derivable from oil exploration in the country (Anele, 2021a: 16). The fishing industry is also adversely affected: about 50,000 jobs and US$600 million in export earnings have been lost due to piracy in Nigerian waters (Anele, 2021a: 16). In terms of military spending, a breakdown of the budgetary expenditure for 2020 shows that the country spent about US$381.90 million (Bell, 2021: 16). Moreover, research has shown that piracy weakens the tourism industry (Anele, 2020b), compromises foreign investments, derails international trade, and undermines the implementation of trade agreements, economic partnership agreements, and other economic initiatives, like the Chinese ambitious Belt and Road Initiative in Nigeria (Anele, 2022a).

Kao (2016: 3) opined that unlike traditional piracy on the high seas, contemporary piracy, epitomized by Nigeria, is demonstrated through various forms depending on the region and "adapt[s] to modern technical, political, economic, and social developments." It ranges from "petty larcenies in territorial waters to sophisticated criminal syndicates whose goal is to capture the vessel itself." In the process, violence is used to achieve this goal. For example, while weapons like RPGs, guns, such as AK-47s, and knives are used in the attacks (Iwunze, 2019), pirates physically and psychologically threaten the crew before the seamen are kidnapped, tortured, and held hostage (Table 2). Again, firing guns at vessels to compel the ship to stop or at seafarers to subdue the crew is a violent act that shows the linkage between the nature of piracy in Nigeria and violence.

In concluding this section, it is imperative to state that the nature of piracy in Nigeria reveals a significant level of violence. The roadmap to the violent nature of piracy in Nigeria is drawn as piratical acts include, but are not limited to: kidnapping for ransom, armed robbery, attacking offshore oil rigs, stealing tankers or cargo, and siphoning oil from tankers (Anele, 2020b). Aside from the empirical evidence of violent piratical acts in Nigerian waters, Nigerian pirates use "military tactics and sophistication in their nefarious activities owing to their link to transnational organized crimes and political patronage" (Anele, 2020b: 619). Additionally, pirates "know how to skillfully maintain and fire their weapons, they ambush security forces, and they board vessels with tactical precision" (Anele, 2020b: 619 quoting Kevin Doherty).

3 Causes of Piracy in Nigeria

The nature of piracy in Nigeria reveals that the prevailing economic stagnation and privation is at the center of the causes of the crime in the country. Most times, responses to such economic deprivation by the Nigerian youths include violent acts, like piracy. Consequently, a dialectical analysis of the economic theory of piracy is crucial in defining and interrogating the causes and nature of piracy in Nigeria. It must be pointed out that the political class and the elite in Nigeria engage in rent-seeking and other forms of corruption which have culminated in the dearth of employment opportunities, facilitated poverty and increased economic inequality that fuels insecurity in the country (Herbert & Husaini, 2018: 1), especially piracy. Also, bad governance, reflected by unproductive and repressive economic policies, exemplified by the policy to close the Nigerian border with Benin Republic, has triggered disaffection among the Nigerian youths towards the government of Nigeria (Oguntoye, 2020).

Some of these pervasive economic policies that directly affect the Niger Delta region include the issue of resource control, lopsided revenue sharing formula, the dearth of infrastructure, which retards entrepreneurial development, and the destruction of the environment due to oil exploration that have prevented the Niger Delta communities from engaging in their age-long professions: farming and fishing (Anele, 2022b; Jacobsen, 2019–2021; Odalonu, 2019). The youths of Niger Delta have continued to respond by threatening and destroying oil installations and subsequently hijacking vessels off the country's waters (Evans & Kelikume, 2019). Thus, poverty and unemployment as a result of bad economic policies by the government of Nigeria and the destruction of the environment, especially farmlands and rivers, due to oil exploration in the Niger Delta communities, culminate in violent piratical acts off the coast of Nigeria (Anele, 2021b).

Another significant theory that highlights the causes of piracy is the failed state theory. Various authors have used the failed state theory to analyze the susceptibility of Nigeria to insecurity, particularly piracy. For example, Rotberg and Campbell (2021) identify Nigeria as a failed state due to the country's inability to guarantee the safety and security of its citizens. Nwalozie (2020) opines that Nigeria is a failed state because rather than engendering good governance, introducing democratic tenets, and instituting "true federalism," the government of Nigeria has stirred the embers of ethnic jingoism. The failed state theory further implies that the Nigerian government has failed to engender economic development, create employment opportunities, secure the lives and properties of its citizens, and suppress corruption in government, the maritime industry, and the oil sector in the country (Ogbonnaya, 2020).

In linking the failed state theory to piracy, Hastings (2009: 213) uses quantitative analysis to suggest that failed state is linked to "less logistically sophisticated hijackings (kidnappings for ransom), while state weakness encourages more sophisticated attacks (those where the ship and cargo are seized and sold)." It is observed that piracy as a result of state failure or state weakness is common in Nigeria, exemplified by the inability of government to monitor its maritime domain (Anele, 2022b). A failed or weak state, like Nigeria, provides an enabling environment "for pirates to operate with low risk of apprehension. As a country becomes politically weaker, the likelihood of piracy increases" (Regan, 2020: 3). Daxecker and Prins (2013a: 942) argue that a weak state, including its economic interests, leads to the adoption of piracy by insurgencies, like the Niger Delta militants, in Nigeria. These assertions suggest that state failure or weakness is central to violent piracy in Nigeria because it creates a friendly environment for other causes of piracy to manifest and thrive in the country.

The geopolitical theory of piracy is predicated on the implication of criminal activities that bolster insecurity in territorial and regional waters, epitomized by maritime terrorism, transnational organized crime, and internal violence in a country. The Gulf of Guinea (GOG) is geostrategically located in terms of the energy supply by some GOG countries, like Nigeria and Angola. It provides access to the sea for six landlocked West African countries and links Africa to Asia and Europe (Ogbonnaya, 2020). The combined effect of heavy vessel traffic due to the geostrategic importance of the GOG and a dearth of maritime domain awareness by Nigeria and other GOG countries has led to the emergence of incessant violent piracy in the GOG waters, especially off the coast of Nigeria. Also, the geopolitics of piracy entails close proximity to waterways, major transportation lanes, and important ports, on the one hand, and the existence of remote coastal villages that are used as hideouts that facilitate kidnap and ransom piracy, on the other hand (Jacobsen, 2019–2021).

Moreover, in addition to questionable government policies, such as the rejection of trained private armed guards (PAGs) on board vessels in Nigerian waters, and the rapacious maritime security architecture (Iheduru, 2023: 140–147) lax coastal and port security and a widespread dearth of maritime governance illustrated by ill-trained, ill-equipped and underfunded maritime enforcement agencies, encourage piracy in Nigeria (Gesami, 2021). The existence of transnational organized criminal syndicates that engage and support the stealing of crude oil and the hijacking of oil tankers to sell their cargo in the black market supports the geopolitical theory of piracy in Nigeria (Gesami, 2021). Similarly, the use of the GOG as a transportation route for weapons and drugs with minimal opposition from West African law enforcement agencies contributes to piracy and the sustenance of the crime off the coast of Nigeria (Gesami, 2021).

Another theory that attempts to adumbrate the causes and prevalence of piracy in Nigeria is the frustration-aggression theory, which postulates that an obstacle to the attainment of a goal culminates in frustration which could lead to aggression (Akahalu, 2014). Similarly, the existence of aggressive behavior implies the existence of frustration and vice versa (Kaloyirou, 2004). Crawford (2016) maintains that the fundamental premise of the frustration-aggression theory is that an individual becomes frustrated if their "goal-directed behaviour" is futile; thereby leading to aggressive behavior. Similar to Aminu (2013) and Inyang (2018), Nwokedi et al. (2020) deploy the frustration-aggression theory to opine that the youths in the Niger Delta region of Nigeria, due to frustration and anger, became pirates to benefit from the lucrative maritime business engagements in their communities through illegal and forceful methods.

Comparably, the theory of greed is significantly relevant to the discourse about piracy in Nigeria. It has been suggested that the economic nature of piracy (ransom) and "the availability or abundance of capturable natural resources rents" (Murshed & Tadjoeddin, 2007: 7) lead to greed that manifests in violent piratical acts. The theory of greed has been used to elucidate the causes of piracy in Nigeria. Lending credence to the theory of greed and its linkage to piracy in Nigeria, Balogun (2018) opines that petro-piracy and other oil-related criminal behavior in relation to oil exploration and production and petro-capitalism to gain access to oil wealth and rents through clientelist networks prompted and sustained piracy in the country. Therefore, the "consideration of conflicts using the greed framework of analysis provides a local basis to" understand and appreciate the motive towards mobilizing rebellious forces, such as the Niger Delta militants, in attacking oil tankers off the coast of Nigeria (Balogun, 2018: 34). The greed theory[3] has been applied in resource-rich countries, like Nigeria, where incessant conflicts and violent confrontations abound because of the quest to control the resource endowments by militant groups, such as the Movement for the Emancipation of the Niger Delta (MEND) (Balogun, 2018). Anele (2021b) is of the view

---

[3] This refers to the personal gains of the militants in the Niger Delta region that use piracy to achieve their economic agendas as opposed to the grievance theory that focuses on the public good. See Hoeffler, A. 2011. "Greed" Versus "Grievance": A Useful Conceptual Distinction in the Study of Civil War? *Studies in Ethnicity and Nationalism*, 11(2): 275.

that narrow economic considerations and greed influence groups to engage in rebellious acts, like violent piracy off the coast of Nigeria.

Identically, the theory of enterprise adumbrates the causes of piracy off the coast of Nigeria, as the convergence of the enterprise model and transnational organized crime, like piracy, is key. Thus, Smith addressed transnational organized crime under the prism of the enterprise model, which perceives entrepreneurial activities as the core basis for organized crime's existence (Balogun, 2021: 3 citing Dwight Smith). Entrepreneurial activities exist because the legitimate marketplace does not serve or satisfy many potential customers (Lyman & Potter, 2015). Also, crime, like piracy, as an enterprise, presupposes illegal entrepreneurs[4] that purportedly bolster macro-economic growth, create employment opportunities where none exist and attenuate poverty in underdeveloped areas, like the Niger Delta region (Edwards & Gill, 2002). Aziani et al., (2021: 3), opine that:

> Illegal enterprise theory springs from general economic theories of crime ... by concentrating on the points of overlap between licit and illicit activities. According to this theory, criminals are rational actors engaged in profit-oriented behavior. They are involved in activities that, albeit illegal, are driven by the same laws of supply and demand that determine the legal market ... This is because there is both a continuum of legal and illegal markets, and a demand for certain goods and services that exists beyond the boundaries of legality.

In buttressing the above point, it is significant to state that the importance of crude oil in the global energy mix makes the supply of crude oil in the black market off the Nigerian coast a lucrative enterprise (Anele, 2021b). As part of transnational organized crime, piracy is a criminal entrepreneurial act that is fundamentally coordinated and organized, which may not be hierarchy-based; however, whose stratagems are coordinated and organized (Balogun, 2018). In terms of the goals of the enterprise regime, it provides a rationale for analyzing illegal enterprises, like piracy. Such rationalization is connected to the notions that the marketplace may oscillate from legal to illegal due to the fluid nature of legal boundaries, including the existence of demand that sustains the marketplace and propels entrepreneurs towards ensuring that demand is met irrespective of being illegal (Balogu,

---

[4] Kleemans suggests that there is a thin line between legal and illegal enterprises. Kleemans, E.R. 2014. Theoretical Perspectives on Organized Crime. In *Oxford Handbook on Organized Crime*. ed. L. Paoli (ed). Oxford: Oxford University Press.

2018; Lyman & Potter, 2007). For instance, oil bunkering, which is a legitimate maritime activity, has become a mechanism to sell stolen crude oil in the black market due to the prevalence of violent piracy.

4 Linkages between Piracy and Violence in Nigeria

From the outset, the violent nature of piratical acts is not in doubt. This is because the use of PAGs by shipping companies to protect vessels suggests that piracy is violent (Ahmed, 2020). Also, Asal et al. (2020) suggest that piracy is violent in nature because pirates attack, loot, and commandeer ships, kidnapping their crews and stealing their cargo in the process. It is imperative to state that though "contemporary piracy occurs in different geographical and environmental locations, some pirates, *exemplified by Nigerian pirates*,[5] are far more violent and even employ far more sophisticated weapons in their operations than others employ" (Nwalozie, 2020. See Table 2). Hastings and Phillips (2015: 570) state that kidnapping for ransom due to piracy "should be seen not as *sui generis* but as an extension of the land-based kidnappings and violence to the sea." Above all, the definition of piracy, under the extant legal instruments, specifically describes it as violent in nature, thereby laying the foundation that piracy is inherently, intrinsically and ordinarily violent (LOSC, art 101; SPOMO Act, s 3). Below is an analysis of some of the theories that, sometimes through proxies, substantiate the thesis that piracy in Nigeria is violent.

It is indubitable that piracy in Nigeria is essentially connected to the oil industry in the country. This is because most Nigerian pirates target oil tankers due to the economic importance of the cargo, crude oil, to the development of the country and most of the pirates are from the Niger Delta region where oil is exploited. Thus, the concept of "petro-piracy" was created by Murphy (2013), and it is germane in theorizing and conceptualizing the linkage between piracy and violence in Nigeria. To buttress the linkage between piracy and violence in Nigeria, Ogbonnaya (2020: 13) notes that four pirate attacks occurred off the Nigerian coast in December 2019 and on 2 January 2020, and pirates killed four security personnel and kidnapped three seafarers on board a dredger off Forcados terminal in Nigeria. Some of the violent activities of Nigerian pirates include armed robbery, hostage-taking, kidnapping and the adoption of military tactics, strategies and

[5] Italicized words by this author.

sophistication in conducting their nefarious acts (Anele, 2020b). Specifically, Nigerian pirates "know how to skillfully maintain and fire their weapon, they ambush security forces, and they board vessels with tactical precision" (Anele, 2020b: 619 quoting Kevin Doherty). Additionally, it is noted that pirates in West Africa, especially Nigerian pirates, use violence as their modus operandi and as "a conscious business model, in which violence and intimidation play a significant role" (Stockfisch, 2017: 74).

Comparably, the theory of resource control links Nigerian piracy, which revolves around the agitation for resource control by the Niger Delta communities, to violence. For instance, a 2021 report from the United States (US) Energy Information Administration states that in the past, MEND, like other militant groups, attacked or threatened attacks on oil infrastructure for political objectives, as they claim to seek a redistribution of oil wealth and resource control (Background Reference: Nigeria 2021. See also Jacobsen, 2019–2021; Nyekwere & Duson, 2020). The implication of this is that the existence of the purported resource control agitation groups, which have morphed into militant groups, exemplified by MEND, links Nigerian piracy to violence (Nwachukwu et al., 2020). Jacobsen (2019–2021) outlines how the militant groups that purport to fight for resource control destroy oil installations and use violence to attack vessels for purely personal gains: kidnapping crew members for ransom. The involvement of the militant groups in the agitation of resource control by the Niger Delta communities bolsters the use of the theory of resource control as a nexus between Nigerian piracy and violence.

Further, the theory of geography is germane in connecting piracy to violence in Nigeria. It has been submitted that long shores and archipelagic configurations provide safe havens for pirates (Daxecker & Prins, 2013b). These geographical locations make it difficult and expensive for maritime enforcement agencies to effectively patrol the waters of riparian states. It is arguable that states located in close proximity to major chokepoints, for example the Strait of Malacca, or heavy vessel traffic, like the Gulf of Guinea, may experience more piracy as a result of their geographical location (Daxecker & Prins, 2013b). Thus, the Niger Delta region as the hub of piracy in the GOG instantiates the use of geographical theory to clarify the linkage between piracy and violence in Nigeria. This theory is crucial because the region is where the natural resources, oil and gas, are exploited. Moreover, the attack of oil tankers and subsequent kidnapping for ransom occur offshore in the Niger Delta region. Therefore, it could be argued that the onshore and offshore activities in the Niger Delta area align with the violent nature of piracy in Nigeria. Pointedly, Tobor (2016) states that the neglect of the region by the multinational oil corporations (MOC) and the Nigerian government led to the emergence of militants that use violence as a strategy of engagement and method to communicate their political objectives.

In congruence with the previous theories, the militant groups' analogy lends credence to the theory that there is a nexus between piracy and violence in Nigeria. It is imperative to reiterate that the linkage between piracy and violence through the vehicle of militant groups is mirrored by the involvement of the militant groups in some of the causes of piracy analyzed earlier in this chapter in the section "Causes of Piracy in Nigeria." For instance, the perennial issue of resource-control agitation is being sustained by various militant groups. It is arguable that the emergence of resource-control agitation is coterminous to the origin of militant groups in the Niger Delta (Tubor, 2016). It has been observed that militant groups that engage in violence against the government and private citizens extend their violent acts to the sea (Kikuta, 2021). Existing literature suggests that insurgents, as well as militant groups, use violence, especially piracy, to fund their activities (Daxecker & Prins, 2013a; Daxecker & Prins, 2019). Moreover, piracy thrives during armed conflict or insurgency as epitomized by the Nigerian pirates (Daxecker & Prins, 2017). In consonance with the above argument, the militant groups that engage in the destruction of oil installations and use violence to drive their point home regarding pollution of the Niger Delta environment due to oil exploration are the channel through which piracy and violence intertwine.

As the name suggests, violent election is another example of the alignment between piracy and violence in Nigeria. Hence, consistent with the theory of the militant groups, violent election supports the theory that piracy and violence are connected in Nigeria. The nexus between piracy and violence is bolstered by the fact that militant groups are used in perpetrating violence to rig elections in the Niger Delta region (Jacobsen 2019–2021; Chinwokwu & Michael, 2019; Hazen & Horner, 2007). Further, in linking politics to piracy in Nigeria, it has been argued that criminalizing politics and politicizing crime contribute to contemporary piracy in Nigeria (De Montclos, 2012). It is important to note that there is a comprehensive research work on the linkage between piracy and violent elections (Daxecker & Prins, 2016). The implication is that militant groups are used by politicians to wreak havoc against their perceived political enemies (rivals) so as to rig elections in the Niger Delta communities. Also, these militant groups are contracted to interrupt activities in the oil industry, including hijacking oil tankers in Nigerian waters (De Montclos, 2012; Nigeria's Dangerous, 2015 Elections: Limiting the Violence, 2014). The elections and piracy linkage in Nigeria is a "feudal system" that has long existed where some politicians are alleged to have covered up and protected pirates in exchange for a share of their loot, which is then used to fund election campaigns (Noack, 2014, citing Hans Tino; Jacobsen, 2019–2021). Suffice to say that the violence the militant groups exhibit during elections is applied as the militants engage in piratical activities.

There is a thin line between piracy and transnational organized crime in Nigeria (Anele, 2022c; Bueger & Edmunds, 2020; Jin & Techera, 2021; Schneider, 2020). The existence of transnational organized crime operating in West Africa has created an enabling environment for piracy to thrive. Owing to the nature of transnational organized criminal groups as organizations that deploy violence in their administration and profits from the sale of violent materials, such as guns, and violence-inducing merchandise, like cocaine; it can be theorized that piracy and violence are intrinsically linked (Adetula, 2015; Shaw et al., 2014; Alemika, 2013). The linkage between piracy and transnational organized crime presupposes the existence of violence as pirates can easily acquire weapons that will be used in hijacking vessels off the coast of Nigeria. Thus, the existence of transnational organized criminal groups that benefit from piracy enterprise lend credence to the consilience between piracy and violence in Nigeria.

5   The Way Forward

The theories of the causes of piracy are expected to succinctly to identify and outline some of and adumbrate some of the root causes of piracy that is violent and circumstances that make the crime intractable. Most of the causes of piracy are land-based, which means that it is imperative to eliminate these onshore causes of piracy. Nonetheless, most countries that have pirate-infested waters, such as Nigeria, lack the political will to suppress piracy because they benefit from the situation that induces people to become pirates. It is noted that piracy acts endure because the conditions driving the crime have not been eliminated as successful attacks against ships still lead to profitable outcomes, and the likelihood of capture and prosecution remain low in most places (Daxecker & Prins, 2015). This chapter suggests that the elimination of the onshore causes of piracy expatiated by some of the theories analyzed above is key to curbing piracy in Nigeria (Anele, 2021c).

To eliminate the onshore causes of piracy, the Nigerian government must, first of all, prioritize the cultivation of political will to suppress piratical acts in its waters. The existence of political will to curb piracy entails the introduction and promotion of policies and programs to eliminate piracy, typified by economic growth, the availability of equipment to maintain maritime domain awareness through regular policing of the waters of Nigeria by maritime enforcement agencies, and the implementation of antipiracy legal instruments. More so, the political will in this regard requires the prosecution of pirates and piracy enablers (the elite, officials of shipping companies, politicians, and government officials), and the promotion and support for regional cooperation as platforms to combat piracy in Nigeria.

Beyond the cultivation of the political will to curb piracy, the elimination of the onshore causes of piracy in Nigeria through good governance is another significant factor in suppressing Nigerian piracy. For instance, the existence of poverty and unemployment in the Niger Delta is one of the major factors that led to the Niger Delta youths becoming violent pirates. Poverty and unemployment are harbingers of insecurity in a country (Desai & Shambaugh, 2021); they arise because infrastructure development is absent in the region where oil is exploited in the country, thereby preventing the youths of the region from engaging in entrepreneurial activities. More importantly, the pollution and destruction of the environment of the oil-producing communities in the Niger Delta prevent the people in these communities from engaging in farming and fishing. Thus, the government of Nigeria must engender good governance by conducting free and fair elections, observing the rule of law principle in its activities, expediting infrastructure development, cleaning up the Niger Delta environment, effectively regulating the activities in the oil industry, especially in the areas of gas flaring and oil spillage, and conscientiously handling the resource control issue to eliminate the frustration and aggression existing among the youths in the region.

There is a need to transform Nigeria, in terms of its economy and security, to overcome its failed or weak state status. It is indubitable that the continued and the heightened level of insecurity in all the geopolitical zones in Nigeria is an indication of a failed state: Boko Haram in the Northeast, bandits in the Northwest, herdsmen in the Northcentral, secessionists in the Southeast and Southwest, and the militant groups in the Southsouth geopolitical zones of the country. A country that cannot protect and secure the lives and properties of its citizens and the resultant economic challenges is susceptible to violent piracy. Consequently, it is imperative for the government of Nigeria to tackle the issue of regional insecurity, specifically providing adequate funds for the training and procurement of modern surveillance and tracking facilities for the maritime enforcement agencies, like the NIMASA and the Nigerian Navy (NN). It is evident that insufficient modern surveillance and tracking facilities by the maritime enforcement agencies is a contributory factor to the recurrent nature of violent piracy off the waters of Nigeria.

Additionally, the government of Nigeria, aside from prosecuting pirates, must prosecute corrupt government officials, politicians, officials of maritime enforcement agencies, the elite, officials of shipping companies, and those that aid and abet pirates, whether for economic or political reason. The absence of prosecution of those culpable in the rising spate of violent piracy in Nigerian waters has encouraged the continued existence of the crime despite the attempts to repress it. To achieve this, the Nigerian government must, among other things, enhance its criminal justice system and strengthen the judiciary through regular training on the intricacies of piracy and procurement of modern adjudicatory equipment. The combined effect of introducing an efficient criminal justice system and bolstering the judiciary would culminate in the prosecution of pirates, those who support pirates and people that benefit from piracy, such as politicians and the elite. More so, those involved in transnational organized crime that supply arms and ammunition to pirates, and facilitate the selling of stolen cargo from hijacked oil tankers, should be prosecuted for money laundering, economic and financial crimes, terrorism and piracy (Money Laundering Act 2022; ICPC: 'Independent Corrupt Practices & Other Related Offences Commission' Act 2004; EFCC: 'Economic and Financial Crimes Commission' Act 2004; Terrorism Act 2013; SPOMO Act 2019; *Federal Republic of Nigeria v Binaebi*).

In concluding this part, the government of Nigeria must engage in regional cooperation in curbing piracy. This is because Nigerian piracy extends to other GOG countries and some of the causes of piracy are transnational in nature. Besides, legal instruments and soft laws encourage the use of regional cooperation as an antipiracy initiative (Anele 2022c). In terms of antipiracy legal instruments, Nigeria should effectively implement provisions of the SPOMO Act that domesticated the LOSC and the SUA Convention. This is important because proper implementation of the antipiracy legislation would immensely contribute to the elimination of piracy in the waters of Nigeria. Regional cooperation is also critical in implementing provisions of antipiracy legal instruments in terms of information sharing, regular joint naval training programs and funding. It is important to state that soft laws enacted by the International Maritime Organization, such as the guidelines for the use of PAGs, can also facilitate the suppression of piracy off the coast of Nigeria. Thus, it behooves the government of Nigeria to implement some of these soft laws to eliminate piracy in the country's waters. The implementation of these measures would strengthen the antipiracy policy of Nigeria.

6 Conclusion

This chapter, after interrogating the nature of piracy in Nigeria that potentially leads to consistent violence, attempted to use theories or their proxies to analyze the causes and the linkages between piracy and violence in Nigeria. It was discovered that the exploration of oil in the country has been characterized by violence. Thus, the emergence of militant groups forcefully demanding for resource control, among other things, culminates in violent piracy in Nigeria, which impedes the country's economic engagements, such as the implementation of trade agreements. In theorizing the causes of piracy in Nigeria, it was revealed that most of the theories also established that violence is coterminous with piracy. For example, the frustration-aggression theory strongly suggests a violent reaction to, inter alia, poverty and unemployment due to pollution arising from oil exploration in the Niger Delta region. Suffice to say that the theories of violent elections, militant groups and geography, among others, demonstrate the piracy/violence nexus in Nigeria. Owing to the consequences of piracy in Nigeria, exemplified by the kidnapping of seafarers and the loss of revenue by the government of Nigeria, the chapter recommended some measures to curb piracy in the country. The chapter noted that the cultivation of political will by the government of Nigeria and the entrenchment of good governance are among the key measures to eliminate violent piracy off the waters of the country.

Bibliography

Books

Alemika, E. E. O. (Ed.). (2013). *The Impact of Organised Crime on Governance in West Africa*. Friedrich-Ebert-Stiftung.

Hazen, J. M., & Horner J. (2007). Small Arms, Armed Violence, and Insecurity in Nigeria: The Niger Delta in Perspective. Small Arms Survey.

Lyman, M. D., & Potter, G. W. (2015). *Organized Crime*. 5th edn. Pearson Education.

Lyman M. D., & Potter G. W. (2007). *Organized Crime*. 4th edn, Prentice Hall.

Transnational Organized Crime in West Africa: A Threat Assessment. 2013. UNODC.

Chapters in books

Kleemans, E. R. (2014). Theoretical Perspectives on Organized Crime. In L. Paoli (Ed.), *Oxford Handbook on Organized Crime*. Oxford University Press.
Armed Forces Act, Cap No A20, Law of the Federation of Nigeria 2004.
Economic and Financial Crimes Commission (Establishment, etc.) Act, 2004
Independent Corrupt Practices and other Related Offences Commission Act No.5 Laws of the Federation of Nigeria 2004.
Money Laundering (Prevention and Prohibition) Act, 2022.
Nigeria Maritime Administrative and Safety Agency Act, 2007.
Suppression of Piracy and Other Maritime Offences Act 2019.
Terrorism (Prevention) (Amendment) Act, 2013.

Conventions/treaties

Convention for the Suppression of Unlawful Acts against the Safety of Maritime Navigation, adopted 10 March 1988, (entered into force 1 March 1992) 1678 UNTS 221.
United Nations Convention on the Law of the Sea, adopted 10 December 1982, (entered into force 16th November 1994) 1833 UNTS 3.

Reports

ICC International Maritime Bureau. (2020). Piracy and Armed Robbery against Ships, Report for the Period 1 January—31 December 2019.
ICC International Maritime Bureau. (2021). Piracy and Armed Robbery against Ships, Report for the Period 1 January—31 December 2020.
ICC International Maritime Bureau. (2022). Piracy and Armed Robbery against Ships, Report for the Period 1 January—31 December 2021.
ICC International Maritime Bureau. (2023). Piracy and Armed Robbery against Ships, Report for the Period 1 January—31 December 2022.

Cases

Federal Republic of Nigeria v Binaebi Johnson & Co, Suit No.FHC/PH/62c/2020 (Unreported).

Journal articles

Adongoi, T., et al. (2019). An Appraisal of Sea Robbery Control in Nigeria's Waterways: Lessons from Niger Delta Region. *International Journal of Criminology and Sociology, 8*, 75. https://doi.org/10.6000/1929-44.2019.08.09

Adongoi, T., et al. (2017). The Impact of Sea Robbery on Artisanal Fishing in Rural Settlements in Niger Delta Region of Nigeria. *International Journal of Innovation and Sustainability, 1*, 32–43.

Ahmed, M. (2020). Maritime Piracy Operations: Some Legal Issues. *Journal of Maritime Safety, Environment Affairs, and Shipping, 4*(3), 63–64. https://doi.org/10.1080/25725084.2020.1788200

Aleksandrov, I., et al. (2015). On Psychological and Psychiatric Impact of Piracy on Seafarers. *Journal of IMAB, 21*(4), 991–994. https://doi.org/10.5272/jimab.201514.991

Aminu, S. A. (2013). The Militancy in the Oil Rich Niger Delta: Failure of the Federal Government of Nigeria. *Interdisciplinary Journal of Contemporary Research in Business, 4*(11), 817.

Anele, K. K. (2020a). Addressing the Issues of Piracy off Indonesia and Nigeria. *The Indonesian Journal of International & Comparative Law, VII*, 247.

Anele, K. K. (2020b). Harvest of Arrests but no Prosecution: Ideation Toward Strengthening the Legal Regime for Prosecuting Pirates in Nigeria. *Commonwealth Law Bulletin, 46*(4), 618–619. https://doi.org/10.1080/03050718.2020.1774402

Anele, K. K. (2020c). The Potential Effects of Piracy on the Art-Craft Industry: A Comparative Analysis of Nigeria and Indonesia. *Indonesian Law Review, 10*(2), 229. https://doi.org/10.15742/ilrev.v10n2.652.

Anele, K. K. (2021a). The Potential Impact of Piracy on the ACFTA: A Nigerian Perspective. *Journal of Territorial and Maritime Studies, 8*(1), 16. https://doi.org/10.2307/JTMS.8.1.5

Anele, K. K. (2021b). Theoretical Analysis of the Causes of Piracy off the Nigerian Coast. *Academia Letters, 2567*, 3. https://doi.org/10.20935/AL2567.

Anele, K. K. (2021c). A Critical Analysis of the Implications of Covid-19 on Piracy off the Nigerian Coast. *Brazilian Journal of International Law, 18*(2), 123–126. https://doi.org/10.5102/rdi.v18i2.7332

Anele, K. K. (2022a). Comparative Analysis of the Impact of Piracy on International Trade in Korea, Indonesia and Nigeria. *Asia Pacific Law Review, 31*(2–3). https://doi.org/10.1080/10192557.2022.2117476.

Anele, K. K. (2022b). Theoretical Analysis of the Linkages between the IOCs' Oil Exploration Activities and Piracy in Nigeria. *Security Journal*. https://doi.org/10.1057/s41284-022-00361

Anele, K. K. (2022c). Reimagining Regional Cooperation as a Springboard for Curbing Piracy off the Coast of Nigeria. *Journal of Comparative Law in Africa, 9*(2), 34. https://doi.org/10.47348/JCLA/v9/i1a2.

Asal, V., et al. (2020). Maritime Insurgency. *Terrorism and Political Violence, 1.* https://doi.org/10.1080/09546553.2020.1761796

Aziani, A., et al. (2021). A Quantitative Application of Enterprise and Social Embeddedness Theories to the Transnational Trafficking of Cocaine in Europe. *Deviant Behavior, 42*(2), 3. https://doi.org/10.1080/01639625.2019.1666606

Balogun, W. A. (2021). Why has the 'Black' Market in the Gulf of Guinea Endured? *Australian Journal of Maritime & Ocean Affairs, 3.* https://doi.org/10.1080/18366503.2021.1876311

Bueger, C., & Edmunds, T. (2020). Blue Crime: Conceptualising Transnational Organised Crime at Sea. *Marine Policy, 119*, 5. https://doi.org/10.1016/j.marpol.2020.104067

Chinwokwu, E. C., & Michael, C. E. (2019). Militancy and Violence as a Catalyst to Kidnapping in Nigeria. *International Journal of Police Science & Management, 21*(1), 19–21. https://doi.org/10.1177/1461355719832619

Daxecker, U., et al. (2019). *Fueling Rebellion. International Area Studies, 122*(2), 129. https://doi.org/10.1177/22338659

Daxecker, U., & Prins, B. C. (2017). Financing Rebellion: Using Piracy to Explain and Predict Conflict Intensity in Africa and Southeast Asia. *Journal of Peace Research, 54*(2), 215–216. https://doi.org/10.1177/0022343316683436

Daxecker, U. E., & Prins, B. C. (2016). The Politicization of Crime: Electoral Competition and the Supply of maritime Piracy in Indonesia. *Public Choice, 169*(3), 375–393. https://doi.org/10.1007/s11127-016-0374-z

Daxecker, U. E., & Prins, B. C. (2015). Searching for Sanctuary: Government Power and the Location of maritime Piracy. *Conflict Management and Peace Science, 41*(4), 699. https://doi.org/10.1177/0738894215594756

Daxecker, U., & Prins, B. C. (2013a). Insurgents of the Sea: Institutional and Economic Opportunities for Maritime Piracy. *Journal of Conflict Resolution, 57*(6), 942.

Daxecker, U., & Prins, B. C. (2013b). The New Barbary Wars: Forecasting Maritime Piracy. *Foreign Policy Analysis, 5.* https://doi.org/101111/fpa.12014

De Montclos, M. P. (2012). Maritime Piracy in Nigeria: Old Wine in New Bottles? *Studies in Conflict & Terrorism, 35*, 535. https://doi.org/10.1080/1057610X.2012.684651

Desai, R. M., & Shambaugh, G. E. (2021). Measuring the Global Impact of Destructive and Illegal Fishing on Maritime Piracy: A Spatial Analysis. *PLoS ONE, 16*(2), 1–2. https://doi.org/10.1371/journal.pone.0246835

Edwards, A., & Gill, P. (2002). Crime as Enterprise? The Case of "Transnational Organised Crime." *Crime, Law & Social Change, 37*, 219.

Evans, O., & Kelikume, I. (2019). The Impact of Poverty, Unemployment, Inequality, Corruption and poor governance on Niger Delta Militancy, Boko Haram Terrorism and Fulani Herdsmen Attacks in Nigeria. *International Journal of Management, Economics and Social Sciences, 8*(2), 62–63. https://doi.org/10.32327/IJMESS/8.2.2019.5.

Ezeozue, C. (2019). Piratical Challenges in the Nigeria Ocean Space: Implications for National Security. *International Journal of Research and Innovation in Applied Science, IV*(X), 58.

Fuchs, I. (2020). Piracy in the 21st Century: A Proposed Model of International Governance. *Journal of Maritime Law & Commerce, 51*(1), 6–7.

Gesami, B. (2021). Maritime Security Threat in Africa. *Academia Letters, 3564,* 3. https://doi.org/10.20935?AL3564.

Hamby, S. (2017). On defining Violence, and Why it Matters. *Psychology of Violence, 7*(2), 168–170. https://doi.org/10.1037/vio0000117

Hastings, J. V., & Phillips, S. G. (2015). Maritime Piracy Business Networks and Institutions in Africa. *African Affairs, 114*(457), 570. https://doi.org/10.1093/afraf/adv040

Hastings, J. V. (2020). The Return of Sophisticated Maritime Piracy to Southeast Asia. *Pacific Affairs, 93*(1), 5–29. https://doi.org/10.5509/20209315

Hastings, J. V. (2009). Geographies of State Failure and Sophistication in Maritime Piracy Hijackings. *Political Geography, 28,* 213. https://doi.org/10.1016/j.polgeo.2009.05.006.

Hoeffler, A. (2011). 'Greed' Versus 'Grievance': A Useful Conceptual Distinction in the Study of Civil War? *Studies in Ethnicity and Nationalism, 11*(2), 275.

Iheduru, O. (2023). Hybrid Maritime Security Governance and Limited Statehood in the Gulf of Guinea: A Nigerian Case Study. *Journal of Military and Strategic Studies, 22*(3), 140–147.

Inyang, B. (2018). Militancy and Youth Restiveness in the Niger Delta Region of Nigeria. *LWATI: A Journal of Contemporary Research, 15*(4), 206.

Jin, J., & Techera, E. (2021). Strengthening Universal Jurisdiction for Maritime Piracy Trials to Enhance a Sustainable Anti-piracy Legal System for Community Interests. *Sustainability, 13*(13). https://doi.org/10.3390/su13137268

Kao, B. M. (2016). Against a Uniform Definition of Maritime Piracy. *Maritime Safety and Security Law Journal, 3,* 3.

Kikuta, K. (2021). A Typology of Substitution: Weather, Armed Conflict, and Maritime Piracy. *Political Science Research and Method, 1,*. https://doi.org/10.1017/psrm.2021.47

Murphy, M. N. (2013). Petro-piracy: Oil and Troubled Waters. *Orbis, 57*(3).

Nwachukwu, P. I. et al. (2020). The Impact of Piracy on Economic Prosperity in Niger Delta Region in Nigeria. *International Journal of Research and Innovation in Social Sciences, IV*(II), 326.

Nwalozie, C. J. (2020). Exploring Contemporary Sea Piracy in Nigeria, the Niger Delta and the Gulf of Guinea. *Journal of Transportation Security, 13,* 165–168. https://doi.org/10.1007/s12198-020-00218-y

Nwokedi, T., et al. (2020). Assessment of Sea Piracy and Armed Robbery in Nigeria Industrial Trawler Fishery Sub-sector of the Blue Economy. *Journal of ETA Maritime Science, 8*(2), 114–132. https://doi.org/10.5505/jems.2020.29053

Nyekwere, E. H., & Duson, N. A. (2020). Fiscal Federalism, Resource Control, and Restructuring in Nigeria: The Contending Issues. *Global Journal of Politics and Law Research, 8*(4), 14.

Odalonu, B. H. (2019). Paradox of Poverty in the Midst of Abundant Resources: The Politics of Oil Resources and Renewed Insurgency in the Niger Delta Region of Nigeria. *International Journal of Scientific and Cultural Innovations and Sustainable Learning, 10*(1), 94–96.

Regan, J. (2020). Varied Incident Rates of Global Maritime Piracy: Towards a Model for State Police Change. *International Criminal Justice Review, 3*. https://doi.org/10.1177/1057567720944448

Schneider, P. (2020). When Protest goes to Sea: Theorizing Maritime Violence by Applying Social Movement Theory to Terrorism and Piracy in the Cases of Nigeria and Somali. *Ocean Development & International Law, 1*. https://doi.org/10.1080/00908320.2020.1781383

Seyle, C. D., et al. (2018). The Long-term Impact of Maritime Piracy on Seafarers' Behavioral Health and Work Decisions. *Marine Policy, 87*, 23–28. https://doi.org/10.1016/j.marpol.2017.10.009

Tobor, J. O. (2016). Terrorism or Clamor for Resource Control: An Analysis of Nigeria's Niger Delta Militants. *Journal of Terrorism, 7*(3), 24.

Ugwueze, M. I., & Asua, S. A. (2021). Business at Risk: Understanding Threats to Informal Maritime Transportation System in the South-South, Nigeria. *Journal of Transportation Security, 14*. https://doi.org/10.1007/s12198-021-00233-7.

Zou, K., & Jin, J. (2021). The Question of Pirate Trials in States without a Crime of Piracy. *Chinese Journal of International Law, 19*, 594–595. https://doi.org/10.1093/chinesejil/jmaa040

Thesis/Conference paper/Research paper

Adetula, V. A. O. (2015). *Nigeria's Response to Transnational Organised Crime and Jihadist Activities in West Africa*. Friedrich Ebert Stiftung, Discussion Paper No X, 13–14.

Akahalu, U. A. (2014). *Interrogating Frustration-Aggression from Environmental Degradation in the Niger Delta Conflict* (Doctoral Thesis), Nottingham Trent University, 86.

Balogun, W. A. (2018). *Crude Oil Theft, Petro-piracy and Illegal Trade in Fuel: An Enterprise-Value Chain Perspective of Energy-Maritime Crime in the Gulf of Guinea* (Doctoral Thesis), Lancaster University, 33–36.

Bell, C. (2021). *Pirates of the Gulf of Guinea: A Cost Analysis for Coastal States*. Stable Seas Report, 16.

Crawford, Jr. W. S. (2016). *The Frustration-Aggression Hypothesis Revisited: A Device Congruence Perspective* (Doctoral Thesis), The University of Alabama, 7.

Herbert, S., & Husaini, S. (2018). *Conflict, Instability, and Resilience in Nigeria. Rapid Literature Review 1427*. GSDRC, University of Birmingham, 1.

Iwunze, F. C. (2019). *The Suppression and Prosecution of Maritime Piracy under International Law* (Master's Thesis), Near East University, 30.

Jacobsen, K. L. (2019–2021). *Pirates of the Niger Delta: Between Brown and Blue Waters*. Global Maritime Crime Programme of UNODC, 7.

Kaloyirou, C. A. (2004). *Bullies in Greek Cypriot State Primary Schools: A Problem or a Challenge?* (Doctoral Thesis), University of Warwick, 47.

Murshed, M., & Tadjoeddin, M. Z. (2007). *Reappraising the Greed and Grievance Explanation for Violent Internal Conflict*. MICROCON Research Working Paper 2, 5.

Ogbonnaya, M. (2020). From Nationalist Movements to Organised Crime Groups: The Trajectory of the Nigeria Delta Struggles. *Research Paper, Issue, 12*, 9–11.

Shaw, M., et al. (2014). *Comprehensive Assessment of Drug Trafficking and Organised Crime in West and Central Africa*. Report prepared for African Union, 10–12.

Stockfisch, H. (2017). *Lifting the Eyepatch: The Business Models of Piracy* (Ph.D Dissertation), Universitat der Bundeswehr, 74.

Online materials

Background Reference: Nigeria. (2021). U.S, Energy Information Administration, U.S. Department of State, 4. https://www.eia.gov/international/content/analysis/countries_long/Nigeria/NigeriaBackground.pdf Accessed: 17 March 2023.

Covid-19 and the Nigerian Oil and Gas Sector—Impact on the Nigerian Economy and Key Mitigation Measures. https://www.opml.co.uk/files/Projects/a0773-covid-19-nigerian-oil-sector.pdf?noredirect=1 Accessed: 16 March 2023.

Nigeria's Dangerous 2015 Elections: Limiting the Violence. 2014. International Crisis Group, African Report No. 220, 15–16. https://reliefweb.int/sites/reliefweb.int/files/resources/220-nigeria-s-dangerous-2015-elections-limiting-the-violence.pdf Accessed: 17 March 2023.

Noack, R. (2014). Why Nigeria's Election Year May See a Spike in Pirate Attacks. *The Washington Post*. https://www.washingtonpost.com/news/worldviews/wp/2014/10/14/why-nigerias-election-year-may-see-a-spike-in-pirate-attacks/ Accessed: 18 March 2023.

Oguntoye, P. (2020). Border Closure: Impact on the Nigerian. *Businessday*, Lagos. https://businessday.ng/opinion/article/border-closure-impact-on-the-nigerian-economy/ Accessed: 17 March 2023.

O'Moore, M. *Defining Violence: Towards a Pupil Based Definition*. http://schoolbullying.eu/doc/Violencedefinition.pdf Accessed: 16 March 2023.

Rotberg, R. I., & Campbell, J. (2021). Nigeria's is a Failed State: The First Step to Restoring Stability and Security is Recognizing that the Government has Lost Control. *FP*. https://foreignpolicy.com/2021/05/27/nigeria-is-a-failed-state/ Accessed 18 March 2023.

Varrella S. (2021). Contribution of Oil Sector to GDP in Nigeria from 4th Quarter of 2018 to the 2nd Quarter of 2021. *Statista*, New

York. https://www.statista.com/statistics/1165865/contribution-of-oil-sector-to-gdp-in-nigeria/ Accessed: 18 March 2023.

What is Violence, 8. https://us.sagepub.com/sites/default/files/upm-binaries/39356_978_1_84787_036_0.pdf Accessed: 18 March 2023.

Insurgency in Mozambique: Can SADC's NATO's Article 5 Treaty Address Future Insurgences in the Region

Victor H. Mlambo, Mandla Mfundo Masuku, and Daniel Nkosinathi Mlambo

1 Introduction

Ever since the September 11 attacks in the United States of America in 2001, countries have had to deal with increased threats internally and externally. Armed Non-State Actors rise and their ability to launch attacks beyond borders has created considerable challenges within the international security architecture (Reyes Parra, 2021). The growth, sophistication, and complexity of Armed Non-State Actors have forced nation-states to reconfigure how they work together to ensure their interests are preserved. Collective defence is when a group of countries come together and agree to work together to advance their interests and also work together to protect those interests. Collective defence is underpinned by the ideology that collectively, countries stand a better chance of advancing and protecting their interests rather than

V. H. Mlambo (✉)
School of Public Management, Governance and Public Policy, University of Johannesburg, Johannesburg, South Africa
e-mail: victorml@uj.ac.za

M. M. Masuku
School of Built Environment and Development Studies, University of KwaZulu-Natal, Durban, South Africa

D. N. Mlambo
Department of Public Management, Tshwane University of Technology, Pretoria, South Africa

unilateral action. The North Atlantic Treaty Organization (NATO) represents the concept of collective defence. Collective defence is at the very heart of NATO's founding treaty. It remains a unique and enduring principle that binds its members together, committing them to protect each other and setting a spirit of solidarity within the Alliance (Mazilu, 2002). Frohlich (2014) outlines that for over four decades during the Cold War, NATO was successful in its central task: avoiding conflict through a system of collective security. Therefore, this begs the question, can a binding collective defence framework be vital in addressing threats posed by Armed Non-State Actors? The insurgency in Mozambique has been crippling for the country socio-economically; it has starved the country of billions in foreign direct investments, increased population displacement, and contributed to the fragility concerning governance (Mlambo & Masuku, 2021).

Mutisi (2016) reflects that from past experiences, the Southern African Development Community (SADC) could be more convincing regarding regional interventions. This chapter contends that collective action is the key to resolving the conflict in Mozambique. While soldiers have been deployed, there is a need to strengthen governance institutions, assist in mediating political differences between the Liberation Front of Mozambique (Frelimo) and the Mozambican National Resistance (Renamo), and, through policy support, to address poverty and inequality. However, the deployment of troops in Mozambique and the subsequent debates on the need for a collective defence framework mirroring that of NATO has become a highly debatable probable policy approach. Article 5 of NATO's founding treaty states that an attack on any of the 30 allies will be considered an attack on them all, and this clause is crucial to the security architecture of NATO (Deni, 2017). The insurgency has devastated socio-economic life in Cabo Delgado. Bartlett (2022) reflects that since the conflict began in 2017, the conflict has left nearly 4,000 people dead and displaced 800,000, half the province's population. However, the Global Centre for the Responsibility to Protect (2023) notes that more than 6,500 people have been killed and nearly one million displaced since October 2017. Apart from civilian deaths and displacement, infrastructure has been another casualty of the conflicts. The conflict significantly reduced civilians' access to essential services across Cabo Delgado. According to the United Nations Development Programme's (UNDP) Infrastructure Damage Assessment of January to May 2022 in Cabo Delgado, the level of damage to public infrastructure is severe in districts that had been under the control of Non-State Armed Groups (NSAGs) (Feijó et al., 2022).

As a result of the conflict, the International Committee of the Red Cross (2021) notes that Mozambique's northern province has put an enormous strain on existing water and health facilities, some of which were previously damaged by extreme weather events. As a result, a concerning shortage of safe water, sanitation, and health services is a looming threat to public health for displaced people and host communities. The extent of the violence was evident in the large-scale displacement, destruction of infrastructure, civilian deaths, and the hastened retreat of multinational cooperation. Such events raised alarm bells in the region. There was fear of regional insecurity. The Mozambican government was criticized for initially downplaying the threat and delaying SADC intervention as the insurgency grew in scope (Cheatham et al., 2022). The fear of the violence spreading to other countries gave an immediate need for a regional response. There were security risks and challenges for SADC countries, as they feared reprisals from the insurgents if they intervened in Mozambique (Vhumbunu, 2021). Therefore, an intervention was needed to ensure stability in the region.

This chapter questions whether a binding collective security framework in the SADC would sufficiently address the insurgency in Mozambique and future regional threats. If such a clause existed in the SADC, how would the SADC respond to the insurgency in Mozambique, and how would collective defence be undertaken in the region? Therefore, this chapter seeks to examine the insurgency in Mozambique and whether a binding security agreement would address the insurgency and ensure regional peace and stability. The chapter also addresses the challenges of establishing a collective binding security framework in the SADC.

2 Methodology

This chapter used a qualitative research approach where a literature review was undertaken to answer the underlying research questions. This approach allowed data collection from a local, regional and international perspective. This approach was employed to further broaden the understanding of conflict and insurgency in Mozambique and how the region (through the SADC) can better react to this growing problem. Political instability and governance issues have driven the conflict in Cabo Delgado province (Mlambo & Masuku, 2021). What has also been worrying is the lack of an effective response to the conflict from Mozambique. Scholars have argued that while a collective defence framework would be essential, the SADC currently does not have a binding framework similar to that of NATO. This, coupled with porous borders, poverty, and rising inequality, contributes to the conflict and the fragmentation of governance in Mozambique. The chapter dwells on the debates, arguments, and theoretical literature informing this contemporary issue, especially the implication for the region should the insurgency spread beyond Mozambique. Considering the pre-colonial, colonial, and current narratives around the development, governance, and the need for collective defence in the SADC, these narratives will, therefore, become integral in allowing the chapter to reach a meaningful conclusion, hence the reasoning for the utilization of this methodological approach.

3 The Concepts of Collective Security and Collective Defence

To put the chapter into its proper context, it is necessary to reflect briefly on the notions of collective security and defence. The concept of collective security can be understood as an agreement between countries that pledge cooperative joint action in the eyes of threat to their economic or territorial sovereignty (Butfoy, 1993). These threats may be addressed using armed forces or economic sanctions. Collective security is a binding agreement between states (that may not be necessarily like-minded) not to resort to force when addressing current or future disputes, and to collaborate against states that break this rule (Jordaan, 2017). Collective security is currently regarded as the most promising approach to international peace. It is regarded as a valuable device of crisis management in international relations. It is designed to protect international peace and security against war and aggression in any part of the world. Collective security responded to the decline of the balance of power system (Jordaan, 2017). Schwarzenberger (1951) understood the balance of power as an equilibrium or a certain amount of stability in power relations that, under favourable conditions, is produced by an alliance of states. For Claude (1989), the balance of power is a system in which some nations regulate their power relations without any interference by any significant power.

Collective security is underpinned by a rule-based system in which collective and overwhelming action is taken against aggressor states. Collective security relies on "the major actors within the system accepting its legitimacy and responding together to punish those who did not" (Papp, 1997: 153, as cited in Jordaan, 2017: 164). However, applying collective security is not without challenges. First, countries must get along with the status quo, respecting present state boundaries and not using force when defending other states or territories (Bennett & Lepgold, 1993). Second, there must be a common understanding of aggression and how the world must respond. Finally, all member states, especially powerful countries, must commit their forces and resources to stop possible aggression (Jordaan, 2017). Therefore, collective security becomes viable when all those involved agree to its operational rules.

However, there are considerable challenges in applying the concept of collective security. For example, states do not regard themselves as members of one society having a common vital interest in protecting and preserving each other's rights (Lindley-French, 2003). Does it matter if Nigeria goes to war with Ghana? What is South Africa's interest if Russia and China go to war? Another challenge to collective security is that its risks are significant. Governments of nation-states can enforce the law against individuals (citizens) with little risk or fear. Internationally, however, the situation is quite different (Jordaan, 2017). Disparities of power are much more significant. Collective security, therefore, is about a global system that involves a significant number of actors. However, the insurgency in Mozambique questions the type of response (apart from the military intervention that has already taken place) that the region should undertake to ensure long-term peace and stability. Therefore, for developing regions, rather than relying on collective security to resolve conflict-related issues, collective defence offers a more effective form of cooperation on issues of commonality.

Collective defence agreements are essential as they protect one's interests and contribute to regional security. The North Atlantic Treaty Organization (NATO) is a classic example of such an agreement. In 1949, because of the need to ensure collective defence for European countries and to provide collective security against the Soviet Union, NATO was created by the United States, Canada, and several western European nations. At the heart of the organization was the need to safeguard the freedom and security of all its members by political and military means (Gazzini, 2003). The Union of Soviet Socialist Republics (USSR) was seen as a threat in terms of military strength and from an ideological perspective. Hence, the West needed to come together to protect their interests (driven by similar ideologies and world views). At the same time, the relevance of NATO today is being questioned, especially its role in international security architecture. The Alliance remains one of the prime examples of a binding collective security framework. Article 5 of the NATO treaty ("an attack on one is an attack on all"), was first applied in the aftermath of the 11 September 2001 attacks in the USA.

Subsequently, several operations were agreed upon, such as: enhanced intelligence-sharing on terrorism; assistance to allies and other states subject to increased terrorist threats as a result of their support for the campaign against terrorism; increased security for facilities on NATO territory; backfilling of selected NATO assets required to support operations against terrorism; blanket overflight clearances for military flights related to operations against terrorism; access to ports and airfields for such operations (NATO Review, 2005). To ensure the prevention of further attacks on the USA, Operation Eagle Assist was launched. The Airborne Warning and Control System (AWACS radar aircraft) that helped patrol the skies over the United States was deployed. Eight hundred and thirty (830) crew members from 13 NATO countries flew over 360 sorties. This was the first time that NATO military assets were deployed to support an Article 5 operation (NATO Review, 2005).

Even though the difference between collective security and defence has been examined, it becomes vital to understand the drivers and complexity of the insurgency in Mozambique, whether it warrants a collective regional intervention, and, if yes, how such will be undertaken.

4 The Insurgency in Mozambique's Cabo Delgado Province: Drivers and Possible Solutions

Scholars have been asking themselves one central question: What drives the Cabo Delgado conflict, and how has it further divided Mozambican society? No single cause explains the current insurgency; instead, there is a combination of issues. For Mlambo and Masuku (2021), the rise in conflict and insurgency in Mozambique is attributed to multidimensional causes: social and economic factors, the influence of radical preachers, and the endogenous process of advancing extremism in the province. The insurgency in Mozambique is being waged by a group that calls itself al-Shabaab—not to be confused with the Somali group of the same name—and is affiliated with the Islamic State's (ISIS) Central Africa Province. Despite al-Shabaab's recent flood of attention in Mozambique, the insurgency is not new. A local religious group called Ahlu Sunnah wal-Jamaa (ASWJ) turned towards militancy around 2015, eventually renaming itself (in whole or in part) al-Shabaab (Ross & Donahue, 2021). The militant group has fought insurgently against Mozambique's government since late 2017. While the militants have pushed for the desire to establish rule by a hard-line version of Islamic law in Cabo Delgado, Mlambo and Masuku (2021) argue that, in the past, the Mozambican authorities have neglected that northern Cabo province, this neglect, coupled with high levels of poverty and inequality made it easy for marginalized youths to be recruited into the arms of militant groups.

The Mozambican government had not previously paid attention to the people's pleas in the Cabo region until the discovery of natural gas. Mozambique has never fully recovered from the civil war, estimated to have killed one million people during a 15-year conflict. This chapter contends that there has never been peace in the Southern African country. Instead, political elites from the Mozambican National Resistance (Renamo) and Frente de Libertação de Moçambique (Frelimo) have cooperated to ensure progress towards peace and cohesion. However, this cooperation was never built on a solid foundation. Shared values and ideological perspectives have never guided it; compromises have had to be made to ensure progress and stability. Reinforcing this, the Africa Report (2021) contends that before the conflict broke out with the Islamist Ansar al-Sunna rebels in the gas-rich Cabo Delgado province in 2017, the Frelimo government had not yet ended its years-long fight with Renamo. Surprisingly, rather than being on the path to peace, both sides in the Cabo Delgado conflict alienate the population. However, Gardner (2021) communicates that this alienation is not a new phenomenon, nor is it isolated; instead, for decades residents complained that they have seen little of this wealth or investment passing down into their community, which prompted the beginnings of the insurgency in 2017, later becoming "internationalized" as they gained support from the Islamic State.

This chapter proffers three main reasons why the insurgency has consolidated its presence in the Cabo province. First, governance in Mozambique is fragmented; while there is unity on paper, decisions often do not reflect this need for cooperation regarding effective partnerships. Second, the Mozambican army has been described as ill-equipped to fight the insurgents, and while President Filipe Nyusi has historically been resistant to foreign boots on the ground, when it became observable that the army was finding it difficult to restore peace and stability without outside assistance, eventually he has accepted outside help. Further, the Mozambican army lacks the financial resources or a coordinated regional approach to effectively stem ASWJ's advances. Chikohomero (2020) notes that while regional troops and those from Rwanda have been deployed in Cabo Delgado, a long-term plan is needed from the SADC and the African Union (AU), especially concerning ensuring civilian protection against attacks and restoring security in Cabo Delgado. Third, it has been revealed that not all those in the ranks of the insurgents are locals; there have been reports of fighters from Tanzania and neighbouring countries in the ranks of the insurgents in Mozambique. This, therefore, reflects that borders cannot stem the inflow of foreign fighters sympathetic to the insurgents. These issues have morphed into a serious challenge to Mozambique's sovereignty and its ability to address the insurgency.

The fundamental question in this deliberation has been: Where is the SADC in all of this? It is undoubtedly clear that the regional body needs to play a role, but there have been questions about the type of role that needs to be played by the body. Regional economic communities (RECs) in Africa have always lacked one important element, namely, cooperation concerning collective defence. While RECs in Africa show noteworthy progress in some areas, they remain hampered by constraints such as overlapping memberships, weak policy coordination, harmonization and fragile political commitment (Uzodike, 2009). Therefore what ought to be the long-term solution in Mozambique? Can a collective defence approach deter potential insurgency or terrorist attacks, and how should SADC coordinate its regional intervention activities?

5 Insurgency, SADC, and the Question of Regional Intervention

Ever since the insurgency began, there have been growing calls for the SADC to intervene in Mozambique to protect civilians and ensure the conflict does not spill over to the rest of the region. However, from the onset, the Mozambican government has hesitated to allow such an intervention, arguing that the country's security forces have the situation under control. This hesitancy cannot be viewed in isolation; instead, there is a history of regional interventions in the SADC that have given rise to more questions than answers, thus consolidating scepticism. Khadiagala (2021) communicated that the SADC does not have a remarkable record of military interventions in civil conflicts in the region. Therefore, it would be misguided to attempt an intervention without an adequate understanding of the political dynamics at play in northern Mozambique. It took years for the Mozambican government to address the need to decentralize power and resources to the provinces. This had been a long-standing demand by the former rebel movement, Renamo. However, Frelimo (the ruling party) depended on a heavily centralized form of governance where provinces were mere outposts of the central government (Khadiagala, 2021).The conflict in the Cabo region is driven by socioeconomic and governance. Hence they require economic and governance solutions. Halakhe (2021) argues that sending more soldiers and weapons to northern Mozambique would only serve to exacerbate the problem. In many conflict-ridden African countries (Nigeria, Central African Republic, Sudan, South Sudan, and Mali), extensive military presence is yet to deliver a decisive victory against the continent's various insurgent groups. At the core of this failure for Halakhe (2021) is that governments across the continent have repeatedly failed to identify and address the underlying socio-economic drivers of insurgency within their territories. Instead, they swiftly labelled all insurgent activity as "terrorism," which needs to be addressed militarily.

This strategy may work in the short term but will likely fuel conflict in the longer term. The insurgency in the Cabo province cannot be observed within the confines of terrorism. However, there is a need to address the socio-economic conditions fuelling the conflict. Despite these observations, on the 23 June 2021, in a summit held in Maputo, the 16-member bloc of Southern African countries approved the deployment of a Standby Force in support of Mozambique to combat terrorism and acts of violent extremism in Cabo Delgado (Al Jazeera, 2021). At the same time, Mozambique was reluctant to allow in foreign troops. However, as the insurgency spread and casualties increased, coupled with the country's inability to address the insurgency, the government eventually allowed foreign troops to help the Mozambique army quell the insurgency and bring about stability in the region. Subsequently, a contingent of 2,000 troops from regional states was deployed, and Rwanda, which is not a SADC member, contributed 1,000 soldiers to Cabo Delgado (Crisis Group, 2023; Mugabi, 2021). Troops on the ground are meant to fight against Islamic State-connected insurgents under the Southern African Development Community Mission in Mozambique, or SAMIM, with support from Rwanda. Other countries that have contributed troops or support officers include Botswana, Lesotho, Angola, Namibia, Tanzania, and Zambia (Stark, 2022).

The deployment has had some achievements. For example, some roads have been reopened, and a semblance of calm has returned in critical locations for liquefied natural gas projects, such as Palma and Mocímboa da Praia (Vaudran, 2022). However, there was concern about the lack of coordination with the AU within the deployment context. The SADC informed the AU only six months after the deployment. This set aside its historical mistrust of the AU and its insistence on the principle of subsidiarity—which means, in this case, SADC leads on security issues (Vaudran, 2022). The EU provide EUR15 million in support of the SADC mission to Mozambique (SAMIM) (Guarascio, 2022). However, while this mission has received support, it has not been without controversy. Fabricius (2023), for example, says there were circulating videos showing soldiers in uniform burning bodies on a pile of what appears to be household items, and this drew widespread condemnation. Nonetheless, there is a need for a long-term plan for peace, inclusive development, and inclusive politics to promote long-term peace and development in the region.

Apart from the above, it becomes essential to note that the SADC region has a Regional Counter Terrorism Centre (RCTC) as "a dedicated structure to coordinate regional efforts" which came into being in at the end of February during a launch function in Dar-es-Salaam in 2022 (Ndebele, 2022). The region faces a threat concerning unpracticable attacks attributed to terrorism. Thus, it became vital for regional states to consolidate resources by sharing information and coordinating their responses to this growing threat (Mambo, 2022). The insurgency in Mozambique gave greater impulse for the region to realize that stability is key to deeper integration and sustainable development, adding that institutions such as the RCTC are critical in promoting peace and stability in Southern Africa (Mambo, 2022). At the core of the RCTC will be: advising SADC on counterterrorism and prevention of violent extremism policies, programmes, and deployments within the SADC region; coordinating the implementation of the SADC regional counterterrorism strategy; and leading the review process of the strategies (Mambo, 2022).

To effectively respond to potential threats, the SADC must adapt their tools and actions to ensure that they counter the terrorists' efforts and stop them in their tracks. The only way to address terrorist threats in the region is if member states work together to fight all forms and manifestations of this real threat (Mambo, 2022). This chapter argues that while the creation of this centre ought to be viewed in a positive light, it remains to be seen how effective it will be from a regional coordination standpoint, especially considering the increasing threats in the region. Regionally, while the Protocol on Politics, Defence and Security Cooperation envisages cooperation on matters of politics, defence, and security that shall at all times promote the peaceful settlement of disputes by negotiation, conciliation, mediation, or arbitration, however when it comes to enforcing such cooperation, there seems to be a lack of commitment and consensus. Article 3 of the Mutual Defence Pact 2003 communicates that as per the United Nations Charter, states shall settle any international dispute in which they may be involved, by peaceful means, so that regional and international peace, security, and justice are enhanced (Ngoma, 2004). Moreover, Article 6 says that an armed attack against a state party shall be considered a threat to regional peace and security. Such an attack shall be met with immediate collective action.

Article 6 of the mutual defence pact resembles that of Article 5 of NATO; however, the difference is the unbinding nature of the SADC defence pact. Apart from respecting the sovereignty of Mozambique, the SADC cannot intervene without adequate knowledge about the parties to the conflict, what drives the conflict, and uncertainties about the outcomes. (Ngoma, 2004). While the conflict has been driven by marginalization, neglect, and poverty, this has coincided with the discovery of one of the world's largest natural gas deposits, attracting French, Italian and American companies. The discovery has re-awoken the debate on the natural resource curse in Africa, where multinational corporations are accused of exploiting natural resources at the expense of local communities who do not benefit from their extraction, thus fuelling rebellion. To protect the infrastructure in the northern region, the government employed the services of Dyck Advisory Group, a private military contractor providing aerial support to Mozambican ground forces battling Islamic State-linked insurgents (Hill & Nhamirre, 2021). One would have thought that the Mozambican government would request support from the SADC rather than spend millions on private security. Hence, this signals a lack of trust in the SADC and paints a picture that Mozambican special forces are incapable of addressing the insurgency.

One cannot blame Mozambique for this hesitancy; there have been mixed reactions to past SADC interventions. The SADC interventions in internal conflicts in its neighbourhood have not worked out well. In 1998, on behalf of the SADC, Botswana, Zimbabwe, and South Africa restored order and constitutional legality in Lesotho (Khadiagala, 2021). However, the haphazard nature in which the mission was put together guaranteed it would not achieve its desired outcomes. As a result, South African troops lost their lives, and SADC troops had to withdraw in ignominy. Another intervention was that of the Force Intervention Brigade (deployed under the United Nations Security Council resolution) composed of Malawi, Tanzania, and South Africa. The goal was to defeat the M23 rebels in the DRC (Khadiagala, 2021). While the force made considerable gains, the militia menace in the region has continued unabated, raising questions about the long-term efficacy of the brigade's work even while the brigade remained in place. The contributing countries have lost enthusiasm for managing the multiple problems in the region (Khadiagala, 2021).

Despite the scepticism concerning SADC intervention, there is no doubt that the SADC needs to take a collective stand.

However, simultaneously, there is a need to consider Mozambique 's position. This chapter critiques Mozambique's regional approach to the conflict. Seemingly, the country's lack of trust in the SADC was observed when the country did not solicit assistance from the SADC in the early stages of the conflict. This chapter believes that while the SADC has intervened militarily in the country, more attention and emphasis should be directed towards addressing the communities' grievances in Cabo Delgado. As argued earlier, regional intervention may reduce violence in the short term, but it does not address the issues that have given rise to this conflict. When one looks at conflict patterns with a military element attached, they have never had peace and stability.

For many years, the discovery of oil in South Sudan encouraged the government in Khartoum to militarize a conflict that was, at heart, about self-determination and dignity for southerners. South Sudan did attain independence in 2011 but after the tremendous loss of lives. A low-level insurgency in Angola's Cabinda oil-rich region has persisted because of Luanda's indifference to the plight of the local population (Khadiagala, 2021). The same has been seen in Delta state, where the Nigerian government has since abandoned its military approach to resolving the oil-related conflicts. Rather, it has learnt to use political approaches in meeting the demands of the Niger Delta oil-producing communities (Khadiagala, 2021). Therefore, many insurgencies in Africa are not isolated but are directly linked to governance, service delivery, poverty, inequality, and marginalization issues. These issues cannot be resolved through force but require political dialogue (Masuku & Jili, 2019).

In the Cabo province region, locals have lost trust in the government. Therefore there is a need to build credible and transparent natural resource governance institutions that meet the yearnings of impoverished communities.). There must be a proper analysis of those problems and a definition of the problem. What we see in Mozambique is a resource conflict reminiscent of what we have seen in other parts of the continent. This includes Liberia, Sierra Leone, CAR (Central African Republic), the Democratic Republic of Congo, and Nigeria. For any decision or intervention, the SADC needs to know the underlying causes and provide the correct definition of the problem (Khadiagala, 2021). The continual exclusion of communities adjacent to those significant investments from any benefit from them is one of the biggest problems we face across the continent. This assertion reinforces the argument that a military intervention will not address the core issues driving the insurgency. Instead, the SADC must focus and make the Mozambican leadership understand that the solution to sustainable peace and security is to resolve the triple challenge of poverty, inequality, and unemployment. Any other solution will be temporary. However, even though arguments around a NATO-like approach to collective defence may be viable, states in the SADC are not developed compared to NATO member states, and the socio-economic challenges differ significantly. Therefore, while the need to ensure a collective defence approach may be vital for long-term development, reflecting on the challenges the region may encounter in establishing a binding collective security framework in the SADC becomes important.

6 The Challenges of Establishing a Binding Collective Security Framework in SADC

While calls for a regional collective security framework have been mirrored on a binding framework like that of NATO, one cannot compare NATO member states and those of SADC. The NATO states are first-world countries characterized by robust economies, stable democracies and governance systems, and have considerable influence within the global security architecture. NATO members are grounded in similar ideologies and values, which bind them together.

One cannot deny that globally, there has been an increase in threats of terrorism (Magen, 2018). In Africa, ungoverned spaces, the breakdown in the rule of law, and the inability of governments to maintain control over the territory has given rise to violent non-state actors. In Southern Africa, the Mozambique insurgency gave new impetus for regional leaders to address what has become a growing threat to regional stability. Considering the socio-economic dynamics in the region, one may argue that rather than going at it alone, a regional collective defence approach may be viable if centred on cooperation and coordination and supported by the establishment of the SADC Regional Counter Terrorism Centre. A regional collective defence approach will ensure that member states can support one another in times of crisis. Nevertheless, it becomes essential to note that because states are obsessed with sovereignty and the fear of supranationalism in Africa (Fagbayibo, 2013), one ponders how the SADC will make this realizable, considering that many states in the SADC tend to put national interests ahead of continental interests. Therefore, for the SADC to ensure collective defence becomes realizable, regional countries need to understand the threat posed by terrorism and insurgency holistically and comprehend that a collective defence approach will ensure that every member is protected in times of crisis. While this will not take away the role of the AU regarding continental security, with growing threats, RECs need to (to some extent at an individual level) be able to ensure their security outside of AU parameters.

The question, therefore, is: Can the SADC establish a binding collective security framework to address threats that threaten the peace and stability of the region? This chapter supports the notion of collective security in the SADC but argues that five challenges stand in the way of such an agreement.

(1) Sovereignty and the Fear of Supranationalism

A binding collective security agreement can only become viable if it can garner the cooperation of all member states, representing a key element in the regional integration agenda. While on paper, regional members agree to cooperate to deepen regional integration, often countries tend to put national interests ahead of regional considerations. This tends to undermine the whole idea of integration (Mlambo & Mlambo, 2018). For example, Mozambique initially told the international community what support it needed to deal with an Islamic State-linked insurgency. However, it would tackle some aspects of the problem unassisted, for reasons of sovereignty. However, this proved very difficult to operationalize. The lack of trust in the SADC was reflected when Mozambique did not immediately seek assistance from the SADC but employed private contractors to assist its army. So important is the element of sovereignty that President Nyusi emphasized that Mozambique alone would decide on the terms and conditions of any international aid it may need. Another challenge to a binding security framework is the fear of supranationalism, where regional states worry that a binding agreement would result in the SADC overriding their national laws (Saurombe, 2012). Regional economic communities in Africa fear supranational structures overriding national institutions.

(2) Resources and Financial Capacity

As of 2020, NATO members spent around €930 billion on defence (Brzozowski, 2021). In contrast, the International Labour Organization reflects that more than 60% of the population in the SADC lacks access to an adequate supply of safe water, a third of the SADC population lives in abject poverty, and about 40% of the labour force is unemployed or underemployed (The International Labour Organization, 2013). To ensure an effective security framework, there is a need for financial, logistical, and human capital resources. The availability of these is essential to ensure that the mobilization can be rapid in the event of an attack. In the SADC, socio-economic challenges must be addressed before the region can consider a binding regional security framework. The SADC is battling to reduce poverty, inequality, and to spur development. It becomes difficult to understand how member states will finance a collective binding security agreement while such challenges persist.

(3) Hegemonic Considerations

Some scholars argue that NATO does not represent the interests of all members but rather those of the United States. Haar (2020) contends that the US uses NATO to pursue its foreign policy agenda, and should the US leave the Alliance, the relevance of NATO will cease to exist. Likewise, there have been continued arguments in Africa that RECs only serve the needs of powerful states rather than those of the collective. In the SADC, Alden and Soko (2005) note that economically powerful countries will likely have a more significant say in the collective agreement as they will be contributing more regarding its operational budget. Therefore, even though regional states may support the notion of collective defence, the fear of a few states having considerable power over others may eventually lead to other states opting out of such an agreement. For example, South Africa, Namibia, and Botswana are economically stable countries. Hence, they may have a more political and economic say on how collective defence needs to be undertaken as compared to other states, hence the fear of hegemonic control.

(4) Governance, Political Will, and Geography

Many countries in the SADC are going through some form of governance, economic, and political challenges, hence, resources have been employed to ensure that such challenges can be addressed nationally. The idea of collective defence is to protect each other from attacks. However, for a collective defence framework to be practical, there is a need for stability and peace in the region; unless governance issues are addressed, collective defence becomes futile. Additionally, as argued earlier, political support in African RECs is compounded by various factors that have hindered their effective functioning. In Mozambique, the mere fact that the government did not seek assistance from the SADC can be interpreted as a lack of political will from Mozambican authorities. In support, Sany (2021) argues that there is a need for the government to restore trust by engaging with communities in a transparent manner. The government waited too long to address these divides and, perhaps more importantly, to tackle the area's systemic poverty and inequality. This demonstrates a great lack of political will.

(5) Borders

The region's long and porous borders pose a considerable threat to peace. Collective defence hinges on the notion that each nation can effectively police its territory to ensure minimal threats emanating from the border. The porosity of borders in the SADC will make it difficult to ensure adequate regional security. For example, it has been reported that fighters have been crossing over from other countries to join the insurgency, signalling a need to reinforce border control to ensure a well-functioning collective security framework. In the DRC, fighters came from neighbouring countries; the poor border management gave rise to weapons trafficking, further fuelling conflict (Anderlini & Conaway, 2004). Therefore, borders and their weaknesses in Mozambique must be addressed to ensure that a collective binding agreement can likely yield positive results.

7 Solving African Issues, the African Way: Pan-Africanism and the Spirit of Ubuntu

Ever since the periods of decolonization in Africa, there have been growing calls for the continent to adopt African ways of addressing African issues. There is a need for the continent to rid itself of over-reliance on external parties to solve African conflicts. Driving this has been the notion that over-reliance on external parties gives rise to external meddling in the affairs of Africa. Pan-Africanism and the spirit of Ubuntu have been seen as alternative approaches to ensure Africans take charge of their destiny. At the core of Pan-Africanism was the need to create a sense of brother/sisterhood and collaboration among all peoples of Africa (and the African diaspora). United, Africa can work together to resolve socio-economic and political development challenges (Mazrui, 1995). Kwame Nkrumah argues that Africans share common bonds and objectives and advocates unity to achieve these objectives. African states cannot sit back while other nations are suffering, as this neglects the sense of unity and brother/sisterhood, which is the core value of Pan-Africanism. This chapter notes that there have been many examples of where Pan-Africanism has been employed to try to resolve African disputes. They joined forces in West Africa, Cameroon, Chad, and Nigeria to fight Boko Haram. In Somalia, African Union Mission to Somalia (AMISOM) was central in reducing violence (International Crisis Group, 2021) in Lesotho, the SADC intervened in 2011 to restore stability and constitutional authority. In the Gambia, Economic Community of West African States (ECOWAS) threatened to invade the country if former president Yahya Jammeh refused to hand over power (Hartmann et al., 2017). These are a few examples from a political perspective of where Pan-Africanism was applied. Therefore, from a Pan-Africanist perspective, the SADC ought to support Mozambique as it cannot sit idly by while another African country is in need. However, it ought to consider Mozambique's concerns.

Ubuntu as a philosophy is another concept which Africans use to emphasize that we are one and we need each to ensure inclusive growth and development. The term Ubuntu refers to behaving well towards others or acting in ways that benefit the community (Lefa, 2015). The term, like Pan-Africanism, advocates togetherness as well as a fight for the greater good. It argues for collaboration, support, upholding values, and coming to the aid of those in need, where people work together, people help each other, and people do good without expecting anything (van Breda, 2019). The spirit of Ubuntu is essentially to be humane and to ensure that human dignity is always at the core of one's actions, thoughts, and deeds when interacting with others. Having Ubuntu is showing care and concern for one's neighbour. Therefore, Africa cannot be comfortable with what is going on in Mozambique and the SADC cannot sit back while one of its members is going through trying times. Ubuntu teaches that one cannot suffer while others are happy. This, therefore, implies that there is a need for Mozambique to be assisted and Africa and the SADC need to take the lead to ensure that peace and stability.

While this chapter agrees that Pan-Africanism and the spirit of Ubuntu are critical concepts in the quest to consolidate peace and development, it acknowledges they do not reflect on the role of external actors as parties fuelling this conflict. Consequently, it becomes difficult for African solutions to African problems while third parties are fuelling the conflict. Second, these concepts speak of an environment where cooperation is key. However, they fail to reflect on how African countries can ensure effective governance to ensure this brother/sisterhood becomes realizable. Third, they fail to reflect on how issues such as poverty, and unemployment can be addressed from a Pan-Africanist and Ubuntu perspective. Nevertheless, they remain essential concepts for African unity.

8 Concluding Remarks

There is no denying that the SADC is not immune to forces that threaten regional stability and social cohesion. This realization warrants the SADC member states to come together and forge a realistic framework that will ensure the region can collectively address threats in the region. From the discussion, it has become clear that a combination of factors are driving the insurgency in Mozambique, and there is no single solution to the problem. However, it has become observable that at the core of the insurgency are governance-related issues that have given rise to marginalization, poverty, and inequality. Even though at the beginning, the Mozambican government argued that the situation was under control, with increasing deaths, and population displacements, a regional intervention became necessary. Therefore, the SADC and Rwanda have since supported Mozambican forces in addressing the insurgency. However, many scholars are against deploying troops, fearing it will only exacerbate an already fragile situation. They argue that at the heart of the conflict are governance issues. Hence, Mozambique should address these issues rather than allowing for the deployment of troops. There have been calls for a binding regional security framework to ensure the region is better prepared to respond to threats quickly. However, while such calls have increased, considerable challenges need to be addressed before such a framework can even be established in the region. It is important to note that the deployment of troops may reduce the violence in the short run. However, troops will not be in the country forever, and unless the socio-economic issues driving this conflict are addressed, conflict will arise again soon.

References

Al Jazeera. (2021, June, 23). *Southern African Nations Agree to Deploy Forces to Mozambique*. https://www.aljazeera.com/news/2021/6/23/southern-african-nations-agree-to-deploy-forces-to-mozambique

Alden, C., & Soko, M. (2005). South Africa's Economic Relations with Africa: Hegemony and its Discontents. *The Journal of Modern African Studies, 43*(3), 367–392.

Amnesty International. (2021, May 14). *Mozambique: Rescue Attempts Jeopardized by Racial Discrimination Following Palma Attack—New Survivors' Testimony*. https://www.amnesty.org/en/latest/news/2021/05/mozambique-rescue-attempts-jeopardized-by-racial-discrimination-following-palma-attack/

Anderlini, S. N., & Conaway, C. P. (2004). Disarmament, Demobilisation and Reintegration. *International Alert: Women Waging Peace, Inclusive Security, Sustainable Peace: A Toolkit for Advocacy and Action* (pp. 125–134).

Bartlett, K. (2022, March 04). *Mozambique's Displaced Recount Brutality of Cabo Delgado Insurgents*. https://www.voanews.com/a/mozambique-s-displaced-recount-brutality-of-cabo-delgado-insurgents-/6470157.html

Bennett, A., & Lepgold, J. (1993). Reinventing Collective Security after the Cold War and Gulf Conflict. *Political Science Quarterly, 108*(2), 213–237.

Brzozowski, A. (2021, March 16). *US Pressure Brings About Rise in NATO Defence Spending, Despite Pandemic.* https://www.euractiv.com/section/defence-and-security/news/us-pressure-brings-about-rise-in-nato-defence-spending-despite-pandemic/

Butfoy, A. (1993). Collective Security: Theory, Problems and Reformulations. *Australian Journal of International Affairs, 47*(1), 1–14.

Cheatham, A., Long, A., & Sheehy, T. (2022, June 23). *Southern African Countries and Rwanda Pulled the Country's North Back from the Brink. It's an Opportunity that must be Seized.* https://www.usip.org/publications/2022/06/regional-security-support-vital-first-step-peace-mozambique

Chikohomero, R. (2020, June 2). *Can SADC Come to Mozambique's Rescue?* https://issafrica.org/iss-today/can-sadc-come-to-mozambiques-rescue

Claude, I. L. (1989). The Balance of Power Revisited. *Review of International Studies, 15*(2), 77–85.

Crisis Group. (2023, January 31). *Making the Most of the EU's Integrated Approach in Mozambique.* https://www.crisisgroup.org/africa/east-and-southern-africa/mozambique/making-most-eus-integrated-approach-mozambique

Deni, J. R. (2017). *NATO and Article 5: The Transatlantic Alliance and the Twenty-First-Century Challenges of Collective Defense.* Lanham, Maryland: Rowman & Littlefield.

Fabricius, P. (2023, January 10). Defence Officials Probe 'Despicable' Video of Soldiers Apparently Burning Insurgent Bodies Like Rubbish. https://www.dailymaverick.co.za/article/2023-01-10-probe-into-video-of-soldiers-apparently-burning-insurgent-bodies/

Fagbayibo, B. (2013). Common Problems Affecting Supranational Attempts in Africa: An Analytical Overview. *Potchefstroom Electronic Law Journal/potchefstroomse Elektroniese Regsblad, 16*(1), 31–69.

Feijó, J., Maquenz, J., Salite, D., & Kishner, J. (2022, November, 30). *Characterization of the Socioeconomic Conditions of Internally Displaced People in Northern Mozambique Throughout the Year 2021.* https://omrmz.org/observador/or-127-caracterizacao-das-condicoes-socioeconomicas-dos-deslocados-internos-no-norte-de-mocambique-ao-longo-do-ano-de-2021-english-version-available/

Frohlich, T. (2014, August 4). *The Future of NATO: More Than Just Collective Security.* https://www.gmfus.org/blog/2014/08/04/future-nato-more-just-collective-security

Gardner, F. (2021, March, 31). *Mozambique: Why IS so Hard to Defeat in Mozambique.* https://www.bbc.com/news/world-africa-56597861

Gazzini, T. (2003). NATO's Role in the Collective Security System. *Journal of Conflict and Security Law, 8*(2), 231–263.

Global Centre for the Responsibility to Protect. (2023, May, 31). *Mozambique.* https://www.globalr2p.org/countries/mozambique/

Guarascio, F. (2022, September 8). *EU Boosts Military Support to Gas-Rich Mozambique Amid Energy Crisis.* https://www.reuters.com/world/eu-boosts-support-southern-african-military-mission-mozambique-2022-09-08/

Haar, R. N. (2020). Why America Should Continue to Lead NATO. *Atlantisch Perspectief, 44*(2), 31–37.

Halakhe, A. (2021, May 6). *Further Militarisation will not end Mozambique's Insurgency.* https://www.aljazeera.com/opinions/2021/5/6/further-militarisation-will-not-end-mozambiques-insurgency

Hanlon, J. (2018, June 19). *Mozambique's Insurgency: A New Boko Haram or Youth Demanding an End to Marginalisation?* https://blogs.lse.ac.uk/africaatlse/2018/06/19/mozambiques-insurgency-a-new-boko-haram-or-youth-demanding-an-end-to-marginalisation/

Hartmann, D., Guevara, M. R., Jara-Figueroa, C., Aristarán, M., & Hidalgo, C. A. (2017). Linking Economic Complexity, Institutions, and Income Inequality. *World Development, 93*, 75–93.

Hill, M and Nhamirre, B. (2021, March 31). Mercenaries Fighting Insurgents in Mozambique Set to Exit. https://www.bloomberg.com/news/articles/2021-03-31/military-contractor-fighting-mozambique-militants-set-to-exit

International Committee of the Red Cross. (2021, October, 11). *Mozambique: ICRC Director of Operations Says Combined Impact of Conflict and Extreme Weather in Cabo Delgado Threaten Public Health.* https://www.icrc.org/en/document/mozambique-icrc-director-operations-says-combined-impact-conflict-and-extreme-weather-cabo

International Crisis Group. (2021). *Ending Nigeria's Herder-Farmer Crisis: The Livestock Reform Plan.*

Jordaan, E. (2017). Collective Security in Africa: The Tension Between Theory and Practice. *Strategic Review for Southern Africa, 39*(1), 1–25.

Khadiagala, G. (2021, May 27). *Regional Military Intervention in Mozambique is a Bad Idea. Here's Why.* https://theconversation.com/regional-military-intervention-in-mozambique-is-a-bad-idea-heres-why-161549

Khadiagala, G. (2021, May 28). *Why Regional Military Intervention in Mozambique is a Bad Idea.* https://www.wits.ac.za/news/latest-news/opinion/2021/2021-05/why-regional-military-intervention-in-mozambique-is-a-bad-idea.html

Lefa, B. J. (2015). The African Philosophy of ubuntu in South African Education. *Studies in Philosophy and Education, 1*(1), 15.

Lefebvre, S. (2003). The Difficulties and Dilemmas of International Intelligence Cooperation. *International Journal of Intelligence and Counterintelligence, 16*(4), 527–542.

Lindley-French, J. (2003). Common Interests and National Interests: Bridging the Values/Interests Gap. *American Foreign Policy Interests, 25*(1), 13–18.

Magen, A. (2018). Fighting Terrorism: The Democracy Advantage. *Journal of Democracy, 29*(1), 111–125.

Mambo, C. (2022, March 11). *SADC Moves to Thwart Terrorism.* https://www.sardc.net/en/southern-african-news-features/sadc-moves-to-thwart-terrorism/

Masuku, M. M., & Jili, N. N. (2019). Public Service Delivery in South Africa: The Political Influence at Local Government Level. *Journal of Public Affairs, 19*(4), 1–8.

Mazilu, D. (2002). NATO Activated Article 5 of North Atlantic Treaty. Romania- An Active Factor of Antiterrorist Coalition. *Euro-Atlantic Studies, 5*, 67–72.

Mazrui, A. A. (1995). Pan-Africanism: From Poetry to Power. *African ISSUES, 23*(1), 35–38.

Miller, L. H. (1999). The Idea and the Reality of Collective Security. *Global Governance, 5*(3), 303–332.

Mlambo, V. H., & Masuku, M. M. (2021). Terror at the Front Gate: Insurgency in Mozambique and its Implications for the SADC and South Africa. *Journal of Public Affairs, 22*(1), 1–8.

Mlambo, V. H., & Mlambo, D. N. (2018). Challenges Impeding Regional Integration in Southern Africa. *Journal of Economics and Behavioral Studies, 10*(2), 250–261.

Mugabi, I. (2021, July 13). *Rwanda's Military Aid for Mozambique Rattles SADC.* https://www.dw.com/en/sadc-upset-by-rwandas-military-aid-to-appease-mozambiques-cabo-delgado-province/a-58250646

Mutisi, M. (2016). SADC Interventions in the Democratic Republic of the Congo. *Conflict Trends, 2016*(3), 27–35.

NATO Review. (2005). *NATO's Response to Terrorism.* https://www.nato.int/docu/review/2005/issue3/english/art1.html

Ndebele, L. (2022, March 2). *SADC Sets up Counter-Terrorism Centre in Tanzania.* https://www.news24.com/news24/africa/news/sadc-sets-up-counter-terrorism-centre-in-tanzania-20220302

Ngoma, N. (2004). SADC'S Mutual Defence Pact: A Final Move to a Security Community? *The Round Table, 93*(375), 411–423.

Papp, D. S. (1997). *Contemporary International Relations: Frameworks for Understanding* (5th ed.). Allyn and Bacon.

Reyes Parra, P. D. (2021). Self-Defence Against Non-State Actors: Possibility or Reality? *RFJ, 9*, 151.

Ross, D., & Donahue, E. (2021, April, 13). *The Evolution and Escalation of the Islamic State Threat to Mozambique.* https://www.fpri.org/article/2021/04/the-evolution-and-escalation-of-the-islamic-state-threat-to-mozambique/

Sany, J. (2021, May 19). *Pathways to Peace in Mozambique.* https://www.usip.org/publications/2021/05/pathways-peace-mozambique

Saurombe, A. (2012). The Role of SADC Institutions in Implementing SADC Treaty Provisions Dealing with Regional Integration. *Potchefstroom Electronic Law Journal/Potchefstroomse Elektroniese Regsblad, 15*(2).

Schwarzenberger, G. (1951). *Power Politics: A Study of International Society* (No. 18). Stevens.

Stark, V. (2022, February 22). *South Africa Sending Fresh Troops to Mozambique to Fight Islamist Insurgents.* https://www.voanews.com/a/south-africa-sending-fresh-troops-to-mozambique-to-fight-islamist-insurgents-/6454195.html

The Africa Report. (2021, February 21). *Mozambique: What Will Happen in 2021?* https://www.theafricareport.com/63782/mozambique-what-will-happen-in-2021/

The International Labour Organization. (2013, November 20). *Inequality in Southern Africa: Options for Redress.* https://www.ilo.org/actrav/WCMS_230181/lang--en/index.htm

Uzodike, U. O. (2009). The Role of Regional Economic Communities in Africa's Economic Integration: Prospects and Constraints. *Africa Insight, 39*(2), 26–42.

van Breda, A. D. (2019). Developing the Notion of Ubuntu as African Theory for Social Work Practice. *Social Work, 55*(4), 439–450.

Vaudran, L. (2022, April 11). *Joint Strategies Needed by SADC and Rwanda in Dealing with Cabo Delgado Insurgency.* https://www.dailymaverick.co.za/article/2022-04-11-joint-strategies-needed-by-sadc-and-rwanda-in-dealing-with-cabo-delgado-insurgency/

Vhumbunu, C. H. (2021). Insurgency in Mozambique: The Role of the Southern African Development Community. *Conflict Trends, 2021*(1), 3–12.

Walt, S. M. (1985). Alliance Formation and the Balance of World Power. *International Security, 9*(4), 3–43.

Mediatized Conflict: A Case of Nigerian Media Reportage of Farmer-Herder Conflict

Ridwan Abiola Kolawole and Babatunde Raphael Ojebuyi

1 Introduction

The role of media in conflict situations has been acknowledged by researchers either in its escalation or de-escalation (Biazoto, 2011) even though the media are saddled with the socially responsible role of enhancing peacebuilding in a conflict situation, evidences have shown that the media are sometimes accomplices in the conflict escalation (Apuke & Omar, 2020; Biazoto, 2011). With a growing population amidst ethnic diversity, Nigerian media, in the recent past, have not created value for their audience who are diverse in their ethnicity, culture, religion, and class (Nwachukwu et al., 2021). This assertion reflects in the picture painted by the media of different groups in Nigeria. Such labelling as: immigrant, settler, native, non-native, foreigner, stranger element, host community, indigene, and non-indigene, among others, which the media have deployed to characterize some groups who Nwachukwu et al. (2021: 57) describe as "other," do not necessarily depict such groups and are the bane of conflict de-escalation in the country.

One of the major challenges Nigeria is currently facing relates to the farmer-herder conflict (Chukwuma, 2020; Nwankwo, 2021). Emanating

R. A. Kolawole (✉)
Department of Mass Communication, Fountain University, Osogbo, Nigeria
e-mail: ridwan.kolawole@fuo.edu.ng

R. A. Kolawole · B. R. Ojebuyi
Department of Communication and Language Arts, University of Ibadan, Ibadan, Nigeria

© The Author(s), under exclusive license to Springer Nature Switzerland AG 2024
O. B. Mlambo and E. Chitando (eds.), *The Palgrave Handbook of Violence in Africa*, https://doi.org/10.1007/978-3-031-40754-3_55

from this conflict is the ethnic colouration which has consistently called into question the togetherness of Nigeria as a country because of the unrest it causes (Nwachukwu et al., 2021). The metamorphosis of the farmer-herder conflict in Nigeria has two distinct causes. The first is the case of herders, predominantly Fulani people, who have lived in the southern part of Nigeria for decades and who, because of expansion in farming activities and urbanization, have limited resources to feed their animals and have resorted to grazing their animals on farmers' crops (Olaniyi, 2015). The second cause stemmed from the climatic conditions which have forces the herdsmen to migrate southwards in search of food for their animals during the dry season. Notwithstanding, Awogbade et al. (2016) attribute the situation to the unrestricted influx of nomadic cattle-rearers into Nigeria. The authors argue that even though the violence is eco-related, they describe the violence as symbolizing an emerging trend of trans-border pastoral terrorism in Nigeria. The herders do not mind grazing on people's farms and are ready to fight whoever dares to confront or prevent them from grazing on farmers' crops (Odunlami, 2017). The destruction of crops and farmlands by these nomads has led to conflict in its violent form resulting in the loss of lives and the displacement of people (Awogbade et al., 2016; Tade & Yikwabs, 2020). The conflict ravages all six geopolitical zones of the country with varying degrees of casualties and loss of property. The United Nations Office for the Coordination of Humanitarian Affairs reports that over 81,000 people have been displaced (Olaleye, 2020).

Meanwhile, as a result of the conflict, Ogbonnaya (2021) reports that more than 2,000 people were reportedly killed in the Middle Belt region (North Central) alone by the last quarter of 2015 while US$13.7 billion was lost to the conflict between 2013 and 2015. In the North-Central region alone, Mercy Corps reports that at least $14 billion in potential revenues has been lost to farmer-herder conflict (Premium Times, 2016). Discussing the way the Nigerian media reported the Anti-Open Grazing Law, particularly in Benue State, Gever (2018) states that the media did more harm than good in reporting the issue. This perspective of the mediatization of the conflict was consequent upon the media narratives of "we" versus "them" which the media have portrayed over the time. The deployment of the Nigerian media space to the farmer-herder conflict has undoubtedly given it more attention, especially in the last decade (Apuke & Omar, 2020; Pate & Dauda, 2015). The attention is not unconnected to the media's penchant for conflict, which is inherently news value that the media cannot overlook (Vladisavljevic & Voltmer, 2017).

This chapter explores the dimension of this publicity and perspectives vis-à-vis conflict (de)escalatory narratives. Specifically, the chapter examines how Nigerian media are implicated in disseminating frames about the farmer-herder conflict and audience stakeholders' perception of the media reportage of the conflict. But, while media reporting of conflict is important to both the media (for performing their surveillance function) and the audience, including the policymakers, a peacebuilding perspective from the point of view of peace journalism is better deployed to explore ways of de-escalating the conflict. Youngblood (2016) opines that conflict reportage should be done out of malice, prejudice, and propaganda such as name-calling or labelling among others. Much as the media play a vital role in making others' opinions and yearnings known to the public, "the centrality of the mass media in defining the direction of conflicts in Nigeria is acknowledged to the extent that a debate is raging on the culpability of traditional and social media in some of the violent disruptions in the country" (Pate & Dauda, 2015: 214). Stemming from this debate, this chapter explores the dimension of media reportage and angles vis-à-vis conflict (de)escalatory narratives through the instrument of the mediatization of conflicts. Existing literature reveals that these aspects have been given scant scholarly attention. Consequently, the chapter attempts to fill the gap by answering two research questions: (1) What is the extent to which Nigerian media are implicated in their reportage of farmer-herder conflict in the country? and (2) What is the audience's perception of media narratives of Nigeria's farmer-herder conflict? To achieve these objectives, we employed Erving Goffman's framing theory as the framework and used both quantitative and qualitative content analyses and in-depth interviews as the methods.

2 Mediatization of Conflict and Reportage of Nigerian Farmer-Herder Conflict

The media's unquenchable thirst for newsworthy events has increased their consistent reportage of seemingly negative happenings, especially in the case of the yet-to-end Nigerian farmer-herder conflict. Reporting conflict is never bad in itself but when the media get themselves involved and present issues from the perspective of a party to the conflict instead of from their expected neutral position, then, mediatization of conflict is being practised. Mediatization of conflict is the process in which the media are implicated in the conflicts they disseminate because of their escalatory narratives that are either manifest or implied in their reportage (Cottle, 2006; Youngblood,

2016). It is the opposite of the mediation role expected of the media, especially during adversities/conflicts. In simple language, it is war journalism (see Youngblood, 2016). Understandably, the media have to carry negative stories, as such, to attract the attention of their audience, while, particularly in the media landscape of Nigeria which is essentially neoliberal, the media's proclivity to report negative happenings is hinged on making profits (Cottle, 2006; Oreglia, 2014; Pinker, 2018). The journalistic tradition, "If it bleeds, it leads" (Cooper & Roter, 2000), appears to characterize media reportage. This mantra is firmly entrenched in journalism practice. In essence, conflict/crisis, destruction, and violence are integral parts of news values which journalism leverages in practice. It, therefore, needs to be stressed that conflict is a news value to which the media ordinarily give preference. According to Harcup and O'Neill (2001), journalists hasten to the call of negative events because their consumers prefer these to non-conflict events. Arguably, Pinker (2018) states that it is news if it is unusual or negative, noting that journalists will be interested in sad or bad occurrences. Pinker contends that as long as there are bad occurrences in society, society will have enough to make up the news content. In his analytical exegesis of mediatized conflict, Cottle (2006: 9) posits that:

> The media...are capable of enacting and performing conflicts as well as reporting and representing them; that is to say, they are actively 'doing something' over and above disseminating ideas, images and information. The media's relationship to conflict, therefore, is often not best thought of in terms of 'reflection' or even 'representation' given its more active performative.

The narrative presented by Cottle, although, suggests what is often the trend in the media's conflict reportage, the pervasiveness of such does not make it a normality because the damage could be monumental. A good instance of the media's role in the escalating of conflict and promotion of war journalism clearly manifested in the Rwandan genocide championed by *Radio Mille Colline* (Hefit & Jonas, 2020). The media reportage (episodic) of farmer-herder conflict has also been established to be feeding into the conflict and thereby leading to its escalation (Gever, 2018), owing to the way they (the media) frame the conflict and its actors. Also, the way actors react to the media narrative of the conflict (thematic) reportedly affects the direction of the media reportage. The two situations illustrated present reciprocity (an exchange) of frames between the media and the actors. Beyond these, the sensitive nature of conflict reporting requires that the media play the role of arbiters (Folarin, 2002).

In another instance, after the passage into law of the Anti-Open Grazing Prohibition Bill by the Benue State Government, the Nigerian mass media framed the 2017 Anti-Open Grazing Law in such a way that the herdsmen were made to feel they were the targets of the new law (Gever, 2018). Reportage of this nature has the potential to turn the herdsmen, who by their nature are nomadic, into endangered species and, thus, spur them into developing means to fortify themselves against any perceived aggression. But as a balance to the tale, researchers (e.g., Tyopuusu, 2019) have reported the woes of the farmers in the hands of the herdsmen who graze their cows on the farms indiscriminately and attack any audacious farmers who tend to protect their farms. In particular, Tyopuusu (2019) states that farmers in some villages were driven from their farms by the herdsmen. From Benue to Plateau, Adamawa, Taraba, and Nasarawa States in the north and Delta, Edo, Anambra, and Enugu in the south, Nigerian media have different dimensions of reporting the clash between the farmers and the herdsmen, thereby making their own contribution to the escalation of the conflict (Gever, 2018). Some scholars (Arowosegbe, 2019; Olaniyi, 2015) have reiterated that this incessant conflict is attributable to the scarcity of resources or what could be regarded as a struggle over limited resources by both the farmers and the nomads. Ranked as the fourth deadliest conflict in the world (Chukwuma, 2020; Ezemenaka & Ekumaoko, 2018), and second to Boko Haram in Nigeria (Amnesty International, 2018), the farmer-herder clash has minimally attracted the committed attention of the Nigerian Government, especially in terms of providing permanent solutions. Even though international attention on the conflict soars every day, insignificant consideration is given, vis-à-vis investigations about the conflict, at home (Ezemenaka & Ekumaoko, 2018).

3   Theoretical Underpinning

The study is guided by framing theory. Specifically, emphasis is placed on the constructionist approach to framing: a perspective popularized by Entman, (1993: 52) who notes that to frame is to "promote a particular problem definition and treatment recommendation for the item described." In the estimation of Entman, the objective framing in the media is to select an aspect of social reality and present such to the media audience in a way (or through the lens) that the media choose to disseminate the reality. In the process, notes Entman, the media conceal some aspects of social reality while disclosing others. The aim is solely to consistently present a narrative about an issue.

The constructionist approach to framing empowers journalists (or the media in general), who Omanga (2016: 26) describes as "information processors", to decide what to report and how to report them, to use their own frames and those of others through their gatekeeping role in news gathering, editing, and dissemination. This process is informed by the four levels of framing as enunciated by Entman, cited by Omanga (2016). These four levels are: (1) the communicator (journalists); (2) the text (the media content); (3) the receiver (the audience); and (4) the culture. Omanga implies that the culture has a way of affecting the other three levels. Within the constructionist paradigm of framing, the communicator, in disseminating the "text" to the audience, incorporates labels, and some identity constructs, among others, which are informed by communicator's cultural environment.

Lee (2010) reports that some scholars consider framing as second-level agenda-setting. Although the Agenda-Setting Theory projects the salience of issues (that is, what to talk about), framing theory presents "indicator salience, illustrating how the media tell the audiences how to think about something" (Lee, 2010: 365) through the journalists "judgemental" frames. The media's consistent presentation of a narrative or perspective on a phenomenon tends to manipulate audience focus towards what the media set out to achieve. This agrees with the proposition of Goffman (1974). Frames are reinforced by the ambience or environment that makes them convenient for the journalist to express. This cultural environment makes it easy for the media to get the audience persuaded or manipulated to accept the message being communicated, or, at worst, make it what should be discussed by the audience. Using the dichotomy of war journalism and peace journalism of Galtung (2003), it is easy to theorize the Nigerian media reportage of farmer-herder conflict in these two directions. Therefore, the constructionist approach to framing will be applied to examine what construction is applied and which actors are involved in the construction of narratives presented in either escalating the conflict or de-escalating it.

4 Methodology

The study was carried out using a sequential exploratory research design. The contents of the media were explored before the perspectives of the audience (including representatives of the conflict actors) were sought. News stories published by *ThisDay*, *The Punch* and *The Premium Times* between 2016 and 2020 were purposively selected from the online version of the newspapers. After the collection of the news stories from the websites of the newspapers through the search section, the first 33 news stories of each newspaper were chosen. 'The copious texts (words) of the news stories were extracted into a Microsoft Word document. A total of 93,263 texts written by the journalists of the newspapers and opinions from the public (letters to editors and public affairs analysts' columns/views) on the conflict were extracted respectively. Out of these, *ThisDay* had a large frequency of 61,294 words followed by *The Punch* and *The Premium Times* which had 17,018 and 14,950 respectively. These texts were further analysed using discourse content analysis (DCA) aided by Voyant-Tool, a corpus textual analysis tool. Outcomes of the analysis were used for the formulation of questionnaire items and an In-depth Interview (IDI) Guide, which were used for the collection of data for the survey and In-depth Interview research methods aspect of the research design. The questionnaire contained closed and open-ended questions and was administered using Google Form.

The respondents to the survey and participants in the IDI were chosen using purposive and available sampling procedures. The purposive technique was considered for getting only the views of the people who had been following the conflict through news media, and people who were the direct/indirect victims or knew the victims of the conflict. The availability technique was chosen on the people's readiness to voluntarily respond to the survey. While the participants of the IDI were largely drawn from the North-Central region, respondents to the survey were from Abia, Edo, Kebbi, Kwara, Lagos, Nasarawa, Osun, Oyo, Rivers States, and Federal Capital Territory. A total of 119 audience members responded to the survey, while IDI had three interviewees.

Corpus discourse analysis was carried out on the news texts and open-ended responses aspects of the data collected using the survey research method. Open-ended responses were categorized into: the escalation of the conflict, truthfulness of the news stories, and victimhood. Escalation of the conflict entailed the views of the respondents which specifically pointed out how the newspapers are contributing to the conflict. By truthfulness of the news stories, respondents' views that established the correctness of the news stories about the conflict were explored. The victimhood detailed experiences of the respondents (affected directly or indirectly) after herdsmen's attacks or invasion in various communities. Emerging themes for episodic and thematic frames from the newspapers and respondents were analysed using textual analysis. Like the quantification of the news texts, these categorizations were also quantified using the discourse analysis tool stated earlier. In the open responses, 971 words were found that aligned with the escalation of the conflict classification, while truthfulness of the news stories and victimhood had 711 and 342 accordingly.

5 Findings and Discussion

The findings of this study are broadly divided into two, namely: (1) episodic (which refers to media frames), and (2) thematic (which implies stakeholders'/audiences' frames of the conflict between the farmers and the herdsmen) even though the results from the two are explored complementarily in the discussion.

Episodic Frames

Episodic frames from the qualitative analysis of the selected newspapers—*The Punch, ThisDay* and *Premium Times* revealed "othering" narratives, labelling, and ethnicization of the conflict. These were significantly projected in the texts of the selected newspapers. The othering narratives are better understood through source attribution and people. That is, the sources used by the newspapers were non-conflict actors who appeared in this study as "self" against the conflict actors who are the "other." The newspapers copiously cited various news sources. These sources were predominantly victims, relatives of the victims, and residents in the communities, states and local government areas where herdsmen were reported to have attacked or invaded. They also cited government sources. In most cases, the government sources were used when the reaction of the state government officials was needed towards attacks or "invasions" of the herdsmen and the public's expectations from the governments at the state level. A significant number of these sources, except government sources, expressed views that could escalate the conflict. For instance, a source who pleaded anonymity and used by *ThisDay*, said:

> During their journey, they frequently trespass farmlands owned by locals in their host communities, destroying crops and valuables. Attempts by farmers to prevent them from causing havoc are met with stiff and violent resistance. Most times, the farmers are overpowered, injured and killed, while others are evicted from their homes.

Another source also noted that "'Heads roll for cows to feed.' The reason for this is not farfetched: In some views, the Fulani herdsmen when interviewed have said that they'd be no option than making sure that their cows feed," (*ThisDay* Newspaper, November 23, 2017).

Labelling and ethnicization of the conflict were mostly conveyed by the newspapers with the frequent use of "Fulani" and "herdsmen." Though the newspapers attributed the mentions to their sources, *The Punch* (from its reporters/editors' perception) largely saw the attackers or criminals as suspected herdsmen, while *ThisDay* based its representation of the herdsmen on what people said about the pastoralists concerning the attacks and killings the sources said they had executed, with the emphasis that the herdsmen were not ready to explore peace options. These positions can be better appreciated from the extract below:

> According to a source that would not want their name mentioned. The solution is not for the herdsmen to leave the communities. There are a lot of political intrigues attached to the development and some people create mischief out of it. The source enthused that some elements want to create an impression that the clashes between herdsmen and farmers are prevalent in the present administration forgetting that from time immemorial, before democracy, herdsmen and farmers have been fighting. (*ThisDay* Newspaper, 2017)

Surprisingly, *ThisDay* noted in one of its news stories that "Alhaji Sale Bayeri, the spokesman of Miyetti Allah Cattle Breeders' Association of Nigeria (MACBAN) in Plateau, the sunshade body of the Fulani herdsmen, said, the herdsmen will not accept ranches; "we shall prefer to explore our traditional grazing routes/reserves." In its representation of the attackers or criminals as suspected herdsmen, *The Premiums Times* explores farmers as sources and victims more than indirect victims. While the newspapers are appropriating activities of the criminal herdsmen to Nigeria's Fulani, one of the security experts notes that the herdsmen are not Nigerians. According to him:

> There has never been problem between Fulani and the Yoruba. We grew up to know them; they had the settlement; their cows don't graze on people's farms. These ones they call herdsmen are not Nigerians. I am saying it emphatically! I am a security officer of international repute. These ones they are calling Fulani herdsmen are not Nigerians. I told them during security summit in Abuja that people should approach these herdsmen and speak Nigerian Hausa-Fulani to them, they don't understand. Ask them if they claim to be Nigerians, where are they from? (IDI/A farmer and head of native security group in Oke Ogun area of Oyo State)

The views of the expert align with the position of one of the farmers that the media hardly interview them when the herdsmen attack. He pointed out that:

> The media need to know the extent of damage done to our farmlands and see how the herdsmen have destroyed our farms. I understand that the journalists are also afraid to come to the affected communities but we like to let the relevant stakeholders hear our voices so that we can get help. (IDI/Male/53 years/Leader of farmers/Benue State)

The views, from the expert and the farmers, resonate with the themes discussed earlier under the episodic frame that newspapers are using secondary sources more than the primary sources (the farmers and relatives of the victims) in their reportage. Therefore, the truthfulness of the news stories about the conflict is expected to be questioned by the respondents of the survey aspect of the study.

6 Thematic Frames

The qualitative views of the audience were discursively analysed. Like the episodic framing, the audience believed that the media were instrumental in the escalation of the conflicts and that believing in the news stories being reported by the Nigerian newspapers is subject to second thoughts. As explained under the episodic frame, the audience also have the views that herders were creating issues that continue increasing the growth of the conflict, while the media could not be exonerated from the conflict growth based on their "biased" reportage. In the victimhood classification, the findings reveal that the conflict affected the farmers more than the herders. The impact, according to the views, has largely been on farmlands and insufficient food production for people (Table 1).

Table 1 Audience perception of parties being supported by the media in relation to rating of the reportage

Conflicting Party	N	Mean	Std. Deviation	P-Value [Equal Variance Assumed]
Farmers	52	2.13	0.841	0.015
Herdsmen	12	1.50	0.522	
None	51	2.57	0.728	0.038
Both	1	1.00	0.000	

Source Researcher's analysis, 2021

Findings presented in Table 1 further substantiate the fact that the media pay less attention to herdsmen as victims of the conflict when farmers and herdsmen are considered as the key primary actors. Analysis shows that a significant number of the respondents believe that Nigerian newspapers are supporting farmers (M = 2.13, SD = 0.841) more than herdsmen (M = 1.50, SD = 0.522). However, when respondents were asked to state if none of the actors or both of them are being supported by the newspapers, analysis reveals a significant inconsistency in their views. They believe that none of the actors is being supported (M = 2.57, SD = 0.728). These results imply that the newspapers' episodic frame cannot be attributed to the audience's perception about which actor is being supported absolutely (Table 2).

While it was difficult for the audience to pinpoint the actor being supported most when the collective categorization approach was employed, they were able to perceive that the government and herdsmen are being held responsible for the conflict. The finding in the thematic frames expounds on this position. However, this also remains a questionable perception based on the fact that more than 62% of 40 and 54% of 59 respondents who believed the news reports about the conflict to a large and the least extent thought that the newspapers are holding the government responsible respectively. These results were not quite different from believing that the newspapers are holding herdsmen responsible. These results, as shown in Table 3, could be more understood based on the fact that a significant number of the respondents were not direct victims of the conflict (Table 3).

Surprisingly, 40.3% of 60 respondents who believed that the government is exhibiting a lackadaisical attitude towards the conflict are not direct victims. A large number (44 = 30.0%) who also said the government is handling the conflict poorly are also not direct victims. There are areas where the views

Table 2 Audience believability of media reportage and stakeholders held responsible

Believing Media Reports	Stakeholders hold responsible						Total
	Farmers	Herdsmen	Government	Security Agencies	NGOs	Others	
Undecided	1(5.0%)	8(40.0%)	11(55.0%)	0(0.0%)	0(0.0%)	0(0.0%)	20(100%)
A least extent	2(3.4%)	21(35.6%)	32(54.2%)	1(1.7%)	1(1.7%)	2(3.4%)	59(100%)
A large extent	0(0.0%)	10(25.0%)	25(62.5%)	5(12.5%)	0(0.0%)	0(0.0%)	40(100%)

Source Researcher's analysis, 2021

Table 3 Audience victimhood by government's attitude and efforts towards resolving the conflict

Direct or Indirect Victim	Lackadaisical	Poor	Good
No	48(40.3%)	44(30.0%)	6(5.0%)
Yes	12(10.1%)	9(7.6%)	0(0.0%)
Total	60(50.4%)	53(44.5%)	6(5.0%)

Source Researcher's analysis, 2021

of the audience align and do not resonate with the episodic frame of the newspapers. These outcomes are explored further as presented in Table 4.

According to the findings in Table 4, the rating of the reportage within the categories of being partisan, unfair, or fair resonates with the extent to which the audience believed that the media contributed to the escalation of the conflict. At 24.204[a] of Pearson Chi-Square and degree of freedom of 2, the rating is significantly associated with the escalation of the conflict ($P < 0.000$). This significance is explored further, and the findings are presented in Table 5, where the percentiles of the respondents who chose partisan, unfair and fair rating categories are analysed along with the media contribution to the escalation of the conflict (Table 5).

According to the findings as shown in Table 5, 50% to 95% of the respondents believe that newspapers were "partisan" and "unfair," and that the conflict is being escalated. On the other hand, 75%, 90% and 95% of those who believe that the media are fair in their reportage also believed that the conflict was being escalated. This escalatory role is captured in an interview with a Peace and Strategic Studies expert thus:

> The role of the media in the conflict is damaging, honestly. The media have over the time played an escalatory role in this farmer-herder conflict. If the media can be mindful of their utterances and their choice of words, the better it is for peace to reign supreme in our country.

Table 4 Association between the rating of the reportage (partisan, unfair and fair) and media contribution to the escalation of the conflict

	Value	df	Asymp. Sig. (2-sided)
Pearson Chi-Square	24.204[a]	2	0.000
Likelihood Ratio	26.189	2	0.000
Linear-by-Linear Association	23.392	1	0.000
N of Valid Cases	119		

[a]0 cells (0.0%) have an expected count of less than 5. The minimum expected count is 11.70
Source Researcher's analysis, 2021

Table 5 Percentage of the audience who believe in media contribution to the escalation of the percentile

		Rating of the media reportage	Percentiles						
			5	10	25	50	75	90	95
Weighted Average (Definition 1)	Media contribute to escalation of the conflict	Partisan	1.00	1.00	2.00	2.00	2.00	2.00	2.00
		Unfair	1.00	1.00	1.00	2.00	2.00	2.00	2.00
Tukey's Hinges	Media contribute to escalation of the conflict	Fair	1.00	1.00	1.00	1.00	2.00	2.00	2.00
		Partisan			2.00	2.00	2.00		
		Unfair			1.00	2.00	2.00		
		Fair			1.00	1.00	2.00		

Source Researcher's analysis, 2022
Key: 1.0 = No; 2.0 = Yes

7 Discussion

Both the episodic and thematic data from this study have revealed that the media failed in their social responsibility because of the blameworthy frames they adopted in presenting the farmer-herder conflict. This is opposed to their being harbingers of peace and playing a mediation role in conflict situations (Cottle, 2006; Folarin, 2002). The choice of words and framing constructs adopted by the media also indicated partisanship, which was also confirmed by the audience and stakeholders. This clearly contradicts objectivity which is a strong value in journalism. This is an instance of mediatized conflicts and war journalism alluded to by Cottle (2006). The media, perhaps evasively, concentrated on sources such as farmers (the victims), police, residents, and the government's spokesperson to the exclusion of the alleged (i.e., the herders). This strategy of exclusion could be alluded to as the "us" versus "them" sentiment propagated by the media according to Youngblood (2016). The media are complicit in the characterization of the conflict actors, even though the news sources also took parts in the constructionist narratives. This resonates with the constructionist framing approach by Entman that the explanations offered by the media are a product of their discretion in deciding what to report out of an array of information at their disposal. The audience did not have an opposing view than to state that the media reportage of the conflict between farmers and the herders shows partisanship just as they maintained that the way the media have reported the matter was capable of escalation. Overtly or covertly the newspapers reportage depicted an ethnicization narrative similar to that narrated by Hefit and Jonas (2020) in the case of the Rwandan genocide. Undoubtedly, there is evidence regarding the atrocities of the herders on farmlands, but Nigerian media need to understand the terrain of conflict reportage better in order to reduce the tension in the land. Another important finding of this study is that media framing of the farmer-herder conflict in Nigeria forms the talking point of members of the public irrespective of whether they are victims or not. In alignment with their "bleeding-leading" narrative, Nigerian journalists tilt towards promoting negatives—conflict, crimes, and odd events—which, according to Harcup and O'Neill (2001), are the media consumers' preference. This further reinforces the culpability of the media in the conflict. Interestingly, this study has established that the audience the media seek to serve in the case of farmer-herder conflict blamed the media for the way they have reported the conflict over time.

8 Recommendations and Conclusion

Stemming from the findings of this study, relevant stakeholders and policymakers, especially governments at all levels, should rescue the country from the perennial farmer-herder conflict. While they need to holistically find a lasting solution to the menace which has claimed thousands of lives and resources, Nigerian media need to equip themselves with sufficient training tailored towards reporting the conflict in a peacebuilding manner. The Nigerian government, through its relevant agencies, should ensure the protection of lives and property of all, as dictated by the constitution. In order to ensure food security, there is a need for the government, particularly, to have a strategic policy on securing people who are in the food production chain, as well as their farms, against any eventuality. Finally, should the media continue its present "us" versus "them" narrative in farmer-herder conflict reportage, SDG goals number two (war against hunger) and 16 (peace and strong institutions) may not be met. Meanwhile, while this chapter essentially focused on the Nigerian newspapers, further studies could incorporate radio stations and a comparison of their reportage could also be explored. This could provide a larger picture of media narratives of the conflict.

Acknowledgements This research publication was made possible by support from the Social Science Research Council's Next Generation Social Sciences in Africa Fellowship, with funds provided by the Carnegie Corporation of New York.

Bibliography

Albert, I. O. (2008). Understanding Peace in Africa. In D. J. Francis (Ed.), *Peace and Conflict in Africa* (pp. 31–45). Zed Books.

Amnesty International. (2018). *Harvest of Death Three Years of Bloody Clashes Between Farmers and Herders in Nigeria* (pp. 1–69). www.amnesty.org

Apuke, O. D., & Omar, B. (2020). Conflict Victims' Assessment and Narratives on the Reportage of Herdsmen-Farmers Conflict. *Conflict Studies Quarterly, 2*(31), 22–40. https://web.b.ebscohost.com/abstract?direct=true&profile=ehost&scope=site&authtype=crawler&jrnl=22857605&AN=142714399&h=xSVI3mxWdeU4VaUiTxRlNYqkePFApikc3IgHFMI7GpM4MEE%2BI2XcIAwxG191HWYOVgn6dxxjoDujL%2BWa%2FF2Rnw%3D%3D&crl=c&resultNs=AdminWebAuth&resultLo

Arowosegbe, J. O. (2019). Hausa-Fulani Pastoralists and Resource Conflicts in Yorubaland. *Interventions, 21*(8), 1157–1187. https://doi.org/10.1080/1369801x.2019.1649182

Awogbade, M. O., Olaniyan, R. A., & Faleye, O. A. (2016). Eco-violence or Trans-border Terrorism? Revisiting Nigerian Pastoral by. In R. A. Olaniyan & R. T. Akinyele (Eds.), *Nigeria's Ungoverned Spaces*. Obafemi Awolowo University Press. https://www.academia.edu/37226000/Eco-violence_or_Trans-border_Terrorism_Revisiting_Nigerian_Pastoral_Nomadic_Fulani_Question

Biazoto, J. (2011). Peace Journalism Where There Is No War. Conflict-Sensitive Reporting on Urban Violence and Public Security in Brazil and Its Potential Role in Conflict Transformation. *Conflict and Communication Online, 10*(2), 1–19.

Chukwuma, K. H. (2020). Constructing the Herder-Farmer Conflict as (In)Security in Nigeria. *African Security, 13*(1), 54–76. https://doi.org/10.1080/19392206.2020.1732703

Cooper, C. P., & Roter, D. L. (2000). "If It Bleeds It Leads"? Attributes of TV Health News Stories That Drive Viewer Attention. *Public Health Reports, 115*(4), 331–338. https://doi.org/10.1093/phr/115.4.331

Cottle, S. (2006). Mediatized Conflict: Developments in Media and Conflict Studies. In *Mediatized Conflict: Developments in Media and Conflict Studies*. Open University Press. http://orca.cf.ac.uk/3982/

Entman, R. M. (1993). Framing: Toward Clarification of a Fractured Paradigm. *Journal of Communication, 43*(4), 51–58. https://doi.org/10.1111/j.1460-2466.1993.tb01304.x

Ezemenaka, K. E., & Ekumaoko, C. E. (2018). Contextualising Fulani-Herdsmen Conflict in Nigeria. *Central European Journal of International and Security Studies, 12*(2), 30–55.

Folarin, B. (2002). *Theories of Mass Communication: An Introductory Text*. Link Publications.

Galtung, J. (2003). Peace Journalism. *Media Asia, 30*(3), 177–180. https://doi.org/10.1080/01296612.2003.11726720

Gever, C. V. (2018). When Solution Triggers More Conflicts: Frames and Tone of Media Coverage of the Anti-open grazing Law of Benue State, Nigeria. *Media, War and Conflict, Journals,* 1–15. https://doi.org/10.1177/1750635218810908

Goffman, E. (1974). *Frame Analysis: An Essay of the Organisation of Experience*. Harper & Row.

Harcup, T., & O'Neill, D. (2001). What Is News? Galtung and Ruge Revisited. *Journalism Studies, 2*(2), 261–280. https://doi.org/10.1080/14616700118449

Hefit, A., & Jonas, A. L. (2020). From Hate Speech to Incitement to Genocide: The Role of the Media in the Rwandan Genocide. *Boston University International Law Journal, 38,* 1–37. https://heinonline.org/HOL/Page?handle=hein.journals/builj38&id=7&div=&collection=

Idowu, O. S. (2018). Causes and Effects of Conflict Between Cattle Herdsmen and Host Community on Food Sustainability in Nigeria. *Albanian Journal Agricultural Science, 17*(2), 119–124.

Kolawole, R. A., & Okiki, A. T. (2019). Proceedings of the 28th RuSAN Conference. In A. Kolawole (Ed.), *"Victims of Unchecked Assaults": Intercultural Communication and Farmers' Narrative of Herders' Invasion in Oke-Ogun Area of Oyo State* (pp. 45–47). Rural Sociological Association of Nigeria.

Lee, S. (2010). Peace Journalism: Principles and Structural Limitations in the News Coverage of Three Conflicts. *Mass Communication and Society, 13*(4), 361–384.

Nwachukwu, C. A., Ajaero, I. D., Ugwuoke, J., & Odikpo, N. (2021). Is There Ethnic Othering in Newspapers' Coverage of Farmers/Herders Conflict in Nigeria? *African Journalism Studies.* https://doi.org/10.1080/23743670.2021.1886962

Nwankwo, C. F. (2021). Discursive Construction of the Farmer-Pastoralist Conflict in Nigeria. *Open Political Science,* 136–146.

Odunlami, D. (2017). Sleeping on the Feet with Open Eyes! Newspaper Coverage of the Fulani Herdsmen/Farmers' Conflict in Nigeria. *AGOGO: Journal of Humanities, 2,* 29–37.

Ogbonnaya, B. M. (2021). *Peacebuilding Agencies and Farmer- Herder Conflicts in Nigeria's Middle Belt Region: Successes and Policy Challenges* (Issue 31).

Olaleye, A. (2020). *81,000 Nigerians Destitute, 73 Dead from Fresh Herder-Farmer Clashes—UN*. Punch Newspapers. https://punchng.com/81000-nigerians-destitute-73-dead-from-fresh-herder-farmer-clashes-un/?amp=1

Olaniyi, R. O. (2015). Bororo Fulani Pastoralists and Yoruba Farmers' Conflicts in the Upper Ogun River, Oyo State Nigeria, 1986–2004. *Journal of Asian and African Studies, 50*(2), 239–252. https://doi.org/10.1177/0021909614522948

Omanga, D. M. (2016). *The Media and Terrorism: Editorial Cartoons, Framing and Legitimacy in the Kenyan Press, 1998–2008*. Lit Verlag GmbH & Co.

Oreglia, E. (2014). The Media in Transitional Democracies. *New Media & Society, 16*(8), 1338–1340. https://doi.org/10.1177/1461444814546303

Pate, U. A., & Dauda, S. (2015). The Media, Responsibility and Conflict-Sensitive Reporting in Nigeria. In I. Oblora & S. Udeze (Eds.), *Emerging Trends in Gender, Health and Political Communications* (pp. 214–229). Rhyce Kerex Publishers.

Pinker, S. (2018). The Media Exaggerates Negative News. This Distortion Has Consequences | Steven Pinker | Opinion | *The Guardian*. https://www.theguardian.com/commentisfree/2018/feb/17/steven-pinker-media-negative-news

Premium Times. (2016). *Nigeria Loses $14 Billion Annually to Herdsmen-Farmers Clashes—Report* | Premium Times Nigeria. https://www.premiumtimesng.com/news/headlines/201829-nigeria-loses-14-billion-annually-herdsmen-farmers-clashes-report.html

Tade, O. (n.d.). Herder-Farmers Conflict: Embracing the Ganduje, Abounu Solution. *Vanguard News*. Retrieved March 25, 2021, from https://www.vanguardngr.com/2021/03/herder-farmers-conflict-embracing-the-ganduje-abounu-solution/

Tade, O., & Yikwabs, Y. P. (2019). "If You Kill Me, You Take the Cow": Victimization Experiences of Farming and Herding Communities in Nasarawa. *Journal of Aggression, Conflict and Peace Research, 11*(4). https://doi.org/10.1108/JACPR-06-2019-0417

Tade, O., & Yikwabs, Y. P. (2020). Conflict Triggers Between Farming and Pastoral Communities in Nasarawa State, Nigeria. *Journal of Aggression, Conflict and Peace Research, 12*(3), 101–114. https://doi.org/10.1108/JACPR-10-2019-0448

Tyopuusu, J. (2019, July 26). Herdsmen Have Made Our Villages Inaccessible—Taraba Residents—Punch Newspapers. *The Punch*. https://punchng.com/herdsmen-have-made-our-villages-inaccessible-taraba-residents/

Udo, A. F., Odey, E. S., & Olofu-Adeoye, A. (2013). The Media and Conflicts in Nigeria. *International Journal of Asian Social Science, 3*(11), 2226–5139. http://www.aessweb.com/journal-detail.php?id=5007

Vladisavljevic, N., & Voltmer, K. (2017). Media Framing of Democratisation Conflicts in Egypt, Kenya, Serbia and South Africa. *Sociologija, 59*(4), 518–537. https://doi.org/10.2298/soc1704518v

Yekinni, O. T., Adeniyi, R. T., & Adebisi, S. A. (2017). Crop Framers' Adaptation Strategies to Mitigate Conflicts with Nomads in Oyo State. *Nigerian Journal of Rural Sociology, 17*(1), 19–26.

Youngblood, S. (2016). *Peace Journalism Principles and Practices: Responsibly Reporting Conflicts, Reconciliation and Solutions* (1st ed.). Routledge. https://doi.org/10.4324/9781315648019

Conclusion

Obert Bernard Mlambo and Ezra Chitando

The chapters in this handbook have sought to make sense of the phenomenon of violence in the vast, historically and culturally diverse and heterogenous geographical landscapes of the African continent. This has opened a window, through multidisciplinary and interdisciplinary approaches, to the study of violence in the African continent's different and diverse spaces. Using various approaches to the study of violence in Africa, despite all its different contours of practice, knowledge, beliefs, cultures, and religions, the chapters have shown that violence in Africa depends on many factors. This was demonstrated by examining the political, social, economic, religious, and cultural functions of the concept of violence in the context of various practices and social processes in different African places and contexts—analysing the phenomenon of violence, and the agents involved, with a view to ascertaining the interpretation of violence in different African settings.

A product of collective work in consultation with various experts, this handbook is a record of various aspects of violence in Africa. Contributors to this volume have tried to look at the occurrence of violence in

O. B. Mlambo (✉)
Classical Studies Section, School of Languages and Literatures, Rhodes University, Makhanda, South Africa
e-mail: obertmlambo@gmail.com

E. Chitando
Department of Philosophy, Religion and Ethics, University of Zimbabwe, Harare, Zimbabwe

© The Author(s), under exclusive license to Springer Nature Switzerland AG 2024
O. B. Mlambo and E. Chitando (eds.), *The Palgrave Handbook of Violence in Africa*,
https://doi.org/10.1007/978-3-031-40754-3_57

Africa from the perspectives of its indigenous people. Although the handbook also explores violence through the lens of European experts, it does so without being confined by Eurocentric understandings of Africa. The distinctive contribution of this handbook is its defamiliarization of violence in Africa within broad approaches, involving intersectionality and interdisciplinary approaches, in which violence is examined in the larger African milieu. Thus, the book interrogates why violence occurs in different parts of Africa within peculiar political economies, while elaborating on the different factors and contexts that can influence violence in African societies. Employing interdisciplinary and multidisciplinary approaches to study violence in Africa's diverse politico-historical contexts also allows for a broader approach to narratives of violence and cultures of violence, as the chapters in this handbook have demonstrated.

Violence is performed. It is a practice. Anthropologists, to understand human actions, have formulated the "practice theory." Members of a society or a group can perform violence by drawing on the existing repertoire of practices in their respective societies. This is a view that has been explored in this handbook in minute detail. Some of the chapters in this volume have demonstrated that the phenomenon of violence in Africa manifests itself through human and non-human agents. The chapters have argued that in practising violence, human players have many objectives, beliefs, and interests, but whatever their objectives and whatever their beliefs about how and why to carry out violence, they will always draw on the existing repertoire peculiar to their context. The chapters have starkly revealed that violence in Africa reproduces itself when its practitioners draw upon forms of repertoires of knowledge, be they religious ideas, political motives, economic motivations, or racial or gender differences, among other things.

Some chapters have asked the necessary question of what causes violence in Africa, or what disposes people in different contexts to perform or practice violence. Such an important question has allowed for an exploration of the logic of the aims of violent actions, and the lived experiences of different human groupings, in which shared and inherited knowledge and beliefs count for something. The performance of violence in specified locations, as the chapters have demonstrated, must be understood not as the mere enactment of a practice, but as its knowledgeable, informed, and goal-directed enactment.

The handbook has offered a window into the various facets of violence and how it is represented, experienced, practised, and performed in Africa. The contributors to the handbook, drawn from across Africa, have examined the complex narratives of violence in different African settings and contexts. Their portrayal of the phenomenon is a means of re-evaluating and responding to previously held understandings of violence in Africa. They have offered rich alternative perspectives—which crucially provide a more organic and indigenous version of narratives and discussions of violence in Africa by scholars who have direct experience with Africa, and are not far removed from the continent's historical and cultural milieu.

Index

A

Agriculture 171, 172, 329, 332, 336, 338, 340, 344, 549, 553, 605, 646, 652, 875, 880, 882
Algeria 111, 127–131, 481, 485, 489, 492, 686, 746
America 30, 78, 87, 88, 91–93, 143, 144, 223, 288, 290, 295, 367, 411, 486, 488, 491, 492, 504, 571, 667, 668, 673, 910, 975, 1111
Angola 99, 227, 266, 329–341, 343–345, 438, 481, 489, 645, 646, 652, 653, 748, 754, 927, 1057, 1058, 1060, 1094, 1119, 1122
Apartheid 4, 6, 53, 56–63, 65, 69–71, 73, 79, 124, 224, 234, 245, 249, 253, 258, 330, 619–624, 626–628, 634, 662, 667, 668, 672, 673, 686, 1073, 1075, 1076, 1080, 1081
Arabs 133, 185
Armed 11, 24, 34, 37, 85, 99–102, 108, 113, 120, 128, 146, 148, 159, 191, 212, 225, 228, 267, 294, 311, 315, 317, 318, 330, 379, 389, 393, 397, 410–412, 419–421, 429, 437–440, 442–445, 447–451, 453, 454, 460, 480–482, 484–486, 488–494, 561, 584, 651, 733, 745, 747, 753, 756, 757, 762–764, 766, 781, 881, 1005–1007, 1055, 1057, 1058, 1088, 1092, 1094, 1097, 1099, 1114, 1120
Armies 110, 491
Art 41, 110, 186, 309, 425, 975, 1097

B

Boko Haram 34, 108, 111–113, 228, 379, 387, 390, 397, 398, 409, 486, 490, 576, 577, 583–596, 725, 749, 760, 1101, 1126, 1137
Borderlands 121, 125

© The Editor(s) (if applicable) and The Author(s), under exclusive license to Springer Nature Switzerland AG 2024
O. B. Mlambo and E. Chitando (eds.), *The Palgrave Handbook of Violence in Africa*, https://doi.org/10.1007/978-3-031-40754-3

Borders 3, 59, 81, 100, 119–135, 153, 158, 160, 222, 224, 229, 233–235, 389, 390, 392, 395, 397, 399–401, 446, 481, 486, 489, 494, 523, 721, 724, 728, 729, 731–738, 746, 760, 831, 886, 918, 1056, 1066, 1079, 1093, 1111, 1114, 1118, 1126, 1134

Border violence 7, 126, 127

Botswana 12, 108, 109, 114, 266, 276, 298, 462, 484, 522–534, 650, 784, 927, 964, 1119, 1121, 1125

Burundi 99, 204, 291, 438, 447, 451, 489, 492, 748, 1055

C

Cabo Delgado 8, 222, 228, 229, 231–233, 235, 236, 1112, 1113, 1116, 1117, 1119, 1122

Cameroon 99, 111, 186, 290, 396, 447, 481, 484, 486, 488, 489, 491, 585, 586, 749, 759, 760, 886, 1023, 1051, 1061, 1126

China 106, 107, 290, 330, 411, 421, 484, 485, 491, 639, 1064, 1075

Coastal 40, 233, 330, 481, 651, 652, 732, 885, 1094

Colonialism. *See* Colonization

Coloniality 77, 78, 81, 87–89, 92, 168, 173

Combatants 101, 112, 113, 147, 150, 159, 422, 423, 427, 429, 439, 440, 448, 449, 491, 757, 758, 763

Culture 1–3, 7, 10, 12, 25, 27, 28, 32, 84, 88, 105, 145, 146, 151, 153, 160, 162, 168–171, 177, 185, 194, 199, 258, 259, 268, 286, 287, 289–291, 298, 300, 301, 318, 319, 368, 371, 375, 380, 391, 414, 430, 479, 521, 532, 542, 543, 555, 556, 560, 562, 565, 568, 583, 584, 603, 604, 614, 615, 619, 629, 630, 634, 760, 766, 786, 795, 807, 823, 827, 828, 837, 838, 843, 849, 853, 855, 887, 894, 897, 900, 912–915, 917, 919, 928, 929, 944–949, 951–954, 963, 969, 983, 985, 987, 995, 1005, 1007, 1008, 1037, 1055, 1079, 1133, 1138

Culturecides 7, 78, 84

D

Dam(s) 272, 647

E

Elections 10, 44, 68, 104, 106, 206, 207, 213, 243, 258, 259, 267, 270, 271, 274, 276, 277, 281, 285, 286, 291–293, 295–297, 301–303, 309, 348–354, 356–359, 361, 364, 368, 370, 372–378, 380–382, 491, 605, 611, 624, 664, 991, 1007, 1008, 1013, 1034–1037, 1061, 1077, 1099, 1100, 1109

Epistemicides 7, 78, 84, 88, 90, 188

Epistemic violence 2, 6–8, 24, 26, 27, 32, 33, 77, 78, 87, 88, 93, 121, 187–191

Eritrea 122, 141–153, 155–157, 160, 162, 447, 489, 747, 749, 1059

Ethiopia 141, 146, 147, 152, 153, 222, 411, 423, 428, 445, 447, 486, 489, 491, 504, 652, 731, 747, 749, 789, 824, 885

Extremism 26, 111, 226, 294, 390, 394, 487, 560, 561, 565–567, 570, 572, 575–577, 580–582,

585, 588, 590, 592–596,
724–726, 729, 733, 735, 737,
1116, 1119, 1120

F

Feminist 78, 80, 89, 90, 92, 641,
752, 765, 825–827, 837, 843,
844, 875, 912, 947
Forests 111, 128, 225, 387,
400–402, 544, 552, 554, 649,
707, 754

H

Harm 29, 30, 34, 35, 42–44,
53–58, 60–63, 65, 66, 68–72,
128, 159, 203, 244, 255, 281,
342, 354, 357, 381, 390, 395,
426, 523, 556, 622, 641, 681,
714, 726, 751, 752, 757,
781–783, 786, 787, 796, 802,
822, 853–855, 868, 869, 881,
903, 905, 947, 995, 1002,
1015, 1028, 1040–1043,
1046, 1047, 1073, 1134

I

Internet 30, 142, 143, 161, 162,
311, 350, 515, 662, 680,
729–731, 736, 952
Islam 2, 105, 229, 560–563,
568–570, 572, 576–582, 586,
590, 595, 596, 721–725, 727,
734

K

Killings 56, 88, 107, 146, 196, 198,
227, 244, 247, 249, 254, 276,
307, 320, 322, 369, 371, 373,
418, 421–423, 426, 427, 450,
463, 465, 544, 547, 549, 552,
561, 584, 601, 623, 650, 688,
689, 691, 701, 702, 709, 713,
730, 759, 764, 969, 970, 972,
983, 1006, 1008, 1011, 1014,
1025

M

Madagascar 104, 665
Malawi 40, 230, 347, 484, 663,
678, 685, 699–701, 703–707,
710, 712–715, 885, 886, 1121
Mali 100, 104, 111, 112, 291, 379,
396, 438, 447, 484, 486,
489–491, 746, 748, 758,
760–763, 1051, 1119
Marine 650, 651
Masculinity 34, 36, 40, 198, 421,
422, 429, 555, 804, 814, 823,
838, 843, 844, 849, 853–855,
857, 860, 872, 881, 894, 896,
897, 901, 904, 909, 910,
912–920
Mecca 563, 564, 577, 578
Military 2, 5, 18, 24, 25, 27, 37, 44,
100–102, 105–107, 109,
111–114, 122, 125, 135, 153,
159, 196, 221, 226, 228–230,
232–236, 251, 252, 266, 267,
269, 272, 290, 295, 309, 310,
312, 313, 315–322, 331, 354,
369, 378, 379, 390–394, 396,
397, 399–401, 410, 411,
416–418, 420–423, 429, 438,
449, 452, 454, 461, 463, 465,
469, 470, 490, 580, 585, 587,
591, 594, 602, 603, 645,
649–652, 727, 746, 749, 764,
981, 985–987, 1006, 1007,
1033–1038, 1041–1045,
1048, 1055, 1062, 1092,
1097, 1115, 1116, 1118,
1119, 1121, 1122, 1130, 1131

Money 54, 56, 68, 70, 108, 124, 128, 130, 135, 208, 210, 213, 215, 230, 288, 312, 370, 377, 416, 470, 473, 474, 508, 509, 514, 515, 594, 702, 706, 732, 733, 787, 823, 841, 872, 885, 918, 942, 1025, 1041, 1058, 1102

Mozambique 19, 100, 107, 110–112, 114, 171, 222, 228–234, 266, 271, 276, 445, 447, 450, 489, 646, 647, 649–653, 663, 701, 757, 884–886, 927, 964, 1051, 1058, 1112–1128

Muslim(s) 158, 229, 307, 564, 566, 568, 576, 579–581, 583, 586, 591, 723, 725, 726, 728, 732, 735

N

Nature 5, 6, 9, 12, 13, 17, 24, 25, 36, 37, 41, 42, 44, 66, 80, 104, 107, 112, 124, 158, 168, 170, 171, 178, 187, 190, 194, 198, 206, 207, 214, 224, 227, 243, 248, 254, 259, 260, 278, 287, 291, 303, 312, 319, 342, 349, 357, 367–371, 374, 375, 392, 394, 396, 400, 418, 469, 480, 541–547, 551, 553–557, 565, 579, 612, 614, 634, 640–652, 654, 655, 680, 681, 684, 687, 713, 722, 729, 736, 737, 752, 800, 803, 814, 827, 850, 853, 866, 867, 875, 880, 883, 886, 894, 901, 909, 912, 962, 966, 969, 981–983, 990, 1006, 1021, 1033, 1038–1040, 1045, 1071, 1088, 1091–1093, 1095–1098, 1100, 1102, 1103, 1121, 1136, 1137

Niger 100, 104, 107, 108, 111, 112, 308, 323, 379, 396, 398, 447, 481, 484, 486, 488, 489, 491, 492, 585, 746, 748, 749, 886, 1051, 1088, 1091, 1093, 1095–1099, 1101, 1103, 1122

Nigeria 9, 10, 13, 18, 19, 34, 37, 43, 44, 67, 100, 108, 111–114, 178, 222, 225, 234, 256, 288, 307–310, 312–316, 318–320, 322, 323, 329, 332, 335, 347, 368, 369, 372–382, 387, 388, 390, 393–403, 409, 438, 445, 447, 480, 481, 484, 486, 488–493, 576, 577, 579, 583–589, 591–596, 649, 653, 665, 689, 725, 747–749, 759, 760, 781, 790, 852, 886, 1051, 1056–1058, 1087–1103, 1115, 1119, 1122, 1126, 1133, 1135–1137, 1141, 1146

Nile 754

P

Politics 1, 2, 5, 11, 13, 17, 26, 27, 35, 40, 44, 83, 93, 107, 125, 143–145, 152, 153, 161, 168, 195, 212, 213, 226, 259, 265, 266, 270, 272, 281, 288, 290, 291, 318, 347, 348, 351, 353, 354, 361, 363, 370, 371, 375–377, 379, 394, 410, 414, 459–461, 463, 464, 466, 468, 472, 473, 475, 480, 489, 491, 492, 582, 583, 591, 595, 602–607, 609–615, 624, 625, 694, 779, 784, 785, 904, 985, 986, 988, 989, 1004, 1034–1036, 1048, 1059, 1071, 1072, 1076, 1081, 1099, 1120, 1131

Postcolony 8, 186, 196

Power 6, 7, 9, 14, 24, 26, 29, 34, 36, 44, 53, 63, 70, 78, 82, 87, 89, 92, 101–107, 111, 112, 114, 119, 121, 126, 134, 142, 145, 146, 149, 151, 152, 154, 156, 162, 168, 169, 174, 177, 185, 186, 195, 196, 198, 203, 209, 221, 225, 231, 232, 234, 235, 243, 245, 246, 256, 257, 266, 275, 278, 285, 286, 288, 289, 292–295, 309, 310, 315, 323, 330, 331, 335, 336, 340, 342, 344, 348, 351, 352, 355, 359, 363, 368–372, 374, 377, 380–382, 390, 392, 393, 395–397, 411, 415, 421, 429, 439, 446, 447, 460, 462, 463, 465, 467–475, 488, 489, 523, 542, 556, 564, 581, 590–592, 595, 602–608, 611, 613, 614, 624, 625, 630, 631, 639, 643, 644, 655, 668, 678–681, 687, 688, 690–692, 702, 705, 712, 725, 728, 746, 751, 752, 755, 760, 780–782, 784, 786, 789, 799, 823, 824, 828, 834, 840, 853, 868, 872, 873, 875, 880, 881, 883, 884, 887, 894, 896, 897, 909, 911, 912, 915–920, 942, 943, 946, 948, 951, 962–964, 966, 967, 979, 982, 983, 985, 986, 990, 995, 1001, 1006–1008, 1010, 1014, 1024, 1035, 1038–1041, 1044, 1045, 1054–1057, 1059, 1063–1066, 1114, 1115, 1118, 1125, 1127

Q
Quran 568, 577, 578, 580–582, 586

R
Religion 5, 12, 13, 26–28, 36, 111, 226, 288, 289, 294, 369, 525, 543, 548, 559–563, 565–567, 569–572, 575–577, 579–583, 590–593, 595, 604, 605, 615, 629, 678, 681, 694, 713, 721–725, 735, 737, 738, 802, 805–807, 809, 812, 820, 823, 825, 899, 944–947, 1046, 1057, 1059, 1074, 1077, 1080–1082, 1133
Resistance 127, 128, 132, 146, 214, 226, 249, 309, 319, 592, 608, 619, 644, 649, 971, 974, 983, 986, 1005, 1140
Revolution 56, 93, 127, 149, 156, 247, 322, 354, 645, 725, 729, 754, 812, 986, 1064
Rivers 65, 66, 322, 329, 331, 554–556, 647, 831, 963
Rwanda 99, 100, 204, 227, 243, 437, 438, 446, 447, 481, 486, 489, 490, 492, 686, 746, 748, 1064, 1117, 1119, 1128

S
Soldiers 10, 11, 24, 83, 101, 102, 112, 113, 147, 149, 159, 191, 193, 194, 196, 222, 257, 268, 272, 273, 275, 276, 316, 320, 321, 355, 358, 360, 409–430, 438–448, 450–454, 461, 481, 492, 502, 594, 750, 757, 758, 761, 764, 991, 1112, 1119, 1120
Somalia 99, 102, 108, 111, 114, 298, 445, 447, 453, 481, 484, 486, 489–492, 587, 723–728, 731–735, 738, 748, 750, 759–761, 852, 1051, 1055, 1059, 1060, 1126
South Africa 33

Structural violence 8, 10, 16, 24, 29, 78, 79, 83, 120, 169, 245–247, 259, 261, 332, 341, 342, 446, 506, 514, 515, 646, 884, 931

Sudan 3, 10, 99, 100, 104, 107, 108, 122, 129, 144, 147, 204, 222, 227, 291, 298, 379, 411, 416, 427, 429, 438, 439, 445, 447, 451, 481, 486, 489, 491, 492, 652, 726, 731, 747, 748, 750, 759, 761, 762, 764, 781, 882, 885, 886, 1055, 1058, 1059, 1119, 1122

T

Torture 6, 7, 35, 43, 79, 103–105, 120, 124, 125, 130, 134, 268, 272, 274–277, 308, 311, 312, 322, 372, 422, 427, 463, 525, 529, 713, 714, 722, 766, 859, 894, 983, 986, 991, 993, 1001, 1011, 1014, 1015, 1036, 1043

Tunisia 111, 121–123, 126–128, 130–135, 481, 486, 725, 746, 784

U

Uganda 3, 10, 13, 36, 43, 100, 104, 110, 111, 114, 204, 411, 417, 422, 425, 429, 437–439, 443, 447, 489, 492, 504, 506, 601–606, 608–612, 614, 615, 678, 726, 747, 748, 750, 756–758, 790, 857, 859, 885, 886, 905

V

Veterans 102, 154, 273, 422, 469, 545, 546, 984

Vigilantes 10, 107, 204, 212–218, 294, 349, 350, 353, 354, 356–364, 474

Violence. *See* Border violence, Epistemic violence, Structural violence

W

War 7, 8, 10, 11, 19, 24, 25, 34, 42, 81, 100–102, 105–107, 110–113, 130, 141, 142, 144, 146–149, 152, 153, 155–160, 162, 191, 193–196, 198, 228, 273, 279, 286, 295, 302, 310, 318, 330–332, 334, 340, 341, 343, 377, 390, 394, 401, 410–414, 416, 419, 421, 422, 424, 426–429, 431, 438, 439, 441, 443, 445, 447, 449, 450, 454, 460, 469, 484, 488, 545, 577–579, 585, 587, 588, 593, 594, 596, 602–604, 641, 645, 649, 651, 652, 669, 722, 747, 750, 753, 755, 758, 760, 762, 765, 766, 779, 781, 786, 971, 972, 983, 986–993, 1002, 1004–1009, 1114, 1115, 1117, 1035, 1061, 1072, 1075, 1136, 1138, 1145, 1146

Weapons 159, 309, 420, 493, 555, 586, 587, 647, 755, 758, 766, 781, 895, 911, 992, 1014, 1098

Y

Youths 7, 9, 10, 101, 214, 271, 311, 315, 317, 322, 323, 356, 357, 362, 363, 389, 390, 412, 464–466, 482, 490, 512, 514, 515, 620, 621, 724, 726, 728, 735, 750, 826, 834, 929, 989, 1093, 1095, 1101, 1117